FIAT IUSTITIA

Essays in Memory of

OLIVER DENEYS SCHREINER

Oliver Deneys Schreiner

Photograph by Leon Levson

FIAT IUSTITIA

Essays in Memory of

OLIVER DENEYS SCHREINER

Edited by

ELLISON KAHN

Professor of Law in the University of the Witwatersrand, Johannesburg

Published for

THE SCHOOL OF LAW
UNIVERSITY OF THE WITWATERSRAND
JOHANNESBURG

by

JUTA & CO LTD

CAPE TOWN WETTON JOHANNESBURG

First Published 1983

PO Box 123, Kenwyn 7790

ISBN 0 7021 1335 2

SET, PRINTED AND BOUND IN THE REPUBLIC OF SOUTH AFRICA
BY THE RUSTICA PRESS (PTY) LTD, WYNBERG, CAPE

D111

PREFACE

Oliver Deneys Schreiner was a great judge, a great man and a great South African. He was born on 29 December 1890 and died on 27 July 1980.

Early in 1981 the Governing Committee of the School of Law of the University of the Witwatersrand, Johannesburg, with which Oliver Schreiner had been closely connected, did me the honour of asking me to make arrangements for and edit a collection of essays in his memory. Gladly I accepted the invitation. This co-operative work is the result. I can only hope that it is a fitting memorial to so distinguished a person.

My warm thanks go to all who responded to my request for a contribution. May they find this volume sufficiently interesting and attractive to recompense them for their labour of love and homage.

There are many whom I should like to thank for their assistance. Bill Schreiner, the elder son of Oliver, and his wife, Pat, were extremely helpful to me all through and particularly when I wrote the biographical part of the book; I spoke to them at length on a number of occasions. Bill was so kind as to arrange the letters found in his father's house on his death and leave me complete freedom as to their use, a freedom he extended to all documents and photographs left by his father. His confidence in my good taste and sense of propriety touched me, and I trust that I have proved myself worthy of it. But not only this—I hope that I have done justice to the magnificent material he put at my disposal. It provided excellent primary matter, together with the letters and documents Oliver Schreiner donated to the University of the Witwatersrand, Johannesburg in 1974, which are lodged in the University Archives, the archivist of which, Joan Biddles, was always her very helpful self.

I also had the advantage of a conversation, during a lunch-hour walk in the midst of a conference, with Oliver Schreiner's younger son, Deneys, and his wife, Else.

Various practitioners and colleagues at my university were good enough to write to me in response to my sending them an offprint of my earlier biographical sketch of Oliver Schreiner published in the November 1980 issue of the *South African Law Journal*. I made use of certain anecdotes they told me, and have mentioned their names where I did so. My friend and colleague, Professor Friedel

Sellschop, Director of the Nuclear Physics Research Unit of the University of the Witwatersrand, kindly lent me the photographs that appear between pages 374 and 375.

I have done my best to track down the copyright in photographs and to obtain the permission of the holders of it in each instance. If in a particular case I have failed to get permission, it has been unwitting, for it was of unknown provenance, and I tender my apologies to the person concerned.

Mrs Fanny Goldman, of the secretariat of the School of Law of my university, typed my awkward—to use a generous adjective—manuscripts in her impeccable way and with her traditional wonderful good humour.

A number of the old photographs which were faded or in sad condition were splendidly touched up and rendered into reproducible form by Mr Mark Hudson, Senior Technician (Photography) of my university. I am most grateful to him.

My wife has helped me immensely with the checking of references in the contributions, the adaptation of manuscripts to the 'house style' I adhere to, and the other finicky, time-consuming duties of an editor.

My deep thanks go to the printers and publishers. Mr Hubert Elffers, of The Rustica Press, was remarkably good to me. His advice was invaluable—on the type of print to be used, the size of the page, the type of binding, the appearance of the dust-jacket, the arrangement of the illustrations and so much else. I had certain ideas but he had the professional knowledge, and that makes the essential difference.

Mr J Douglas Duncan, managing director of Juta and Company Limited, my old friend—not simply my publisher, but my friend—has, as always, been behind me. He committed his firm to this hazardous enterprise, with no more financial support than a guarantee of R4 000 from the Board of the *Annual Survey of South African Law*, an underwriting of part of the cost of production for which I am most grateful, but which is only a fraction of the total cost.

As producer, director, editor, sub-editor, financial controller, proof-reader (second string), office-boy and general factotum, I thank, finally, you who have read this preface, if you are the purchaser of the work. I cannot say that without you it would not have been born; but—with the support of many like you—it will have been born without an entry in the debit column in the register of births of books.

ELLISON KAHN

School of Law
University of the Witwatersrand, Johannesburg
15 November 1982

CONTENTS

		Page
PREFACE		v
LIST OF ILLUSTRATIONS		ix
TABLE OF PRINCIPAL ENACTMENTS		xiii
TABLE OF PRINCIPAL CASES		xv
LIST OF PRE-PUBLICATION SUBSCRIBERS		xix
PART ONE	Biographical	
ELLISON KAHN	*Oliver Deneys Schreiner: A South African*	1
ELLISON KAHN	*Father and Son—W P Schreiner and Oliver*	100
PART TWO	Tributes	
LORD DENNING	*Reminiscences of a Visit to South Africa*	127
H R HAHLO	*In Memory of Oliver Schreiner*	130
ARTHUR SUZMAN	*Oliver Schreiner—Some Reminiscences and an Appreciation*	131
R S WELSH	*Oliver Schreiner—A Personal Tribute and Recollection*	134
PART THREE	Legal Essays	
P Q R BOBERG	*Uncommon Cause*	145
†EXTON BURCHELL	Aberratio Ictus	165
J M BURCHELL	*The Administration of Justice and the Defence of Privilege in Defamation: The Balancing of Interests: The Administration of Justice and the Protection of Reputation*	172
M M CORBETT	*Discretionary Trusts, Powers of Appointment and the Rule Regarding the Delegation of Testamentary Power*	188

		Page
W H B DEAN	*Reason and Prejudice: The Courts and Licensing Bodies in the Transvaal* ..	211
JOHN DUGARD	*International Human-rights Norms in Domestic Courts: Can South Africa Learn from Britain and the United States?*	221
H R HAHLO	*Cohabitation, Concubinage and the Common-law Marriage*	244
A J KERR	*Customary Law in the Appellate Division 1945–1960*	264
C S MARGO	*Reflections on Some Aspects of the Judicial Function*	282
A S MATHEWS	*The Rule of Law—A Reassessment* ...	294
H C NICHOLAS	*The Two Cardinal Rules of Logic in* Rex *v* Blom	312
S A STRAUSS	*Clinical Independence of the Doctor in the Treatment of Prisoners: A Critical Survey of our Law*	329
J D VAN DER VYVER	*Law and Morality*	350
ROGER WHITING	*Factual Causation in Perspective*	370
MARINUS WIECHERS	*The Fundamental Laws behind our Constitution: Reflections on the Judgment of Schreiner JA in the Senate Case*	383
D ZEFFERTT	*Pointing Out*	395

LIST OF ILLUSTRATIONS

Oliver Deneys Schreiner .... Photograph by Leon Levson	*Dust-jacket and frontispiece*
	Between pages
W P Schreiner, father of Oliver	12–13
Fanny Schreiner, mother of Oliver	12–13
W P Schreiner and his wife Fanny	12–13
W P Schreiner, High Commissioner, with Otto Beit (*left*), at the opening of workshops for South African wounded servicemen at Richmond on 30 September 1917 ...	12–13
W P Schreiner with his son Bill early this century	12–13
Oliver, his sister Ursula and W P Schreiner on the *Edinburgh Castle* June 1911 *en route* to England	12–13
W P Schreiner Cartoon by D C Boonzaier 1901	46–47
Oliver Schreiner's success in the June 1912 Cambridge law examination, with the congratulations of Professor Courtney S Kenny	46–47
Eights Week at the University of Oxford 25 May 1912, showing Oliver with Gerrit (later Mr Justice) Maritz and Walter Power	46–47
Eights Week, showing Oliver with Gerrit Maritz and others	46–47
Captain O D Schreiner during the Great War	78–79
Oliver with his sister Ursula in London during the Great War	78–79
W P Schreiner, Fanny, Frances and Ursula in London during the Great War	78–79
Oliver, WP and Fanny in London during the Great War	78–79

Between pages

General J C Smuts on receiving the freedom of the city of Manchester 14 May 1917, showing Walter Long (Colonial Secretary) and W P Schreiner 78–79

Dinner at the Savoy Hotel, London, on 23 May 1917, in honour of General J C Smuts, showing Smuts, W P Schreiner, Viscount Milner, the Earl of Selborne and Lord Gladstone 78–79

Oliver as a boy 110–111

Oliver in the blazer of the South African College 110–111

Oliver Schreiner on his appointment to the Bench in 1937 110–111

Oliver Schreiner in early middle age 110–111

Oliver Schreiner in middle age 110–111
Photograph by Leon Levson

Oliver Schreiner in middle age 110–111

Oliver Schreiner in 1972 at the time of the Golden Jubilee of the University of the Witwatersrand 110–111

Oliver Schreiner in 1972 in the robes of the Chancellor of the University of the Witwatersrand 110–111

Edna Schreiner, wife of Oliver, in her thirties 142–143

Edna Schreiner and her daughter Jean, with the Schreiners' Packard ('Packie') 142–143

Oliver and Edna Schreiner with their first motor car, a Rugby 142–143

Mrs Fanny Schreiner with her four children, Frances, Bill, Ursula and Oliver 142–143

Oliver Schreiner with his family, about 1939 142–143

Oliver Schreiner at the family fishing shack . . . 142–143

Mrs Fanny Schreiner with Oliver and his family, about 1928 142–143

Edna and Oliver Schreiner at the entrance to their house 'Lyndall' 142–143

Oliver and Edna Schreiner at the front door of their house 'Lyndall' 190–191

	Between pages
The Transvaal Bench 1940, 1941 or 1942. Magnificently composed photograph by Leon Levson	190–191
Pre-World War II Johannesburg Bar Golf Cup Tournament, showing Oliver Schreiner with Tilson Barry KC	190–191
Pre-World War II Johannesburg Bar Golf Cup Tournament, showing Oliver Schreiner with 'Sonny' Ettlinger, J G N Strauss and Tilson Barry KC	190–191
The Appellate Division 1945 or 1946	270–271
The Appellate Division 1949 or 1950	270–271
The members of the Appellate Division September 1954, with Sir Alfred Denning LJ (subsequently Lord Denning MR)	302–303
The Appellate Division's Wednesday afternoon bowls in the early fifties	302–303
The entire Appellate Division at the Wednesday afternoon bowls in the early fifties	302–303
Oliver Schreiner receiving the honorary degree of Doctor of Laws at the graduation ceremony of the University of Cape Town 27 June 1958	342–343
On the occasion of the conferring of the honorary degree of Doctor of Laws on Albert Centlivres by the University of the Witwatersrand 4 April 1964, showing Oliver Schreiner as Chancellor of the University	342–343
Oliver Schreiner being capped by Richard Feetham, Chancellor of the University of the Witwatersrand, on receiving the honorary degree of Doctor of Laws 8 April 1961	342–343
Reception during the session of the Court of Appeal of Lesotho, Maseru, April 1971, showing Oliver Schreiner (President of the Court), Chief Leabua Jonathan (Prime Minister), Mr Justice H R Jacobs CJ, Mr Justice A Milne JA and Mr Justice I A Maisels JA	342–343

Between pages

Official opening on 6 December 1967 of the Neutrino Laboratory of the University of the Witwatersrand at ERPM 11 000 feet below the surface; Oliver Schreiner looking at the MO, who is pretending to be another type of MO—a mine official 374–375

Oliver Schreiner inspecting the equipment at the Neutrino Laboratory 374–375

Oliver Schreiner with Charles Stallard QC on Stallard's 95th birthday on 4 June 1966; also present Brother Norwood E Coaker (Coaker QC) and the Hon E R Roper 374–375

Oliver Schreiner talking to the former Chief Justice, Sir James Rose Innes 374–375

TABLE OF PRINCIPAL ENACTMENTS

(Only enactments specially discussed are listed. References are to South African enactments unless otherwise stated.)

No	*Year*	*Short title*	*Page*
27	1955	Appellate Division Quorum Act	36, 99
34	1956	Apportionment of Damages Act	146ff
38	1927	Black Administration Act	
		s 11(1)	265ff, 275ff
		s 11(3)	275
		s 22(6)	272ff
		s 23(2)	278, 279
		s 23(3)	279ff
		s 23(10)	279ff
142	1910	[Black Marriages and Estates] Proclamation	278
35	1952	High Court of Parliament Act	36
74	1982	Internal Security Act	332, 338n
7	1958	Police Act	332ff
	1964	Police Regulations GN R203	333ff
8	1959	Prisons Act	332ff
32	1961	Republic of South Africa Constitution Act	
		s 2	363n, 391
53	1955	Senate Act	37, 384, 392
46	1951	Separate Representation of Voters Act	35
9	1956	South Africa Act Amendment Act	42
83	1967	Terrorism Act	337ff

TABLE OF PRINCIPAL CASES

(Only cases specially discussed are listed.)

A

Page

Attorney-General *v* British Broadcasting Corporation [1981] AC 303 (HL), [1980] 3 All ER 161 .... 224, 226

B

Basner *v* Trigger 1946 AD 83 .... 78, 173, 183, 186
Boerne *v* Harris 1949 (1) SA 793 (A) 76
Botes *v* Van Deventer 1966 (3) SA 182 (A) 155

C

CIR *v* Lukin's Estate 1956 (1) SA 617 (A) 192, 197
CIR *v* Sive's Estate 1955 (1) SA 249 (A) 203, 210
Cohen *v* CIR 1946 AD 174 71
Collins *v* Minister of the Interior 1957 (1) SA 552 (A) 42ff, 47, 383ff
Commissioner for Inland Revenue *v* City Deep Ltd 1924 AD 298 217
Cooke *v* Head [1972] 2 All ER 38 (CA), [1972] 1 WLR 518 259
Cowburn *v* Nasopie (Edms) Bpk 1980 (3) SA 547 (NC) 389
Crookes NO *v* Watson 1956 (1) SA 277 (A) 78
Crown Mines Ltd *v* CIR 1922 AD 91 216

D

Dessels, *Ex parte* 1976 (1) SA 851 (D) 250
Die Spoorbond *v* SAR 1946 AD 999 70
Drummond *v* Drummond 1979 (1) SA 161 (A) 249, 250

E

Essa *v* Divaris 1947 (1) SA 753 (A) 70

F

Fernandez *v* Wilkinson 505 F Supp 787 (1980) 230, 232, 242
Filartiga *v* Pena-Irala 630 F 2d 876 (2d Cir 1980) 229, 232, 242
Findlay *v* Knight 1935 AD 58 182
Frankel's Estate *v* The Master 1950 (1) SA 220 (A) 69, 136

G

Gaudras *c* Dangereux *Cours Ch Mixte* 27 fev 1970, [1970] *Semaine Juridique* 16305 251

H

Harris *v* Minister of the Interior 1952 (2) SA 428 (A) 35, 127, 384
Herschel *v* Mrupe 1954 (3) SA 464 (A) 138

J

Jooma *v* Lydenburg Rural Licensing Board 1933 TPD 477 217

K *Page*

Kakamas Bestuursraad *v* Louw 1960 (2) SA 202 (A) 147, 154
King NO *v* Pearl Insurance Co Ltd 1970 (1) SA 462 (W) 149
Kroomer *v* Johannesburg Municipality 1928 TPD 69 .... 213, 214

L

Lareau *v* Manson 507 F Supp 1177 (1980) 231

M

Malone *v* Metropolitan Police Commissioner [1979] Ch 344 226
Manisty's Settlement, *In re* [1974] Ch 17, [1973] 2 All ER 1203 .... 208, 210
May *v* Udwin 1981 (1) SA 1 (A) 173ff, 186
Mdolo *v* Vanda 1969 BAC 25 (S) 269
Michelle Marvin *v* Lee Marvin 557 P 2d 106 256
Minister of Native Affairs, *Ex parte*: *In re* Magqabi *v* Magqabi and Mngonjane *v* Mngonjane 1955 (2) SA 428 (A) 278
Minister of Native Affairs, *Ex parte*: *In re* Molefe *v* Molefe 1946 AD 315 274
Minister of Native Affairs, *Ex parte*: *In re* Yako *v* Beyi 1948 (1) 388 (A) .. 265ff
Minister of the Interior *v* Harris 1952 (4) SA 769 (A) 36, 384, 388
Myburgh, *In re* (1896) 13 SC 218 191

N

Nkambula *v* Linda 1951 (1) SA 377 (A) 275

O

Orpen, Estate *v* Estate Atkinson 1966 (4) SA 589 (A) 197

P

People *v* O'Brien [1965] IR 142 404
Pettkus *v* Becker (1981) 117 DLR (3d) 257 (SC) 260
Pogrund *v* Yutar 1967 (2) SA 564 (A) 184
Portwood *v* Svamvur 1970 (4) SA 8 (RAD) 161
Preston *v* Luyt 1911 EDL 298 181
Pretoria North Town Council *v* A1 Electric Ice-cream Factory (Pty) Ltd 1953 (3) SA 1 (A) 76, 218

R

R *v* Blom 1939 AD 188 .... 312ff
R *v* Britz 1949 (3) SA 293 (A) 72
R *v* Davies 1956 (3) SA 52 (A) 73
R *v* De Villiers 1944 AD 493 319
R *v* Duetsimi 1950 (3) SA 674 (A) 397
R *v* Erasmus 1945 OPD 50 321
R *v* Ismail 1952 (1) SA 204 (A) 326
R *v* Karg 1961 (1) SA 231 (A) 74
R *v* Krull 1959 (3) SA 392 (A) 73
R *v* Kuruma, son of Kaniu [1955] AC 197 (PC), [1955] 1 All ER 236 403
R *v* Mabena 1968 (2) SA 28 (RAD) 169
R *v* Mlambo 1957 (4) SA 727 (A) 75, 322ff
R *v* Nhleko 1960 (4) SA 712 (A) 402
R *v* Samhando 1943 AD 608 396
R *v* Tebetha 1959 (2) SA 337 (A) 75, 398ff
R *v* Thibani 1949 (4) SA 720 (A) 72
Ratsialingwa *v* Sibasa 1948 (3) SA 781 (A) 277
Robertson *v* Robertson's Executors 1914 AD 503 .... 193, 202

S

Page

S *v* Adams; S *v* Werner 1981 (1) SA 187 (A) 239
S *v* Bock 1968 (2) SA 658 (A) 238
S *v* Ismail (1) 1965 (1) SA 446 (N) 402
S *v* Mbele 1981 (2) SA 738 (A) 396
S *v* Mtshiza 1970 (3) SA 747 (A) 167
S *v* Raisa 1979 (4) SA 541 (O) 168
S *v* Tissen 1979 (4) SA 293 (T) 167
Sachs *v* Dönges NO 1950 (2) SA 265 (A) 75
Shidiack *v* Union Government, Minister of the Interior 1912 AD 642 ... 215
Sterling *v* Cupp Or 625 P 2d 123 231
Suid-Afrikaanse Nasionale Trust en Assuransie Maatskappy Bpk *v* Fondo 1960 (2) SA 467 (A) 276
Swart NO and Nicol NO *v* De Kock and Garner 1951 (3) SA 589 (A) ... 32

U

Umvovo *v* Umvovo 1953 (1) SA 195 (A) 267
Union Government (Minister of Finance) *v* Olivier 1916 AD 74 192

V

Venutolo *c* Dlle Bertoit D 1960 515 note Malaurie 258
Vitoria *v* Union National South British Insurance Co Ltd 1980 (4) SA 406 (T) 149ff
Vorster *v* AA Mutual Insurance Association Ltd 1982 (1) SA 145 (T) .. 149, 152

W

Watkins-Pitchford, Estate *v* CIR 1955 (2) SA 437 (A) .. 190, 192, 195, 199, 205
Westminster Bank Ltd NO *v* Zinn NO 1938 AD 57 .... 194, 199

LIST OF PRE-PUBLICATION SUBSCRIBERS

Mr A J Aaron
Adv S Aaron SC
The Hon Mr Justice L W H Ackermann
Mr M W Adcock
Adv Gerald Alexander SC
Adv Bernard Ancer
Andrew & Lister Inc
Mr P A Anscombe
Mrs Theresa Antrobus
Mr J A Arderne
Mr M Lewis Arenson
Mr M G Ashworth
Association of Law Societies of the Republic of South Africa

The Hon Mr Justice P W E Baker
G Bakker
Adv B R Bamford SC, MP
Mr G Barlow
Barlow Rand Limited
Prof A H Barnard
Mr Benjamin Baron
Mr James M Barry
Mr G A Barton
Baskin & Partners
The Hon Mr Justice J J Basson
Prof L G Baxter
Mr A C Beck
The Hon Mr Justice C E L Beck
Mr Ernest Beder
Mrs Susan Bedil
Mr David Behr
Mr A J Behrmann
Mr F C S Bell
Mr Lionel Benjamin
The Hon Mr Justice H J Berker
Dr B L Bernstein
Adv E Bertelsmann
The Hon Mr Justice K Bethune
Prof R C Beuthin
Adv George Bizos SC
Adv P Blieden
Adv A P Blignault
Adv M Bliss SC
Alderman A Bloomberg
Adv Karen Blum
Blyth & Coetzeé
Mr M C J Bobbert
Prof P Q R Boberg
Mr Ronald Bobroff
Prof H Booysen
Mr W H Booysen
Mr Jeffrey Bortz
The Hon Mr Justice W G Boshoff
Mr P H Bosman
Mr A L Bostock
Adv L G Bowman
Bowman, Gilfillan & Blacklock, Inc
Prof G R Bozzoli
Dr E P Bradlow
Mr R A Brady
Brand van Zyl Law Library, University of Cape Town
Adv M S M Brassey
Adv D A Bregman
Mr A J Brink
Prof P E J Brooks
Adv E B Broomberg
Adv Jules Browde SC
Adv Carol E Bruyns
Mr G M Budlender
Prof J M Burchell
Mr Timothy D Burrell
Mr D W Butler

Mr Edwin Cameron
Carlston & Co
Mr N D Carmen
Mr F H I Cassim
Prof R W Charlton
Mr Halton Cheadle
Chernin & Partners
Prof Joan Church
The Hon Mr Justice P M Cillié
Prof A C Cilliers
Mr Charl Cilliers
Sir John Clayden
Clemmans & Johnston, Inc
Adv T D Cloete
The Hon Mr Justice J D Cloete
Adv Petrus Coetsee
The Hon Mr Justice G A Coetzee
Mr J A Coetzee
Adv J H Coetzee SC
Mr N W Coetzee
Adv C Z Cohen SC
Mr Jack I Cohen
Mrs Ann Cohen
Prof Leslie Cohen
Mr Roy Cohen
Mr J L Cooper
Dr W E Cooper SC
Prof A J C Copeling
The Hon Mr Justice M M Corbett
Mr A M Costa
Couzyn, Hertzog & Horak
Mr Ian S Cox
Mr K T Cremer
Mr P M Crossley

Mr C H A Damant
Adv S A Danilowitz
Dazana & Masiza
Prof W H B Dean
De Beers Consolidated Mines Limited
Mr S P de Beer-Strydom
Mr C de Heus
The Hon Mr Justice M R de Kock
Prof Henk J Delport
The Rt Hon Lord Denning
Adv I W B de Villiers SC
Mr M M de Villiers
Mr René M de Villiers
Prof J C de Wet
Mr Derek P Dexter
The Hon Mr Justice J M Didcott
The Hon Mr Justice M A Diemont
Adv L R Dison SC
Adv B Doctor
Dr J A v S D'Oliveira
Mr K J Douglas
Downes Sullivan & Clulow
Prof John Dugard
Mr Andrew Duncan
Prof J R du Plessis
Prof Lourens M du Plessis
Adv Stephan du Toit
Adv W R E Duminy
Mr David Dyzenhaus

Prof A B Edwards
The Hon Mr Justice J P G Eksteen
The Hon Mr Justice C F Eloff
Adv Hilda Ellison
Adv G Essey
Prof H J Erasmus
Adv D M Ettlinger

Adv I G Farlam SC
Mr M Favish
Feinsteins Incorporated
Mr P L Ferreira
Adv Melville H S Festenstein
Adv V G Fevrier
Mr C B H Fincham
Mr C F Forsyth
Adv Karin I Foulkes-Jones
Adv J G Foxcroft
Adv S Frank
The Hon Mr Justice B L S Franklin
Mr M G Fredman
Mr R J Friedland
Friedland Hart & Partners
Mr C Friedman
The Hon Mr Justice G Friedman

Adv P A L Gamble
Adv J J Gauntlett
Mr Carveth H Geach
Adv Basil Georgiou
Senator A Getz
Prof J T R Gibson
Mr G S Giles
Mr Henry C Ginsberg
Adv P Ginsburg
Adv L I Goldblatt
Adv E L Goldstein SC
The Hon Mr Justice R J Goldstone
Adv Gerald Gordon QC
Adv A M Gottlieb
Sir de Villiers Graaff
Mrs Zilla Graff
Mr Stanley Green
Mr H A Groenewaldt
Adv B Griesel

Prof H R Hahlo
Mr M H Hales
Hammicks, Sweet & Maxwell
Mr B B Hardman
Mr B G A Harris
Prof G F Hartford
Mr N R L Haysom
Mr Anselm Herrmann
The Hon Mr Justice V G Hiemstra
Dr F G Hill
Mr C J Hinrichsen

Adv P B Hodes SC
Mr L H Hodes
Mr G G Hoexter
Adv R P Hoffman
Mr S G Hoffman
Adv Gys Hofmeyr SC
Mr R T Hofmeyr
The Hon Mr Justice G N Holmes
Mr Michael Eric Hood
Adv Martin Horwitz SC
Prof W J Hosten
Mr J W Hubbart
Mr A Hyman

Adv I Isaacs QC
Mrs Lila E Isakow
Mrs Joyce Jackson
Prof Stanley Jackson
Adv M S Jacobs
Mr C A Jaffe
Jagger Library, University of Cape Town
The Hon Mr Justice Neville James
Mr T I Jika
Adv M M Joffe
Johannesburg Public Library
Mr David John
John & Kernick
Mr D E Jooste
The Hon Mr Justice C P Joubert
Prof D J Joubert
Mr David Judah
Director General: Justice

Prof G C Kachelhoffer
Prof Ellison Kahn
Mr Morris Kaplan
Mr Louis Kane-Berman
Mr M M Katz
Mr Adriaan Kennedy
Adv S W Kentridge SC
Mr W R Kerfoot
Prof A J Kerr
Adv E L King SC
Mrs J G Kinghorn
Adv T E Kleynhans
Dr P J Kloppers
Adv D B Knight SC
Mr R C Knight
Mr J E Knoll
Mr J V Knoll
Prof D S Koyana
The Hon Mr Justice G P C Kotzé
Mr James H Kotzé
Adv J C Kriegler SC
Mr Konrad Kritzinger
Mr J M Kron
The Hon Mr Justice M E Kumleben
Adv M D Kuper
Adv Ruth Kuper

Adv M B Labe SC
Mr Andrew Ladley
Adv P Lakier SC
Mr William Lane
Mr M P Larkin
Mr Robert J Lashansky
Mr P J Laubscher
Law Faculty, University of Cape Town
Law Faculty, University of Port Elizabeth
The Law Shop
Adv J V Lazarus SC
Legal Resources Centre Johannesburg
The Hon Mr Justice R N Leon
Mr Edwin M Letty
Adv G Leveson SC
Mr H R Levin
Mr Jack Lewsen
Prof Phyllis Lewsen
Mrs Carole H Lewis
Dr P R B Lewis
Mr D B Lewis
Mr O G Lewis
Adv E A Limberis
Adv D J Lombard SC
Mrs Cheryl Loots
Prof J G Lotz
Prof M M Loubser
Adv A W S Louw
Prof G F Lubbe
Adv J Lubbe
Miss Stephanie Luiz
Prof J R Lund

Mr Cameron Madikizela
Adv I Mahomed SC
Adv Clifford R Mailer
Adv I A Maisels QC
Mr K D H Maisels
Prof F R Malan
Mr Joseph H Malherbe
Adv J P Malherbe SC
Malherbe, Saayman & Vermaak
Adv H E Mall SC
Mr Peter J Mansell
Mr V G Mansell
W C M Maqutu & Co
Adv R M Marais SC
Adv G J Maree
The Hon Mr Justice C S Margo
Mr J F Massyn
Prof A S Mathews
Mr Neville Matterson
The Hon Mr Justice W S McEwan
Mr E S Mchunu
McKechnie, Hugo & Strampe
Prof J S McLennan
Adv Herbert McKenzie SC

Prof D J McQuoid-Mason
The Hon Mr Justice D A Melamet
Mr L S Melunsky
Adv A Mendelow QC
Mr Isaac Mendelow
N Mendelow & Co
Mr John J Mendelsohn
Mr Joel Mervis MPC
Adv D Meyerowitz SC
Mr J J Meyersohn
Michael Krawitz, Donenberg & Co
The Hon Mr Justice S Miller
Prof S M Miller
The Hon Mr Justice A J Milne
Prof J R L Milton
Mr Andrew Mitchell
Mobil Oil Southern Africa (Pty) Ltd
Prof J T Moelwyn-Hughes
Mr Johann D Möller
Mr Malcolm Moodie
Mr C E Mosdell
Prof D W Morkel
Mr Ian Morrison
Adv Anton W Mostert SC
Mr Frederick Mostert
Adv C J Mouton
Mr C J Mouton
K K Mthiyane & Co
Mr E Mureinik
Miss Christina Murray
Adv J F Myburgh
Mr J Myers
Adv S J Mynhardt

Prof F R N Nabarro
Mr J J N Nabarro
Nasboek Bpk
The Hon Mr Chief Justice C J M Nathan
Prof Carmen Nathan
Prof S J Naudé
The Hon Mr Justice H H Nestadt
Mr T M Newsome
The Hon Mr Justice H C Nicholas
The Hon Mr Justice P M Nienaber
Mr A R S Norval

Adv M W Odes SC
Mr M C O'Dowd
Prof N J J Olivier
Prof M J Oosthuizen
Mr H J J Orkin
Prof J M Otto

Mr Andrew Paizes
Pagden, Christian, Hanley & Parkin
Dr Pieter Pauw
Adv C J Pearson
Mr R H Peart
Mr Philip Pencharz
Mr Xola M Petse
Adv J D Pickering
Mr Jacques Pienaar
Mr V T Pienaar
Adv C Plewman SC
Mr D Pont
A S Powell & Kelly
The Hon Mr Justice H J Preiss
Pretoria Bar
Adv Errol Price
Mr B J Prinsloo
Prisman & Wilson
Mr J T Pretorius
Mr Neville J Pretorius
Mr Neville R Pudney

The Hon Mr Chief Justice P J Rabie
Mr W A Ramsbottom
Prof W A Ramsden QC
Prof B G Ranchod
Adv George Randell
Prof John Redgment
Rhodes University Library
Mr A J Richard
Adv F G Richings
Rink Estates
Mr R J Rohan-Irwin
Mr Denis J Rondi
Mr N J Roodt
Adv C Rosenthal SC
Mr A M Rosettenstein
Mr Hugo Rosettenstein
Adv D P J Rossouw
Mr M L Rostowsky
Mr Harold Rudolph
Rushmere Noach & Partners

Adv L J Saad
Mr J D K Saayman
Mr D H Sampson
Mr A J G M Sanders
Adv Stanley W Sapire
Mr W P N Sceales
Dr I Schäfer
Mr Arthur Schoeman
Mrs Else Schreiner
Prof G D L Schreiner
Mrs Pat Schreiner
Adv W H R Schreiner SC
Adv W P Schutz SC
Mr Michael Schneider
Prof K G J Schwietering
Prof J P F Sellschop
Adv R L Selvan SC
Prof G Seymour-Wood
Mr Louis Shakenovsky
Mr M L Shakinovsky
Adv J L Sher
Mr Morris Sher
Mr Paul M Shilubane
Mr T J Shilling
Adv S K M Sibanda
Adv Jonathan Silke
Adv J A Shortt-Smith
Mr Kenneth C Simon
Prof June Sinclair
Mr A St Q Skeen
Adv H Z Slomowitz SC
Sloot, Broido, Hesselson & Liknaitzky
Mr N L Smailes
Mr Alan Smiedt
Prof Catherine Smith
The Hon Mr Justice E A T Smith
Mr Raphael Smith
Col Steward Smith
Adv H Snitcher QC
The Hon Mr Justice R A Solomon
Mr M N Soondka
Adv B R Southwood
Adv B S Spilg
Mr P R Spiller
Dr E Spiro
Spoor & Fisher
The Hon Mr Justice H G Squires
Standard Bank Library
Mr K W Standenmacher
Mr G H Stein
Adv Jan F Steyn
The Hon J H Steyn
The Hon Mr Justice L C Steyn
The Hon Mr Justice M T Steyn
Prof S A Strauss
Dr N Stutterheim
Adv Roland Sutherland
Prof W G Sutton
Adv Arthur Suzman QC
Adv A J Swersky SC

Prof Louise A Tager
Adv Anver Omar Tayob
Mrs Jeanne McKie Thomson
Frank R Thorold (Pty) Ltd
Mr J K S Thorpe
Adv K S Tip
Prof Karl Tober
Mr Stanley Treisman
Mr I J Trengove
The Hon Mr Justice J J Trengove
Adv W H Trengove
Mr A P Trichardt
Mr A E G Trollip
Adv A T Trollip
The Hon Mr Justice W G Trollip
Mr T N Truran
Adv Michael Tselentis
Mr E S K Tucker
Mr Solly Tucker

Mr A Tugendhaft
Prof P D Tyson

University of Durban-Westville
Adv J Unterhalter SC

Prof Adrienne van Blerk
The Hon Miss Justice Leo van den Heever
The Hon Mr Justice H J O van Heerden
Van Heerden & Co
Prof L F van Huyssteen
Prof F F W van Oosten
Dr O T van Schalkwyk
Adv Rex van Schalkwyk
Mr R E van de Pol
Mr F J van Rensburg
Prof P van Warmelo
Mr N van Wezel
Dr D H van Zyl
Prof C G van der Merwe
Prof J D van der Vyver
Mnr André J van der Walt
The Hon Mr Justice P J van der Walt
Prof R verLoren van Themaat
Mr Louis Venter
Mr W M Venter
Mr Kenneth A Verhage
The Hon Mr Justice G Viljoen
The Hon Mr Justice W Vivier
Mr H V Vorster
Mr Henry Vorster
Prof M P Vorster

The Hon Mr Justice C J Waddington
Webber, Wentzel & Co
Adv R S Welsh QC
Adv E M Wentzel SC
Mr Nathan Werksman
Werksmans
The Hon Mr Justice and Mrs P J Wessels
Prof Roger Whiting
Prof Marinus Wiechers
Prof N J Wiechers
Mr D G Williams
Adv A B M Wilson SC
Mr D C S Wimble
Mr R A F Winchester
Adv Mannie Witz
Monique Woods
Adv P M Wulfsohn SC
Mr Basil Wunsh
Mr R E Worroll

Adv P Yutar SC

Prof D T Zeffertt
Prof R Zimmermann
Mr R H Zulman SC

PART ONE

Biographical

OLIVER DENEYS SCHREINER: A SOUTH AFRICAN[1]

ELLISON KAHN*

Youth (1890–1911)

It has been said of R A Butler that he was the greatest Prime Minister Britain did not have. So it may be said of Oliver Deneys Schreiner that he was the greatest Chief Justice South Africa did not have.

Some of us in the latter part of our allotted span look back on a person or a few people whose nobility of character vibrates in the memory. I am among those fortunate enough to be able to look back in this way on Oliver Deneys Schreiner; and I should like to

[1] Inevitably, this article will repeat some part of what I wrote in 'Oliver Deneys Schreiner—The Man and his Judicial World' (1980) 97 *SALJ* 566. Fortunately, Mr W H R Schreiner SC, the elder son of Schreiner, has been so kind as to place at my disposal additional documents. In my *SALJ* article (see at 567n5) I had access to the material Oliver Schreiner donated in 1974 to the University of the Witwatersrand, consisting of numerous letters, the diary he kept on his travels abroad on long leave in 1947 and 1952, and sundry other papers from 1947 to 1974, together with duplicate originals, carbon copies or corrected drafts of many letters written by him. The new material consists in the main of letters sent by him to his wife Edna, by his wife to him, and by relatives, friends and colleagues to him from the beginning of 1952 to his death. There is a dearth of copies or drafts of letters written by him. A good deal of correspondence appears to have been lost or destroyed; possibly it was torn up before Schreiner went on leave in 1952. But much other material was kept, including the diary he wrote from 2 August 1918 to 19 April 1919, which I call his war diary. The University papers I call the 'ODS papers Wits' and the family papers the 'ODS family papers'.

I have deliberately quoted extensively from the letters and diaries. As far as I know, this is the first time anyone has had access to this type of material relating to a member of the South African judiciary and his relationship with his colleagues and the Government.

I trust that I have been circumspect in my citation of expressions of sentiments by Oliver Schreiner and his wife Edna. In my view any embarrassment that might otherwise exist is more than offset by the value of showing an aspect of the 'human' side of their relationship and of Schreiner himself. The same problem confronts many biographers, and I decided to try to follow the courageous example of David Fraser in his *Alanbrooke* (1982) in his use of intimate letters and diaries of the protagonist of his book.

I have tried to give a three-dimensional portrait, bearing in mind what Dr Anthony Clare, of the Institute of Psychology, said in an article in *The Listener* (vol 108 no 2772 p 4 (5 August 1982)): 'Many public figures are never portrayed save one-dimensionally. The athlete, the artist, the judge and the actress are rarely discussed in any terms other than the particular profession or public ability which summarizes and labels them. Divorced from the impulses, motivations, values and emotions which fuel them, such individuals appear truncated and partial, half-human rather than superhuman, and seeming to inhabit a world which is not bound by remorseless demands of a more mundane order involving the often competing claims of career, family, home, marriage and other personal relationships.'

* BCom LLB (Witwatersrand) LLM LLD (Natal) Hon LLD (Cape Town), Advocate of the Supreme Court of South Africa, of the Middle Temple, Barrister, Professor of Law in the University of the Witwatersrand, Johannesburg.

paint a portrait of him, as it appeared to one who had a fair deal to do with him in the last three decades of his life of near ninety years. He died on 27 July 1980. His life is part of our history. As far as fairness to the living and near descendants of those who have departed allows, I shall try to tell all, as I know it. I bear in mind the words of Dr Samuel Johnson: 'If we owe regard to the memory of the dead, there is yet more respect to be paid to knowledge, to virtue and to truth.'[2]

Oliver Schreiner was born on 29 December 1890, the third of the surviving children of William Philip Schreiner and his wife Fanny.[3] William (Bill) was the eldest; Frances (Dot) came next; and the youngest was Ursula. With all three Oliver was on affectionate terms the whole of his life.

His father's parents were Gottlob Schreiner (1814–76), born in Germany and trained in England as a missionary, and Rebecca Schreiner (1818–1903), born Lyndall, daughter of a London Congregational minister. 'Lyndall' was a name the family was attached to. The heroine of the immortal novel *The Story of an African Farm*, by Oliver's aunt, Olive (1855–1920), is Lyndall. The house that WP and his family occupied in 1905 in Newlands opposite Kelvin Grove bore that name. It was the second Christian name of Oliver Schreiner's sister Frances. It is the third Christian name of his younger son, Deneys. It was the name given to Oliver's last house, 24 Sixth Avenue, Lower Houghton, Johannesburg. It was the given name of a daughter of Schreiner's sister Ursula and of a grandniece of his.

W P Schreiner (1857–1919), after a distinguished academic career at the South African College and in England, where he took a first in both parts of the Law Tripos at Cambridge and in the LLB of the University of London, had been at the Cape Bar since 1882. At the time of Oliver's birth WP's practice was firmly established. Three years later he became Attorney-General in Rhodes's ministry. The Jameson Raid at the close of 1895 led to his resignation and finally to his complete break with Rhodes. WP was to become Prime Minister of the Cape from October 1898 to June 1900. In 1899, after a visit to the Ciskei and Transkei, he had been transformed from a person with a belief that the Blacks are to be 'kept in their place' to a champion of the rights of persons of colour. For long he was Leader of the Cape Bar. From 11 November 1914 to his death on 28 June 1919 WP filled the important post of High Commissioner for the Union in London. If one word had to be chosen to epitomize the wealth of WP's many admirable qualities, it would be 'integrity'.

[2] *The Rambler* No 60.

[3] For further details of Schreiner's ancestry, see 'Father and Son: W P Schreiner and Oliver' 100 below.

Oliver Schreiner's mother was of a long line of distinguished Cape stock, this time on the Afrikaner side. She had been Fanny Reitz, second youngest child of F W Reitz senior, prominent agriculturist and politician, whose seventh child, bearing the same Christian names as his father, achieved fame as a judge, President of the Orange Free State, politician, and champion of the advance and development of the Afrikaans language.

WP and Fanny called their second son 'Oliver' after an elder brother of WP's, who had—like four other of his brothers and sisters—died in infancy; and 'Deneys' after the family of Fanny's mother, born Cornelia Magdalena Deneys.

Oliver considered himself to be a South African. Eric Walker's biography of his father, published in 1937, bears the apparently dull, yet truly inspiring, title *W. P. Schreiner: A South African*, and it is one that I should like to adopt for this biographical sketch of his son. In a letter written to T B Bowker MP on 23 November 1961, Schreiner said: 'Only one fourth of me is British, one fourth being German and one half Dutch, including Huguenot. Perhaps it is for this reason that I have no feeling of group loyalty towards any particular section of the South African nation.'

With his parents Oliver had the warmest of relations. Both he loved deeply. He had a very close bond with his father, whose uprightness, dedication to duty and lack of racialistic feeling he admired greatly. To the end of his life Oliver carried in his fob the gold hunter his father gave him when he went up to Cambridge. WP saw in Oliver's character and career the expression of all he held dear and all the hopes a father can dream of being realized in the life of a child. There were a number of traits common to the two of them; and they had a resemblance of facial feature, especially with the large, square forehead.

Oliver was a special favourite of his aunt Olive, whose only child had died the day after her birth, a tragedy from which Olive never fully recovered. Her ardent maternal instincts turned towards her nieces and nephews. As a young boy, Oliver was pro-Boer in the Anglo-Boer War, as she was, whereas WP, though he had sympathy for the Boer cause, believed that his duty compelled him to side with the British. Years later Oliver Schreiner wrote to Henry Fagan (1889–1963),[4] his former colleague on the Appellate Division: 'During the Anglo-Boer War I used to fight with fists in support of the Boer Republics on the school playground at Rondebosch.' That took courage.

Oliver had a deep regard for Olive, and they corresponded regularly. An entry in his war diary of 16 March 1919, written while he was with his parents in England, awaiting a ship back to

[4] On 14 February 1960. ODS papers Wits.

South Africa, reads: 'My Aunt Olive (usually Olivet or Vetski) was here—she comes every Sunday. A strange person this, with much, very much that is lovable, and prejudices. She takes a little knowing.' He defended her memory from detractors. In 1950 a writer who had published a work on Olive submitted to him for comment a play she had written that involved her. His reply,[5] pointing out inaccuracies, shows him in his occasional icy mood. In particular he objected to the suggestion that she was 'vain or vainglorious. . . . She seemed to me, like any really big person, incapable of attaching the slightest importance to being thought great.'

Oliver went initially to Rondebosch Boys' High School, but he completed his pre-university education at the South African College School (SACS). Both were and are today leading educational institutions. In 1874 SACS had become separate from the South African College, founded in 1829, and it had gradually taken over all secondary schooling from the parent body, which from 1900 confined itself to university teaching for the degrees of the University of the Cape of Good Hope, which had been created in 1874 as a degree-conferring body without a teaching function.[6] A fellow student was the prodigy, Jan H Hofmeyr (1894–1948), three and a half years younger than Oliver. The two were Victoria Scholars in 1905.[7] They matriculated at the same time. Hofmeyr came first in the school and third in the colony; he won the English prize, Schreiner coming second, and sixteenth in the matriculation in the colony.[8] Both proceeded to the South African College in Orange Street on the edge of the centre of Cape Town, where WP had gone too. Among their lecturers was the scholarly and beloved Professor William Ritchie (1854–1931), Professor of Classics from 1882 to 1903, and of Latin from 1903 to 1918 and thereafter in the University of Cape Town, which the South African College then became,[9] until 1929.[10] There is an interesting story told by his daughter Vera that reveals Schreiner's early outlook on racial prejudice. 'I got a letter from Vera Ritchie (now Mrs Forrest)', runs a letter to Schreiner from Albert Centlivres (1887–1966) in his retirement on 22 April 1959.[11] 'She says that her father would have been horrified to see the developments of modern times and she

[5] On 23 October 1950. ODS papers Wits.

[6] The University Incorporation Act 16 of 1873 (C). See, generally, W Ritchie *The History of the South African College, 1829–1918* (1918); Eric A Walker *The South African College and the University of Cape Town, 1829–1929* (1929); John Linnegar *SACS—150 Years. A History of the South African College Schools* (1979); Maurice Boucher *Spes in Arduis: A History of the University of South Africa* (1973).

[7] Linnegar op cit previous note at 216. Oliver's brother Bill was a scholar in 1900: ibid. A special examination was written for the scholarship.

[8] Alan Paton *Hofmeyr* (1964) 10.

[9] In terms of the University of Cape Town Act 14 of 1916.

[10] On Ritchie, see Boucher op cit note 6 at 57, 106–9, and *Dictionary of South African Biography (DSAB)* I 671.

[11] ODS family papers.

adds "It was in one of his classes, I believe, in the old 'SACS' that a chief's son who was always unobtrusive & studious happened to be late and slipped into a bench with two 'whites' who believed in apartheid & they ostentatiously moved out refusing to sit beside him. At once Oliver Schreiner came forward & sat with him. After class Father asked the two students to stop behind & told them plainly that the colour of the skin was not what counted in university students, & if they could not behave with ordinary courtesy in his classes he would dispense with their attendance."'

Among the students at the South African College taking the BA was an attractive and intelligent woman, Edna Lambert Fincham. Six months older than Oliver (she had been born on 8 July 1890), from 1820 Settler farming stock of the Eastern Cape, like Dot she had attended the well-known girls' school in Cape Town, Rustenburg School at Rondebosch, which she did not care for, and now was happy at the co-educational South African College. Both she and Oliver were on the Students' Representative Council. She obtained her BA Honours degree in 1909, and subsequently her MA in philosophy. Thereafter she taught at a number of schools, including the Good Hope Seminary at Sea Point, where she took classes in Latin and English, and Potchefstroom Boys' High School; ill health and home-sickness, however, caused her to spend much time at the family farm 'Hopewell', Imvani, near Butterworth.

Hofmeyr was a superior scholar to Schreiner, but then he had quite extraordinary intellectual gifts coupled with a daunting capacity for work; and he did not live the rounded life that Schreiner did, with full participation in social activities and in sport. Oliver played rugby at school and college, being captain of several junior teams. Hofmeyr tried to play cricket. Schreiner, wrote Paton in his *Hofmeyr*,[12] was one of the most popular and influential of the students. Hofmeyr was awarded the SACS Rhodes Scholarship for 1910, being then only 15 years old. Albert van de Sandt Centlivres, who was to become Schreiner's colleague on the highest court, had obtained it three years before; and it could have been Schreiner's, for he passed his examinations for the BA with Honours in 1910, being placed first in Classics, and in every way fulfilled the qualifications laid down in Cecil John Rhodes's will. Whether there was any contemplation of his applying for the scholarship is not known; Paton[13] makes out that after the scandal of the Jameson Raid there was a family understanding that no Schreiner would accept anything from such a tainted source. Very likely, however, there had been no intention on the part of WP or Oliver to look to Oxford. WP had gone to Cambridge, and in 1905 he and his son had paid a visit to it, where Oliver, to his father's disappointment, fell for the

[12] Op cit note 8 at 16, 20. [13] Op cit 16.

charms of Trinity College and decided against Downing College, of which WP had been a student. It is not as though the Rhodes Scholarship was something the two of them regarded as beyond the pale of discussion. In 1912, when Oliver was at Oxford, they had expressed to each other disappointment that the SACS Rhodes Scholarship for the next year had been awarded to Theo Haarhoff and not to Cecil Steyn. They had nothing against Haarhoff, but felt that Steyn had sacrificed his scholastic record for the sporting reputation of the school, the College and the province; he had played for the College's first rugby team when still a schoolboy, and when at College had been capped for Western Province, the champion team.[14] To them Steyn came closer to Rhodes's ideal.

At all events, Oliver sought and succeeded in winning the Jamison Scholarship[15] of £400 for oversea study for four years. J W Wessels (1862–1936), later Chief Justice, another South African College man, had won it in 1882. Armed with this sought-after award, in early June 1911 Oliver set sail for England with his father and his sister Ursula, who was to go to Newnham College at Cambridge. A trip in August to Norway by the three was an ever-remembered prelude to the beginning of term in October.

Cambridge (1911–14)

From the start at Trinity Schreiner worked very hard, determined to justify his father's financial support of him and to maintain the reputation his father had gained at the university. Constantly WP warned him not to overdo things.[16] On his father's advice, Schreiner decided ultimately not to go for the Whewell Scholarship in International Law, which the brilliant J E R (Etienne or Oefie) de Villiers (1875–1947) had won in 1898; a first in both parts of the Law Tripos was the crucial thing. And there were also the Bar examinations to keep in mind. WP much regretted his son's refusal to take up rowing, which he had found so thrilling and healthy a sport when he was at Downing thirty years before; and, for all his love of rugby, he was worried that Oliver had decided to play that game, which he considered to be dangerous. 'But you are a stubborn dog, too', he wrote affectionately on 15 October 1912. Oliver, sturdily built, indeed inclined, like his father, to stoutness (at the time a relation, John George Silke, an attorney practising at Benoni, addressed letters to him as 'Fatty'), became a member of the Trinity rugby fifteen.

[14] See Paton op cit 19.

[15] It had been created in 1873 in terms of a bequest by Mrs Sophia Jamison; it had nothing to do with Dr (later Sir) L S Jameson of the Raid.

[16] For the correspondence of WP to Oliver, see 'Father and Son: W P Schreiner and Oliver' 100 below.

Soon after his arrival at Cambridge, Oliver Schreiner resolved to become a total abstainer from intoxicating liquor. He once told me that he had seen a student at Cambridge hopelessly drunk, which distressed him, and decided that there was no purpose in drinking. In his war diary he wrote on 18 February 1919 that it was a 'very splendid' thing that the whole of North America was 'dry'; South Africa of all countries should abolish the sale and consumption of drink. Possibly the failure of Prohibition later gave him second thoughts. At no time, however, was he an avowed teetotaller in the sense of an advocate of abstinence and prohibition; he did not follow the example of his father's older brother Theo (1844–1920) and older sister Het (1850–1912), who were so fanatical in the cause as once to open the stopcocks of the vats of a viticulturist and wine producer they were visiting, resulting in enormous financial loss to him.

Aunt Olive, too, warned him to take care of his health. 'As to sports and exercise generally', she wrote on 21 February 1913[17] to him from Muizenberg in her execrable hand, 'not only do I believe in exercise for the young & strong, but I believe it should be regarded as a duty by all persons of whatever age or condition to take it daily, if possible; strength and activity are great ends in human life to be strived after. Horse riding, mountain climbing & rowing have been the three joys of my life. What I mean is that where sport or exercise of any kind cease as in the modern world to be undertaken purely for their own sake, . . . the danger does rise of forcing the body so far, you weaken instead of strengthening it. It isn't shortening life that matters a bit—a man may live more in twenty years than another in forty—what *does* matter is going on living where the power to work has gone from one. Death is nothing—to go on living with a broken wing you are always trying to raise for flight & can't—is everything.' She ended, as so often, with the words 'Smallest Aunt'.

Courtney Kenny (1847–1930), WP's teacher and mentor, was now Downing Professor of the Laws of England, having been given the chair on Maitland's death in 1907. He and his daughters were very kind to Oliver, and Ursula looked after him with tender care.

There were a number of South Africans studying law at Cambridge at the time, among them (at St John's) Norman Ellis Rosenberg, who became a leading silk at the Johannesburg Bar, and Peter Clouts, who had befriended Jan Hofmeyr at SACS and the South African College, and was to practise at the Cape Bar. Schreiner outshone them academically.

He sent letters, asking for advice on his syllabus and the future of Roman-Dutch law, to C G Maasdorp (1848–1926), Judge President of the Cape Provincial Division, and Sir James Rose Innes (1855–1942), judge of appeal. Maasdorp wrote on 3 April 1912:[18]

[17] ODS family papers. [18] ODS family papers.

'You need have no fear that Roman Dutch law will pass away in your time. . . . It will occupy the full attention of students for generations to come as the common law of this country.' Innes, replying to 'My dear Oliver', suggested in a letter of 17 April 1912[19] that he 'make a special feature of Roman law. Ground yourself thoroughly in that and your Dutch law will present few difficulties.' He went on: 'As to your second question, I do not know who your authority is, but I beg to differ from him. It would be a sad day for S. Africa if the common law of our country were changed in favour of English law, but that change is not likely to come in my time & in yours; nor in my judgment will it ever be effected. In special departments like Life Insurance & Bills of Exchange the tendency will of course be to assimilate our law to that of England or other modern countries, but the main principles of our Jurisprudence will I trust always remain what they are. . . .'

The advice of Innes on Roman law was followed. The copy of Rudolf Gneist's *Syntagma* in the possession of the family, which is entirely in Latin, containing parallel texts of the Institutes of Gaius and Justinian, is heavily annotated by Schreiner.

Work coupled with intellect had its reward. The *Cambridge University Reporter* of 11 June 1912, under the heading 'Intercollegiate Examination in Law. June, 1912', shows two names under Class I: in order of merit, 'Schreiner Trin.' and 'McNair Cai.'. McNair was William McNair, called Willie by Schreiner, a student of Gonville and Caius College.[20] Rosenberg was third in the list of those with seconds, and Clouts ninth. The same journal on 17 December 1912 set out the results in the 'Intercollegiate Examination in Law. December, 1912'. This time Schreiner stood alone under Class I (apparently McNair did not enter). Rosenberg was second among the second classes, and Clouts ninth again.

In the long vacation of 1912 Schreiner went back to Cape Town to stay with his proud parents, and to have a rest.

In March 1913 Schreiner was elected to a Senior Scholarship at Trinity. The Master of Trinity, H Montagu Butler, sent him this letter:[21]

[19] ODS family papers.

[20] McNair, two years younger than Schreiner, also served in the infantry throughout the Great War, and also became a captain. He was a judge of the Queen's Bench Division of the High Court of England and Wales from 1950 to 1966.

What was the 'Intercollegiate Examination in Law'? Mr W H R Schreiner SC kindly wrote for an explanation to Professor P W Duff, who was Regius Professor of Civil Law in the University of Cambridge from 1945 to 1968, and a fellow of Trinity College from 1925 and Vice-Master from 1960. His answer was 'a preliminary to the Tripos because the University did not provide it'. Presumably this means a precursor to the Tripos. It cannot mean a substitute for Part I of the Tripos, for that did exist.

[21] ODS family papers. Butler was the uncle of R A Butler's father, and Master of Trinity from 1886 to 1918. R A Butler's father—Sir Montague Butler—became Master of Pembroke College, and that is the college to which 'Rab' went.

'Dear Mr Schreiner,

'It was a great pleasure this morning to hear from our two skilled examiners their very favourable report on your work in Law.

'We had not a moment's hesitation in electing you to a Senior Scholarship.

'This must, I am sure, give great pleasure to your father and your sister as well as yourself. . . .

'Believe me most truly yours,

'H. Montagu Butler.'

(Butler was the Master when Bertrand Russell was an undergraduate at Trinity from 1890 to 1893. In his autobiography, published in three volumes in 1967–9,[22] Russell said that Butler 'came straight out of Thackeray's *Book of Snobs*',[23] and was unctuous and evil. The letter to Schreiner is only a pale reflection of Butler's 'epistolatory style' that Russell found exemplified in the letter he received in June 1893[24] congratulating him on being seventh wrangler.)

Kenny, naturally, was delighted. In offering his congratulations to WP he said: 'Not to speak of the present advantage of the society of the Scholars' table in that college—the intellectual élite of the undergraduate world—there is the lifelong advantage he will reap from the testimony which that position bears to his mental capacity.'[25] Henry A Hollond (1884–1974), a young Fellow of Trinity,[26] for whom Oliver had considerable regard, in conveying his congratulations in a letter of 15 March 1913 to Oliver, wrote: 'I think that you are the first member of the College who has ever been elected to a scholarship in Law.'[27]

From Hopewell came a letter from Edna Fincham,[28] with whom he had been corresponding, who had been teasing him about his seriousness and sage advice, and dwelling, in a striking way, on the conditions of the Coloureds, the literary gifts of George Gissing and other novelists, and Afrikaner–British attitudes: 'It is splendid & you have the sincere congratulations of an aforetime classmate, who once in your company plodded dazedly through the labyrinthine intricacies of Thucydides. . . .'

More triumphs were to come. In June 1913 Schreiner obtained the top first in Part I of the Law Tripos, and was awarded the George Long Prize in Roman Law and Jurisprudence.[29] From the Master of Trinity came an epistle more in his customary style:[30]

[22] Schreiner read it, I like to think at my suggestion. He wrote to a friend on 25 June 1971 that he had found it very interesting. 'A remarkable man if ever there was one.' What Schreiner thought of Russell's attitude to adultery can well be imagined.

[23] *The Autobiography of Bertrand Russell 1872–1914* (being vol I) (1967) 66–7.

[24] Ibid. [25] Letter of 2 April 1913. ODS family papers.

[26] Appointed Reader in English Law in 1919, and Rouse Ball Professor of English Law in 1943.

[27] ODS family papers. [28] Of 1 April 1913. ODS family papers.

[29] Schreiner repeated the performance of J W Wessels thirty years earlier.

[30] ODS family papers. All the further letters in this part of my paper are from the same source.

Regiment and South Wales Borderers. He saw service in France with his regiment, becoming a captain. Bored, awaiting action, he enrolled for a course of lessons in drawing with a firm in England. He had for long dabbled in art. On 2 April 1912 WP had written to Oliver that Dr Mellé of Robertson had given him Oliver's 'old Caesar, illuminated seven years ago with your quaint conceits of men & things'. The drawings he did in France, Schreiner used to say, never led to a complimentary reply, though the few that have survived show some ability; but he continued his art in desultory fashion down the years, and the record of one of his protracted trials shows in the margins sketches of wonderfully strange animals.

In June 1916 the degree of Bachelor of Arts was conferred by proxy on Schreiner under special regulations applicable to men on military service. Thus Part II of the Law Tripos was never written by him.[32]

The Battle of the Somme commenced on 1 July 1916, and Schreiner's regiment took part in the dreadful series of engagements that followed. Schreiner was wounded in the right arm at Trônes Wood. While he was recuperating in hospital in England, he received the news on 10 October that he had been elected to a fellowship at Trinity in recognition of his outstanding intellectual ability. W P Schreiner received a letter on 24 October from Daniele Spring-Rice:[33] 'Dear High Commissioner, & Lord High everything else. How pleasant to have so distinguished a son! I never suspected Trinity of being so intelligent.' Fifteen days later Oliver was awarded the Military Cross. Those were two shafts of light in the gloom.

After Schreiner had recuperated he left England to rejoin his regiment, which was stationed in Mesopotamia (Iraq). He set sail on a Friday the 13th; it was the worst week of the war for the sinking of Allied ships by German submarines; his ship was torpedoed, but fortunately a destroyer close by rescued Schreiner. Thereafter he saw action in the Near East. In his war diary he wrote that while he was no fire eater, he was pleased he had not missed his share.[34] As throughout his army career, he was always in the attacking party and never involved in the difficult operation of a counter-attack. In mid-1918 he sailed home to Cape Town on furlough. He went to see Edna Fincham, who had been in correspondence with him, and at Hopewell they became engaged. Then on 3 August he boarded ship to return to his regiment. He decided to keep a diary for the first time, which he wrote up in pencil day

[32] *The Times* 10 October 1916.

[33] I am beat as to who she was; no reference book available to me gives me a clue. Probably she was related to Sir Cecil Spring-Rice, Ambassador to the United States. Certainly she was not his wife or daughter.

[34] 22 August 1918.

W P Schreiner, father of Oliver

Fanny Schreiner, mother of Oliver

W P Schreiner and his wife Fanny

W P Schreiner, High Commissioner, with Otto Beit (*left*), taken at the opening of the workshops for South African wounded servicemen at Richmond, England, on 30 September 1917

W P Schreiner (*left*) with his son Bill (*seated*) early this century

Oliver, his sister Ursula (Kay) and W P Schreiner on the *Edinburgh Castle* June 1911 *en route* to England

by day. It is an interesting document, revealing a good deal of Schreiner's character and outlook at a relatively young age. The diary was composed for his fiancée, as Sir Alan Brooke's diary in World War II was composed for his wife, and was addressed to her. Not all the contents could have reached Edna in the form of letters. The diary, which carries on until Oliver's return to Cape Town on 19 April 1919, merits some attention. As with his writings generally, it is shot with humour, irony and wit; even in the most serious contemplation of events past, current or expected his sense of fun tended to come through. Constantly he wryly confessed his own shortcomings, in manifestly hyperbolic terms—'a very groovey [*sic*] person', who feels happiest when moving stupidly in an uneventful routine, and who should have been a bank clerk'. (17 November 1918; 1 April 1919.) It contains much of Oliver's love for Edna, very well put. There is also a good deal on what he read; for there was time for reading, as he was not involved in any further engagements in Mesopotamia, and all his regiment did during the two and a half months that he was with it until the end of the war was to pursue—in vain—fleeing and dispirited Turks; and months passed from the armistice until he was demobilized. The books ranged widely—Carlyle's *Sartor Resartus*; Charlotte Brontë's *Villette*; Gilbert Murray's recently published *Faith, War, and Policy*; Tolstoy's *Resurrection*; *War According to Clausewitz*; some of E V Lucas's essays; George Gissing's *Born in Exile* (wearisome: 'He is a snob at heart, I feel sure': 30 October 1918); *Ons Land*; the *Manchester Guardian* ('a healthy antidote to the prevailing Toryism of the army officers': 20 September 1918); Dickens's *Tale of Two Cities*; Tennyson's *The Princess* (which may have prompted Schreiner to try his hand at writing poetry: the two sonnets in the diary are of some literary merit); O Henry's short stories; J B Bury's *History of Free Thought* (which upset Schreiner by its account of the prosecution of Galileo and others for daring to use their reason); William James's *Pragmatism*; F S Oliver's *Alexander Hamilton* (which he found very fine, though some critics have thought it partisan); Herbert Spencer's *Education* (with which, for all the flaws he could see in it, he was in general sympathy); and much else of scholarly or literary standing.

In late February Schreiner read Bertrand Russell's *Principles of Social Reconstruction*, which had been published in 1915. This work, which had a considerable popular appeal, urged reform through the liberation of the creative impulses in man—education, marriage and religion. Russell had been a pacifist during the war, and had gone to prison in May 1918 for publishing an article condemning the rejection of the German peace offer and the continuation of the war, and for saying that if it continued the American army would intimidate English strikers. In 1916 Russell had been fined £100 for writing an anti-conscription leaflet, and as a consequence the College Council of Trinity had resolved to deprive him of his lectureship. On 1 March 1919 Schreiner wrote in his diary: 'Any qualifications I have in my impertinence introduced into my approval of it I withdraw penitently. It is a very fine book and I am more than ever ashamed of my College for persecuting the wise and big hearted author. Yet I *will* believe we were right in going to war and sticking it out.'

Return and Qualification for the Bar (1919–20)

It was not until early March that Schreiner managed to get back to England—on a boat with 160 nurses on board, 'so it won't do to get ill'. (21 February 1919.) The wait had made him desperate, so much so that, quite out of character, he was prepared to tell a lie: he would not mention repatriation until he was demobilized, as the regulations stated that, pending decision on a claim for repatriation, a member of the services had to stay with his unit; he was even prepared to deny that South Africa was his country. (19 February 1919.) All went well, however, and he was aboard the *Llanstephan Castle* when it set sail from Cape Town on 28 March 1919. He was never to forget his old regiment. Every year or so he and his signals NCO, Alan Young, wrote to each other, and they met whenever Schreiner was in England. As late as 1974 Young was still addressing his letters to 'Capt. O. D. Schreiner'. Then he changed to 'Mr Justice O. D. Schreiner'. This exchange of letters, which ended only with Young's death early in 1980, testified to Schreiner's innate courtesy and his interest in the well-being of people, whatever their stations in life. He had a phenomenal memory of individuals and the course of their lives.

On 17 March Schreiner had paid a visit to Alfred Zimmern (1879–1957)[35] at the Foreign Office—'that dear chap whose translation of Pericles you have. . . . We had a fine talk, at least I loved it, whether he was bored or not.' *En route* to Cape Town he read Zimmern's *Nationality and Government.* 'It is extremely interesting and original. I should like to present a copy to each Nationalist member of our house. I wonder if you will love Zim as I do; a little

[35] Sir Alfred Eckhard Zimmern was born in Surbiton of a Jewish family of liberal outlook that had migrated to England from Germany after the 1848 revolution. He went to Winchester and New College, Oxford, where, after obtaining a first in Greats, he became a lecturer and fellow. His book *The Greek Commonwealth* (1911) gave him an international reputation. The Great War changed his career. He joined the political intelligence department of the Foreign Office. From 1919 to 1921 he was Wilson Professor of International Politics at the University College of Aberystwyth. After a sojourn at Geneva, he became the first Montague Burton Professor of International Relations at Oxford in 1930, which position he held until 1944. He was knighted in 1936. During World War II he again served in the Foreign Office. Lord Salter (*Dictionary of National Biography 1951–1960* 1096) describes him as unimpressive in physical appearance but making a deep impression by his vitality, lucidity and sincerity.

fat, partly-German, Jew, with eyes that beam on you, all kindness. I don't think I ever made friends with any man so quickly, and tho' there's more in his little finger than in the whole of me he never makes me feel a worm. In his book he says he read Mazzini's essays when he was a boy. Lucky Zim.' (31 March 1919.)

It was not that Schreiner was at all jingoistic. Having heard that a passport had been refused to De Wet to attend the Peace Conference, he wrote that 'passport refusing is cowardly, like shouting down an antagonistic speaker'. (2 February 1919.) Like Botha, Smuts and many others, he hoped that Germany would not be bled white, for that would produce 'undying resentment'. (3 December 1918.)

Schreiner's views on religion were by then settled, and they were never to soften—indeed, perhaps they hardened somewhat towards the end of his life. They were like those of his father. 'At the back of my mind I have the feeling that only by believing some things that we cannot know . . . can we be our best. But when it comes to believing any of the ordinary creeds one is offered—I can't manage it. . . .' (3 December 1918.) 'How far is one justified in trying to refute a genuine believer in Christ?'—with the implicit answer: not at all. (17 January 1919.) '. . . [T]hough I cannot believe what Christians believe, I think we are in danger of losing the advantage that the story of Jesus may have for us and the moral strength derived from a faith in his perfection.' (8 February 1919.) After reading Oliver Lodge's *Substance of Faith* he remained quite unconvinced that science and Christianity are reconcilable. (5 March 1919.) Church services he attended when in the army for reasons of discipline only; and the church parade on 10 November 1919, on the eve of the anticipated armistice, nauseated him: he had looked for an impressive occasion with a sermon to 'remind one for what one took up arms, to emphasise the ideals that must not be obscured in the time of settlement, possibly to confirm a belief in God's care for humanity in this great test'. Instead—'the sickliest note of thanksgiving that the damned thing was over. . . . God be praised who has confounded our enemies!'

In his diary Schreiner stated that he had for long been in favour of co-education. (6 February 1919.) The complete absence of any feelings of racialism or class distinction is evidenced in two entries in the war diary. Just before he had left Iraq he had spoken often to an Indian officer in the mess whom the White officers were not speaking to; in fact he was afraid that the officer would see that he was making a point of speaking to him, one of the first to receive a commission in the combatant units as opposed to the medical service—'the thin end of the wedge, a wedge, I think, of gold'. (9 December 1918.) The second entry was on 30 March 1919, just two days after the ship had left port. There is a discussion of the difficulty of being both rich and good; and the unfortunate effect of wealth 'on the impecunious ministers to its comfort. Now the waiter at our table, or steward, to give him his title, might from one point of view be regarded as perfect of his kind. But often I want to hit him on the back and shout, "Remember you're a man, with a soul. For God's sake don't cringe like a dog. Damn it! We're all servants of our fellows and there's nothing nobler about collecting fees or selling wool than about providing others with food. But the lawyer and the farmer don't fawn on their customers. Why should you?" Edna, dearest, I hate politeness, except between equals.' Schreiner wrote in his war diary of loneliness—'surely the worst fate that can befall a man. Hardly can it be justifiable to put a poor scoundrel of a criminal into solitary confinement, except for a very short period.' (2 March 1919.) On the very day of the armistice (though that was not then known for certain—the official confirmation came only a couple of days later) he was trying soldiers for minor offences and disliked it immensely: 'I'm not cut out for being a magistrate.' This proved to be wrong.

On board was Sir David de Villiers Graaff MP (1859–1931),[36] who had kept the position of High Commissioner in London warm for WP to accept soon after the outbreak of the war, and who had been in the Union Cabinet until 1916. Then 58, he was thirty years older than his wife, who was with him—a contrast that amused Schreiner. Despite Graaff's enormous wealth, Schreiner refused to play bridge with him until he learned that Graaff played for love: 'for all Sir David's millions they could not stand the drain if they played for high stakes. . . . I think I could make more at cards than at the Bar. I think the devil loves me; but so long as someone else does too, I'll try and keep the old fellow at bay.' (29 March 1919.)

On 19 April 1919 the *Llanstephan Castle* docked at Cape Town. Edna was there. She and Oliver were married at Hopewell on 6 May 1919.

To practise at the South African Bar, Schreiner, as the law stood in 1919, had still to qualify as a barrister in England; and he considered that he ought to get some practical experience in the workings of the law. So it was that he and Edna soon went to England. On the water they got the sad news from the captain of the ship of the death of WP in England on 28 June; it was a great shock.[37]

In England, ex-servicemen were given special concessions and short courses. On occasion Schreiner, with a wisp of a smile, used to say that he had not completed the whole of a law examination in his life, and had attended only one lecture on Roman-Dutch law.

[36] Father of Sir de Villiers Graaff, prominent politician of later times.

[37] See Schreiner's letter of 27 August 1942, reproduced in 'Father and Son: W P Schreiner and Oliver' 100 below at 124.

He eat his dinners as a student of the Inner Temple, where he won the Yerburgh-Anderson Scholarship. Within a few months he had qualified for admission to the English Bar. Already he felt he ought to read in chambers; he had written to Sir John Simon (1873–1954), who some years earlier had been Attorney-General and then, up to 1915, Home Secretary, and had known WP, to ask him if he could arrange a pupillage for him. The result was that Schreiner spent six months reading in chambers with Wilfrid Greene (1883–1952), who later graced the Bench as Lord Greene MR, and thereafter six months with Geoffrey Lawrence (1880–1971), later Lawrence LJ, and finally Lord Oaksey. While he was with Lawrence he worked with his pupil-master when he acted as a junior in a complicated appeal to the Privy Council. On 23 July 1947, when Schreiner was abroad on long leave and attended the dinner at Lincoln's Inn at the first Grand Night since World War II began, he met Simon again. The entry in his diary reads:[38] 'I introduced myself to Simon (who had recently been Lord Chancellor); after twenty-seven years I don't suppose he knew me from a packet of Lux, but he didn't show it.' He also met Greene and Oaksey again.

While Oliver and Edna were in England, their first child was born on 15 February 1920. They gave her the names Jean Frances Fincham. Olive Schreiner, then in England, was very fond of Edna;[39] Oliver she adored; and she wrote pathetically to him on 22 January 1920, in anticipation of the birth of his child: 'When you get old, you are not as utterly alone in the world as a childless woman.'[40]

The Johannesburg Bar (1920–37)

Schreiner decided to practise at the Johannesburg Bar, where the prospects of a young advocate with his background seemed brightest. In October 1920 he was admitted as an advocate of the Transvaal Provincial Division. He took chambers in 13 Sauers Buildings in Johannesburg, where the Bar was then housed. On 27 October he opened his fee book with two briefs to draw declarations, from a leading firm of attorneys, Webber, Wentzel, Solomon & Friel, at three guineas each; and a brief from another prominent firm, Findlay & Niemeyer, a consultation for a trial (another three guineas), which led to a big fee on trial on the 29th of 70 guineas, followed by refreshers on 2 and 3 February of 20 guineas each. The value of money in those days, according to the

[38] ODS papers Wits.

[39] Olive Schreiner papers South African Library Cape Town (SAL). Letter to Ruth Alexander, then married to Morris Alexander MP, of 7 September 1919; letter to Jessie, Lady Rose Innes, 7 January 1920.

[40] Olive Schreiner papers SAL. Olive Schreiner died at Wynberg in the Cape on 11 December that year.

consumer price index, was about seven times its present value, and the incidence of income tax was lower. But the statement that briefs amounting to a considerable sum awaited him on being called[41] is an exaggeration. A trial a month, most at a far smaller fee, was standard in Schreiner's first year; the work otherwise was the usual small stuff that an inexperienced junior with support from a range of attorneys could expect. The end of his first year of practice saw a gross income of £714; as expenses in those days were very low, this was a most satisfactory start. And he had been given briefs by some of the largest firms—apart from the two mentioned, Van Hulsteyn & Ford, Bell & Dewar, Hayman & Godfrey, and Hutchinson, Bowen & Sessel among others. All told, in his first year twenty firms had supported him. The future looked bright.

In his second year Schreiner earned £1 310; it rose, with occasional dips, to £1 937 in his sixth year and £3 620 in his thirteenth year (27 October 1932 to 26 October 1933, the last full period covered by his surviving fee books), when he was receiving briefs from some forty firms of attorneys.[42] In that year he received twenty-three guineas for drafting the Bill that became the Rand Water Board Statutes 1903–1932 Amendment (Private) Act 1933,[43] and one hundred guineas for a general retainer by Anglo American.

While his practice was consolidating, Schreiner lectured to the law classes of the University College, Johannesburg, and then the University of the Witwatersrand, Johannesburg, which the College had become in 1922. The classes were held in part-time hours, at first in the 'Tin Temple' in town, near Park Station. Initially three others lectured the students: J Colin (later Professor) Murray, a well-known attorney, and two colleagues at the local Bar, N E Coaker (later a silk) and W H (later Mr Justice) Ramsbottom, a close friend of Schreiner's. The remuneration was £60 a year for a lecture a week for about thirty weeks. In 1925, the records of the University show, Schreiner lectured in the Law of Evidence, Roman Law I and II, and Criminal Law, delivering four or five lectures a week. In 1926 he gave the courses in Procedure and Evidence and in Sale; in 1927 the course in Procedure and Evidence; and in 1928 the course in the Law of Evidence. By now Robin McKerron (1900–1973) had arrived as the first professor of law at the University and the only full-time member of the staff of the Department of Law. The following year the extent of Schreiner's practice demanded that he cease to lecture; he left with the warm appreciation of the Board of the Faculty of Law, of which he continued to be a member until his death; his service of fifty-eight years will never be equalled.

[41] 'C.R.P.' 'Hon. Mr. Justice O. D. Schreiner' (1938) 55 *SALJ* 1.

[42] His carefully written-up fee books show the following gross income for the first thirteen years in pounds: 714, 1 310, 1 510, 1 368, 1 247, 1 937, 2 568, 3 856, 3 115, 3 288, 2 996, 3 873, 3 620.

[43] Act 21 of 1933.

Mr Arthur Suzman QC, the doyen of the Johannesburg Bar, in this collection of essays recollects Schreiner as an outstanding teacher, most lucid in exposition.[44] He was no orator, however, and disliked making public speeches.

Schreiner participated fully in the spirit of camaraderie and helpfulness at the Bar. Mr Twemlow said in *Our Mutual Friend* of the House of Commons that it was 'the best club in London'; so one might say of the local Bar that it is the best club in Johannesburg. As he grew more experienced and as his practice became heavier, Schreiner was asked ever more for guidance by younger colleagues; and, as Mr I A Maisels QC said in his tribute in court to the memory of Schreiner on his death, he was always ready to help a junior over difficult points. But more: he was ready to assist financially. One young advocate, for instance, who was struggling to get recognition, was coming to the end of the road. Schreiner, then by no means wealthy, made him a loan; unfortunately, it only postponed his colleague's departure from the Bar.

His practice was almost entirely civil, very mixed, with a good deal of opinion work, and not many protracted trials. The 'cab rank' attitude at the Bar caused Schreiner to have to participate in some matters unpleasant to him. He disliked dirty language intensely, and never used it, an attitude that was always respected. But he accepted a brief in an action for damages for *injuria* in which the foulest of epithets were the basis of the complaint; and he forced himself to refer to them.

What assisted Schreiner greatly in his practice was what Mr Justice H C Nicholas once referred to as 'a phenomenal knowledge of case law, and an ability, which was legendary, to rise from his desk during a consultation, take down a law report, and open it at a case' in point.[45] (This attribute, it seems to me, is precisely the one R B Haldane (later Lord Haldane LC) had, which he alludes to in his fine autobiography published in 1929.)

The law reports are not peppered with cases in which Schreiner appeared.[46] Possibly this is because it was not long after he took silk in September 1935 that he accepted an appointment as acting judge after he had been urged to do so by Philip Millin, his senior, to whose claims he wished to defer—an episode that will be discussed later. So on 15 February 1937 Schreiner AJ sat until 1 August that year, when he was given a permanent appointment. He was 46; though he was the youngest member of the judiciary at the time, he was not by any means the youngest ever to be appointed to it. But he could look back with satisfaction to the success he had attained,

[44] 'Oliver Schreiner: Some Reminiscences and an Appreciation' 131 below.

[45] In his speech at the opening of the Oliver Schreiner Law Library of the University of the Witwatersrand, Johannesburg on 25 August 1976. See (1980) 97 *SALJ* 577.

[46] There are a few important cases, such as *Wynn NO and Westminster Bank Ltd NO* v *Oppenheimer* 1937 TPD 91.

despite five lost years through the Great War. After all, even some very good men had not made a go of it at the Bar. Schreiner was under no illusions as to the capacity of attorneys to discern talent among the young. 'Attorneys are often slow to see who are the best men', he was to say in a letter to his wife years later.[47] 'I've seen lots of cases of their mistaken assessments both favourable and unfavourable.' And he concurred in what Albert Centlivres wrote to him on 15 October 1953[48] on the death of A J ('Sport') Pienaar KC (1884–1953), the Parliamentary Draftsman, who in 1951[49] had given a closely reasoned opinion that the legislature was bound by the entrenched sections of the South Africa Act, an opinion which the Government, to its cost, had disregarded: 'I have always thought that attorneys are very undiscerning. In 1923 Sir Henry Juta in giving the judgment of the Court of Appeal paid a very warm tribute to Sport's marked ability and candour in arguing a case and Sir James Rose-Innes [*sic*] repeated the compliment in another case a year later. One would have thought that these high encomiums would have caught the eye of the attorneys but I don't suppose that they troubled to read the Appeal Court reports. Sport's rugged independence in the performance of his duties as Parliamentary draftsman should be an inspiration to his successors in office.'

There was, of course, quite a drop in Schreiner's income through his accepting a position on the Bench. The salary of a puisne judge was £2 750.[50] Schreiner never thought there was in any manner a duty on members of the Bar to join the judiciary when asked to do so unless there was a very good reason for refusal, such as conscientious objections to imposing the death sentence; yet he believed that only senior members of the practising Bar should be selected for the Bench. In discussing the matter with him—for I was puzzled by the apparent inconsistency in his attitude—I could get no satisfaction. Once Schreiner had made up his mind, he was like Sigmund Freud, whose personality, as depicted in Ernest Jones's biography,[51] in many respects corresponded to Schreiner's: he would listen politely, even make some helpful comments, but remain immovable.[52]

Oliver's family had grown in size. On 21 March 1922 his son William (Bill) was born, and on 9 December 1923 his younger son Deneys (whose first name George, after that of his mother's father, is not used). But tragedy had hit Schreiner and his wife. At the age of 11 Jean suddenly began to have epileptic fits; there was no reason

[47] On 16 September 1953. ODS family papers. [48] ODS family papers.

[49] Tabled on 18 May 1951. See *The Star* 19 May 1951.

[50] Judges' Salaries (Amendment) Act 30 of 1934; the previous salary (unchanged from 1912 (Judges' Salaries and Pensions Act 16 of 1912)) was £2 250.

[51] *The Life and Work of Sigmund Freud* (1953–7; abridged edition 1961).

[52] Op cit abridged edition (Pelican Books 1964 reprint) 476.

to expect them, unless it was that she had tended when very young to have convulsions on running a high temperature. At that time the drugs available to control epilepsy were not very efficacious. Edna Schreiner sought medical advice from all quarters, in South Africa and abroad; but little could be done in the early days. It was a harrowing time until the improvement in methods of control years later. Jean was very clever. She was sent to Parktown Girls' High School, the principal of which was a close friend, Miss Kathleen Ramsbottom, one of the three sisters of Hal Ramsbottom who became headmistresses of leading schools. With determination and help from Miss Ramsbottom and others, Jean obtained a first-class pass in the matriculation examination in 1937, and went to the University of the Witwatersrand, where she read successfully for the degree of BA. But unfortunately, though she subsequently qualified as a librarian, she was never able to hold down a job for long; the drugs took a heavy toll. In the latter part of her life she stayed at home; and her condition appeared to deteriorate. The burden initially fell largely on Edna; after her death it fell entirely on Oliver. They shouldered it magnificently.

While he was at the Bar Schreiner worked very hard, but he was not a slave to work as his father had been. He lived a balanced life, seeing a good deal of his family, reading widely and well, and taking a good deal of exercise—for some years he used to walk from his home in Rhodes Avenue in Parktown West, Johannesburg, to chambers in the morning, a distance of about three miles. Always he was keen on participating in sport. For golf he showed considerable aptitude, being a six-handicap player for many years. When the family home was in Observatory, in the eastern suburbs of Johannesburg, at times he would walk, golf-bag on his back, across town to the Country Club in the west, play eighteen holes, and walk back with his golf-bag, covering all told about fifteen miles on foot. On three occasions he won the annual competition for the Johannesburg Bar Golf Cup, played over 36 holes in one day. Perhaps that is not remarkable; the heavy, deliberate-moving Walter Pollak (1903–1971) also won it several times, hitting the ball only a short distance but always down the middle of the fairway; he and Schreiner benefited by not consuming hard liquor at lunch-time.

The Schreiners lived quite well, despite the virtual absence of any taste for luxuries. His sons went to St John's College, a leading private school in Johannesburg, the University of the Witwatersrand and, after the Second World War, in which they served in the armed forces, to Trinity College, Cambridge. It appears that Schreiner believed, as Freud did, that there were three things one should never economize on: health, education and travel.[53] The

[53] Op cit 456.

family went on regular holidays, quite often to the Kruger National Park, for Schreiner took pleasure in wild life. True, in the early thirties their home had been moved to 24 Sixth Avenue, Lower Houghton, in what was becoming a very select suburb to the north, yet close to town. To the acre plot on which the house stood was soon added another acre. The house, spacious as it was, cost only £4 500; and Schreiner bought the plot on the corner of Fourth Avenue for £300. The owner of the empty plot next to Schreiner's house was very happy to make an exchange. This was Schreiner's residence for the rest of his life. The downstairs veranda—a kind of palm court—was closed in to make an enormous study when Schreiner was appointed to the Bench and moved his law library to his home. The additional acre, which Edna used to cultivate as a garden while her health permitted, was sold in 1956 for over £5 000, a price that gave the Schreiners considerable satisfaction.

The one real extravagance was the purchase during middle age—but not in later life—of fairly expensive motor cars, of which the best loved was a Packard, known affectionately as 'Packie'. Schreiner was inclined to drive rather fast, though in his letters he occasionally expressed amazement at the speed at which some of his friends drove. It may be that in England people tend to drive more slowly; at all events, when Sir Alfred Denning (subsequently Lord Denning) (1899–) visited my university in 1954, he returned from a trip to the Kruger National Park[54] in a pensive mood, saying quietly to me that until his children were qualified in their careers he would prefer not to be driven by Oliver Schreiner again. Up to 4 March 1956 Schreiner was fined for exceeding speed limits three times; on that day he wrote to his wife 'it is sweet of you to speak of my second conviction for speeding but actually it is my third—one opposite the Central Prison, Pretoria (£5), one just past Swartkops Aerodrome (£2) and now this one. Not bad though over a period of over 30 years' driving.' The Pretoria conviction was probably the one recounted to me over forty years ago by a former clerk of his. Schreiner was driving from Johannesburg to the Palace of Justice in Pretoria. The car was stopped by a traffic officer, who wrote down the particulars in his 'spot fine' book, and then asked the driver his name. The clerk interrupted, saying, 'Mr Justice Schreiner'; the traffic officer was about to tear up the 'ticket' when Schreiner said 'Don't you do that'. He would never pull rank; when he wrote to an official he did not use official or headed paper, but wrote on an ordinary lined pad and signed himself 'O D Schreiner'. The one thing he did object to was the distance from the built-up section to the uninhabited borders of some villages; that the whole of it should be subject to a low speed limit he felt was misleading and unfair.

[54] See Lord Denning 'Reminiscences of a Visit to South Africa' 127 below at 128 and H R Hahlo 'In Memory of Oliver Schreiner' 130 below.

Unlike his father, Schreiner had no interest in participating in active politics, the art of the possible, which, because of the time it took up and, for one not at the Cape Bar, the distance between Parliament and the place of one's practice, was a kiss of death in his time (as it is today) to an advocate wishing to advance in his profession in South Africa. Jan Hofmeyr, his old companion in SACS and South African College days, approached him in the late nineteen-twenties to enter politics, but he declined. In any event, even if he had been returned to Parliament, he would not have lasted long there, for his absolute honesty, his complete lack of racism or racialism, and his old Cape liberal belief in integration and equal rights for all civilized men and women would rapidly have put an end to his career in politics. Political strategy and the making of concessions would have been quite unacceptable to him. When, of all people, the liberal and self-righteous Jan Hofmeyr in 1929 in a contest for a seat in the House of Assembly tried to get an advantage from the colour prejudices of voters by making capital out of a statement by the Minister of Labour that Indians would be admitted to the Typographical Union, Schreiner was upset. He wrote to Hofmeyr: 'I feel that the platform is not the place for compromise; it is the place for saying what one really feels and what one hopes to persuade other people to feel.'[55]

Fortunately, this did not spell a break in his friendship with Jan Hofmeyr, who was a frequent visitor to 'Lyndall', arriving, clad in dustcoat, in his own motor car; being about private affairs, he would not use the ministerial car or chauffeur.

In 1930 in the book *Coming of Age: Studies in South African Citizenship and Politics*, produced by a group of South Africans to mark the forthcoming twenty-first anniversary of unification, Schreiner published an essay on 'South Africa and the Commonwealth'. He deprecated the type of imperialism redolent of Anglo-Boer War days, and approved the absence of any racial basis in the structure of the Commonwealth. Perhaps, he wrote, looking forward, as almost always he did, in hope, one day it would be replaced by a wider association of nations freely co-operating. Another essay, written with Hal Ramsbottom (1894–1960), on 'The Franchise', spelt out the association of the depressed economic condition of those who were not White with their lack of voting power: an association then not so widely appreciated as today. The authors dismissed the ideals of territorial segregation and communal representation in Parliament; they pleaded for a common society and colour-blind electoral roll, though they were prepared, for practical reasons, to leave the franchise for Whites without qualifications, and have qualifications for others adjusted to prevent

[55] Schreiner to Hofmeyr 7 December 1929, quoted in Paton *Hofmeyr* 168.

the White vote from being swamped. In his retirement, thirty and more years later, this indefensible attitude was expressly abandoned by Schreiner,[56] who by then had become converted to a belief in a general, non-racial qualified adult franchise on a common roll, introduced gradually. No one could ever persuade him to favour a universal adult franchise.

Before his elevation to the Bench, Schreiner had been Chairman of the old Johannesburg Joint Council of Europeans and Africans for two years, and had held office as Vice-chairman of the South African Institute of Race Relations. He was known as a man of liberal outlook.[57] While on the Bench he studiously refrained from publicizing any political views he might have. He also avoided becoming an office-bearer of any organization that could be thought to have a political tinge. It was obviously quite in order for him to be President of the South African Red Cross Society, which he was from 1942 to 1945; and for him to accept appointment as a Governor-General's nominee on the Council of the University of the Witwatersrand for a four-year term in 1938, an appointment that was to be renewed by the Government every four years for the rest of his life.

The story of Schreiner's attitude to the failure of the Cabinet to offer a judicial appointment to Philip Millin instead of himself must be told, well known though it is in general outline. The Millins were friends of the Schreiners, and they visited one another's homes from time to time, though more in the twenties, when they both lived in Rhodes Avenue, than in the thirties, when the Schreiners were in Houghton and the Millins in their magnificent house in Pallinghurst Road, Westcliff. Sarah Gertrude Millin (1888–1968), the novelist, biographer and social historian, was a formidable woman with an abrasive personality, and her views on the question of colour did not coincide with those of her husband or Schreiner. In the early thirties, when Edna Schreiner was abroad, Oliver stayed with the Millins. At the time Sarah Millin was writing her biography of Smuts,[58] whom she could hardly see as being capable of acting wrongly. Vainly did Oliver and Philip try to get her to acknowledge the most improper nature of Smuts's deportation of the nine strike leaders in 1914, which had been described by a Transvaal judge as lawless kidnapping by the executive.

Philip Millin (1888–1952) was scarcely more than two years older than Schreiner, but he had been in practice over seven years longer; for he had not joined the armed forces during the Great War,

[56] See, for example, his second presidential address, 'Political Power in South Africa', to the South African Institute of Race Relations on 14 January 1963 (republished in his *The Nettle: Political Power and Race Relations in South Africa* 55).

[57] See 'C.R.P.' 'Hon. Mr. Justice O. D. Schreiner' (1938) 55 *SALJ* 1 at 3.

[58] *General Smuts* (1936).

perhaps because his wife Sarah was then a pacifist and also felt that two men in the army from each family was enough. He was one of the men of whom Schreiner asked whether he was right in his intention to set up practice in Johannesburg; and he had said yes. Millin had taken silk in 1927, and had appeared in many important trials; his reputation as an advocate stood very high. Years later, on hearing of his death, Schreiner confided to his diary[59] that 'Philip was a very dear friend to me. There never was a more generous helper to the young advocate than he was to me and others.'

In February 1937 the Millins received a shock. John Murray (1888–1976), who had gone to the Bar in 1913 had taken silk in 1931, they learned was to become a judge on the 15th, and Oliver to be an acting judge from that day. Sarah Millin wrote to Oliver Schreiner on 31 January 1953, telling him that she proposed to deal with the matter in the autobiographical work she was writing and to let him know that she would express her gratitude for the attitude he took at the time. The book was published in 1955 as *The Measure of My Days*. In it Sarah Millin said that her husband had thus been passed over five times since 1929, when he ought to have had the offer of an acting judgeship. She had got her facts muddled, if by being passed over she meant that before 1937 those who had received their patents as silks in the Transvaal after Philip had been given preference over him.[60] But now it had indeed happened. Piecing together the account in her letter and the subsequent autobiographical work,[61] according to Sarah Millin Oliver Schreiner came to the Millins' house one evening to tell Philip about the offers to Murray and himself. He knew that Philip desperately wanted an appointment, even though it meant his income would drop to one-third of what it had been. For years he had found Wessels CJ intolerable to appear before, regarding him as a bully; Wessels' behaviour in the appeal in the famous *Doornhoek* bribery prosecution[62] had been such that Millin, who had a large

[59] 16 April 1952, when he was aboard the SS *Vergelegen en route* to the United States to undergo an operation on his pharynx. ODS papers Wits.

[60] The three previous appointments had been those of Grindley-Ferris (born 1876, silk 1922, appointment 1933), N J de Wet (born 1873, silk 1912, appointment 1932) and G J Maritz (born 1889, silk 1926, appointment 1930). Agreed, Millin, when Maritz got the nod, had a much larger practice, and was a much better lawyer. It may be that the Millins felt that Grindley-Ferris had taken Philip's rightful place. He was appointed an acting judge in 1929 when Philip 'had reason to expect an Acting Judgeship' (letter of Sarah Millin), and again in 1932, receiving a permanent appointment in 1932. Grindley-Ferris had taken the most roundabout route in the history of the country to ascend the Bench: acting judge in South West Africa in 1924; acting judge in the Transvaal from March 1927 to March 1928; acting judge in the Natal Native High Court for a few weeks in 1929; President of the Special Court for Income Tax Appeals in March and April 1930; acting judge in Natal from May 1930 to 18 January 1931; Judge President of the Natal Native High Court from 19 January 1931 to 14 February 1933.

[61] *The Measure of My Days* 162–9. See also Martin Rubin *Sarah Gertrude Millin: A South African Life* (1977) 187ff. There are factual errors in her account, which I have disregarded.

[62] *R* v *Alexander and others* 1936 AD 445, where Millin had appeared for the Crown.

practice before the Appellate Division, vowed that he would never appear before him again; and though Wessels had died in September of the previous year, the wound still hurt. Years before, Maritz, according to Sarah Millin, had told Philip that it was his negrophilism that was the cause of his claims being overlooked; but Philip believed it was because he was a Jew. Philip Millin had vehemently opposed his wife's writing the biography of Smuts, but she could not resist the great opportunity, though she promised not to let Philip see a word of it, so that there could be no embarrassment with Smuts. The all too flattering biography appeared in 1936. She now felt she had been a fool and let her husband down. 'Negrophilism had nothing to do with it this time, for, if there was a passionate negrophilist, it was Oliver', she wrote in her autobiography in rather exaggerated terms.[63] Sarah Millin immediately concluded that the real reasons were anti-Semitism in the country, associated partly with the immigration of German Jewish refugees, which had led to the passing of the Aliens Act 1937,[64] and the fear of Smuts, the Minister of Justice, which Philip had expected, that he would be suspected of doing a favour to his biographer in return for her kind work. Oliver Schreiner told Philip Millin that evening that he could not accept a seat on the judiciary because it was Millin's due; but Millin would not hear of it, saying that Smuts would not appoint a Jew, and if Oliver refused the offer it would go to someone whom he would not be so glad to see on the Bench. Oliver, convinced, went home. The Millins did not approach Smuts, which Schreiner agreed was correct: 'But I still expect to see Philip on the A.D. Bench, if I live so long', he told them.[65] (This did not happen, which Schreiner regretted; on hearing of Millin's death he wrote in his diary that the Transvaal Bench on which he 'worked so well and unselfishly . . . gave insufficient scope for his outstanding reasoning power, and strong sense of justice'.) Later Smuts wrote to Millin confirming what he and his wife had believed were the reasons, and saying the promotion would come in happier times. Jan Hofmeyr, then in the Cabinet, sent a letter to Sarah Millin, saying that he knew nothing of judicial appointments until they had been made, and that he was most distressed at Smuts's weakness.[66] Smuts, who had received a diplomatic response from Philip and a devastating one from Sarah, then decided that the next vacancy would be filled by Millin; so he ascended the Bench on 4 September that year, barely a month after Schreiner's permanent appointment had come through.

When Sarah Millin discussed her proposed autobiography with Schreiner in 1953, he asked her what Philip would have thought had

[63] *The Measure of My Days* 162.
[64] Act 1 of 1937, aimed at restricting the entry of Jewish immigrants.
[65] Letter to Sarah Millin of 12 February 1937.
[66] See *The Measure of My Days* 166 and Paton *Hofmeyr* 262.

she made him out to be a place-hunter. She replied that she would 'try not to dishonour Phil', and in this she succeeded in large measure.

Already, she said in her letter to Schreiner, 'it is many years since you ceased to approve of me. . . . We may as well clear the air generally. You have long felt my attitude towards colour to be bad.' That was true. Sarah Millin had become obsessed with a belief that the future of Whites the world over was being threatened by persons of colour. She became a strong supporter of apartheid, being both fearful of and disliking Blacks. Ultimately, ever ruder and more intolerant and egocentric, she broke with Schreiner, as she did with almost all her friends and acquaintances. That must have been in 1961 or 1962.[67] Schreiner understood that she regarded her life as being in ruins after the death of Philip in April 1952, forgave her behaviour, except where it was vindictive, and kept affectionate memories of her.

THE TRANSVAAL BENCH (1937–1944)

As a trial judge Schreiner was as painstaking, conscientious, hard working, reliable, patient and courteous as he had been as counsel. He kept in mind the desire of litigants and accused and their legal representatives not to have the outcome of a case delayed; throughout his judicial life he was renowned for not sitting on reserved judgments long. True, during his career on the Bench, as in his private affairs, when he had come to a provisional conclusion he was difficult to move; but his mind was not shut. As far as the function of a judge in our system permitted, he tried to ensure that justice was done, and he frequently asked a pointed and penetrating question.

In criminal cases he always bore in mind the oft-quoted dictum of Curlewis JA in *R* v *Hepworth*,[68] which sometimes led to the discomfiture of defending counsel: 'A criminal trial is not a game where one side is entitled to claim the benefit of any omission or mistake made by the other side, and a judge's position in a criminal trial is not merely that of an umpire to see that the rules of the game are observed by both sides. A judge is an administrator of justice, he is not merely a figure-head, he has not only to direct and control the proceedings according to recognized rules of procedure but to see that justice is done.' Particularly in cases involving dishonesty or where there was real moral reprehensibility, such as great brutality, or premeditated killing, the accused was in a poor

[67] From internal evidence in my diary. On 29 December 1960 I attended a function at her house in honour of Sir John Clayden. Schreiner was there. On 5 May 1963, after she had quarrelled with me, Schreiner told me that she would no longer talk to Leopold Greenberg or him.

[68] 1928 AD 265 at 277.

position if he did not give evidence after a prima facie case of guilt had been established.[69] For Schreiner uprightness and candour were among the cardinal virtues. He gained the reputation of not being an 'easy' criminal judge. That was certainly the view of one of the several counsel who appeared for the accused before Schreiner in the special criminal courts established during World War II in terms of the Criminal Code to try charges of treason, or the special high court created then under war measures in terms of the War Measures Act 1940[70] to try cases of alleged serious crimes, aimed at sabotage or hampering the prosecution of the war. That advocate said to me many years ago that it was almost impossible to persuade Schreiner that the Crown had not proved its case, and he had told him so.

In an address delivered in June 1945,[71] after he had become a judge of appeal, Schreiner said: 'It may be better that ten guilty men escape rather than one innocent man is convicted, but it remains a serious evil when guilty men avoid the consequences of their crimes.'[72] But he went on to find great merit in the accusatorial system in 'the sense of freedom that it inevitably engenders'.

With criminal punishment he took a traditional line. The deterrence of others he could see was open to the moral objection that a man must be treated as an end in himself and not as a means of benefiting others; still, it was a practical, common-sense justification of punishment; and retribution was, to some extent, also justifiable to allow expression of social indignation.[73] It was a theme he was to return to in one of his last judgments.[74]

Schreiner was not opposed in principle to capital punishment, as were Maritz and Krause, for instance, nor did he shrink from imposing it, as his father might have, where the dictates of his stern sense of duty demanded it. To him it was the ultimate penalty that the public demanded if it was not to take the law into its own hands. The fear of lynching, ever with him, was one of the reasons, he told me, for his deciding to impose the death sentence for rape in the one instance that he did so: it was a horrifying cross-colour case, where there were two victims. The most famous trial in which Schreiner sat where an accused was sentenced to death was that of Robey Leibbrandt and others for alleged treason. He presided over the special criminal court constituted in terms of the Criminal Code; the other members were Ramsbottom and

[69] On the foregoing, see R S Welsh 'Oliver Schreiner—A Personal Tribute and Recollection' 134 below at 138.

[70] Act 13 of 1940.

[71] 'The Prisoner in Court', delivered at the National Conference of the South African Institute of Race Relations and the Social Services Association and published in (1945) 12 *Race Relations* 51.

[72] Idem at 55. [73] Idem at 58.

[74] *R* v *Karg* 1961 (1) SA 231 (A). See 74 below.

De Beer JJ. The trial, the actual hearing of which lasted ten weeks, apart from preliminary applications, stretched over six and a half months in 1942 and 1943. It was a very trying case. Leibbrandt did not go into the witness box, which counted against him, the Crown having built up a very strong case. Shortly after the conclusion of argument on both sides, Schreiner delivered what the Appellate Division on appeal[75] called 'a very carefully prepared judgment', which ran to 70 000 words and took seven hours to deliver. After he had been found guilty, Leibbrandt delivered an address from which Schreiner tried unsuccessfully to eliminate the flights of Nazi propaganda.[76] The court thereafter sentenced him to death. His appeal to the Appellate Division was unsuccessful, but the Smuts Government commuted the sentence to life imprisonment. When the National Party came to power in 1948 he was released.[77]

A finding of extenuating circumstances where an accused was guilty of murder in Schreiner's view had to rest on proper grounds. Some of the senior members of the Johannesburg and Pretoria Bar remember this well. Two of the stories told to me will suffice. One young advocate was defending in a murder case where the crime was a shocking one. After the finding of guilty had been returned, he asked Schreiner J if he might put forward a plea to the jury that there were mitigating factors. The answer was that he might, but that the jury would be instructed that the ultimate decision was that of the presiding judge. The jury, perhaps taking the hint, found that there were none; most assuredly there were none. The accused was sentenced to death, and subsequently hanged. *R* v *Blyth*[78] went differently, but only just. In what is still a leading case, the Appellate Division upheld the decision of Schreiner J on several aspects of the requirement of the Criminal Code that conviction on a confession requires confirmation or otherwise evidence *aliunde* that the crime has been committed. The accused had written to 'The Superintendent of Police, Marshall Square, Johannesburg' that ten months earlier she had murdered her husband by arsenical poisoning. He had been an alcoholic and maltreated her. There was evidence to show that she had probably bought arsenic. The corpse contained a considerable amount of it. The accused, though she now claimed that her confession was false, did not give evidence. A student at my university[79] listened to the trial. There were two assessors, one of whom was Walter Pollak, who, I imagine, would have found it difficult to sentence anyone to death. Schreiner

[75] *R* v *Leibbrandt and others* 1944 AD 253 at 288, per Watermeyer CJ.

[76] See C P Bresler, who had been counsel for six others of the eight accused, in his *Tilt the Sack* (1965) 136–7. Subsequently Bresler was a Transvaal judge.

[77] He died on 1 August 1966: *Rand Daily Mail* 2 August 1966.

[78] On appeal 1940 AD 355.

[79] I hope Mr Charles Rosenthal SC will not mind my mentioning his name. I am indebted to him for telling me about it.

announced that his assessors had persuaded him that there were extenuating circumstances, but, he added, his chin jutting out characteristically with indignation, had he sat alone he would have found there were none and sentenced the accused to death. He said: 'I sentence you to imprisonment for the rest of your natural life.' Some years later she was released.

Not all of Schreiner's decisions that went on appeal were upheld. *R* v *Hennig*,[80] a case of alleged treason, was one where the Appellate Division set aside his ruling on the law. It concerned the meaning of the then requirement of the Criminal Code that a conviction required the evidence of two witnesses.[81]

As a trial judge, Schreiner showed a consummate ability to master the details of the most protracted evidence. Mention has been made of the trial of Robey Leibbrandt, in which there were 189 witnesses.[82] It was a quality that was to serve him and his colleagues well after 1944, in the years when he was a judge of appeal. Long after he had retired, a former colleague of his, in a letter expressing a feeling of unhappiness at the prospect of hearing an appeal set down for a six-week hearing, said: 'I wish you were here to make it seem all so simple, as you, in the end, did for us lesser mortals!'

On the enunciation of a rule of law Schreiner had shown a deep regard for the considerations of social advantage and public advantage that should be borne in mind by a judge. *Botha* v *Assad*[83] affords a good illustration. He held that the doctrine of *laesio enormis*, which had not then been abolished by legislation in the Transvaal, was not applicable to contracts of letting and hiring; and he elaborated on the undesirable practical consequences that would follow if it were. In his judgment Schreiner showed his ability to deal with the old authorities if in his view the occasion called for him to do so. When, four years later, he sat on the Appellate Division bench that had to consider the doctrine,[84] he said that it was out of place in the modern world, stated in an *obiter dictum* that it should not be applied beyond sales of immovables, and (here agreeing with his three colleagues who held that the doctrine was still extant) expressed his view that it ought to be abolished by the legislature. Parliament gave it its quietus in 1952.[85]

Inevitably many of the reported judgments of Schreiner's when he sat on the Transvaal Bench—there were some 160 of them—dealt with minor matters or pieces of legislation that have since been repealed, or have been overtaken by later decisions of a larger

[80] 1943 AD 172.

[81] It is no longer the law. The Criminal Procedure Act 51 of 1977 has no such provision.

[82] Bresler op cit note 76 at 132.

[83] 1945 TPD 1.

[84] *Tjollo Ateljees (Eins) Bpk* v *Small* 1949 (1) SA 856 (A).

[85] General Law Amendment Act 32 of 1952 s 25.

court in the division or by judgments of the Appellate Division. One judgment that used to be cited frequently, but no longer is, was that in *Klaassen* v *Benjamin*.[86] When it was delivered, it was welcomed for throwing light on the nature of the expression *res ipsa loquitur* and of the onus of proof. Nowadays still more clarity has been attained by the judiciary on the distinction between the onus of proof and the evidential burden of rebutting a prima facie case established by the other side;[87] and the illustration that Schreiner J gave[88] of the principle that the onus does not shift is not an accurate reflection of the present-day law of defamation.

The analysis by Schreiner in *Stern* v *Kuper*[89] of the nature and effect of remuneratory donations and the meaning of the maxim that donations are not presumed is still of value.

The Appellate Division (1945–60)

The first ten years. On 21 November 1944 Richard Feetham (1874–1965) reached the retirement age of 70, resulting in a vacancy on the Appellate Division, then five members strong. Promotion to the highest court had never been on seniority, and rightly so, for not all trial judges make good judges of appeal. South Africa had always followed the English model, not the Scottish.

Schreiner was sixth in seniority on the Transvaal Bench. Of those ahead of him, only Murray was really of the quality required.[90] There were a number of judges in other divisions who had had longer service than Schreiner: Fischer JP (1878–1957) and Van den Heever J (1894–1956) in the Free State; H S van Zyl JP (1876–1955), Percy Jones J (1876–1954), Sutton J (Schreiner's cousin) (1880–1955) and R P B Davis J (1881–1948) in the Cape; Lansdown JP (1874–1957), Pittman J (1878–1964), Gutsche J (1876–1947) and Gane J (1874–1963) in the Eastern Districts; A A R Hathorn JP (1882–1957) in Natal; and Bok J (1880–1956) in Griqualand West. Van den Heever and Davis would have been excellent appointments. The choice of the Smuts Government, however, was Schreiner, who was appointed on 1 January 1945. This elevation met with wide satisfaction.

The highest court was a powerful one: Watermeyer CJ (1880–1958) and Tindall (1879–1963), Centlivres, Greenberg (1885–1964) and Schreiner JJA. Tindall retired in April 1949, and his place was taken by Van den Heever. Watermeyer CJ retired in

[86] 1941 TPD 80.

[87] See, for example, *South Cape Corporation (Pty) Ltd* v *Engineering Management Services (Pty) Ltd* 1977 (3) SA 534 (A) at 548.

[88] See L H Hoffmann and D T Zeffertt *The South African Law of Evidence* 3 ed (1981) 389.

[89] 1941 WLD 223.

[90] The order of seniority was: Barry JP and Solomon, Maritz, Grindley-Ferris, Murray and Schreiner JJ.

October 1950, and the Appellate Division was then enlarged to six members, the new ones being Oscar Hoexter (1893–1970) and Henry Fagan. The composition of the court remained the same for the next four and a half years, until Greenberg retired in March 1955. The vacancy was filled by L C Steyn (1904–1976). The following year saw the death of Van den Heever and additional appointments to bring the court to eleven members, resulting in the appearance of six new judges of appeal; but these happenings call for consideration later. There were several acting appointments. Davis, in particular, filled temporary vacancies.

Up to the time when it was announced that L C Steyn would join the court, things ran smoothly and the atmosphere in Bloemfontein was a pleasant one. The terms straddled mid-February to the end of March, the month of May, mid-August to the end of September, and mid-November to mid-December—five months in all. During the vacation there were some reserved judgments to write, and records to read; but there was also time for a holiday and a rest. Term meant strenuous work; Sunday morning was an ordinary working morning, conferences being regularly held then. Schreiner did not like leaving his wife and daughter behind in Johannesburg; but there was a job of work to be done with intense concentration, efficiently and expeditiously, and isolation in what he called this 'sort of monastic grove'[91] was conducive to these ends. To the outsider it seems rather like being a schoolboy at boarding school. And if the weather of Bloemfontein was inclined to extremes—well, at least it gave something to talk about over the telephone or by letter to those at home. Edna Schreiner found the separation hard; in the last few days before he had to attend the next session the heightening unhappiness was to an extent limited by the realization that 'your terms in Bloemfontein are interesting and well occupied and that you are well companioned by your Brothers of the Bench'[92]—sentiments that were to change to deep sympathy when the court was enlarged and her husband's rightful expectancy of office of Chief Justice dashed. She found some solace in the contemplation of his love and constancy, and her pride in him—and yet it made his absence all the more painful.

Conferences at times tended to grow rather heated, as one judge of appeal tried to bring another or others around to his point of view. Schreiner told me many years after he had retired[93] what long, arduous and even at times acrimonious discussions there had been in the very important so-called *Language Ordinance* case—*Swart NO and Nicol NO* v *De Kock and Garner*,[94] where by a

[91] Letter to Edna S of 19 September 1952. ODS family papers.

[92] Letter of Edna S to ODS of 23 February 1955. ODS family papers.

[93] On 23 September 1966, when I was at his house giving him the little assistance I could with the Hamlyn Lectures he was preparing.

[94] 1951 (3) SA 589 (A).

majority of three (Centlivres CJ, Van den Heever JA and Fagan JA) to two (Schreiner JA and Hoexter JA) the Appellate Division upheld the validity of a Transvaal ordinance compelling the use as medium of instruction in private schools of the official language in which the pupil was more proficient. The majority found that a law which did not discriminate against either official language did not fall within the embrace of the provision in the Constitution guaranteeing the equality of the official languages. But to Schreiner, who delivered a great dissenting judgment, the provision guaranteed 'not merely equality of treatment of the two official languages but also the free use by all persons of whichever of the languages they choose to use. Equal freedom is not the same as equal absence of freedom. . . .'[95] In the discussions Schreiner found Centlivres and Van den Heever immovable. Yet he found their reasoning utterly unconvincing. The invocation by Centlivres of the provision in the Defence Act on the language of instruction Schreiner used as an example of what he believed the irrelevant considerations they took into account. Hoexter tried to persuade Fagan, who was wavering, to go with him and Schreiner; but ultimately (so Schreiner told me) the prospect of the little boy deprived of education in the tongue his mother taught him proved too appalling for Fagan.

In October 1953, during the vacation, Schreiner wrote to Centlivres that on a certain occasion during the discussions in the last session he had 'rudely dragged in the use of historical matter & the Language Ordinance case'. (It was unusual for Schreiner to apologize; in this regard he had the same failing as R P B Davis: that he was sorry he would show by conduct, but rarely by words.) Centlivres replied[96] that he was not 'conscious of any "rudeness" on your part—brusqueness, perhaps, but that—if it be a fault—is, I'm afraid, one of my characteristics'—which was really not true. Centlivres continued: 'The fact that there are occasionally differences of opinion among the six old men of Bloemfontein is a healthy sign. God forbid that we should be ja-broers. Can you imagine anything more horrid than that we should hold a caucus meeting & that the minority should have their mouths shut by the majority? During the meetings we hold the keenness sometimes leads one to become excited & what is said during a spasm of excitement is, I hope, never taken seriously.' Then Centlivres recounted a tale which shows that Schreiner was exaggerating in saying that Centlivres could not see the ordinary comedy of human existence. 'And this reminds me of a story told me by Percy Jones yesterday. [He would be Jones J of the Cape Bench.] He was up in Bloemfontein in connection with an appeal in the spacious days of Wessels J & was staying at an hotel where the judges were also

[95] At 612. [96] On 15 October 1953. ODS family papers.

staying. He had a room opposite the judges' sitting-room & in those days the judges held their conferences in this room at night-time. Percy told me that Wessels' voice was heard all over the hotel: there was apparently a heated argument going on about the merits of Percy's appeal which was down for hearing the next day. Percy bravely decided to knock on the door of the judges' sitting-room & tell them he did [? not] want to hear them discuss the merits of his appeal!'

Still, to Schreiner[97] Centlivres lacked an ordinary sense of humour. Wit and the quirks of life, he once told me, would leave Centlivres cold, yet he would burst into laughter at a feeble joke. He had a bad ear for languages; for instance, he pronounced 'farcical' as 'farsisal'; and Hoexter, whom Schreiner regarded as a very clever man and found an amusing companion, would take Centlivres off behind his back. But Schreiner was very fond of Centlivres: he had a very strong sense of duty, was very kind, was as devoid of vanity as it is possible for man to be, had an engaging shyness, and was quick to make friends and popular not only at home but also abroad, where after his retirement he attended conferences in the United States and Australia. Agreed, Schreiner told me, he was not out of the top drawer of intellectual quality, and he was no literary stylist, but his judgments were well organized, especially where legislation was involved: he would cite all the relevant provisions, so that the judgment was admirably self-sufficient, and Schreiner tried to follow his model.

For the intellectual qualities of Leopold Greenberg Schreiner had the greatest admiration and respect, but, he told me, he often disagreed with him in the decision of appeals.

One other colleague was mentioned by him: Davis, who sat so frequently as an acting judge of appeal from 1944 to 1947. Davis had told Schreiner that he had never disagreed with his great friend Watermeyer in the decision of a case, which Schreiner found an amazing statement.

Two anecdotes relating to appeals in which Schreiner sat call for recounting. In a case involving the *contra fiscum* rule Walter Pollak KC was arguing that the rule applied. Schreiner JA made the observation that it could operate for and against the taxpayer, according to the circumstances; it was six of the one and half a dozen of the other, in fact a 'toss-up'. To which Pollak replied: 'Whatever your lordships may do in the privacy of your chambers, in open court one has to give reasons!'[98]

The other anecdote was kindly related to me by Mr Eric Morris SC.[99] It concerns what occurred during argument in the case of *Big*

[97] Private communication on 23 September 1966.
[98] See D Meyerowitz in (1971) 88 *SALJ* 532, whose wording I have largely followed.
[99] Letter to me of 27 May 1981.

Ben Soap Industries Ltd v *CIR*.[100] I take the liberty of quoting Mr Morris, with his inimitable style: 'The company had, prior to the outbreak of war, and anticipating both the war and excess-profits duty, inflated its earnings as reflected in the balance sheet, the object being to establish a high "pre-war standard" and so to reduce the excess profits. It was duly taxed on the inflated income. Later the secretary was ignominiously dismissed, and his wandering (minstrel's) feet led him to the Receiver of Revenue, where he sang his dreamy lullaby—or maybe it was a ballad, song or snatch. The chorus was "treble tax". Comes the appeal and Rosenberg KC (with him EM) is busy explaining very nicely to the court that if Big Ben wanted to pay more tax for 1939 (or 1940) than it should have, well that's all there is to it, and a pre-war standard, once determined, would make the Medes and the Persians look like a woman motorist who is hunting for a parking place. All is going very nicely until Schreiner JA leans forward and says "Mr Rosenberg!" "Yes, m'Lord?" "I thought that the business of this company was boiling soap, not cooking books." "As your lordship pleases." Oliver sat back, almost as if embarrassed at his sarcasm, and uttered not another word during the appeal. His standards were such that he could not countenance or forgive anything which did not measure up to those standards.'

1951–60: The constitutional crisis, the enlargement of the Appellate Division, and the passing over of Schreiner as Chief Justice. The period between 1951 and 1956 will go down in history as the lustrum in which the Government, after a long struggle, eventually achieved its aim of removing the Coloured voters from the common roll. A bare outline of the oft-told story will suffice. The Appellate Division declared the Separate Representation of Voters Act 1951,[101] which provided for Coloureds to elect their own MPs and MPCs, to be invalid as it had been passed by the legislature by the ordinary bicameral procedure instead of the unicameral two-thirds majority entrenched procedure.[102] Centlivres CJ delivered the judgment, with Greenberg, Schreiner, Van den Heever and Hoexter JJA

[100] 1949 (1) SA 740 (A).

[101] Act 46 of 1951.

[102] *Harris* v *Minister of the Interior* 1952 (2) SA 428 (A), overruling *Ndlwana* v *Hofmeyr NO* 1937 AD 229. Argument took place on 2–3, 25 and 26 February 1952, and judgment was delivered on 20 March. On 22 January 1952 Centlivres had written to Schreiner from his home at Kenilworth, Cape Town, that 'I quite agree with you that the Status Act has as much to do with the issues raised in the Franchise case as the flowers that bloom in the spring'. He went on to deal with the questions that the case raised, all of which were traversed in the judgment later. Centlivres said that the Appellate Division would 'have to listen to an argument lasting probably six days (as contrasted with the hour's argument that took place in *Ndlwana's* case) & then make up our minds which way the judgment should go—a process which will take considerably longer than was the case in *Ndlwana* v *Hofmeyr N.O*'. In *Ndlwana's* case argument took place on 23 March before Stratford ACJ, De Villiers JA, De Wet JA and Watermeyer AJA. The appeal was dismissed immediately, reasons being given in the judgment of the court delivered by Stratford ACJ on 5 April.

concurring. (The sixth, and most recently appointed, judge of appeal, Fagan JA, did not sit in the case.[103])

Parliament then passed the High Court of Parliament Act 1952[104] by the ordinary bicameral procedure. It stated that any Appellate Division decision invalidating an instrument purporting to be and enrolled as an Act of Parliament had to be brought before the High Court of Parliament for review. The members of the High Court were the members of the two Houses of Parliament. When the Bill was before Parliament, Oscar Hoexter, in a letter of 30 April 1952, expressing the hope that Schreiner had fully recovered from the operation in the United States on his pharynx, could not resist giving vent to his Puckish sense of humour: 'If I were an M.P., I would propose an amendment that no member of the [High] Court [of Parliament] having a law degree should be allowed to vote, provided that any Cabinet Minister having a law degree would be allowed to vote if he filed an affidavit that, in spite of his degree, he had no knowledge of law.' He went on to remark that he had been told that 'Hennie van Zyl, the ex J.P. of the C.P.D., is particularly bitter against me; he says that he never thought that I could associate myself with such a judgment. I am tickled because I do not know the old bird at all.'

The Appellate Division, sitting with the same members, declared the Act to be invalid.[105] This time there were five separate judgments. The common ground was that the High Court was Parliament in disguise, which was not the protection of the court implicit in the Constitution. Schreiner JA went furthest in stating what was the protective judicial system envisaged: it was not even any type of court of law—for instance, possibly not a specified magistrate's court empowered to hear a final appeal from the Appellate Division in a case concerned with the validity of an enactment.

The Government then secured the passage of the Appellate Division Quorum Act 1955[106] by the ordinary bicameral procedure, requiring eleven judges of appeal to sit when the validity of a purported Act was in question. By now L C Steyn had taken the place of Greenberg on the highest court; Greenberg had reached the age of retirement of 70 on 21 March 1955. Lucas Steyn had been appointed to the Transvaal Court only on 8 August 1951, and at the time of his promotion was twelfth in seniority on a provincial

[103] He has been leading counsel for the Government in *Ndlwana* v *Hofmeyr NO*. Leslie Blackwell (1885–1976), a judge in the Transvaal from 1943 to 1955, years later wrote that Fagan had told him shortly before his death that he was in entire agreement with the judgment declaring the Separate Representation of Voters Act invalid: *Sunday Times* 25 September 1966.

[104] Act 35 of 1952.

[105] *Minister of the Interior* v *Harris* 1952 (4) SA 769 (A). Argument took place on 27 to 29 October 1952, and judgment was delivered on 13 November.

[106] Act 27 of 1955. See Appendix at p 99 below.

division bench sixteen strong. The most senior member after the Judge President was John Murray and the second Ramsbottom, two most eminent jurists: Murray had been appointed on 15 February 1937 and Ramsbottom on 15 September 1938. Both had been acting judges of appeal, Murray for some time in 1949 and 1950, and Ramsbottom for several months in 1950. And there were outstanding judges in other divisions, all with much greater judicial experience than Steyn, some of whom had been acting judges of appeal in the past. I do not wish to suggest for a moment that Steyn was not a brilliant jurist; but his promotion did not meet with universal approval. Greenberg wrote to Schreiner on 2 January 1955, when he was on his last leave, that 'to me it seems a long way the worst that has been done in the demoralization of the Bench'. Schreiner took it calmly, saying in a letter to his wife of 15 March 1955, 'I must learn to call him Lukas [*sic*]'.

In the same session of Parliament, again by the bicameral procedure, the Senate Act[107] was passed, which so enlarged the upper House as to give the Government the two-thirds majority of both Houses it needed. The plan was obvious.

Who were the five new judges of appeal to be? They turned out to be, in order of seniority of appointment, E M de Beer (1892–1961), Judge President of the Orange Free State Provincial Division, who had been a judge since 19 September 1939; F G Reynolds (1887–1968), Judge President of the Eastern Districts Local Division, who had been a judge since 31 October 1948; C P Brink (1897–1964), senior judge in the Free State after De Beer, who had been a judge since 1 October 1948 and acted as a judge of appeal for a period in 1953 and 1954; H W R ('Hein') de Villiers (1891–1973), senior judge in the Eastern Districts after Reynolds, and previously on the Transvaal Bench, who had been a judge since 1 January 1946 and spent a period in 1951 as an acting judge of appeal; and C G Hall (1886–1979), sixth in seniority in the Cape Provincial Division, who had been a judge since 1949. Price J (1887–1970), sixth in seniority in the Transvaal Court, took the place of Reynolds as Judge President of the Eastern Districts Court—a step on his part that disappointed Schreiner. D O K Beyers (1909–1974) was moved from the Griqualand West Local Division, where he was the sole judge, to head the Free State Court.

The existing members of the Appellate Division were not consulted. Schreiner wrote to his wife on 26 March 1955:[108] '. . . you can take it that you heard about the appointment of our five new

[107] Act 53 of 1955.

[108] ODS family papers. All the correspondence from Oliver Schreiner to Edna Schreiner, and from Edna Schreiner to Oliver Schreiner, that is quoted hereafter is from the same source.

colleagues as soon as we did; certainly their names were first reported to us by the Registrar as having been announced over the wireless.' He went on in typical vein: 'There it is—and the only course is to take things philosophically, reminding oneself of the relative unimportanceness of the affair in the general scheme of things. One can forecast what is likely to happen during the next few years if one feels that way inclined, but my own view is that the best plan is just to go quietly along doing our stuff at home and here and not getting het up about what developments there may be. I've always thought that Sir William Osler's[109] advice, which I culled from a little book that I found by my bedside at Ralph Houghton's place, was very sound—that we shouldn't dwell either on the past or on the future unduly. A bit of each is of course necessary but mainly one does best to carry on with the affairs at hand. It is likely to result in a more composed approach and better health. . . . The big tides are not much affected by the stirrings on the surface. And the big tides are mainly in the right direction.'

Shortly thereafter Schreiner was approached to take the post of Chief Justice of Southern Rhodesia. He wrote to his wife on 10 May 1955: '. . . a man from Rhodesia named Stumbles, who is the Minister of Justice of Southern Rhodesia, came here today and offered me the job of Chief Justice there.[110] I told him at once that however much pleasanter and easier it might be to live there I had to carry on here. Actually, of course, it was no great plum that was being offered, since it was only the C.J'ship of S.R. and not of the Federal Appeal Court, on which Jack [Clayden] will be sitting. But apart from that, there could be no question of leaving this Court, could there? He was quite a pleasant chap, Stumbles—a feller perhaps I should say rather than chap! Don't tell anyone. . . . I've told Albert [Centlivres—the Chief Justice] under a pledge of secrecy, but none of the others. It isn't fair to let it be known that the job is being as it were hawked around. Now for a job of work.'

Edna replied on the 13th: 'My dearest love . . . of course there was no need at all to consult me. . . . Indeed, it is quite clear to me that this is the very juncture when circumstances must dictate to any man of courage & honour. You could not possibly pull out at this moment without taking the easy—the too easy—path. . . . I am in full agreement that this course could not be adopted without sacrifice of the very qualities that make you what you are. We must just stay and battle on and take what may be coming to us with courage and dignity.'

109 1849–1919, eminent physician and medical historian, Professor of Medicine at McGill, thereafter Pennsylvania, Johns Hopkins and finally Oxford (1905–11).

110 See A R W Stumbles *Some Recollections of a Rhodesian Speaker* (1980) 60–1 on the appointment of Murray: 'Judge Murray was like a breath of fresh air. He completely changed the outlook which in the past had been handed down from a rather frozen and rigid judiciary. He knew men and affairs and was very human and understanding' (p 61).

Subsequently Stumbles offered the post to John Murray, who accepted it with some qualms, which his wife, a strong-willed lady, managed to overcome. He had been disheartened by being overlooked for promotion to the Appellate Division and, with Ramsbottom, having had to carry the burden of running the Transvaal Provincial Division, where Maritz (1889–1964), the Judge President, was a lazy and inept administrator. Murray, who was 67, assumed office on 1 August 1955. He took a little while to settle down in his new position; but it was not long before his considerable legal and delightful personal qualities were greatly appreciated.[111] On 28 November 1956 Edna wrote to Schreiner that she 'hears on all sides that happiness beams' from John Murray, and that his wife says 'that John is much respected up there' and his appointment 'has had such a good effect on his "ego" which was a bit shaken & undermined by his treatment down here'.[112]

Clearly Schreiner was unhappy about the appointment of the five newcomers to the Appellate Division, not only because in the case of some of them he was worried about their having broken faith with their brethren, or been so foolish or egotistical as to think they had been promoted on merit, but also because he doubted their capacity and willingness to do the work of the court. On 28 August 1955, before the newcomers had sat, Schreiner, then Acting Chief Justice, wrote to Edna: 'It makes one feel a little sick when one has to arrange for courts that do not look like the stuff that used to be

[111] Murray was knighted on 14 August 1958. His period of office was extended to 3 March 1961. He retired to Plettenberg Bay, where he died on 10 May 1976. See (1976) 93 *SALJ* 324. Murray was a good friend of Schreiner's, who, accompanied by Jean, stayed with him and Lady Murray in the early seventies on at least two occasions. There are some amusing letters from Murray in the Schreiner family papers, a few extracts from which call for quotation. On 18 March 1956 he wrote: 'One spot of bother awaits me at Umtali—the local Church of England parson appears on several counts of tampering with boys. Shall I tell my assessors (two magistrates) the well known epitaph, familiar I imagine, of a gentleman of similar proclivities, "Here lies a man accursed of God, Not earth to earth, but Sod to Sod, For men of great wickedness, Hell was created bottomless"?'

The death of Toon van den Heever on 29 January, he said, was 'a great loss. . . . I think he felt as much as anyone the way the glory has departed.' Murray found the appointment of D O K (Otto) Beyers in Van den Heever's place as having 'the one merit of being really funny. . . . Still he's an amusing card & very companionable & even if he never did very much work he was invaluable at a Bar Dinner.' He continued: 'The only reason why I felt really sad about Hal [Ramsbottom] being disregarded is that if or when Gerard Maritz goes, he will have to face the insult of being passed over. . . .' (This did not happen, as Ramsbottom was appointed to the Appellate Division at the beginning of 1959, Maritz JP retiring on 7 December that year.) Letters to Schreiner from Murray in old age show no falling away of his renowned ability as a raconteur. One anecdote starts teasingly: 'I don't usually inflict improprieties on you—but last week I heard one which might possibly raise a faint smile. . . .' (12 November 1972: the story is not worth recounting). In the same letter he said: 'I don't think I feel disposed to follow your advice re inflicting myself on the bowling fraternity—possibly my 18 years on the TPD & 6 in Rhodesia gave me an aversion to any form of bias.'

[112] But in a letter of 30 November 1956, in which she said that the Murrays had told her in confidence that John has been asked to stay on for three years, having made such a success at his job, Edna Schreiner wrote: '. . . it is well deserved, for John was never soured or embittered by his long spell in the desert.'

there. . . . I've little doubt that most of the cases will be decided fairly rightly—the job isn't so difficult that every case calls for high quality, thank Heaven. But it isn't going to be a court to be proud of being on or its being one's country's highest court. But we'll live through these interesting unattractive times—at any rate in the long run the country is fairly certain to come right.' And on 18 October that year: 'Dearest Pallikin, we've had our first day of the 11 judge system—Toon [van der Heever] sat out and Albert [Centlivres] took the top court and I the bottom one. One can't help thinking of the shades of Innes and Solomon and the other giants of the past; I wonder if they are looking down on us or in on us, without our knowing it.'

Initially Schreiner was averse to having anything to do with the newcomers socially or in sport. Referring to the old practice of the judges of appeal playing bowls together, especially on Wednesday afternoons, he told Edna (18 October 1955): 'I really don't feel inclined to team up with the new boys. But I think Albert may favour keeping the crowd together as much as possible. Though not as gentle as Henry [Fagan] he is less nasty than I am.' Edna's response appears from Schreiner's letter to her four days later: 'I was glad to get your support for the view that we should be reasonably firm about extra judicial associations with the newcomers. Whether there will be modifications over the years remains to be seen; but for the present, and especially with the most thickskinned of them, it is clearly necessary to maintain a reasonable distance. . . . My dear, the ivory tower isn't so blissfully secluded as it was, in your representation, but it has its amusing aspects. We'll get the stuff done though not as easily or as efficiently as heretofore.' On the 24th Schreiner reported to Edna that '[t]hings proceed reasonably here—there has not been undue appeasement so far as the Chief, Toon [van den Heever], Oscar [Hoexter] and I are concerned. Henry is such a kindhearted chap that if the devil himself dropped in for a friendly chat Henry would bring him a footrest for his cloven hooves and a peg to hang his tail on. It is instinctive with him. The only one towards whom the rest of us have gentler feelings is Brinkie [Brink]. He is a sick man and naturally kindly and modest. How he came to be mixed up in the racket I do not know. But we are sorry for him. . . .' Hein de Villiers particularly seemed to arouse the ire of Schreiner and his wife. 'I've just heard Hein', he wrote to her on 25 October, '—who has strolled into the [Bloemfontein] Club—ask the Chief whether there was bowls arranged for tomorrow—which is a non-Court day. Albert said nothing had been arranged yet! I shall do my best to stiffen the C.J.'s back, but it isn't easy to tell H. straight out that he isn't wanted, and never will be!' On 27 November he reported to Edna: 'We have not yielded so far as Hein is concerned —he played this morning—presumably with Reynolds.'

On 29 January 1956 Toon van den Heever died, at the tragically early age of 61. It was out of term, and Schreiner was in Johannesburg; but he went to Bloemfontein to attend the funeral. Van den Heever's daughter Leonora (now Miss Justice Van den Heever) thanked him for his telegram, letter and wreath, 'and even more for the fact that you came down for Toon's funeral. He was the hub of our universe, not only husband and favourite father, but guide, philosopher and friend, jester, handyman—everything.'[113]

The Appellate Division had lost a brilliant member. Centlivres, whose tenure as Chief Justice was to end on 31 January the following year, was pessimistic. 'It looks as if when you and Oscar retire', Centlivres wrote on 6 February, 'the A.D. will have the distinction of being the weakest Bench in the country. What a terrible contrast to the Bench presided over by Innes C.J. It will take years to build up a strong Bench again & you and I will not live to see that.'[114]

D O K Beyers was promoted to the empty chair; Ramsbottom was again overlooked. Schreiner did not find the newcomers particularly able colleagues. On 27 October 1955 he wrote to Edna: 'Work is not very heavy but I have to do a lot of judgments these days—one doesn't know whom to put jobs on to yet awhile. In fact I would rather do them myself—that doesn't apply to the old crowd of course. There have not been any differences of opinion yet—the cases have been completely straightforward. But there will be the times when one will look for help and may not get it.' He denied that he was doing more than his old colleagues: 'We finished our long case just before 1 p.m. today—I produced the first smile in the long drawn out affair by saying that in view of the lateness of the hour we would not give judgment immediately. . . . This afternoon we have a talk about the lines of the judgment, which is now committed to Henry's care. You mustn't think that I do more than my fair ration of judgments. The new boys naturally can't be entrusted with the heavy stuff, but Albert, Toon and Oscar do just as many as I do—Albert more.' (19 November 1955.) Again: 'There is the problem of dealing with the judgments of the new men—they take a good deal more working at than do those of the old hands. . . . [M]ost of the burden falls on Albert. . . . [W]hen one thinks of the number of people who believe that the additional appointments must at least lighten the work for the seniors it makes one laugh a bit sourly.' (22 November 1955.)

In early 1956 the social boycott of the newcomers in games of bowls began to be relaxed. 'I feel a little bad about Reynolds', wrote Schreiner to his wife on 5 March, 'as he is very civil to me.' Later that month he and Otto Beyers were admitted to the game: 'I

[113] Letter of 7 February 1956. ODS family papers.

[114] ODS family papers.

think we've shown long enough how we feel about the packing [of the court].' (11 and 14 March 1956.) Hein de Villiers was fortunately away—'he takes things for granted so unattractively.' (14 March 1956.) But it was 'going to be difficult to maintain' the boycott of him. (1 September 1956.)

Schreiner was still concerned about the quality of work of the newcomers. 'Albert . . . does far more work than anyone else. The new boys can not (between ourselves) for the most part be entrusted with the writing of judgments. But when Albert goes there will have to be some relaxation of the practice.' (20 March 1956.) 'Some of the new boys are very conscientious about reading all the records from cover to cover but it doesn't necessarily produce better results.' (25 March 1956.)

Meantime the South Africa Act Amendment Act 1956[115] had come into operation on 1 March. It had been passed by the two-thirds majority unicameral procedure, the swollen Senate giving the Government its necessary majority. The Separate Representation of Voters Act of 1951 was thereby revalidated and the entrenchment of all votes was removed. 'Dearest Chum', Schreiner had written to his wife the previous year ('chum' was the old-fashioned term of endearment he frequently used), 'Just a line apropos of (Modern English Usage[116]) the new legislation in regard to the Senate. Don't get downhearted, my beloved; this is what we expected and it just has to be gone through. . . . [O]ne can't do anything about it and so must just do the ordinary chores and keep smiling.' (10 May 1955.)

The validity of the 1956 statute was immediately challenged by two Coloured voters. The full bench of the Cape Provincial Division, in a judgment delivered on 18 May,[117] upheld it. The inevitable appeal to the Appellate Division was argued on 15 to 19 October, judgment being delivered on 9 November.[118] Meanwhile the passing over of Schreiner as Chief Justice was entering into its first phase; and he was trying to keep his wife from too great distress at a time when the state of her health was causing ever-increasing concern. She was suffering from high blood pressure and from other serious complaints; she had written to Schreiner on 22 March: 'I fear my days of any active gardening are over: a saddening thought, for I did love it.' He dropped a long letter to her from Bloemfontein on 17 May: 'Here is some information for your own

115 Act 9 of 1956.

116 H W Fowler *A Dictionary of Modern English Usage* 1 ed (1926, used by Schreiner) 28; 2 ed (1965; revised reprint 1978) 33.

117 *Collins* v *Minister of the Interior* 1956 (1) PH K54 (C), *coram* De Villiers JP and Newton Thompson and Van Winsen JJ.

118 *Collins* v *Minister of the Interior* 1957 (1) SA 552 (A), *coram* Centlivres CJ, Schreiner, Hoexter, Fagan, Steyn, De Beer, Reynolds, De Villiers, Brink and Beyers JJA and Hall AJA. At the time there were only ten permanent judges of appeal.

ears alone. Albert got a letter from Swart [the Minister of Justice] asking him to stay on for another year as Acting Chief Justice. Albert had turned it down. Hall, who turns 70 in July, has been invited to stay on for another year and has accepted. I told Albert that he must not refuse on any view that he would be keeping me out of the job, as I am satisfied that the Government doesn't plan to offer it to me; this suggestion to Albert, of course, only confirms it. But what I think may be in their minds is that Lukas [*sic*] might find it easier to take on the job after another year's experience, and the Government might feel that it wouldn't be so likely to lose them the odd country attorney's vote. Anyhow, I am glad that Albert has turned it down, not for any effect on my prospects of being appointed—these are anyway about nil and it is neither an honour nor an amusement to be in charge of the Court as at present constituted—but for the effect it may have in making it difficult for the Government. I wonder how Swart had the nerve to write asking Albert to do it in the interests of the administration of justice after what he has said about and written to Albert in the past and after what he has done to this Court. Anyhow, my love, it is something to laugh quietly to yourself about and certainly nothing to feel indignant about on my behalf. The little worries of old men are not of much importance in this world, or the next.'

The reply of his loyal wife could not have been unexpected. It was written on the 19th. She said that 'when I think of that most despicable manoeuvre, I tremble with rage. Does he imply that the interests of the Administration of Justice would not be safe in *your* hands? Well, he might well suffer some confusion of mind. . . . I can imagine he will be puzzled by Albert's reaction. . . . It must be puzzling to Swart to have to deal with a man of the old school of integrity and honour. . . . For myself, you know that I don't care whether this preferment comes to you. Sufficient that I know no one could deserve it more or bring greater powers of mind & rectitude to the holding of it. . . . But . . . it isn't much use to talk to me of treating the whole thing as a joke. It is infamous.' She ended by saying 'meanwhile, the love of you and the pride in you grow & grow, and you are the whole centre & meaning of my life'.

Two days later Schreiner replied in the same vein as before: 'I was afraid that despite my attempts to keep you calm you would get het up. But really, my darling, it isn't a thing to be distressed about—only interested and amused. Assume in advance that I will not be appointed C.J. and feel perfectly happy about it. . . . Now thank you, my darling, for having become indignant, but don't do it again.' The appeal was in vain.

On 22 June Centlivres wrote to Schreiner from his home in Cape Town with an interesting piece of news: that he had been approached that day 'for a set-down of the Senate case for October

15th. I was told that the case might last two weeks as the Govt. intends to contest the correctness of the two previous Constitutional decisions of the A.D. So much for the assurance which Swart gave Eddie de Beer when the latter accepted a seat on the A.D.!' This reflection presaged an extraordinary outburst in court on 15 October.

Schreiner continued with his work undeterred, determined as ever to do it expeditiously and well. In mid-September he wrote to his wife of records he had to read, including the record of the Senate Act case. 'But I never think it does to look too far ahead. Sometimes one has a sense of pressure, as if one fears one will not be able to deal with all the stuff properly or in time. But these occasions are rare and fleeting. One finds that the prospective troubles iron themselves out to a large extent when one reaches them, and a tough looking proposition more often than not turns out to be a mild affair.' (16 September 1956.) He kept reasonably cheerful and optimistic—at least on paper. 'It is said that they are busy preparing the Raadsaal for the eleven of us to sit there next month. I remember that old Ben [Tindall],[119] when I first came to this court, used to speak of "The Big Five". I always felt it was a trifle pompous. Can one now talk of "The Big Eleven", without a mixture of laughter and tears? But time will put these things into proper perspective—not our time may be, but the country's time.' (19 September 1956.)

On no occasion did Schreiner give any details about the appeals he was hearing. This will explain the opening of an affecting letter to him from Edna on 20 September on the constitutional question. 'What your views as to the ultimate position are of course I don't know. But I just want to say that if such a position arises that you feel a drastic step on your part is the right course, please remember that your family is solidly behind you. I can live as a poor man's wife very easily, and it would probably be good for me, and very good for our Jean . . . in our easy sheltered way of life. . . .'

In the evening of 15 October Schreiner wrote to his wife in detail on the events of that opening day of the argument in the Senate Act appeal. '. . . [T]he Government advocates had filed heads which appeared, though not quite clearly, to accept the correctness of the previous decision of this Court in which we held the Act removing the Cape non-European voters from the roll to be invalid. But the Government advocates apparently served further heads of argument yesterday on the appellants' counsel in which they attacked the previous decision. [Graeme] Duncan, the appellant's counsel, asked

[119] B A Tindall (26 April 1879–2 February 1963); judge of the Transvaal Provincial Division from 1 December 1922 to 31 July 1937; Judge President from 1 August 1937 to 28 February 1938; judge of appeal from 1 March 1938 until his retirement on 26 April 1949.

at the start of the hearing that he be given a clear indication by the other side as to whether they were going to persist in this attack on the earlier judgment and [D P] de Villiers, for the Government, said, in effect, that he planned to wait and see how things developed. Then Eddie de Beer said that wouldn't do as he and others had accepted appointment only on the understanding that the earlier decision was not to be challenged. After consulting the Government—Dönges, I believe—de Villiers then withdrew his threat to attack the earlier judgment. You can imagine, can't you, what a bombshell Eddie's announcement was. But can you picture people accepting a position on this Court on condition that certain issues will not be raised before them? The inference is natural that they were prepared to consider any other issues of a related kind and were consulted as to whether they felt prepared to deal with such issues. One assumes they were not invited to express their views in advance, but fancy any sort of talk of that kind. It just shows what we have come down to. It must be said in Eddie's favour that he spoke up quite frankly and was not prepared to let himself be forced to deal with the issue that he had been promised would not be raised. The others have not shown their hands except, between ourselves, Brinkie [Brink JA] has told us that he was given a similar undertaking by Swart, who was the one who spoke to Eddie. The whole thing is horrid but interesting. Well, enough of that. . . . Don't worry about our cares and tribulations. Things aren't really so bad and in fact Oscar [Hoexter] has enjoyed himself immensely today over Eddie's effort. He reckons it's great fun: But what a poor show for our Court's prestige.'[120] The next day Schreiner sent another letter, saying that 'Oscar is still happy over yesterday's disclosure by Eddie. It has made all the difference to him! . . . Hou moed.' On the 17th he wrote: 'There were no new bombshells by Eddie, though he did slip in a reference to the scramble for seats in the Senate—quite irrelevantly. Oscar regards him, generally and not in relation to the present case, as wholly unpredictable, and I think he is about right.'

Argument ended on the 19th, and on the 21st Schreiner was unusually revealing in a letter to Edna: 'Whether I shall write a

[120] The episode was reported in the press. See, for example, *Rand Daily Mail* 16 October 1956. An explanation was given by the Minister of Justice, Mr C R Swart, in the House of Assembly on 25 January 1957 (*Debates* cols 189–91): Mr Justice De Beer had told him, said the Minister, that he had on several occasions expressed the opinion that the 1952 decision of the Appellate Division on the Separate Representation of Voters Act had been wrong; and would he not be in an awkward position if the issue should be raised again? He (the Minister) had said that it was unlikely that it would. There had never been any intention of a conditional appointment, for the Government does not impose conditions when appointing a judge, nor does a judge accept appointment on certain conditions; he (the Minister) had only tried to help Mr Justice De Beer with a personal problem, and the judge had subsequently stated that if he had thought this to be a condition of his appointment, he had been mistaken. Mr Justice De Beer had been the only judge concerned in the matter.

judgment or not will depend on the circumstances; I will not do so unless I think it is necessary or helpful. Albert is busy on one but his will not be the only one. I wish I could write more fully. Anyhow, between ourselves don't expect the appeal to be allowed or you will be disappointed. It is a question of what division there will be in the court. This is, of course, for you alone. Don't let it worry you. These things will iron themselves out in the long run, and it doesn't help to get het up about them.' On the 26th he told her: 'To date there are three judgments prepared or preparing . . .'; and went on to say of a letter from John Murray: 'You never read such a gossipy letter with frank comment—almost all very kindly —on his brethren. He thinks the world of Jack's [Clayden's] work, and I don't wonder; what a difference it would make to this court if we had Hal [Ramsbottom], John and Jack here. . . . Well, my love, this is certainly a time for patience and yet more patience, isn't it?'

Two days later he wrote: 'I've done about all that has fallen to my lot in the Senate case and for the rest it will take its course. Our job is a funny one. When there is a difficult, worrying case there is a great feeling of relief when one has got a judgment off one's chest—whether it is a majority or a minority judgment. The danger of this is that once one achieves a judgment that can hang together logically, and the result of which is not unsatisfactory, one naturally feels that that is that and that the further exploration of the matter is no longer of such importance. And even the fact that one has had the judgment typed out and circulated [among the other judges], though it should, of course, be an irrelevancy, tends to make reconsideration and recall more difficult. We are all mighty human and judgment is not always, or perhaps even often, a matter of precision. [Oliver Wendell] Holmes once said that most legal problems resolved themselves into questions of degree.'

At the end of October Schreiner informed his wife what was about to happen, in a typical self-depreciative tone: 'We did conferences, including the final one on the Senate case. As I forewarned you the appeal is going to be dismissed. Keep this under your hat, of course. . . . You shouldn't be kept in suspense. Also, strictly between ourselves, I've written a dissenting judgment but no one else agrees with me, so I must be wrong. It happens that way and one mustn't think that the sky is going to fall because of the result of the appeal.' To this Edna replied on 4 November, saying that she, like all who were acquainted with him, was filled with great pride and knew that his judgment was completely impartial and objective. It was amusing to think that the Government 'need not have gone to the expense of packing the A.D. with their minions'. While any prospect of Oliver's being appointed Chief Justice had now gone, she was grateful, for 'it would have just about broken your heart to preside. . . . And it won't do the Gov't any good to

Mr. W. P. Schreiner, K.C.

BETWIXT AND BETWEEN.

From D C Boonzaier's *Owlographs: A Collection of South African Celebrities in Caricature* (1901) 50. See pages 3 and 105 below. (W P Schreiner and Boonzaier were both members of the Owl Club, the social, literary and musical society in Cape Town)

1268 *CAMBRIDGE UNIVERSITY REPORTER* [JUNE 11, 1912

Intercollegiate Examination in Law. June, 1912

CLASS I.	
Schreiner	Trin.
McNair	Cai.

CLASS II.	
Curtois	Queens'.
Thompson	Joh.
Rosenberg	Joh.
Lightbody	Trin.
Parks	Queens'.
Fream	Trin. H.
Powell	Joh.
Hopkins	Trin.
Clouts	Joh.
Lim	Cla.
Goodman	Pemb.
Wilson	Girton
van Druten	Joh.
Baxter	Pemb.
Heatley	Pet.
Evans	Trin. H.
Hill	Girton
Parham	Trin. H.

CLASS III.	
Watson	King's.
Das	Jes.
Jennings	Queens'.
Moulden	Non Coll.
O'Brien	Trin.
Rees	Cla.
Walker	Cai.
{Seys-Phillips	Trin.
{Stockwood	Joh.
Sington	Trin.
Banister	Jes.
{Langley-Smith	Queens'.
{Misra	Cai.
Payne	Jes.
Oppenheimer	Jes.
{Duthie	Trin.
{Ellicott	Trin.
{Milner	Pet.
{Pradit	Cla.

Hurrah! My best congratulations to you and to all. C. S. Kenny.

10 *June* 1912.

Oliver Schreiner's success in the June 1912 law examination, with the congratulations of Professor Courtney S Kenny, the eminent Downing Professor of the Laws of England in the University of Cambridge, friend and mentor of W P and Oliver Schreiner. See pages 7–11 and 112

Eights Week at the University of Oxford 25 May 1912. *From left to right:* Gerhardus (Gerrit) J Maritz, later a Transvaal judge, then a Rhodes scholar at Trinity College, Oxford (see page 58); Walter Power, a South African Rhodes scholar; Oliver Schreiner

Eights Week at the University of Oxford, 25 May 1912. *From left to right:* 'Beak' Steyn, Oliver Schreiner, Eric Thomas, Gerhardus (Gerrit) Maritz

have to take the step of passing over the only judge that stood out against their manoeuvring. Not every one will know that such a step was contemplated before the judgment was given.' To this Schreiner sent his answer on 10 November, a day after judgment had been delivered: 'You musn't say you're proud of me for disagreeing with my brethren. It isn't a cause for pride at all. If one is wrong well that is not anything to be proud of, and if one is right it only shows how miserably unconvincing one's way of putting it must be! Anyhow that's all behind us. There is quite enough in front of us to keep us out of mischief. . . . Now I must get to work on a long case we have next week about flooding in Germiston. I must restrain the impulse to remark on the fact that the name of the township was Wadeville!' (It was a temptation that was not resisted; his judgment in the case began:[121] 'In the year 1946 the appellant . . . established the industrial township of Wadeville (*absit omen*) on land belonging to it.')

The main judgment in the *Senate* case was delivered by Centlivres CJ, who held that the validity of the Senate Act and the South Africa Act Amendment Act was not affected by the legislative scheme. Nine members of the court concurred in his judgment; Steyn JA delivered a separate concurring judgment, holding that if a Senate was reconstituted, for whatever object, it was still a Senate for all purposes. Schreiner JA, dissenting, concluded that a legislative plan was not necessarily valid through being split into separate valid stages; the new Senate could act bicamerally, but not in the unicameral procedure, which contemplated real protection against parliamentary majorities acting bicamerally. It was a closely reasoned judgment, a classic dissent; to some South African lawyers it had a thrilling visionary quality, born of a mental power given to only a few judges, and not necessarily to everyone with a fine quality of mind. Opinions of commentators have differed on the result of the *Senate* case: possibly most have favoured the view of the majority, on the theory that the South African Parliament had been cast in the British mould, and that it is difficult to declare null an Act, prima facie lawful, on the ground of motive. But there has been powerful support for Schreiner's penetrating the form to find the substance. At all events, it would not be unfair to say that those who have hitherto disagreed with the judgment of Schreiner JA remind one of what John Randolph, American statesman, once said of a judgment of the great Marshall CJ:[122] 'Wrong, all wrong, but no man in the United States can tell why or wherein.' In this memorial volume Professor Marinus Wiechers gives the first detailed critical appreciation of Schreiner's judgment.[123]

[121] *Germiston City Council* v *Chubb & Sons Lock and Safe Co (SA) (Pty) Ltd* 1957 (1) SA 312 (A) at 316.

[122] Cited in C Warren *The Supreme Court in United States History* II (1922) 273n.

[123] 'The Fundamental Laws Behind the Constitution: Reflections on the Judgment of Schreiner JA in the *Senate* Case' 383 below.

The time was now approaching for Centlivres to retire as Chief Justice. There had been vague talk about the possibility of Dr T E Dönges KC,[124] the Minister of the Interior, being appointed Chief Justice. He had taken silk in 1939, had enjoyed a large practice, and had promoted the ultimately effectual legislation that had led to the removal of the Coloured voters from the common roll. This move was not in the mind of the Government, however, unless, possibly (there is no available documentation on the question) as a weapon of persuasion of others. On 21 November 1956 Schreiner warned Edna of an impending happening that he knew would distress her; he tried, once more, to make her reach a mood of calm resignation. '. . . [T]here are further talks going on about the C.J.-ship. As you know already there is no question about my ever being appointed. And let me say between ourselves that there are quite a lot of advantages in not doing that job in these days. In fact probably by the time this reaches you I will have told you [over the telephone] who has been appointed. At the moment his acceptance has not been sent to the Government but it will be, in all probability tomorrow. As he has not yet quite finally decided to accept I withhold his name. But actually it is a cert. All I suggest is that you take it calmly and don't be angry with him. We all know that I would not be appointed and he did his best to get the Government to appoint me. We won't have to act as GG & Her Ex next year when the Jansens go overseas!!'

Later that day he wrote again, but did not post the letter until the next day, when he sent two further letters. 'About the C.J.-ship, this has now been offered to Henry Fagan who, after much heart searching and after trying on the telephone and by letter to get Swart [the Minister of Justice] to change his and the Cabinet's mind, has accepted less worse befall. That is not a view that one could possibly criticise. You and I have long realised that I would not be appointed and we must both look at the advantages, which are undoubted. I will not have the administrative work to do and there will be no question of ever having to act as G.G. Anyhow, chum, I know you won't be sorry or angry at all. Dear old Henry is very miserable and one must try to keep his pecker up for him.'[125]

The first letter of the 22nd expanded a little on the matter. 'Just a note written in the morning to let you, in advance I hope of publication in the newspaper, know that Henry Fagan has agreed to

[124] 8 March 1898–10 January 1968; member of the National Party Cabinet from 1948; Minister of Finance 1958; President-elect in 1967, but suffered a brain haemorrhage on 11 May, completely incapacitating him mentally, and leading to his curators successfully applying to court to authorize them to lay down his office on his behalf.

[125] According to the report of an interview with him by a well-known writer, Charles Eglington (see *The Star* 10 December 1963), Fagan said that he had written to the Minister of Justice that if the rumour were true that the offer was to be made to him, he would like the matter to be reconsidered, in view of the seniority of Schreiner and Hoexter. It is widely believed that Hoexter, who had been a friend of Swart's, refused to take the appointment over Schreiner's head, but I have no documentary proof of this.

be our new C.J. He has been mightily exercised in his mind and tried to get the Government to change its mind and appoint me. But of course they wouldn't dream of that. I know you will have wifely feelings of indignation near the surface but you know that we have for long been quite clear that I would not be appointed and in many ways Henry's appointment will make things more comfortable here than if the next man [L C Steyn] had been appointed or anyone had been brought in from outside. The only argument against his acceptance would be that it may make things easier for the Government; it probably will. But perhaps that is an argument that one should take into account. Anyhow, belovedie, no regrets. In many ways it will save us bother. No need to act for the G.G. when they go on leave next year and so on. Now me for a job of work.'

The second letter added still more detail. 'Henry . . . only finally sent off his letter of acceptance today. Although he knows for certain that I would not in any circumstances have been appointed he is very miserable about it, especially as Albert and Oscar were for his turning it down. But honest Injun, chum, I am really happy not to have the job. In other circumstances I should have enjoyed it, but not now. It is much better to be freed from the responsibility of running this Court and working with the present Minister. There would certainly have been a lot of unpleasantness and worry. Henry will be a kind boss and I'm sure we'll get along very well.'

On the 23rd Edna answered the first letter, expressing her indignation. She agreed that they had known for some time that his appointment 'was, shall we say, extremely improbable' and said that there are 'reasons too, personal reasons, why one is very, very glad that you did not have to accept this appointment. Yet, in spite of all this, I find myself shaking with rage. I've been walking backwards and forwards in the garden trying to get myself under control, but not very successfully. That this slur should be cast on you, the best man in the world, this imputation of incompetency or dishonesty, still seems impossible to believe. I have to make myself remember that, coming from where it does, this slight is an honour to you. They are afraid of your strength & integrity, that everyone must realize that knows you at all, these mean & ignoble men. And so their despicable action just adds to one's pride in you and joy in the honour of being close to you. If things were otherwise, how keenly one would feel on your behalf this loss of an appointment which should normally have been the finish of your career. Now, from that point of view, there are no regrets for the position, only the feeling that your grand career is indeed finishing on its highest note—a great, full note that should inspire all who have ears to hear. . . . No—I am not angry with the man who is supplanting you. . . . I just despise him, as a little, little man. Blessing, my best and dearest one. I burn with pride in you.'

The next day Schreiner replied in terms that are to his everlasting credit. '. . . Your letter, my darling, breathes the fiery sweetness of the dear protective chum you are. But, belovedie, it isn't a case for either pride or anger. What reason have you to be proud of me beyond the fact that I am one of the generation of judges that go on doing their jobs with more or less success? Some of them get appointed to the highest job in their line, others don't. Think of Ben [Tindall] and Leopold [Greenberg] who did not become C.J. And think of John [Murray], Hal [Ramsbottom] and many other fine judges who didn't even become judges of appeal. After all, chum, you will agree that I am only as senior as I am by having lucky appointments at earlier stages. In front of Philip [Millin] to the T.P.D., in front of R.P.B. Davis to the A.D. . . . Helped by this advancement I certainly was by the fears of governments that their followers were more anti-semitic than themselves. Had there been a perfect choice of the best men all the way through I should not have been in a position to be passed over now. And as for Henry, he only took it when he was certain that I would not be appointed. It is not perhaps exactly the same as my taking the appointment ahead of Philip but it was not very different. Really my only regret is that if Henry had not been appointed the position of the government might have been a little shaken by the probable next one on the taxi rank [L C Steyn], while there won't be any objection in the general mind of unprejudiced voters, if such exists, to Henry's appointment. So, my darling, no regrets or bitterness. These are after all just troubles. One doesn't work for them and they don't mean a thing really. . . .'

Edna Schreiner replied in a series of letters:[126] 'Your career is not just founded on fortunate promotions. If I had any doubts on the matter, I need only ask the local members of the Bar.' Hal Ramsbottom 'told me of your letter trying to exonerate Henry on the grounds of his efforts to get Swart & the Cabinet to change their minds, but said that his opinion remained unchanged'. She referred to Oliver's having told her of Fagan's 'dreams of doing something really important for S. Africa, of the fact too that his nervous excitability & instability had led already to a couple of nervous breakdowns in his life: and it was possible there might be a recurrence'; but if he was unhappy, 'and if, as Leopold [Greenberg] thinks, he will prove unequal to carrying out efficiently his ordinary job, let alone his confused dreams',[127] he had brought his troubles on himself by his weakness. 'I cannot & will not follow you in your pity for "poor old Henry" and his heartburnings. . . .

[126] Edna S to ODS 25, 26 and 28 November and 1 December 1956.

[127] Edna's letter of 26 November said that Leopold Greenberg still felt that Fagan had acted wrongly; and that he regarded him as 'a born muddler & mucks up everything he touches'. Greenberg, though he never made public pronouncements on politics or personalities, had strong private views.

He must know, if he looks at things honestly, that . . . he was making it much easier for the Govt. to put through an action that nothing could excuse—nothing. . . . We will carry our heads high . . . but I could not bear it if a mistaken loyalty made you carry on to the end of your time, propping up & helping along that poor Henry. I know that you are sorry for him: but remember that never, never would either Albert or Oscar have done what he has done.' (Edna did not then realize that Fagan was older than her husband, and would reach the age of retirement in April 1959.[128]) But Schreiner was not a person who would show outwardly such inner feelings as he had by resigning.

The passing over of Schreiner had been unprecedented, though since then the appointment as Chief Justice of a judge of appeal not senior in the hierarchy has occurred three times. There was no convention in 1956, however, that the position went to the judge of appeal who had the longest service on the court; indeed, on the death of Lord De Villiers CJ (1842–1914) Innes JA appeared to entertain the belief (a mistaken one) that N J de Wet (1873–1960), the Minister of Justice, had some claim to fill the vacancy.[129] On the other hand, there had been a practice by the executive of deferring to seniority in the Appellate Division, though certainly not in provincial divisions in the appointment of judge presidents, who sometimes were appointed directly from the Bar or from other divisions or from judges lower in the provincial hierarchy. A number of designations to the office of Chief Justice had been of very elderly judges, who might justifiably have been overlooked (no member of the Bench in office prior to the coming into operation of the Judges' Salaries and Pensions Act 1912[130] was subject to an age of retirement). J W Wessels was 70 when he was appointed Chief Justice on 4 October 1932, holding the position until his death on 6 September 1936; J S Curlewis was 73 when he received the appointment on 21 October 1936, retiring voluntarily on 1 March 1938; James Stratford, who fell under the 1912 Act, was 68 on his appointment on 1 March 1938, and held office for little more than a year, reaching retirement age on 19 July 1939.

The English-medium press, though laudatory of Fagan as a man

[128] Henry Fagan (4 April 1889–6 December 1963) was a very versatile man—*inter alia* promoter of the cause of the Afrikaans language and culture; prominent poet and playwright in Afrikaans; Professor of Law in the University of Stellenbosch 1919–20; advocate; member of Hertzog's Cabinet in 1938; follower of Hertzog in his refusal to support Smuts on the war issue; member of the Cape Bench in 1943; Chairman of the Native Laws Commission 1946–8, which in its report (UG No 28-1948) concluded that total segregation was impracticable, and made detailed proposals for continual consultation between racial groups—the recommendations being rejected by the National Party Government; judge of appeal in 1950; Chief Justice from 1957 to his retirement on turning 70; subsequently (1962) a United Party senator. He was a gifted, cultivated, gentle, humane and courteous man. He was not a member of the Broederbond (see Professor T J Haarhoff's tribute in *The Star* 10 December 1963).

[129] See James Rose Innes *Autobiography* (1949) 257.

[130] Act 16 of 1912.

and a jurist, was scathing about the Government's action.[131] Naturally, Schreiner received many private communications commiserating with him, from members of his family, friends, members of the Bar and colleagues on the Bench. Ramsbottom was very upset.[132] Two others may be mentioned. 'Eddie de Beer . . . has expressed grief at my not being appointed and so has Otto Beyers. The latter may still turn out to be a satisfactory judge in time. Well, my love, hou moed and keep smiling.'[133]

The reason or reasons for the snub to Schreiner have never been revealed. No suggestion was made that it was because he was not entirely at home in Afrikaans and did not write judgments in it. His mother, of long and distinguished Afrikaner lineage,[134] never spoke Afrikaans to the family. Schreiner's view was that a judge should give judgment in the language in which he was most fluent, so that he could express his views as precisely as possible. As a trial judge he had chosen Afrikaans-speaking clerks (some of whom later were elevated to the Bench themselves) to put him on the right path when he spoke Afrikaans, which he did at times, such as when summing up to a jury. Schreiner, however, certainly read and understood Afrikaans and spoke it with fair ease.

Any man of honourable ambition and with confidence in his own ability, supported by the views of his peers, feels distress at having his legitimate hopes of getting to the highest position in his chosen field turn to ashes. It must have been so with Schreiner, no matter what he said to his wife or did not say to others—he never raised the matter in public or private, and if anyone did raise it he would turn the conversation with his customary charm and smile. He simply carried on, if anything, working harder than ever. One of his colleagues wrote to him during this period that 'you want to help the A.D. to recover, whatever the circumstances may be'—despite concern about certain appointments—whereas he, the writer, had reservations. It goes greatly to Schreiner's credit that he bore no animus towards Fagan. Whenever Fagan was absent—acting as Governor-General or on leave—Schreiner accepted the offer

131 See, for example, *The Star* 27 and 28 November 1956. The breaking of a long-established tradition naturally produces a reaction in certain quarters. For instance, Bora Laskin was appointed Chief Justice of Canada in 1974 over the heads of seven of his nine fellow judges on the Supreme Court of that country, ending a practice of fifty years to appoint the senior member. Though Laskin's reputation as a scholar was very high, there were some comments that his outlook on constitutional questions was congenial to the Prime Minister, Pierre Trudeau, whereas that of the senior judge, Martland J, was not. Others said that the promotion was unwise because it would create hard feelings in the court.

132 Edna S to ODS 26 November 1956: 'I wish Hal looked better. He was poorly over the weekend, after having been better, and I'm afraid that it was worry and concern over your A.D. position that brought on the trouble again. He is very white & drawn & thin, our poor old Hal.' However, on 12 December Ramsbottom wrote to 'Dear old Oliver' that he was almost his old self again.

133 ODS to Edna S 27 November 1956. The mercurial De Beer again!

134 See 'Father and Son: W P Schreiner and Oliver' 100 below at 102.

of the acting chief justiceship. There was a rumour, however, that Steyn would be asked to act when Fagan went on his last leave prior to retirement. This gave deep concern to Hoexter;[135] to his relief the rumour proved to be unfounded. But there was something behind the rumour. Once Schreiner had been rejected for the highest position on the judiciary, it was bound to occur on the next occasion. On 4 April 1959 Fagan would turn 70. Despite gloomy predictions, he had coped quite well; he had delivered erudite judgments—he read Latin with ease—and had shown considerable capacity to deal with complex facts.[136]

On 7 February 1959 the newspapers announced that Lucas Steyn, next in seniority on the Appellate Division to Schreiner and Hoexter, would be the new Chief Justice. The reaction of a considerable number of Schreiner's colleagues or former colleagues, of many members of the profession and of the English-medium press was possibly even stronger than in 1957. The very appointment of Steyn, from the start of his working life a member of the public service, had been controversial, and the Bar had protested publicly, on the ground that elevations to the Bench should be only from the ranks of practising advocates of the highest standing, and the Minister of Justice had undertaken that this would be so.[137] Furthermore, Steyn had been on the Bench for only eight years.

On the very day the news appeared in the press Albert Centlivres sent Schreiner a letter of commiseration,[138] saying that he found it difficult to remain calm. There will be 'intense resentment in the legal (& other) circles', he said. Could Oliver find consolation in the deep appreciation of his great services to the law? Centlivres reflected on the time they were colleagues. 'We found our differences of opinion stimulating in the sense that each of us delved more deeply into the matters at issue. . . . I always found you a tower of strength. Up to the time of Leopold's retirement we were a happy lot in the A.D. After that there was strain and stress but your being on the Court meant everything to me.' A leading public servant told me that he went to see Schreiner that day in his chambers in the Appeal Court to convey his distress and that of so many others; Schreiner said nothing, but tears welled in his eyes. The normally phlegmatic Ben Tindall, of great ability and devoid of prejudice,[139] Schreiner's colleague in his first four years on the

[135] Hoexter to Schreiner 31 April and 29 May 1958. ODS papers Wits.

[136] See (1959) 76 *SALJ* 117. On 13 March 1959 Schreiner wrote to his wife: 'Our Henry [Fagan] is full of beans now that he has only a fortnight to go before he escapes into the real world out of the judicial academy. He's really itching to be at his old game of politics, or semi-politics. . . . He is a good-hearted chap whatever folk may say about him.'

[137] See, for example, *The Star* 30 July and 2 and 22 August 1951; *Rand Daily Mail* 31 July and 2 and 3 August 1951.

[138] Letter of 7 February 1959 to ODS. ODS family papers.

[139] See the elegant tribute to his memory by Steyn CJ published in (1963) 80 *SALJ* 164, extracts of which appear at 283–4 below.

Appellate Division, was moved to write:[140] 'Reading my paper at 6 this morning I saw the disappointing news of the injustice of which you have now been the victim for the second time. The step taken is against the interests of the A.D. and of the Bench as a whole and is damaging to the public interest.' But he begged 'my dear Oliver' not to resign, because 'the loss to the A.D. would be almost irreparable' and he would not like to see the Government get the additional satisfaction of Oliver's departure. 'What a world! It is difficult to be optimistic in the South Africa of today.' Some other colleagues or former colleagues on the Bench were even more indignant. The forthright Hoexter wrote on 11 February 1959 that he had not congratulated 'Lucas . . . and do not intend to do so. Indeed I shall have to restrain myself from saying even more emphatically what I have said to him on numerous occasions, in 1955, 1956 and 1958. . . . Apart from van Blerk I can think of no colleague who would want Lucas as C.J., but I daresay I shall be the only one expressly to say so.'

The Bar and the attorneys' profession made no statement, but a question was asked in the House of Assembly on 13 February, to which the Minister of Justice, Mr C R Swart MP (1894–1982), replied that two judges of appeal had been passed over when the vacancy in the chief justiceship had been filled, 'because the person appointed was considered by the Government to be the best person in all respects for the post'.[141] *The Star* on 7 April 1959 published a lengthy anonymous article (now known to be by Arthur Suzman QC), saying that no one could seriously claim that the passing over had been on the merits, and that the 'inference is irresistible that political motives and sectional considerations' had come into play. The theme was taken up by some newspapers the next year, in their appreciation of the work of Schreiner on his imminent retirement. They attributed the ignoring of the rightful claim of one of our most distinguished judges to petty political considerations flowing from the liberal opinions he had expressed before he had been appointed to the judiciary, and the humanistic values and fearless independence of mind he had shown on the Bench.[142]

The disregard of Schreiner has not been forgotten. It was referred to by Mr Justice H C Nicholas, of the Transvaal Bench, at the opening of the Oliver Schreiner Law Library of the University of the Witwatersrand, Johannesburg, on 25 August 1976. 'In 1956 he could legitimately have expected appointment as Chief Justice, but

[140] From the Civil Service Club on 7 February 1959. ODS family papers.

[141] *House of Assembly Debates* 13 February 1959 col 794. On 20 April, in reply to another question, the Minister stated that he had not consulted the outgoing Chief Justice about the appointment of his successor, as the 'exclusive prerogative of appointing a Chief Justice is vested in the Governor-General-in-Council' (*Debates* col 4304).

[142] For example, *Rand Daily Mail* leader 31 December 1960; *Sunday Times* leader 11 December 1960—'the most eminent and distinguished Judge of his generation'.

that eluded him. This statement may create a wrong impression, because it suggests that he sought the appointment; he has an inherent and intractable modesty and humility, and he never sought offices or honours. . . . The whole legal profession was disappointed and dismayed. . . . His judicial stature placed him among the giants of the past: Lord De Villiers, Sir James Rose Innes and Sir William Solomon. . . . In 1959 he was passed over again. Once more the profession was deeply disappointed. It was suggested that the reason was a political one. If that is so, it was a reproach on a system which could allow political considerations to bear upon the appointment of the Chief Justice. But after sixteen years we can see that it is unimportant to his prestige that Schreiner JA did not become Schreiner CJ. What is important is that the authority of his judgments remains undisturbed, and that the esteem, the respect, the reverence in which he was universally held remain unimpaired. Machiavelli said that titles do not reflect honour on men, but rather men on their titles.' Early in 1981 a judge who had been on the Bench for many years, in giving evidence before the Commission of Inquiry into the Structure and Functioning of the Courts, under the chairmanship of Mr Justice G G Hoexter, said that it was a 'skandalige episode', undermining the independence of the judiciary, and a piece of political revenge.

Meantime, there had been another appointment out of the ordinary course, to fill the vacancy caused by the retirement of Centlivres on 31 January 1957 and make up the then complement of ten in the Appellate Division. The information was conveyed by Schreiner to his wife on 3 December 1956. 'Well, today came the news that you will have received by now that your friend "the Butcher" [A C Malan] is to take Albert's place. Curiously I had a note from "the Butcher" this morning condoling with me but reminding me that others too had been passed over! He then spoke of looking forward to collaborating with me in the future. And yet it never struck me that he was coming here, so that when Albert came in a few minutes later and offered me 5/- if I could give the name of the new man in three guesses I couldn't do it! Money chucked away! . . . I reckon there will be some disharmony when the Butcher comes. He has ability but not gentleness. Poor old Henry [Fagan] is very distressed. He did try to get Hal [Ramsbottom] and I think he expected the Government to respond.' A week later Schreiner wrote to his wife: 'It isn't quite clear why he [Malan] was appointed. He is of course next puisne of the Transvaal after the unacceptable Rammie. But as far as I know he is not *persona grata* with the Government.' He speculated on the possibility that some of Malan's colleagues had been anxious to get rid of him. 'He certainly has ability and if he is prepared to work he may be a useful member as things go. Useful but hardly clubbable!' It was a fair appraisal, for at the beginning of term the next year Malan was annoyed at being given an inferior room, and some shuffling had to be done, Schreiner told his wife on 25 February 1957. '"A.C."', he continued, 'will certainly liven up things. He has his own way of disposing of problems—a quick way, and not necessarily a mistaken way. But it remains to be seen whether he will do the solid sort of work that is required here. He has merits, like all of us, even the humblest.'

It was indeed a surprising elevation. Malan (25 December 1889–19 August 1963) had been appointed to the Transvaal Bench on 15 February 1939. Schreiner had been his colleague there for six years. Malan was next in seniority to Ramsbottom among the judges of the Transvaal after Maritz JP. While, in Bar parlance, he was good on fact, he had given little indication of the quality called for in a judge of appeal, whereas Ramsbottom had the stamp of greatness. Moreover, it was said that Malan at the time was making quite plain his lack of regard for certain appointees to the Transvaal and Appeal Benches. Most junior counsel and many silks were terrified of appearing before Malan, for not only would he refuse to tolerate papers out of order or ill-prepared or unsupportable contentions (no bad thing)—he was so often rude, sardonic, impatient, overbearing and a bully.[143] Yet, like almost all men, he was not of a piece, and he had his praiseworthy points. Some years later, in paying tribute to his memory in the Appellate Division,[144] L C Steyn CJ said that Malan was one of the strongest and most colourful personalities he had known, with well-defined convictions, unafraid, dynamic and immovably independent. On Malan's death a moving letter appeared in the press by a man who had been his clerk in the Transvaal Court for seven years, in which he spoke of his inner kindness, his carefully hidden but keen sense of

[143] There is a little hitherto untold tale that I should like to tell. Malan, who had started working life as a schoolteacher, prided himself, with some justification, on his mastery of English. Shortly after the last war junior counsel appeared in a criminal trial before him. During the proceedings he received the customary tongue-lashing from Malan; but this time counsel was not prepared to accept it without protest—he had been an officer and then a prisoner of war who had escaped and led a hard life on the run thereafter; furthermore, he was about to leave the Bar. In the course of increasingly unpleasant exchanges, Malan said to the advocate: 'Are you trying to be truculent, Mr——?', mispronouncing 'truculent' as 'true-sue-lent'. 'No, my lord', came the answer, 'I am not trying to be truculent'—the word being pronounced correctly. For once Malan had no reply.

Some entertaining stories of Malan are told by Isaac Goodman in his *Judges I Have Known* (1969) ch 12. There is one story I should like to add that has, to my knowledge, never been put into writing: I heard it told by the victim in an after-dinner speech. The victim, who never made a claim to being an Adonis, was appearing in a running-down trial. He was attempting to show Malan J with the aid of models how the collision had occurred, and said: 'If your lordship would now watch me.' To which Malan J answered, with his famous stress on every word: 'Mr——, must I *look* at you as well as listen to you?' Later he said to Malan J: 'I wish to change my argument. I am not happy with it.' Turning his familiar purple and smiling his familiar freezing smile, Malan replied: 'By all means Mr——, by all means. Nothing is closer to my heart than your happiness.'

[144] On 22 August 1963; see *Rand Daily Mail* 23 August 1963.

humour, his fortitude in the face of ill health, his dislike of publicity (unlike some of his colleagues, but exactly like Ramsbottom) and his very careful consideration of all factors before deciding on punishment of criminals ('the Butcher' was not fair), to which one should add his efforts to prevent his rebukes to counsel receiving publicity in the press. If a man can be a hero to his clerk, there must be good in him.

So once more Ramsbottom had been overlooked. A few years earlier, Schreiner, dwelling on certain appointments to the Bench and the consequences that are 'inevitable when people are given jobs that are far beyond their capacities' and saying: 'Perhaps it will begin to dawn on some of the less wild ones that to weaken the judiciary is to weaken the whole fabric of the state', reflected: 'I really don't know what would happen to the T.P.D. if Rammy fell ill.'[145] Now Ramsbottom's health had begun the decline that was to end in his early death on 30 November 1960.

On 3 December 1956 Schreiner wrote also to his old, dear friend Ramsbottom to tell him the news about Malan. 'I'd rather like to know what went on', came the reply on the 12th. 'At any rate it has saved me a lot of bother. I doubt whether the Govt. would want me to succeed Gerard [Maritz]. He is not going to create a vacancy if he can help it—and what may be the position in 3 years[146] time we don't know, but I fancy they have plans. Don't let A.C. [Malan] or the fact of his appointment worry you. That is Fagan's trouble, & if he is miserable it serves him right. He will probably be more miserable before long.' There was a limit to the tolerance of the saint-like Ramsbottom, of whom no man ever spoke ill and whom all regarded with esteem and affection.

There was some evidence that had Ramsbottom been offered the vacant seat, he might have refused to accept it out of protest at the treatment meted out to Schreiner, a step that would have been most painful to Schreiner and his wife.[147] Things had calmed down, however, by the end of 1958. By then Ramsbottom had witnessed three further appointments to the Appellate Division: in 1958 that of P J van Blerk (1906–1980), a member of the Free State Court since 1952 and from 1955 its Judge President; in 1958 also that of N Ogilvie Thompson (1904–), who had been appointed to the Cape Court in 1949; and at the beginning of 1959 that of Andrew B Beyers (1903–1975). But Beyers left the highest court in June 1959 to take the judge presidency of the Cape Provincial Division over the head of Herbstein J, the senior judge, who had been appointed in 1947 and had been acting Judge President during the long illness of J E (Jackie) de Villiers (1894–1960). De Villiers, who retired on

[145] ODS to Edna S 25 October 1955.
[146] Maritz JP would reach the retirement age of 70 on 7 December 1959.
[147] Edna S to ODS 3 December 1956.

28 June 1959, well before the statutory age limit, was an able judge; but though he had sat on the Cape Bench since 1 March 1939, he had also been overlooked for elevation to the Appellate Division. He had been chairman of the commission appointed after the war to decide on which enemy aliens who were sympathetic to the Nazis should be deported from South West Africa.[148]

Ramsbottom accepted a seat on the Appellate Division early in 1959, and the problem that might have arisen over the judge presidency of the Transvaal was solved. When Maritz retired on 7 December, Rumpff J, third in seniority on the Transvaal Bench, was appointed to fill the vacancy. Maritz's style of dispensing justice in criminal cases and appeals and in the divorce court had frequently attracted the attention of the press, which delighted in his, to put it kindly, unorthodox behaviour.[149] Schreiner, who had known Maritz in his student days in England, where he had been a Rhodes scholar at Trinity College, Oxford, found one final accolade too much to stomach. 'I read the "Star" leader of Saturday night cracking up Gerrit Maritz. One doesn't want to be hard on Gerrit but when one thinks of how first John [Murray] and then Hal [Ramsbottom] carried him over the years it makes one feel that such fulsome flattery as the "Star's" is rather out of place. But newspapers are that way—whichever judge plays up to them is their hero. Still one musn't be sour. Gerrit has his points.' It reflected Schreiner's balanced outlook. He was never savage in his condemnation of others; he tried to find the good points in them, while always being aware of the bad.

Centlivres wrote to Schreiner on 7 January 1959 that he 'was very pleased, both for your sake and Rammy's, to hear that he had been appointed to the A.D. You will no doubt find him a tower of strength and, relieved as he will be of carrying on his shoulders the burden of the T.P.D., his health will no doubt improve. And how absurd that he should have to walk into Court after others who have had far less judicial experience. . . . What a blow to the T.P.D.'

Ramsbottom in the short spell of life left to him was as painstaking as ever. Towards the end of 1959 Schreiner told his wife[150] that 'Hal is in good shape and is I think enjoying the work. . . . [He] has been working away at a judgment that is giving him some trouble. He is so thorough and conscientious that it takes it out of him more than it does out of a rhinocerous hide cuss like me. I haven't seen much of the team this morning—I expect they are working at home or perhaps not.' The last reference to Ramsbot-

[148] See *Minister of the Interior* v *Bechler* 1948 (3) SA 409 (A).

[149] See, for instance, 'Die ,,Kamerhof-Koning"' *Dagbreek* 1 November 1953; 'Mr. Justice Maritz on the Bench—And 15 Men Go Free' *The Star* 1 April 1959.

[150] Letter of 12 November 1959.

tom in the correspondence was on 5 June 1960: 'It was the usual sort of Sunday with Hal and me alone in the [Appeal Court] building. It used to be quite different when I came here first—we used to be all working and conferring. Now [he added ironically] we get through our work more easily it seems.'

On 30 November 1960 Ramsbottom, after a long sick-bed, died in Johannesburg. Schreiner attended the funeral on 3 December at the crematorium. It was a time of sadness.

The four years that Schreiner had to suffer the indignity of having been passed over for the position of Chief Justice, before he retired from the judiciary, must have been a period of trial, though he never lost his sense of humour and fun. His attitude is revealed in a letter of 8 January 1966 sent to him, when he was on leave, by Hoexter: 'Enjoy your well-earned rest & remember that as far as I was concerned you have been the real C.J. since Albert retired. I think that Lucas [Steyn] has now realised that what he wants is not a politically orientated but a strong bench and that with your departure he will have to do twice as much as before. And both Cora [Mrs Hoexter] and I get the impression that he was also asking himself whether he would not have been happier if he had refused to become C.J. He does not worry about me because, as you know, I have told him his fortune so often; but you never said anything; all you did was to work harder than ever, and I certainly think that he has a feeling of guilt. At least, I very much hope he has. I shall miss you not only in court & in conference but at the Club. If anything happens to annoy me in the future I shall retire without any misgivings.'

Indeed, Schreiner seems to have resolved from the start to do his duty with, if possible, even greater determination. Only Hoexter and he, and Ramsbottom after he had joined the court, worked on Sunday mornings. 'Oscar [Hoexter] . . . and I', he wrote on Sunday 7 December 1958 to his wife, '. . . were the only members of the Court here this morning. It is really an unsatisfactory position that we can't collect a team for a conference on a Sunday morning as we used always to do before the Court was enlarged. Now they go to church or their farms or their golf courses. For the first ten years that I was here we always had everyone here on Sunday morning—it was an ordinary working morning. But I suppose that one was spoilt in those days.'

Shortly after Centlivres retired he warned Schreiner that he was overdoing things.[151] 'I am sorry to hear that you have given up Saturday evening bridge and now go to Chambers every night of the week. That sounds too much like excessive work. However elementary the bridge of some of us was, it provided a welcome

[151] Centlivres to ODS 1 April 1957. ODS family papers.

relaxation from work on at least one night a week. Don't go & work too hard & ruin your health. Rather sit a little longer to polish off the judgments & give yourself more relaxation during the actual term.'

To his wife Schreiner explained how he lived during the five months taken up by the court terms. His life was virtually confined to board and lodging at the Bloemfontein Club and work in the Appeal Court building. 'You ask about my routine. It is very simple. I walk up by the north or the south route and reach chambers at 8.15–8.30. Work and potter till 9.45—then court till lunch with a ¼ hour tea break. Then afternoon court till 4.30 as normal. But often the cases end earlier and sometimes they end later. Then tea at the club and back to work till near 7. Then back to the club and back to court about 7.45. Till about 9.15 at the court. Wednesdays it is work including conferences in the morning, but normally no court. Bowls in the afternoon. Evenings as on other days. Saturdays same as Wednesdays except that no bowls. Sunday morning work in chambers and bowls in the afternoon. Evening as before. So it goes. Dull but practical. One gets through the stuff.'[152]

Four matters worried Schreiner in those years. The first, as had been the case ever since the court was enlarged in 1955, concerned the ability, diligence and sense of duty of some of his colleagues. Letters to his wife show his attitude to various of them. Of the two courts that would sit in the Appellate Division: 'It will all pan out quite well, I expect. We'll make more mistakes than this court used to make forty years ago, or perhaps more recently, but we must just do our best to prevent the sky from falling.' (24 February 1957.) 'There are two or three to whom easy cases can be assigned without causing one more trouble than if one did the judgments oneself, but mostly the latter course is the easiest. Really it would be easiest of all if one sat by oneself, but naturally the results wouldn't be satisfactory.' (8 May 1957.) 'Oscar [Hoexter] has just gone off—he is the only one that works here at night now. The others I suppose take their work home. Sez you!' (13 May 1957.) 'I've just been going through a judgment of Oscar's with him. . . . There aren't many of us that really go through the judgments carefully. And it needs to be done. . . . Ogilvie [Thompson] is in good health again and does his stuff well. . . . Oscar has just 'phoned me from his room to read out a proposed amendment—I must get him down to the Club. He is a rapid and efficient worker.' (25 September 1957.) 'We are getting into our stride here. If only we had more solid workers it would go more easily, but we manage. . . .' (5 November 1957.) 'We had conferences this morn-

[152] ODS to Edna S 4 March 1958.

ing— . . . they are not the old battlefields they used to be. It is just a matter of spelling and punctuation. When we dissent—and in two of today's cases I was in a minority of 1—we don't argue but just stay put with our views. Not good.' 'There will have to be an acting or permanent appointment for next term to take Reynolds's place. . . . We could do with a good 'un.' (22 May 1958.) 'The rest of the day I've spent doing the judgment in the case we heard on Monday and Tuesday. I've finished it now but it still has to be vetted by my brethren. There may be some dissent, if they have the energy to write dissenting judgments, which is doubtful.' (5 June 1958.) Of Hall's trying to leave before the end of term: he 'will probably have to wait—these blokes are always in a hurry to get away—provides the Government with an excuse for making us (or trying to make us) live in Bloemfontein.' (6 December 1958.) 'Oscar is quite a mad boy about playing things. After bowls he played bridge and since dinner he has been playing slosh—a form of billiards that old Bill [Oliver's brother] played a good deal of in his later years. If Oscar didn't have such an exceptionally quick mind he would never get through his work. As it is he dashes it off in half the time that I take.' (Wednesday 3 June 1959.) 'Our brother Malan went off today. He leaves early and makes it rather inconvenient for us.' (28 September 1959.) '. . . [T]omorrow two more appeals—one for me to write and the other I've asked Otto [Beyers] to do. He is one of those who can get a judgment done in reasonable fashion and with fair expedition. . . . I wish that they would send us a couple of good men. . . . Ain't we got fun!' (7 December 1959.) 'It will be good to have Oscar's active brain at work again. . . . A.C. Malan has left. . . . There always seems to be something at the end of term that makes it difficult for him to stay to the bitter end. Cattish, eh?' (10 June 1960.)

The second troublesome matter was the appointment of acting judges of appeal, or acting judges, from the ranks of retired judges. Schreiner and Centlivres had identical views on the practice: in principle it was wrong, and should not be resorted to except for very short periods. It reduced the efficiency and prestige of the Bench, and was inconsistent with the preservation of judicial independence. The executive should not have the 'discretion to extend the working lives of some judges [those on pension] at an increased rate of pay'.[153] But Schreiner had to witness a number of appointments of retired judges of appeal in an acting capacity. Hall had turned 70 on 13 July 1956 but had been given a further year as an acting judge of appeal; and then, to Schreiner's dismay, the acting appointment was extended for another year. 'It is quite, quite wrong but I'm afraid that is irrelevant.'[154] Norman Price, who

[153] ODS to Centlivres 4 May 1958. ODS papers Wits. Similar sentiments are expressed in a letter by Centlivres to Schreiner of 18 November 1957. ODS family papers.

[154] ODS to Edna S 24 March 1957.

had retired as Judge President of the Eastern Districts Court on 1 May 1887 on reaching 70, became an acting judge of appeal, Hein de Villiers moving to the post Price vacated, and the Appellate Division being reduced from ten to nine permanent members. 'I would have been glad', Schreiner wrote home, 'if Price had been able to rise to the occasion and turn down the job.'[155] Malan stayed on for a year in an acting capacity after his retirement on 25 December 1959, to Schreiner's surprise—'I am sure he doesn't like it here', he had written to his wife on 28 September 1959. 'So why should he stay?' It must have also astonished and grieved Schreiner some years later that Hoexter, who had been 'horrified'[156] by the extension of tenure of office of Hall and Price, and had on several occasions spoken to Schreiner of resigning, was also prepared to be an acting judge of appeal after he reached the age of retirement on 6 March 1963.

The third issue was his relationship with his colleagues. He was on good social terms with all save those who had accepted appointment in 1955 when the court was enlarged. Hoexter was a special friend, and he found him amusing. Schreiner wrote about Oscar's 'delving into the old authorities not because he thinks it necessary to do so but to satisfy Lucas [Steyn] that the decision which the rest of us are agreed on is right. . . . Oscar quite enjoys himself hunting about in the dusty old tomes of various sizes and finding, every now and then, something to laugh at.'[157] On another occasion: 'Oscar is chuckling because he has assigned to Hall the job of overruling Hein's judgment. It is the sort of occasion for Schadenfreude that delights Oscar's heart.'[158] But a typical remark of Hoexter's posed the issue of the 1955 appointees and of Price, who, in Schreiner's eyes, had also been a pawn in the Government's game to remove the Coloured vote through accepting the judge presidency of the Eastern Districts Court, and so facilitating the elevation of Reynolds and Hein de Villiers to the Appellate Division. 'Albert's departure', he wrote to his wife on 24 February 1957, 'raises a problem—I think we shall probably allow the barriers to fall away, provided, as Oscar reminds me, the other blokes are agreeable to their removal!' On 8 May 1957 Reynolds and De Villiers—'that strange, complacent fellow'[159]—were admitted to the bowls game. But there was a limit to forgiveness. Five days later he wrote to Edna that Price was to stay at the Bloemfon-

[155] ODS to Edna S 29 May 1957. [156] ODS to Edna S 2 November 1957.

[157] ODS to Edna S 27 November 1956.

[158] ODS to Edna S 6 March 1956. Hoexter's behaviour puzzled Schreiner. Every day, even bowls day, he rushed off to the Bloemfontein Club to play bridge—of a low order, the players being much inferior to Hoexter: he did not play in a studious way, however, but simply dashed 'from hand to hand. It would almost amuse him as much to deal out the hands and then count which had the most picture cards to see who wins!' (ODS to Edna S 8 May 1957).

[159] ODS to Edna S 8 May 1957.

tein Club: '. . . a problem arises. At present I sit at one table, Reynolds sits alone at another. Price may expect to sit with me but I intend that he shall sit with Reynolds or alone at a third table. . . . I have just as little respect for his acceptance of this post as I have for Reynolds's acceptance with the other four.'

Last of all there were the official functions. Schreiner, like his father, had never been one to care much for them, and he understandably found them particularly irksome in the last four years. When the Minister of Justice paid a visit to Steyn CJ on 5 June 1959, and all the judges of appeal were asked to tea, he told Edna that 'Oscar, Hal and I weren't there', adding jokingly, 'You don't think we're wrong, do you?' The functions in May 1960 to celebrate fifty years of Union he found depressing. 'I agree with those who think the occasion is rather one for sober reflection on the disappointments of the past than one for whoopee.'[160] He declined every invitation that in all conscience he could, agreeing, and then 'with long teeth', to attend only the civic dinner ('Ugh!') and 'the blasted Garden Party'—'Fortunately Neville Holmes has a grey topper and doings to match, and so will set the tone for our party. I'll wear my 13 year old best suit!'[161]

Throughout his letters to his wife, so warm and informative, Schreiner's sense of humour shines. 'I have . . . the grandest pair of gloves—surely the poshest in Bloemfontein, if not in S.A.! Many thanks, chum; it is a lovely present and they fit like gloves.' (9 May 1955.) 'My darling chum, some people say this is the solidest rain that Bloemfontein has ever had—others only that it is the solidest since Noah's time.' (28 March 1956.) 'It is a rather heavy [case] and I may not get the judgment done before we leave. But I'll do my best. Ludwig Mond, Alfred Mond's father, reckoned it was no excuse if he was told that a man who had messed something up had done his best. In fact he thought it made things worse, as there was then no prospect of improvement! A tough old bloke.' (25 September 1960.) Of a certain medical practitioner he had met: 'Apparently he has almost lost the gift of speech owing to the extreme loquacity of his wife who talks endlessly.' (9 March 1958.) 'My brethren . . . have left me as a dissenter on more than one occasion . . . so I must have misunderstood a couple of the cases.' (21 March 1958.) 'Henry [Fagan] . . . went to church this morning. I asked him to pray for me but I think he forgot. Pity.' (23 March 1958.) On an appeal that turned out to be unexpectedly difficult: '. . . to get the judgment done timously (no "e", according to Fowler![162]) I have had to do it myself.' (22 September 1958.) 'I have written yesterday's judgment

[160] ODS to Edna S 26 February 1960.

[161] ODS to Edna S 14, 16 and 17 May 1960.

[162] See H W Fowler *A Dictionary of Modern English Usage* 1 ed (1926, used by Schreiner) 654; 2 ed (1965; revised reprint 1978) 640.

and "imped" today's.' (4 November 1958—'imp' was a term he had coined as short for an impromptu judgment of the court dismissing a wholly unmeritorious appeal.) 'I decided to "imps".' (7 June 1960.) Towards the end of his judicial tenure Edna's health became steadily worse, and she suffered the first of the series of cerebral haemorrhages that were to leave her bedridden and ultimately virtually unconscious. Her handwriting became ever unsteadier, and finally her letters ceased. But Schreiner retained his courage and tried to cheer her up. 'It won't be long now', he kept saying in his correspondence. He could so easily have resigned, and so heeded Edna's pleas—for ever since he had gone to the 'monastic grove' in Bloemfontein she had felt desperately lonely during the court terms; and now she was clearly entering the last phase of her life; but his unyielding sense of duty—and perhaps pride—drove Schreiner on to the last day.

Several other issues engaged Schreiner's attention privately during his final period on the Bench. In 1958 he told Fagan of his sorrow at the proposed abolition of the recognition of foreign qualifications for admission to practice:[163] 'a narrow-minded coterie is resolved to sacrifice the interests of our country and of those individuals who believe that broadening the mind by foreign study is a good thing and not evil. It is the old idea, inherent in the caste system, that you lose caste if you go overseas.' In another letter to Fagan[164] he expressed the belief that, apart from subsistence and travel allowances based on actual expenditure, and an entertainment allowance for the Chief Justice and judge presidents, salaries of all judges should be the same, and be 'sufficient to maintain them in the dignified comfort that their high office requires'. Once the prestige of the Bench had been restored and it was again an honour to be appointed to it, and a still greater honour to be appointed to the Appellate Division, the question of judicial salaries would again become a rightly minor one. The best men were not becoming judges, not because of underpayment but because they were not being asked. To Schreiner the ideal method of appointment was by an independent body.[165]

Pro Deo defences by newcomers to the Bar caused Schreiner concern. Of a case in which the death sentence had been imposed for murder and leave to appeal refused by the trial court, he wrote:[166] 'Yet we were all perfectly clear that the conviction was

[163] Letter of 18 November 1958. ODS papers Wits. The proposal came to fruition in the Admission of Advocates Act 74 of 1964.

[164] Of 27 September 1957. ODS papers Wits.

[165] Set out in a memorandum of 4 May 1958 on the Bill that was to become the Supreme Court Act 59 of 1959. (ODS papers Wits.) It could consist of the Prime Minister, the Minister of Justice, the Leader of the Opposition, and a representative of each of the two branches of the legal profession.

[166] To Edna S on 1 May 1956.

wrong. . . . The defending counsel was youthful and ineffective; it isn't satisfactory that such should be the weak shields of persons on capital charges. It would be better if, say, five years experience were required.'

The second last letter Schreiner was to write home from the Appellate Division—it was on 23 November 1960—sums up his long spell in that court: 'Now, me for Charles Street and Room No 7 at the Club—my room for 16 years.'

The long pull was over. Mr Justice Schreiner had seen it through. There had been work to do; he had sacrificed one long leave towards the end of his service on the Appellate Division to do it. A number of lawyers anticipated Schreiner's seventieth birthday on 29 December 1960. Among them was that outstanding advocate, Walter Pollak, who had started practice at the Johannesburg Bar in 1927, taken silk in 1945, and, at the height of his powers, left a year before Schreiner's retirement to try to break into the closely-knit ranks of the London tax Bar.[167] Pollak expressed his regret at Schreiner's retirement and dwelt on the 'tremendous loss to the Bench'. 'I am deeply grateful for your friendship and for the example you set. Thank you. But the debt . . . is owed to you by South Africa and by all who value the great judge. Not the least blot on the Government's record is its disgraceful treatment of you. It may be of some consolation to you to know that in the hearts of the Johannesburg Bar you were for long primus inter judices.'[168]

[167] See my obituary in (1971) 88 *SALJ* 280. It was Schreiner who had put me in touch with Sir John Clayden (see page 286).

[168] Centlivres sent Schreiner a letter on the 26th, which is strangely naïve in places. He remarked that had Schreiner been born when he was, and he when Schreiner was, Schreiner would have retired as Chief Justice and he as an ordinary judge of appeal. 'By the accident of birth I happened to be your senior in years and became "ripe" for the CJ-ship at a time when a divinely appointed Govt had a slender majority in Parliament and had not hit on the device of appointing public servants to the Bench. . . . When I was appointed [Chief Justice] in 1950 I had the uneasy feeling that Leopold [Greenberg], who had had far more judicial experience than I had had, should have been chosen if he hadn't had the misfortune of having been appointed to the A.D. after I was appointed.' Leslie Blackwell (1885–1976), who was elevated to the Transvaal Bench in 1955, because Smuts did not want to have him in his Cabinet, puts the matter in proper perspective in his book *Are Judges Human?* (1962) 7. He points out that in 1924 Tielman Roos had offered Greenberg a seat on the Transvaal Bench when Greenberg was only 39 and had just taken silk. Though Blackwell does not say so, there can be no doubt that Roos had in mind attracting the Jewish vote. Blackwell says that he advised Greenberg to accept, despite the financial sacrifice, as it was difficult for a Jew to reach the Bench. Then Blackwell makes the valid statement: 'On seniority and on merit Greenberg should have reached the Appeal Court some years earlier, and would then in the ordinary course have become Chief Justice. But a large section of political South Africa, though willing to accept an occasional Jewish Judge, could not, so it seemed, view with any favour the idea of a Jewish Chief Justice, and at the appropriate moment another Judge much his junior [Centlivres] was placed on the Court of Appeal ahead of him. So Greenberg never reached the actual top, but for many years, like Oliver Schreiner after him, he was the outstanding Judge of the Appellate Division' (the last statement goes wrong on the time element at least).

F N Broome (1891–1980), a judge in Natal from 1939 and Judge President from 1950 until his retirement in 1961, gives another story in his memoirs, *Not the Whole Truth* (1962) 174–6. He says that Richard Feetham (1874–1965), who had been on the Bench

On the day of his retirement Schreiner gave what was probably his first interview to a newspaper reporter. It was published the next day[169] with a photograph showing him with his whimsical smile. '"What have I to say? My cases as a judge. There they are . . ." and he waved to the law reports. "No, I have no idea of going into politics. Write a book? What talent have I for that? . . . I mean to live quietly here. My wife is an invalid. . . . A man works, and he becomes 70, and what is there to congratulate him on? Becoming 70 is something that happens to a man. . . ."'

But he was to live a full life in his many years of retirement. And he could look back on sixteen years of notable achievement on the highest court of the country. It would be as well at this stage briefly to survey his contribution to the enunciation and development of the law in his judgments in the Appellate Division, of which some 355 were reported.

Schreiner as jurist. Oliver Schreiner was deeply impressed by the judgments and writings of the American judge and jurist, Oliver Wendell Holmes. Sometimes in judgments and in conversation he would quote Holmes's celebrated sentiment, 'The life of the law has not been logic; it has been experience';[170] and he referred to it in

since 1923, and Judge President of the Natal Provincial Division since 1930, ought to have been appointed to the vacancy on the Appellate Division caused by the unexpected resignation of Sir J E R (Oefie) de Villiers on 14 February 1939. (De Villiers (1875–1947) had undergone a mental decline, and had already become a pathetic figure.) But this would have meant the appointment of Broome to the Natal Bench, and Broome was the member of the House of Assembly for Pietermaritzburg District, an unsafe seat. So Centlivres was elevated. But Stratford CJ retired on 19 July 1939, on becoming 70 years of age (Broome speaks of 'another unexpected vacancy . . . on the Appeal Court Bench'—if it was unexpected, then the Department of Justice had slipped up badly); and this time Feetham simply could not be passed over. Frank Broome, whose frank book was published while Centlivres was alive, said that when he asked Senator Clarkson, the only Natal member of the Cabinet, 'whether Centlivres's claims were really regarded as superior to Feetham's, . . . he replied that Centlivres was a better Roman-Dutch lawyer. I am afraid I laughed in his face. From an intellectual and judicial point of view there could be no comparison between the two men, and Feetham's scholarship could have led him easily along the by-ways of Roman-Dutch law to fastnesses which Centlivres would have found it difficult to penetrate' (p 175). (Although I have the highest regard for Feetham, least honoured of the great men who have served this country, I find this statement exaggerated in the extreme.) Broome goes on, however, to pay tribute to the dignity and distinction with which Centlivres filled his years on the Appellate Division. (Of course, if Centlivres had been appointed after Feetham, he still would have become Chief Justice at the time he did, for Feetham reached the age limit on 22 December 1944.)

Let us be honest. Greenberg was the only professing Jew in the history of this country to have been made Judge President of a provincial division. R P B Davis, Judge President of the Cape Provincial Division from 14 May 1948 until his death on 6 December that year, though by birth a Jew did not profess to be one; married to Irene Marais, he was a conforming member of the Dutch Reformed Church. (Private information; see also *Dictionary of South African Biography* II 160.) At least two Jews have been passed over for no rational reason. I do not wish to mention their names. Lawyers will know who they are.

[169] *Rand Daily Mail* 30 December 1960.

[170] *The Common Law* (1881) 1, cited by Schreiner JA in *Daniels* v *Daniels* 1958 (1) SA 513 (A) at 522. Could Holmes have borrowed it from Rudolf Jhering's *Geist des römischen Rechts*, which he had read in a French translation in 1879? The passage from Jhering translated into English runs: 'Life is not here to be a servant of concepts, but concepts are here to serve life. . . . What will come to pass in the future is not postulated by logic but

the Hamlyn Lectures he delivered at Cambridge in 1967.[171] He would have appreciated Holmes's statements that, as to law reports, 'the last twenty years takes up most of the law unto itself';[172] that it 'is better that the law should be commonplace than that it should be eccentric';[173] and that 'in fifty years we shall have it in a form which no man could have dreamed fifty years ago'.[174] No doubt the members of the present-day judiciary will be just as appreciative of the possible applicability to them of the last passage. In the twenty-two years that have passed since Schreiner left the South African judiciary, the face of the common law has changed appreciably, especially in criminal law and the law of delict. The Appellate Division has been in a creative mood. At the risk of overstatement, it may be said that it has been trying to make the law more logical and internally coherent, sometimes leaving it to the legislature to decide whether dents should be made in the attractive resultant structure to meet a social need: thus, for instance, with the decisions that self-induced intoxication can be a defence to a criminal charge[175] and that ignorance of the law can be an excuse,[176] with neither of which conclusions it is at all likely Schreiner would have been party to. It has also taken an entirely subjective attitude to criminal intention, probably far beyond where Schreiner would have been prepared to go, in trying to attain justice for the accused. And, unless decisions of our courts have so settled the matter that in all conscience it is not possible to take another view, or unless (possibly) the result would be to break the symmetry of the law, it has tried to avoid the twisting of Romanistic principles, concepts and basic rules of law as a consequence of the invasion of the common law of England. Finally, the tendency (though it has not been universal) has been to expand the scope of the Aquilian action and the *actio injuriandi*, and give relief where it was denied in the past.

Schreiner belonged to an earlier era, into which he fitted exceptionally well; it may be that he would not have made the same impact in a more static or a more mobile society. It is strong testimony of the extent of his intellect that while some of his decisions no longer represent the law, so many still do. He achieved for his time a nice balance between the demands of certainty and desirable change, the pull of historical forces and the accepted standards of right conduct. He had a remarkable gift of synthesis,

by life. . . .' See Konrad Zweigert and Kurt Siehr 'Jhering's Influence on the Development of the Comparative Legal Method' (1971) 19 *American J of Comparative Law* 215 at 225–6.

171 *The Contribution of English Law to South African Law; and the Rule of Law in South Africa* (1967) 14.

172 In a letter to Sir Frederick Pollock: *The Holmes–Pollock Letters* II (1942) 20.

173 *Collected Legal Papers* (1920) 276.

174 *Speeches by Oliver Wendell Holmes* (1913) 34.

175 *S* v *Chretien* 1981 (1) SA 1097 (A).

176 *S* v *De Blom* 1977 (3) SA 513 (A).

finding common threads in decisions that at first sight seemed irreconcilable. So many of his judgments show the grand sweep. Others cut down the ambit of a supposed rule that on closer analysis is found too widely couched to do justice to the individual or to be socially desirable. By nature he was not a black-letter lawyer, and his approach was analytical and teleological rather than historical; but he was fully equipped to explore Roman law and the tomes of the writers on Roman-Dutch law, though he was apt to content himself with the citations of counsel or one of his brethren sitting on the court.[177] In his search for the just, reasonable and convenient answer to a legal issue, the expression of human needs and values in a civilized community—these were crucial criteria in his eyes—he was not averse to taking a line from Anglo-American law[178] or (occasionally) another legal system.

The stress he placed on justice and the felt needs of the time has already been illustrated in his attitude to the doctrine of *laesio enormis*. He frequently alluded to the need for modification and growth of the law, so essential to its life. One could look, for instance, at his treatment of the *culpa compensatio* principle in relation to condonation of the adultery of the plaintiff suing for divorce,[179] now of historic interest only; his rejection of eighteenth-century forms of criminal punishment;[180] his remarkable extension of the buyer's remedy against eviction;[181] his appealing tentative solution to the perplexing question of the liability of the dealer–seller for consequential damages flowing from a latent defect[182] that subsequently proved too radical for the Appellate Division,[183] which plumped for a narrow formulation that is inadequate for modern commerce;[184] and his realistic holding[185] that a soldier can acquire a domicile in an area in which he is not stationed, with *obiter dicta* suggesting (indeed, it follows virtually *ex hypothesi*) that the capacity extends to the area in which he is stationed.

177 For example, *R* v *Milne and Erleigh (7)* 1951 (1) SA 791 (A) at 877 (citations by counsel); *R* v *Davies* 1956 (3) SA 52 (A) at 59–60; and *Ex parte Minister of Justice: In re R* v *Gesa; R* v *De Jongh* 1959 (1) SA 234 (A) at 240 (authorities dealt with by another member of the court).

178 See, for example, his Hamlyn Lectures, *The Contribution of English Law to South African Law; and the Rule of Law in South Africa* (1967) 17; *Fletcher* v *Fletcher* 1948 (1) SA 130 (A) at 145.

179 *Harris* v *Harris* 1949 (1) SA 254 (A) at 266; *Daniels* v *Daniels* 1958 (1) SA 513 (A).

180 *R* v *Kumalo* 1952 (1) SA 381 (A) at 385.

181 *Lammers and Lammers* v *Giovannoni* 1955 (3) SA 385 (A), criticized by D F Mostert 'Uitwinning by die Koopkontrak in die Suid-Afrikaanse Reg' 1968 *Acta Juridica* 5 at 43–9 as being out of accord with the Roman-Dutch law and resulting in the seller's suffering an undeserved loss and the true owner's getting an undeserved gain.

182 *Hackett* v *G & G Radio and Refrigerator Corporation* 1949 (3) SA 664 (A) at 692–3.

183 *Kroonstad Westelike Boere-Ko-operatiewe Vereniging Bpk* v *Botha* 1964 (3) SA 561 (A), especially at 571.

184 See Jean Davids in (1964) 81 *SALJ* 419; H R Hahlo and Ellison Kahn *The South African Legal System and its Background* (1968) 312–14; J C de Wet in *De Wet en Yeats Die Suid-Afrikaanse Kontraktereg en Handelsreg* 4 ed (1978) 303.

185 *Baker* v *Baker* 1945 AD 708.

Schreiner, however, was no judicial revolutionary; he was resistant to appeals to change the law, mainly justified on civil-law grounds, that would overturn the settled legal order. Thus he was with the majority in holding that an unauthorized taking for a temporary purpose is not theft.[186] 'There should if possible be a high degree of rigidity in the definition of crimes. . . . It should not be left to judges to decide whether a particular act was done with evil intent or furtively.'[187] The definition of a crime, he said, is not an area for growth in the common law. 'If there are acts similar to theft which should be punished the legislature must intervene.' That the legislature did, by an unclear statute[188] that creates many anomalies.

To give three further illustrations: The Appellate Division had settled the liability at common law of local authorities for omissions, and if the result was unsatisfactory, he said, the remedy lay in legislation.[189] It would not be right to import via English law the doctrine of laches, despite its probable civil-law origin.[190] The court would not now consider a submission that it should apply the test of reasonableness to provincial ordinances.[191]

Like all judges, if pressed, even those most wedded to legal symmetry,[192] Schreiner denied that rules of our law are always dictated by considerations of logic.[193] 'Relevancy', commences a classic statement of his in the law of evidence, 'is based upon a blend of logic and experience lying outside the law.'[194] And in a clear, helpful analysis of a problem of multiple causation, he said: 'Causality often raises difficult legal questions which cannot always be answered by strict adherence to logic.'[195] In *Frankel's Estate* v *The Master*,[196] in which the Appellate Division held that in the absence of an antenuptial contract the matrimonial property regime is determined by the law of the husband's domicile at the time of marriage, and not by the law of the intended matrimonial domicile, Schreiner JA rejected the explanation of certain of the old authorities as resting on the latter ground because the underlying principle of generally applying the law of the country of the matrimonial

[186] *R* v *Sibiya* 1955 (4) SA 247 (A). The reaction of academics was mixed.

[187] At 256–7.

[188] General Law Amendment Act 50 of 1956 s 1.

[189] *Moulang* v *Port Elizabeth Municipality* 1958 (2) SA 518 (A), especially at 523.

[190] *Zuurbekom Ltd* v *Union Corporation Ltd* 1947 (1) SA 514 (A), especially at 543.

[191] *Joyce & McGregor Ltd* v *Cape Provincial Administration* 1946 AD 658.

[192] See, for example, Steyn JA (dissenting) in *R* v *Davies* 1956 (3) SA 52 (A) at 74, on attempts to commit the impossible: 'Logika, hoe belangrik ook, is per slot van rekening nie die enigste rigsnoer nie. Nòg die bestaande reg, nòg die praktiese eise van die regsverkeer, nòg die regsgevoel van die mens is altyd logies.'

[193] For instance, *Ex parte Minister of Justice: In re R* v *Gesa; R* v *De Jongh* 1959 (1) SA 234 (A) at 239.

[194] *R* v *Matthews* 1960 (1) SA 752 (A) at 758.

[195] *Kakamas Bestuursraad* v *Louw* 1960 (2) SA 202 (A) at 220. See P Q R Boberg 'Uncommon Cause' 145 below at 147.

[196] 1950 (1) SA 220 (A).

domicile is the fact that generally the spouses will live there. 'The practice of seeking wider, underlying, principle behind a recognized specific rule is a valuable means of improving the form of the law, by making it more logical and harmonious, but the practice may, if pursued incautiously, have unsatisfactory effects on the law's substance', he said.[197] He expanded on this sentiment, and concluded: 'The certainty of a generally accepted rule should not, without good cause, be weakened by doubts as to the reasons that may have led to its establishment.'[198]

In a masterly concurring judgment in *Die Spoorbond* v *SAR*[199] Schreiner JA elaborated on the caution to be observed in arguing by analogy. Assuming a trading corporation was entitled to sue for defamation, it did not follow that the state (the Crown then) could bring such an action against a subject. '. . . [G]reat care should be exercised in arguing by analogy from the rights of one person to the rights of another whose qualities are not identical with those of the first.' The Crown was a very different kind of person from other persons, natural or artificial. '. . . [T]here is no reason in common sense or logic for concluding that wherever a subject would have a right of action there the Crown must have one too.' The judgment continues on these lines, and is instinct with a belief in fairness, convenience, social advantage and freedom of expression.

Another splendid judgment along the same lines is that in *Essa* v *Divaris*,[200] in which he rejected the argument that the Praetor's Edict relating to *nautae*, *caupones* and *stabularii* should be extended to the keeper of a parking garage on the ground that it had been extended by our courts to cover the common carrier. There were important differences between a dead thing like a motor car and a living creature like a horse. No reason existed to extend 'by analogy the argument from analogy'. Once more considerations of fairness, convenience and social advantage proved paramount.

On the other hand, Schreiner JA was prepared to use this tool of reasoning where he considered it appropriate. Thus he invoked the law of theft by false pretences as an analogue to demonstrate that in principle there can be no objection to holding that there can be theft and so robbery where there is a voluntary handing-over under threat of physical harm—'the law may treat the vitiated will as if it were non-existent'.[201] In that case he showed a typical refusal to be hamstrung by legal dogmatics, and a conscious desire to decide in accordance with the prevailing sense of justice and the dictates of common sense.

[197] At 237. [198] At 238. [199] 1946 AD 999 at 1011–12.

[200] 1947 (1) SA 753 (A).

[201] *Ex parte Minister of Justice: In re R* v *Gesa; R* v *De Jongh* 1959 (1) SA 234 (A) at 240. This decision of Schreiner's has frequently been quoted as a model statement of the problem and its solution.

The logical principle of argument *ad absurdum*, pregnant with the danger of over-generalization, was evaluated in *Cohen* v *CIR*,[202] where it was held that the term 'ordinarily resident' in terms of the Income Tax Act could relate to a person physically absent for the entire tax year. The appellant's contention that there had to be physical presence for part of that year was shown by the respondent to produce surprising results in hypothetical cases. 'No doubt', concluded Schreiner JA, 'the posing of hypotheses that lead to absurdity does not necessarily and in all cases provide a sure guide to the meaning of a statute. But the method is of value and may be decisive when related to the slender basis for the contention from the acceptance of which such anomalous results would flow.'[203]

Two criminal cases may be cited to show Schreiner JA robustly rejecting the siren call of *elegantia juris* and giving what he considered to be a decision in accordance with common sense and social needs. Naturally, they have resulted in some academic criticism (though the first has also evoked support) on the basis that they violate legal principle in order to punish the wicked. The first was *R* v *Scoulides*,[204] in which it was held that a seller who intentionally gives less change than he knows is due is a thief; if the law said he was only a breaker of a contract it would be gravely deficient. The second was *R* v *Gani*.[205] Here Schreiner JA held that in a charge of murder against co-accused, even if it is uncertain who committed the crime, nevertheless each one who co-operated with the others, knowing that the deceased had been murdered, could be found guilty as an accessory after the fact.

Two further attempts by Schreiner to ensure that morally reprehensible acts do not escape punishment as falling outside the symmetrical net of the principles of the criminal law[206] were subjected to considerable adverse criticism by commentators. One has been rejected by the Appellate Division. He had twice[207] expressed the view—though it had not become the *ratio decidendi* of either case—that in 'joining-in' crimes X, who, after Y has inflicted a fatal injury on Z, 'joins in' while Z is still alive, is guilty of murder as a *socius* (a co-perpetrator in current terminology). Schreiner JA found that considerations of policy and the practical needs of the administration of the criminal law called for this conclusion, which could find a theoretical basis in the doctrine of ratification. But in *S* v

[202] 1946 AD 174. [203] At 186. [204] 1956 (2) SA 388 (A).

[205] 1957 (2) SA 212 (A).

[206] He clearly expounded this outlook as President of the Court of Appeal of Swaziland in *R* v *Mathenjwa* (17 March 1971 (unreported)), analysed by B van D van Niekerk in (1971) 88 *SALJ* 145.

[207] *R* v *Mtembu* 1950 (1) SA 670 (A) at 677–9 and *R* v *Mgxwiti* 1954 (1) SA 370 (A) at 381–3; accepted as correct by Tredgold CJ in *R* v *Chenjere* 1960 (1) SA 473 (FC) at 474–5, but criticized in the second edition of J C de Wet and H L Swanepoel *Strafreg* (1960) 168–70 as wrong in principle and 'absolutely cynical' in its invocation of 'practical advantage'.

Thomo[208] the Appellate Division—though very likely only *obiter*—concluded that a verdict of murder could not be reached, as this calls for conduct that caused or causally contributed to the death of the victim, and causation cannot be replaced by ratification, which has no place in our criminal law.

The other attempt by Schreiner JA was in *R* v *Britz*.[209] Here, giving the judgment of the court, he held that where A has killed B and seeks to raise the very special protection of justifiable homicide given by the Criminal Procedure Act[210] in certain circumstances to a person who kills another who is fleeing from or resisting arrest, the implied intention of the legislature is to place on A the onus of proving the requirements of the Act. Schreiner was concerned about the grave risk of the misuse of firearms and the protection of the sanctity of human life. It was a courageous decision in view of its derogation from the general principle that the onus of proof is on the prosecution. But its days seem numbered; Rumpff CJ and Jansen JA have stated *obiter* that it is wrong.[211]

It was only after Schreiner had retired that the Appellate Division rejected the *versari in re illicita* principle,[212] insisted that the accused had the requisite *mens rea* for the very crime alleged, delivered its crucial judgments on the meaning of criminal negligence, and held that for murder the *mens rea* is *dolus* and for culpable homicide *culpa*. With some of these decisions it is very likely that Schreiner would have disagreed. Still, it ought to be remembered that he delivered one of the judgments in *R* v *Nsele*[213] that settled the principle of the subjective test for criminal intention.

His views on provocation[214] have had a mixed reception and fate. There is much to be said for the view that the new direction in which he struck out in *R* v *Thibani*[215]—taking into account the

[208] 1969 (1) SA 385 (A) at 399. Young J in *R* v *Masuka* 1965 (2) SA 40 (SR) had already come to the same conclusion. See J H Hugo in (1969) 86 *SALJ* 391 and M A Rabie 'The Doctrine of Common Purpose in Criminal Law' (1971) 88 *SALJ* 227, 334, especially at 237–8, 335–43. In *S* v *Khoza* 1982 (3) SA 1019 (A) the majority of the court, on their reading of the facts, did not find it necessary to go into the question. Corbett JA in his dissenting judgment (at 1037–8) was not convinced that the statement in *Thomo* was *obiter*, but in any event supported the statement. On the other hand, Botha AJA (now JA), in a striking dissenting judgment, concluded that the statement was *obiter* (at 1056–7), and vigorously supported the decision of Schreiner JA as soundly based pragmatically and correct in legal principle apart from its reliance on ratification, which there is no need to have recourse to: the active association with the murderous act suffices.

[209] 1949 (3) SA 293 (A).

[210] Now s 49 of the Criminal Procedure Act 51 of 1977.

[211] *Matlou* v *Makhubedu* 1978 (1) SA 946 (A) at 956, 962.

[212] *S* v *Van der Mescht* 1962 (1) SA 521 (A), especially at 530; *S* v *Arenstein* 1964 (1) SA 361 (A) at 365; *S* v *Bernardus* 1965 (3) SA 287 (A) at 296; *S* v *Qumbella* 1966 (4) SA 356 (A) at 364; and *S* v *Mtshiza* 1970 (3) SA 747 (A). They probably would not have appealed to Schreiner: see *R* v *Mathenjwa*, decided by the Court of Appeal of Swaziland on 17 March 1971, discussed in (1971) 88 *SALJ* 145.

[213] 1955 (2) SA 145 (A).

[214] In *R* v *Thibani* 1949 (4) SA 720 (A) and *R* v *Krull* 1959 (3) SA 392 (A).

[215] 1949 (4) SA 720 (A).

provocation, had the accused had the intention to kill?—though it could have been more clearly stated, set the tone for development of the switch to the subjective test of intention.[216] In *R* v *Krull*,[217] speaking for the majority of the court, he held firmly that provocation cannot reduce intentional killing to culpable homicide; being in accordance with principle, this decision holds its ground. But in the same case Schreiner made a statement, really *obiter*, inconsistent with the first holding, that, for 'practical reasons', where the state of mind of the accused arises from mental abnormality short of legal insanity, or from idiosyncracies within the limits of normality, his conduct must be tested against the objective standard. In *S* v *Mokonto*[218] this approach was rejected in favour of the subjective one.

Time has been much kinder to the judgment of Schreiner JA in *R* v *Davies*[219] on that most debated of subjects, attempts to commit the impossible. Carrying all members of the court except Steyn JA with him, he rejected the distinction between absolute and relative impossibility, resting his conclusion in part on the basis of the 'weight of juristic opinion' and the 'current of legal decisions' abroad, and came down firmly on the side of a purely subjective test: at common law an attempt will exist even though the means used were inadequate or the object was unattainable, provided what the accused was aiming at was a crime. In *Haughton* v *Smith*[220] the House of Lords refused to take this line, finding that the law could not be so 'asinine'; but later it had to try to eat some of its words, and its decision was subjected to a devastating attack by H L A Hart[221] and by the Law Commission;[222] the upshot was the passing by the United Kingdom Parliament of the Criminal Attempts Act 1981, as a result of which *Haughton* v *Smith* is buried and the law of England in all important respects is the same as our law.

In general, it has been seen that Schreiner's attitude to common-law crimes was not a restrictive one,[223] though there are

216 E M Burchell and P M A Hunt *South African Criminal Law and Procedure* I: *General Principles* (1970) 120. But according to J C de Wet en H L Swanepoel *Strafreg* 3 ed (1975) 133, matters are completely confused in the decision.

217 1959 (3) SA 392 (A). See now also *S* v *Bailey* 1982 (3) SA 772 (A).

218 1971 (2) SA 319 (A) at 326.

219 1956 (3) SA 52 (A). Reaffirmed in *S* v *Palmos* 1979 (2) SA 82 (A) at 87–8.

220 [1975] AC 476 (HL), [1973] 3 All ER 1109.

221 'The House of Lords on Attempting the Impossible' (1981) 1 *Oxford J of Legal Studies* 149, written before the publication of the report of the Law Commission. He agreed substantially with the wording of art 5 s 501 of the American Law Institute Model Penal Code: Proposed Official Draft.

222 *Report on Attempts and Impossibility in Relation to Attempt, Conspiracy and Incitement* Law Com No 102 (HMSO 1980).

223 As exemplified by cases already discussed: *Ex parte Minister of Justice: In re R* v *Gesa; R* v *De Jongh* 1959 (1) SA 234 (A); *R* v *Scoulides* 1956 (2) SA 388 (A); *R* v *Gani* 1957 (2) SA 212 (A); *R* v *Davies* 1956 (3) SA 52 (A). To these may be added *R* v *Milne and Erleigh (7)* 1951 (1) SA 791 (A), where he applied a wider test than the majority of the court to the nature of theft of money.

decisions going in the other direction, such as *R* v *Sibiya*[224] on temporary unauthorized taking not being theft. Nor did he as a rule permit technical points to loom large in allowing criminal appeals,[225] though again one must be careful not to overstate his approach.[226] His attitude to the principles to be followed in imposing punishment for crime was on orthodox lines; as would be expected, he made valuable contributions to their understanding,[227] in particular the expression 'extenuating circumstances' in relation to a sentence for murder.[228] Many of his most dearly held views were given expression to in one of the last judgments he delivered, that of the court in *R* v *Karg*.[229] This very carefully reasoned opinion was delivered only three days after the conclusion of argument, which was typical of the speed at which Schreiner worked—always at full throttle. It is proper for a judge to take into account the consideration that aggrieved persons must not be tempted to seek private vengeance, he said; justice must be done not only to the community, but also to the complainant or to the parents of a person wrongfully killed. While the object of deterrence in the imposition of a sentence remains as important as ever, the element of retribution, recognizing the indignation of interested persons and the community, rightfully reduced in importance in modern times, is not absent, though '[n]aturally, righteous anger should not becloud judgment'.

When it came to fair treatment of the accused, Schreiner, for all his distaste for discharging a manifestly guilty person, was adamant that it be observed. It has been shown that he was in favour of our broadly accusatorial system of criminal procedure for its fairness to accused persons. He said that 'the presumption of innocence is recognized as a fundamental safeguard of the rights of the individual'.[230] '[T]o give an innocent accused real protection against false incrimination by an accomplice a new cautionary rule [was] . . . created almost single-handed' by him.[231] His was a lonely dissent in

[224] 1955 (4) SA 247 (A). [225] For instance, *R* v *P* 1957 (3) SA 444 (A).

[226] See, for instance, *R* v *Mathlau* 1958 (1) SA 350 (A), where he alone would have allowed the appeal completely; *R* v *Parker* 1958 (2) SA 639 (A), where, dissenting alone, he would have allowed the appeal; *R* v *Tebetha* 1959 (2) SA 337 (A).

[227] *R* v *Mzwakala* 1957 (4) SA 273 (A) at 277–8 (an important disquisition); *R* v *Barnardo* 1960 (3) SA 552 (A) at 557; *R* v *Karg* 1961 (1) SA 231 (A) at 236. See too *R* v *Sachs* 1953 (1) SA 392 (A) at 412ff (dissenting with Hoexter JA).

[228] *R* v *Fundakubi* 1948 (3) SA 810 (A); *R* v *Odendaal* 1949 (3) SA 1114 (A); *R* v *Taylor* 1949 (4) SA 702 (A).

[229] 1961 (1) SA 231 (A), especially at 235–6.

[230] *R* v *Britz* 1949 (3) SA 293 (A) at 302.

[231] L H Hoffmann in (1961) 78 *SALJ* 431n19, referring to *R* v *John* 1943 TPD 295 and *R* v *Ncanana* 1948 (4) SA 399 (A) (a classic statement), to which may be added *R* v *Mpompotshe* 1958 (4) SA 471 (A) and *R* v *Nhleko* 1960 (4) SA 712 (A). This rule has survived despite the absence from the Criminal Procedure Act 51 of 1977 of the provision found in its predecessors that the evidence of an accomplice had to be supported by confirmation or proof *aliunde* that the offence had actually been committed: C W H Schmidt and D T Zeffertt in *The Law of South Africa* IX (1979) para 559.

R v *Tebetha*[232] on the meaning of the statutory provision corresponding to s 218(2) of the Criminal Procedure Act 1977,[233] that evidence is admissible of anything pointed out by an accused or of any fact or thing discovered in consequence of his information, even though the pointing out or information is part of an inadmissible confession or other statement. Schreiner JA gave the provision a narrow construction, because he considered that the literal construction of the majority let in dangerous and very prejudicial evidence. His view is strongly supported in an essay in this memorial volume.[234] He once told me that he was convinced that the majority in the case were quite wrong, and that he would rather have the typical Continental inquisitorial system than a South African rule which gives so much power to a policeman.

For all the popular belief that Schreiner was a 'convicting judge' in criminal cases, there is at least one decision in which, approving the attitude of Steyn CJ and D O K Beyers JA, he took a very strict view of the burden cast on the prosecution to close all roads that might lead to facts consistent with innocence.[235] Passages from the sharp dissenting judgment of Malan JA (with whom Price AJA concurred), which was more down to earth, have since been cited with approval in two unanimous judgments of the Appellate Division.[236]

In the other large branch of public law, constitutional and administrative law, the most famous of Schreiner's decisions—those in the *High Court* and *Senate* cases[237]—have already been discussed. Mention has also been made of his striking dissent in the *Language Ordinance* case[238] and his decision in *Die Spoorbond* v *SAR*[239] that the state cannot sue for defamation.

The prerogative came for consideration in *Sachs* v *Dönges NO*.[240] Concurring with the majority decision that the passport in question could not be revoked by the executive, and with the reason given by Watermeyer CJ that it was issued in terms of a contract, Schreiner JA denied that prerogative powers 'form an almost mystical field in which the executive is free not only to do whatever it wills, but also to undo whatever it has done'.[241] The decision of Watermeyer and Schreiner goes further in the protection of individual rights than any decision on the nature of a passport in the Western world.

232 1959 (2) SA 337 (A). 233 Act 51 of 1977.

234 D Zeffertt 'Pointing Out' 395 below.

235 *R* v *Mlambo* 1957 (4) SA 727 (A) at 728–9. Note also the 'soft' attitude of Schreiner JA in *R* v *Dube* 1948 (3) SA 360 (A) at 364–5.

236 *S* v *Rama* 1966 (2) SA 395 (A) at 401; *S* v *Sauls* 1981 (3) SA 172 (A) at 182–3. See H C Nicholas 'The Two Cardinal Rules of Logic in *R* v *Blom*' 312 below at 323–4.

237 Respectively *Minister of the Interior* v *Harris* 1952 (4) SA 769 (A) and *Collins* v *Minister of the Interior* 1957 (1) SA 552 (A).

238 *Swart NO and Nicol NO* v *De Kock and Garner* 1951 (3) SA 589 (A).

239 1946 AD 999. 240 1950 (2) SA 265 (A). 241 At 307.

Schreiner, it is clear, had a deep concern for the protection of the individual's liberty of action against unwarranted invasion, so necessary in a country in which three-quarters of the people have no say in the election of their governors. But if a rule of common law or the legislation in point was quite clear, he did not hesitate to apply it, no matter how grievously it trenched on human freedom. 'The [value] of the maxim *audi alteram partem*', he once said,[242] '. . . would be lessened rather than increased if it were applied outside its proper limits.'

The validity of subordinate legislation was always carefully considered by Schreiner JA.[243] He took a rather rigorous attitude to it. And he warned against the dangers inherent in conceptualism in administrative law; of the supposed distinction between judicial, quasi-judicial and purely administrative functions and discretions: '[O]ne must be careful not to elevate what may be no more than a convenient classification into a source of legal rules.'[244]

Let me turn now to private law. In the field of contract he was, by and large, an upholder rather than a destroyer of apparent bargains. In a leading decision on mistake[245] he spoke of 'the generally objective approach to the creation of contracts which our law follows. . . . No other approach would be consistent with fairness or practicality.' But here he quoted cases frequently cited for the reliance theory (the theory of belief), which is sometimes linked to the doctrine of estoppel. The *obiter dicta* of Jansen JA in the only case in which the majority of the Appellate Division have considered the basic theory of contract do point in the direction of the reliance theory.[246] This theory, it could be argued, is really in support of the subjective (consensual) approach, but supplies the necessary limitations to its operation through the reliance principle. Very likely, however, once the law relating to operative error is invoked, both theories will normally lead to the same result.

In *Boerne* v *Harris*,[247] alone in a five-judge court, Schreiner JA held that a letter, purporting to exercise an option to renew a lease, but containing an incorrect date of reference to the renewal, was

[242] *Laubscher* v *Native Commissioner, Piet Retief* 1958 (1) SA 546 (A) at 549.

[243] A good illustration is afforded by *Arenstein* v *Durban Corporation* 1952 (1) SA 279 (A). A frequently cited judgment of his is that in *Amoils* v *Johannesburg City Council* 1943 TPD 386, on the test of reasonableness.

[244] *Pretoria North Town Council* v *A1 Electric Ice-cream Factory (Pty) Ltd* 1953 (3) SA 1 (A) at 11. Professor W H B Dean in his essay 'Reason and Prejudice: The Courts and Licensing Bodies in the Transvaal' 211 below at 218 calls the judgment in that case by Schreiner JA (in which the other members of the court concurred) a 'reassertion of rationality'.

[245] *National and Overseas Distributors Corporation (Pty) Ltd* v *Potato Board* 1958 (2) SA 473 (A) at 479.

[246] *Saambou-Nasionale Bouvereniging* v *Friedman* 1979 (3) SA 978 (A). In *Mondorp Eiendomsagentskap (Edms) Bpk* v *Kemp en De Beer* 1979 (4) SA 74 (A) he was even clearer in his views, but his was one of the dissenting judgments.

[247] 1949 (1) SA 793 (A).

effectual. To him it was an obvious error in expression that should have been seen by any reasonable lessor, and '[o]ne must not introduce into the modern law of contract a formalism that is foreign to its spirit'.[248]

Schreiner's attitude to the now defunct doctrine of *laesio enormis*, to the Pothier rule on the liability of the dealer–seller for consequential damages flowing from a latent defect, and to the liability of the proprietor of a parking garage has been mentioned.

There are several other illuminating analyses. Two may be referred to: cession in relation to offers and options,[249] and the ratification or confirmation of a contract compared with the conclusion of a new one (possibly by implication).[250]

On the law of interpretation of contracts the synopsis by Schreiner JA in *Delmas Milling Co Ltd* v *Du Plessis*[251] of the classes of evidence that can be used and when they can be used has been frequently cited; but recently courts have tended to find the principles he enunciated somewhat restrictive, and academic criticism has become rather adverse.[252] Mention should also be made of his stress in another case[253] that rules of construction should not be allowed forced entry.

Some of the judgments of Schreiner JA on delict have not weathered that well. His analysis of the controversial concept of the 'duty of care'[254] has been found by the Appellate Division to suffer from being used in relation to fault and not—if that 'onding' (monstrosity) of a concept is to be used at all—in relation to wrongfulness.[255] On the other hand, his masterly concurring judgment in *Die Spoorbond* v *SAR*[256] holding that the state cannot sue for defamation remains a classic.

On liability for an omission Schreiner JA took the narrow view of the majority in *Silva's Fishing Corporation (Pty) Ltd* v *Maweza*[257] that it calls for prior positive conduct. This is no longer acceptable, and the Appellate Division now invokes the wide criterion of the legal convictions of the community.[258] There are other cases where Schreiner took a very cautious attitude to the extension of the

248 At 810.

249 *Hersch* v *Nel* 1948 (3) SA 686 (A) at 691ff.

250 *Covary* v *Registrar of Deeds* 1949 (2) SA 719 (A) at 734–5.

251 1955 (3) SA 447 (A) at 454.

252 See, *inter alia*, *Swart* v *Cape Fabrix (Pty) Ltd* 1979 (1) SA 195 (A); *List* v *Jungers* 1979 (3) SA 106 (A); A J Kerr in (1969) 86 *SALJ* 8 and frequently thereafter in that journal, and also in his *The Principles of the Law of Contract* 3 ed (1980) 246–51. But see R H Christie *The Law of Contract in South Africa* (1981) 176–80, who clearly finds it valuable.

253 *Kliptown Clothing Industries (Pty) Ltd* v *Marine and Trade Insurance Co of SA Ltd* 1961 (1) SA 103 (A) at 107–8.

254 *Union Government* v *Ocean Accident and Guarantee Corporation Ltd* 1956 (1) SA 577 (A) at 585.

255 *Administrateur, Natal* v *Trust Bank van Afrika Bpk* 1979 (3) SA 824 (A) at 833, per Rumpff CJ. See also *Shell & BP South African Petroleum Refineries (Pty) Ltd* v *Osborne Panama SA* 1980 (3) SA 653 (D).

256 1946 AD 999 at 1011–12.

257 1957 (2) SA 256 (A).

258 *Minister van Polisie* v *Ewels* 1975 (3) SA 590 (A) at 596–7.

Aquilian remedy,[259] in marked contrast to the Appellate Division in its current mood.

Since Schreiner left the Bench the law of defamation has shed much of its English-law garb, and *animus injuriandi* has been lifted from a practically fictional to an essential component of defamation.[260] The stock defences have been allocated to their correct niches, either rebutting the 'presumption' of fault arising from the publication of defamatory matter or the 'presumption' of unlawfulness so arising. The liability without fault of the media of communication has been established.[261] The Appellate Division, in its long course of reframing the law of defamation, has had occasion to deal rather critically, yet not unappreciatively, with the judgment of Schreiner JA in *Basner* v *Trigger*.[262]

There remain some very fine judgments on delictual questions by Schreiner that are still cited: among them, those on the justification of a limited scope for vicarious liability,[263] and on the factors to be taken into account in deciding on the quantum of care called for in the determination of negligence.[264]

The nature of a trust *inter vivos* was the subject of a remarkable display of realistic analysis by Schreiner JA in his dissenting judgment in *Crookes NO* v *Watson*.[265] There he went into the serious objections to treating it, as the majority did, as a *stipulatio alteri*. It was a courageous but vain attempt to stem the tide. In his Hamlyn Lectures in 1967 he again expressed his regret at the result of the decision in the case. It was a pity, he wrote, that 'we have been so hesitant about taking into our law enough of the English law of trusts to satisfy the needs of modern South Africa. One can borrow too much, but one can also borrow too little.'[266]

On the law of persons there is one passage that abides in the memory. That is where, in considering a dispute on the custody of

[259] For instance in *Union Government* v *Ocean Accident and Guarantee Corporation Ltd* 1956 (1) SA 577 (A)—see criticism by P Q R Boberg in 1972 *Annual Survey of South African Law* 133, *inter alios*. Compare the robust extension of delictual liability for pure economic loss caused by a negligent misstatement in *Administrateur, Natal* v *Trust Bank van Afrika Bpk* 1979 (3) SA 824 (A).

[260] See, *inter alia*, *Jordaan* v *Van Biljon* 1962 (1) SA 286 (A); *Craig* v *Voortrekkerpers Bpk* 1963 (1) SA 149 (A); *Nydoo* v *Vengtas* 1965 (1) SA 1 (A); *Benson* v *Robinson & Co (Pty) Ltd* 1967 (1) SA 420 (A); *Suid-Afrikaanse Uitsaaikorporasie* v *O'Malley* 1977 (3) SA 394 (A); *May* v *Udwin* 1981 (1) SA 1 (A); *Marais* v *Richard* 1981 (1) SA 1157 (A).

[261] *Pakendorf* v *De Flamingh* 1982 (3) SA 146 (A).

[262] 1946 AD 83. Schreiner JA (at 95) drew a distinction between *animus injuriandi* and the malice or improper motive that is relevant to defeat the defence of privilege—a distinction that the Appellate Division accepted in *May* v *Udwin* 1981 (1) SA 1 (A), where the views of Schreiner are shown to have clear authority in Roman-Dutch law. But cases after *Basner* v *Trigger* are against Schreiner's opinion that privilege rebuts the inference of *animus injuriandi* and that an onus of *proof* is placed on the defendant to establish the defence: see Hoffmann and Zeffertt op cit note 88 at 389. See, generally, J M Burchell 'The Administration of Justice and the Defence of Privilege in Defamation' 172 below at 173, 177, 183–4.

[263] *Carter & Co (Pty) Ltd* v *McDonald* 1955 (1) SA 202 (A) at 211.

[264] *Herschel* v *Mrupe* 1954 (3) SA 464 (A) at 477.

[265] 1956 (1) SA 277 (A) at 291ff.

[266] Op cit note 171 at 47.

Captain O D Schreiner during the Great War

Oliver with his sister Ursula (Kay) in London during the Great War

ft to right: WP, Fanny, Frances (Dot) and sula (Kay) in London during the Great War

Left to right: Oliver, WP, Fanny and a colleague of Oliver's in London during the Great War

General J C Smuts signing the register after receiving the freedom of the city of Manchester 14 May 1917. *Left to right:* The Town Clerk (Thomas Hudson), General Smuts, the Lord Mayor (Alderman Smethurst), Walter Long (the Colonial Secretary), W P Schreiner, Sir Daniel McCabe

Dinner given at the Savoy Hotel, London, on 23 May 1917 in honour of General J C Smuts. *Left to right:* W P Schreiner, Lord Harris, Viscount Milner (High Commissioner for South Africa 1897–1905, and Governor of the Cape Colony 1897–1901 and of the Transvaal and Orange River Colony 1902–5), General Smuts, the Earl of Selborne (High Commissioner for South Africa and Governor of the Transvaal and Orange River Colony 1905–10), Lord Gladstone (High Commissioner for and Governor-General of the Union of South Africa 1910–14), Lord Sandhurst, Lord Sydenham

minor children, he spoke of a need to instil in children 'a due regard for the superlative virtues of truthfulness and kindliness'.[267]

The view of Schreiner[268] that a revoked will can be revived by a subsequent valid will has proved attractive to some commentators,[269] though the question is still an open one.

Schreiner made some valuable contributions to our understanding of the rules of interpretation of legislation. His statement[270] on the correct approach to the topic has been frequently quoted. In various judgments he pointed to difficulties in the operation of the constitutional rule that in the event of conflict the signed copy of an Act or ordinance prevails;[271] expatiated on the distinction between true retrospectivity of legislation and interference with vested rights;[272] and analysed the *ejusdem generis* rule.[273]

On Black customary law Schreiner delivered a number of leading judgments that clarified aspects of this complex subject.[274]

In the sphere of jurisprudence his analysis of the nature of the *ratio decidendi* of a single judgment[275] met with the commendation of Sir Rupert Cross.[276]

. Schreiner had a reputation for being hard on the taxpayer. Perhaps some of his decisions unconsciously reflect his private attitude that the citizen must yield his due to the state; but on at least one occasion[277] he was a dissentient who favoured the taxpayer. A judgment of his,[278] divorced from that question, remains as a valuable analysis of the distinction between questions of fact and questions of law in adjective law as a whole.

Looking over Schreiner's twenty-four years' service on the Bench, one can see why judges and writers on the law, especially where they express disagreement with a decision of his, are apt to pay deference to him by using such expressions as 'a great judge',[279] 'so eminent a judge',[280] or 'a most distinguished judge of appeal'.[281] In our legal tradition, based on that of England, an important function of a judge is to give an authoritative statement of the scope of a rule of law and, where this is appropriate, its possible limitation or extension. There is also some room in appropriate circum-

267 *Fletcher* v *Fletcher* 1948 (1) SA 130 (A) at 146.
268 *Moses* v *Abinader* 1951 (4) SA 537 (A).
269 For instance, M M Corbett *et al The Law of Succession in South Africa* (1980) 100.
270 *Jaga* v *Dönges NO* 1950 (4) SA 653 (A) at 662ff.
271 *R* v *Silinga* 1957 (3) SA 354 (A) at 358–9.
272 *Shewan Tomes & Co Ltd* v *Commissioner of Customs and Excise* 1955 (4) SA 305 (A) at 312.
273 *Grobbelaar* v *Van de Vyver* 1954 (1) SA 248 (A) at 254.
274 See A J Kerr 'Customary Law in the Appellate Division 1945–1960' 264 below.
275 *Pretoria City Council* v *Levinson* 1949 (3) SA 305 (A) at 316–17.
276 *Precedent in English Law* 3 ed (1977) 79.
277 *CIR* v *Epstein* 1954 (3) SA 689 (A).
278 *Morrison* v *CIR* 1950 (2) SA 449 (A) at 455.
279 For example, Hoffmann and Zeffertt op cit note 88 at 389.
280 A J Kerr *The Principles of the Law of Contract* 3 ed (1980) 247.
281 C P Bresler (formerly a Transvaal judge) *Tilt the Sack* (1965) 135.

stances for *obiter dicta* on a matter fully argued, which Schreiner JA appreciated, though he was always careful not to give approval in a remark by the way to a proposition generally accepted as law but still devoid of the imprimatur of the Appellate Division. On the width of the *ratio* of a decision a judge may, as Greenberg was inclined to do, keep within the narrowest confines necessary to reach a decision. Schreiner, however, was apt to go out of his way to settle a disputed point, which often is of great service to those involved in the administration of justice. For example, in *Essa* v *Divaris*[282] he said that the important question whether the keeper of a parking garage was included in the term *stabularius* in the Praetor's Edict had been fully canvassed in argument; that an early solution was desirable; and that 'although it would . . . be possible to decide the case on the more conservative lines preferred by my brother Greenberg, I think that it is more satisfactory to follow the lines of the argument and deal with the applicability of the Edict'.

A reading of Schreiner's decisions as a judge of appeal leaves a strong impression of three convictions of his: first, that the Appellate Division has its own ethos—'this court', he would frequently say, with the stress on 'this', as being a court distinct from and on a higher plane than provincial and local divisions; secondly, that the Appellate Division has a duty to be loyal to the characteristic spirit it has evolved for itself; and thirdly, associated with the first two convictions, that, in general, it is the function of a judge of appeal to look at matters afresh, untrammelled by decisions of courts lower in the hierarchy—Schreiner did not often expressly consider or cite the decisions of those courts.[283]

His style of writing was generally spare, with only an occasional flourish. Almost all his judgments were lucid, leaving no loose threads to flaw the appearance of the fabric. One of the last letters to his wife from Bloemfontein is revealing: 'We finished our case today just after lunch time and I have since then been busy trying to frame the judgment with the proper precision. It is one of those cases where there is no doubt about the result but one has to be very careful in the choice of the right words. The fewest words the better is often the right rule, but then one has to be mighty careful that the few are just what the doctor ordered. Our brethren are there to help of course by vetting one's language but primarily one has to do it oneself. Words! Words! What a strange thing that they should be so potent!'

The Last Phase (1961–80)

Schreiner may have told the newspaper reporter in the garden of his home in Johannesburg, after he had heard his last case in

[282] 1947 (1) SA 753 (A) at 775.

[283] See my article 'The Rules of Precedent Applied in South African Courts' (1967) 84 *SALJ* 175 at 188.

Bloemfontein, that he meant to live quietly at home. Certainly he had no wish to be appointed an acting judge of appeal, and no offer came anyway. There was work to hand, however. For the first ten years or so his was not the conventional retirement of a man who was in debit to life, having reached is allotted span. True, there was bowls, a game he loved; but his arthritis, which had started in his early sixties, became increasingly incapacitating, and eventually he had to have a serious operation to replace his hip joint. Even then he continued being plagued with the illness. Never had he worked with his hands. 'It just goes to show how things get handed on in a family', he once wrote to his wife,[284] expressing his pleasure on hearing that his younger son was doing carpentry. 'I don't suppose I was born to be a waster of time on golf courses and bowling greens; it was just that my father worked terribly hard with his brain but not at all with his hands, and Bill and I just carried on.' But there was activity for Schreiner's brain. The press[285] had already revealed that he had accepted the position of a judge of appeal in the High Commission Territories—Basutoland, Bechuanaland Protectorate and Swaziland. The President of the court was Sir Walter Harragin, a former colonial judge, who is perhaps best known as the Attorney-General of Kenya who in 1941 unsuccessfully prosecuted Sir Delves Broughton for the murder of the Earl of Errol.[286] Harragin had served a spell as Chief Justice of the territories and thereafter settled in Johannesburg in 1952. He had been on the Court of Appeal of the High Commission Territories since 1955, and remained on it until 1965. The other members of the court, appointed initially for a year as from 1 January 1961, were, in order of seniority, Mr Justice E R Roper (1886–1974), a retired Transvaal judge, Schreiner and Sir John Murray. After Harragin left, Roper became President. As the territories became independent (Botswana in September 1966, Lesotho in October 1966, Swaziland in September 1968) and acquired their own courts of appeal, Schreiner served on each. His colleagues changed from time to time as incumbents retired, resigned or died. When Roper retired in 1969, Schreiner took his place at the head of the three courts of appeal. Leo Caney, who had been on the Natal Bench, sent this letter to Schreiner on 22 October:[287] 'My dear Oliver . . . Would I mind having you as my Chief? What a question! I shall be honoured and delighted (sorry though I am that Roper is leaving us) to serve under you. Long may it be so.' Schreiner retired from the courts of appeal at the end of 1973. He was 83 years of age, and though the sessions were not long—all told they stretched over

[284] ODS to Edna S 24 September 1956. ODS family papers.

[285] See *The Star* 20 December 1960.

[286] See the entertaining account by the leader for the defence, H H Morris KC, in his memoirs, *The First Forty Years* (1948) ch XXVI.

[287] ODS family papers.

about six weeks a year—they entailed some travelling, and it was time to call a halt. Moreover, he had had a stroke in April, while driving his car; he had looked very ill for some months, and though he recovered fully from it, he resolved never to drive again, lest he be a danger to others.

Schreiner was shortly to see one of his wishes fulfilled:[288] a Black judge. In January 1974 Mr J G Mapetla (1931–75), head of the civil service of Lesotho, was appointed Chief Justice of that state. He died after a long illness in December the following year.

For a few years Schreiner's services were in demand as an arbitrator. In the month after his retirement he started the important and very protracted arbitration hearing arising out of damage caused by the floods at Kariba Dam.

There was also educational, social and charitable work for him to do. He did not merely think, speak and write about such matters: he did something about them.

In education his main interest lay in the University of the Witwatersrand, Johannesburg. When Richard Feetham, in old age, resigned as Chancellor of that institution in 1961, Schreiner was elected unopposed to succeed him from the beginning of 1962. The University followed the example set by the University of Cape Town in 1958, and conferred an honorary degree of Doctor of Laws on him in 1961. Rhodes University in 1963 granted him his third honorary doctorate in law. Schreiner remained Chancellor, even after he had had his stroke;[289] in those days the position was for life or until resignation. At the end of 1974, however, he was persuaded that he had done all that could be expected of any man. The duties of the office were proving burdensome; for though it is largely a titular post, it calls for considerable service, particularly in the conferring of degrees and the granting of certificates, and in attendance at numerous official functions. His period of chancellorship had been outstanding. In academic proceedings he was dignified, calm, perfect in his observance of protocol, and yet at the same time warm and genial. For every graduand there were the

[288] On 25 July 1973 Schreiner, at a reception for the judges of appeal of the Court of Appeal of Swaziland, of which he was President, said that he looked forward to the time when African judges would be appointed to the judiciary of the country, but that the Government should not hasten this process: *The Star* 25 July 1973.

[289] On 14 April 1973. He replied in typical courteous and brave style, but with shaky hand, to a letter of mine expressing my delight that I had heard he was well on the way to recovery, and would have paid him a call but for doctor's orders forbidding it. The reply was sent on the same day. After thanking me and my wife for our wishes for a speedy recovery, he said: 'It was a disconcerting incident and has cast a burden on you chaps, especially Bozz [Prof G R Bozzoli, the Vice-Chancellor, who had to act for him] that I very much regret. I didn't do it on purpose!

'I write rottenly but (you may not believe me) better than I did a week ago. You have been doing the citation for [the honorary degree for] Anna Scheepers this morning. I wish I had been there.'

'. . . I mean to get well and do a job again.'

riveting of attention that is the essence of a gentleman, a smile, words of congratulation, and the bone-crushing handshake for which he was famous and, among the weaker of us, notorious. There was hardly an official function that he did not attend; and always he was the soul of good manners and good humour. Whenever it was feasible, he brought Jean with him; he looked after her with touching care.

Although he was Chancellor, he remained on the Council, as Feetham had done—not really a desirable thing in practice. When it was announced at a meeting of the Council in 1977 that the State President had appointed him for yet another four-year term, Schreiner chuckled: 'It is ridiculous. I'll be over 90 at the end of the period.' He did not live to see it out.

On the Council he did not speak often; but when he did it was always to the point. He could alight on something the others had missed. Great reliance was placed on his wise and balanced opinions. Always ready to see the force of arguments on both sides, nevertheless he was as a rule firm in his conclusions, which were couched in the moderate terms typical of him. Of late years he used to lean forward on his seat, a hand frequently cupped over one ear, so as to hear better, absorbing all that was said. Never did he deviate from his high democratic principles or belief that academic freedom is the hallmark of a true university.

Those who knew him best are of the opinion that in the last three years of his life his mental powers began slowly to decline. To me, associated largely with him in University work, they remained undimmed with the passage of time. How well I remember how, towards the end of 1979, I served with him on a committee of three appointed by the Council to go into a legal question relating to it. He did not agree with certain professional advice that had been given, for reasons he stated clearly. A case in point decided fifty years ago came immediately to his lips. Then he mentioned something that Tilson Barry KC had once said to him, that if in an opinion counsel stated that there was no essential difference between the problem posed in the papers and one decided in a particular reported decision, it was not *likely* that counsel would be wrong—it was *certain* that he would be.

Schreiner's social and charitable work was concerned mainly with two organizations. The first was the Alexandra Health Centre and University [of the Witwatersrand] Clinic, of which he was Chairman for many years, and in which his wife took a deep interest in the days she was a well person. Situate as it was on the periphery of the Black slum of Alexandra, so shamefully neglected by the authorities, the clinic, a voluntary society, gave medical help in an area where it was desperately needed. By helping run it, Schreiner could find practical expression for his lifelong concern with the interests of the Black population, his deep humanity, his compassion and his charity, and his belief that every person should do his share for the needy.

The second organization was the South African Institute of Race Relations, of which he had been elected an honorary life member in 1960, being one of ten so honoured, and on the Council of which he served for many years, attending its long annual meeting—stretching over several days—religiously, though grumbling at times at the speeches of the young radicals. From 1961 to 1963 he was President of the Institute. He had had doubts about his accepting the post, fearing that it might do the judiciary no good for a retired member to associate himself prominently with the public controversies the Institute would necessarily be engaged in; it might lead the public to think that in the past his judicial functions had been influenced by a point of view now classed as semi-political.[290] Centlivres reassured him,[291] referring to the support the eminent and upright Sir James Rose Innes had given in his retirement to the Non-racial Franchise Association in its opposition to Hertzog's Representation of Natives Bill.

For the last thirty years of his life Schreiner was an Honorary President of the South African Institute of International Affairs, an organization that even in this country could not be stigmatized as political. To the end he was a regular attender at its monthly meetings at Jan Smuts House in the University grounds.

There were a couple of societies that he felt compelled to dissociate himself from because they had introduced a colour bar. There was always a stage when he had to make a mute protest. In his last year on the Appellate Division, for all his love of sport he declined to attend the trials to pick the Springbok rugby team to meet the New Zealanders, as he did not ever attend the local sports stadium, because only Whites were allowed to be spectators.[292] In 1970 he refused to accept renomination as President of the Cripple Care Association of the Transvaal, since it had amended its constitution to restrict membership to Whites, failing which its grant by the Government would have been stopped; and in 1972 he declined to become a sponsor of another worthy social-service organization, as it worked on a colour-bar basis in order to get an essential subsidy from the Department of Social Welfare. 'I think that I understand and sympathise with your point of view', he wrote to the Chairman of the latter body.[293] 'The problem has arisen before, many times since Naaman worshipped in the temple of Rimmon. . . . Where people are active and do good work they

[290] Letter to Quintin Whyte, Director of the SAIRR, of 7 November 1960. ODS papers Wits.

[291] Letter of 8 November 1960. ODS papers Wits.

[292] ODS to Edna S 13 May 1960. ODS family papers.

[293] On 3 January 1973. ODS papers Wits.

have to compromise. But where one is a mere figure-head, like a sponsor, one has greater freedom. Then one may indulge in the otherwise hateful practice of handwashing.'

He also washed his hands of seats at municipal bus stops and parks as long as they were marked for different races. On 1 February 1974 I was taking him home in my car at the end of a meeting of the University Council; this was after he had had his stroke and no longer drove, frequently caught buses and was suffering grievously from arthritis. We discussed the removal by the Johannesburg City Council of a good deal of 'petty apartheid', opening up to all racial groups the municipal rates hall, the Rand Show and seats at bus stops. We agreed that this was a most commendable step. To my surprise he said that now he could sit at the bus stop and in a park. Never had he sat on a seat there marked 'Europeans Only' or 'Whites Only': 'I always felt ashamed at the thought of sitting when some elderly African washerwoman had to stand.'

Agreeing with Centlivres that this was the right thing,[294] he kept away from party politics. He did, however, in his near two decades of retirement state his outlook on political matters, though he was not prepared to participate in public protest, as was Centlivres; to him Schreiner wrote:[295] 'I remain . . . a poor protester. . . . When you protest you pull a trigger and if there is only a flash in the pan you have shown your weakness.' To some onlookers Schreiner, as is so often the case with the aged, became more conservative with the advance of years; perhaps a more accurate assessment would be that he abided by views he had held from his youth that looked ever more conservative as the outlook of the liberals became more radical. In his presidential addresses to the South African Institute of Race Relations[296] and in a highly praised article he published in 1961[297] he expressed an understanding of the desire for partition or total separation as a natural, though far from ideal or even commendable, expression of national group feeling: but it was politically and economically out of the question. Group loyalties had to be subordinate to loyalty to the country as a whole, which called for just and kindly treatment for all 'national groups'. Modern standards happily rejected racial domination or privilege. It was a

[294] '. . . I think on the whole that it is better for an ex-judge not to get mixed up with party politics': Centlivres to Schreiner in a letter of 8 November 1960. ODS papers Wits. Earlier that year Schreiner had written to his wife: 'Some folk think that not all he does is sufficiently non-political for a retired C.J. but we live in unusual times and I don't blame him for going a little further than he would otherwise go. He has been a valuable figure in his postretirement period.' Letter of 7 June 1960. ODS family papers.

[295] On 16 March 1964. ODS papers Wits.

[296] 'Realism in Race Relations' (16 January 1962), 'Political Power in South Africa' (14 January 1963) and 'South Africa—United or Divided?' (14 January 1964), all republished in his *The Nettle: Political Power and Race Relations in South Africa*.

[297] 'Building Real Nationhood in South Africa' *Optima* September 1961 p 125 (republished in *The Nettle*).

grave injustice to debar a man on account of his race or colour from using his capabilities to the full. Nor, for all his personal strict moral code, did Schreiner uphold the anti-miscegenation and certain other parts of the immorality law. They had not been enacted to prevent the 'intrinsic heinousness' of the conduct they condemned; often the punishment they led to increased the hardship to the offender's family, and it resulted in many suicides by Whites. His conclusion twenty years ago was that some form of power sharing is essential, if Whites are to survive; an immense immediate advancement in education and equal access of all to it is necessary; economically the welfare state is acceptable, but the essentials of individual freedom must be preserved.[298] The rising generation of Whites must stay in South Africa, be unafraid of change, and help the country overcome its problems.

Henry Fagan after his retirement published what had for so long been on his mind in two small books, *Our Responsibility* (1960) and *Co-existence in South Africa* (1963), in which he expounded his policy of White control of the vote but government through consultation. He asked Schreiner for his opinion of them. Schreiner[299] praised the skill with which Fagan had marshalled his arguments, but rejected his solutions outright. The letters of Schreiner are striking. Had he written Fagan's books, he said, he would have sternly opposed and not supported racial segregation in universities. 'I should have spilt a bibful over the Natives Land Act 1913 as the *fons et origo mali*, which set us whites firmly on the road to making snug.' Consultation would not wash with the Non-White, even 'if he has never heard of Washington's dictum that Influence is not Government . . .'. There was no alternative to the counting of heads; 'the important thing, of course, is to see that they have the right stuff inside them and not that they have the right external appearance. . . . [I]n the end, and I believe the sooner the better, we shall be driven back to the one sound basis of a common roll with a civilisation test. That is the only system . . . that is defensible before any tribunal in the world. If adopted before it is too late it could avoid voting by races at a stage dangerous to civilisation in South Africa.' As for Hertzog's two-stream policy for Whites, Schreiner wrote, he had condemned it from the outset; a single stream would have led to our being 'happier and more united. Probably we should have been more bilingual too. Heaven knows when we are going to get the one stream now.'

In his inner heart Schreiner, for all the patriotism he and his family had shown to the country, believed in one world. 'I wonder whether the day will come when the peoples of this world will

[298] On the last question, see his Hamlyn Lectures op cit note 171 at 83.
[299] In letters to Fagan of 14 February 1960 and 27 October 1963. ODS papers Wits.

glory in the *weakness* of their states', he confided to his diary[300] on 17 April 1947, when he was in Boston in the United States, and was suffering from a surfeit of military films and sights.

Various invitations were extended to Schreiner during the first ten years or so of his retirement to deliver a public lecture or series of lectures of high standing. Because of Jean's ill health and his advanced age he refused almost all. The Hon Joseph Herbstein (1897–), who had retired from the Cape Bench at the age of 65 in 1963 and settled in Israel, conveyed an invitation to him in 1966 to give the 'Greenberg Memorial Lecture' of the Leopold Greenberg Institute for Forensic Medicine, named in honour of Schreiner's colleague on the Bench, who had died not long before. Schreiner would have liked to go to honour the memory of 'one of our great judges and a much beloved friend'; in addition, he would have liked to see Dr Charles Fincham, the Ambassador of South Africa to Israel, who was Edna's nephew. But he could not manage it; had he been able to, almost surely the Hebrew University of Jerusalem would have conferred on him an honorary LLD. As it was, he had only with great reluctance and much persuasion accepted an invitation to deliver the Hamlyn Lectures, significant a mark though it was of his distinction; and these he was preparing.[301] His choice of subjects, following a suggestion of the trustees of the Hamlyn Trust, was 'The Contribution of English Law to South African Law; and the Rule of Law in South Africa'. He delivered the lectures at his beloved Cambridge. It is a pity that that institution did not see fit to award him an honorary degree, as Oxford had awarded its alumnus, Albert Centlivres. Shyly, he approached me for advice on recent publications he should read in order to prepare the lectures. Later he asked me to go through his manuscript, and to 'pull no punches'. It was a great pleasure to render him a little assistance. In the result there was a manuscript in pencil that must have been hard on the hand to write but convenient for rubbing out desired changes; there was, however, no typist immediately available to the author. Again I was approached diffidently: had I any suggestion? Immediately I said that the University would be delighted to do the typing. Schreiner took a bit of convincing that this was so, and had, as always, to be prevailed on to allow anyone to do him a small service. It was done.

The lectures were given and published in 1967. They were generally well received, though one critic[302] commented that

300 In the ODS papers Wits.

301 Letter from the Hon Joseph Herbstein to me of 26 May 1981.

302 Leonard Lazar (a former member of the Johannesburg Bar) in (1968) 31 *Modern LR* 582. Alec Samuels in (1968) 17 *International and Comparative LQ* 1072, however, complimented the author for 'fearless objectivity' and a 'balanced approach to a most sensitive problem'.

For an appreciation of what Schreiner said in the Hamlyn Lectures about the Rule of Law, see A S Mathews 'The Rule of Law—A Reassessment' 294 below at 303, 311.

Schreiner's analysis of the Rule of Law was too legalistic, being based on the nineteenth-century concepts of Dicey. That was fair enough. Schreiner was not prepared to link the Rule of Law with universal panaceas.

There were sorrows and tragedies in Schreiner's private life. His older brother Bill, who never married, had lived alone in 'Eastcliff' in St James after the death of his mother in the mid-thirties. As the years went by he suffered more and more from arthritis and other illnesses. When Oliver had been appointed to the Bench, his biographer in the *South African Law Journal* had referred to Bill as his 'better-known brother'.[303] That was because Bill had made a name for himself in the world of rugby football, not the world of the Bar. He had become a member of the South African Rugby Board in 1909, when he was 23 and while still a player and a student. Two years later he played for Western Province. Showing great qualities of leadership and judgment of players, he was appointed to the South African Selection Committee in 1912, and he served on it until 1952, being chairman from 1920 on. Generous, wise, fair, kind if teasing, Bill would not tolerate anyone taking advantage of another person. At the Bar he had a very modest practice; his heart lay elsewhere. His heart lay with people. A most popular person, he once boasted that he had been best man at fifty weddings. Like all the male Schreiners, he loved fishing from the rocks. Oliver was very concerned at Bill's decline in health, and grieved when he died on 13 April 1957.

More immediate was the condition of his wife Edna. By the time he returned home from Bloemfontein the last time in mid-December 1960, she was bedridden, and, stricken by a series of strokes, entering the twilight world between life and death in which she was to linger so long. In the evenings Oliver would read to her, hoping, against his better judgment, that she would understand.

On 5 March 1962 Edna died. She was a remarkable woman, intelligent, well educated and well read, selfless, and a loving wife and mother. Her high principles emerge from a simple statement she made in a letter to Oliver,[304] that she had taught her children and grandchildren 'that one of the greatest things in life is to be honest and true in every little detail'. There were dozens of letters and telegrams of condolence,[305] many of which revealed aspects of Edna's personality, uprightness, helpfulness and charm. Oliver's widowed sister Ursula Scott, known as Kay, wrote from Rondebosch to 'my dear brother', saying that they were both 'blessed to have had such long happy years, and memories of such fine upright

[303] 'C.R.P.' 'Hon. Mr. Justice O. D. Schreiner' (1938) 55 *SALJ* 1 at 3.
[304] Of 23 February 1955. ODS family papers.
[305] All are in the ODS family papers, kept in a file by Schreiner.

loving companions'. A friend of Edna's[306] who had worked with her in the Alexandra Clinic wrote: 'I don't think I have ever known anyone else who combined so beautifully intellectual ability with absolute integrity, a loving heart and a sense of humour.' Theo Haarhoff, who had been Professor of Classics for so long at Wits, a convinced spiritualist, tried to console Oliver: '. . . my thoughts went back to the old days at SACS when both you and she were on the S.R.C. . . . There are things in life that do not perish with the body. You have reason to be proud of her, as she was proud of you. For my part, I have reason to believe that life is continuous and that she will continue to be near you. . . . You and your children will understand the meaning of the Roman "pietas" and you will continue to cherish her memory.' But Schreiner had no religious faith or real belief in the hereafter to sustain him in his suffering.

A lady[307] who had been at school with Edna remembered her as 'one of the big girls who had a friendly word for the little sister—at an age where a few years' difference is world's apart'. Joan Raikes, the principal of Roedean School, widow of Humphrey Raikes, for so long Vice-Chancellor of Wits, reflected on the Alexandra Clinic days: 'What wonderful work she did at the clinic and the crèches. I remember so well the fun we used to have in the committee. Edna was always the peacemaker when we used to quarrel.' She also recalled that Edna had been one of the pioneers in the establishment of clinics, nursery schools and crèches in the Transvaal.

One of Oliver's nieces begged him to 'remember Aunt Edna as she used to be—gay and so full of love and life. . . . She who loved you so much would not want to cause you any sadness.'

Enid Ramsbottom, one of the three sisters of Hal who became headmistresses of leading schools, tried to console him: '. . . the long months of illness are over and her beautiful spirit free.' Her sister Kathleen, who had been principal of Parktown Girls' High School when Jean was a pupil there, wrote words of comfort that leave an indelible impression: 'This means a release for that bright spirit—clouded and shut away for so long. . . . There are two pictures of her that I specially love to remember because they seem to express essential aspects of her personality. One morning, long ago, we had gone round to your house. It was early spring and she took us into a part of the garden which has, I think, since been sold. The first daffodils were coming out—pure yellow amidst the soft greens of new leaves all about them—and she gave us some. There was sunlight on her garden and on her hair and on her

306 Elsie Moodie, sister of a well-known attorney.

307 Mrs Marjorie Charlton, wife of a Johannesburg medical specialist, and mother of Professor R W Charlton, today a Deputy Vice-Chancellor of Wits and head of the Department of Experimental and Clinical Pharmacology.

joyous, loving face—she was part of the hope and freshness of a new summer. On the other occasion she was going out to dinner. She wore a black taffeta dress and some soft wrap—furs, I think—about her shoulders. There was the same happy friendliness, but graciousness and dignity too, in keeping with a more formal engagement. And how lovely she was to look at.'

In the midst of the collection of letters and telegrams of condolence that Schreiner kept in a file is a cutting of an article from the *Reader's Digest*,[308] on the wrongfulness of the taboo on the harmless and natural method of dissolving tension—tears.

His sisters Ursula and Dot were to go next. His younger son Deneys had moved from Wits to take a chair of chemistry at the University of Natal in Pietermaritzburg. Bill, his elder son, and his wife Pat, both so close to Oliver, sustained him in his days of sadness, and were a great consolation to him for the rest of his life. He and Jean continued staying at 'Lyndall'. They lived modestly. Schreiner was concerned that he should leave enough for Jean to live on if he were to die first. Fortunately, he had invested in sound shares from the time he had managed to save. He was one of those who put money into Blyvoors. Though Keynes may have called the stock exchange a glorified casino, Schreiner had no qualms about playing in it. Not that he tried to analyse the market; he followed the advice of his stockbrokers. In the last part of his life one of his main delights was to watch the movements of share prices, and he phoned his broker practically every day. Things went right, and he died a wealthy man. He could have left much more had he gone in for an estate-planning scheme, so commonly used to damp down death duties. But that would have been against his principles: he owed his tribute to the state.

One by one his old dear colleagues departed. Henry Fagan, of whom he had been so fond, died on 6 January 1963, and Ben Tindall on the 2nd of the next month. Leopold Greenberg went on 12 September 1964 at the age of 79. At his cremation at the Braamfontein Crematorium on Monday the 14th Schreiner delivered a memorial address. He spoke of their long and intimate friendship, of Greenberg's probity, modesty and humanity. As a citizen and Jew, a family man and a friend, his life had been a shining exemplar, Schreiner said.[309]

Albert Centlivres followed on 19 September 1966; the detailed correspondence between him and Schreiner had continued to the last. Oscar Hoexter, so long his amusing companion on the Appellate Division, was the next of his colleagues in Bloemfontein to go. It was on 25 July 1970. That, apart from Schreiner, meant the passing of the old guard.

[308] The cutting reveals no date of the issue of the magazine.
[309] *Southern African Jewish Times* 18 September 1964.

On 19 March 1974 Jean had an epileptic fit in her bath and drowned. It was a tragic end to a blighted life. Those of us who have lost a child can appreciate what Sigmund Freud meant when he said that it is the most monstrous thing that can happen to man. At the cremation tears ran down Schreiner's face.

Later he wrote to Alan Young, his signals NCO in the Great War, telling him the sad news, saying that she had been spared the parting had she been left after he had died.[310] It was almost word for word from the famous book by Viktor E Frankl, *Man's Search for Meaning*,[311] though whether Schreiner had read it I cannot say.

Four years later, in very old age Schreiner had to suffer another shock. The brilliant elder son of Deneys (who was now a Vice-Principal of the University of Natal), named Oliver after his grandfather, who had been awarded the high honour, the nearest equivalent to a South African Rhodes Scholarship at Cambridge, of the Elsie Ballot Scholarship, and was the fourth generation of Schreiners to go to Cambridge and the third to Trinity, had taken a first in his LLB. At the age of 27 he was about to be accorded the signal honour of being offered a fellowship at his college, as had his grandfather. On Tuesday 7 March 1978, while he was riding his bicycle along a narrow street in Cambridge, he was tipped off, fell on his head, and died. No one saw the accident. All that was found was some paint on the bicycle. Almost certainly a truck or large motor car had knocked him off, but the driver may not have been aware of this. An outstanding scholar, sportsman and leader of men, a person imbued with a deep social conscience who would have done so much for his country and its people, had suddenly gone.[312] The old judge had undertaken to propose a resolution at a meeting of the University Council on the following Friday. I did not think he would appear. But he did. He stood up and spoke to the proposal; he engaged more in the deliberations of the body than he usually did. All were moved by his courage and stoicism.

W P Schreiner had commenced practice at the Bar on 17 August 1882. His two sons had followed his example; leaving aside the Great War, when WP had been High Commissioner and Bill and Oliver in the armed forces, Bill being invalided out after service in East Africa, there had been no break in the continuity of Schreiners as advocates since then; for during the Second World War, in which Oliver's two sons served, Bill the elder was at the Cape Bar. While young Oliver was alive, old Oliver could look forward to the prospect of a fourth generation at the South African Bar; as it turned out to be, the centenary of the family in the profession took

310 See letter from Alan Young, now addressed to 'Mr Justice O.D. Schreiner', of 12 January 1975. ODS family papers.

311 Originally published in German in 1946. See the eighth impression (1977) of the English version of the revised edition of 1972, pages 114–15.

312 See the tributes in (1979) 96 *SALJ* 203–4.

place in 1982, but when Bill Schreiner SC of the Johannesburg Bar retires the connection of the family with law will cease.

Oliver Schreiner grieved at his losses, but he did not indulge in the egoism of self-pity or suffer the depression that so frequently stems from self-dislike. He regarded himself rightly as having a nature not particularly sensitive, which helped him sustain his burdens. Nor, until perhaps near the end of his life, did he lose that specially significant relationship which the advance of years makes it so difficult to sustain—the relationship with oneself.

His outward demeanour can best be described by the cliché—a cliché for all its Shakespearean origin—that he did not wear his heart upon his sleeve. He would have shared William Plomer's belief that good manners demand a certain reticence. Sarah Gertrude Millin once said to me that someone close to Oliver had told her that there was a door in his soul through which no one had ever passed; to which I replied that Sigmund Freud had written that there are secret recesses of a man's soul that will not be revealed even to his psychoanalyst.

Schreiner had sentiments in the sense used in the expression that often came to his lips, usually with a smile, 'them's my sentiments'; but he was not sentimental in the sense of tending to be swayed by feeling or emotional weakness rather than by reason. This will be apparent from a reading of the two obituaries he was good enough to write at my request for the *South African Law Journal*. They were of S S ('Toby') Taylor and Charles Stallard.[313] Taylor attained the age of 90, and Stallard 100. Both were silks when Schreiner came to the Bar. Taylor left in 1930 at the age of 55 to take a post with a mining house in London, and even the charitable Schreiner could scarce forbear to hide his sense of disappointment thirty-five years later. Stallard at the age of 58 went into politics, and became a member of Smuts's World War II Cabinet. Clearly Schreiner did not care for his colour prejudice. Still, the University Archives house an interesting correspondence between the two when Stallard was in his nineties.

Perhaps I have been a little hard. Most of Schreiner's letters of condolence or commiseration on a sad episode in the life of a relation, friend or acquaintance are couched in touching terms. His phenomenal memory of individuals and their lives, his deep interest in their well-being, and his instinctive good manners led to his writing a very large number of such letters. And no bitterness or hatred entered his mind, or outright condemnation of failings or weaknesses of others, except where grave moral reprehensibility was clear. A vivid picture comes to my mind of him, in his eighties, rising from his chair at a gathering, and alone going up to

[313] Respectively (1965) 82 *SALJ* 421 and (1971) 88 *SALJ* 275.

meet and shake the hand of a man who had entered the room, a man of whom a judge had said harsh things in passing a few days before, remarks that had received considerable publicity in the media.

His outlook was broadly optimistic. To all, his advice was to keep smiling, and he followed his own advice. I thought his attitude was that of Viscount (Sir Herbert) Samuel, the British statesman, who described himself as a 'meliorist' (a term he borrowed from George Eliot), 'meaning one who believes that the present is on the whole better than the past and that the future may be better still, but that effort is needed to make it so'.[314] There was one reservation, however, which he expressed in a letter to Centlivres:[315] 'the programme of apartheid is unjust and will come to a bad end, carrying us with it, unless there is an early change.' In years closer to his death he found that encouraging changes were taking place. The only time anyone can remember his being uncalm and despairing of the future was in June 1940, when France fell and it seemed that Britain would be invaded and conquered.

Frequently there is dissonance between a person's life and his work. W B Yeats wrote in a poem that 'a man must choose perfection of the life or of the work'. That may apply more to poets and novelists than to lawyers and judges; disorder and lack of magnanimity could follow from feeding one's work on one's instincts and emotions. It can, however, also happen in the law: a man may be charming and thoughtful in his personal life but not in his working life; or the reverse; or in both lives. Schreiner was in both.

He had pride, pride not in the sense of an unduly high opinion of his qualities or arrogant bearing or conduct—far from it; but pride in the sense of what befits one's position, what prevents one doing anything unworthy. And he had the humility that clothes a person who is seeking for knowledge, not only in the natural sciences but also in the social sciences. He was not always self-assured, and when he was embarrassed a low whistle would escape his lips, though I could never catch the tune.

Schreiner's life had its full measure of pain. His triumphs he waved aside like a gentleman; his disappointments and burdens he bore like a man. He met Dostoevsky's hope, that he would be worthy of his sufferings.

What made him meet any situation were those crucial qualities in the make-up of a complete human being, a sense of humour and a well of fun. He would rarely allow them rein in his judicial work, for it might be at the expense of the litigants, the accused or counsel. But in private they would bubble forth. He loved a joke,

314 Viscount Samuel *Memoirs* (1945) 251.
315 Of 6 March 1964. ODS Wits papers.

provided it was clean. The nearest he ever got beyond cleanliness was at the last Oxford–Cambridge Dinner that was held at the old Pretoria Club.[316] He was the guest of honour. After speaking for half an hour he said: 'you expect a *risqué* joke. I know none. But I will tell you a story. When I was last in England I went first to Oxford, and found the students were interested in *Lady Chatterley's Lover.* Then I went to Cambridge and found it quite different. They were interested in Lady Chatterley.' At an official dinner he tried playfully to insist that I, who was in the best of health, accept his proposal that I take one of the pills he was swallowing to relieve his arthritis. 'They are really excellent', he said with the ghost of a smile. On 8 July 1978 I approached him for information about George Schreiner Findlay QC, whose obituary I was writing for the September issue of the *South African Law Journal.* Oliver was the cousin of George Findlay's father, through the Schreiner line. Chuckling, he said that Findlay had been interested in the law, and when he (Schreiner) was a judge used to write to him about legal questions—as if he were interested in such questions! When the University Council considered a proposal that the revamped Law Library be named after him, he began (perhaps it was half-seriously) 'I have not been consulted', but overwhelmed by the acclaim that followed the proposal, he gave a rueful grin and succumbed. Even his peculiar quiddities had humour associated with them. He told me that he had never insured the contents of his house: 'And I've never had a burglary. Look at the money I've saved!' Nor did he have burglar bars on the windows, let alone a burglar alarm. Late one evening I took him home. He felt in his pocket for his keys; they were not there; they had been left in his bedroom, and he was locked out, for no servant was available to let him in. It was quite simple for me to open a window catch by inserting a forked stick I found in the garden through an open fanlight. Again he had proved his point! Then, like many people of advanced years, he would not wear a seat-belt in a motor car, even after it became compulsory to do so. When anyone drove him home, and he was in the passenger's seat in front, he would drape the seat-belt over his shoulder, but not fasten it. The reason he gave was that if the car should catch on fire he would be trapped. Not for a moment did I believe that he really thought the chances of this happening were other than insignificant compared with the chances of the car's being involved in an accident and his failure to be strapped in leading to injuries that could have been avoided. When he told me, in that throaty voice so utterly his, why he took the attitude he did, there was a glint of devilment in his eyes. Like many persons hard of hearing, he found some amusement in

[316] I am indebted to my friend Professor Friedel Sellschop for the story.

pretending to be deafer than he really was. He caught me once mispronouncing 'kilometre'; only he, I and a colleague of mine at the Law School of a large number of guests realized that an eminent visitor with the most English of names, who spoke an apparently impeccable standard BBC English, must have been born on the Continent, and spent his early life there, as was the case.

Oliver Schreiner's sense of humour would sometimes be interlocked with his modesty and dislike of publicity. Shortly after his retirement I wrote an article on his life and work for the *South African Law Journal*. It was due to be published in the May 1961 issue. He got to hear about it, and he said to me: 'No, no. You must not publish it until I am dead.' Then he added, with his characteristic deep chuckle: 'I promise you I will not keep you long.' I could only reply that I very much hoped he would; and he did.

What struck everyone who met Oliver Schreiner for the first time was his exquisite politeness. Even those who saw him frequently were still at times moved by his courtliness, as it were from a gentler age. There is a passage in Bertrand Russell's autobiography[317] describing a friend of his, Crompton Davies, who had been with him at Cambridge, and subsequently became a prominent solicitor, which, translated into the South African scene, seems to me to apply in all essentials to Oliver Schreiner: He 'was truly democratic. He always spoke to his clerks or his servants with the same tone that he would have used to an important person such as one of the Indian Rajahs whose affairs he handled, and his manner in a two-roomed Irish cabin was exactly the same as in a party of celebrities. I remember with what grave courtesy he rose to bow and shake hands with our parlourmaid, on hearing that she came from the same district as his family.'

Associated with Schreiner's innate courtesy, one felt, was his fierce independence. He would shrug aside any offer of physical help, and any other offer of assistance was usually politely declined. At a time when he was Chancellor of the University, in his mid-seventies and limping badly—it was before the operation on his hip—the Nuclear Physics Research Unit was conducting its neutrino experiments in the uttermost part of ERPM, the deepest mine in the world. Schreiner went along with the University party which was being shown the experiments *in situ*. Mr Peter Anderson, head of Corner House, took one look at Schreiner and blanched. He told the mine manager to get the MO right away. The MO was dressed as if he was an official; he walked after Schreiner with tin hat on head—and medicine bag tucked behind his back.[318] Two other illustrations: When one drove him home late

[317] *The Autobiography of Bertrand Russell 1872–1914* (1967) 71.

[318] Again I am indebted to Professor Sellschop, this time for the details. It was on 6 December 1967. The occasion was the official opening of the Neutrino Laboratory at 77 level Hercules Shaft ERPM Boksburg, at 11 000 feet below the surface. See the photographs that appear between pages 374 and 375.

at night, after his driver had ended his day's work, he would always insist on being dropped at the corner so as not to take one out of one's way. After I had given up assuring him that it was not out of my way, and if it had been it would have been my pleasure, I had to resort to telling him that if he insisted I would be upset. In 1979, when he was in his eighty-ninth year, and walked with difficulty, because of age and arthritis, he attended a Council meeting. During the period for refreshments after the meeting it was discovered to the general consternation that the lifts were not working. Schreiner's car, his driver in it, was in the basement, fourteen floors down. While I was talking to a colleague, I had a feeling something was amiss. I looked round and could not see the old judge. Though he could give me thirty years in experience of life, I was still fly enough to realize what had happened. I caught up with him three flights down on the stairs, steadily limping down. We walked the rest together.

In the last stages of his life Schreiner grew ever more lonely—and loneliness was a sore trial to him. He went alone to England in mid-1978, when he was 87. At Cambridge he attended a dinner at Trinity College given by the Master and Fellows. There is a document[319] setting out the names of the guests, and the year they first came into residence. Near the head were Sir Ronald Francis Roxburgh (1908), the former judge of the English High Court, and Schreiner (1911). On the document, in Schreiner's hand, is an extraordinary note dealing with his religious beliefs—or, rather, absence of them. It came to this, putting the matter delicately: The concept of the divinity of Christ, though noble, is historically unacceptable, and gravely unfair to persons who do not believe in it. But it does not follow from disbelief that one should declare it, thereby hurting the feelings of others and depriving them of the comforts of religion, and also reducing the support the belief gives to morality. 'So one should zip one's lips except to persons who could not be prejudiced.'

There it was. He was not going to seek a crutch that he had had no faith in before. More firmly than ever, despite death being round the corner, Schreiner was sticking to his unbelief. His mother had had him baptized in the Dutch Reformed Church; as a boy he had accompanied her on Sunday mornings as she wandered from church to church, including the Anglican one. But he was as unconvinced as his father had been. Down the years he had written of his doubts. After the earthquake in the Ionian Islands, for instance, he told his wife: 'A disaster like that must make it difficult for the churches in the area to keep their flocks.'[320] 'How can such grim things fall upon one and heaven's powers stand aside and do

[319] In the ODS family papers.
[320] Letter of ODS to Edna S of 27 September 1953. ODS family papers.

nothing?'[321] This of the news of the painful death of a child. 'As far as we *know* it all comes to an end. Of course we can't be certain and it may be that it is otherwise.' So he wrote home on 16 October 1956.[322] Much later he told the audience listening to his opening address at the Conference on the Mental Health of the Family on 27 June 1972: 'The fear of death . . . is one of the commonest nuisances, for we most of us seem to be unable to accept the wise reflection that Shakespeare put into the mouth of Julius Caesar, that there is nothing sillier than fearing the inevitable. . . .[323] Sometimes I wonder whether one could not [reach] a really firm conclusion that eternal life, if it were possible, would be so unendurably dull that one would long for its end.'

After Jean's death he made a fresh will, adding two minor codicils in later years. He remained alone in the big house, 'Lyndall'. Having given the matter serious thought, he decided not to move to a flat. Where would he put his large library? Why should he adjust at his age to a new life style? He engaged a driver, so that he could attend meetings, see relations and friends, and go to bowls at the Country Club three times a week without causing people too much trouble.

Bowls he enjoyed greatly, although he could not bend fully to throw a wood in orthodox fashion.

Reading took much of Schreiner's time. Towards the end of his life he told me he was tackling Macaulay's *History of England* again, a daunting task for anyone.

He took care of his health, consulting the leading specialists. Don Craib, the former part-time Professor of Medicine at Wits, had long since retired to the Cape, but there were other eminent men. Craib, who died in May 1982, wrote from time to time to Schreiner. Early in 1937 Oliver had given Craib a copy of Eric Walker's biography, which he greatly enjoyed reading. 'It's high time somebody wrote a book entitled "The Three Schreiners and South Africa 1880–1980"', ran a passage in what appears to be Craib's last letter. 'Our history needs such a book.'[324] In a letter of 28 May 1979[325] Craib, speaking of two octogenarians exchanging thoughts, stated that 'we both now know that we were more often than not dealing with affairs over which we never really had any significant control; that we were the pawns rather than the players, and that we are now merely outsiders looking into a human turmoil far more shocking than anything we ever believed could or would be possible in our time.' He concluded: 'When I think of you I call to mind a man who has spent his life in the practice of virtue,

[321] Letter of ODS to Edna S of 14 June 1955. ODS family papers.
[322] Letter of ODS to Edna S. ODS family papers.
[323] *Julius Caesar* act II scene 2 line 30.
[324] N d. ODS family papers.
[325] ODS family papers.

based on an unblemished idealism that found an outlet in the contemplation and worship of the Goddess of Justice; a religious way of life that has awarded you a calm spirit in this world, with a high regard awaiting you in the world to come. As I once told Hal [Ramsbottom]: Should there come a day for me to stand trial on a capital charge, I would calmly mount the gallows in the firm belief that human justice was about to be done, provided that Oliver Schreiner were the judge in charge of the case.'

At the beginning of 1980, after he reached his ninetieth year, Oliver Schreiner began saying to his family 'My friends have gone; I have lived too long'. In April he had a heart attack and spent several weeks in hospital. On his return home visitors were initially forbidden, and thereafter discouraged. He started to stroll about the suburb, as had been his habit; and in typical fashion he began to test himself by walking longer distances. On Sunday morning the 27th of July he sat down on his easy chair, intending soon to go for a walk. He never rose from it.

In his will he left 46 small legacies to relations, friends and servants; no one close to him appears to have been forgotten. There were fourteen small legacies to schools and charities. Juta and Company, Limited, was left R200; this expressed Schreiner's thanks for receiving law reports gratis for years. (The firm donated the sum to the Wits Law School, which bought Daumier legal prints in Schreiner's memory.) Many of his books went to the South African Institute of Race Relations. The total value of all these bequests was nearly R40 000. Some R320 000 went in eleven large legacies. The beneficiaries were the Universities of Cape Town and the Witwatersrand, and the South African Institute of Race Relations (nearly R52 000 each), the University of Zimbabwe, Rhodes University, the Inner Temple, the Hebrew University of Jerusalem and Trinity College, Cambridge (nearly R26 000 each), and the Universities of Botswana, Lesotho and Swaziland (some R8 650 each). The balance of the estate went in almost equal shares to his sons.

It was a will so typical of him.

Appendix to note 106: The Appellate Division Quorum Act 27 of 1955

This statute, which replaced s 110 of the South Africa Act 1909, in addition to requiring eleven judges of appeal to sit when the validity of a purported Act was in question, changed the quorum in other appeals to five judges of appeal. The previous position was, broadly, that in an appeal from a single judge (such as in a criminal or civil trial) the quorum was three judges of appeal, but otherwise was four. The Minister of Justice, Mr C R Swart MP, had written to Centlivres, the Chief Justice, on 23 March 1955 to say what the Government's intentions were as regards the quorums, and that its further intention was to appoint five additional judges of appeal, so that the Appellate Division would sit in two divisions; any comments would be welcome. On the 26th Centlivres replied, saying that he was pleased that comments would be welcome even though the Government had decided on its course. There was no need for five additional judges of appeal. The Appellate Division was not behind with its work. Two divisions might result in conflicting decisions. Previously the Government had consulted the Chief Justice before reaching a decision affecting the Appellate Division. Yet a couple of hours after the Minister's statement had reached him, the press had been notified of the decision. His colleagues and he regarded this as 'laakbaar en afkeuringswaardig'—reprehensible and objectionable. The letter concluded that Steyn JA wished to state that because of his short spell on the Appellate Division he was in no position to comment.

This letter evoked a stinging, confidential reply from Swart on 1 April, to the effect that it was for Parliament and the Government to prescribe legislation, and the comment by Centlivres had transgressed permissible limits.

In the ODS papers Wits, in which the documents can be found, is lodged a holograph memorandum by Schreiner, dated 27 March, apparently meant for his own eyes only. It contains this passage: 'The immoral political device of the fait accompli was much used by Hitler. Only less unworthy than those who use it are those whose inertia permits it to be used. A country whose citizens cannot perceive when they are being subjected to its use or cannot rouse themselves to repudiate and prevent it is heading for the destruction that befell Germany.'

In a letter written by Centlivres in his retirement from his home 'The Haven' in Crescent Road, Claremont, Cape Town on 26 December 1960, to welcome Schreiner 'to the select band of septuanarians'—Centlivres's spelling of 'septuagenarians'—the following appears: 'By far the most painful experience I had during my legal career was the conference we held to discuss our reply to the Minister of Justice's letter announcing that the Govt. had decided to enlarge the A.D. It came as a shock to me that one of my colleagues took the view that it was our duty to accept meekly the decision of the Govt. That colleague did not realize then (I hope that he realizes it now) that there is a vast difference between a judge and a public servant. Perhaps one should be charitable, especially at this time of the year, and ascribe his failure to realize the difference to the fact that he himself had been a public servant for so many years and a judge for so few years. It is no doubt difficult for a man whose life-training was to accept without question the decisions of the Executive to throw off what had become a habit on his part.' (ODS family papers.)

FATHER AND SON—
W P SCHREINER AND OLIVER

ELLISON KAHN*

On the death of Oliver Schreiner an old-fashioned document case, popular in the early part of this century, was found in his dressing-table. It contained a large number of letters, most of them from his father, WP, sent to him almost every week when he was at Cambridge from October 1911 until the outbreak of the First World War, and thereafter while he was with the 6th Northamptonshire Regiment in the British Expeditionary Force in France in 1914 to 1916. The British Expeditionary Force letters, written when WP was High Commissioner in London, as would be expected are almost entirely confined to family affairs; but the Cambridge letters are splendid—informative, shedding light on political, legal and personal events, and, above all, shining with the light of deep parental love. On reading the Cambridge letters one feels exhilarated and uplifted, with renewed faith in the innate goodness of man. No author has hitherto had access to them.[1] It is clear that Eric Walker in writing his biography *W. P. Schreiner: A South African*[2] had not seen them. They call for an appreciation, no matter by how poor a hand, in showing the close bond between two great members of a remarkable South African family.

The story of the life of William Philip Schreiner (30 August 1857–28 June 1919) is known to all who have an interest in our history;[3] but it would be as well to trace it briefly here, dwelling in particular on events alluded to in the Cambridge letters.

He was the tenth child of twelve children of Gottlob (1814–76) and Rebecca Schreiner (1818–1903), only seven of whom survived

* BCom LLB (Witwatersrand) LLM LLD (Natal) Hon LLD (Cape Town), Advocate of the Supreme Court of South Africa, of the Middle Temple, Barrister, Professor of Law in the University of the Witwatersrand, Johannesburg.

[1] I am grateful to Mr W H R Schreiner SC, son of Oliver Schreiner, for making them accessible to me, and giving me complete discretion as to their use. They are in the Schreiner family papers, which I shall refer to as ODS family papers. The W P Schreiner papers in the South African Library, Cape Town, will be referred to as the WPS papers SAL.

[2] London: OUP 1937. Cited hereafter as Walker.

[3] Apart from Walker's biography, mention may be made of the good biographical sketch by Professor T R H Davenport in *Dictionary of South African Biography (DSAB)* II 636 and the short account by Edgar H Brookes in *Standard Encyclopaedia of Southern Africa (SESA)* IX 529.

childhood. Gottlob, immortalized in his daughter Olive's *The Story of an African Farm* as Otto, was born in Swabia (Suabia), Germany, of a humble family (his father was a shoemaker). He trained in London for the Church Missionary Society, but transferred to the London Missionary Society. In 1837 he married Rebecca Lyndall, daughter of a Congregational minister. A year later the Schreiners moved to South Africa, where finally they settled at the Wittebergen reserve in the north-east Cape, near the border of Basutoland. Their first child, Catherine, was born on 23 July 1838. In 1860 she married John Findlay (1839–1902); among their twelve children was John H L, attorney of Pretoria, whose son, George Schreiner Findlay QC, was to become a striking, if rather unorthodox, member of the legal profession.[4] Two of the children of Gottlob and Rebecca were to make undying names for themselves: Olive (1855–1920), the novelist, writer on political affairs and feminist, the ninth child—that turbulent spirit with a streak of genius, whose life and work are too well known to need recounting here; and WP. Two others, also powerful characters with strong convictions, were to serve their country well. They were Theophilus (Theo) (1844–1920)[5] and Henrietta (Het) (1850–1912). Theo, schoolteacher and temperance worker, selflessly helped educate Olive and WP at a time when Gottlob, dismissed by the London Missionary Society, could not provide for them. Quite unlike the two of them, however, Theo was avowedly, almost fanatically, pro-British (a sentiment that caused a long family estrangement,[6] especially between him and Olive), pro-Rhodes and religious. Like the two of them (though WP only later in life), he was a champion of the rights of Non-Whites. In 1915, after WP had been appointed High Commissioner in London, Theo took WP's place as one of the senators nominated, in terms of the South Africa Act, 'on the ground mainly of their thorough acquaintance . . . with the reasonable wants and wishes of the coloured races in South Africa'; he had been elected to the first Parliament as the member of the House of Assembly for Tembuland, with a large Black electorate. Het (Mrs Stakesby-Lewis) was, if anything, more devoted to the temperance movement, rights of Blacks[7] and religion than Theo, and did much for these causes; but, above all, she was adored by so many for the help she gave the poor and distressed.

After attending the small government school in Cradock, of which Theo was then headmaster, WP went to the Rev Robert Templeton's[8]

[4] On the early history of the Findlays, see Joan Findlay (ed) *The Findlay Letters 1866–1870* (1954). On George Findlay, see my obituary in (1978) 95 *SALJ* 415.

[5] See Edgar H Brookes in *DSAB* IV 546 and *SESA* IX 529.

[6] See letter by Theo to WP of 24 December 1906 (WPS papers SAL), making reference to it.

[7] In a letter to Het of 29 January 1900 (WPS papers SAL), WP refers to her 'cruelly unjust' allegation in the *Methodist Times* of the brutal treatment of the Natives in South Africa.

[8] On Templeton, see *DSAB* I 786; Ellison Kahn 'James Rose Innes' in R M de Villiers (ed) *Better Than They Knew* II (1974) 57 at 61.

celebrated school at Bedford, just after Richard Solomon[9] had left, and while William Solomon[10] and James Rose Innes[11] were still there; and when in 1873 Templeton was appointed principal of the Grahamstown boys' public school, WP followed him. Templeton regarded him as the most intellectually gifted pupil he had ever had. At the age of 16 WP passed his matriculation examination and, armed with a school scholarship, in 1874 enrolled at the South African College in Cape Town for the degree of Bachelor of Arts. The College, founded in 1829, had prepared candidates for the certificates in arts, science and law of the Board of Public Examinations; but in 1874 the Board had been replaced by the University of the Cape of Good Hope, a degree-conferring but non-teaching body. Among his colleagues and friends were Henry Juta[12] and (towards the end) J W Wessels.[13] WP was the top student for the BA in both literature and science, and was awarded the Porter Scholarship, which helped finance his going to Cambridge in 1879 and studying law: pursuing his real love, medicine, a five-year course of study, was beyond the means of his family.

Meanwhile he had met and become privately engaged (though the news soon leaked out) to Frances Hester (Fanny) Reitz, of other remarkable Cape stock. The Reitz family tree has been traced back to Jacobus von Reutz, born in 1510, burgomaster of a German town. In the seventeenth century the ancestors of Fanny moved to Holland. Jan Frederick Reitz (1761–1824), a Dutch naval officer, settled in the Cape in 1794, and married Barbara van Reenen, who came from a prominent family. His sixth child was Francis William senior (1810–1881), a leading agriculturist and politician, member of the House of Assembly for Swellendam from 1869 to 1873, and then Gentleman Usher of the Black Rod, who married Cornelia Magdalena Deneys, and had twelve children. The seventh child, named after his father, was to attain fame as a judge, President of the Orange Free State, leading contributor to the recognition of Afrikaans as a language, and politician.[14] The youngest child, a

[9] 1850–1913. Brother of William; politician and advocate; member of W P Schreiner's ministry of 1898–1900; legal adviser to the Transvaal Administrator 1901; Attorney-General of the Transvaal 1902–6; Agent-General in London 1907; High Commissioner in London from Union to his death.

[10] 1852–1930. A judge in the Cape 1887–1902, then in the Transvaal; judge of appeal after Union, and Chief Justice 1927–9.

[11] 1855–1942. Held high political office in the Cape; Chief Justice of the Transvaal 1902–10; judge of appeal on Union and Chief Justice 1914–27. See Kahn op cit note 8.

[12] 1857–1930. Advocate in Cape; Attorney-General 1894; Speaker 1896–8; Judge President of the Cape Provincial Division 1914–20; judge of appeal 1920–3.

[13] 1862–1936. Advocate in the Transvaal; judge in the Transvaal 1902–20; Judge President of the Transvaal Provincial Division 1920–3; judge of appeal 1923–32; Chief Justice 1932 to his death.

[14] F W Reitz (1844–1934), a lifelong republican; Chief Justice of the Orange Free State 1874–88; President 1888–96; State Secretary, Transvaal 1898; President of the Union Senate 1910–20; senator thereafter until 1929. Among the fifteen children born of his two marriages were the prominent politicians Deneys and Hjalmar. Generally on the Reitz

daughter, Kitty, became the wife of the Rev Joseph Sutton, and the second son of this union, George Gerhard, born in 1880, was appointed a judge of the Cape Provincial Division in 1929 and Judge President in 1946, retiring early on 14 May 1948. So George Sutton[15] was a cousin of Oliver Schreiner's. He married Agnes Watermeyer, sister of E F Watermeyer, later the eminent Chief Justice; the close relationship of so many distinguished members of legal families in those days is remarkable. The second last child was Fanny. In an affectionate letter written on 25 January 1925 by her from 'Eastcliff', St James, the family seaside residence where she and her son Bill lived after WP's death, to Oliver at his chambers in Corporation Buildings, Johannesburg, she said 'but dear son, I often feel that I have not been the right mother for your Father's children. You needed someone cleverer, stronger, who would have been more of a help to you all than I was. You see, my Father had a large family, and Aunt Kitt and I, who were the two youngest, came when he had had heavy losses through drought, & horsesickness . . ., so that when the time for our education came he could not afford to send us to school. We just got taught by dear old Aunt Keetjie, with my father to take us for arithmetic, at which she was weak, and old Dr White who lived in a cottage on our Farm, to give us lessons in French, and that was the sum total of our education. Later on being with Dad helped me greatly, he was so patient with my ignorance and so helpful to me in every way.'

In England WP won a minor mathematics scholarship at Downing, so to that college (for Oxbridge) relatively new (it was founded in 1800), and somewhat unfashionable, he went, simultaneously eating his dinners at the Inner Temple and studying for the LLB of the University of London. At Downing he did well in rowing and his June examination, and benefited from the guidance of that inspiring law teacher, Courtney Stanhope Kenny (1847–1930), who had become a Fellow of the college in 1875, a

family, see *DSAB* II 575ff and Conrad H Reitz *The Reitz Family: An Annotated Bibliography* (University of Cape Town School of Librarianship 1964). See also the famous work by Deneys Reitz, *Commando* (1929; 2 ed 1931) ch I. There it is said that when F W Reitz senior went to Scotland in 1816 (this is an error—it was much later) to study agriculture, he met Sir Walter Scott, to whom he presented a lion skin as a gift from the poet Thomas Pringle; and that he loved to tell the story of his being present at the banquet when Scott admitted that he was the author of the Waverley novels (this was in 1827). Can his imagination have run away with him? In chapter 5 of Edmund H Burrows's *Overberg Outspan* (1952), which is on F W Reitz senior, it is stated that he went to Scotland only in 1829 (see page 118). In the ODS family papers there is an amusing letter by J F Reitz, of the then firm of attorneys of Lionel G Murray and Reitz, Cape Town, of 9 April 1959, addressed to 'Dear Uncle Oliver', answering some of Oliver Schreiner's questions about the 'familie'. The ODS family papers also contain a splended photograph of the Reitz family taken at FW senior's farm Kliprivier, near Swellendam, in December 1877, with the old couple and eleven of their children, including Fanny and Kitty, and twenty-two grandchildren, among them Hjalmar, a baby in the arms of his father. The photograph is reproduced on a plate facing page 191 of Burrows's book, with a guide on page 191 to all present.

[15] On Sutton, see (1929) 46 *SALJ* 383 and 1934 *SALT* 10.

man only ten years older than WP, who was Downing Professor of the Laws of England when Oliver was at Cambridge.[16] Inns of Court scholarships followed, and Schreiner's academic reputation was established. At the time he was an imperialist, conservative and anti-Black. He obtained a first in both parts of the Law Tripos and the Chancellor's medal, and a first in the LLB of the University of London, and was called by the Inner Temple on 3 May 1882. On 17 August that year he was admitted as an advocate of the Cape Supreme Court; he started at the local Bar and rapidly built up a large practice, so that he was able to marry Fanny on 3 January 1884. The ceremony was at the Dutch Reformed Church at Swellendam, the bride being given away by her brother, the Chief Justice of the Free State. Their first child, a daughter, died soon after birth towards the end of the year. The tempting offer of a fellowship at Downing came at the same time, but Fanny's opposition and financial considerations—he was helping support a number of relatives—precluded his accepting it.

In April 1886 his son William Francis Reitz (Bill) was born; there followed Frances (Dot) in 1888, Oliver Deneys in December 1890, and Ursula Hester (Kay, Kate or Kite) in June 1892.

All the while WP's legal career advanced. From 1885 to 1890 he was Parliamentary Draftsman. He participated in political negotiations, being made a Companion of the Order of St Michael and St George (CMG) in 1891 for the work he did in drafting the Swaziland Convention of 1890. A year later he took silk. But he drove himself too hard and collapsed. A voyage to England in 1892 restored his health. A disciple of Rhodes at the time, he accepted the position of Attorney-General in Rhodes's ministry of May 1893, being returned to the House of Assembly as the member for Kimberley in June. But a collapse began to threaten again, and he resigned, only to take up the position once more in September 1894, after being returned, with Rhodes, for Barkly West. Schreiner had the general support of the Afrikanerbond. The Jameson Raid at the end of 1895 led to his resignation from the Cabinet. Ultimately there was a complete break with Rhodes. After he had given evidence, with the utter candour he always showed, in London before the commission of inquiry, which cross-examined him mercilessly, Schreiner found himself with his old chief aboard the *Tantallon Castle*. They thrashed matters out. That was enough for Schreiner: Rhodes wanted war.[17] After the election of late 1898

[16] See the obituary by A L Goodhart in *Dictionary of National Biography 1922–1930* 466. MP 1885–8 for Barnsley, concurrently with his fellowship; in 1888 succeeded F W Maitland as Reader in English Law, and in 1907, on Maitland's death, succeeded him as Downing Professor of the Laws of England, filling the chair until 1918. His *Outlines of Criminal Law*, first published in 1902, has become a legal classic. There is a striking tribute to Kenny by Stanley French in *Justice of the Peace* 5 April 1980 p 205.

[17] See Walker 94.

Schreiner was appointed Prime Minister on 14 October, as leader of the South African Party, a loose grouping composed of the Afrikanerbond (of which he was never a member, though he was its leader in Parliament) and its allies. The Bondsmen preferred him to the maverick Merriman. They found him more likeable than the caustic-tongued Merriman and less liberal on the colour question; and they trusted him. It was only in April 1899 that WP's views on Non-Whites came to be similar to those of Olive. He returned from a long visit to the Ciskei and Transkei a champion of the rights of persons of colour. What a change from the man who, in 1893 as Attorney-General, had spoken in favour of the Constitution Ordinance Amendment Bill, which was duly passed, against the opposition of Merriman, Innes and Sauer, to end the 'plumping' system of voting in the Cape Town constituency, by which an elector could cast all his four votes for one candidate; a measure obviously aimed at preventing the return of a distinguished Muslim, Ahmed Effendi; in the debate in the House of Assembly on which he had dwelt vehemently on the basic inequality of White and Black and on the likelihood of the need for the change in the Constitution were a Coloured person to be elected. It was truly a Pauline conversion.

Schreiner's Cabinet could hardly hang together for long: John X Merriman, J W Sauer, A H Herholdt and Dr T N G te Water were pro-Boer; Richard Solomon was imperialistically inclined; and Schreiner himself was torn, with sympathy for the Boer cause yet rightly convinced of the legal constitutional rights and power of the British Government, and, believing that, while he was responsible to the Cape House, he was a 'minister of the Crown' in the literal sense, unable to comprehend Merriman's contrary view, so divorced from law and practicality, that he was a servant of the people only.[18] Schreiner worked very hard for peace, and after the Anglo-Boer War had begun tried to prevent a Boer rebellion in the Cape. Certainly he helped quieten things; and there was no outbreak by the Blacks. The Cabinet split on the punishment of the rebels, Schreiner, Solomon and Herholdt, to meet the Imperial Government's wishes, agreeing not to propose a general amnesty for the rank and file. Schreiner resigned as Prime Minister and subsequently his seat in the House. In 1901 he was offered the judge presidency of the Eastern Districts Court, of which S T Jones and William Solomon were puisne judges; he declined, though he agreed to act in that position for some six weeks from late August. On a number of other occasions he was to refuse a judicial

[18] This comes out well in Phyllis Lewsen's *John X. Merriman: Paradoxical South African Statesman* (1981) 189, 225–6, 229. This work (cited hereafter as *Merriman*) is a shortened version of Professor Lewsen's unpublished DLitt thesis presented to the University of the Witwatersrand in 1981, and which will be cited as *Merriman* (thesis). See, too, the cartoon by Boonzaier between pages 46 and 47, and James Rose Innes *Autobiography* (1949) 187.

appointment; at least so far as it was to a trial court, one of the reasons was that, with his inherent tender-heartedness, he doubted if he could sentence a man to death. The work of a judge, he found, was about a sixth of that called for by private practice.[19] Jones was appointed Judge President after Schreiner's departure.

April 1905 saw WP, accompanied by Oliver, aboard the *Briton*, *en route* to Europe, to seek the 'cure' at Bad Nauheim. The two explored the Rhineland, and then went to England, where Oliver, to WP's disappointment, was attracted by the spacious glories of Trinity College at Cambridge. In 1908 Schreiner won one of the Queenstown seats in the House. Already he had agreed to defend Dinizulu for alleged high treason arising out of the 1906 Bambatha rebellion; and his sense of professional ethics and conscience would not allow him to withdraw from this exacting though ill-paid commitment in order to accept the invitation of Merriman, Prime Minister of the Cape, to represent the colony at the National Convention. To a large extent Schreiner prevented a miscarriage of justice in the Dinizulu trial, where Carter, the Attorney-General, typifying Natal Whites in their most vindictive mood, had launched a prosecution of extraordinary width. And it is hardly likely that Schreiner would have been able to do more than raise at the National Assembly some additional arguments in favour of federation and give some help to the weak Natal delegates; unification had the support of all the powerful figures at the discussions. Possibly he might have secured a modicum more recognition of Non-White political rights; he fought valiantly but in vain for guarantees against political discrimination on grounds of colour, both in the Cape Parliament, where the draft legislation was approved, and in Britain, where he led an unsuccessful mission to plead the cause of the Non-Whites.

Just before Union on 31 May 1910 Merriman, Prime Minister of the Cape, offered Schreiner, who would not stand for the House of Assembly, either a seat on the Bench or a position in the Senate as one of the four members nominated for their knowledge of 'the reasonable wants and wishes of the coloured races'. Schreiner greatly desired the latter appointment; only if the recommendation were not forthcoming would he join the judiciary.[20] The decision lay with Botha, of whose policy towards Blacks Schreiner had been highly critical. But Botha, who believed that Dinizulu was innocent and was about to release him from prison, was grateful to Schreiner for his noble efforts in the case. So Schreiner became a senator. Almost immediately the segregationist and racial policies of the Government aroused his opposition. In 1911 the Immigration Bill was introduced, which was not to be passed until 1913. He co-

[19] Walker 244. [20] Walker 336.

operated with Gandhi in opposing it, for it was aimed primarily at ending the entry of Asians; but he achieved scant success.

In early June 1911 WP set sail with Oliver and Ursula on the *Edinburgh Castle* for England. Both children were to go to Cambridge—Oliver to Trinity College and Ursula to Newnham. But first came a trip in August to Norway, which remained vivid in Oliver's memory to the end. Then WP returned home alone. The correspondence with Oliver was soon to start. It is time to take stock of the character, qualities and failings of WP, whom Eric Walker has said,[21] with some exaggeration, Oliver so closely resembled 'in build and spirit'.

Intellectually he was very gifted, and he was a cultivated person. His letters contain occasional quotations, flowing naturally, not only from the English classics but also from the authors of ancient Greece and Rome and from writers in French. As far as an extremely busy professional and political life allowed, Schreiner read widely.

A generally quiet and dignified demeanour normally hid a nervous, excitable, sentimental temperament; he was inclined to obstinacy, melancholy, depression and a feeling that he was isolated; and—save in legal matters—self-questioning. His temper was somewhat short, and when, as so often was the case, he was suffering from overwork, strain, worry or ill health, he was inclined to lose it. This tendency did not serve him well when he was conducting a case or arguing in court. The most celebrated outburst came relatively early in his career, in 1895, when he was Attorney-General. It was in the case of *Cook Brothers* v *The Colonial Government*,[22] in which, leading Juta QC, Schreiner succeeded in defending an action by the Cook brothers to have their rights sustained to certain concessions granted to them by Sigcau, the Paramount Chief, before the cession of East Pondoland to the Crown. Richard Solomon QC led for the plaintiffs. There was considerable interjection by members of the court, composed of De Villiers CJ and Buchanan and Upington JJ. The Chief Justice found for the Government on the law; but he expressed the court's sympathy for the moral claims of the plaintiffs, which, he said, the Government ought to bear in mind, the importance of the decision in law, and the considerable expense that could have been saved had the defendant excepted, as it should have, to the plaintiffs' declaration. In the circumstances, he said, each party should bear its own costs. Whereupon Schreiner burst out that he hoped the order as to costs was not associated with the personality of leading counsel for

[21] At 342.

[22] (1895) 12 SC 86; also reported in 5 CTR 107, where the evidence and interruptions by the court are set out in fair detail, but the outburst by Schreiner is not mentioned. For certain details, see Walker 62–3.

the Government. De Villiers CJ, stunned momentarily by this unprecedented reflection, turned pale, then said crisply that personalities did not colour his judgments, and strode out of court.

Henry Juta, his old friend, whom he had found such a solace in England in his loneliness when he arrived at Cambridge, at times would trade on this weakness. Still, this baiting did not excuse an outburst in court on 22 August 1912, at a time when WP was weary, carrying—as so often—too much weight, suffering from a heart complaint and beginning to become deaf. The incident is vividly portrayed in a dignified letter to WP from Henry Juta:[23]

'Chambers 22.8.12

'Sir,

'You stated in Court today with regard to a remark I made to the Judge as to the calling of Mr Bosman that it was imperfect. . . . You are entitled to your own recollection which differs from that of my junior and myself. But you proceeded to make the following public statement: "It is not only incorrect but it is false—and my friend knows it." This is so serious a matter that unless you are prepared to withdraw it—made I believe when you were very heated—as publicly as you made it it is obvious that our life-long friendship must be at an end.

'I cannot [? bring] myself to write any more. I can hardly write this: that is much too obvious.

'H Juta.'

Next morning the contrite Schreiner made *amende honorable*, explaining that the 'statement was made in haste. . . . I wish to be permitted to express my regret to your lordship and to my friend and to withdraw the unjust remark, which but for the strain of protracted work and of this heavy case would never have been made.'[24]

But the episode was not typical of Schreiner in his court work. True, he fought his cases hard; he put his clients and witnesses through a gruelling time at pre-trial interviews; his cross-examination was rigorous in the extreme; and he was apt—increasingly so with the passing years—to be laborious and over-meticulous in detail, and to adopt the tone of a lecturer rather than a persuader when arguing a legal point or addressing the court on the evidence. Still, he was for long the leader of the Bar; and though his chamber work was very large, once his practice had been established he never was in want of court work. There were able men at the Cape Bar in his time; competition was keen; even good advocates occasionally could not make a livelihood; fees by modern standards, even allowing for the fall in the value of money since the Great War and the absence of any tax on income in almost

[23] WPS papers SAL.
[24] The WPS papers SAL contain a holograph draft of the reply.

all the years when Schreiner practised,[25] were low. It says much for WP's forensic ability that, starting without any financial resources, and simultaneously with the performance of much largely unpaid public service, he could maintain a practice that kept him and his family in a comfortable style of life.

Outside court Schreiner was normally sweet tempered, and was always considerate, with great charm of manner. Never did he refuse help to colleagues at the Bar who sought his advice; but not only to them—to anyone who came to him in distress. Young relatives were assisted by him financially, especially with their education. But he was a pretty easy mark for all. One letter will suffice. It was written by the unfortunate Melius de Villiers on 12 March 1914[26] from 'Blanckenbergh' in Wynberg to 'My dear Mr Schreiner'; it stated that previously he had made an arrangement with WP to look up authorities for him; that after the work of the University Commission was over, he (Melius) would have nothing to do, and did Mr Schreiner care to enter into such an arrangement again?

Schreiner was a warm-hearted and kindly person, hard on himself but soft towards and trusting of others; but once his trust was betrayed by a person, he never relied on his word or deed again. Constantly he wrote letters of congratulation, encouragement or sympathy to others, a practice Oliver was to follow. In his professional, political and private life he was the soul of honour, renowned and beloved for his utter integrity.

In politics he tried to be a moderate, so difficult at a time when political feelings ran high. Like Merriman, he disliked the stratagems of political life and the opposing demands that politics makes on men. One of his weaknesses was an inability to delegate; another was his verboseness and undue devotion to minutiae. In her biography of Merriman[27] Phyllis Lewsen gives this view of Merri-

[25] The first country-wide income tax was introduced by the Income Tax Act 28 of 1914, the maximum marginal rate being 7½ per cent. But the Cape Colony imposed an income tax from 30 June 1904 (Additional Taxation Act 36 of 1904), the initial maximum marginal rate being 5 per cent, a rate maintained by the annual renewals of the tax (Additional Taxation Act 26 of 1905; Income Tax Continuance Act 9 of 1906; Income Tax Continuance and Mining Profits Act 26 of 1907), but increased to 8,75 per cent for 1908–9 in respect of incomes of £10 000 and above—in present-day terms, say, R300 000 (Income Tax Act 21 of 1908) and maintained at that level for 1909–10 (Income Tax Act 20 of 1909).

[26] WPS papers SAL. On Melius de Villiers (1849–1938), brother of Lord De Villiers, see M Wiechers in *DSAB* II 184 and V G Hiemstra in *SESA* III 660. Judge of the OFS 1876–89, Chief Justice 1889 to March 1900. Refused an offer in 1902 by Milner of the Chief Justiceship of the Orange River Colony, as he had sworn to help regain the country's independence. From 1905 to 1909 Professor of 'Zuid-Afrikaansche Recht' at the University of Leyden. Thereafter, apart from serving on a number of commissions, he confined himself to writing on law, at which, a true, if self-taught, scholar, he excelled.

[27] At 201. But Merriman was fond of Schreiner. In a letter to Innes of 3 June 1910 Merriman, referring to his failure to secure the appointment as Prime Minister of the Union and his subsequent decision not to accept ministerial office under Louis Botha, wrote: 'Schreiner behaved *very well*. He wrote me a most manly honest letter—just one of

man—no easy person himself—as a minister in Schreiner's Cabinet: 'Merriman knew that Schreiner was an admirable man with great refinement of character and intellect, but his monologues and cosmic pessimism were irritating, and he was often unintentionally rude and overbearing.'

Schreiner always prepared with much care any major statement he was to make; and he could make a great speech in Parliament. James Rose Innes in his autobiography[28] commented on the magnificence and moving quality of his speeches in the House on the report of the Cape committee of inquiry into the Jameson Raid and on the so-called Treason Bills of 1900 concerned with the punishment of the Cape rebels and related matters.

In private life Schreiner was far more a family than a club man, though he was a Freemason and an ardent follower of sport, especially rugby, a keen fisherman from the rocks and an occasional, though very poor, golfer. He devoted loving attention to his wife and children, and he was most affectionate towards the young generally. After dinner he would work on his papers amid the noise of the family gathered together—a gift of concentration that Oliver did not have; during the week he carried on toiling at home until after midnight; he did a good deal of legal preparation each Saturday; and on Sundays he tried to recover by sleeping late, his wife and children frequently being at a Dutch Reformed or other church, but he, being no orthodox Christian, not.

WP did not care to be the centre of attraction on official occasions. Though he was as flattered as any ordinary man of honourable ambition by invitations that signified a compliment, he shrank from the public gaze. Thus he would not accept the invitation of Lord Milner to represent South Africa at the coronation durbar of Edward VII in Delhi in 1903.[29] His attitude is reflected in a comment in a letter to Oliver written on 1 October 1912, in which he said that he was to be a guest at the dinner of the Council and Senate of the South African College: 'Then I am to speak, and it's "all but half of what I cares for", as I prefer the quiet of home.'

Oliver Schreiner was at Trinity College, Cambridge, until the outbreak of the Great War, when he immediately enlisted, breaking his law studies. During the long vacations of 1912 and 1913 he went back to Cape Town to stay with his parents. To their great joy he did extremely well at Cambridge, gaining the George Long Prize in Roman Law and Jurisprudence and being one of only two to get a first class in Part I of the Law Tripos in 1913. (The other

those that with all his eccentricities makes one love him.' See Phyllis Lewsen (ed) *Selections from the Correspondence of John X. Merriman 1905–1924* (Cape Town: Van Riebeeck Society 1969) 196.

[28] Op cit 189. See also Walker 82–3, 236. But Merriman (Lewsen *Merriman* 231) regarded the Treason Bill speech as 'long and rambling'.

[29] Walker 247.

Oliver as a boy

Oliver in the blazer of the South African College

Oliver Schreiner at the time of his appointment to the Bench in 1937

Oliver Schreiner in early middle age

Oliver Schreiner in middle age

Photograph by Leon Levson

Oliver Schreiner in middle age

Oliver Schreiner in 1972 at the time of the Golden Jubilee of the University of the Witwatersrand, Johannesburg

Oliver Schreiner in 1972 in the robes of the Chancellor of the University of the Witwatersrand, Johannesburg

was William McNair of Caius, who went on to sit Part II in 1914; after the Great War McNair took an LLM and got the Whewell Scholarship in International Law. He was a judge of the Queen's Bench from 1950 to 1966.) Schreiner was awarded a Trinity College Senior Scholarship and, in 1916, while he was on active service, a fellowship. But WP, in advising him on his studies, warned him not to work too hard. There are many letters in this vein, varying in opening, as was the case with all the letters, from 'Dear old Son', 'Dear Boy', 'Dear old Fellow', 'Dearest old Fellow', 'Dear old Chum', 'Dear old Pal' to 'Dear old Chap', and always ending 'Your old Dad'. The handwriting, though very small and rather spidery, is clear, save for an occasional word.[30]

On 17 October 1911 WP urged Oliver to find a '*good coach* for some subjects, especially the English law things, Real Property, Contracts, and perhaps for Jurisprudence'. This would save time and guide reading. Already WP was speaking of Oliver's going for the highly regarded Whewell Scholarship in International Law. (It had been won by the brilliant J E R (Etienne or Oefie) de Villiers, later De Villiers JA, in 1898; the scholar in 1912 was Ronald Roxburgh, who was a Chancery judge from 1946 to 1960.) He returned to the subject in a letter of 27 December 1911. 'It must rest with you and your advisers what you do in the matter. I should almost have thought that without endangering the place in either the second part of the Tripos or the Bar Final, you could scatter the Whewell work over the three years, and write for it about the end of your fourth year. There is no doubt that if you secured it, and had also done the trick in your Tripos, both parts, you would stand a fair chance for a Trinity fellowship, which would be a grand platform for your future. No haste to get to practice is prudent, though I love the spirit which you have in the matter. But I shall not worry you, dear boy, about the scheme. I only want you to have before you for consideration the possibilities that lie near your hand.'

The next mention of the Whewell Scholarship in the letters is on 25 February 1913. 'Your taking that course of lectures [in political science], I am delighted to hear of: these side studies are of a nature which young men too rarely discern,—nor did I take the right steps in those ways at Cambridge. Such intellectual exercises, the thought they breed, broaden the basis of legal education, which has a narrowing tendency if taken alone. Moreover, when you come to the Whewell, your bread will come back from the waters.' It was followed by advice on 4 March that year: 'I think you are right, *pace* dear Dr. Kenny, in your plan and purpose about the Whewell.

[30] Schreiner's handwriting was to cause difficulties to subordinates and typists during his period in London from 1914 to 1919; several had to have their eyes tested and obtain spectacles; and some typists requested magnifying glasses. See Walker 366.

The benefit of that line of study will be great in later years. But, above all, don't overwork: keep reserves of strength always.' But a letter of 18 March urges Oliver to drop his Whewell studies, in order to concentrate on the Law Tripos; otherwise there would be too much strain. '*You must not overdo things*', take on too heavy a load so as not 'to disappoint the old man. Now, dear, realise at once that you will not, cannot, disappoint me. I have that confidence in both your purport and discretion that I should absolutely not feel at all bumped if you changed your course, took up this, or dropped that. . . . I trust you altogether, as much as I love you.'

So the Whewell studies were dropped. It must have caused WP relief. Some time before he had urged Oliver not to overdo his work. He had heard, he wrote on 23 April 1912, that Oliver was working seven days a week, which is dangerous. 'Festina lente, old chap'—do not 'overtax your endurance'. 'I once had the unpleasant experience at Cambridge of taxing my powers beyond their bearing point, largely because (ass that I was!) I burnt the candle at both ends making later (early) hours pay for mild social dissipations in the evenings—but I don't want you ever to reach that point, or have a similar experience. . . . I love your self-control and spare habits of life. All I must suggest is that you should not deny yourself a reasonable measure of expenditure where social exigencies point that way.'

A letter of 4 February 1913 discusses Oliver's problems with his studies for his Bar examinations and Odgers's lack of sympathy. 'I think you can hope to do fairly well without the lectures: at any rate in my day I simply read up the Common Law without attending lectures, and yet was lucky enough to win a 100 pound Junior Inner Temple fellowship. *See Kenny*. He will give you good advice on broad lines as to this reading.' (In fact, Kenny and his daughters proved staunch friends to Oliver.)

WP returned to the topic in a letter of 7 November 1913. 'Your remarks about lectures remind me so much of my experiences and sentiments. Barring Kenny and Clark, I took no realised benefits from *lectures*,—but I found great advantage in *coaching* from several men, especially Kenny again, Scrutton, and (in Ethics) Caldecott.'

At the end of 1913 WP was again urging his son to take it easy. 'You are going it at an immense pace, and there is danger of a break down. *That must not be*. Don't take an evil example from the old man's later years.' (5 December 1913.) Again: 'You must not tax your powers too heavily, my dear; that is the thing I am most anxious about. Remember you have a long road before you, also that you should make use of social opportunities and meeting men of the time while you are at Cambridge. Dont be too centred in your work.' (19 December 1913.)

W P Schreiner's love for, concern about and close personal relationship with Oliver came out vividly from his letters. 'Dear lad', he wrote on 1 October 1912, after Oliver had returned from Cape Town to England, 'it has been such a joy to me to have you near me during the three months. I may be a very foolish but I am a fond old man: and you bare [*sic*][31] many of my best eggs in your basket.' Shortly thereafter: 'Do write to me at length, old man: I know that nothing that concerns you will be trivial to me. You and I have a tie between us that is very exceptional: we have been so much about together, and we have so much in common by temperament and proclivities. Let me be your eldest brother rather than only the old father. You may think you know, but you dont, *how* it strains my very heart strings to part from you.' (11 October 1911.)

On 12 December 1911 WP wrote at 'one-thirty a.m.!' so that the mail would reach Oliver shortly after he had become of age on the 29th. 'My dear Man: For when you read this you will have passed the big day . . . and will be emancipated in law from the guardianship of the old man. It seems incredible that twenty-one years have all but passed since the nurse of Pine Grove introduced me to that quaint morcel [*sic*] of humanity with the specially flexible and gappy mouth,—that dear being who has positively never been a source of anything but joy to me ever since. I see you, old chap, in all the stages looking backwards, and upon my word I have a lump in my throat.'

This moving letter is matched by one written on 8 October 1912, in which WP touches very delicately on the topic of women. 'The only danger I see is perhaps a creature of my own imagination, —the dread of your being bit by the opposite sex. There I think is the heel of my Achilles. Let me be in all things your friend, my dear. Never let anything in the way of a trouble be unshared with me; but regard me as a sort of old brother who has been through the mill, and can sympathize.'

On 29 December 1912 WP wrote: 'My dearest old Pal: It is the evening of your birthday, and I must write a bit of my letter now to wish you all the blessings that the best of lives can hold for my dear son. . . . [T]he old Pale Face [wants] to tell of his love for you. . . . Your letters show me that you are taking a keen and close interest in the public events which are crowding thick upon a dissolving era, and I dont doubt that you will have your share in the shaping of destiny in your own country in due course. My opportunity came to me in specially troublous & stormy times, & I must not grumble that my career may be regarded as a failure. Indeed I am conscious of faults of temperament & character & errors of conduct to which in great measure my collapse as an influence in this country may be attributed.'

31 WP's spelling was not always correct. For instance, he consistently spelt 'develop' 'develope' (for example, letter of 14 January 1913).

In similar vein was a letter of 14 November 1913. 'The state of affairs, as to the parties, the Indians, & the workers of this country is not happy; it is not possible to regard with contentment the harsh attitude of the Government on the great problems. . . . Some day you will have to take a place in our affairs, and I wish I could be here to see how you will influence your time. My own efforts, burdened by a very difficult personality, have always been poor & ineffective. May you keep always consistently broad humane views in . . . your actions & policy. Now, old boy, I have rambled sadly, but I am sad. I love you & I want to see you again.'

After another success in examinations that Oliver modestly attributed to good fortune, WP wrote in ironic vein on '29/30/4/13'—'near 1 a.m.' (many of his letters spoke of the time of writing as being after midnight, and that he was 'dead beat', 'most fagged' or the like): 'Another accident! Of course I dont remember how some 30 odd years back, a certain young man, also a Cambridge undergrad, used to feel quite sure things would go awry till the list came out! So you have by chance scored another first,—a good foundation dear, very good. I wonder whether you can *quite* grasp what you are to me, & how I long that I could be more to and do more for you.'

WP frequently spoke of his disappointment at Oliver's decision not to take up rowing, 'that noble sport' (5 October 1912), and at his playing rugby, which WP regarded as a dangerous game. Rowing was 'valuable exercise, and one could row every day, wet or fine' (13 February 1912). Would Oliver not take up rowing as well as rugby? 'But you are a stubborn dog, too' (15 October 1912). Meantime, he ruefully reflected on the nature of his own prowess at golf. 'Eighteen holes in 129!' (19 November 1912), and 'in *only* 127'—but Ralph Close, his colleague at the Bar, took 135 (1 April 1913); 35 strokes for the small six-hole links at Newlands—'only 14 above bogey' (14 November 1911).

Professional work was very heavy for the 'old man'—who was only in his fifties, but weary beyond endurance, with his 'legs terribly crook' (2 January 1912). 'I am beyond ordinary fagged', he wrote on 13 February 1912, from 'Eastcliff', the family seaside home at St James. 'But the old sea comes to me through the window with its soothing cadence.' In less than six months, he told Oliver on 16 April that year, 'I have made £3,000 at the Bar, largely in consulting practice'. He had to turn away briefs (29 October 1912). Fanny Schreiner was worried. 'Ol boy', she pleaded on 4 March 1913, 'I wish you would write & persuade Dad to go across & take the treatment at Nauheim again this coming season. He wants bracing up. . . . He ought not to be working so hard at his time of life, & it is not necessary from a monetary point of view.' Sometimes sleep overcame Schreiner. He wrote to Oliver from 'Villa Flandre', their home in Newlands, on 20 May 1913: 'I slept 21 hours between 1 a.m. Sunday and 9 a.m. Monday. So I did myself well!' But he really was overdoing things. Typical of certain letters is the following: 'I feel at times terribly jaded. Moreover I weigh 214 lbs, which is at least a stone too much. And my poor legs are more groggy than ever!' (20 March 1914.)

Schreiner dwelt on some of his cases. On 19 January 1914 the Appellate Division gave its important decision in *Green* v *Fitzgerald.*[32] Four days later WP wrote: 'Fitzgerald & Green we won: a big victory. Old vindictive Roman Dutch Law obsolete in its expansion to adulterine offspring of the Roman Law doctrine of the Constitutions regarding those born of incestuous & nefarious unions. "Consideration" *vs.* "*justa causa*", *alias* "redelijke oorzaak", still pending, but a hollow fight . . . which we need not fear.' The prediction was warranted when the judgment on *Conradie* v *Rossouw*[33] was delivered on 27 June 1919, a day before the death of WP.

In a letter of 12 September 1913 from the Hotel Imperial, Bloemfontein, he wrote: 'Dearest old Pal: . . . I am most fagged, & must get some sleep before tomorrow's resumption of the big McCabe case[34] which loiters painfully & I may be unable to bolster up a correct but *weak* judgment of Maasdorp J.P. Make a note, dear boy, if you are one day a Judge, always to find your facts fearlessly & plainly, & to discredit where discredit is due!'

Schreiner deeply regretted his lack of success in persuading the judiciary that women were eligible to enter the attorneys' profession. True, Mahatma Gandhi's clerk, Miss Sonya Schlesin, had failed to secure registration of her articles, on the ground that the Admission of Justice Proclamation of 1902 of the Transvaal referred to male attorneys only.[35] With J E R (Oefie) de Villiers as his junior, Schreiner persuaded Maasdorp JP that that Transvaal decision was wrong.[36] But on 22 October 1912 the Appellate Division (before whom D M Buchanan appeared for the unfortunate woman) reversed the decision, holding—in Orwellian terms—that s 20 of the Cape Charter of Justice used 'persons' with ref-

[32] 1914 AD 88. The court held that the crime of adultery had been abrogated by disuse, and so had the indirect consequence that the guilty parties could not bequeath to an adulterine child more than was required for its maintenance.

[33] 1919 AD 279.

[34] *Rubidge* v *McCabe & Sons* 1913 AD 433, a case on servitudes, on appeal from the decision of Maasdorp JP in the CPD. The decision of the court *a quo* was upheld with modifications, costs to be paid by the appellant. The argument took place on 12 and 13 September. On 19 September all three members of the Appellate Division bench—Lord De Villiers CJ, Solomon J and J de Villiers JP (of the TPD)—delivered judgment. Sir Henry Juta KC led for the appellant. Lord De Villiers (at 439) referred to Juta's contention that Maasdorp JP did not state that he disbelieved certain witnesses whose evidence was favourable to Juta's client, but concluded that Maasdorp JP's judgment was founded on his belief in the correctness of evidence of witnesses on the other side.

[35] The case was *Schlesin* v *Incorporated Law Society* 1909 TS 363, and the legislation Proc 14 of 1902 (T) s 11.

[36] *Wookey* v *Incorporated Law Society* 1912 CPD 263.

erence to males only. Innes ACJ and Solomon J were regretful that they had closed an honourable calling to one half of the citizens because of their sex alone; but relief had to be sought from the legislature.[37] This relief came only in 1923, and then through a private member's Bill.[38]

Schreiner told the sad tale to Oliver. 'Today I placed before Maasdorp J.P. a fairly reasoned argument for the registration of the articles of clerkship of a young lady [Madeline Una Wookey] who wishes to become an attorney. . . . It will be as narrow as old Cambridge if the Court falls back upon doctrines of the dark ages in order to refuse women that career. I think, old fellow, of the injustice to many women who *must* make their own livings if the avenues to honourable professions are closed to them; & think, too, of the noble work done by them as doctors, nurses, inspectors. . . .' (9 April 1912.) Dot was sitting her law examinations, and WP must have been happy by the decision of Maasdorp JP. Then came the blow of the reversal on 22 October 1912. 'Whatever your views may be as to the broad question', he wrote to Oliver the next day, 'you will feel with Dot in her disappointment at the decision (at which I cannot cavil from a legal point of view) that women cannot become attorneys. . . . To me the objections to opening all fields of useful energy to men and women alike do appear mistaken, & often narrow. But Dawn breaks gradually.' Oliver must have agreed, for WP's letter of 3 December on the subject reads: 'I am *so* glad you regret Miss Wookey's failure to get admission as an articled clerk. Nothing but the growth of healthy public opinion on true democratic lines can now help the matter.'

It has been said that 'Dot Schreiner [was] the first South African woman barrister'[39] and that Minnie de Villiers, Oefie's wife, was

[37] *Incorporated Law Society* v *Wookey* 1912 AD 623. On 29 July 1913 Olive Schreiner, showing her feminist side, wrote from De Aar to Oliver, then in Cape Town during the long vacation from Cambridge:

'I don't think there is much fear of Dot's not being able to practise, if not at once, at least very soon. If ever Hertzog comes in, you may be sure he will pass the Act legalizing woman legally.

'Is it not rather strange that we in the Cape Colony are bound by the old Roman Dutch laws which in Holland were all done away with in I believe *1806*. At present women are allowed to be both barristers & attorneys. There are 34 women lawyers in little Holland, 18 of whom are in full practice, the rest being newspaper editors, political workers, atc, as is often the case with barristers in England. There is no law against their being judges though one has not yet been appointed. Tell Dot this as it may interest her.

'Good bye, dear Laddie. I'm so glad you're having a good lot of exercise.'

[38] Women Legal Practitioners Act 7 of 1923, passed without opposition. Subsequently it was replaced by the Women Legal Practitioners Act 11 of 1963, which was repealed by the Attorneys Act 53 of 1979, a consolidation Act in which no mention is made of the topic. Apparently it was cold mutton and not served up again, being unpalatable to the female sex. The Act of 1923 opened the door for women to all branches of the profession. On the history of the question and the quaint views of Melius de Villiers and R P B Davis (later Davis J), see my note in (1969) 86 *SALJ* 351.

[39] *The Argus* Supplement 'Argus 125' 26 February 1982 p 37. As she was married to a professional soldier during the Great War and became Mrs Gregg, something has gone wrong.

the first woman to obtain the degree of LLB in South Africa—this was in 1915, she having studied at the South African College.[40] *Se non è vero, è molto ben trovato.*

For all his protestations of being aged, Schreiner was still only in his fifties. But, being the last of twelve children to survive infancy, and having lost all political power when he was in his early forties, after having been a leader of men far older than himself, he began to witness the decline or death of many who had been dear or close to him. Het—the warm-hearted Het, whose marriage had been childless but who had adopted the many children of her sister Alice Elizabeth (1845–1884) (Mrs Hemming)—in 'the clutches of dropsy' was slowly dying. 'I am so glad to see something of that dear soul, who was my girl mother when I was a small boy & went to school at Cradock. It is very sad to see how frail & worn she has grown; & to feel that probably she has not much longer to be with us. She is the most loving, altruistic spirit I have ever met. Some day when you have a spare half hour drop her one of your breezy letters: she will value it immensely.' (7 November 1911.) 'Her life, old boy, has been one long proof of the possibility of giving oneself up entirely for others. A more absolutely unselfish tireless worker for all sorts & conditions of men & women has not lived. To me, as a boy, she was a little mother,—even if I was rather a bad son. So you will feel with me in this time of shadow.' (9 December 1911.) In August the following year she died.

The life of Gordon Sprigg,[41] old, in political obscurity, came to an end on 4 February 1913, and in his letter to Oliver on that day Schreiner wrote: '. . . today is sad, as my old friend Sir Gordon Sprigg passed away this morning. I am to be a pall-bearer tomorrow, & must break away from Court for the purpose. Only two [he and Merriman] now remain of the roll of Cape Prime Ministers & one [he] is very groggy on his pins. I am sending you an Argus with a good article on Sir Gordon's career. Read such things, they give you touch with the near past which is so important in keeping true historical perspective. There is too much tendency to treat History as "something that happened long ago"—& I like to note that you are always keenly alive to the current world events, & think out the positions as they arise.'

The following month Schreiner had found it difficult 'to sort the phrases' in his valedictory to Sir Perceval Laurence,[42] who had

[40] V G Hiemstra in *DSAB* III 22. See also J J Oberholster in *SESA* III 658.

[41] 1830–1913. MLA 1869; PM 1878–81; member of Upington's Cabinet of 1884; PM 1886–90; member of Rhodes Cabinet 1893–6; PM 1896–8 and (replacing Schreiner) 1900–4. Conceited, covetous of power, wily, a master of political and parliamentary tactics, but in general a man of integrity. See J A Benyon in *DSAB* II 698.

[42] 1854–1930. Judge of High Court of Griqualand 1882–8; JP 1888–1900; second puisne judge of CPD 1910; AJA during 1911; AJP of NPD April–September 1912. Author of considerable ability, educationist and pioneer of public libraries. Never married. See R F Kennedy in *DSAB* III 500.

retired from the judiciary at the age of 59, after thirty-one years on the Bench. When he did sit he was 'quite a judicial ornament. . . . But it is best that he resign, both for family reasons, and because lately we have had little value from his being nominally on the strength of this Bench.' (11 March 1913.)

The death on 10 November 1913 of 'Dick' Solomon, then High Commissioner in London, upset Schreiner greatly.[43] Four days later he wrote to Oliver of Solomon with fond recollections of his former colleague, thanking Oliver for acting on his cable and sending flowers on his behalf to the funeral. 'He was one of the finest minds we have produced, and a good friend always. The intellectual quality was so predominant that he was never a strong partisan, since parties are always based on poor reasons: & thus he had the experience of being appreciated to the full by few who could grasp the grounds of apparent inconsistencies in his political career. He did the work to hand, & did it thoroughly, & he loved working for work's sake so much that he would forgo the temptation, itself natural, to refuse opportunity to labour because accepting it might involve at times activity on lines not personally approved by him, *e.g.* in connection with the Chinese importation into the Transvaal. I could not go in such lines, but I never judged him harshly.' 'Now', he went on, 'it seems to me that my old Cabinet is getting sadly reduced; Te Water is a crock, old Herholdt is frail, and I am expecting John X. to remain years after the last of us.' He was right; Merriman lived until 2 August 1926, being then in his eighty-sixth year.

Almost immediately came one of the several offers of a position of honour that were made to Schreiner after his premiership had ended—he was never a forgotten man, like a former American President tends to be—and that he was to decline. It would appear that the offer is not known to historians of the period. On 5 December 1913 he told Oliver: 'Between ourselves Botha wrote to ask me to take the post emptied by the death of Sir Richard Solomon. It was an unexpected compliment, but of course I did not entertain acceptance. My few years must, while health permits, be spent in my own country, doing I fear little active forward work, but still exercising a little influence and bearing some weight against worrying experiments in policy & legislation.' Merriman, knowing full well that Botha was trying to get him out of the legislature, where his sharp speeches were trying to the Prime Minister, had

[43] In the ODS family papers is a cutting from the *Christian Express* of 1 December 1913 containing a detailed, touching and honest obituary of Solomon by 'R.W.R.I.'—from the detailed account of the famous trial of the Rev J D Don in 1885 for criminal defamation, in which Richard Solomon conducted a brilliant and successful case for the defence, clearly Richard Rose Innes (brother of James), the prominent attorney of King William's Town who briefed Solomon. (On 'Dick' Rose Innes, see George Randell *Gentlemen of the Law of the Eastern Cape* (1982) 41.)

already rejected the offer[44]—he was too old to leave home, in effect to become an exile, and perhaps he could do something for South Africa 'before I go to the land where all things are forgotten'. The gap was filled temporarily by Sir David de Villiers Graaff.[45] But it was not to be long before Schreiner took his place.

At times Schreiner looked back wistfully on his days of political power. 'I now and then wish I were in the House again,—but *only* now and then: for I realise how far from young & strong I am, & how still impossible it would be, holding my strong view as to the root evil of our constitution, to become a force again where prejudice is so rampant.' (To Oliver 29/30 April 1913.) Still, 'I can't feel yet that I should go on the Bench, mainly because I fancy, probably an idle dream, that my being in the Senate does still give some sense of satisfaction and security to the natives & coloured folk who trust me—& so contribute to prevent the movement of things in the wrong direction.' (8 April 1913.) And this despite the fact that 'I am not in either Caucus. . . . In Caucus secrets are preserved very well in these un-Parliamentary days, when the destinies of measures & Cabinets are not, as they should be, fought for and decided on the floor of the House.' (4 February 1913.)

The lack of harmonious relations in the Cabinet, the want of proper control of the Ministers by Botha, the burden of administration cast on Smuts: of these WP wrote with concern. (21 May 1912.)

The policy of Botha's Cabinet on relations between Whites and persons of colour continued to distress Schreiner greatly. The Natives Land Bill, imposing segregation in land ownership, which became law in 1913,[46] had understandably caused great apprehension among the Blacks—and J W Sauer, colleague of WP in his old Cape Cabinet, who had piloted it in Parliament, had 'always been regarded as a particular friend' of theirs. (11 March 1913.) The departure of Hertzog from the ministry in December 1912 caused Schreiner to say: 'This country is, unhappily, not more bent upon a sane evolutionary policy as to the Natives & Coloured people, but a

[44] Lewsen *Merriman* (thesis) 490. The text of Botha's letter (unfortunately without the date) can be found in Sir Perceval Laurence's disappointing *The Life of John Xavier Merriman* (1930) 351. Merriman wrote in his diary on 20 November 1913: 'On my return home I found a letter from Botha pressing me to take the High Commissionership. Very civil and gentlemanlike.' And on 21 November: 'Wrote reply to Botha declining offer. . . .' See Phyllis Lewsen (ed) *Selections from the Correspondence of John X. Merriman 1905–1924* op cit note 27 at 236. I cannot resist quoting from his letter to Innes offering his congratulations on Innes's appointment as a judge of appeal (op cit 196): 'I *know* what intrigues these were and how everything is subordinated to the desire to get awkward opponents, or rather candid friends, out of the way.'

[45] 1859–1931. Member of Merriman's Cabinet of the last days of the Cape Colony; member of Botha's Cabinet 1910–13 and 1915–16. In 1913 he married Magdalena (Eileen) van Heerden, thirty years younger than he; Sir De Villiers Graaff, the political figure of our time, was one of their three sons. See *DSAB* II 267.

[46] Act 27 of 1913.

majority in the Union are prone towards rash experiments which could result in great evils and long regrets.' (7 January 1913.) He warned Oliver of the danger of 'colour prejudice. Dear Boy, fight against narrowness till you trample it under foot. I love your broad-minded view of things.' (24 October 1913.)

In the struggle between labour and capital in South Africa and England from 1912 to 1914 WP had sympathy with the former. 'Dont be hasty in conclusions against the workers. Their only chance is in union & firm cohesion.' (5/6 March 1912.) 'Things can only get worse until the fact is recognised & applied that Capital & Labour are partners.' (2 April 1912.) 'Profits *to capital* must greatly diminish or the solution will not work.' (16 April 1912, a letter in which WP expressed his liking for Oliver's 'tone of sympathy for the workers in the recent big skirmish'.) Smuts's unlawful deportation of the nine strike leaders in 1914 led to great concern by Schreiner of the danger of converting workers from constitutional methods to the 'direct method' of the general strike, and of trying the patience of Blacks and Coloureds. (15 February 1914.) In the Senate he fought in vain the Bill to declare the nine prohibited immigrants retrospectively.[47] 'We shall perhaps have eleven votes against twenty five or thereabouts in favour of the doctrine of liberty & fair trial, even of the devil himself! . . . Well, old boy, I have made a fair fight. . . . We are on the right side, few or many, as time will show. . . .' (13 March 1914.)

In April 1914 Schreiner at last took the advice of his wife and friends and set out, alone, for England and the 'cure' at Bad Nauheim; he was never to return. Abroad, he travelled at different times with Olive, and with Oliver and Ursula, in Germany. His health improved, but the outbreak of the Great War was imminent, he could see. Back at Cambridge just before the fateful 4th of August, he looked with horror on the outbreak of hostilities. Unlike Olive, he was wholeheartedly behind Britain. Oliver immediately went on an officers' training course; he received his commission on 13 September. Ursula was doing VAD work in Cambridge, and soon joined the South African Anglo-French Ambulance at Cannes. Dot arrived at the beginning of 1915; and Fanny in the middle of that year, allowing Dot to join Ursula. Bill, in the Union Defence Force, was to see service in East Africa. WP, too, was to render service. On 2 September 1914 Lord De Villiers, the Chief Justice, who was then acting Governor-General, died. A few days later N J de Wet MP, the Minister of Justice, called on Sir James Rose Innes, senior judge of appeal and Acting Chief Justice, to offer him the Chief Justiceship. Innes, with a vague, though unjustifiable, belief in a 'right' of succession to that position of a

[47] It became the Indemnity and Undesirables Special Deportation Act 1 of 1914.

Minister of Justice or his counterpart,[48] asked whether De Wet—who was only 40—had considered his own position. De Wet said he had no ambitions to ascend the Bench.[49] That left an opening in the Appellate Division, which then had only three permanent members, William Solomon being the second. Despite his never having held judicial office, Schreiner was immediately offered the vacancy. It was a temptation to sit with Innes and Solomon. But the prospect of having to spend at least five months a year in Bloemfontein was most unappealing: the town which his friend Innes was to describe to him in a letter of 12 October 1916[50] (addressed to 'My dear Schreiner'—a Sherlock Holmes–Dr Watson type of absence of first names was prevalent in those days) as 'that dust-ridden spot, which a light-hearted Convention decreed should be the judicial Capital of the Union—a more unsuitable centre for legal work it would be impossible to have selected; inconvenient for judges & litigants alike'. But nevertheless, unlike several persons in later years who had been offered but refused a seat on the highest court, this did not actually deter Schreiner from accepting, once telegrams from De Wet, through the office of Sir David Graaff, had assured him that Innes would be Chief Justice, and Solomon would remain as a judge of appeal. Nor did the fact that his pension would be on the ungenerous basis fixed by the Judges' Salaries and Pensions Act 1912[51] lead him to reject the invitation. The deciding factor was an oddly minor one. Two telegrams by Graaff to De Wet summarize the issue. 'Schreiner called today stop Willing to accept position appellate judge offered but only on same terms as Innes & Solomon regarding travelling allowance please cable decision.' (23 September 1914.) 'Your telegram 25th September Schreiner really sorry law precludes his being placed on same footing Solomon stop Whilst thanking Government Schreiner regrets in foregoing circumstances unable to accept offer.' (29 September 1914.)[52]

Thereafter Schreiner was naturally concerned about his future. Fortunately, salvation was just around the corner. It was the renewal by Botha of the offer of the High Commissionership in London. This time the proposal proved most acceptable. Schreiner

[48] See my essay, 'James Rose Innes' (op cit note 8) at 74–5, and references there.

[49] He became a judge of the TPD in 1932, a judge of appeal in 1937, and Chief Justice from 1939 to 1943. On De Wet (11 September 1873–16 March 1960), see (1960) 77 *SALJ* 133 and *DSAB* IV 128.

[50] WPS papers SAL.

[51] Act 16 of 1912. The annual salary of a judge of appeal was £2 750, and the pension at the rate of £120 for each year of service, with a maximum of £1 200 (s 4). Although he would be subject to the compulsory retirement age of 70, being appointed to the Bench after the commencement of that statute (s 6), Schreiner could have reached the maximum. But the previous rights of Innes and Solomon under the Judges' Pensions Ordinance 35 of 1903 (T) were preserved (s 3), which would give them up to two-thirds of the average salary of the last three years of service.

[52] For all the foregoing, see the WPS papers SAL.

admired Botha's attitude to the war and his handling of the rebellion; and now he could play his part in the world conflict. So it was that on 11 November 1914 Schreiner assumed office for an indefinite period, perhaps until the end of hostilities. As had happened on a previous occasion,[53] he declined a knighthood: to him his CMG should not be converted to a KCMG.[54] He was not the first South African, nor was he to be the last, to decide not to become 'Sir'. But he greatly desired to be made a Privy Councillor, an unusual distinction for a South African. It came his way rather late, at the New Year of 1917.[55] Now, if he did not bear the appellation 'Sir', he was the 'Right Honourable'.

The appointment of Schreiner was made at a time when the status of the dominions was rising, and the work required of a High Commissioner of a dominion in England becoming more demanding. Never trained and devoid of natural skill as an administrator, unaccustomed and hesitant to delegate, over-meticulous, temperamentally unable to dictate letters or documents, Schreiner was a trial to himself, his subordinates and, frequently, those who had an appointment to see him. But his warmth, kindness, thoughtfulness and probity made him a much-loved chief. In addition to his official duties, he devoted himself to the welfare of South African soldiers and war workers.

At the end of the Great War, when he was only 61, Schreiner was clearly declining rapidly in health. Innes was in London with his wife, trying desperately to see his daughter Dorothy, Countess von Moltke, who had been in Germany and stood by her adopted country during the war. There is a revealing passage in Innes's outstanding autobiography.[56] '. . . I knew that he had been working against the collar. Soon after my arrival, he told me that his

[53] Walker 364.

[54] Most of the South African knighthoods appear to have been that of the KCMG—Knight Commander of the Order of St Michael and St George. The highest class of the order—Knight Grand Cross (GCMG)—was rarely given; Sprigg (KCMG in 1886) became GCMG in 1902. The ranking of the orders of knighthoods at the time was: the Garter, the Thistle, St Patrick (all three with a very limited membership), the Bath, St Michael and St George, the Star of India, the Indian Empire and the Royal Victorian Order. (The Order of the British Empire was created only in 1917.) Thereafter came the Knights Bachelor, who were not members of any order. Some South Africans were Knights Bachelor. Henry de Villiers became one in 1877, just over three years after his appointment as Chief Justice of the Cape Colony. He was made a KCMG in 1882. On his appointment as Chief Justice of the Union in 1910 he became a peer, the only one in our history. The peerage was an hereditary one. Laurence J was made a knight in 1908 and a KCMG in 1911. There are similar examples. Richard Solomon was created a Knight Commander of the Order of the Bath—KCB—in 1905, and a GCMG in 1911.

Baronets, whose eldest sons succeed to the title, unlike knights, and who take precedence over knights, were very rarely created in South Africa. Graaff was an exceptional case.

In accordance with a resolution of the House of Assembly on 26 February 1925, titles were not thereafter conferred on South Africans.

[55] Walker 365, who makes the strong suggestion that it was because of his German ancestry and name.

[56] At 266.

heart was very unsatisfactory and I urged him to ease off. We had lunch together, I remember, and he lit one of those strong cigars that his soul loved. In reply to my remonstrance he quoted from *David Harum*:[57] "When a dog is really ill an extra flea or two is of no account." There had been a touching conversation at our first meeting; I had corresponded with him about Dorothy's welfare, and he handed me the office file to read. I found that every cable and letter had been drafted by himself, and the instructions at every stage had been written in his own hand. Deeply grateful though I was, I pointed out that if he insisted upon giving personal attention to every detail of the papers that came before him, he would kill himself in the end. "I dealt with your daughter's case as if she were my own child", was his reply. It was the crown of well-nigh fifty years of friendship, and the fragrance of it is with me still.'

To Schreiner's joy he heard in June that Ursula had had a son—his first grandchild. On the 28th of that month, the day the Treaty of Versailles was signed, worn out, he died.[58]

At the time of his father's death, Oliver was on the water, *en route* with his bride to England. In his war diary, composed in the form of letters to his fiancée, Edna Fincham, Oliver had written on 30 August 1918: 'My old man's birthday today—he must be 62 or 63.[59] Do you remember at Hopewell, dear Hopewell,[60] when I told you I loved the old man better than anyone else in the world?'[61] Many years later, when he was on the Transvaal Bench, he wrote a typically kind letter of condolence to Felix Landau (son of Professor Rabbi J L Landau[62]), a junior member of the Bar:

[57] 1898. Written by Edward Noyes Westcott (1846–98), an American banker. The protagonist is a country banker, wise and full of wit.

[58] Olive Schreiner, who was to die before the next year was out, wrote to Lucy Molteno, wife of J C Molteno MLA, on 14 August 1920: 'My brother's death was the hardest blow I have had in my life. It seems to have ended everything for me.' To Smuts she wrote on 5 July 1920: 'Don't overwork yourself and kill yourself as my brother did. Terrible to live on when passionate will & desire to work are there but machine won't work.' (Olive Schreiner papers SAL.)

[59] A revealing error. WP was 61.

[60] The Fincham family farm in the eastern Cape, near Queenstown.

[61] To which he added: 'It was in the first place a wrong thing to say, for of course I love my parents equally. Secondly it was to say the least a tactless remark to make on such an occasion: but in truth all through that memorable strange morning none might accuse me of brilliant generalship. Well is it that in this conflict of hearts victory is not always with the clever. But, my dear, you dont mind my old dad a lot do you? Of course you dont. For you know that I could not love you more than I do if I had no other friend in the world.'

[62] 4 May 1866–26 August 1942. Eminent Hebrew scholar and Chief Rabbi of the United Hebrew Congregation of the Witwatersrand. Oliver had paid a fee to Felix Landau, in his early struggling years at the Johannesburg Bar, to note up his law reports, and felt very close to him. Felix Landau practised at the Johannesburg Bar until 1953, when he emigrated to Israel. In 1961 he was appointed a district judge in that country. In due course he became President of the Jerusalem District Court, from which he retired on reaching the age of 70 on 27 July 1981—three days before I met him, after many years, at a reception at the Knesset. I am indebted to him for giving me a copy of the letter.

'24 6th Avenue
Lower Houghton, Jhb.
27-8-42

'My dear Felix,

'Just a note to express the sympathy which we all feel with you in the loss of your father. We know that his condition has for long been so serious that the end was not wholly unexpected; nevertheless the finality is necessarily a great shock. I was about your age when my father died and I shall never forget receiving the tidings from the ship's captain when I was returning to England. It is a big break, this one that every generation has to go through. Intellectually I have never been convinced of the immortality of the soul and yet I think that at the back of my mind there lives a half-assumption that when I pass out I shall see my parents again. I do not believe there will ever be a satisfactory substitute for family life. Those of us who have lived our early years in happy family surroundings have gained something permanent, something that no subsequent disasters can take away. Please give our sympathetic regards to your mother who has fought such a gallant fight for so long. You and your brother will be a great stand-by to her now.

'Yours

'O.D.S.'

PART TWO

Tributes

REMINISCENCES OF A VISIT TO SOUTH AFRICA

LORD DENNING*

It was in August and September 1954 that we came first to South Africa. It was to visit all the universities. We travelled by sea on the Union-Castle liner, the *Athlone Castle*. We had our two teen-age sons with us, John and Robert. It took 13 days. We played deck tennis with the first Viscount Leathers. He had done much to win the war by organizing the shipping. I also prepared lectures I was to give in South Africa. Approaching the Cape, we sailed through the Cape 'rollers'. We had one of the most beautiful views in the world—Table Mountain—clear in the sunshine with no 'tablecloth' of cloud upon it.

Almost first up the gangway to meet us was the Chief Justice of South Africa himself—Albert van de Sandt Centlivres—cheerful and welcoming. He presided over the Supreme Court of South Africa. It was its golden age. Two years before in 1952 it had decided the great case of *Harris* v *Minister of Interior*.[1] It is reported in England in the Times Law Reports as *Harris* v *Dönges*.[2] It was epoch-making. It was of great constitutional importance. The court held that an Act of the Parliament of South Africa (about separate voting for Whites and Coloureds) was invalid because it offended against the entrenched clauses of the Constitution. It also was a significant departure from the strict doctrine of precedent. It overruled the previous decision of the Supreme Court in *Ndlwana* v *Hofmeyr NO*.[3] I have often used *Harris* v *Dönges* in support of my campaign to do away with the strict doctrine of precedent in the English courts.

After a day or two we took the 'Blue Train' to Johannesburg—about 1 000 miles. It took 24 hours. To greet us, there were Oliver Schreiner and his wife Edna, along with 'Bobby' Hahlo and his

* The Rt Hon Lord Denning of Whitchurch, MA (Oxon) Hon LLD (Ottawa, Glasgow, Southampton, London, Cambridge, Leeds, McGill, Dallas, Dalhousie, Wales, Exeter, Columbia, Tilbury, Western Ontario, British Columbia, Sussex), Hon DCL (Oxon), Judge of the High Court of Justice of England and Wales 1944–8, Lord Justice of Appeal 1948–57, Lord of Appeal in Ordinary 1957–62, Master of the Rolls 1962–82, Honorary Fellow of Magdalen College, University of Oxford, DL Hants, Honorary Bencher of the Middle Temple, Honorary FBA.

[1] 1952 (2) SA 428 (A). [2] [1952] 1 TLR 1245. [3] 1937 AD 229.

wife Hanna. They made our stay one of the most memorable of our lives. We met all the best people in Johannesburg—the judges and the professors. They were the most able and the most accomplished of any we have met in all our travels. We have good photographs to bring back to us memories of them—Oliver Schreiner and Edna, Bobby Hahlo and Hanna, Mr Justice and Mrs Ramsbottom, Professor and Mrs Ellison Kahn, and Professor J E Scholtens. You will know, too, with me that they are of the very best.

The Schreiners and the Hahlos took us—and our two sons—on the most exciting expedition that we have ever undertaken. In two cars we drove the 600 miles or so to the Kruger National Park. Picnics on the way. Three days driving through the Park. Three nights in a 'luxury' cottage in a rest camp. Seeing elephants, giraffes, lions, tigers, hyenas, monkeys, impalas—everything. We have fine photographs to this day to remind us of it all. Beneath one of three giraffes I wrote that they are 'the Court of Appeal sticking their necks out'. We went up to the Kaapsehoop and looked down from the 'top of the world'. On the way back by night, one of the cars broke down on a very lonely stretch of the road, miles from anywhere. We waited anxiously in the dark—fearing trouble—but Oliver came up in time to save us. He was always a good man to have on your side in time of trouble.

I gave my addresses in the Great Hall of the University of the Witwatersrand. I am glad to say it was full. There is nothing more discouraging to a speaker than to have a hall half empty with the audience rattling about in their chairs.

We went to Bloemfontein and saw the Appellate Division of the Supreme Court at work. We met all the judges. There were only six of them at that time—Centlivres (Chief Justice), Greenberg, Schreiner, Van den Heever, Hoexter and Fagan. They did fine work in bringing together the principles of Roman-Dutch law with those of the common law of England—taking the best of each.

We went to Durban and thence by the Garden Route—through the Transkei—to Grahamstown—the beautiful town with its old university—and on to Cape Town. The university there has the most magnificent site of any university in the whole world. It has still in the foreground the acres of camellias planted by Cecil Rhodes.

We thought—and still think—that South Africa is a wonderful country. Its people are a wonderful people. It has its problems—as do we all—but it is wrong for outsiders to criticize when they do not know the true facts.

To come back to Oliver. He was a true South African. His father had been Prime Minister of the Cape. He himself went to Cambridge and took a first class. He had a mind of the highest calibre.

As a judge, he was the foremost of his time. He contributed much to the discussion in the court itself. His judgments were very clear and well expressed. He took the greatest care over them. They rank with the best of judgments anywhere.

Apart from his judicial work he took a great interest in the University of the Witwatersrand and in the students. He became the Chancellor, and presided over the deliberations with all his usual skill and firmness. He was an outdoor man too. He loved his golf and played whenever he had the opportunity.

He rarely came over to England, except a few years back when he came to give the Hamlyn Lectures at Cambridge, his old university. They were very well received.

We went once more to South Africa—and that was in 1974. Oliver had retired as a judge, but he was still Chancellor of the University. His dear wife Edna had died—and he was bereft. He was getting older and could not do as much as before, but he still had the same keenness of mind and sense of humour.

Oliver Schreiner was truly a great man and a great judge—and to us a great friend. The people of South Africa should hold his memory in honour for ever after.

IN MEMORY OF OLIVER SCHREINER

H R HAHLO*

Feeling privileged and honoured at having been asked by Professor Kahn to contribute to this volume in memory of the late Hon O D Schreiner, I wish to add my personal tribute to that of Professor Kahn.

Oliver Schreiner was one of my earliest personal friends in South Africa, and we continued to correspond until shortly before his death. During my twenty odd years as Dean of the Faculty of Law of the University of Witwatersrand, he served as a member of our Faculty and faithfully attended as many meetings as his judicial duties permitted. His, and the late Mr Justice Ramsbottom's, wise counsel contributed greatly to keeping the Faculty on the right path.

When Lord Denning visited South Africa, and I took him, his wife, and their sons to the Kruger National Park, Mr Justice Schreiner and his wife Edna, who predeceased him by many years, came along. Nothing shows up a man's true character as well as a visit to the Game Reserve. Both Lord Denning and Mr Justice Schreiner showed what they were made of. Without putting on any airs, they 'pitched in', taking their share of all chores.

I shall never forget the first morning in Skukuza, when, at six o'clock in the morning, Oliver Schreiner knocked at the door of my bungalow, calling urgently 'come quick, Bobby, we must go to see the lions'. I somewhat reluctantly got up, and we drove to the road where the lions were supposed to be, but never saw one. When, after our return to the camp, I had the car filled up, I talked to the attendant about the lions. 'Oh, they never put in an appearance before ten o'clock', he said. And so they did.

While in camp we met the late Professor Robin McKerron, who also happened by chance to be there at the same time. He joined us in the evening, but only after he had promised 'not to talk law', which he loved to do. Oliver Schreiner never casually talked law, at least with me.

Oliver Schreiner will go down in history as one of South Africa's great judges. He also was one of nature's gentlemen. May his soul rest in peace.

* Dr Jur (Halle) LLB LLD Hon LLD (Witwatersrand), Advocate of the Supreme Court of South Africa, Associate Member of the International Academy of Comparative Law, Paris, Visiting Professor of Law, University of Toronto, formerly Director, Institute of International and Comparative Law, McGill University, Montreal, Professor of Law Emeritus in the University of the Witwatersrand, Johannesburg.

OLIVER SCHREINER—SOME REMINISCENCES AND AN APPRECIATION

ARTHUR SUZMAN*

It was in 1924—now approaching sixty years ago—that I first came into contact with Oliver Schreiner—then a junior advocate at the Johannesburg Bar and a part-time lecturer in law at the University of the Witwatersrand. I was a second-year student, reading for the legal BA degree.

At that time all the lecturers in the Department of Law were part-time incumbents, and lectures were held in the late afternoons in a wooden and corrugated-iron building in Plein Street, affectionately known as the 'Tin Temple'.

It was not until 1927 that our Faculty of Law was able to boast of its first full-time professor, Robin McKerron. Initially we had no law library, though we were permitted to make use of the Supreme Court Library.

Each subject of study was virtually coterminous with a single prescribed textbook, with occasional reference to an article in the *South African Law Journal*. Thus, Roman-Dutch Law was R W Lee's *An Introduction to Roman-Dutch Law* and J W Wessels' *History of the Roman-Dutch Law*. Jurisprudence was Thomas Erskine Holland's *The Elements of Jurisprudence*, Public International Law was W E Hall, Conflict of Laws was A V Dicey, and so on. This made study less demanding, but less interesting.

Schreiner lectured on Roman Law and on Evidence. The first course in Roman Law was based on R W Leage's *Roman Private Law: Founded on the Institute of Gaius and Justinian*; the second course was based on J B Moyle's *Institutes of Justinian*.

Other lecturers included W H Ramsbottom, Harry Rissik, Sybrand ('Laddie') Rissik, Norwood Coaker (all juniors at the Johannesburg Bar) and J Colin Murray, the well-known attorney.

Ramsbottom, who lectured on Roman-Dutch Law, wrote out his lectures on the blackboard—albeit in a magnificent hand—which we assiduously copied out. Another lecturer, who shall be

* QC BA LLB (Witwatersrand) BCL (Oxon), Advocate of the Supreme Court of South Africa, of the Middle Temple, Barrister, Member of the Johannesburg Bar.

nameless, customarily interrupted his short journey from the since demolished Corporation Buildings (where the Bar then had its chambers) to the 'Tin Temple', for the pause that refreshes, which tended to enliven his lectures.

Though Schreiner had no pretensions to being an academic or a Roman-Dutch-law scholar, he ranked, in my respectful estimation, amongst the outstanding teachers of law I was later privileged to encounter, including such eminent figures as G C Cheshire, Sir William Holdsworth, R W Lee, C K Allen, Felix Jolowicz and C H S Fifoot at Oxford; and Roscoe Pound, Felix Frankfurter and Samuel Williston at the Harvard Law School.

In expounding the basic concepts of the law Schreiner had the rare gift of lucidity of exposition. If I were to venture one criticism, it would be that he did not actively promote discussion in class—but perhaps paucity of time, the lateness of the hour and length of the syllabus all militated against resort to the Socratic method.

After my call to the Bar in 1928 I was privileged to appear with Schreiner as his junior, and against him as opponent. Incidentally, I seem to have been the sole person admitted to the Transvaal Bar in that year: today they come in droves.

In those far-off halcyon days everything was on a less grand scale than today, and life was far more leisurely. Chambers were far smaller and so were fees.

In 1928 the South African judiciary, including the Appellate Division, numbered only some thirty judges in all, of whom eight sat in the Transvaal; while the Johannesburg Bar then numbered only some seventy-five members. Both Bench and Bar have since mushroomed enormously: our Bench today numbers close on one hundred while the Johannesburg Bar now has some 270 members.

The then leader of the Bar was that venerable Victorian figure, Colonel C F Stallard. His court presence was the most dignified and impressive I have witnessed. In 1971 I was privileged to attend his hundredth birthday celebration, enlivened by the skirling of one hundred pipers drawn from various regiments.

The other silks at the Johannesburg Bar in 1928 were Manfred Nathan, 'Toby' Taylor, Patrick Duncan, Harry Morris, Leslie Blackwell, Tilson Barry, Jack Brink and Philip Millin. Among the leading juniors were Maurice Franks, Angus Mulligan, Norman Rosenberg, Ramsbottom and, of course, Schreiner.

In those days, when work was far from plentiful, briefless conscientious juniors occupied themselves with unpaid 'devilling'. It was an education to work for and with Schreiner.

After his appointment to the Transvaal Bench in 1937, Schreiner soon revealed his abilities as an outstanding judge. Both as a puisne judge and later, as a member of the Appellate Division, he was ever courteous, seldom impatient, and never hectoring or condescending. Counsel seldom quaked before Schreiner as they did before Greenberg (his immediate senior on the Appellate Division), whose questioning of counsel in the course of argument was always penetrating and often devastating. If Greenberg was the more incisive, Schreiner was the more stubborn. Greenberg's razor-like intellect contrasted sharply with Schreiner's doggedness. Their approach to the law, too, was different. Greenberg's approach was 'The result is Gilbertian, but it is the law'; Schreiner's approach was 'The result is Gilbertian, it cannot be the law'. If Greenberg could be likened to Cardozo, Schreiner was more in the mould of Brandeis.

In criminal matters Schreiner was not noted for his leniency, while in tax matters the taxpayer almost invariably came second.

Schreiner must clearly rank amongst the great South African judges of the past, including Lord De Villiers, Innes and Greenberg. His passing over as Chief Justice was a reflection not on Schreiner, but on those responsible for judicial appointments.

Schreiner had the marks of a great man: he had humility without being humble; he was disarmingly modest, and displayed an unswerving integrity, without exuding rectitude. For him, when things were ill done, silence was not an option. He had a profound sense of rightness but was never an absolutist. He was blessed with a sense of balance and a quiet engaging sense of humour. I have long regarded Schreiner as perhaps the most outstanding all-round judge our country has produced and would liken him, in many respects, to that great English judge, Lord Denning. His outstanding contributions to our law will ever remain our *lucrativa hereditas*.

OLIVER SCHREINER— A PERSONAL TRIBUTE AND RECOLLECTION

R S WELSH*

It was of another Oliver that Dr Johnson wrote: '*Nullum quod tetigit non ornavit.*'[1] Oliver Schreiner, too, in the course of his long life, did nothing without distinction: at two schools in Cape Town; at two universities (a Fellow of Trinity College, Cambridge, at an early age); on the field of battle in the First World War (wounded on the Somme in 1916 and decorated); at the Inner Temple after the war, with Greene and Lawrence; at the Johannesburg Bar between the two wars; as a judge: first, for eight years, of the Transvaal Provincial Division, and then, for fifteen years, of the Appellate Division; as President of the South African Institute of Race Relations; and as Chancellor of the University of the Witwatersrand. What an incomparable record of devotion to duty and distinguished unselfish service to his profession and his country! In 1957 he should obviously have succeeded Centlivres as Chief Justice. The fact that he did not merely enhances his judicial fame and reputation: who now recalls even the names of the politicians of those times who, not once but twice, would not have him as Chief Justice of South Africa?

In the tribute by Professor Kahn which appeared a few months after Schreiner's death,[2] there is a discussion of his qualities as a judge and an analysis of some of his more important judgments. My purpose is less ambitious and more personal. I never appeared before Schreiner in the Transvaal; for by the time I started practice at the Johannesburg Bar in 1947 he was already a judge of appeal. Between 1948 and 1960, however, it was my good fortune to appear often in Bloemfontein before courts of which he was a member: usually (although not always) with a leader, since it was only in 1959 that I took silk. What an education that was for a

* QC BA (Pret) LLB (Witwatersrand) BCL (Oxon), sometime Vinerian Scholar, Advocate of the Supreme Court of South Africa, of the Inner Temple, Barrister, Member of the Johannesburg Bar, Judge of the Court of Appeal of Swaziland.

[1] Epitaph on Oliver Goldsmith (1776), *Boswell's Life of Johnson* (Clarendon Press 1934) III 82.

[2] (1980) 97 *SALJ* 566.

young practitioner! I therefore confine this brief memoir to recollections of some appeals in which he sat and I appeared during those years.

Despite this very limited and arbitrary basis of selection, the appeals which I remember cover quite a broad field. There was only one criminal appeal; but it was an important and laborious one for all concerned.[3] The rest were civil matters. They dealt with such diverse topics as the validity of a *lex commissoria* in a contract for the sale of immovable property[4] (long before the Conventional Penalties Act[5]); the applicability of the *Turquand* rule to corporations other than limited liability companies and the scope of that rule;[6] the question of *mora debitoris*;[7] the meaning of an obscure provision in the Usury Act,[8] which does not form part of the present and even more incomprehensible legislation commonly known as 'LADOFCA';[9] the equally obsolete award of interest *a tempore morae* at the rate of 6 per cent per annum (this in 1949);[10] the inadmissibility of ministerial speeches and parliamentary select committee proceedings in aid of statutory interpretation;[11] the rules of the conflict of laws governing the matrimonial property regime of spouses whose intended matrimonial domicile differs from the husband's actual domicile at the time of the marriage;[12] the still vexed question of civil liability for pecuniary loss sustained by reason of a negligent misstatement;[13] the interpretation of patent specifications;[14] the continuing interpretation of the testamentary dispositions of Sammy Marks;[15] the defence of statutory authority in a municipal flooding case;[16] the interrelationship of the Motor Vehicle Insurance Act[17] and the Workmen's Compensation Act;[18] the test of trade-mark infringement under the 1916 Act;[19] the interpretation of some difficult provisions relating to discoverers' certificates in the Precious Stones Act;[20] the 'source', for income-tax

[3] *R* v *Milne and Erleigh (6)* 1951 (1) SA 1 (A); *R* v *Milne and Erleigh (7)* 1951 (1) SA 791 (A).

[4] *The Mine Workers' Union* v *Prinsloo* 1948 (3) SA 831 (A).

[5] Act 15 of 1962.

[6] See note 4.

[7] *Microutsicos and another* v *Swart* 1949 (3) SA 715 (A).

[8] Act 37 of 1926.

[9] *Mavromati* v *Union Exploration Import (Pty) Ltd* 1949 (4) SA 917 (A).

[10] Ibid.

[11] Idem at 927.

[12] *Frankel's Estate and another* v *The Master and another* 1950 (1) SA 220 (A).

[13] *Herschel* v *Mrupe* 1954 (3) SA 464 (A).

[14] *Power Steel Construction Co (Pty) Ltd* v *African Batignolles Constructions (Pty) Ltd* 1955 (4) SA 215 (A).

[15] *O'Dwyer* v *Estate Marks and others* 1957 (1) SA 287 (A).

[16] *Germiston City Council* v *Chubb & Sons Lock and Safe Co (SA) (Pty) Ltd* 1957 (1) SA 312 (A). Schreiner's judgment in this case contains one of his rare judicial jokes; but he took care to veil it in 'the decent obscurity of a learned language'.

[17] Act 29 of 1942.

[18] Act 30 of 1941. See *South British Insurance Co Ltd* v *Harley* 1957 (3) SA 368 (A).

[19] Patents, Designs, Trade Marks and Copyright Act 9 of 1916. See *Greenblatt* v *Hirschson* 1958 (4) SA 371 (A).

[20] Act 20 of 1927. See *Rabinowitz and another* v *De Beers Consolidated Mines Ltd and another* 1958 (3) SA 619 (A).

purposes, of profits derived by a local stockbroker from dealings in London;[21] and a variety of questions relating to death duties.[22]

I remember *The Mine Workers' Union* v *Prinsloo*[23] very well, for it involved my first appearance before the Appellate Division. The judges were Tindall, Greenberg and Schreiner. I was led by Pollak KC, and Ettlinger KC led J D Schwartz for the appellants. The debate about the validity of a *lex commissoria* is now obsolete, in view of the Conventional Penalties Act.[24] The discussion of the *Turquand* rule is not. It was, for some time at least, regarded in some quarters as controversial, especially in view of an earlier Natal judgment which was not referred to and of a later English judgment.[25] It may no longer be so.[26] Anyhow, Greenberg's judgment (in which Tindall and Schreiner concurred) is still authoritative in this country and is not affected by s 36 of the Companies Act.[27]

The issue in *Frankel's Estate and another* v *The Master and another*[28] was, as Schreiner said,[29] 'whether, where a man and woman at the time of their marriage intend to settle in a country other than that of the man's domicile, that country's law, and not the law of the man's domicile, governs the proprietary rights of the spouses'. The answer was an emphatic No, both in Natal and in Bloemfontein; but for a variety of reasons. Pollak KC, who led me in both courts, cited much Roman-Dutch and civilian authority and developed the argument with that logical and persuasive force and skill of which he was a master. This, however, merely called forth four separate judgments in the Appellate Division, all against us. Of these the most notable was Schreiner's. He expressed what continued, until the end of his life, to be his own approach to an argument that, however intellectually attractive and logically unassailable, offended his practical and judicial instincts:

> 'The practice of seeking wider, underlying, principle behind a recognized specific rule is a valuable means of improving the form of the law, by making it more logical and harmonious, but the practice may, if pursued incautiously, have unsatisfactory effects on the law's substance. If some reason for a rule of law has appealed to the fertile brain of an early writer and has been accepted, possibly without re-examination, by later writers it may take the place of the rule itself, although it was not

[21] *Commissioner for Inland Revenue* v *Black* 1957 (3) SA 536 (A).

[22] *Hansen's Estate* v *Commissioner for Inland Revenue* 1956 (1) SA 398 (A); *Commissioner for Inland Revenue* v *Lazarus' Estate and another* 1958 (1) SA 311 (A); *Commissioner for Inland Revenue* v *Loewenstein NO* 1959 (1) SA 319 (A); *Commissioner for Inland Revenue and another* v *Isaacs NO and others* 1960 (1) SA 126 (A).

[23] 1948 (3) SA 831 (A).

[24] Act 15 of 1962.

[25] *Insurance Trust and Investments (Pty) Ltd* v *Mudaliar* 1943 NPD 45; *Rama Corporation Ltd* v *Proved Tin and General Investments Ltd* [1952] 2 QB 147, [1952] 1 All ER 554. Cf *Mahomed* v *Ravat Bombay House (Pty) Ltd* 1958 (4) SA 704 (T) and *Wolpert* v *Uitzigt Properties (Pty) Ltd and others* 1961 (2) SA 257 (W).

[26] Cf *Freeman & Lockyer* v *Buckhurst Park Properties (Mangal) Ltd* [1964] 2 QB 480 (CA), [1964] 1 All ER 630 and a note by R J Rohan-Irwin in (1964) 81 *SALJ* 382.

[27] Act 61 of 1973.

[28] 1950 (1) SA 220 (A).

[29] At 237.

in fact the reason or the only or most important reason for the adoption of the rule into customary or statutory law. If the result is a better, fairer, clearer rule it may be of no importance that the modification rested on a weak foundation. But unless the result is good it is difficult to see why the rule should be changed because a writer or writers conceived a plausible but possibly erroneous reason for its introduction.'[30]

The same pragmatic theme emerges from the Hamlyn Lectures which Schreiner delivered at the University of Cambridge in 1967,[31] long after his retirement from the South African Bench.[32] Speaking of 'borrowing' by South African law from English law, he suggested that practising lawyers and judges 'may be expected to look . . . to the benefits to be derived by litigants and the community if the borrowing takes place, compared with the position if it does not'. He contrasted an 'interest in the harmony of the law' with 'providing ever more appropriate and convenient rules—if one is more concerned with the practical service of the community'. There was never any doubt as to his own preference for considerations of practical convenience, or as to his own overriding concern with 'the practical service of the community'.

This is not to say that Schreiner was not a master of our common law. He shared the prejudices of Stratford no more than he did the narrow doctrinaire inflexibility of L C Steyn. He read Latin and Nederlands fluently and readily. Anyone who may doubt his command in this field should read his masterly judgment in one of the last cases he heard before going to Bloemfontein, about the now obsolete doctrine of *laesio enormis*.[33] Moreover, he delivered this judgment only a fortnight after the hearing. He would have regarded the reservation of judgment—any judgment—for a year as unthinkable.

In 1950 there was an appeal by two Johannesburg financiers against convictions and severe sentences which had been imposed on them after a long trial, preceded by a protracted preparatory examination.[34] The appeal was heard by Centlivres, Greenberg and Schreiner. It went on from early in October until late in November 1950 during a very hot Bloemfontein summer. The record occupied almost 15 000 pages. I was junior junior junior counsel for the Crown. Williamson KC (with whom I shared what was said to be the honeymoon suite at the old Polleys Hotel) is dead; so is Bekker;

[30] At 237–8.

[31] *The Contribution of English Law to South African Law; and the Rule of Law in South Africa* (1967) 17, 105.

[32] After his retirement from the South African Bench in 1960, he sat on the Court of Appeal of the old High Commission Territories and, when they became independent states, presided over the separate Courts of Appeal of Botswana, Lesotho and Swaziland.

[33] *Botha* v *Assad* 1945 TPD 1.

[34] *R* v *Milne & Erleigh (6)* 1951 (1) SA 1 (A); *(7)* 1951 (1) SA 791 (A).

so are Rosenberg KC and Lowen, who appeared for Milne; so is A B Beyers KC, who led for Erleigh; and so are all the judges. The only survivors are Watermeyer (who recently retired as Judge President of the Cape); Theron (who is now the senior puisne judge in the Transvaal); J C de Wet (who has retired from the University of Stellenbosch); and myself.

In all this I played an entirely unfamiliar role. Even in those early days I knew very much less about criminal law than about company law. The appeal nevertheless presented some interesting questions of company law. Centlivres was always patient and kindly. Greenberg was profound, inscrutable and somewhat taciturn; but when he asked questions they were always to the point, and he was not content with a smooth or evasive answer. Schreiner was different from them both. He was somewhat younger and perhaps more tenacious of a first impression. It used to be said—indeed, Beyers said it in the Appellate Division to Schreiner's face—that Schreiner was biased against persons accused of crimes involving dishonesty. Waving his glass [of water] at Schreiner on a hot summer's afternoon, he said: 'Your lordship is trying to create a new common-law offence—dishonesty.' These are my no doubt imperfect recollections of events that happened more than thirty years ago. It is certainly true that Schreiner had a strong preference for straightforwardness. Certainly, also, he did not view with favour the failure of an accused person to give evidence after a prima facie case of theft or fraud had been made out against him. He dissented against the allowance of the appeals on some of the common-law charges. In the result, however, it made little difference. The severe sentences which the trial judge (Lucas) had imposed were considerably reduced; but both men went to prison for some years; and now they and all those who judged them and most of those who prosecuted and defended them are dead.

Herschel v *Mrupe*[35] was a different kettle of fish: a claim for damages for pecuniary loss caused by negligent misstatement. The action started in a magistrate's court, the amount in issue being £112 10*s* 10*d*. The magistrate found for the plaintiff. His judgment was reversed by a two-judge court in the Transvaal Provincial Division,[36] which granted leave to appeal to our highest court. I appeared in that court for the appellant. The appeal was heard by Centlivres, Schreiner, Van den Heever, Hoexter and Fagan. They took two months and a half (in those days an unusually long time) to deliver their several judgments. The appeal was dismissed by four to one, Centlivres (to my own surprise) dissenting. Each of them delivered a separate judgment, of which Schreiner's is prob-

[35] 1954 (3) SA 464 (A). I wish that I were free to tell a tale which would reduce this case to its proper proportions. Alas, not yet!

[36] *Mrupi* v *Herschel* 1953 (3) SA 553 (T).

ably the most helpful and, nowadays, the most usually quoted. But too much was made of this trivial case, which could have been decided much more simply. In retrospect, I think that it should never have been allowed to go to the Appellate Division at all. In 1967 Schreiner himself acknowledged that our law on this difficult subject was not 'clear' or 'satisfactory'.[37] Nor, despite more recent judicial pronouncements, can a practitioner yet give his clients confident advice on this branch of the law.

Schreiner knew a great deal about the complex mining laws of South Africa. He had had experience in this field at the Bar. Soon after he went on the Transvaal Bench, he gave a judgment[38] which, although afterwards somewhat watered down by the Appellate Division[39] and affected by legislation,[40] remains the starting-point for anyone wishing to investigate the difficult questions that arise when there is a conflict between surface rights and mineral or mining rights. As far as I can recall, only two important cases concerning the mining laws came before Schreiner whilst he was a judge of appeal.[41] The first of these was heard before my time at the Bar. The second was a complex matter concerning discoverers' rights in respect of diamonds and the cession of them under the Precious Stones Act.[42] Schreiner, who presided over a five-judge court, gave, as usual, a lucid exposition of the subject. He received me kindly when, on the morning of the appeal, I went to tell him that my leader (Pollak QC) would not be appearing, since he had fallen ill on the previous day. Luckily, I had appeared in both the courts below (with Pollak before the court of the first instance and with Maisels QC before the full court in Pretoria); and Pollak and I had gone through the heads of argument thoroughly together (as was Pollak's wont) some days before the appeal was to be heard.

About tax: it was sometimes said that Schreiner regarded taxpayers and criminals in much the same light. This generalization was not accurate. What *was* true was that Schreiner did not greatly care for dishonesty or deviousness, in regard to tax or anything else. But he knew and observed the rules. In *Black*,[43] for instance, as Acting Chief Justice he delivered a judgment dismissing an appeal by the Revenue against a judgment of the Income Tax Special Court in favour of my client the taxpayer, a Johannesburg stockbroker who had derived profits from share dealings in London. This judgment is still sometimes referred to in connection with the 'source', for income-tax purposes, of trading profits.

[37] *Hamlyn Lectures* 54.

[38] *Transvaal Property and Investment Co Ltd and Reinhold & Co* v *SA Townships Mining and Finance Corporation Ltd and the Administrator* 1938 TPD 512.

[39] *Nolte* v *Johannesburg Consolidated Investment Co Ltd* 1943 AD 295.

[40] Expropriation of Mineral Rights (Townships) Act 96 of 1969.

[41] *Zuurbekom Ltd* v *Union Corporation Ltd* 1947 (1) SA 514 (A); and *Rabinowitz and another* v *De Beers Consolidated Mines Ltd and another* 1958 (3) SA 619 (A).

[42] Act 44 of 1927. [43] *CIR* v *Black* 1957 (3) SA 536 (A).

As to death duties: *Hansen's Estate*,[44] in which Schreiner sat as the second of five judges and Hoexter delivered the judgment, was decided in favour of the Revenue mainly on the authority of a Scottish case.[45] *Lazarus' Estate*[46] was at the time thought to be more controversial; for if a right to receive trust income was a 'usufructuary or other like interest' for estate-duty purposes under the 1922 Act,[47] there was admittedly what Schreiner called an 'awkwardness' in determining the value of the benefit arising from the cessation of such an interest. But that did not deter Schreiner. He cited English authority for 'the principle that assessment provisions in taxing statutes receive a large, liberal, generous interpretation'[48] and for the view that '[o]nce that it is fixed that there is liability, it is antecedently highly improbable that the statute should not go on to make that liability effective'.[49] Ettlinger QC, a very experienced tax practitioner, thought this reasoning 'unconvincing';[50] and very soon after Schreiner's retirement, Steyn CJ was predictably critical of the English authority on which Schreiner had relied.[51] But all this is now water under the bridge. There is nowadays no doubt that the cessation of a right to income under a trust attracts estate duty.[52]

The Revenue did not, however, always win death-duty cases in Schreiner's court. In *Loewenstein*[53] an estate-duty scheme involving the dilution of a company's share capital was upheld by a full court over which Schreiner ACJ presided. In *Isaacs*[54] Schreiner delivered a concurring judgment upholding another estate-duty scheme, of a kind which was not unknown in the 1950s, and must have cost the Revenue many millions of pounds, involving the transfer of assets to a foreign private company in exchange for a claim not enforceable in the South African courts. It was no doubt this decision that precipitated the drastic amendments to the estate-duty legislation which were almost immediately afterwards enacted by Parliament in 1960.

What emerges from this hotch-pot of personal recollections? At least, I would hope, an impression of the wide range and power and impartiality of Schreiner's judicial work during his last twelve

[44] *Hansen's Estate* v *CIR* 1956 (1) SA 398 (A).

[45] As Schreiner said in his *Hamlyn Lectures* (at 22), '[i]t is perhaps a reproach to South African lawyers that we have not made a greater use of Scottish cases and textbooks than we have, for Scottish law has a civilian background not very different from our own'. He added that 'the technical legal vocabulary of Scotland may sometimes be discouraging': a remark which illustrates his own disinclination to indulge in any sort of overstatement.

[46] *CIR* v *Lazarus' Estate and another* 1958 (1) SA 311 (A).

[47] Death Duties Act 29 of 1922.

[48] At 326.

[49] At 326, citing Lord Dunedin in *Whitney* v *Inland Revenue Commissioners* [1926] AC 37 at 52.

[50] 1958 *Annual Survey of South African Law* 243–4.

[51] *CIR* v *MacNeillie's Estate* 1961 (3) SA 833 (A) at 838.

[52] *Sekretaris van Binnelandse Inkomste* v *Jordaan en 'n ander* 1967 (3) SA 329 (A) at 335. Cf the Quebec case of *Laverdure* v *Du Tremblay and others* [1937] AC 666 (PC).

[53] *CIR* v *Loewenstein NO* 1959 (1) SA 319 (A).

[54] *CIR and another* v *Isaacs NO and others* 1960 (1) SA 126 (A).

and a half years on the Appellate Division, as it affected only one young practitioner during those years. And of course my account hardly touches on his contribution to the development of our criminal law and does not refer at all to the part which he took in the great constitutional cases of the 1950s, or to his attitude towards the doctrine of apartheid. Schreiner did not greatly care for doctrines: least of all that one.

I suppose that as one grows older, one is increasingly prone to become *laudator temporis acti*. But I continue to think that Schreiner was one of the great judges of the twentieth century. He was also a very fine man. He was a generation older than I; but during the last forty years of his life I received, in one way and another, abundantly of his friendship, kindliness, counsel and encouragement, in bad times as well as good. 'Hou moed', he used to say. I am proud to be allowed to record this tribute to him and in honour of his memory.

Edna Schreiner, wife of Oliver, in her thirties

Edna Schreiner and her daughter Jean, with the Schreiners' Packard ('Packie'). See page 22

Oliver and Edna Schreiner with their first motor car, a Rugby

Mrs Fanny Schreiner with her four children: Frances (Dot), Bill, Ursula (Kay) and Oliver

Oliver Schreiner and his family, about 1939. Jean (*kneeling*), Deneys, Edna, Bill and Oliver

Oliver Schreiner at the family fishing shack at Nutzi, district Bredasdorp, Cape Province

Mrs Fanny Schreiner with Oliver and his family, about 1928. *Left to right:* Deneys, Jean, Edna, Oliver, Bill

Edna and Oliver Schreiner at the entranc to their house 'Lyndall' in Lower Houghton, Johannesburg

PART THREE

Legal Essays

UNCOMMON CAUSE

P Q R BOBERG*

I The Nature of the Problem

Multiple causation has appeared in South African law. Unfortunately, like a wolf in the night, it has come in the sheep's clothing of contributory negligence.[1] And the shepherds of our jurisprudence have sometimes been deceived.

If causation is a difficult subject, it may seem that multiple causation can only be worse. Yet simple manifestations of the phenomenon are of everyday occurrence, and give no trouble. The liability of joint wrongdoers is based on multiple causation; so is the defence of contributory negligence. Why, then, the mystery?

In principle, the issue of multiple causation arises whenever a totality of harm results from the operation of two or more causes. But its recognition and resolution are hampered by its ability to assume a variety of forms. Damage may flow from a combination of the forces of nature and the hand of man, from the acts of two or more defendants, or from the acts of a defendant and of the plaintiff himself. A cause may be responsible for the whole harm, in the sense that none would have happened without it;[2] or it may merely have increased the harm initiated by another cause. This diversity of presentation tends to obscure the homogeneity of the solution: the same simple principles determine liability in all these cases.

* BA LLB LLM LLD (Witwatersrand), Advocate of the Supreme Court of South Africa, Professor of Law in the University of the Witwatersrand, Johannesburg.

[1] I refer to the cases in which it had to be decided whether failure to wear a seat-belt when travelling in a motor car can amount to contributory negligence. They are discussed later in this article.

[2] This does not mean that it is the sole cause of the harm; it means only that its causative effect operated in relation to all the harm that resulted. Thus negligent driving without which a motor accident would not have occurred is *a* cause of *all* the injuries sustained in that accident, although *some* of the injuries were *also* caused by the victim's failure to wear his seat-belt. There is a distinction between a *part cause* of the damage and a *cause of part* of the damage: the negligent driving falls into the first category, the failure to wear a seat-belt into the second. This distinction seems to have been overlooked by A J Kerr when he criticized the present writer in (1980) 97 *SALJ* 541 at 545. It is not correct to say, as he does, that '[i]f the plaintiff's total damage is R10 000 and it is proved that had he worn a crash-helmet . . . the total damage would have been R6 000, it seems that he will be liable for 100 per cent of the amount of the damage which results from the causal factor for which he is responsible, that is R4 000'. For the negligent driving of the person responsible for the accident remains *a cause* of the R4 000 damage that would have been avoided by wearing a crash-helmet, notwithstanding that this was *also* caused by the plaintiff's failure to wear a helmet. In truth the R4 000 damage is a product of multiple causation.

They are easily stated: *(a)* a person is liable only for the damage that he caused; *(b)* a person does not escape liability for damage that he caused merely because it also had other causes; *(c)* damage is presumed to be indivisible, so that a person proved to have participated in causing damage is liable for all of it unless he proves that he caused only part of it.

Where it is self-evident that all the causes in a particular case operated to produce the whole harm and not merely a part of it—as in the ordinary collision case involving joint wrongdoers or contributory negligence—we apply these principles unconsciously and without even bothering to characterize the issue as one of multiple causation.[3] But it is important to realize that the obvious indivisibility of the damage in such cases is the foundation of our whole approach. This is expressly stated in relation to joint wrongdoers by s 2(1) of the Apportionment of Damages Act 1956, which speaks of being 'liable in delict . . . for the same damage'. If A breaks C's arm and B breaks C's leg, it would be unthinkable to label them 'joint wrongdoers' and hold each liable *in solidum* for both injuries, unless indeed one were accountable for the act of the other.[4] Otherwise each, having caused C a distinct item of damage, is liable only for the damage that he caused (an application of principle *(a)* above). And though s 1(1)(*a*) of the Act does not expressly speak of 'the same' damage in relation to contributory negligence, it clearly implies this. Hence we may conclude that the application of the Apportionment of Damages Act—whether to joint wrongdoers or to contributory negligence—presupposes the prior resolution of the divisibility of damage issue. It is only *after* we have reduced the plaintiff's total harm to its indivisible elements and established the causes of each that the Act can determine the legal liability for each. In short, the Act must be fuelled with information as to the 'persons [who] are . . . liable in delict . . . for the same damage' (s 2(1)), or as to whether a person has suffered 'damage which is caused partly by his own fault and partly by the fault of any other person' (s 1(1)(*a*)). To derive that information from the facts is an antecedent process in which the Act plays no part. Because most cases involve obviously indivisible damage, it is a process that tends to pass unnoticed. But it clamours for con-

[3] Thus in the case of joint wrongdoers, since each has caused the whole harm, each is liable for all of it, despite the fact that others also caused it. The statutory possibility of a divided judgment (in terms of s 2(8)(*a*)(ii) of the Apportionment of Damages Act 34 of 1956) and the right of contribution between joint wrongdoers *inter se* do not detract from this basic principle.

With contributory negligence one of the causes is the plaintiff's own fault. Here the equivalent of holding him 'liable' for the harm is to make him bear an equitable proportion of it himself in terms of s 1(1)(*a*) of the Apportionment of Damages Act.

[4] For example, if A created the foreseeable risk of B's conduct, as in the trial court's view of the facts in *Van den Bergh* v *Parity Insurance Co Ltd* 1966 (2) SA 621 (W) (see too *Parity Insurance Co Ltd* v *Van den Bergh* 1966 (4) SA 463 (A)), and as in *Sadomba* v *Unity Insurance Co Ltd* 1978 (3) SA 1094 (R). Likewise if A is vicariously liable for the acts of B.

scious recognition where a cause operates only to increase harm that would in any event have been sustained—though to a lesser degree—without it.

These, then, are the manifestations of multiple causation that require closer consideration: situations involving, not a part cause of the whole harm, but a cause of only part of the harm. Paramount in such cases is the issue of divisibility of the harm. Can it be established which part of the harm is attributable to which causes? Who bears the onus of doing so? If the onus is discharged, how is liability determined? If the onus is not discharged, how is liability determined? Typically, these are questions that arise when it is alleged that a motorist's injuries were aggravated by his contributory negligence in failing to wear a seat-belt. The first is a question of fact, the other three are questions of law. To show that they may be answered by applying the simple principles stated above is the purpose of this article.

II Mr Justice Schreiner's Contribution

Twenty-two years ago a question of multiple causation came before Mr Justice Schreiner in *Kakamas Bestuursraad* v *Louw*.[5] It appeared that the plaintiff's pump site had become silted up, partly through natural forces and partly because of the way in which the defendant had constructed a dam. With characteristic lucidity the learned judge of appeal enunciated propositions of considerable value in solving the seat-belt problems of today:[6]

> 'Causality often raises difficult legal questions which cannot always be answered by strict adherence to logic. Recourse may sometimes be had to what Lord Wright in *Smith, Hogg and Co Ltd* v *Black Sea and Baltic General Insurance Co Ltd* [1940] AC 997 at 1003 and 1004 called the law's "empirical or common-sense view of causation", in order to select one or more of the co-operating causes for the purpose of deciding the particular case. Excesses of nature like flooding and silting may do damage without human assistance, but sometimes one man's actions may make the position worse for another. Whether that has happened or whether the human intervention must be regarded as an irrelevancy, since it could not have contributed materially to the causing of the damage, will often be a question of degree, to be decided upon a broad estimate of the probabilities. . . .
>
> 'It was, however, argued on behalf of the defendant that as the plaintiff had not attempted to show what proportion of the silting up [of the plaintiff's pump site] was due to the faulty methods of construction [of the defendant's dam] he was not entitled to recover any damages. I do not agree. We were referred by counsel for the plaintiff to the case of *Bonnington Castings Ltd* v *Wardlaw* [1956] 1 All ER 615, where a workman had been injured by inhaling noxious dust, part of which only

[5] 1960 (2) SA 202 (A).
[6] At 220, 222.

was caused by machines in respect of which the defendant employer had been negligent. It was held by the House of Lords that since that part was a material part of the whole body of inhaled dust the defendant was liable. That decision illustrates the principle that a plaintiff can hold a defendant liable whose negligence has materially contributed to a totality of loss resulting partly also from the acts of other persons or from the forces of nature, even though no precise allocation of portions of the loss to the contributing factors can be made. (See also *New Heriot* case [*New Heriot Gold Mining Co Ltd* v *Union Government* 1916 AD 415], and *Silva's Fishing Corporation (Pty) Ltd* v *Maweza* 1957 (2) SA 256 (A) at 264.)'

Had these remarks come to the attention of courts dealing with the seat-belt cases, they might have facilitated a finding that contributory negligence can consist in a plaintiff's omission to wear a seat-belt which materially contributes to the totality of his loss, even though that loss also results partly from another person's negligent driving. They also place the onus of proof where it belongs. As Schreiner JA said, in a case of the type before him (that is, where the plaintiff's loss has been caused partly by the forces of nature and partly by the conduct of the defendant) it is not for the *plaintiff* to prove *which part* of the loss the defendant caused. But the learned judge might have added (though in the circumstances it was unnecessary for him to do so) that the *defendant* can escape liability for the whole loss by proving *which part* he caused. In short, the harm is presumed to be indivisible, and the plaintiff need prove only that the defendant contributed materially to the totality of it. The onus is then on the defendant to rebut the presumption by proving that the harm is in fact divisible and that he did not cause all of it—which he does by proving which part he *did* cause.

The same principle as to onus, it will be shown, applies *mutatis mutandis* in the contributory negligence seat-belt cases.

III The Seat-belt Cases

Three hurdles confront a defendant who seeks a reduction in the plaintiff's damages for failure to wear a seat-belt. He must satisfy the court: *(a)* that contributory negligence can consist in conduct which merely increases the quantum of loss without having any causative effect upon the accident or event which leads to that loss in the first place; *(b)* that it was *negligent* not to wear the belt, that is, a reasonable man in the plaintiff's position would have worn it; and *(c)* that the plaintiff's failure to wear the belt *materially contributed* to the totality of his loss (to use the language of Schreiner JA), that is, it was a cause (together with the defendant's negligent conduct) of the loss in the sense that the loss would have been reduced or even avoided entirely had the belt been worn.

In only one of the four seat-belt cases thus far appearing in our jurisprudence did the defendant manage to surmount all three hurdles. That was *Vorster* v *AA Mutual Insurance Association Ltd*,[7] where the damages awarded to a plaintiff in respect of that portion of her injuries which the parties had agreed would probably have been avoided by wearing a seat-belt were reduced by 20 per cent.[8] Previously, in *King NO* v *Pearl Insurance Co Ltd*,[9] followed in *Sparg* v *AA Mutual Insurance Association Ltd*,[10] the defendant had been unhorsed at the first hurdle by the erroneous view that conduct which did not have a causative effect upon the accident or event leading to the damage could not constitute contributory negligence either at common law or for the purposes of s 1 of the Apportionment of Damages Act.[11] And in *Vitoria* v *Union National South British Insurance Co Ltd*[12] it was the second hurdle that unhorsed the defendant when the trial court refused to regard the plaintiff's failure to wear her belt as negligent in the circumstances.[13] Though

[7] 1982 (1) SA 145 (T).

[8] The unbelted plaintiff sustained injuries to her foot, rib, scalp, face and knees. It was common cause that her foot injury, for which R3 000 were the agreed damages, would have occurred whether or not she had worn the belt. It was also common cause that her other injuries, agreed at R1 000, would probably have been averted by wearing the belt. Thus the third hurdle—causation and its attendant issue of divisibility of damage—had already been surmounted by the parties' pre-trial consensus, leaving only the first two for the court's attention. In a judgment that would, if one may respectfully say so, have done credit to the Appellate Division, Goldstone J held that the plaintiff's failure to wear the belt had been negligent, and that it sufficed that this had contributed to the quantum of her loss although it had had no causative effect upon the collision. Being already presented with divided damage, he awarded the plaintiff the R3 000 in full and reduced the R1 000 by 20 per cent to R800.

[9] 1970 (1) SA 462 (W). The case concerned failure to wear a crash-helmet, not a seat-belt, but that is immaterial.

[10] Unreported; ECD case no 1517 of 1978.

[11] The reasoning of Colman J in *King's* case was criticized by the present writer in 1970 *Annual Survey of South African Law* 174–9, who pointed out that '[l]iability in delict is for causing damage, not for causing "accidents" or "events" leading to damage' (at 176). Overseas authorities showed that causation affecting only part of the harm was well known to the common law, and raised the issue of the divisibility of the harm, ie whether its elements could be apportioned to their respective causes. Likewise critical were N J van der Merwe and P J J Olivier *Die Onregmatige Daad in die Suid-Afrikaanse Reg* 4 ed (1980) 160n46 (cited hereafter as *Die Onregmatige Daad*) (see too previous editions), who found Colman J's decision unfair to the defendant and incompatible with the wording of s 1(1)(*a*) of the Apportionment of Damages Act, which speaks of *damage*, not an accident, caused partly by each party's fault. See too J C van der Walt *Delict: Principles and Cases* (1979) § 44n36 (cited hereafter as *Delict*), Louise Tager (1970) 87 *SALJ* 156 at 158, and Kemp J Kemp 1979 *Obiter* 18 at 56. These criticisms commended themselves to Addleson J in *Bowkers Park Komga Co-operative Ltd* v *SAR & H* 1980 (1) SA 91 (E) (a case not involving failure to wear a seat-belt), who found additional support for them in *South British Insurance Co Ltd* v *Smit* 1962 (3) SA 826 (A) and *Froom* v *Butcher* [1976] QB 286 (CA), [1975] 3 All ER 520, and declined to follow *Sparg's* case (see the preceding note), although it had been decided in his own division. (For notes on *Bowker's Park Komga*, see P Q R Boberg (1980) 97 *SALJ* 204, A J Kerr (1980) 97 *SALJ* 541 and J Y Claasen 1980 *De Rebus* 384.)

In *Vorster* v *AA Mutual Insurance Association Ltd* (*supra*, notes 7 and 8) Goldstone J declined to follow *King* on the ground that it had been clearly wrong (see at 162F–G). That decision finally made its quietus when it was overruled in *Union National South British Insurance Co Ltd* v *Vitoria* 1982 (1) SA 444 (A) at 460B–C.

[12] 1980 (4) SA 406 (T).

[13] Spoelstra AJ's reasoning that the risk of a collision had not been sufficiently real to require the plaintiff to take precautions against it because her father, with whom she had

the Appellate Division rejected both the view in *King's* case and the trial court's finding of no negligence on appeal from this decision in *Union National South British Insurance Co Ltd* v *Vitoria*,[14] it nevertheless unhorsed the defendant at the *third* hurdle by finding that causation had not been established.[15] And this despite the parties' agreement—similar to that in *Vorster*—that the plaintiff would probably not have sustained her injuries had she worn the belt![16] With this divergence of judicial opinion, and particularly the question of onus of proof in relation to causation raised by the *Vitoria* appeal, it is evident that the seat-belt situation requires closer examination.

The importance of the *Vitoria* decision should not be underestimated. By overruling the *King* doctrine that causation affecting only the quantum of loss is irrelevant, and by affirming as a general proposition that it is negligent not to wear a seat-belt, the Appellate Division eliminated the first two hurdles facing defendants in these matters. It thus cleared the way for a full consideration of the third hurdle—the requirement of causation. Why had the defendant failed to discharge the onus of proving that the plaintiff's failure to wear a seat-belt had materially contributed to the totality of her loss? Was this finding correct? How can future defendants surmount this final hurdle? Upon what basis are the unbelted plaintiff's damages to be apportioned? The answers to these questions, it is believed, will determine the future of our law in relation to seat-belts and indeed in relation to multiple causation affecting quantum in general.

As to the first question, the words of Rumpff CJ speak for themselves:[17]

> 'Weens bogenoemde oorwegings was appellant dus geregtig om te pleit dat respondente luidens art 1(1)(*a*) van die Wet [op Verdeling van

been travelling, had been a careful and competent driver, was criticized by the present writer in (1981) 10 *Businessman's Law* 153. He pointed out that the learned judge overlooked the other two factors that a reasonable man considers when determining the degree of care required of him, viz the gravity of the harm that might ensue (which is considerable in a motor collision), and the ease of guarding against it (merely by wearing a seat-belt). See too J Neethling and J M Potgieter (1981) 44 *THRHR* 204, J Y Claasen (1981) 44 *THRHR* 207 and A J Kerr (1981) 98 *SALJ* 22. On appeal in *Union National South British Insurance Co Ltd* v *Vitoria* 1982 (1) SA 444 (A) (see further the text above), the Appellate Division rejected this finding of Spoelstra AJ and laid down a general rule that drivers of and passengers in motor vehicles are negligent if they do not wear seat-belts (at 458, 460).

[14] 1982 (1) SA 444 (A).

[15] Rumpff CJ reasoned that, because the evidence showed that persons who wore only a lap-belt of the kind with which the vehicle in question had been fitted usually jack-knifed forward and hit their heads on the dashboard, the defendant had not discharged the onus of proving that the plaintiff's injuries would probably have been less severe had she worn the belt. See further the next note and the text below.

[16] The judgment in *Vorster* v *AA Mutual Insurance Association Ltd* 1982 (1) SA 145 (T) was available to, and was considered by, the Appellate Division. How Rumpff CJ disposed of the parties' agreement as to causation appears from the quotation in the text 150–1 above.

[17] At 463. Jansen JA, Rabie JA, Joubert JA and Trollip AJA concurred.

> Skadevergoeding] skuld gehad het. Die bewyslas om die skuld te bewys het op appellant gerus en in die onderhawige geval is die skuld bewys. Appellant moes egter ook bewys dat die skadevergoeding wat respondente bewys het wel verminder behoort te word. Weliswaar het respondente deur die partye se voormelde ooreenkoms erken dat, indien sy die gordel gedra het, sy waarskynlik nie die gesigsbeserings sou opgedoen het nie. Maar *in casu* is die erkenning nie voldoende om appellant van sy bogenoemde bewyslas te kwyt nie. Die rede is dat volgens die getuienis in hierdie saak respondente selfs met die skootgordel waarskynlik haar kop teen die paneelbord sou gestamp het. Daar is geen getuienis oor hoe hard die stamp waarskynlik sou gewees het nie, of oor hoe die paneelbord presies gemaak is, en daar is geen getuienis oor watter kopbesering sy waarskynlik sou opgedoen het nie. Sou haar brein permanent beskadig kon gewees het? In so 'n geval sou haar skade miskien groter kon gewees het as die letsels aan haar gesig wat sy wel opgedoen het.'

It is tempting to argue that the possible injuries mentioned by the learned Chief Justice are matters of mere speculation that the defendant was not called upon to exclude. The defendant's case was that, had she worn the belt, the plaintiff would not have sustained the injuries that she *did* and for which she sued: it was not required to show also that she would not have suffered some other unspecified injury. Such an onerous burden few defendants could hope to discharge, for the belt might have caused internal injuries, or prevented the plaintiff from escaping if the vehicle caught fire. Such an onus would deprive the new defence of all practical value.

Nevertheless, it is submitted that the decision is in truth correct, and that it does not have the effect deplored in the preceding paragraph. The facts are distinguishable from those of *Vorster* (*supra*), for the car had been fitted with a simple lap-belt, whereas in *Vorster*[18] the belt had been a 'three-point type' which crosses one shoulder as well as encircling the hips, thus overcoming the jack-knifing deficiency of the lap-belt. Since lap-belts do not comply with the legislation making the fitting and wearing of seat-belts compulsory, this cardinal reason for the actual outcome in *Vitoria* is unlikely to recur. Now as to that outcome, the court did not in fact saddle the defendant with an onus of eliminating imponderables. It did not find itself in a state of utter uncertainty as to the plaintiff's fate had she worn the belt. What it found on the evidence was that the plaintiff would *probably* have jack-knifed forward and struck her head on the dash-board. It is true that her consequential injuries were speculative, but the point is that, far from establishing a probability that the plaintiff's loss would have been less had she worn the belt, the evidence established a *probability* that there would

[18] See 1982 (1) SA 145 (T) at 148A–B.

still have been a loss without revealing any clue as to its probable gravity. Hence the defendant could hardly claim to have proved that the plaintiff's hypothetical loss would probably have been less than her actual one[19]—the onus of doing which the court had correctly placed upon it. The key to the decision lies in the italicized words '*probably*' and '*probability*' above. The proven inadequacy of lap-belts removed the case from the realm of mere speculation as to possible injury and created a probability of some injury of unknown gravity. This is also the limitation of the decision: it has no application to three-point belts, for, as the evidence in *Vorster* showed, the wearing of those belts creates an overwhelming probability of less or no injury being sustained.[20]

This answers the first three questions posed above. The fourth, relating to the proper basis of apportionment, will now be considered.

In *Froom* v *Butcher*[21] Lord Denning MR sought to avoid protracted and expensive disputes as to degrees of fault in seat-belt cases by proposing a rough working rule: where wearing a belt would have prevented all injury the plaintiff's damages should be reduced by 25 per cent; where some injury, though substantially less, would still have been sustained, the reduction should be 15 per cent. This approach commended itself to Goldstone J in *Vorster*, but the Appellate Division would have none of it in *Vitoria*. Having offered a variety of hypothetical situations to show that the comparative culpability of the unbelted passenger and the negligent driver depends on the circumstances, Rumpff CJ concluded that ''n klakkelose beroep op wat Lord Denning in die *Froom*saak gesê het nie in ons reg geregverdig is nie'.[22] He continued:[23]

> 'In die geval waar daar in ons reg 'n versuim was om 'n veiligheidsgordel te dra, en daar bewys word dat die eiser weens hierdie versuim meer skade gely het as wat hy sou gely het indien hy wel 'n veiligheidsgordel gedra het, is daar geen probleem oor kousaliteit nie. Sowel die nalatigheid van die bestuurder van die motor wat die botsing veroorsaak het, as die versuim van die eiser om die gordel te dra, het daardie ekstra skade veroorsaak. Hoe moeilik dit ook al mag wees, moet, in ons reg, in elke geval die omvang van die skuld van die eiser en die omvang van die skuld van die nalatige bestuurder bepaal word. Alleen dan kan die vordering vir skadevergoeding ten opsigte van die ekstra skade op 'n billike en regverdige wyse verminder word.'

[19] Logically, the reasoning is as follows: if x (the plaintiff's actual injuries) is of a known value greater than 0, and y (the plaintiff's hypothetical injuries had she worn the belt) is of unknown value but also probably greater than 0, it cannot be inferred that x is probably greater than y.

[20] See 1982 (1) SA 145 (T) at 149H–fine: 'If a front seat passenger is not wearing a seat-belt the probability of injury is six times greater than if such passenger was wearing a seat-belt. . . . If a person is thrown out of a motor vehicle in consequence of a collision there is a five times greater risk of fatal injuries being sustained by such person.'

[21] [1976] QB 286 (CA), [1975] 3 All ER 320.

[22] 1982 (1) SA 444 (A) at 462B–D. [23] At 462–3.

With the greatest respect, in none of these judgments did the court come to grips with the real question—whether the plaintiff's damage is divisible into that part which would have been averted by wearing a seat-belt, and that part which would have occurred in any event. One must join issue with Rumpff CJ when he says that these cases raise no problem of causation. The learned Chief Justice himself spoke twice of the '*ekstra* skade' (my italics) that a belt would have prevented. Correctly he said that this *extra* damage had been caused both by the negligent driving and the plaintiff's failure to wear the belt, and that *it* would have to be apportioned by comparing their degrees of fault. But he did not express the implicit corollary: it is *only* in respect of this *extra* damage that a seat-belt would have prevented that the plaintiff's failure to wear the belt had any causal significance; the failure had no causative effect whatever upon damage that would have occurred in any event. Such damage, having been caused solely by the negligent driving, is not subject to apportionment and the plaintiff is entitled to full compensation for it. As principle *(a)* above states, a person is liable (or subject to apportionment) only for the damage that he caused.

And so, since not all the damage should be apportioned, it is clear that apportionment cannot take place before its subject-matter has been ascertained. In short, the issue of divisibility of the damage is logically anterior to the issue of apportionment.[24] This is not made clear in any of the above judgments.[25]

[24] Of course, the issue of divisibility has no relevance in the great majority of cases where it is obvious that all the causes operated in respect of all the harm. For divisibility means the capacity of the totality of loss to be divided into those separate elements that have different causes—the 'apportionment of harm to different causes', the American *Restatement of the Law of Torts* calls it (see quotations in 1970 *Annual Survey of South African Law* 177–8). And it is important to realize that this kind of apportionment has nothing whatever to do with the ordinary apportionment in terms of s 1(1)(*a*) of the Apportionment of Damages Act. The latter is an apportionment of *fault* between the parties (the title of the Act is a grievous misnomer—the 'damages' are not apportioned: the totality of fault that caused the harm is first apportioned between the parties to determine each's share of it, and then the plaintiff's damages are *reduced* in proportion to his share). It is an apportionment that can take place only in those jurisdictions where a statute authorizes it, and, as has been shown 146 above), such statutes presuppose that the harm is indivisible, ie that each party's fault had causal effect upon the whole of it. The former kind of apportionment, on the other hand, requires no statutory justification. It is simply the process of determining what harm a party's conduct caused, and the need for it follows logically from the principle that a party is liable only for that harm which he caused.

[25] The parties may, however, remove the issue of divisibility from the court's adjudication by agreeing upon it themselves. This is what happened in *Vorster's* case (*supra*), where the parties agreed that, of the plaintiff's total loss of R4 000, R3 000 had been caused solely by the driver's negligence and R1 000 had been caused partly by that negligence and partly by the plaintiff's failure to wear her seat-belt. It was therefore unnecessary for Goldstone J to advert to the question of divisibility, and he correctly reduced only the R1 000. Nor does divisibility arise where it is proved or agreed that *no injuries* at all would have been sustained had the plaintiff worn a belt, for then the *whole* of the plaintiff's loss had the same causes, ie the driver's negligence and the plaintiff's failure to wear a belt. It would have been helpful had the Appellate Division clarified these matters in *Vitoria's* case, instead of dismissing the whole causation issue as presenting no problem (see quotation in the text at 152 above).

It is therefore submitted that the correct approach in the seat-belt cases is as follows: A defendant who seeks a reduction in the plaintiff's damages for failure to wear a seat-belt bears the onus of establishing his defence of contributory negligence. To do this he must prove *(a)* negligence, and *(b)* causation. In the light of *Vitoria*, *(a)* should be easy enough. As to *(b)*, it suffices to prove that the plaintiff's failure 'materially contributed to [the] totality of [his] loss', as Schreiner JA put it in *Kakamas Bestuursraad* v *Louw* (*supra*)—which is achieved simply by proving that, had the plaintiff worn the belt, the totality of his injuries would probably have been less severe than it in fact was. This is the equivalent, in a contributory-negligence case, of the onus placed upon the *plaintiff* in the *Kakamas* case, namely, that of proving that the *defendant's* conduct had materially contributed to the totality of his loss, though it had also been caused by the forces of nature. The parties are reversed, but the principle is the same: a plea of contributory negligence is essentially the defendant's allegation that the negligent plaintiff's conduct materially contributed to the totality of his loss, though the loss was also caused by the negligent defendant's conduct. Nor is there any reason to require more than this. Just as the plaintiff in *Kakamas* did not have to show *which* part of his loss the defendant had caused, so a defendant who pleads contributory negligence need not show *how much* of the total loss the plaintiff's due care would have averted: it is enough that the loss would have been materially less. Likewise there is no onus on the defendant to exclude the merely speculative *possibility* that the belted plaintiff might have suffered some other—perhaps even greater—injury:[26] the plaintiff in *Kakamas* did not have to exclude the possibility that his pump site might in any event have been destroyed by lightning or a storm of unusual violence.

Upon proof of the negligent plaintiff's material contribution to the totality of his loss, the defendant has established his plea of contributory negligence and is prima facie entitled to a reduction in the damages awarded to the plaintiff in respect of the whole of the loss. (The *Kakamas* equivalent is the defendant's liability for *all* the plaintiff's loss, including the indeterminate portion attributable to the forces of nature.) This conclusion may be expressed by saying that damage is presumed to be indivisible (see principle *(c)*, 146 above), which is simply another way of saying that the onus of proving divisibility rests upon the party who seeks to reduce his liability by alleging it (in a case like *Kakamas*, the defendant; in contributory-negligence cases, the plaintiff). If authority for such a presumption be demanded, the answer must be that it is implicit in

[26] This, as is pointed out at 151–2 above, distinguishes the present general submission from the facts of *Vitoria's* case, for the evidence there established a *probability* of some other injury with no indication of its extent.

Schreiner JA's reasoning in *Kakamas*, that it is acknowledged overseas,[27] that it is the very substratum of all applications of the Apportionment of Damages Act, and that it is in any event a proposition of ordinary common sense.

Thus far the waters of our jurisprudence have been charted. There is no direct authority for the last submission, which is that the unbelted *plaintiff* is entitled to prove—if he can—that his contributory negligence did not have causal effect upon the totality of his loss, but only upon an identifiable part of it, so that only the damages awarded for that part should be reduced. He does this by satisfying the court that he would probably have sustained some loss of a determinate amount even if he had worn the belt. In short, he proves that the damage is divisible. The dearth of South African authority is surely no impediment to this conclusion. Apart from the support it enjoys overseas,[28] it is merely an application of the principle that a person is liable only for the damage that he causes.

IV The Case of the Valuable Horses

Botes v *Van Deventer*[29] presented an unusual problem which, it is believed, received an unsatisfactory solution. The plaintiff's horses had been killed in a collision which, the trial court found, had been caused solely by the negligent driving of the defendant's servant. The animals had, however, been valuable racehorses, and the court found that the plaintiff had been negligent in allowing them to roam freely in a paddock traversed by an unfenced public road, upon which the accident had occurred, though apparently it would not have been negligent to treat ordinary, less valuable, horses in this way. But the trial court did not regard this as contributory negligence, because in its view the plaintiff's 'negligence' had not been a cause of the collision, but only of the quantum of the harm suffered. The court's approach was to hold that the plaintiff had

[27] See quotations and citations in 1970 *Annual Survey of South African Law* 177–9, H L A Hart and A M Honoré *Causation in the Law* (1959) 210 and John G Fleming *The Law of Torts* 5 ed (1977) 188 (cited hereafter as *Torts*).

[28] See especially Fleming *Torts* 187:

> '[W]here each of several defendants causes only part of the total damage and it is practically feasible to split up the aggregate of loss and attribute identifiable parts to each of them, liability will ordinarily [footnote: 'ie, except in the case of so-called "joint" tortfeasors who have acted in accordance with a common plan'] be confined to that portion for which each is separately responsible. . . . Finally, apportionment [of damage to causes, not of fault] may be possible even between a plaintiff and defendant, as when the former's own carelessness contributed to some, but not all, of his injuries.'

This appears under the heading 'Apportionable Damage'. Later, under 'Contributory Negligence: Causal Irrelevance', Fleming says (at 264–5):

> '[A] particular plaintiff's negligence may be found to have been contributory to only part of the damage, but not to all. Thus a moped rider with extensive head injuries aggravated by his negligent failure to wear a crash-helmet suffered a reduction only with respect to such additional injury.'

[29] 1966 (3) SA 182 (A).

negligently created a hidden hazard for the defendant's driver, who could not reasonably have foreseen the presence of unattended horses of exceptionally high value upon the road. Accordingly, said the court, the plaintiff was entitled to compensation only on the basis of the harm that the driver could have foreseen, that is, the value of the horses as ordinary horses rather than as racehorses—which led to an award of R600.

Not surprisingly, this approach was rejected by the Appellate Division. Van Blerk JA said:[30]

> 'Dit blyk . . . die sienswyse van die verhoorhof te wees dat eiser se "nalatigheid" slegs inwerk op die omvang van die skade, wat veroorsaak is deur die botsing, en niks te doen het met die oorsaak van die botsing self nie. Die bevinding is nie dat eiser bydraend nalatig was nie, of dat hy die risiko van skade aanvaar het nie, asof dit 'n geval is van *volenti non fit injuria*. Dat dit so is blyk uit die sinsnede dat eiser "niks gedoen het om die skade—nie die botsing nie—te verhinder nie", en uit die verwysing na die feit dat die vragmotorbestuurder nie kon voorsien het, of verwag het, dat perde van buitengewone hoë waarde op die pad sou wees nie. Hierdie benadering is onhoudbaar, en is strydig met ons regspraak. Waar dit eenmaal bevind is dat die botsing geheel en al aan die nalatigheid van die vragmotorbestuurder te wyte is, kan hier geen sprake wees van nalatigheid (skuld) aan die kant van die eiser wat die verweerder onthef, hetsy gedeeltelik of in die geheel, van aanspreeklikheid vir die skade wat veroorsaak is deur die botsing nie. Hy kan ook nie aanspreeklikheid vryspring deur bewys dat die omvang of afmetings van die skade nie voorsienbaar was nie. Dit is genoeg as hy die aard van die skade moes voorsien het—in hierdie geval skade wat uit die botsing met diere voortvloei.'

His lordship then quoted a passage from Centlivres CJ's judgment in *Herschel* v *Mrupe*[31] where the textbook example of the Ming vase appears:

> 'Assuming that the respondent could not reasonably have foreseen the extent of the loss which the appellant would suffer, it does not follow that the appellant is not entitled to be reimbursed to the full extent of the loss occasioned to her by the respondent's negligence. If through my negligent driving of a motor car I crash into another car containing valuable china and that china is smashed I cannot be heard to say that I am not liable for the loss of the china because I was not aware of the presence of the china, or that a reasonable man would not have foreseen the presence of the china.'

Van Blerk JA also quoted his own earlier epitome of the proposition in *Ocean Accident and Guarantee Corporation Ltd* v *Koch*:[32]

> 'He [the wrongdoer] would be liable for damage of which the nature, although not the extent thereof, was foreseeable.'

[30] At 190–1.
[31] 1954 (3) SA 464 (A) at 474.
[32] 1963 (4) SA 147 (A) at 152.

The court therefore concluded that the plaintiff was entitled to compensation on the basis of the actual value of his horses as racehorses, and increased his damages to R1 200.[33]

No one would quarrel with the hallowed proposition for which the decision is authority: the reasonable-foresight test of negligence requires only that the *nature* or *kind* of harm suffered be foreseeable; there is no need that its *extent* be also foreseeable. Thus if personal injury is foreseeable it matters not that its gravity exceeds normal expectations; if damage to property is foreseeable it matters not that the property actually damaged is of unusually high value.

But is this all that there was to the case? If one accepts the factual finding—which seems reasonable—that the plaintiff had not taken reasonable care of his horses *in the light of the fact that they were valuable racehorses*,[34] why was he not adjudged guilty of contributory negligence and his damages reduced accordingly? Both courts seem to have rejected this course on the ground that the plaintiff's negligence had causative effect, not upon the collision, but only upon the quantum of the damage suffered. This led Van Blerk JA to make a statement with which one must respectfully disagree, for it conflicts with the law in the seat-belt cases. It appears in the above-quoted portion of his judgment, and reads:

> 'Waar dit eenmaal bevind is dat die botsing geheel en al aan die nalatigheid van die vragmotorbestuurder te wyte is, kan hier geen sprake wees van nalatigheid (skuld) aan die kant van die eiser wat die verweerder onthef, hetsy gedeeltelik of in die geheel, van aanspreeklikheid vir die skade wat veroorsaak is deur die botsing nie.'

If this means—as it seems to do—that there cannot be contributory negligence which has causative effect only upon the quantum of the

[33] Ogilvie Thompson JA and Botha JA concurred in the judgment of Van Blerk JA; Rumpff JA delivered a concurring judgment; Williamson JA, concurring with Van Blerk JA on the substantive law, dealt in his judgment only with the evidence point that arose in the case.

[34] This is a perfectly acceptable conclusion, for the degree of care that a reasonable man takes of his property is influenced by the value of that property. One does not take the same care of a box of matches as one does of a gold cigarette-lighter. As Fagan JA remarked in *Herschel* v *Mrupe* 1954 (3) SA 464 (A) at 497, the reasonable man would not 'be expected to hold a cheap toy in his hand as securely as he should hold a valuable watch, or to keep a borrowed novel locked away in his safe as he would a pearl necklace entrusted to his custody'. J C van der Walt (1967) 30 *THRHR* 70 at 78–9 argues convincingly that, since negligent conduct is conduct which creates an unreasonable risk of harm to others, precautions required in caring for animals are affected by characteristics of the animal which increase the risk of injury to others (for example, a vicious temperament), but cannot be affected by a merely economic quality such as the high value of the horses in *Botes's* case, for that is not a factor increasing the risk of injury to others. But this argument looks only at negligence as a ground of liability for harm caused. It has no relevance to *contributory* negligence, which is based, not upon a wrongful act creating an unreasonable risk to others (see Van der Merwe and Olivier *Die Onregmatige Daad* 153, Van der Walt *Delict* § 44), but simply upon the equitable consideration that a person who fails to take reasonable care of himself or his property should not recover full compensation. Certainly the economic value of an animal is relevant in determining the care that ought to be taken to protect it from injury.

damage suffered and not upon the collision giving rise to the damage, it was contradicted by Rumpff CJ when he said in *Vitoria*:[35]

> 'Daar kan dus in bepaalde gevalle van bydraende nalatigheid skuld wees ten opsigte van die handeling of versuim wat die skade veroorsaak en in bepaalde gevalle van bydraende nalatigheid kan daar skuld wees ten opsigte van die skade sonder dat daar skuld was by die skadeveroorsakende gebeurtenis.'

Accepting, then, that the plaintiff's failure to care properly for his racehorses *could* amount to contributory negligence although it had causative effect only upon the quantum of his loss, one may be tempted to regard *Botes* as falling within the principle of the seat-belt cases, and calling for a reduction in the plaintiff's damages only in respect of that portion of his loss which his negligence aggravated (that is, the 'extra' value of his horses as racehorses). But this is wrong. It is not true that the plaintiff's 'negligence' was not a cause of the *collision*. If factual causation is to be determined by the *sine qua non* test,[36] surely the test is satisfied here. For if the plaintiff had taken such care of his horses as was reasonable in the circumstances (including the circumstances that they were valuable stud racehorses), the collision would not have occurred.

Why, then, did the court *a quo* hold (and the Appellate Division apparently accept) that the plaintiff's 'negligence' was not causally connected with the collision? Perhaps the explanation lies in the notion that 'fault'—in the sense of 'verwyt' or imputation of blameworthiness—attached to the plaintiff only because his horses

[35] *Union National South British Insurance Co Ltd* v *Vitoria* 1982 (1) SA 444 (A) at 456; see further 150ff above. Unfortunately, there are passages in the judgment which imply that this conclusion is based on an unfettered, literal reading of s 1(1)(*a*) of the Apportionment of Damages Act, and that it was not also the position at common law. Thus Rumpff CJ twice rejected the holding of Colman J in *King NO* v *Pearl Insurance Co Ltd* 1970 (1) SA 462 (W) at 466–7 (see 149 above) that s 1(3) defines 'fault' in relation to the plaintiff to limit its meaning to conduct that would have amounted to contributory negligence at common law (see Rumpff CJ at 456C; and at 460B he says: 'Dit was mi die bedoeling dat art 1(1)(*a*) gelees word soos dit daar staan. Daar is, mi, geen rede om dit na aanleiding van art 1(3) te beperk nie, soos in die *King*saak gedoen is.') But at 458B Rumpff CJ himself concludes from the authorities he cites that the common law included within the ambit of contributory negligence conduct causative only of the damage: 'Uit bogaande aanhalings blyk dit dat volgens die reg bydraende nalatigheid ook in verband kan staan met die eiser se versuim om gevolglike skade of verlies te vermy deur die uitoefening van die nodige redelike sorg. Dit is nie noodwendig beperk tot die vermyding van die skadeveroorsakende voorval self nie (bv 'n motorbotsing). Kyk bv die *Lennon*saak [1914 AD 1 at 6].'

That this was indeed the common law the present writer attempted to show in his discussion of *King's* case in 1970 *Annual Survey of South African Law* 174–9. One may therefore accept Colman J's view that s 1(3) gives to 'fault' of the plaintiff the same meaning as contributory negligence at common law. That was not where Colman J erred: his error lay in believing that conduct causative only of the damage would not have constituted contributory negligence at common law.

[36] As it was held in *Minister of Police* v *Skosana* 1977 (1) SA 31 (A) and *Standard Bank of South Africa Ltd* v *Coetsee* 1981 (1) SA 1131 (A).

were valuable (his precautions would have been adequate had they been ordinary horses), and it therefore seemed to follow that, because the collision would still have occurred had they been ordinary horses kept in the same way and hence without negligence on the plaintiff's part, his 'negligence' was not a cause of the collision.

But this reasoning is fallacious. It confuses fault with conduct. The question was not whether the plaintiff's 'fault'—in the sense of culpability—was a cause of the collision: the question was whether the plaintiff's *conduct*, already adjudged culpable in the light of the circumstances (including the value of his horses), was a cause of the collision. And indeed it was. For the fact was that the horses *were* valuable stud racehorses, and if the plaintiff had taken reasonable care of them they would not have been killed. To say that the plaintiff's 'negligence' did not cause the collision because he would not have been negligent if he had kept ordinary horses in this way and the collision would nevertheless have occurred, is as illogical as to say that, because it would not be negligent to run for a train with a newspaper under one's arm and drop it, one's negligence in running for a train with a Ming vase under one's arm and dropping it is not a cause of the vase's destruction because the object under one's arm would have been dropped in any event. The court misapplied the test of causation. The question was not whether the accident would have happened in *different* factual circumstances in which the actor would not have been negligent (that is, had the horses been ordinary horses); it was whether the accident would have happened in *the same* circumstances had the actor exercised due care.

If, then, the plaintiff's negligence *was* indeed a cause of the collision, and hence of the whole of his loss, it may seem that the seat-belt cases are distinguishable, and that the reduction for contributory negligence in terms of s 1(1)(*a*) of the Apportionment of Damages Act should affect the whole of his damages, no question of divisibility arising. Yet it appears unjust to apply the reduction to the whole of the plaintiff's compensation, for his conduct was culpable only because his horses were exceptionally valuable, and even ordinary horses would have been killed had he kept them in the same way, which it would not have been negligent to do. In this quandary the doctrine of the 'relevance' of negligence, as explained by Van Rensburg,[37] comes to our aid. Although the

[37] See A D J van Rensburg 1977 *TSAR* 101 at 106ff. Taking arms against the misuse of 'negligence' in a causal context (for example, the oft-heard formulation 'Did the actor's negligence cause the harm?'), Van Rensburg declares: '*Nalatigheid* is slegs 'n juridiese aspek van die handeling, en . . . die juridiese aspek as sodanig kan nie iets feitelik veroorsaak nie' (at 110). The question is whether the actor's *conduct*, not his negligence, caused the harm. But this does not mean that the operation of the negligent quality of the act in relation to the harm is ignored, for once a causal link between conduct and harm

plaintiff's negligent *conduct* caused all his loss (for none would have occurred had he acted carefully), the *negligence aspect* of that conduct (that is, the reason for labelling it negligent) was *relevant* only to that part of his loss attributable to the exceptionally high value of his horses, that is, the difference between his actual loss and the loss he would have sustained had the horses been ordinary ones. Since legal responsibility arises only from *relevant* negligence, the plaintiff should have been awarded full damages for that part of his loss to which his contributory negligence was irrelevant (that is, the R600 that ordinary horses would have been worth), plus reduced damages (in terms of s 1(1)(*a*) of the Act) for that part to which his contributory negligence was relevant (that is, the additional R600 that his racehorses were apparently worth). Inasmuch as this conclusion invokes the principle of divisibility of the damage, it may seem similar to that reached in the seat-belt cases. But, otherwise than in those cases, it is founded, not upon *causation* of only part of the loss, but upon the *relevance* of the plaintiff's *negligence* to only part of the loss.

And so we return to the valuable Ming vase, beloved example of teachers and textwriters. It has long been accepted that the defendant is liable for all its value, because he need not have foreseen the extent of the damage he might cause. This is certainly correct as far as it goes. But it does not go far enough. The defendant's legal responsibility is assured, but what of the plaintiff's contributory

has been established, another question arises: Was the negligent quality of the actor's conduct *relevant* in bringing about the harm complained of?

Van Rensburg explains this by posing the following problem: A, a chemist, sells B a quantity of poisonous pills for photographic purposes. A negligently omits to mark the container 'Poison'. B's wife, C, who is blind, mistakes the pills for a headache remedy, takes them, and dies. Some would say that A is not liable because his 'negligence' did not cause C's death (she could not have read the label in any event). But the issue is not one of causation at all, says Van Rensburg—it is a question of the *relevance of A's negligence*. A's *conduct*—the entire act of supplying unmarked pills—*did* cause C's death. But the *negligence aspect* of it was irrelevant in the circumstances. Van Rensburg explains (at 112):

> 'Waar dit reeds vasstaan dat 'n bepaalde nalatig verrigte handeling oorsaak was van 'n bepaalde gevolg, is dit 'n sinvolle vraag om daarbenewens te vra of die gevolg ook sou ingetree het, indien daardie handeling van sy nalatige aspek ontdaan was, dit wil sê indien die dader 'n handeling verrig het wat van die werklik verrigte handeling slegs sover verskil as wat nodig is om dit 'n nie-nalatige handeling te maak. "Handeling" word hier gebruik in die wye betekenis wat ook 'n late insluit. Hierdie werkwyse is nie 'n toets vir feitelike kousaliteit nie maar 'n toets vir die *relevansie van die nalatigheid*.'

(See too A D J van Rensburg *Juridiese Kousaliteit en Aspekte van Aanspreeklikheidsbeperking by die Onregmatige Daad* (unpublished LLD thesis University of South Africa 1970) 3–65; *Normatiewe Voorsienbaarheid as Aanspreeklikheidsbegrensingsmaatstaf in die Privaatreg* (byvoegsel tot die *Tydskrif vir Hedendaagse Romeins-Hollandse Reg* November 1972) 4.)

That this doctrine of the relevance of negligence is no iconoclasm appears from the fact that it is recognized also in Anglo-American law. Thus Fleming *Torts* 263 tells us that 'a causal relation must exist not just between the injury and the relevant act or omission, but specifically between the injury and that aspect of the conduct which is wrongful' (ie negligent, in this context). Another way of putting it is to say that the plaintiff's injury must be 'within the risk' that made the defendant's conduct negligent, i e the harm must be caused by the materialization of the risk that the defendant was required to guard against.

culpability in thus casually conveying so valuable an article? Should he not be penalized for it by suffering an appropriate reduction in the damages awarded to him? The above discussion shows that he should.

V The Case of the Ferocious Dog

We come now to the last member of this trilogy of teasers. It is *Portwood* v *Svamvur*,[38] in which the plaintiff was severely bitten when he attempted to extricate the defendant's dog from a gate that had entrapped it. The evidence showed that, although the defendant's dog had had a particularly vicious temperament, even a 'normal' dog would probably have bitten the plaintiff (a total stranger) in those circumstances. The court therefore found that the plaintiff's injury was attributable to two factors: the vicious nature of the dog—for which the defendant was legally responsible, and the fact that it had become enmeshed in the gate—for which no blame could be laid at the defendant's door. At this point things started to go wrong. Since the defendant's negligence consisted in keeping a dog which he knew to be vicious, reasoned Beadle CJ, he could be liable only for harm attributable to that viciousness. Certainly the viciousness had converted the mere probability of the plaintiff's being bitten (by a 'normal' dog) into a certainty of being bitten (by a savage dog such as the defendant's). Moreover, it had aggravated the plaintiff's injury, for the defendant's dog, not content with merely biting the plaintiff once as a 'normal' dog might have been, had gratified its savage disposition by biting him four times and gnawing his finger so badly that it had had to be amputated. On the other hand, the causal criterion of *sine qua non* did not seem to be satisfied. Inasmuch as even a 'normal' dog would have bitten the plaintiff, it could not be said that the 'accident' would not have happened but for the defendant's 'act of negligence'.[39]

At this stage Beadle CJ simply threw up his hands. Adopting a common-sense 'juryman's view of the case', he expressed himself satisfied that the dog's savage nature *had* been a cause of the plaintiff's injury, and refused to be 'deterred from maintaining this view by the fact that such ingenuity as I may possess cannot assist me to arrive at the same conclusion by employing any of the accepted tests beloved by lawyers'.[40]

[38] 1970 (4) SA 8 (RAD). The plaintiff's main claim, based upon the *actio de pauperie*, was dismissed because the dog had not acted *contra naturam sui generis*. It is with his alternative claim, based upon the *actio legis Aquiliae*, that we are concerned.

[39] See the judgment at 14–15.

[40] At 15F–G. The learned Chief Justice went on to find that the causal role of the dog's savage nature had been material because it had 'caused the plaintiff to receive injuries which were more severe than those he might have expected to have received from a normal dog', and had 'converted what was a probability of being bitten into a certainty of being bitten' (at 15–16). Having rejected arguments that the dog's getting caught in the

Of course this conclusion was correct. It is a pity that the learned Chief Justice felt himself betrayed by the *sine qua non* test, for that test did not dictate a contrary result. In truth Beadle CJ misapplied it. The question was not whether the harm had been caused by the dog's *vicious nature*: it was whether the defendant's *conduct*, already adjudged negligent in the light of the dog's vicious nature, had caused the harm.[41] Indeed it had, for if the defendant had kept the dog under proper control no harm would have occurred.[42] Nor can one accept Beadle CJ's inquiry whether the dog's vicious nature had caused the *accident*: it was entirely sufficient that it had caused part of the plaintiff's injuries in the sense that they were more severe than those which a 'normal' dog would probably have inflicted.[43]

If, then, the criterion of causation was satisfied, was it correct to hold the defendant liable for the whole of the plaintiff's damage, as Beadle CJ did? This seems unjust, for if the dog had been 'normal' and hence the defendant without negligence in allowing it to roam freely, the plaintiff would still have been bitten, though less severely. It could be argued that the defendant's 'negligence' caused only the 'extra' injury attributable to the dog's vicious nature, so that, if the damage were divisible, he should be liable only for that extra part of it, on analogy with the seat-belt cases.

But the analogy with the seat-belt cases is a false one. As we have seen, the question is not whether the defendant's *negligence* caused the harm, but whether his *conduct* caused the harm, and it is clear that the defendant's conduct caused the whole harm, because if he had controlled his dog properly no accident and hence no harm at all would have occurred. The position is different in those seat-belt cases in which even the belted plaintiff would have sustained some injury.[44]

The conclusion may seem inevitable that the defendant was indeed liable in full. But it is not. The true analogy, it is submitted, is with *Botes* v *Van Deventer*.[45] As it did in that case, the solution

gate had been a *novus actus interveniens*, and that the plaintiff had been guilty of contributory negligence, Beadle CJ held the defendant liable for the whole of the plaintiff's damage.

[41] As Van der Walt *Delict* § 48n4 puts it, 'Beadle CJ obviously erred in attempting to establish a causal relationship between the vicious nature of the particular dog and the plaintiff's injuries. The correct approach would have been to determine the existence of a causal relationship between the owner's omission to control the dog properly and the plaintiff's injuries. On the facts of the case such a causal relationship is fairly obvious.'

[42] The defendant's duty, held Beadle CJ (at 12G–H), had been 'to keep a dog of that nature under proper control and not to allow it to be at large at night unmuzzled'. Had he discharged this duty—ie acted without negligence—the dog would either not have become enmeshed in the gate at all or, if it had, would have been unable to bite the rescuer. Hence the harm would not have occurred.

[43] See the discussion of the seat-belt cases 154 above.

[44] There is, however, a true analogy with those seat-belt cases in which the belted plaintiff would not have been injured at all, but those cases do not raise the issue of the *relevance* of the negligence which *Portwood's* case raised, and which is discussed in the text above.

[45] 1966 (3) SA 182 (A), discussed at 155 above.

turns on the *relevance* of the defendant's negligence. Though his *conduct* caused all the plaintiff's damage, the *negligence aspect* of that conduct was relevant only to the extra part of it attributable to the vicious nature of his dog. For it was only that viciousness that made his conduct negligent. Thus had the defendant been able to show that the damage was divisible by proving how much injury a 'normal' dog would probably have inflicted, he should have escaped liability for that part of the plaintiff's damage—not because his *conduct* did not cause it (and here we part company with the seat-belt cases), but because his *negligence was not relevant* to it.

No doubt divisibility would have been difficult to establish in *Portwood's* case, and so, since the onus lay upon the defendant, the decision that he was liable in full may well have been correct on the facts. But it is important to realize that the possibility of avoiding liability for part of the damage was in principle available to the defendant.

VI Conclusion

This brief adventure in some of the byways of causation illustrates the principle that liability depends upon the existence of a causal connection between the defendant's negligent conduct and the harm for which the plaintiff seeks compensation. This the plaintiff must establish, and he does so merely by proving that the harm would not have occurred had the defendant acted carefully. He is then prima facie entitled to compensation for the whole harm. But the defendant is entitled to show, if he can, that the harm is divisible, and that the plaintiff would still have suffered part of it even if the defendant had acted carefully. He then escapes liability for that part, because his negligent conduct did not cause it. Or he may show that, although his conduct was a cause of all the harm, there was another cause of it—the plaintiff's own negligent conduct. The defendant is then prima facie entitled to a reduction, applied to the whole of the plaintiff's compensation, in terms of s 1(1)(*a*) of the Apportionment of Damages Act. This is the situation in ordinary contributory-negligence cases, and in those seat-belt cases where the plaintiff would have suffered no injury at all had he worn the belt. But the plaintiff is entitled to show, if he can, that the harm is divisible, and that he would still have suffered part of it even if he had not been guilty of contributory negligence. He then avoids a reduction of his compensation in respect of that part, because his contributorily negligent conduct did not cause it. This is the situation in those seat-belt cases where the plaintiff proves (or it is admitted) that he would still have suffered some injury of determinate lesser degree had he worn the belt.

Then there are cases where, although the defendant's negligent conduct caused the whole harm, in the sense that none would have occurred had he acted carefully, the negligence aspect of his conduct was not relevant to part of it. By this we mean that part of the harm was not attributable to the materialization of the risk that the defendant was required to guard against—the reason for calling his conduct negligent. He then escapes liability for that part, not because his *conduct* did not cause it (for it did), but because he was not *negligent in relation* to it. This would have been the position in *Portwood* v *Svamvur* (*supra*) had the defendant established what injuries even a 'normal' dog would have inflicted. And the same principle applies to the plaintiff's contributory negligence. The contributorily negligent conduct of the plaintiff in *Botes* v *Van Deventer* (*supra*) was a cause of the whole harm, for no accident and hence no harm at all would have occurred had he taken proper care of his horses. But since the only reason for calling his conduct negligent was the exceptionally high value of his horses, the negligence aspect of his conduct was not relevant to that part of his harm represented by the value of the horses as ordinary horses. And so, though the plaintiff's contributory negligence called for a reduction of his damages, the reduction should not have been applied to that part, but only to the part of his harm flowing from the 'extra' value of the horses as racehorses.

The distinction between 'negligence' and 'conduct' as a cause of harm may strike some as pedantic.[46] It seems that the common inquiry into whether the actor's 'negligence' caused the harm telescopes two issues which the above approach seeks to separate: *(a)* whether his *conduct* caused the harm; and *(b)* whether the *negligence aspect* of his conduct was *relevant* to the harm. As always in the law, to combine distinct issues within a single concept is potentially confusing. Their separation, it is believed, would have facilitated the proper disposition of the cases discussed above, and would have saved Beadle CJ the frustration of having to resort to a 'juryman's view' of a situation in which the tests of causation 'beloved by lawyers', properly applied, would not really have failed him.

[46] But cf Rumpff CJ in *Union National South British Insurance Co Ltd* v *Vitoria* 1982 (1) SA 444 (A) at 455–6:

> 'In art 1(1)(*a*) [van die Wet op Verdeling van Skadevergoeding] praat die wetgewer van "skade" wat aan "skuld" te wyte is. In die Engelse teks is dit "damage . . . caused . . . by fault". Artikel 1(3) bepaal dat by toepassing van die artikel (d w s wesenlik art 1(1)(*a*) en 1(1)(*b*)) skuld ook 'n "handeling of versuim" is. Op sigself beskou is "skuld" of "fault" nie 'n handeling of versuim nie. Dit is 'n morele attribuut wat 'n regsbetekenis kan verkry en dan is dit wesenlik blaam of verwyt in regsverband. In art 1(1) is dit implisiet dat hierdie verwyt verbind is met 'n handeling of omissie wat skade veroorsaak. . . .'

ABERRATIO ICTUS

†EXTON BURCHELL*

I regard it as a great honour to be associated with this tribute volume in memory of the late Mr Justice Oliver Schreiner. I met the judge when I was appointed to my first lecturing post, in the Faculty of Law of the University of the Witwatersrand, in 1947. In addition to his being a senior member of the Board of the Faculty at that time, he was by then a judge and jurist of considerable stature, having served with distinction for some eight years on the Transvaal Bench and two years on the Appellate Division. And yet he had 'an inherent and intractable modesty and humility',[1] a quality of the truly great. For my part, I deeply appreciated that, from the very beginning and throughout my seven years at Wits, he showed a genuine concern for my well-being and was always willing to discuss a legal problem with me as if I were his equal. At that time the Appellate Division was engaged in a re-examination of *mens rea*, and concepts such as legal intention (*dolus eventualis*) were emerging. On more than one occasion I recall the judge's discussing with me the issue of *mens rea* in the *aberratio ictus* situation;[2] and I felt, therefore, that it would be appropriate to devote this essay to that subject.

The classic *aberratio ictus* (literally, 'deflection of the blow') situation is where X, intending to kill Y, fires a rifle at him, but the bullet misses Y and kills Z. In terms of what could be described as the '*aberratio ictus* rule', which derives support from two 1949 Appellate Division decisions (*R* v *Kuzwayo*[3] and *R* v *Koza*[4]), because of his intention to kill Y, X is guilty of the murder of Z, without the prosecution's having to establish an intention to kill Z specifically. Thus in *Koza* Centlivres JA held that 'where a person commits an act intending to murder one person and kills another he is guilty of murdering that other person'.[5]

On the other hand, if *mens rea* in respect of Z's death is insisted upon, the result is very different. If the possibility of Z's death

* MA (Cantab) LLB (SA) LLD (Natal), James Scott Wylie Professor of Law, University of Natal, Pietermaritzburg. Professor Exton Burchell died on 21 July 1982.

[1] Mr Justice H C Nicholas at the opening of the Oliver Schreiner Law Library of the University of the Witwatersrand on 25 August 1976; see (1980) 97 *SALJ* 577.

[2] From the reported cases it seems that Mr Justice Schreiner did not himself sit in an *aberratio ictus* case.

[3] 1949 (3) SA 761 (A). [4] 1949 (4) SA 555 (A). [5] At 557.

could not reasonably have been foreseen, X would not be liable therefor at all.[6] If X foresaw the death of Z as a real possibility,[7] he would be guilty of the murder of Z; and if he foresaw Z's death as a remote possibility,[8] or if he did not foresee that possibility but a reasonable man would have foreseen it,[9] X would be guilty of culpable homicide.

To take two case examples where this approach was adopted. In *R* v *Ncetendaba*[10] the accused, with the object of killing birds, placed poison in puddles of water that had overflowed from a cattle drinking-trough on Z's farm. Some of Z's cattle drank the poisoned water and died. The accused was acquitted of malicious injury to property, because the prosecution failed to establish that he intended to harm the cattle. In *S* v *Nkombani*[11] X and Z, who were armed with revolvers, took part in a robbery. During the struggle that ensued Z was killed by a shot fired by X at the victim of the hold-up (Y) with the intention of killing him. X was found guilty of the murder of Z, since he foresaw the possibility of the death of Z and was reckless as to whether his death resulted or not.

It will be noticed that the sole question in these cases was whether the accused had actual or legal intention[12] in respect of the eventual result which was the subject-matter of the charge. Adopting this approach, in the court *a quo* in *R* v *Mabena*[13] Young J held that if A wishes to shoot B, but misses and kills C, of whose presence he was not aware, and who quite unbeknown to him happens to be in the line of fire, then A is not guilty of the murder of C, but at most of the attempted murder of B and culpable homicide in respect of C, if danger to C's life was reasonably foreseeable by A.[14]

Although the diametrically opposite view (that is, the '*aberratio ictus* rule') has been strongly contended for,[15] the *mens rea* approach

[6] X would, of course, be guilty of an attempt to murder Y.

[7] A case of legal intention (*dolus eventualis*).

[8] A case of conscious (or advertent) negligence.

[9] A case of inadvertent negligence; see *R* v *Mabena* 1967 (3) SA 525 (R), but contrast the decision in this case on appeal (1968 (2) SA 28 (RAD)), which is considered below.

[10] 1952 (2) SA 647 (SR).

[11] 1963 (4) SA 877 (A). For further cases of *aberratio ictus*, see *R* v *Tshabala* 1921 AD 13; *R* v *Chikokonya* 1938 SR 122; *R* v *Longone* 1938 AD 532; *R* v *Xulu* 1943 AD 616; *R* v *Kuzwayo* 1949 (3) SA 761 (A); *R* v *Koza* 1949 (4) SA 555 (A); *R* v *James* 1960 R & N 159 (SR); *S* v *Mtshiza* 1970 (3) SA 747 (A); *S* v *Songo* 1971 (1) PH H51 (R); *S* v *Zukelwa* 1971 (2) PH H150 (T); *S* v *Tissen* 1979 (4) SA 293 (T); *S* v *Raisa* 1979 (4) SA 541 (O); and *S* v *Mavhungu* 1981 (1) SA 56 (A) at 67F–H.

[12] Or, had he been charged with a crime of negligence, whether he was negligent.

[13] 1967 (3) SA 525 (R); cf *R* v *James* 1960 R & N 159 (SR).

[14] In arriving at this conclusion Young J relied upon the views expressed by J C de Wet and H L Swanepoel *Strafreg* 3 ed (1975) 142–6 (cited hereafter as De Wet and Swanepoel). However, a different conclusion was reached by Beadle CJ on appeal in *Mabena* (1968 (2) SA 28 (RAD)); see below.

[15] J H Pain '*Aberratio Ictus:* The Doctrine and its Reception in Botswana, Lesotho and Swaziland' (LLM dissertation University of Natal 1977). See also his article '*Aberratio Ictus:* A Comedy of Errors—and Deflection' (1978) 95 *SALJ* 480, based upon his dissertation.

derives support from the judgment of Holmes JA in *S* v *Mtshiza*,[16] and was applied in the recent cases of *S* v *Tissen*[17] and *S* v *Raisa*.[18] Moreover, it seems now to have been finally accepted by the Appellate Division in *S* v *Mavhungu*.[19]

Strictly speaking, *Mtshiza* was not a case of *aberratio ictus*, since the accused did not intend to kill Y when, by deflection, he struck and killed Z. Moreover, the majority of the court of appeal (Wessels JA and Trollip JA) found[20] that the trial judge had not been influenced by any principle laid down in the earlier Appellate Division case of *R* v *Kuzwayo*.[21] Nevertheless, in his minority judgment Holmes JA criticized the *ratio* in *Kuzwayo* and in *R* v *Koza*[22] and, having neatly described *aberratio ictus* as no more than 'a convenient Latin expression descriptive of the situation where a blow aimed at A misses him and lands on B', drew attention to the fact that *Kuzwayo* and *Koza* were decided 'before this court had moved away from the old doctrine of *versari in re illicita*' and 'before this court had finally formulated the principles of *dolus eventualis*, in the form in which it is now applied';[23] and Holmes JA concluded:

> 'The result is that nowadays criminal liability is not regarded as attaching to an act or a consequence unless it was attended by *mens rea*. . . . Accordingly, if A assaults B and in consequence B dies, A is not criminally responsible for his death unless—
>
> *(a)* he foresaw the possibility of resultant death, yet persisted in his deed, reckless whether death ensued or not; or
>
> *(b)* he ought to have foreseen the reasonable possibility of resultant death.
>
> 'In *(a)* the *mens rea* is the type of intent known as *dolus eventualis*, and the crime is murder; in *(b)* the *mens rea* is *culpa*, and the crime is culpable homicide.'[24]

In both *Tissen*[25] and *Raisa*[26] this statement of the law by Holmes JA was followed and the '*aberratio ictus* rule' of the earlier Appellate Division decisions (which, as we have seen, per se resulted in liability for harm to, or death of, the 'unintended' victim) was rejected on the ground that it was not in conformity with the present-day insistence upon proof of *mens rea* for the very crime charged in respect of the 'unintended' victim.

Thus, in *Tissen* Margo J concluded:

> 'Here the appellant, in shooting at his intended victim in a crowded street, . . . must have foreseen subjectively the possibility of killing or injuring some person other than the intended victim and he was reckless as to whether death or injury resulted or not.'[27]

[16] 1970 (3) SA 747 (A).
[17] 1979 (4) SA 293 (T).
[18] 1979 (4) SA 541 (O).
[19] 1981 (1) SA 56 (A) at 67F–H.
[20] At 756; see Flemming J in *S* v *Raisa* 1979 (4) SA 541 (O) at 547D–E.
[21] 1949 (3) SA 761 (A).
[22] 1949 (4) SA 555 (A).
[23] At 751E–F, 752–3.
[24] At 752pr–C.
[25] 1979 (4) SA 293 (T).
[26] 1979 (4) SA 541 (O).
[27] At 295E–F.

With respect, the phrase 'some person other than his intended victim' would be too wide[28] in any *aberratio ictus* situation except that of the kind which occurred in *Tissen*, where the accused, in a crowded street, fired several shots at Y, one of which hit Z. The accused clearly had legal intention (*dolus eventualis*) of the *indeterminatus*[29] variety, since he foresaw the possibility of missing Y and hitting a member of the crowd. But for 'the crowded street', however, *dolus eventualis* would be dependent upon proof that the accused foresaw the possibility of killing or injuring the very person killed or injured.

In *Raisa*[30] the accused tried to stab a mother, who warded off the blow by putting her child in front of her, as a result of which the child was stabbed. Flemming J concluded[31] that the accused could not be made liable for assaulting the child with intent to do grievous bodily harm simply on the ground that he had this intention in relation to the mother, but only if such intent, whether in the form of *dolus directus* or *dolus eventualis*, could be proved in respect of the child.[32] The learned judge took the view that even if the '*aberratio ictus* rule' had been applied by the Appellate Division in some of the earlier cases, like the *versari in re illicita* doctrine before its abolition, it had not gained such wide recognition as to become an entrenched principle of our law;[33] and, in any event, relying particularly on *Mtshiza*,[34] he held that the rejection[35] of the *versari in re illicita* doctrine by the Appellate Division meant that the '*aberratio ictus* rule' can have no further application.[36] Moreover, it is respectfully submitted that the following observation of Flemming J cannot be gainsaid:

> 'In modern South African law, where attempt is a criminal offence and is generally punishable with the same penalty as the permissible punishment for the crime itself, there appears to be no juridical or social need for the *aberratio ictus* rule.'[37]

Although *aberratio ictus* and *error in objecto* are not easy to distinguish, difficulty arises if the two are confused.[38] It is a case of *error*

[28] The same comment applies to the following expression that Margo J used earlier (at 295A–B): 'some person other than his intended victim, though not necessarily the deceased'.

[29] See note 41.

[30] 1979 (4) SA 541 (O) (see J M T Labuschagne (1980) 4 *SACC/SASK* 68).

[31] At 548.

[32] Since such intent in regard to the assault on the child had not been established, the matter was remitted to the magistrate for decision on this point (at 548B–C).

[33] At 547–8. [34] 1970 (3) SA 747 (A) at 752–3.

[35] *S* v *Van der Mescht* 1962 (1) SA 521 (A); *S* v *Bernardus* 1965 (3) SA 287 (A).

[36] *Supra* note 30 at 547E–G.

[37] At 543D–E. Thus, where, intending to kill Y, X fires a rifle at him but the bullet misses Y and kills Z, even though X is not liable in respect of the death of Z because of lack of *mens rea*, he will be guilty of attempt to murder Y and can be punished accordingly.

[38] De Wet and Swanepoel 142–3; W A Joubert (ed) *The Law of South Africa* VI (1981) para 94; C R Snyman *Strafreg* (1981) 179–80. *Aberratio ictus* and *error in objecto* were

in objecto where A, intending to kill B, shoots and kills C, whom he mistakenly believes to be B. In these circumstances A is clearly guilty of the murder of C.[39] A's intention is directed at 'a specific predetermined individual, although he is in error as to the exact identity of that individual. In other words, he intends to kill the individual regardless of whether the name of the individual is B or C. There is thus in the case of *error in objecto*, so to speak, an undeflected *mens rea* which falls upon the person it was intended to affect. The error as to identity is thus . . . irrelevant to the question of *mens rea*.'[40] On the other hand, in the *aberratio ictus* situation A intends to kill B but misses him and kills C. A's intention is 'directed at one whom he knows and recognizes to be B. It is through unforeseen and unintended factors that the blow falls upon C.'[41] It follows that A has *mens rea* in the form of intention in respect of C only if he foresaw the possibility of C's death. In the absence of such foresight, A can only be found guilty of the murder of C upon an application of the English law doctrine of 'transferred malice',[42] the doctrine of *versari in re illicita* or the objective test of intention.

Since neither of these doctrines[43] nor the objective test of intention[44] is part of present-day South African law, it is respectfully submitted that the decision of the Rhodesian Appellate Division in *R* v *Mabena*[45] is incorrect. In this case Beadle CJ partially rejected

sometimes confused by the old authorities; see, for example, Voet 48.8.2, and contrast Matthaeus *De Criminibus* 48.5.3.12. Without using the Latin terms, our courts distinguish the two, but in *Mabena* 1968 (2) SA 28 (RAD) at 36 Beadle CJ referred to the distinction as 'rather academic' and 'somewhat unrealistic'; cf Pain (1978) 95 *SALJ* 500–3.

[39] De Wet and Swanepoel 142; J R L Milton (1968) 85 *SALJ* 118.

[40] Milton ibid; cf De Wet and Swanepoel ibid. Where A, intending to kill B, fires at C, whom he mistakenly believes to be B, but misses and happens to kill B, it would seem that A may be guilty of the murder of B (see Milton op cit 119). The deflection of the blow being in the direction of, rather than away from, A's intention, seems to make it a case of *error in objecto* in reverse as it were, rather than *aberratio ictus*.

[41] Milton ibid. Where A does not have a particular person (or object) in mind, it is a case of general intent (*dolus indeterminatus*: see *S* v *Nkombani* 1963 (4) SA 877 (A) at 892; *S* v *Tissen* 1979 (4) SA 293 (T) at 295E–F; and *S* v *Mavhungu* 1981 (1) SA 56 (A) at 66; cf *S* v *Nhlapo* 1981 (2) SA 744 (A) at 751B–C, and De Wet and Swanepoel op cit 146), and no problem arises—for instance, where A throws a bomb into a crowd.

[42] According to the doctrine of 'transferred malice', if A shoots at B and kills C he is automatically guilty of the murder of C if it would have been murder of B had he been killed. A's malice (that is, his intention) is by a legal fiction transferred from the one object to the other. This automatic transfer of the accused's intention without consideration of whether he intended the consequence which is the subject-matter of the charge savours strongly of the *versari in re illicita* doctrine, which has now been rejected in South Africa.

[43] Support for the doctrine of 'transferred malice' is found in *R* v *Chikokonya* 1938 SR 122. On the other hand, apart from the fact that the doctrine is an application of the now rejected *versari* rule, in *R* v *Mabena* 1967 (3) SA 525 (R), which involved an *aberratio ictus* situation, Young J held that 'in my judgment . . . the theory of transferred malice has no place in our criminal law' (at 527). On appeal Beadle CJ took the view that 'English law is . . . unreliable authority on this aspect of Roman-Dutch law' (*R* v *Mabena* 1968 (2) SA 28 (RAD) at 34).

[44] Since the early 1950s the test of intention has been invariably subjective, and it is clear that the objective test can no longer be applied.

[45] 1968 (2) SA 28 (RAD). In *S* v *Songo* 1971 (1) PH H51 (R) the court was bound by the decision in *Mabena*.

the statement of the law relating to *aberratio ictus* by the court *a quo*.[46] The appeal was limited to a consideration of whether it was correct to say (as Young J did in the court *a quo*) that where A as a result of *aberratio ictus* kills C in circumstances in which 'danger to C's life was reasonably foreseeable', A is guilty of culpable homicide in respect of C's death and not of murder. In rejecting this proposition Beadle CJ held that

> 'if A attacks B in circumstances which show that he *must* have realized that what he did was likely to kill B but by mistake kills C instead in circumstances which show that he *ought* to have realized that what he did was likely to cause serious injury to C, he is guilty of the murder of C'.[47]

In arriving at this conclusion Beadle CJ relied upon certain of the old authorities and the earlier decisions of the Appellate Division. In regard to the former, it is respectfully submitted that the learned Chief Justice did not appreciate that the Roman-Dutch writers to which reference was made either failed to distinguish between *error in objecto* and *aberratio ictus*[48] or were influenced by the *versari in re illicita* doctrine,[49] or both.[50] Moreover, apart from the fact that there are traces of *versari* in several of the decisions which were relied upon,[51] they support the Chief Justice's conclusion only because the objective test of intention was applied in those cases.[52] Beadle CJ did emphasize that his formulation of the law was 'peculiar to cases of this sort' and that it did 'not affect the nature of the intent which the Crown must establish in cases of murder which are not cases of *aberratio ictus*'.[53] But, with respect, the invariable application of the subjective test of intention by our courts since the early 1950s does not warrant a departure from it in any circumstances.[54] Indeed, to recognize an exception in the *aberratio ictus* situation is to reaffirm support for the now rejected *versari in re illicita* doctrine.[55]

On the other hand, the decision of the Rhodesian Appellate Division in *Mabena* would meet with the approval of Professor J H Pain, who, after a penetrating analysis, submits that

[46] See above. [47] At 36.

[48] For example, Voet 48.8.2. Beadle CJ regarded the distinction between *error in objecto* and *aberratio ictus* as 'rather academic' and 'somewhat unrealistic' (at 36).

[49] For example, Voet ibid, Matthaeus 48.5.3.12 and Damhouder 85.7: see De Wet and Swanepoel 143.

[50] For example, Voet ibid. Moreover, the Roman-Dutch writers relied upon in *Mabena* (*supra*) judged intention objectively; see especially Beadle CJ's interpretation of Moorman 2.1.20 (at 31).

[51] *R* v *Xulu* 1943 AD 616 (see 'NM' (1944) 8 *THRHR* 53); *R* v *Kuzwayo* 1949 (3) SA 761 (A); *R* v *Koza* 1949 (4) SA 555 (A) at 558, 559–60; cf *R* v *Chikokonya* 1938 SR 122, which, although referred to, was not relied on in *Mabena* (at 33–4).

[52] See, for example, *R* v *Longone* 1938 AD 532 at 538, 539, 541, 542; *R* v *Xulu* 1943 AD 616 at 619.

[53] 1968 (2) SA 28 (RAD) at 36.

[54] It is significant that in *S* v *Nkombani* 1963 (4) SA 877 (A), which was itself a case of *aberratio ictus*, although *Kuzwayo* and *Koza* (*supra*) were referred to (at 889–90, 894), the Appellate Division insisted on proof of subjective intention as the basis of liability.

[55] Milton op cit note 39 at 121.

> '. . . allegations of *versari*, emotionalism and sophistry, dicta taken out of context, and a failure to grasp the purport of the Roman-Dutch writers and what has been decided in the Appellate Division,[56] do not amount to a convincing argument that, for murder to be committed [in the *aberratio ictus* situation], the intention of the accused to kill must relate to the very person killed'.[57]

Pain contends strenuously for what has been referred to above as the '*aberratio ictus* rule', but, with respect, even if this was the position in 1949 when *Kuzwayo* and *Koza* were decided, it seems that it is no longer our law in view of subsequent Appellate Division insistence upon a subjective test of intention, the removal from our law of the doctrine of *versari in re illicita*, and the present-day requirement in every situation, even one of *aberratio ictus*, of proof of *mens rea* for the crime charged in respect of the very person killed or harmed.[58]

Indeed, the following dictum of Trollip JA in the recent Appellate Division case of *S* v *Mavhungu*[59] confirms that in the *aberratio ictus* situation X's liability for murder or culpable homicide in respect of Z's death depends upon the ordinary principles of *mens rea*:

> '[E]ven if the problem is regarded as being one of or analogous to *aberratio ictus* as far as the appellant himself is concerned (i e the mortal blow that he intended Ndou should direct at the mother-in-law having been deflected to the deceased) . . . [t]he State did not prove the initial, fundamental requirement that the appellant subjectively foresaw the possibility that Ndou, in carrying out the agreed common purpose of killing the mother-in-law, would instead kill someone else.'[60]

The learned judge of appeal added that the later Appellate Division dicta relating to *aberratio ictus*[61] 'accord with modern thought and the trend of recent decisions of this court generally on the need for the above-mentioned subjective test to be always satisfied before any accused can be convicted of murder'.[62]

[56] That is, in *R* v *Tshabala* 1921 AD 13, *Longone* (*supra*), *Xulu* (*supra*), *Kuzwayo* (*supra*) and *Koza* (*supra*).

[57] (1978) 95 *SALJ* 480 at 503.

[58] De Wet and Swanepoel 144–6; Joubert op cit note 38 para 94 p 74; Snyman op cit note 38 at 181–2.

[59] 1981 (1) SA 56 (A).

[60] At 67F–H.

[61] *S* v *Nkombani* 1963 (4) SA 877 (A) at 887G–H and *S* v *Mtshiza* 1970 (3) SA 747 (A) at 751D–753A; cf *S* v *Tissen* 1979 (4) SA 293 (T) and *S* v *Raisa* 1979 (4) SA 541 (O).

[62] At 67H–fine.

THE ADMINISTRATION OF JUSTICE AND THE DEFENCE OF PRIVILEGE IN DEFAMATION

THE BALANCING OF INTERESTS: THE ADMINISTRATION OF JUSTICE AND THE PROTECTION OF REPUTATION

J M BURCHELL*

It is generally accepted that in the interests of the administration of justice certain defamatory statements uttered in the course of judicial proceedings[1] ought to be considered as published on a privileged occasion. The extent of this privilege, however, is not subject to the same degree of unanimity.

As long ago as 1881, in a case involving defamatory remarks made in court by a magistrate referring to a person who was a prospective witness, De Villiers CJ stated:

> 'It is the clear policy of our law, as it is that of the English law, to impose no unnecessary fetters upon the freedom of judges and magistrates to comment upon all cases brought judicially before them, and upon the conduct of all persons concerned in those cases.'[2]

The learned Chief Justice, however, recognized that there were limits to this privilege accorded to judges and magistrates, and he found authority for these limits in a passage from Voet.[3] In the course of analysing the judgment of De Villiers CJ, Sheil J in *Clark*

* BA LLB (Natal) LLB Diploma in Comparative Legal Studies (Cantab), Advocate of the Supreme Court of South Africa, Professor of Law in the University of the Witwatersrand, Johannesburg.

[1] This article will deal primarily with judicial proceedings and so will not specifically consider what other occasions (for instance, quasi-judicial proceedings) may qualify as privileged. The article will, however, cover matters intricately linked with judicial proceedings, for instance, the drafting of pleadings.

[2] *Bosman* v *Bisset* (1881) 1 SC 319 at 323. The defence of privilege in fact succeeded in this case.

[3] 47.10.2. This passage has now received approval by the Appellate Division in *May* v *Udwin* 1981 (1) SA 1 (A) at 16–17, and will be considered in detail later.

v *Gadd*[4] stated, *obiter*, that the privilege attaching to judges and magistrates was qualified, not absolute as under English law.[5]

One hundred years since the Chief Justice of the Cape Colony was confronted with determining the bounds of judicial privilege, the Appellate Division in *May* v *Udwin*[6] has authoritatively laid down the principles applicable to this field.

The Appellate Division also drew the same distinction that the late Mr Justice Schreiner had drawn as early as 1946 in *Basner* v *Trigger*[7] between malice or improper motive which is relevant to defeat the defence of privilege, and *animus injuriandi*. Although the late Mr Justice Schreiner's most memorable judgment in defamation was his impressive defence of freedom of expression in *Die Spoorbond* v *SAR*,[8] it is perhaps an appropriate tribute to him to analyse the decision of the Appellate Division in *May* v *Udwin*, where his view on the distinction between motive and *animus injuriandi* is shown not merely to have clear Roman-Dutch authority, but also to be correct.

A practising attorney, one Udwin, instituted an action against a magistrate, one May, for damages flowing from alleged defamatory remarks made by May in written reasons for judgment supplied in connection with certain litigation in which Udwin was concerned as an attorney. The import of the words was that Udwin had been dishonest, amoral and professionally unethical in the conduct of the case. The words were admitted by May to be defamatory but it was alleged that the words had been published on an occasion of qualified privilege.

Van Winsen J, who delivered judgment in the Cape Provincial Division,[9] held that the privilege was not absolute but qualified, and he then enumerated the following factors (which he held were not exclusive) that would lead to a forfeiture of the protection of the defence: *(a)* if the words are not germane to the subject with which the witness or judicial officer is required to deal,[10] or *(b)* if the publisher does not act reasonably in the use of the words,[11] or

[4] 1910 EDL 278.

[5] W S Holdsworth maintains that 'it was settled by the first quarter of the seventeenth century that no action lay against judges, witnesses or counsel for defamatory statements made in the conduct of litigation': *A History of English Law* VIII (1952) (edited by A L Goodhart and H G Hanbury) 376. For a short comparison of the approach of English and South African law to 'privilege', see O D Schreiner *The Contribution of English Law to South African Law; and the Rule of Law in South Africa* (1967) 61–2.

[6] 1981 (1) SA 1 (A).

[7] 1946 AD 83 at 95. Subsequent case law, however, does not favour Mr Justice Schreiner's view that privilege rebuts the inference of *animus injuriandi* (ibid) and that a burden of *proof* rests on the defendant to establish the defence; see the cases cited in notes 22 and 38, and L H Hoffmann and D T Zeffertt *The South African Law of Evidence* 3 ed (1981) 389.

[8] 1946 AD 999 at 1012–13.

[9] *Udwin* v *May* 1978 (4) SA 967 (C).

[10] Van Winsen J cited as authority for this proposition *Basner* v *Trigger* 1946 AD 83 at 97, *Penn* v *Fiddel* 1954 (4) SA 498 (C) at 500 and *Moolman* v *Slovo* 1964 (1) SA 760 (W) at 762.

[11] The learned judge cited as authority for this proposition *Preston* v *Luyt* 1911 EDL 298 at 309, *Richards* v *Kuranda* 1914 WLD 43 at 48, *Findlay* v *Knight* 1935 AD 58 at 75, *Gluckman* v *Schneider* 1936 AD 151 at 161, *Moolman* v *Slovo* (*supra*), *King* v *Neale* 1936 EDL 236 at 250, Voet 47.10.20 and Huber *Hedendaegse Rechtsgeleerdheyt* 6.8.12.

(c) if the publisher was actuated by an indirect or improper motive, that is, by malice.[12]

The learned judge concluded that the words had been germane to the matter with which the judicial officer had been required to deal in his judgment. He further held that no reasonable grounds had existed for publishing the defamatory words, 'nor were there any facts known to the defendant [the judicial officer] from which he could reasonably have concluded that his allegations against plaintiff were well-founded'.[13] Van Winsen J therefore concluded that the defamatory words had not been protected by reason of the privileged occasion. However, the learned judge also considered the possibility of the judicial officer's having been activated by an improper motive in publishing the words. As regards the effect of proof of an improper motive, Van Winsen J held that, as it is now accepted that privilege rebuts the unlawfulness element, the effect of proof of an improper motive (or malice) must be reassessed. Originally, so it was held, proof of improper motive revived the element of *animus injuriandi* which had been negatived by proof that defamatory words had been published on a privileged occasion. Van Winsen J held that '[s]uch an enquiry would now appear to be inapposite when the question to be posed is whether defendant's action in publishing the defamatory words is or is not unlawful'.[14] With respect, the learned judge correctly summarized the position as follows:

> 'If a defendant is motivated by an improper motive it would seem that he has abused the occasion by using it for a purpose other than that for which it was intended and that in so doing he has acted unlawfully, and accordingly falls outside the ambit of the protection contemplated by the law.'[15]

On the facts of *May's* case Van Winsen J held that the judicial officer's attack on the integrity of Udwin had not been actuated by malice, but was attributable to 'an ill-considered and uncalled-for officiousness on his part assayed without a proper regard for all the relevant matter in issue before him'.[16] The court therefore came to the conclusion that the defamatory remarks were not protected by the privileged occasion on which they were published.[17]

May appealed to the Appellate Division against the judgment of Van Winsen J in the Cape Provincial Division awarding Udwin R1 000 damages for defamation. The central question which the Appellate Division had to decide was whether the court *a quo* had

[12] The learned judge cited as authority for this proposition *Basner* v *Trigger* (*supra*) at 95; cf *Jordaan* v *Van Biljon* 1962 (1) SA 286 (A).

[13] *Udwin* v *May* 1978 (4) SA 967 (C) at 974A–B. [14] At 974G–H.

[15] At 974H–fine. [16] At 976A–B.

[17] The decision in *Udwin* v *May* is considered more fully in 1978 *Annual Survey of South African Law* 265–7.

been correct in holding that May had abused or exceeded the ambit of qualified privilege and in consequence had forfeited this protection.

THE DECISION OF THE APPELLATE DIVISION IN MAY v UDWIN[18]

Before turning to the specific issue of the extent of the qualified privilege which applied to a judge or magistrate, Joubert JA, who delivered the unanimous judgment of the Appellate Division,[19] stated:

> '. . . when the publication by a defendant of defamatory matter concerning a plaintiff is proved or admitted two rebuttable presumptions of fact arise, viz a presumption of intent, ie that the defendant intentionally published it with knowledge of its defamatory meaning[20] (*animo injuriandi*) as well as a presumption of unlawfulness, ie that the publication of the defamatory matter was unlawful. See *Suid-Afrikaanse Uitsaaikorporasie* v *O'Malley*.[21]. . . Once the presumptions of *animus injuriandi* and unlawfulness have arisen from the publication of the defamatory matter an onus (in the form of a "weerleggingslas") rests on the defendant to rebut them. The presumption of *animus injuriandi* may be rebutted by proving a defence (a so-called "skulduitsluitingsgrond") which negatives the inference of *animus injuriandi*. See *O'Malley's* case *supra* at 403B–C. A defendant may rebut the presumption of unlawfulness by proving a defence (a so-called "regverdigingsgrond" or justification ground) which is directed at establishing that the publication of the defamatory matter was lawful. One of the ways in which a defendant may rebut the presumption of unlawfulness is by proving that the publication of the defamatory matter was made on an occasion of qualified privilege. The publication of the defamatory matter is then regarded as being in the interest of public policy, and, therefore, as being lawful. See *O'Malley's* case *supra* at 402–3.'[22]

[18] The judgment is reported *sub nom May* v *Udwin* 1981 (1) SA 1 (A).

[19] Wessels JA, Trollip JA, Kotzé JA and Botha AJA concurred.

[20] Holmes JA in *Nydoo en andere* v *Vengtas* 1965 (1) SA 1 (A) stated that the defence of privileged occasion has 'in it the flavour of confession and avoidance (which traditionally affects the incidence of the onus of proof on the pleadings) . . .' (at 21C–D). The words 'proved or admitted' used by Joubert JA in *May's* case indicate that even where the publication of defamatory matter referring to the plaintiff is admitted, a presumption of unlawfulness and *animus injuriandi* arises, and this casts a mere evidentiary burden on the defendant to rebut these presumptions. Incidentally, there is authority for the view that an *onus of proving* a privileged occasion rests on the defendant: see, for instance, *Monckten* v *British South Africa Co* 1920 AD 324 at 331–2; *McLean* v *Murray* 1923 AD 406 at 414; *De Waal* v *Ziervogel* 1938 AD 112 at 120; *Young* v *Kemsley* 1940 AD 258 at 276–7; *Nydoo en andere* v *Vengtas* (*supra*) at 20–1 and 23 (per Holmes JA and Wessels JA); and *Benson* v *Robinson & Co (Pty) Ltd* 1967 (1) SA 420 (A) at 432F (per Holmes JA). In stating that knowledge of the defamatory meaning is required, Joubert JA in *May's* case acknowledges that a mistake of law (whether matter is defamatory or not would appear to involve, in part, a question of law—see *Sutter* v *Brown* 1926 AD 155 at 163 and *National Union of Distributive Workers* v *Cleghorn and Harris Ltd* 1946 AD 984 at 996–7) may negative *animus injuriandi*.

[21] 1977 (3) SA 394 (A).

[22] *Supra* at 10C–G. The Appellate Division in *Marais* v *Richard en 'n ander* 1981 SA 1157 (A) has clearly stated that fair comment excludes the unlawfulness element of defamation, not *animus injuriandi* (at 1166–7).

May's counsel (Mr L R Dison SC and Mr I G Farlam) argued in the Appellate Division that the qualified privilege applying to a judicial officer's exercise of his judicial functions is of a special kind, inasmuch as the judicial officer is liable for defamatory statements made in the course of his judicial functions only where he published them maliciously, that is, where he was actuated by a dishonest or an improper motive.[23]

Joubert JA then embarked on a scholarly analysis of the Roman and Roman-Dutch authorities to determine whether they supported counsel's contentions. The learned judge of appeal, after pointing out that the Roman texts[24] did not draw the clear distinction between defences directed against fault and defences directed against unlawfulness, concluded that neither the *magistratus* nor the *judex* of the Republic or the Principate, referred to in these texts, were judicial officers in the contemporary sense.

The Roman-Dutch writers, according to Joubert JA, also failed to draw the distinction between defences directed against fault and those directed against unlawfulness. However, relying essentially on Voet[25] and Van der Keessel,[26] the learned judge of appeal held that there is a rebuttable presumption that a judicial officer who defames someone in the exercise of his judicial authority is presumed to have acted lawfully within the limits of his authority. In determining the criterion by which it is possible to assess whether a judicial officer in defaming someone in the course of judicial proceedings has abused or exceeded the privileged occasion, Joubert JA relied heavily on a passage from Voet, from which it appears that both a magistrate and a judge may be liable '. . . if in defiance of good morals . . . [they] have loaded someone with insulting words, or have chastised him without reason or beyond the limit, not with a view to upholding the sovereignty of the people, and not for the purpose of advising or instructing him, but with a view to the stirring up of ill-will and evil report (though such a thing is not readily presumed) . . .'.[27]

Joubert JA pointed out that in this passage no express reference is made to *animus* or *dolus*,[28] and that a judicial officer will have abused or exceeded the privilege where he is actuated by 'personal spite, ill will, improper motive, unlawful motive (ongeoorloofde oogmerk

[23] At 12B–D. [24] D 47.10.13.1,5,6; D 47.10.32,33.

[25] 47.10.20 and 47.10.2. [26] *Praelectiones ad Jus Criminale* 47.10.1,6.

[27] 47.10.2. It is interesting that this passage contains the phrase 'without reason or beyond the limit'—could this not be interpreted to mean 'not founded on some reasonable cause' or 'irrelevant'?

[28] P R MacMillan has contended that the defence of privilege is defeated not by malice or improper motive but by *dolus directus*, ie where the defendant's aim and object was to defame the plaintiff ((1975) 92 *SALJ* 144). Joubert JA, in drawing attention to the fact that Voet nowhere refers to *animus* or *dolus* and by later concluding that malice or improper motive rebuts privilege, is impliedly rejecting MacMillan's contention.

of motief) or ulterior motive, that is to say, by malice . . .'.[29] In this way the learned judge of appeal gave approval to the distinction which Schreiner JA had drawn as early as 1946,[30] between malice, which is relevant to defeat the defence of privilege, and *animus injuriandi*. Malice, so Joubert JA held, is a subjective concept, but can be established by inference from the facts. Regard can be had to the defamatory matter, its relevance to the privileged occasion, the nature of the judicial function, the presence or absence of enmity between the parties and, generally, the circumstances relevant to the publication of the defamatory matter.[31]

Joubert JA held that there was an essential difference between the qualified privilege attaching to judges and magistrates on the one hand, and to witnesses, litigants, advocates and attorneys on the other hand. In words reminiscent of those of De Villiers CJ in *Bosman* v *Bisset*,[32] the learned judge of appeal stated that the 'public interest in the due administration of justice requires that a judicial officer, in the exercise of his judicial functions, should be able to

[29] At 19pr–B (italics omitted). Malice is often referred to in the earlier cases as 'express' or 'special' malice; see, for instance, *A Nicholson* v *A Roberts* (1904) 25 NLR 278 at 284, *Reynolds* v *Ainsley* 1904 TS 868 at 870 and *Love* v *Garcia* 1916 EDL 44. The terminology of express or special malice appears to have been adopted from English law. 'Express' or 'special' malice, in English law, is 'ill will or spite towards the plaintiff or any indirect or improper motive in the defendant's mind at the time of the publication, which is his sole or dominant motive for publishing the words complained of. This must be distinguished from legal malice or malice in law which means publication without lawful excuse and does not depend upon the defendant's state of mind'—*Halsbury's Laws of England* 4 ed vol 28 § 145. Corbett JA in *Borgin* v *De Villiers* 1980 (3) SA 556 (A) left open the question whether the term 'express malice' is still appropriate in dealing with a plea of lawful publication of defamatory matter (at 579F–G). (*Borgin's* case also dealt with the defence of qualified privilege, but not in the setting of judicial proceedings.) However, it is submitted that a clear distinction is drawn in our law between malice (the English 'express malice') and *animus injuriandi*, and so there can be no confusion in terminology. Furthermore, Joubert JA's unqualified acceptance of the term malice (covering improper motive, spite and ill will) places the matter of terminology beyond doubt. Jansen JA in *Marais* v *Richard* 1981 (1) SA 1157 (A) has stated that ''n onbehoorlike motief' can defeat what would otherwise be fair comment (at 1170C–D).

[30] *Basner* v *Trigger* 1946 AD 83 at 94–5.

[31] It is interesting that Mr L J Blom Cooper QC submitted a learned 91-page memorandum to the committee considering the law of defamation in England under the chairmanship of Mr Justice Faulks ((1975) Cmnd 5909) and that this memorandum concluded as follows:

> 'The privilege of judges for defamatory remarks made in the course of judicial proceedings should be maintained. It should be neither absolute nor qualified. It should be a generic privilege for those exercising judicial functions. There should be immunity from legal suit for anything said in judicial proceedings by any judicial officer, except where there is established express malice in the defamatory utterance. There would be, in law, a presumption of the absence of malice; malice would therefore have to be proved clearly and conclusively' (p 49).

This conclusion is amazingly similar to that reached by Joubert JA in *May* v *Udwin*. The Faulks Committee, however, decided that the principle of absolute immunity had worked for the last 250 years and more and should not be departed from. The criterion of malice has also been suggested as the correct test in the United States: see (1978) 64 *American Bar Association J* 740. Douglas K Barth, writing in (1977) 27 *Case Western Reserve LR* 727–70, after analysing the German and French law on the topic, suggests a qualified immunity of judges based on a principle of good faith.

[32] (1881) 1 SC 319.

speak his mind freely without fear of incurring liability for damages for defamation'.[33] Unlike English and American law, which confers an absolute privilege upon a judicial officer, in South Africa this privilege is qualified by the fact that the judicial officer must not have been actuated by malice, so Joubert JA held. The irrelevance of the defamatory matter to the proceedings or the absence of reasonable foundation for the statement is at the most only indicative of malice, so far as a judicial officer is concerned. So far as a witness, litigant, attorney or advocate is concerned, because of the fear of the courts being 'wantonly used by those who resort to them . . . for the illegitimate purpose of defaming others',[34] qualified privilege will be accorded only if the defamatory words were relevant[35] to the case and founded on some reasonable cause, according to Joubert JA. The judge of appeal distinguished the cases cited in the court *a quo* by Van Winsen J[36] on the basis that they dealt with witnesses, litigants, attorneys or advocates.

The law as stated in *May* v *Udwin* can be crisply summarized as follows: Privilege rebuts unlawfulness.[37] As a general rule, a 'weerleggingslas' or burden of introducing or adducing evidence of a privileged occasion rests on the defendant.[38] Judges, magistrates, witnesses, litigants, advocates and attorneys have the protection of a qualified, not absolute, privilege regarding defamatory statements made in the course of judicial proceedings. This privilege can be forfeited in certain ways. As far as judges and magistrates are concerned, there is a rebuttable presumption that they acted lawfully within the limits of their authority, ie without malice (it would appear from *May's* case that they do not even have to introduce or adduce evidence of absence of malice). The existence

[33] At 19H–fine. [34] At 20A–B.

[35] A vivid example of a defamatory statement lacking relevancy to the case in hand is to be found in *Cohen* v *Carn* (1904) 14 CTR 362 at 366, where a witness was asked the question: 'Where did you see Miss Cohen speaking to Pross?' To which the witness replied: 'Pross had connection with her mother.' Such a statement was held not to be relevant or pertinent to the issue before the court. The statement attacked the reputation of a third party unconnected with the suit. *Cohen's* case is referred to in *Rubel* v *Katzenellenbogen* 1915 CPD 627 at 633.

[36] See the cases referred to in notes 10, 11 and 12.

[37] See also *Borgin* v *De Villiers* 1980 (3) SA 556 (A) at 571F–G.

[38] At 10. Joubert JA specifically mentions the evidentiary burden or 'weerleggingslas', but unfortunately also refers to 'proving' a defence and 'establishing' lawfulness (ibid). The Appellate Division in *Mabaso* v *Felix* 1981 (3) SA 865 (A) has recently held that, in a situation of alleged self-defence, the defendant must normally prove facts substantiating such defence on a balance of probabilities. The recent Appellate Division decisions on defamation (see, for instance, *Borgin's* case (*supra*) at 571E–G, *May's* case (*supra*) at 10 and *Marais* v *Richard* 1981 (1) SA 1157 (A) at 1166) indicate that the defendant need only adduce evidence of lack of unlawfulness or *animus injuriandi* (for the approach in some of the earlier cases, see note 20). This is not the appropriate place to consider whether the attitude of the Appellate Division to self-defence can be reconciled, in logic or on grounds of public policy, with the defamation cases. A consideration of this problem deserves comprehensive attention, because the solution offered will have a ripple effect on many other areas of the law of delict. See also *Ramsay* v *Minister van Polisie en andere* 1981 (4) SA 802 (A).

of a presumption of lawfulness favouring judges and magistrates means that a special kind of qualified privilege is established. The privilege can be forfeited only if the plaintiff proves on a balance of probabilities that the judge or magistrate had been actuated by malice or improper motive. This malice, which is a subjective concept, is not equivalent to *animus injuriandi*,[39] and can be proved by inference from certain objective factors, utilizing both extrinsic and intrinsic evidence. As far as witnesses, litigants, advocates and attorneys are concerned, privilege will be accorded to them only if the defamatory words were relevant to the case and founded on some reasonable cause.

Applying these principles to the facts, Joubert JA held that, weighing up the factors which might point towards an inference of malice and those militating against such an inference, Udwin had not proved on a balance of probabilities that May had exceeded the ambit of the privileged occasion.

D L Carey Miller,[40] commenting on the court *a quo's* decision in *Udwin* v *May*, has criticized the absolute approach of the Scots and English law and suggested that the middle course might be to adopt the test of reasonable relevance of the statement to the matter before the court. The learned author does not approve of the criterion of malice as the decisive element, because 'it is all too easy to allege malice' and 'it is undesirable that judges should be subject to the threat of such actions [ie defamation actions] which would allow too much scope for subjective factors'.[41] Joubert JA in *May* v *Udwin* has, however, stated that the primary onus is on the plaintiff, who must prove malice on a balance of probabilities, and has also stated explicitly that objective factors, such as irrelevance to the issue before the court and lack of some reasonable cause, can be utilized to draw an inference of malice.

The judgment of Joubert JA in *May's* case is to be welcomed on many counts. It is clearly stated that it is malice or improper motive which leads to the forfeiture of qualified privilege.[42] The importance of judicial independence to the pursuit of the truth and administration of justice is emphasized. The absolute privilege applying to judicial proceedings in other countries is plainly

[39] In *Maskowitz* v *Pienaar* 1957 (4) SA 195 (A) at 203 De Beer JA, after quoting Schreiner JA in *Basner* v *Trigger* 1946 AD 83 at 95–6, expressed the hope that this distinction had been finally settled. See, however, *Jordaan* v *Van Biljon* 1962 (1) SA 286 (A) at 296 and *Nydoo* v *Vengtas* 1965 (1) SA 1 (A) at 13. It is now beyond doubt that malice and *animus injuriandi* are different concepts: see *Suid-Afrikaanse Uitsaaikorporasie* v *O'Malley* 1977 (3) SA 394 (A) at 403A–B; *Borgin* v *De Villiers* (*supra*); and *May's* case at 10.

[40] 'Defamation by a Judge' 1980 *Juridical Review* 88.

[41] Op cit 109. Lord Denning also does not approve of the malice criterion; see *Sirros* v *Moore* [1975] QB 118 (CA) at 136D–E, [1974] 3 All ER 776 at 785.

[42] See the cases cited in note 39 above. Jansen JA in *Marais* v *Richard* 1981 (1) SA 1157 (A) has also stated that an improper motive can defeat what would otherwise constitute fair comment (at 1170C–D).

rejected, and, although it may be very difficult for an individual to prove malice or improper motive on the part of a judge or magistrate, there nevertheless exists some avenue of redress for a person whose reputation is injured by a remark from the Bench. The traditional arguments put forward for absolute immunity, namely, the need for finality in judicial proceedings, the need for an independent judiciary and the diminishing of respect for judges by putting them on trial, are not entirely convincing and certainly do not preclude the possibility of a qualified 'good-faith' immunity.[43]

The possibility of a remedy is particularly important, as it is necessary for judges to side-step any criticism that they are placing themselves in an 'ivory tower'.[44] An additional reason for retaining the possibility of an action against a judge or magistrate for defamation in judicial proceedings is that an unfortunate remark made by such judicial officer without reasonable cause and not relevant to the issue before the court might be reported fairly and accurately in a newspaper and receive wide publicity. It is also perhaps fair to say that the reasonable reader of this newspaper report might well endow the statement with an added degree of veracity in that it emanated from the Bench.

From an academic standpoint it is most pleasing to see the blend of policy considerations and principle that Joubert JA achieves in *May's* case. Roman-Dutch principles are applied in a situation where there is very little contemporary case authority, while at the same time the considerations of public policy pertaining to frankness in judicial proceedings receive explicit attention.

There are, however, certain aspects of the judgment that call for comment.

The judgment centres on the privilege attaching to judges and magistrates, but Joubert JA also made certain *obiter* remarks on the privilege attaching to other parties to judicial proceedings, namely, advocates, attorneys, witnesses and litigants. Other countries do not appear to draw a distinction between the various participants in judicial proceedings.[45] It is the occasion (that is, judicial

[43] See Douglas K Barth in (1977) 27 *Case Western Reserve LR* 727 at 741–3.

[44] Similar arguments have been raised against the immunity of counsel from actions for negligent misstatements. See (1966) 83 *SALJ* 363, (1968) 85 *SALJ* 320 and (1979) 96 *SALJ* 118. In fact, it is interesting to note that the House of Lords in one of the leading decisions on an advocate's immunity from suit for negligent misstatements (*Rondel* v *Worsley* [1969] 1 AC 191 (HL), [1967] 3 All ER 993) relied heavily on the analogy with counsel's immunity from suit for defamation; see Lord Morris of Borth-y-Gest at 252–3, 1014–15, Lord Pearce at 266–7, 1023–4 and 271, 1026, and Lord Upjohn at 283, 1034.

[45] For the position in England, see, generally, Colin Duncan and Brian Neill *Defamation* (1978) 83ff, *Gatley on Libel and Slander* 7 ed (1974) 161–2, *Halsbury's Laws of England* 4 ed vol 28 § 98 and *Winfield and Jolowicz on Tort* 11 ed (1979) at 312–13 (although, at 639, Winfield and Jolowicz treat witnesses separately). For the position in the United States, see *Restatement of the Law: Torts 2 d* (1976) § 585. Although the *Restatement* treats the different parties to judicial proceedings separately, Carey Miller op cit note 40 at 99–103 has pointed out that in the final analysis the test for each is the same. See also Douglas K Barth in (1977) 27 *Case Western Reserve LR* 727.

proceedings), not the communication, which is privileged,[46] and so one might wonder whether it is justifiable to draw a distinction between judges and magistrates on the one hand, and other parties to judicial proceedings on the other hand. It may be valuable to analyse the authorities in order to assess the extent of the difference, if any, in the treatment of advocates, attorneys, witnesses and litigants, as opposed to judges and magistrates.

Advocates and Attorneys

In *Preston* v *Luyt*[47] Kotzé JP set out in detail the principles applying to defamatory remarks made by counsel in the course of judicial proceedings. The Judge President pointed out that there was authority in Roman law to the effect that 'all advocates should give their services to the litigant parties in such a way that they do not avail themselves of slanderous speech and abuse, beyond what the interest of the case demands, and that they abstain from injurious conduct'.[48] Turning to the Roman-Dutch law, Kotzé JP summarized the position as follows:

> 'The privilege, then, of the advocate is qualified in the Roman-Dutch law to this extent that he is to refrain from unnecessary defamation and insult unconnected with the case.'[49]

Kotzé JP cited a passage from Voet[50] to support the conclusion that 'an advocate is protected where he makes a defamatory statement in the interests of his client, pertinent to the matter in issue, even though it be false, provided he has some reasonable cause for his conduct. But if he acts maliciously and says anything altogether unjustifiable and not pertinent to the cause in any respect, even although upon instructions of his client, he exceeds the privilege which the law affords him.'[51] In *Preston* v *Luyt* the English cases conferring an absolute privilege on parties in judicial proceedings were distinguished, and it is clear that the privilege in our law is qualified. There was, however, held to be a presumption of lack of intent favouring the defendant,[52] that is, in current terminology, a presumption of lawfulness.

In *Briscoe* v *Benson*[53] the court stated that an advocate must have great latitude in conducting his case, but that the privilege protecting defamatory communications made in the course of a case is not unlimited. In the words of Wessels J:

[46] See Lord Shaw of Dunfermline in *Adam* v *Ward* [1917] AC 309 (HL) at 348; R G McKerron *The Law of Delict* 7 ed (1971) 188. Incidentally, N J van der Merwe and P J J Olivier also do not distinguish between the participants in judicial proceedings. But they do distinguish between different occasions, for instance, drafting pleadings, cross-examination, etc (*Die Onregmatige Daad in die Suid-Afrikaanse Reg* 4 ed (1980) 423–5).

[47] 1911 EDL 298. [48] Idem at 308. [49] Ibid. [50] 47.10.20.

[51] At 320.

[52] Idem at 309.

[53] 1914 TPD 598.

> 'An advocate may ask a witness any question which goes to his credit. He may ask him if he has committed any crime, however heinous it may be, provided—and this proviso must always be borne in mind—that he has instructions that his client possesses some proof to that effect.'[54]

In *Findlay* v *Knight*[55] the question that arose was whether this privilege extended to an advocate or attorney drafting pleadings. The Appellate Division held that the privilege extended to these matters. The court also analysed the public-policy reasons for a wide latitude being given to an advocate in drafting pleadings, in examination, in cross-examination and in arguing his client's case in court. Wessels CJ stated that the 'welfare of society' and the 'administration of justice' demanded some form of privilege.[56] This privilege had to be qualified, however. In addition, so the Chief Justice held, public policy demanded that the

> '. . . [c]ourts shall not be wantonly used for the purpose of defaming either litigants or third parties. The courts cannot allow advocates or attorneys to use the process of the courts for an illegitimate purpose; "for manifestly the law cannot countenance an abuse of privilege. And where the privilege is abused, malice is inferred."'[57]

Wessels CJ, quoting passages from Voet[58] and Van Leeuwen,[59] stressed that there must be 'a reasonable foundation for the defamatory charges' and the defamatory allegation must be 'relevant to the case'.[60] If the allegation is not relevant to the case, the 'usual presumption is that [it is] made *animo injuriandi*'.[61] Malice was described in terms of spite or improper motive, and it was stated that such malice defeats the privilege. Wessels CJ also maintained that a pleader who does not care whether his defamatory charge is true or false, and who knows or ought to know that no evidence will be produced to support his charge, is 'manifestly abusing the process of the court'.[62] The defendant in *Findlay's* case did not know that the allegations were false, but he did know at the time he made them that he had no proof of the truth, and in this way he published the defamatory matter recklessly, without caring whether it was true or false. The Chief Justice concluded that the defendant had been 'reckless' and 'careless' in making the allegations, and therefore was presumed to be acting *animo injuriandi*. It is clear, however, from the judgment of the Appellate Division in *Gluckman* v *Schneider*[63] that by *animus injuriandi* Wessels CJ in fact was referring to malice or improper motive.

[54] At 600. [55] 1935 AD 58. [56] At 71.
[57] Ibid. See also De Villiers ACJ in *Kleynhans* v *Usmar* 1929 AD 121 at 126.
[58] 47.10.20.
[59] *Het Roomsch Hollandsch Recht* 5.4.3, incorrectly cited as 4.4.2 in the judgment.
[60] At 72. [61] Ibid. [62] Ibid. [63] 1936 AD 151 at 158–60.

Stratford JA in *Gluckman* adopted the test set out in *Preston* v *Luyt* which was quoted earlier in this article.[64] The learned judge of appeal in *Gluckman's* case approved of the view that the relevancy or irrelevancy of the defamatory statement to the issue at hand is vital in determining whether the privileged occasion has been properly used or abused.[65]

Taking into account, amongst other things, the reliability of the source of the information on which the defendant based his allegation and the persistent use of the allegation in the face of 'so much that should have made him pause', the defendant's conduct was designated by the court as 'reckless'.[66] It was held that an inference could be drawn that the defendant was not activated by an honest belief in the truth of the statements, and so published the defamatory matter 'recklessly without caring whether it was true or false and without reasonable grounds for believing it to be true'.[67] Malice was therefore correctly inferred.

In *Basner* v *Trigger*[68] the appellant attorney had presented evidence before a commission of inquiry. During the course of his evidence the appellant made remarks which, in essence, meant that the respondent had been guilty of disgraceful and illegal conduct in causing spying to be done on a trade union, on members of Parliament in the precincts of Parliament and on the public. One of the appellant's defences was privileged occasion. Schreiner JA, in delivering judgment, clearly distinguished between malice (that is, improper motive) and *animus injuriandi*, and emphasized that malice leads to the forfeiture of qualified privilege, not to *animus injuriandi*.[69]

As far as 'relevancy' was concerned, Schreiner JA indicated that whether the statement was relevant to the purpose of the occasion was important in determining whether a privileged occasion existed. All that was required here was that the statement was 'in some measure relevant to the purpose of the occasion'.[70] However, the faintness of the connection between the alleged defamatory statement and the purpose of the occasion was also important in possibly leading to an inference of malice. But Schreiner JA added the following qualification:

> 'Malice is not to be attributed to him merely because he does not think his submissions well founded or because they are pitched too high for reasonable acceptance. Although overstatement is generally an unprofitable practice in the arguer, even far-fetched and fantastic contentions can hardly, in themselves, provide evidence that they were advanced from an improper motive. . . . It seems to me that in respect to matters stated in argument their relevancy must, save perhaps in the most exceptional cases, be decisive whether there is intrinsic evidence of malice. The plaintiff might, of course, be in a position to provide evidence outside

[64] See text to note 51. [65] At 159. [66] At 163. [67] At 165.
[68] 1946 AD 83. [69] At 93–6. [70] At 97.

the statement to show that the defendant was acting from an improper motive in introducing the defamatory matter into his argument, but at least, as a general rule, he will not be able to prove malice by pointing to the extreme or even outrageous lengths to which the defendant went in submitting his case.'[71]

In *Pogrund* v *Yutar*[72] D O K Beyers JA pointed out that this wide language used by Schreiner JA in *Basner* 'is possibly open to misconstruction', and stated that Schreiner JA would not have intended to convey the impression that an advocate has a 'licence to speak ill of others'.[73] Beyers JA held that before the defence of privilege will apply to a statement made by counsel in the course of judicial proceedings, the statement must *(a)* be pertinent or germane to the issue before the court, and *(b)* have some foundation in the evidence or circumstances surrounding the trial.

The judge of appeal in *Pogrund's* case concluded that, although some of the remarks made by the advocate in court had been germane to the issue and had some foundation in the evidence, there was positive evidence that other remarks had been inspired by *animus injuriandi*. Beyers JA was, in fact, referring to malice or improper motive that leads to a forfeiture of privilege.

WITNESSES

In *MacGregor* v *Sayles*[74] the Chief Justice, Sir James Rose Innes, set out the law applicable to witnesses as follows:

> 'Under the Roman-Dutch law the privilege enjoyed by a witness giving evidence in a court of law, in reply to questions regularly and properly put to him, was a very real one. But it was not absolute; that is to say, the fact that defamatory statements were made under such circumstances did not constitute a complete defence. It did destroy the presumption regarding *animus injuriandi*, the existence of which otherwise the law would imply; and it raised a counter presumption that the words were spoken without malice. But the plaintiff might still succeed if he established certain propositions. According to the authorities, it was necessary under such circumstances to the success of the plaintiff that he shall satisfy the court of three things: First, that the witness was actuated by express malice; second, that the words spoken were false; and third, that the witness who uttered them had no reasonable grounds for believing them to be true.'[75]

Kotzé J in *Rubel* v *Katzenellenbogen*[76] (another case relating to the privilege attaching to a witness), in speaking of the relevance of the statement to the case, quoted a passage from Cockburn CJ's judgment in *Seaman* v *Netherclift*[77] which clearly indicates that 'relevance' is important in determining whether a privileged occasion in fact existed.

[71] At 107. [72] 1967 (2) SA 564 (A). [73] At 570C–D.
[74] 1909 TS 553. [75] At 556. [76] 1915 CPD 627 at 632.
[77] (1876) 2 CPD 53.

Kotzé J did suggest that a distinction might be drawn between the case of a witness who appears under subpoena and is compelled to answer questions put to him, and the party who swears an affidavit containing defamatory matter (as in *Rubel's* case).[78] The learned judge stated that both types of witness would be subject to a *qualified* privilege, but the indication is that a wider qualified privilege might attach to a witness under subpoena. Kotzé J stated that a presumption favours the defendant.[79] In other words, to use modern terminology, there is a presumption that he acted lawfully within the limits of privilege.

The witness in *Rubel's* case was held to have had reasonable grounds for believing in the communication made by him, and the court was satisfied that he honestly believed in its truth. The court further stated that excess of language was not proof of malice. Kotzé J specifically stated that under certain circumstances malice can be inferred from lack of reasonable and probable cause, but that such an inference could not be drawn in this case.[80]

Litigants

In *Penn* v *Fiddel*[81] it was stated that a litigant enjoys the same privilege when conducting his case in a court of law as his counsel would possess. Diemont AJ, after mentioning that he could see no reason why this privilege should also not apply to proceedings of a rent board, concluded that the privilege extends only to questions put and comments made by litigants in good faith that are relevant to the proceedings.[82]

Voet clearly states that if a litigant makes a defamatory statement in court proceedings he is presumed to have done so without an intention of wrongdoing, 'but rather with the plan of defending himself'.[83] In contemporary terminology, there is a presumption of lawfulness in the litigant's favour.

Conclusion

The common threads running through the judgments dealing with advocates, attorneys, witnesses and litigants are *(a)* the privilege that these persons enjoy in regard to defamatory statements made in judicial and certain other proceedings is qualified; *(b)* the relevance (pertinence or germaneness) of the defamatory matter to the issue at hand is important in determining whether objectively a privileged occasion existed. Relevance is a broad concept, wider than that embraced by the technical rules relating to relevance in the

[78] 1915 CPD 627 at 633. [79] Ibid. [80] At 635.
[81] 1954 (4) SA 498 (C).
[82] At 500B. See also *Preston* v *Luyt* 1911 EDL 298 at 319.
[83] 47.10.20 (Gane's translation).

law of evidence, and is well expressed in Schreiner JA's words—'in some measure relevant to the purpose of the occasion';[84] *(c)* malice or improper motive defeats privilege (that is, if malice is present there is an excess or abuse of the privileged occasion). Such malice can be proved by inference, using both extrinsic and intrinsic evidence. The following factors, although not exclusive, are important in drawing an inference of malice: the irrelevance of the statement to the matter in hand or to the judicial proceedings, lack of reasonable foundation in the evidence for the allegation, and lack of honest belief that some evidence exists which supports the statement.

It would appear that there is authority for the proposition that in regard to counsel, witnesses and litigants a rebuttable presumption of lawfulness exists, that is, a presumption that the words uttered were within the limits of the privileged occasion. This presumption was in the past referred to as a presumption of lack of *animus injuriandi*, but this was at a time when privilege was regarded as rebutting the inference of *animus injuriandi*. Now that it is clear that privilege rebuts unlawfulness, we can refer to this presumption as a presumption of lawfulness. Furthermore, although this was not considered in *May's* case, the plaintiff would appear to bear an onus of proving abuse of a privileged occasion on the part of an advocate, attorney, witness or litigant on a balance of probabilities. This is because, if there is a presumption of lawfulness, the defendant does not even have to introduce or adduce evidence that he did not exceed the limits of the privilege. One is, therefore, thrown back on the primary onus that rests on the plaintiff to prove facts establishing unlawfulness on a balance of probabilities (the presumption of fault, of course, remains).

If, however, a court in a future case were to decide that the advocate, attorney, witness or litigant does not have the help of a presumption of lawfulness, but has to adduce evidence of absence of malice, then it is submitted that a wide test of relevance, similar to that put forward by Schreiner JA in *Basner* v *Trigger*, should be utilized. If the court favoured a presumption of lawfulness—and there is clear authority for this approach—then the distinction between judges and magistrates on the one hand, and advocates, attorneys, witnesses and litigants on the other hand, stressed by Joubert JA in *May's* case in order to determine the scope of the defence of privilege, would be non-existent.

From the point of view of public policy and the administration of justice, it is surely desirable that judges, magistrates, counsel, witnesses and litigants should all have a similar degree of latitude in their common pursuit—that of truth. In fact, as far as the position

[84] *Basner* v *Trigger* 1946 AD 83 at 97.

of a witness under oath is concerned, it has been stated by Menzies J in *Norden* v *Oppenheim*[85] that the claim of a witness to privilege for what he has said under oath, and while under examination, 'is much stronger than that of either a judge or a party'.[86] The policy reasons for a wide privilege attaching to witnesses is aptly stated by Kotzé JP in *Preston* v *Luyt*[87] as being that the administration of justice requires that witnesses 'should testify with minds absolutely free from the apprehension of being annoyed by civil actions . . .'.

Joubert JA was concerned about the courts being 'wantonly used by those who resort to them'. However, one could hardly say that witnesses under subpoena, who are compelled to attend the proceedings, and advocates, who, at least by etiquette, would appear to be obliged to accept a brief,[88] can wantonly resort to the courts.

There are obvious drawbacks in the concept of malice or improper motive which the Appellate Division has used to strike the balance between the administration of justice (including judicial independence) and the protection of reputation. Different criteria have been suggested in other jurisdictions.[89] None of these is perfect. The malice criterion, which is subjective but can be proved by inference from objective factors, at least accepts the principle that a judicial officer and other participants in judicial proceedings should be liable if they have abused the right or exceeded the privilege accorded by the law, even if it may be difficult to prove liability.

The judgment in *May's* case has ensured that the balance is tilted in favour of the administration of justice and independence of the judiciary, and away from the protection of reputation. Just as press freedom has as its corollary the right of the public to be informed, so the privilege attaching to judicial and certain other proceedings can be regarded not so much as a privilege attaching to the parties themselves, but as a right of the public to have the independence of judicial officers preserved and the administration of justice fostered.[90]

[85] (1846) 3 Menz 42 at 54.

[86] In fact, Kotzé JP in *Preston's* case argued by analogy from the position of judges, magistrates and witnesses in Roman-Dutch law to the position of counsel.

[87] 1911 EDL 298 at 319.

[88] See Salmon LJ in *Rondel* v *Worsley* [1967] 1 QB 443 at 519, [1966] 3 All ER 657 at 675–6: 'A barrister cannot pick and choose his clients. He is by the etiquette of the Bar obliged to appear, certainly in the criminal courts, for anyone prepared to pay his normal fee.' Lord Reid in the House of Lords in *Rondel* v *Worsley* [1969] 1 AC 191 (HL), [1967] 3 All ER 993 stated:

> 'There is no doubt about the position and duties of a barrister or advocate appearing in court on behalf of a client. It has long been recognised that no counsel is entitled to refuse to act in a sphere in which he practises, and on being tendered a proper fee, for any person however unpopular or even offensive he or his opinions may be, and it is essential that that duty must continue' (at 227D–E, 998).

G H Treitel *The Law of Contract* 4 ed (1975) 5n35 is of the view that it is 'by no means clear that the barrister is "bound" by law (as opposed to etiquette)' to accept a brief.

[89] See, for instance, D L Carey Miller op cit note 40.

[90] *Winfield and Jolowicz on Tort* op cit note 45 at 638.

DISCRETIONARY TRUSTS, POWERS OF APPOINTMENT AND THE RULE REGARDING THE DELEGATION OF TESTAMENTARY POWER

M M CORBETT*

> '. . . [O]ur modern law of trusts should not be unduly hampered by views regarding its association with other branches of our own law which may not be historically justified and which, in any event, should not govern, though they may sometimes assist, the development of the law of trusts. . . . [T]rusts are an established feature of our legal landscape . . .': per Schreiner JA in *Crookes NO and another* v *Watson and others* 1956 (1) SA 277 (A) at 290.

The Delegation of Testamentary Power

I commence with the rule regarding the delegation of testamentary power. The Digest[1] records the following opinion of Gaius:

> '*Illa institutio "quos Titius voluerit" ideo vitiosa est, quod alieno arbitrio permissa est: nam satis constanter veteres decreverunt testamentorum iura ipsa per se firma esse oportere, non ex alieno arbitrio pendere.*'[2]

This expresses succinctly the fundamental rule that a testator must himself institute his heir: he cannot in his will delegate this testamentary power to someone else. If he does so, the institution is invalid and devoid of legal effect. The same rule applies to the appointment of a legatee.

This rule was received into Roman-Dutch law. Johannes Voet thus refers to it in his *Commentaries*:[3]

> '*Denique ratae non habendae institutiones illae, quae directo in arbitrium tertii collatae sunt . . .*'[4]

* BA LLB Hon LLD (Cape Town) MA LLB (Cantab), Judge of Appeal, Appellate Division of the Supreme Court of South Africa.

[1] 28.5.32.

[2] 'The appointment of an heir, as follows, "Those whom Titius may wish", is defective, for the reason that it depends upon the desire of another. For the ancient authorities very frequently decided that the validity of wills must be derived from themselves, and not depend upon the wishes of others' (Scott's translation).

[3] 28.5.29.

[4] 'Finally institutions are not to be considered valid if they have been referred directly to the discretion of a third party. . .' (Gane's translation).

and proceeds to illustrate the rule and state the rationale thereof, using the language of Digest 28.5.32.[5] Voet adds, however,[6] that under the law of Holland the institution of an heir may validly be made conditional on the performance of an act by a third party and thus be dependent indirectly on the discretion of that third party. The rule is also mentioned by, for example, Pothier and Domat. In his treatise on *Legacies*, Pothier states the reason for the rule as follows (I quote from the translation of J van der Linden):[7]

> 'De reden is, om dat de aart en het wezen der uiterste willen van een Testateur medebrengt, dat zij vooral *zijnen* wil, en niet dien van een ander bevatten. . . .'

Domat[8] gives substantially the same reason, stating that if a testator, instead of choosing and naming his heir himself, should leave the choice of his heir to another person, the institution would be lame and of no effect, for it would lack the character that is essential to a testament, namely, of containing the proper will of the testator, and not that of another person.

J Brunnemann, in his *Commentarius in Leges Pandectarum*, dealing with Digest 28.5.32, states the general rule that an institution (of an heir) ought not to be handed over to the discretion of a third party, because the last wishes of the testator ought not to depend on the discretion of another. The writer adds, however, that there are limitations to the rule. A condition that Titius shall be heir if Sempronius travels to Rome is not ineffective.[9] It is nevertheless possible for the choice of an uncertain heir from a specified class of persons to be entrusted to another. Next, that which is left for a charitable purpose (*ad piam causam*) may be entrusted to the discretion of a third party. And finally it may be left to the free will of the heir whether he wishes to be heir.

Broadly, this expresses the current approach of our law. One of the early cases in which the point arose was *Pritchard's Trustee* v *Estate Pritchard*,[10] in which the testators (husband and wife), having bequeathed the residue of their estate to their children (and the descendants of any deceased child) and having reserved a usufruct of the estate to the survivor, sought to impose, by way of a codicil, what has been termed a 'protective trust'[11] in respect of the shares accruing to their heirs. The provision was to the effect that should

[5] And citing Digest 28.5.32, 28.5.68 and 35.1.52.
[6] Citing Digest 28.5.68 and 35.1.52.
[7] *Verhandeling van Legaten* § I xiv (p 27).
[8] 2.3.1.1 (William Strachan's translation, Cushing edition (1850) § 2994).
[9] This is the conditional institution referred to by Voet (see above).
[10] 1912 CPD 87.
[11] See, for example, Tony Honoré *The South African Law of Trusts* 2 ed (1976) 109–11; and in English law see D B Parker and A R Mellows *The Modern Law of Trusts* 4 ed (1979) 114ff; Philip Pettit *Equity and the Law of Trusts* 4 ed (1979) 95ff; A Underhill *The Law of Trusts and Trustees* 12 ed (1970) 96ff.

an attempt be made, by reason of insolvency or otherwise, to attach the share of an heir who had become entitled to his inheritance but had not received it, such share should not be payable to the heir, but the executors should 'expend the same in such way as they may deem best, and at their discretion entirely'.[12] The codicil contained a similar provision in the event of an heir's share being adjudged by a competent court to be liable to attachment. The purported conferment on the executors of a discretionary power to expend an heir's share upon these eventualities occurring was held to be of no effect. In coming to this conclusion, Maasdorp JP referred to and relied upon the rule, as stated by Voet,[13] that the institution of an heir which is left directly at the will of a third person is invalid.[14]

Considerably later, in the case of *Estate Watkins-Pitchford and others* v *CIR*,[15] Van den Heever JA stated the general rule as follows:

> 'The general policy of our law is that a testator must himself make his will and cannot commit the discretion as to who shall be beneficiaries under his will to others. There are a few exceptions such as bequests to *piae causae*, which are deemed to be bequests to the administrators of such funds and the case where a fiduciary is charged with the duty of allocating the bequest at his discretion to one or more persons belonging to a limited class, or allocating the bequest in unequal proportions.'

Although at the time no other member of the court concurred in the judgment of Van den Heever JA, this statement of the rule has been cited with approval in several subsequent cases, including judgments in the Appellate Division.[16] The two exceptions mentioned by Van den Heever JA relate to bequests to *piae causae* and to what are generally termed 'powers of appointment'. In conjunction with the above-quoted statement of the rule in regard to the delegation of testamentary power, the learned judge of appeal also remarked that the rules of our law in regard to powers of appointment granted by will required reconsideration and restatement, and he referred in particular to an unfettered power of appointment, such as was to be found in the case there under consideration.

The purpose of this essay is to examine, in the light of the rule prohibiting the delegation of testamentary power, testamentary powers of appointment and particularly discretionary trusts (and their relationship *inter se*), and to determine as far as possible what

[12] 1912 CPD 87 at 93. [13] *Commentaries* 28.5.29.

[14] See also *Vickers' Trustees* v *Cloete and others* 1914 CPD 575; *Arkell* v *Carter NO and others* 1971 (3) SA 243 (R).

[15] 1955 (2) SA 437 (A) at 458H–459A.

[16] See *Standard Bank of South Africa Ltd NO* v *Betts Brown and others* 1958 (3) SA 713 (N) at 721pr–A; *Estate Orpen* v *Estate Atkinson and others* 1966 (4) SA 589 (A) at 593G–H, 596G; *Ex parte Henderson and another NNO* 1971 (4) SA 549 (D) at 552G–H. See also *Harter* v *Epstein* 1953 (1) SA 287 (A) at 293C–D; *Arkell* v *Carter NO and others* 1971 (3) SA 243 (R) at 245D–H.

Oliver and Edna Schreiner at the front door of their house 'Lyndall' in Lower Houghton, Johannesburg

The Transvaal Bench 1940, 1941 or 1942. *Seated, left to right:* Leopold Greenberg JP, Charles E Barry J, I Grindley-Ferris J. *Standing, left to right:* Philip Millin J, A C

Malan J, Saul Solomon J, Oliver D Schreiner J, G J Maritz J, W H Ramsbottom J, John M Murray J. This magnificently composed photograph was taken by Leon Levson

Pre-World War II Johannesburg Bar Golf Cup Tournament. In centre Oliver Schreiner with Tilson Barry KC. See page 21

(Photograph by courtesy of the *Rand Daily Mail*)

Pre-World War II Johannesburg Bar Golf Cup Tournament. *Left to right:* Oliver Schreiner, B A (Sonny) Ettlinger (later KC), J G N Strauss (later a Cabinet minister in Smuts's ministry and subsequently Leader of the Opposition), Tilson Barry KC. See page 21

limitations the law imposes on the conferment of a discretion upon the grantee of a power and upon a trustee. In doing so I shall endeavour to follow the analytical and teleological approach favoured by the illustrious jurist in whose honour this essay is offered, rather than the historical.[17]

Testamentary Powers of Appointment

Although it is strictly a term of art of English law, the phrase 'power of appointment' has become current in our law to describe, *inter alia*,[18] a provision in a will whereby the testator confers upon a person the power to dispose of his (the testator's) property[19] after his (the testator's) death, either by will or by act *inter vivos*. When the grantee of the power exercises it, he in effect makes a selection of beneficiaries on behalf of the testator, and the selection has the same effect as if the testator had made it in his own will. In fact the selected beneficiaries are regarded as having been instituted by the will of the grantor of the power.[20]

The common-law origins of this power to select beneficiaries on behalf of the testator (*potestas elegendi*) were fully researched by Joubert JA in his concurring judgment in the recent case of *Smit* v *Du Toit*.[21] In addition, the one limitation on the rule against the delegation of testamentary power mentioned by Brunnemann in the above-mentioned passage from his *Commentarius in Leges Pandectarum* would seem to be a terse reference to this *potestas (vel facultas) elegendi*.

An early case in our courts which had reference to a power of appointment was *In re Myburgh*.[22] There the testator had created a trust, directed that the trustees should pay the income derived from the trust property to his daughter, A, and on her death to hold the property in trust for the child or children of A in such shares and in such manner as A should by deed or will appoint. De Villiers CJ had this to say about the power conferred upon A:[23]

> 'Where a testator has conferred on a person, to whom he has bequeathed a limited interest in property, the power of selecting the persons on whom such property shall devolve at the expiration of such limited interest, the due exercise of such power has the same effect as if the

[17] See Ellison Kahn 'Oliver Deneys Schreiner—The Man and his Judicial World' (1980) 97 *SALJ* 566 at 591.

[18] It is also used in conjunction with powers created *inter vivos*.

[19] See, for example, *Westminster Bank Ltd NO and others* v *Zinn NO* 1938 AD 57 at 65; *Estate Watkins-Pitchford and others* v *CIR* 1955 (2) SA 437 (A) at 449–51, 453, 458–9; *CIR* v *Lukin's Estate* 1956 (1) SA 617 (A) at 623; *Estate Orpen* v *Estate Atkinson and others* 1966 (4) SA 589 (A) at 594, 596. Cf *Smit* v *Du Toit en andere* 1981 (3) SA 1249 (A) at 1256H–fine, 1259H–1263; *Ferreira NO* v *Smit NO* 1981 (3) SA 1264 (A) at 1276ff.

[20] *Westminster Bank Ltd NO and others* v *Zinn NO* 1938 AD 57 at 66; *CIR* v *Lukin's Estate* 1956 (1) SA 617 (A) at 623F–G.

[21] 1981 (3) SA 1249 (A) at 1259ff. [22] (1896) 13 SC 218. [23] At 224.

testator had himself made the selection in the will. I am not aware that any cases relating to the exercise of such power have ever arisen in this court, but the practice of conferring such powers on fiduciary heirs and legatees was a common one under the Roman as well as the Dutch law. In support of the proposition which I have stated, I need only refer to *Digest* xxxi. 67, and the *Dutch Consultations*, vol. i., Cons. 165.'

In this formulation of the principle the learned Chief Justice was careful to describe the grantee of the power simply as a person to whom 'a limited interest in property' had been bequeathed. Nevertheless, in 1916 Juta AJA, when delivering one of the judgments of the court in the case of *Union Government (Minister of Finance)* v *Olivier*,[24] stated that a power of appointment granted to an heir to bequeath his portion to one or more of his children as he should think fit could be exercised in our law only by way of a fideicommissum, so that the heir or legatee to whom the power of appointment is given is the fiduciary, and the persons selected by the grantee of the power are the fideicommissaries, under the will of the testator. This statement was cited, apparently with approval, by Curlewis CJ in *Westminster Bank Ltd NO and others* v *Zinn*.[25] Fortunately the *potestas elegendi* was rescued from this fideicommissary strait-jacket by the Appellate Division in *CIR* v *Lukin's Estate*,[26] Centlivres CJ (who delivered the judgment of the court) holding that 'what is commonly known as a power of appointment' can be conferred by will on a beneficiary who is a mere usufructuary. The above-quoted dictum from the judgment of Van den Heever JA in *Estate Watkins-Pitchford and others* v *CIR*[27] must, therefore, be read subject to this. Naturally, in many instances the limited interest enjoyed by the grantee of the power is a fiduciary one in the context of a fideicommissum, but, as *Lukin's* case demonstrates, this need not always be the case.

The conferment of a power of appointment necessarily vests the grantee with a discretion. Normally it is in essence a twofold discretion: (i) whether or not to exercise the power, and (ii) if the power be exercised, how and in whose favour an appointment is to be made. In regard to the latter, the testator often circumscribes the ambit of the discretion by nominating or specifying the potential beneficiaries[28] or by limiting them to a specific class of persons.[29] At the same time the testator may widen the discretion by giving the

[24] 1916 AD 74 at 89–90. [25] 1938 AD 57 at 66.

[26] 1956 (1) SA 617 (A). See also *Estate Orpen* v *Estate Atkinson and others* 1966 (4) SA 589 (A) at 594A–E.

[27] 1955 (2) SA 437 (A) at 458H–459A.

[28] See, for example, *Stanley* v *Botha's Executors* (1900) 17 SC 48; *Estate Smith* v *Estate Gourlay and another* 1935 CPD 161.

[29] See, for example, *In re Myburgh* (1896) 13 SC 218 (the children of the grantee); see also *Ex parte Mulder and others* 1924 TPD 755; *Arkell* v *Carter NO and others* 1971 (3) SA 243 (R) at 247A–D; *Smit* v *Du Toit en andere* 1981 (3) SA 1249 (A); *Ferreira NO* v *Smit NO* 1981 (3) SA 1264 (A).

grantee the power to allocate the property which is subject to the power in such proportions as he may deem fit among the selected or nominated beneficiaries,[30] and also the power, in his discretion, to impose conditions or limitations on the bequests to the beneficiaries.[31] In some instances, however, the power of choice granted is a very wide one indeed. And, bearing in mind that a power of appointment constitutes an exception to the general rule forbidding the delegation of testamentary power, the limits to which a testator can go in conferring a wide power of choice upon the grantee of a power is a moot point and one which has not yet been pertinently and authoritatively settled by our courts.

In *Robertson* v *Robertson's Executors*[32] the testator had bequeathed the residue of his estate to his executors as trustees to pay the income to his widow during her life and directed that after her death they should deal with the residue as his widow 'may by will or otherwise in writing have appointed'. The trustees were given powers to sell or retain and hold the whole or any portion of the residue as they in their discretion deemed fit, it being the testator's expressed intention that his widow should have no control over the property during her lifetime. The widow instituted action, claiming an order of court declaring her to be entitled to the corpus of the residue of the estate and directing the trustees to transfer the capital of the estate to her and to render account to her of their administration of the estate. An exception that the declaration disclosed no cause of action was upheld by the provincial division, and this decision was confirmed on appeal. On the widow's behalf it was contended that the testator had in effect bequeathed her the full *dominium* in the residue and that the provisions of the will withholding from her control of the property should not be allowed to cut this down. The Appellate Division (per Innes ACJ) held that the words of the will withholding control could not be ignored; and, in regard to the contention that in effect the testator had bequeathed full ownership, the court stated (the widow being referred to as 'the plaintiff'):[33]

> 'But that is exactly what he has not done. The naked ownership has been vested in the trustees, subject to the plaintiff's life interest, and the property will in due course be passed on by them to future beneficiaries, not yet ascertained. But, it was urged, the plaintiff has the income for life, she can will away the capital, and she can sell it; therefore she is in effect full owner. Well, her rights of disposition are no doubt extensive; with the interest she could deal as she pleased, and she could contract,

[30] See, for example, *In re Myburgh* (1896) 13 SC 218; *Savory* v *Savory and others* (1903) 24 NLR 315; *CIR* v *Estate Hollard* 1925 TPD 154 at 166.

[31] See, for example, *Lindsay's Estate* v *McBride's Curator and others: In re Cuthbert's Estate* 1939 CPD 426; *Ferreira NO* v *Smit NO* 1981 (3) SA 1264 (A). The power to impose conditions may be implicit: *Ex parte Bowie and another NO* 1955 (2) SA 641 (O) at 644–5.

[32] 1914 AD 503 at 505.

[33] At 507.

for valuable consideration, to allocate the capital after her death to an ascertained third party. . . . But in whatever way the law might allow her to dispose of her future rights to the capital, the will would still prevent her from having present possession and control.'

There are two points of significance to be derived from this decision. The first is that, although the validity of the power of appointment given to the testator's widow does not appear to have been put in issue, the court seems to have proceeded on the supposition that it was valid. Had it been invalid and, therefore, *pro non scripto*, the restrictions placed on the rights of the widow to the corpus would surely have been *nuda praecepta* and consequently no legal impediment to her acquiring full ownership of the property.[34] Secondly, it is to be noted that, although the power of appointment is a wide, general one, there is no provision for a gift over in the event of the grantee failing to exercise the power. The significance of this factor will appear from what I have yet to say about general powers of appointment.[35]

A wide and general power of appointment also came to be considered by the Appellate Division in *Westminster Bank Ltd NO and others* v *Zinn NO*.[36] Here the issue was whether or not the power had been validly and effectively exercised. The testator, Henry Reid, had bequeathed to his son, Courage Reid, a share in his estate, subject to a fideicommissum in favour of Courage's issue, and had further provided that should Courage die without issue it should be lawful for him to bequeath his share in such manner as he might by last will or other testamentary writing direct, and that, failing such will or other testamentary writing, the share was to devolve upon his lawful heirs. The testator was domiciled in South Africa, both when he made his will and when he died. His son, Courage, died domiciled in England without issue and having made a will in England, which was valid according to English law. The question (which arose by way of an exception to a declaration) was whether this will, which made no specific reference to the fideicommissary property or the power of appointment, but contained a general devise of the residue of Courage's estate to trustees on certain trusts, was an effective exercise of the power of appointment. It was conceded that judged by South African law the English will, executed by Courage, was not an effective exercise of the power, but it was argued that English law, and in particular a certain English statute, applied to the interpreta-

[34] Cf *Estate Freedman* v *Freedman and others* 1962 (3) SA 79 (W); *Morley and others* v *Standard Bank Trustees Department* 1970 (4) SA 299 (W).

[35] It is to be noted that a similar decision on similar facts was arrived at (by Watermeyer and Sutton JJ) in the case of *Van Niekerk* v *Van Niekerk's Estate* 1935 CPD 359, to which these two comments are equally applicable.

[36] 1938 AD 57.

tion of the English will; and that in accordance therewith the English will was an effective exercise of the power. The Appellate Division held, however, that the English statute was not applicable and that the power had not been effectively exercised. Again it does not appear from the judgments[37] that the validity of the power of appointment was put in issue; but its validity seems to have been accepted by the court. Thus, Curlewis CJ stated in the course of his judgment that in default of issue Courage[38]

> '. . . had the right to bequeath his share in such manner as he may by last will or other testamentary writing direct, and failing such will his share shall devolve upon his lawful heirs. . . . [I]f he died without issue and bequeathed it [his share] by will to some person or persons, such person or persons would take the property not as his heirs but as heirs of Henry Reid.'

It was also pointed out by Curlewis CJ[39] that our law does not draw a distinction, as does English law, between a 'general' power of appointment and a 'special' power of appointment; and it further appears from his judgment that a general power, in the English sense, whereunder the grantee can exercise it in favour of such person or persons as he pleases, including himself or his executors or administrators, does not have any place in our law. Nevertheless, I would point out that the term 'general power of appointment' is sometimes used in our law to denote the case where the grantee of the power has a wide and unfettered discretion to appoint anyone (other than himself).[40]

Next, I would refer to the case of *Estate Watkins-Pitchford and others* v *CIR*,[41] which also came before the Appellate Division. The case was essentially concerned with the applicability of certain provisions of the Death Duties Act of 1922[42] to the dispositions made under a certain will. In this will the testator bequeathed the residue of his estate to his four children in equal shares. In a codicil, executed three years later, the testator stated that, whereas under his will he had bequeathed the residue of his estate to his four children equally, he now declared it to be his wish and intention, and he instructed his executors and trustees accordingly, that the shares of the residue falling to each of his four children should not be paid out to them, but should be retained and invested by his trustees and the income paid to each of them during their respective

[37] See, however, the remarks of Centlivres CJ in *Estate Watkins-Pitchford and others* v *CIR* 1955 (2) SA 437 (A) at 451H–452A, which are referred to below.

[38] At 68–9. [39] At 66, 70.

[40] *Ladies Christian Home and others* v *SA Association* 1915 CPD 467 at 474; *Van Niekerk* v *Van Niekerk's Estate* 1935 CPD 359 at 362; *Estate Watkins-Pitchford and others* v *CIR* 1955 (2) SA 437 (A) at 450, 451. It is in this sense that I shall use the term when speaking of South African law.

[41] 1955 (2) SA 437 (A). [42] Act 29 of 1922.

lives. He further directed that on the death of each child the trustees were

> 'to dispose of his or her share of the residue held by them on his or her account as he or she by last will and testament shall have provided, power to so dispose being hereby conferred upon him or her, and failing any such disposition in his or her will, to pay the corpus of his or her share to his or her lawful issue and failing lawful issue to his or her next of kin'.

One of the testator's four children, a Mrs Watkins-Pitchford, survived the testator and left a will in which she exercised, in favour of certain nephews and nieces, the power of appointment conferred on her by the testator's codicil. The question which arose was whether the interest held by Mrs Watkins-Pitchford immediately prior to her death under the testator's will was a 'fiduciary interest' or a 'usufructuary or other like interest' in terms of s 3(4) of the Death Duties Act 1922. Two members of the court (Centlivres CJ, with Fagan JA concurring) held the interest to have been a fiduciary one; two (Schreiner JA, with Greenberg JA concurring) held it to have been a usufructuary or other like interest; and the remaining member of the court (Van den Heever JA) held that Mrs Watkins-Pitchford had enjoyed full ownership of her share of the corpus (though administration of it was divorced from the ownership and vested in the trustees) and that the interest was consequently neither a fiduciary one nor a usufructuary or like interest.

In all three judgments reference was made to the validity of the general power of appointment granted by the testator to his children. Centlivres CJ referred to Steyn *The Law of Wills in South Africa*[43] and expressed the view that the learned author correctly stated the law when he said that save in excepted cases the grantee's power of choice must not be unlimited, nor can he have an unfettered discretion. Centlivres CJ also referred to Steyn's treatment of the *Westminster Bank* case as an example of one of the excepted cases, and went on to quote from the appellant's heads of argument in that case. From this it appears that the appellant contended that the fideicommissum in Henry Reid's will failed altogether on Courage Reid's dying without issue; that as there was no fideicommissum there could be no power of disposition given, and hence none could be exercised; and that by his will Courage Reid disposed of what had become his own property inherited from Henry Reid. Centlivres CJ concluded:[44]

> 'In holding that Courage Reid's will had not disposed of the property he inherited under his father's will the court must be taken to have

[43] 2 ed (1948) 319. [44] At 452pr–A.

rejected the view that a general power of appointment, followed by a gift over in case of the non-exercise thereof, is void.'

Schreiner JA also referred to the discussion of the subject of powers of appointment appearing in Steyn on *Wills*, and continued:[45]

> 'The learned author, after saying that, with two exceptions, the grantee of a power of appointment cannot effectively be given an unlimited power of choice or an unfettered discretion, states the two exceptions to be where the testator provides for alternative beneficiaries in the event of non-exercise of the power of appointment, and where he divests the grantee of all control during his or her lifetime. It is unnecessary to consider whether all grants of powers of appointment that do not fall within one or other of these classes are invalid if they purport to give an unlimited power of choice or an unfettered discretion, for the authorities cited by the learned author support the validity of at least these two classes, and the provisions of the codicil bring the power of appointment within each of the classes.'

I have already referred to the remarks of Van den Heever JA in his judgment in this case concerning the need for reconsideration and restatement of the rules in regard to powers of appointment granted by will. His conclusion, namely, that the interest held by Mrs Watkins-Pitchford at the time of her death amounted to full ownership, in effect rendered a consideration of the validity of the power granted in that case unnecessary. As the learned judge of appeal stated:[46]

> 'The conferment of a right already enjoyed is a nullity. It is therefore unnecessary to inquire into the validity *per se* of an unfettered right of appointment, such as we have in this case. I am not aware of any case in South Africa in which a thorough investigation of Roman Dutch authority on the subject has been made and I cannot help but surmise that dicta relating to the subject in our decided cases were unconscious echoes of English precedents.'

Later in his judgment Van den Heever JA described the power as a 'nullity'.[47] As I understand the position, he so held, not because he accepted that a power conceived in such wide terms was necessarily per se invalid, but because the grantee of the power, Mrs Watkins-Pitchford, enjoyed full ownership of the property over which the power had been conferred, and thus the grant of it amounted to the conferment of a right already enjoyed, which was a nullity.

There are two other cases in which wills conferring general powers of appointment were considered by the Appellate Division, namely, *CIR* v *Lukin's Estate*[48] and *Estate Orpen* v *Estate Atkinson*

[45] At 453C–E. [46] At 459pr–B. [47] At 459E.
[48] 1956 (1) SA 617 (A).

and others.[49] *Lukin's* case again raised the issue whether an interest bequeathed by will was a fiduciary one or a usufructuary or other like interest for the purposes of the Death Duties Act 1922. The testator, Sir Henry Lukin, had bequeathed 'the usufruct or income' of the residue and remainder of his estate to his wife for the term of her natural life, 'giving her the right of disposition of the said residue and remainder by will'. There were various further dispositions of the residue in the event of the testator's wife's surviving him and dying without having made a will, and appointing executors and trustees and administrators. The contingency of his wife's surviving him and leaving a will, but not having properly exercised the 'right of disposition', does not appear to have been provided for. In the event, Lady Lukin (who survived the testator) left a will in which she exercised the right of disposition over the residue of the testator's estate. On the issue raised it was held by both the provincial division and the Appellate Division that the interest enjoyed by Lady Lukin immediately prior to her death was, despite the conferment of the power of appointment, a usufructuary or other like interest. The width of the power of appointment did not occasion comment; nor was its validity questioned.

And finally, in *Estate Orpen* v *Estate Atkinson and others*, the question which arose was whether the purported exercise by will of a power of appointment by the grantee of it, where this occurred during the lifetime of the testator and the grantee predeceased the testator, was a valid and effective exercise of the power. The court held that it was not. The will provided that the property subject to the power, which was in favour of the daughter of the testator, an income beneficiary, was to devolve (upon a certain eventuality) on 'such person or persons, and in such shares or proportions as she may by last will and testament or other writing direct'. There was a gift over in the event of the power of appointment not being exercised. In holding that the purported exercise of the power was not valid or effective, the Appellate Division appears to have proceeded on the supposition that had the grantee of the power survived the testator she could have made a valid appointment under the power.

Upon reflection, I think that the following conclusions may be drawn from the five Appellate Division decisions to which I have referred:

(a) In no case has that court been pertinently required to prescribe the general limits to which a testator may go in conferring a discretion on the grantee of a power of appointment; nor has the court done so.

(b) Save in certain excepted cases, the grantee's power of choice must not be unlimited, nor can he have an unfettered discretion. This

[49] 1966 (4) SA 589 (A).

general rule was adopted by both Centlivres CJ and Schreiner JA in the *Watkins-Pitchford* case and since each judgment was concurred in by a fellow judge, this represents the view, albeit perhaps an *obiter* one, of four members of the court.[50]

(c) One such excepted case is where the testator has made provision for a gift over in the event of the grantee of the general power of appointment not exercising his power. In this respect, too, the judgments of Centlivres CJ and Schreiner JA (with their respective concurrences) in the *Watkins-Pitchford* case make common ground. Moreover, in the view of Centlivres CJ the decision of the court in the *Westminster Bank* case is direct authority for this proposition. And the *Estate Orpen* case is a further illustration of a general power, coupled with a gift over, which was apparently accepted as being valid.[51]

(d) Another suggested exception is where the grantee has been divested, during his lifetime, of all control over the property which is subject to the general power of appointment. This was approved by Schreiner JA (Greenberg JA concurring) in the *Watkins-Pitchford* case. It would also seem to be supported by the decision in *Robertson's* case, in which, it will be recalled, the property in question was vested in trustees and the grantee of the power was to have no control of it, but in which there was no gift over. In *Lukin's* case, too, the gift over did not actually cover the contingency of a non-exercise of the power of appointment (where the grantee left a will), but the custody and control of the property in question was vested in trustees.

(e) The two cases mentioned in *(c)* and *(d)* above are not necessarily exhaustive of the exceptions to the general rule stated in *(b)* above. This appears from the judgment of Schreiner JA in the *Watkins-Pitchford* case.

Decisions regarding general powers of appointment in the provincial divisions have also been on a somewhat *ad hoc* basis and do not greatly advance the inquiry as to criteria for validity. Most of them have been referred to above,[52] but brief mention should, perhaps, be made of the cases of *Von Schulein's Executors* v *Biesel's Executors and others*[53] and *Ex parte Bowie and another NO.*[54]

Von Schulein's case is noteworthy in that there was no gift over in the event of a non-exercise of the power of appointment (which was a general one), and the will did not specifically divest the grantee of control, during her lifetime, of the property concerned.

[50] See also *Arkell* v *Carter NO and others* 1971 (3) SA 243 (R) at 245D–H, 247A–D.

[51] See also *McEwan's Estate* v *McEwan's Estate* 1933 CPD 489; *Standard Bank of South Africa* v *Myers and others* 1965 (4) SA 268 (D) at 270F–G, 271H–272pr.

[52] See notes 28, 29, 30, 31 and 40 above.

[53] 1940 CPD 168.

[54] 1955 (2) SA 641 (O).

On the other hand, the court did find that the grantee had merely been bequeathed the use and rents of the property, and that the testator had imposed a fideicommissum over it. A will by the grantee of the power bequeathing her assets to various charities was held, in the particular circumstances, to constitute a valid exercise of the power, and effect was given to it.[55]

In *Bowie's* case the testatrix had bequeathed a farm to her sisters subject to the conditions (i) that on the death of either sister her share should pass over to the survivor and (ii) that the farm should not be sold, and that when the survivor became the owner of it she should also be prohibited from selling or otherwise disposing of it except by will, and the heir or heirs so instituted should be regarded 'as the residuary heir or heirs of the appearer herein'. De Villiers J held that the testatrix had created a valid fideicommissum, with the persons appointed by the will of the last-dying sister as the fideicommissaries. In regard to the consideration that it is not a valid fideicommissum when it is left to the discretion of the fiduciary whether or not to restore it, De Villiers J stated with reference to the facts *in casu*:[56]

> 'This is, therefore, not the case where the testator gave the surviving fiduciary an unlimited discretion to institute heirs or not in the sense that she had a discretion whether she would retain the farm for herself or pass same over to another in her will. She was bound to pass on the farm. The fact that the testatrix did not specifically mention what should happen in the event of the surviving fiduciary not exercising her power of appointment, does not alter the position, because where a power of appointment is not exercised a gift-over in favour of the intestate heirs of the fiduciary is implied (*Handley & others* v *Handley & others*, 1919 NPD 154; Nadaraja *Roman-Dutch Law of Fideicommissa*, pp 80–1).'[57]

It is no easy matter to determine, from the decided cases, the basic rationale for these rules and principles concerning general powers of appointment. Questions that immediately spring to mind are: Why should there be a general rule in our law against the conferment of a general power of appointment? What is the basis, legal and logical, of the two excepted cases mentioned above? Are there any other permissible exceptions? In none of the judgments to which I have referred is there a wide-ranging discussion of these matters. Decisions tend to have been arrived at casuistically. The so-called excepted cases appear to be based on the fact that certain general powers of appointment found to be or accepted as being valid or the general dispositions of which the powers formed part

[55] See also *Ex parte Estate Orford* 1924 EDL 316. [56] At 644A–B.

[57] *Bowie's* case appears to have been in effect overruled by the full bench in the case of *Ex parte Roads* 1978 (4) SA 649 (O); but see the criticism of this latter decision in 1978 *Annual Survey of South African Law* 358–63.

displayed certain characteristic features. Limitations of space preclude a thorough treatment of these problems, but a few brief, and somewhat tentative, observations may be appropriate.

Although the rule against the delegation of testamentary power is sometimes mentioned with reference to the legal limitations upon the conferment of a general power of appointment,[58] I am not sure that this rule, to which the grant of a power of appointment is an admitted exception, actually plays a governing role in fashioning the permitted limits of a general power of appointment. The *ratio*, if any, for these limits may rather have to be sought in the principles governing the types of legal institution in which a general power finds itself placed. These institutions are principally the fideicommissum and the trust. In the case of the fideicommissum, the power is usually conferred on the fiduciary. In the case of the trust, the authorities to which I have so far referred are instances where the power has been conferred on an income beneficiary under the trust.

The excepted case based on the existence of a gift over is peculiarly appropriate to the general power of appointment conferred on a fiduciary, of which the *Westminster Bank* case represents a typical example. A gift over would not appear to be essential to the valid conferment of a special power of appointment, that is, where the fiduciary's power of choice is limited to certain specified beneficiaries or a specific class of persons.[59] Why then should it be essential where the power is general? And why should there be this difference between a special and a general power?

A power of appointment is a form of substitution. A gift over is a further substitution and, if successful, prevents the bequest from failing in the event of the non-exercise of the power. Generally speaking, the grantee is not obliged to exercise the power. In the absence of a gift over and in the event of the power not being exercised, the substitution based on the exercise of the power will fail. But is this sufficient ground for holding that a general power vested in a fiduciary, without a gift over, is invalid *ab initio*? It hardly seems to be. Fideicommissary substitutions, of all kinds, may fail for a variety of reasons (including, for instance, a substitution based on a special power of appointment which fails through want of the exercise of the power), but such failure does not necessarily visit them with initial invalidity.

Another possible, and perhaps more plausible, reason for requiring a gift over in the case of such a general power is the contention that, in the absence of the exercise of the power and of a gift over,

58 See, for example, *Estate Watkins-Pitchford and others* v *CIR* 1955 (2) SA 437 (A) at 458H–459A; *Estate Orpen* v *Estate Atkinson and others* 1966 (4) SA 589 (A) at 596; *Ex parte Henderson and another NNO* 1971 (4) SA 549 (D) at 552.

59 See J Voet *Commentaries* 36.1.29; *Ex parte Mulder and others* 1924 TPD 755; *Loock en 'n ander* v *Steyn NO* 1968 (1) SA 602 (A) at 610.

the property in question would vest in the estate of the grantee as fiduciary.[60] Since the exercise of the power is a matter of discretion, this would then mean that in effect the fiduciary was vested with a discretion whether to pass on the property or not. This is a situation that is contrary to the very nature of a fideicommissum and would result in the fiduciary's being regarded as untrammelled owner of the property.[61] It would be different, so the contention goes, in the case of a special power, for there, on the non-exercise of the power, the nominated beneficiaries or class of beneficiaries from whom the grantee was to make his selection could claim the property by the *fideicommissi petitio*;[62] and thus there could be no question of the fiduciary having, in effect, a discretion whether to pass on the property or not, or being, in effect, untrammelled owner of it. On the other hand, if the reasoning in *Bowie's* case[63] be correct, and the position is that a fiduciary with a general power of appointment is bound to pass on the property, either to the person appointed under the power or, in the event of the non-exercise of the power, to the intestate heirs of the fiduciary by reason of an implied bequest in their favour, then this ground of distinction between special and general powers disappears; and thus the question why there should be a difference between the two of them remains unanswered.

The excepted case, based upon the grantee of the power having been divested, during his lifetime, of all control over the property which is subject to the general power of appointment, seems to have special reference to the case of an income beneficiary under a trust, where *dominium* in the capital of the trust is vested in the trustees, but the income beneficiary has a power of appointment in regard to it. *Robertson's* case would typify this. In such a case a gift over of the capital would apparently not be essential to the validity of the general power.[64] The embracing institution not being a fideicommissum *stricto sensu*, and the grantee not being a fiduciary, the problems just discussed in relation to the rule requiring a gift over in the case of a general power granted to a fiduciary would not necessarily be relevant. It would be contrary to the trust to regard the income beneficiary (grantee of the power) as untrammelled owner of the trust capital. Another possible distinction in this respect (that is, the need for a gift over) between a general power conferred on an income beneficiary under a trust and one conferred

[60] *Ex parte Bowie and another NO* 1955 (2) SA 641 (O).

[61] J Voet *Commentaries* 36.1.29; see, for example, *Pritchard's Trustee* v *Estate Pritchard* 1912 CPD 87 at 96; *Nelson* v *Nelson's Estate and another* 1932 CPD 395; *In re Estate Grayson* 1937 AD 96 at 100; cf *Estate Smith* v *Estate Gourlay and another* 1935 CPD 161.

[62] *Ex parte Mulder and others* 1924 TPD 755 at 758; *Loock en 'n ander* v *Steyn NO* 1968 (1) SA 602 (A) at 610.

[63] See passage quoted above from the judgment, to which note 56 has reference.

[64] *Robertson* v *Robertson's Executors* 1914 AD 503; *Van Niekerk* v *Van Niekerk's Estate* 1935 CPD 359; *Estate Watkins-Pitchford and others* v *CIR* 1955 (2) SA 437 (A) at 453B–E.

on a fiduciary may be that on the non-exercise of the power by the income beneficiary, the capital would vest, not in the estate of the grantee, but in the testator's estate, the disposition having failed. On the other hand, if the true construction of the trust is that upon the death of the grantee without having made an appointment the capital vests in the grantee,[65] then this distinction disappears.

Having regard to these problems, there is much to be said for the view that a general power of appointment is valid, provided that there is no uncertainty as to the grantee's power of selection, irrespective of whether there is a gift over or whether the grantee has been divested, during his lifetime, of all control over the property.[66] The function of the law is to give effect to the wishes of the testator, unless prevented by some rule or law from doing so.[67] Where a testator has conferred upon another a clearly expressed general power of appointment, is there any cogent reason for regarding the grant as *pro non scripto* and thus disregarding the wishes of the testator? It is true that, if the power is not exercised and there is no gift over, then the substitution will fail, but in that event the law will decide how the property is to devolve; and, in any case, as I have said, that may happen in the case of a special power, apparently without there being any question of invalidity. And, looking on the other side of the coin, why in the case where such a general power has been properly exercised by the grantee should the grant of the power be held to be invalid and the selected beneficiaries denied the right to succeed to the property? To do so would certainly frustrate the wishes of the testator; and, incidentally, would seem to be contrary to the decisions in *Von Schulein's* case and *Bowie's* case.

Discretionary Trusts

Trusts are today unquestionably 'an established feature of our legal landscape', to quote the words of Schreiner JA cited in the epigraph to this essay. Many trusts are created by will. In doing so testators often confer wide discretionary powers on the trustees (or administrators),[68] not only as to the administration of the trust assets, but also as to the application of the income and capital of the trust. An example illustrative of this is the case of *CIR and others* v *Sive's Estate.*[69] There the testator bequeathed the residue of his estate

[65] Cf Honoré *The South African Law of Trusts* 2 ed (1976) 417–19.

[66] A view expressed in 1949 by Tambyah Nadaraja *The Roman-Dutch Law of Fideicommissa* (1949) 78–81.

[67] *Robertson* v *Robertson's Executors* 1914 AD 503 at 507; *Harter* v *Epstein* 1953 (1) SA 287 (A) at 293C–D; *Estate Orpen* v *Estate Atkinson and others* 1966 (4) SA 589 (A) at 595C–D.

[68] Although the persons vested with the administration of a testamentary trust are often called 'administrators', I shall for the sake of brevity refer merely to trustees.

[69] 1955 (1) SA 249 (A).

to his children (of whom there were four at the time of his death). This bequest was made subject to a number of provisos, or conditions, as to the distribution of both the capital constituting, and the income derived from, the residue. In regard to the capital, the testator provided that each child would become entitled to a one-fourth of his share of the residue when he attained the age of 32 years and to a further one-fourth on attaining 40 years of age. In regard to the remaining half of the share of the residue to which each child was entitled, the testator left it 'entirely to the discretion' of his administrators to decide whether and, if so, when the whole or any portion of it be paid over to the child entitled thereto. In the event of the death of a child before becoming entitled to his share of the residue, various substitutions were provided for. Similarly, in regard to the income the administrators were given a wide discretion whether to pay to the child concerned the income derived from that portion of his share of the residue not yet paid over to him, and, if so, as to how much of the income to pay over to him. Again substitutions were made in respect of this right to income in the event of the death of a child prior to his receiving the capital. Certain questions arose as to the rights of the executors of a deceased child to claim, under the will of the testator, accrued income from the administrators of the trust and as to the liability of the estate of the deceased child to pay estate and succession duty in terms of the Death Duties Act 1922. In regard to this latter issue there was a difference of opinion on the court, but all members of the court appear to have approached the case on the basis that the dispositions of income were valid and the majority on the basis that the dispositions of capital were valid,[70] despite the wide discretion vested in the administrators.

A trust such as the one exemplified by *Sive's* case is often termed a 'discretionary trust'. This is not a precise term of art, but is used generally to denote a trust under which the trustee is given discretionary powers in regard to the application of the trust income or capital or both.[71] In the case of a discretionary trust the question arises: How far can the testator go in conferring a discretion on the trustee without running foul of the general rule against the delegation of testamentary power or the basic requirements for a validly constituted trust? And in this connection one is prompted to ask: May a trustee be vested with a power of appointment, and, if so, can it be a general power of appointment? In considering these questions I shall leave aside, for the moment, the charitable trust,

[70] On the minority view, which was that the children obtained vested rights to their shares of the residue on the death of the testator, the administrators did not have a power of disposition over the capital. See also 1966 *Annual Survey of South African Law* 240–1 and Ian B Murray (1955) 72 *SALJ* 220–1.

[71] See Honoré op cit note 11 at 10; *Scott on Trusts* 2 ed (1956) 935ff; Pettit op cit note 11 at 25, 92; Parker and Mellows op cit note 11 at 18, 62ff, 81.

which, because it is the result of a bequest *ad piam causam*, receives an especially benevolent treatment at the hands of the law.[72]

In the *Watkins-Pitchford* case Van den Heever JA mentioned only two exceptions to the rule prohibiting the delegation of testamentary power: bequests *ad pias causas* and 'the case where a fiduciary is charged with the duty of allocating the bequest at his discretion to one or more persons belonging to a limited class, or allocating the bequest in unequal proportions'. It is not clear to me whether the learned judge of appeal intended to include within this latter exception the case of a testamentary administrator under a discretionary trust. If not, then it seems that the exception must be widened to include such a case. The validity of such a discretionary trust appears to have been accepted in *Sive's* case, and, in any event, the denial of validity in such a case would, it is suggested, stifle to an unnecessary degree the proper development of our law of trusts. Assuming that the discretionary trust is to be regarded as a recognized exception to the rule concerning the delegation of testamentary power, the question is, as I have indicated, how wide and all-embracing can the discretion be?

Here one immediately encounters the second inhibiting factor—the basic legal requirements for a properly constituted trust. In *Ex parte Executors Estate Kemp*[73] Greenberg J quoted from an old English case, *Cruwys* v *Colman*,[74] a cryptic statement of the requisites of a valid trust: 'sufficient words to raise it; a definite subject; and a certain or ascertained object.' 'Object' in this context was used to denote the persons to be benefited in the case of a personal trust or the objects to be achieved in the case of an impersonal trust.[75] Although the statement speaks of the object being 'certain or ascertained', it would seem to be sufficient if it is 'ascertainable'.[76] Does a trust which leaves the disposition of the trust estate, to a greater or lesser degree, to the discretion of the trustee measure up to the requirements of a valid trust?

Two extreme positions seem to be reasonably clear. A testamentary disposition whereby the testator leaves the residue of his estate 'to the discretion of [his] executors'[77] or whereby property is bequeathed to X 'to distribute as he thinks fit'[78] does not raise a trust. The object is too uncertain, and even the intention to create a trust seems to be lacking. Similarly, a disposition which leaves it to the discretion of trustees whether or not to apply the property entrusted to them to the purposes indicated in the will is also a

[72] *Marks* v *Estate Gluckman* 1946 AD 289 at 297–311. [73] 1940 WLD 26 at 32.

[74] (1804) 9 Ves 319 at 323 (32 ER 626 at 627).

[75] *Standard Bank of South Africa Ltd NO* v *Betts Brown and others* 1958 (3) SA 713 (N) at 720G–H. See also Parker and Mellows op cit note 11 at 56, 60.

[76] Ibid at 720F–G. [77] *Harter* v *Epstein* 1953 (1) SA 287 (A) at 287.

[78] *Arkell* v *Carter NO and others* 1971 (3) SA 243 (R) at 243; *Ex parte Henderson and another NNO* 1971 (4) SA 549 (D) at 554C–E.

nullity.[79] On the other hand, there appears to be no objection to a discretionary trust which, as in *Sive's* case,[80] vests a discretion in the trustee to distribute to or withhold from nominated trust beneficiaries trust income or capital. But what of a trust which purports to give the trustee a power of selection?

In *Ex parte Henderson* it was stated:[81]

> 'The precise limits within which a power of appointment may be validly conferred have perhaps not been finally set in the decisions of our courts but there would appear to be no warrant or authority for holding that the power of appointment, in the sense in which the phrase is used in the decisions to which I have referred above, may be validly conferred upon one who has no beneficial interest in the estate. Any purported conferment of the power upon such a grantee (ie one without beneficial interest) would be invalid and in the absence of other indications in the will as to the destination of the assets concerned, such assets would devolve as on intestacy.'

This would not apply to a testamentary trust for charitable purposes. In the case of such a trust, provided that the objects of the trust are specified or indicated with sufficient clarity, the conferment of a power on the trustees to select suitable beneficiaries within the scope of the testator's general intent is valid.[82] In so far as the powers conferred on a trustee under a discretionary trust, such as that typified by *Sive's* case, may be regarded as powers of appointment, this dictum may also be too widely couched in regard to non-charitable trusts.

As we have seen, our courts have recognized as valid powers of appointment incorporated in trusts and conferred upon trust beneficiaries, even where the powers have been cast in wide terms. Is there any reason in principle why a testamentary trustee should not also be endowed with a power of appointment in the form of a discretion to select beneficiaries from a class, or even generally? And, if the law does not allow the conferment of such a power, the further question which suggests itself is: Why should a trustee under a trust be in a different position in this respect from a fiduciary under a fideicommissum or an income beneficiary under a trust?

In this connection the Anglo-American approach is of more than passing interest and may give some guidance as to the future

[79] *In re Estate Grayson* 1937 AD 96; *Villet's Estate* v *Villet's Estate* 1939 CPD 152 at 155.

[80] See also *Estate Smith* v *Estate Gourlay and another* 1935 CPD 161.

[81] 1971 (4) SA 549 (D) at 552H–553A. Cf *Standard Bank of South Africa Ltd NO* v *Betts Brown and others* 1958 (3) SA 713 (N) at 721A–C. The formulation by De Villiers CJ in *In re Myburgh* (1896) 13 SC 218 at 224 (quoted above) also seems to presuppose the grantee of the power being vested with a beneficial interest in the estate.

[82] *Ex parte Henderson and another NNO* 1971 (4) SA 549 (D) at 553B–D. See also *Standard Bank of South Africa Ltd NO* v *Betts Brown and others* 1958 (3) SA 713 (N); *Ex parte Thomson* 1959 (4) SA 528 (D).

development of our law of trusts in this sphere. English law draws a basic distinction between a power and a trust: a power is discretionary, a trust imperative. One type of power is a power of appointment. A power of appointment may be general or special or intermediate. It is general if it is exercisable in favour of anyone, including the grantee; special if it is exercisable in favour of some or all of a limited class of persons; and intermediate if it is exercisable in favour of anyone, with certain exceptions. In the context of trusts—and by reason of the very nature of a trust—only special and intermediate powers (which exclude the donee himself) appear to be relevant.[83]

In a particular instance it may be a matter of some difficulty to determine whether a power given under a trust is a power of appointment (either special or intermediate) or what is known as a 'trust power'. If it is a power of appointment, then the donee of the power can choose whether to make an appointment or not; and if by the end of the period during which the power can be exercised he has failed to make a valid appointment, the objects of the power (that is, those eligible to benefit by the exercise of the power) can do nothing about it, and the court has no jurisdiction to intervene. A trust power, on the other hand, even though it may import a measure of discretion, must be exercised by the grantee, and, should he fail to do so, the court may be approached by potential beneficiaries for an appropriate order. Whether a particular power granted under a will is a power of appointment or a trust power is a question of intention to be derived from the language of the will.[84] Since the decisions of the House of Lords in *McPhail* v *Doulton*[85] and of the Court of Appeal in *Re Baden's Deed Trusts (No 2)*,[86] which made it clear that where the validity of the power is in issue the same test for certainty must be applied to both powers of appointment and trust powers, the main reason for the distinction between powers of appointment and trust powers lies in the consequences that flow from a failure by the grantee to exercise the power.[87] In a discretionary trust both powers of appointment and trust powers may be found.[88]

Under English law a power of appointment may be conferred upon a trustee. This tends to blur the line of distinction between a power and a trust, for in such a case, though the trustee is not obliged to exercise his power, he is by reason of his fiduciary position under a duty to consider whether and in what way he

[83] Pettit op cit note 11 at 20–1; Parker and Mellows op cit note 11 at 62–3, 65, 74, 98ff.

[84] Pettit op cit note 11 at 22–4; Parker and Mellows op cit note 11 at 65ff.

[85] [1971] AC 424 (HL), [1970] 2 All ER 228.

[86] [1973] Ch 9 (CA), [1972] 2 All ER 1304.

[87] Pettit op cit note 11 at 30; John Hopkins 'Certain Uncertainties of Trusts and Powers' (1971) 29 *Cambridge LJ* 68ff.

[88] Parker and Mellows op cit note 11 at 81.

should exercise the power.[89] In regard to the objects of the power the English courts have recognized as valid both special[90] and intermediate[91] powers of appointment vested in a trustee. It would seem that, provided that there is a valid gift over or trust in default of appointment, a mere or bare power of appointment among a class is valid if one can say with certainty whether any given individual is or is not a member of the class; one does not have to be able to ascertain every member of the class.[92] The case of *In re Manisty's Settlement* illustrates how far the English courts appear to be prepared to go[93] in the recognition of wide discretionary powers of selection vested in a trustee. In that case the settlor had conferred on his trustees power to apply the trust funds for the benefit of a class of beneficiaries, who were all present or future members of his family. Certain persons, including the settlor, his wife and certain other persons referred to as 'the excepted class', were excluded from benefiting under the trust. The settlement empowered the trustees in their discretion to add to the class of beneficiaries any person, corporation or charity, other than a member of the excepted class. Action was instituted to determine whether this power to add to the class of beneficiaries (which power had been exercised by the trustees) was valid or void. The court held that it was valid. Two main arguments against validity were raised: (i) that the power of appointment was invalid because it infringed the principle of non-delegation; and (ii) that it was void for uncertainty. With reference to the former argument, Templeman J said:[94]

> 'The argument based on the principle of non-delegation stems from the proposition that a testator must not delegate to other persons the right to make a will for him. It is, however, established by authority that a testator, and a fortiori a settlor, may create powers of disposition exercisable by individuals or by trustees without thereby infringing any rule against delegation. If delegation is the vice then delegation to an individual is as bad as delegation to a trustee.'

As to the second argument, the court held that, on the authorities, a power cannot be uncertain merely because it is wide in ambit. Nor was the power in the instant case invalid on the ground of vagueness. In the course of his judgment the learned judge remarked:[95]

[89] Pettit op cit note 11 at 30; Parker and Mellows op cit note 11 at 81; John Hopkins in (1971) 29 *Cambridge LJ* 68 at 87.

[90] See *In re Gulbenkian's Settlements [Whishaw* v *Stephens]* [1970] AC 508 (HL), [1968] 3 All ER 785.

[91] *In re Manisty's Settlement* [1974] Ch 17, [1973] 2 All ER 1203.

[92] See *In re Gulbenkian's Settlements [Whishaw* v *Stephens]* [1970] AC 508 (HL) at 521E, [1968] 3 All ER 785 at 790C–D; *Halsbury's Laws of England* 4 ed (1981) vol 36 § 815.

[93] Subsequent history may show that the court went too far in this case. For a critical appraisal of this decision, see John Hopkins in (1974) 33 *Cambridge LJ* 66.

[94] At 21–2, 1206.

[95] At 27A–B, 1211C–D.

> 'Logically, in my judgment, there is no reason to bless a special power which prescribes the ambit of the power by classifying beneficiaries and at the same time to outlaw an intermediate power which prescribes the ambit of the power by classifying excepted persons.'

Templeman J pointed out that a power (or trust power) is valid if it can be said with certainty that any given individual is or is not a member of the class of eligible beneficiaries specified by the trust. This test does not invalidate an intermediate power, provided that, having regard to the definition of excepted persons, it can be said with certainty that any given individual is or is not an object of the power. In the instant case the excepted class was certain and consequently there was no difficulty in establishing who qualified as eligible beneficiaries. It is evident that in England much water has flowed under the bridge since *Cruwys* v *Colman*.[96]

Considerations of space permit only brief reference to American law. It would seem that in the United States a trust for the members of a definite class is valid and enforceable, even though a discretion is given to the trustee (or to another person) to select the member or members of the class who are to take and to determine in what proportions they take.[97] Where, on the other hand, the class is an indefinite one, then the general trend of American authority appears to hold that the trust is unenforceable on grounds of uncertainty. It is suggested, however, that if in such a case the trustee is authorized or directed to convey the trust property to such members of the indefinite class as he may select, then he has the power (though he cannot be compelled) to do this, subject to the rule against perpetuities and provided that the class is not so indefinite that it cannot be ascertained whether any person does or does not fall within it; and that, if he exercises the power, the persons so selected become entitled to the property.[98]

It is not easy to predict how South African courts will react when confronted with issues and problems of this nature. The discretionary trust is an instrument often favoured by testators.[99] It would seem to be sound legal policy to give effect, as far as possible, to the last wishes of a testator; and to refuse to do so only when compelling reasons of policy or legal principle dictate such a course. Recognition of the validity of a testamentary trust under which the trustee is given a discretionary power to select beneficiaries, as to either the income or the capital of the trust, from among the members of a limited and clearly defined class of persons should, it is suggested, present no real problem. As far as the rule prohibiting the delegation of testamentary power is concerned, it is accepted

[96] (1804) 9 Ves 319 (32 ER 626). See reference to this case at note 74 above.

[97] *Restatement of the Law: Trusts 2d* §§ 120, 121; *Scott on Trusts* 2 ed II 836ff; 76 *American Jurisprudence 2d* s v 'Trusts' §§ 135, 140.

[98] *Restatement* op cit previous note at § 122; Scott op cit previous note at 844ff.

[99] And settlors.

that a special power of appointment conferred on a fiduciary or an income beneficiary under a trust constitutes a valid exception to the rule. *Sive's* case would also seem to establish that a testamentary provision under which a trustee is given a discretionary power to distribute or withhold from nominated trust beneficiaries trust income or capital also does not offend against the rule, presumably on the basis that it too is recognized as an exception. In the circumstances there seems to be no compelling reason, either in logic or principle, why a provision in a will conferring on a trustee the power to select either income or capital beneficiaries or both from among the members of a limited and clearly defined class should not also qualify as an exception to the rule.

Nor does there seem to be any reason why such a provision should not be regarded as conforming to the basic requirements of a valid trust. While it would probably be inadvisable and unnecessary to introduce into our law the technicalities and subtleties of English law regarding the distinction between a power of appointment and a trust power, it may be necessary for certain purposes to determine whether a power of selection conferred on a trustee is one in respect of which the trustee is obliged to make a selection (that is, a trust power) or one in respect of which he enjoys a free discretion (that is, a power of appointment *stricto sensu*). In either case the provision for a power of selection from a limited and clearly defined class would pass the test of certainty and otherwise conform to the requirements of a valid trust according to Anglo-American law; and in this regard our courts could safely follow the same course as the English and American courts.[100] While, as Mr Justice Schreiner indicated, the development of our law of trusts should not be unduly hampered by views concerning the possible association of the trust with the fideicommissum, in this instance, I believe, some assistance is to be derived from the analogy of the power of appointment vested in a fiduciary.

When, however, it comes to a power vested in a trustee to select beneficiaries from a wide and indefinite class, our courts may well be chary about following the course pointed to in English law by a case such as *In re Manisty's Settlement*. Consideration may, nevertheless, have to be given to the question whether, even though the conferment of such a power placed no binding obligation on the trustee, the actual exercise of the power by the trustee in favour of an eligible beneficiary should not be legally recognized.

[100] Though where the power of selection is a power of appointment *stricto sensu*, in certain instances it may be necessary for there to be a valid gift over.

REASON AND PREJUDICE: THE COURTS AND LICENSING BODIES IN THE TRANSVAAL

W H B DEAN*

In 1925 a significant change occurred in the law relating to the issue of general dealers' licences in the Transvaal. These licences had previously been issued as a matter of course on payment of a prescribed fee, but the General Dealers (Control) Ordinance of that year[1] required every applicant for such a licence to obtain a certificate from a local authority or rural licensing board,[2] and gave these bodies a discretion to refuse certificates on certain specified grounds.[3] Although the decision on the application for a certificate for a new licence was to be 'final' and not 'liable to review, reversal or alteration by any court of law',[4] refusal to renew a licence was subject to appeal to the Supreme Court,[5] and in such a case the evidence and the reasons for the refusal had to be recorded.[6] That part of the ordinance which dealt with the licensing boards was almost immediately declared *ultra vires*,[7] but, after appropriate enabling legislation had been passed,[8] the whole ordinance was substantially re-enacted in 1926.[9] This was only the beginning, however, for over a period of six years, until the repeal of the latter ordinance,[10] there were at least twenty-seven reported cases in which the ordinances were considered. As a result of these decisions, the grant of the limited right of appeal was also declared *ultra vires*,[11] as was the exclusion of the courts' review jurisdiction.[12]

* BCom LLB (Cape Town) PhD (London), Solicitor (Honours) of the Supreme Court of Judicature (England and Wales), Advocate of the Supreme Court of South Africa, Professor of Public Law in the University of Cape Town.

[1] Ordinance 11 of 1925 (T). [2] Idem s 2(1). [3] Idem s 6.

[4] Idem s 9. [5] Idem s 10.

[6] Idem s 8. Substantially similar rights were given to applicants for new licences by subsequent judicial decision; see text to note 22.

[7] *Said & Co* v *Receiver of Revenue Pietersburg* 1926 TPD 302. The validity of the remainder of the ordinance was upheld in *Lambat* v *Receiver of Revenue* 1926 TPD 520.

[8] Local Government (Provincial Powers) Act 1 of 1926 s 1(1).

[9] Ordinance 12 of 1926 (T). Some of the section numbers were changed—ss 9 and 10 of the 1925 ordinance, for example, became ss 10 and 11 respectively of the 1926 ordinance.

[10] Ordinance 3 of 1932 (T) s 1.

[11] *Moola* v *Potchefstroom Municipality* 1927 TPD 522.

[12] *Bignaar* v *Municipal Council of Rustenburg* 1927 TPD 615. On this somewhat 'curious' result, see the remarks of De Waal JP in *Moola* (*supra*) at 524.

More significantly, having saved their inherent power to review administrative action under the ordinance, the courts proceeded to invalidate the refusal of certificates in almost every reported case[13] and, in the process, to set increasingly high standards for the exercise of the discretion granted.

The background to these cases is, of course, the controversy over the position of Indian immigrants and their descendants in South Africa.[14] The controversy was particularly acute in the period spanned by the life of the ordinances, which almost exactly coincided with the period between the first and second Cape Town Agreements between the South African and Indian Governments that were supposed to solve the 'problem'.[15] It was a period of heightened expectations on both sides, and the resulting tension was increased by growing urbanization and severe economic depression.[16] Racial prejudice against Indians was rampant. The granting of trading licences was a major issue in the controversy.[17] Trading was virtually the only occupation that could be followed by Indians in the Transvaal, and the denial of trading rights was one of the ways of pressurizing Indians to leave the country.[18] The ordinances could, of course, be used to achieve this purpose, and the reported cases are evidence that they were. Not unnaturally, Indian traders turned to the courts for protection.

The cases are, therefore, an example of how South African courts reacted when they were called upon to arbitrate in disputes that were not only emotionally charged, but also of national and international significance. Moreover, in view of the comparative willingness of the courts to set aside the exercise of discretionary powers, the cases also represent an interesting stage in the development of administrative law in South Africa. It is for these reasons that this analysis has been undertaken.[19]

[13] The licensing authority's decision was upheld in only three of the reported cases.

[14] The fullest description of the position of Indians during this period is to be found in P S Joshi *The Tyranny of Colour* (1942; reissued in 1973). See also H Chattopadhyaya *Indians in South Africa, A Socio-Economic Study* (1970) and S B Mukherji *Indian Minority in South Africa* (1959).

[15] The terms of the first Cape Town Agreement are fully set out in Chattopadhyaya op cit 212–15.

[16] For a general perspective on these issues, see David Welsh 'The Growth of the Towns' in Monica Wilson and Leonard Thompson (eds) *The Oxford History of South Africa* II (1971) ch IV.

[17] The first Cape Town Agreement dealt expressly with trading licences, the South African Government undertaking to give 'all due consideration to the suggestion made by the Government of India delegation to limit the power of local authorities to refuse licences' (Chattopadhyaya op cit 215).

[18] See the remarks by J H Hofmeyr, Tielman Roos and D F Malan quoted in Joshi op cit note 14 at 113, 119 and 138 respectively.

[19] The topic also appeared to me to be appropriate for inclusion in a series of essays in honour of the late Mr Justice Schreiner, not only because he appeared as junior counsel in two of the cases, but also because the approach adopted by the courts seems to reflect his own views and to underlie the decision in *Pretoria North Town Council* v *A1 Electric Ice-cream Factory (Pty) Ltd* 1953 (3) SA 1 (A).

The reported cases on the 1925 ordinance were principally concerned with its validity[20] and with procedural matters,[21] the most significant decision being to the effect that even where a new licence was being sought, the applicant had to be informed of any objections and given an opportunity to make representations.[22] This put him in a substantially similar position to the applicant for renewal of an existing licence.

Under the 1926 ordinance the courts became more concerned with the basis on which certificates were refused. The principal ground for refusal was that the 'locality of the premises [was] not one in which it [was] desirable that the business contemplated should be carried on by the applicant or at all'.[23] This provision was used in a variety of ways. It was argued, for example, that the locality was primarily residential, that the existing businesses were of a 'better class' than the one proposed and that there were already sufficient traders in the locality. The latter argument was rejected outright, the courts holding that the authorities had no power 'to restrict trade in such a manner as would have the effect of virtually granting a monopoly to certain traders in certain areas'.[24] The other arguments were treated in a more pragmatic fashion, the courts deciding whether, on the evidence available, the conclusion was justified.[25] The impression gained from the cases is one of judicial scepticism, Tindall J remarking in one case: 'There seems to me no justification for the main street in Wolmaransstad laying claim to an exclusiveness which is not found in the main streets of similar villages in the Transvaal.'[26]

Although racial prejudice was clearly an underlying factor in most of these cases, the racial character of many of the objections and refusals became more obvious after the decision in *Kroomer* v *Johannesburg Municipality*.[27] There the court held that the fact that a business would attract African custom could properly be taken into account in deciding whether that business was 'desirable' in a

[20] Note 7 above.

[21] *Ahmed Mohamed & Co* v *Balfour Village Council* 1926 TPD 235; *Hassan & Co* v *Potchefstroom Municipality* 1926 TPD 699; and *Nanabhay* v *Potchefstroom Municipality* 1926 TPD 483.

[22] *Nanabhay* (*supra*) at 491–4. The same was held to be true under the 1926 ordinance: *Bignaar* (*supra* n 12) at 619.

[23] Section 6(2).

[24] *Dangor* v *Ermelo Rural Licensing Board* 1927 TPD 795 at 799, which was applied in *Nathoo* v *Lydenburg Rural Licensing Board* 1927 TPD 922, *Dungarshi Morajee & Co* v *Zoutspansberg Rural Licensing Board* 1927 TPD 987 and *Nanabhay* v *Municipal Council of Johannesburg* 1928 WLD 153. The racist character of the objections in these cases is clear from the evidence in *Dungarshi* at 990. An amendment to the ordinance in 1927 (s 4 of the General Dealers (Control) Amendment Ordinance 10 of 1927 (T)) allowed this argument to be made where the application related to a 'kaffir eating house or native restaurant'.

[25] *Tala* v *Village Council of Wolmaransstad* 1927 TPD 425. The same approach is apparent in *Nathoo*, *Dungarshi* and *Nanabhay* v *Municipal Council of Johannesburg* (*supra*).

[26] *Tala* (*supra*) at 432. This was an appeal under s 11 of Ord 12 of 1926 before it was declared *ultra vires*.

[27] 1928 TPD 69.

particular locality where Whites resided or whether it would cause a 'nuisance or annoyance to persons residing in the neighbourhood'.[28] The courts applied this approach in two cases,[29] but in others were more critical, scrutinizing very carefully both the evidence given and the inferences drawn from it. Thus in *City Council of Johannesburg* v *Turf Stores (Pty) Ltd*[30] the court held that no reasonable man would infer that a business would cause 'natives' to 'congregate' merely because it was owned by an 'Asiatic'. In *Moosa and Sidat* v *Town Council of Springs*[31] the court held that the evidence established only that 'Asiatic' traders, unlike their White counterparts, did not take it upon themselves to disperse Africans 'who had congregated' around their shops. As this had nothing to do with the nature of the business, and as the control of pedestrians was a matter for the police, a refusal on the ground that the business would be 'undesirable' in the locality was set aside. In *Fakir and Son* v *City Council of Johannesburg*,[32] although there was evidence that Africans 'congregated' around the applicant's shop, the court found that this state of affairs was 'too remotely connected with the carrying on of the business to be a nuisance or annoyance within the meaning of the subsection'.

The decisions reveal a curious contradiction in the attitude of the judges. On the one hand, the legislation was strictly construed, normally in a way which would favour the applicant who had been unsuccessful, and it is quite clear that, although reluctant to recognize explicit racism,[33] the courts were not prepared to tolerate decisions based purely on the applicant's race: 'the mere fact . . . that [the applicant] is an Asiatic cannot affect the question. . . . No doubt the committee was acting in what it considered to be the best interests of the locality in an endeavour to prevent commercial penetration by Asiatics as a class but this object cannot be attained under the provisions of the Ordinance.'[34] On the other hand, even these remarks are somewhat ambiguous, implying a tolerance for the committee's endeavours. Such apparent tolerance of racial prejudice is also evident in the approach adopted in *Kroomer*.[35] It is clear, however, that it had its limits. It did not extend to the

[28] Under s 6(*b*) of the 1926 ordinance.

[29] *Pitts* v *Municipal Council of Johannesburg* 1929 WLD 33 (in which the refusal of the certificate was upheld) and *Patel* v *Witbank Town Council* 1931 TPD 284 (in which the refusal was set aside for another reason—that a ground which substantially influenced the committee concerned to refuse the certificate was, as Tindall J put it, 'so fantastic' as to suggest sheer rationalization).

[30] 1930 TPD 593.

[31] 1930 WLD 48.

[32] 1932 TPD 233 at 241.

[33] Even where racial prejudice was expressly alleged, the courts tended to decide the issue on other grounds; see, for example, *Ahmed Mohamed* (*supra* n 21) at 240.

[34] Per Greenberg J in *Nanabhay* v *Municipal Council of Johannesburg* 1928 WLD 153 at 157–8.

[35] 1928 TPD 69. The needs of African customers received no attention in the reported judgments, although the issue was obviously relevant (see the evidence on this point in *Dungarshi* (*supra* n 24) at 990).

'grosser' forms of discrimination—such as the arrogant assumption by White shopkeepers of the 'right' to disperse African pedestrians.[36] Nor did it extend to unfounded generalizations about the personal qualities of individual members of racial groups. The courts were apparently not prepared to think in terms of crude racial stereotypes:

> 'The evidence amounts to this that no matter what class of business the Asiatic trader carries on, . . . the result is to cause a congregation of natives outside the place of business. No reasonable man could attach any importance to such evidence. A reasonable man would realize that such evidence, on the face of it, does not justify any inference.'[37]

If there was evidence, however, the courts would not reject it simply because of its racial character:

> '. . . if it were proved that all Asiatics indulged in some objectionable custom which made their presence in a certain locality a nuisance, the inference might be drawn that a particular Asiatic's presence would be a nuisance. The difficulty, of course, is to establish your major premise. . . .'[38]

The apparent tolerance for racial prejudice also did not extend to the acceptance of reasons that were either irrelevant or had no real foundation in the evidence. Wolmaransstad was not allowed to claim an exclusiveness which it did not possess.

This qualified rejection of racism is not only consistent with the case law in general,[39] but also seems to reflect the basic tenets of the then current 'liberal' approach to racial prejudice, which emphasized the danger of thinking in stereotypes and the counter-productive character of frontal attacks on prejudice and, above all, saw a solution to the whole problem in an appeal to reason.[40]

It is this emphasis on reasoned decision-making that makes the cases of interest to the administrative lawyer. Relying principally upon his own decisions in the pre-Union Transvaal,[41] Sir James Rose Innes had, in decisions such as *Shidiack* v *Union Government*,

[36] *Moosa and Sidat* (*supra* n 31) at 52–3 and 55. In *Mphahlehle* v *Springs Municipality* 1928 TPD 50 the court held a by-law prohibiting 'natives' from using pavements void as being discriminatory (cf *Zackey* v *Boksburg Municipality* 1930 TPD 211).

[37] *City Council of Johannesburg* v *Turf Stores (Pty) Ltd* 1930 TPD 593 at 598.

[38] Idem at 597.

[39] For example, see *Williams & Adendorff* v *Johannesburg Municipality* 1915 TPD 106 at 117, 122–3 and 127–8. Unqualified statements of principle that differentiation on the grounds of race was per se unreasonable and invalid have to be treated with caution.

[40] See, for example, R F A Hoernlé 'On the Future of the Native Peoples in South Africa' in I D MacCrone (ed) *Race and Reason* (1945) 111, which reproduces a paper delivered in 1937. That this was the attitude of the eleven or so judges involved in these cases would be pure speculation. Although some of the same techniques are apparent in these cases as were used by nineteenth-century American judges who were called upon to apply the Fugitive Slave Law (Robert M Cover *Justice Accused* (1975)), the present writer finds it difficult to draw any conclusions from them.

[41] For example, *Judes* v *District Registrar of Mining Rights, Krugersdorp* 1907 TS 1046 at 1051.

Minister of the Interior,[42] set honesty rather than rationality as the standard by which the proper exercise of discretionary powers was to be determined by the courts. Under this standard, apart from cases where there was evidence of mala fides, a decision taken in the exercise of a discretionary power would not be set aside unless the court was satisfied that there was no conceivable reason (however unpersuasive) to support it. The fact that the decision was in part based on irrelevant considerations or that the process of reasoning by which it was reached was in some way defective could not affect its validity.[43] In short, a decision would not be set aside simply because no reasonable man would have reached it. As Krause J pointed out in *City Council of Johannesburg* v *Turf Stores (Pty) Ltd*,[44] an official's decision may be totally prejudiced and yet bona fide. On the *Shidiack* approach, such a decision, because it was bona fide, would be valid. There is some evidence[45] to suggest that by the mid-nineteen-twenties the Appellate Division was beginning to have doubts about this approach. Thus in *Crown Mines Ltd* v *Commissioner for Inland Revenue*[46] Innes CJ himself observed that 'if the facts were so clear that no reasonable man could doubt that there had been an excess payment of tax, that . . . might go to show . . . that [the Commissioner] had not really applied his mind to the point'. Although guarded, this change of emphasis began to make itself felt in decisions in the lower courts. The cases on the ordinance are a good example. Even though some of these decisions can be explained in terms which are consistent with the *Shidiack* approach, it is quite clear that they involved a judicial scrutiny of the evidence on and the process of reasoning by which the decision had been reached which was inconsistent with the 'honesty standard'. The clearest expression of the change is to be found in the following passage from the judgment of Tindall AJP in *City Council of Johannesburg* v *Turf Stores (Pty) Ltd*:[47]

> 'It is clear, of course, that the grounds on which the courts are entitled to interfere with the decisions of administrative bodies . . . are limited. . . . Mr Taylor . . . contended that . . . if it is shown that the body . . . based its conclusion on evidence of such a nature, that no reasonable man could have come to that conclusion . . ., it could be said that the committee did not really consider the application. . . . The remarks of Rose Innes, C.J., in . . . *Crown Mines* . . . lend colour to that view.'

[42] 1912 AD 642.

[43] See, for example, the judgment of Stratford JA in *Union Government (Minister of Mines and Industries)* v *Union Steel Corporation (South Africa) Ltd* 1928 AD 220 at 236–7. 'The law does not protect the subject against the merely foolish exercise of a discretion by an official, however much the subject suffers thereby': per Schreiner JA in *Sinovich* v *Hercules Municipal Council* 1946 AD 783 at 802–3.

[44] 1930 TPD 593 at 598.

[45] See, for example, *Britten* v *Pope* 1916 AD 150 at 167; *Crown Mines Ltd* v *Commissioner for Inland Revenue* 1922 AD 91 at 101; and the dissenting judgments of Innes CJ and Kotzé JA in *R* v *Padsha* 1923 AD 281.

[46] 1922 AD 91 at 102.

[47] 1930 TPD 593 at 596–7.

The law was in a state of flux, and Tindall AJP did not find it necessary to determine the correctness of this contention. That the courts were moving in a new direction is clear from *Patel* v *Witbank Town Council*,[48] where the refusal of a certificate was expressly set aside on the ground that the committee had been substantially 'influenced by a consideration which ought not to have weighed with it'. This is in striking contrast to the decision in *Commissioner for Inland Revenue* v *City Deep Ltd*,[49] where, on the *Shidiack* approach, it had been held that as long as the official 'honestly [held] the view he [did] . . . the fact that he [might] have been, or [had been] influenced by other considerations, some of which might not have been proper for the exercise of his discretion, [did] not matter'.

In part, this trend towards looking more closely at the process of reasoning followed in exercising a discretionary power can no doubt be explained by the nature of the ordinances, which not only granted limited discretion, but also ensured that the evidence, and in the case of a refusal, the reasons for the decision were available to the court.[50] This cannot be the whole answer, however, for in principle the courts treated the powers with the restraint normally accorded to discretionary powers,[51] and it is clear from *Patel* that the standards for the proper exercise of such powers were gradually being raised.

This trend came to an abrupt halt in 1932 with the repeal of the 1926 ordinance. No grounds for the decision to grant or refuse the certificate were stipulated in the new ordinance. In *Jooma* v *Lydenburg Rural Licensing Board*[52] a full bench held that not only was the licensing authority no longer obliged to give reasons for its decisions, but also that it was not even required to disclose the prejudicial evidence on which they might be based. 'The passage of the Licence Control Ordinance spelt the victory of the Transvaal municipalities',[53] and the courts were aware of this. As Tindall J admitted in *Jooma*:[54]

> 'It is of course, generally speaking, impossible for an applicant to make out a . . . case if the board cannot be compelled to disclose its grounds

[48] 1931 TPD 284 at 290–1.

[49] 1924 AD 298 at 307. Some feeling for the difference in emphasis can be gained from comparing the approach adopted by the majority in *Padsha* (*supra* n 45) with that adopted in *Turf Stores* (*supra* n 47) to inferences of personal qualities to be drawn from racial characteristics.

[50] The honesty standard had been adopted in the Cape under legislation which more closely resembled the 1932 ordinance, but this was under the influence of *Shidiack*: see *Perbhoo* v *King William's Town Municipality* 1915 CPD 137 and *Jaffer* v *Wynberg Municipality* 1915 CPD 155, the latter being cited in *Jooma* v *Lydenburg Rural Licensing Board* (*infra* n 52 and the text thereto).

[51] See, for example, *Pitts* (*supra* n 29) at 36–7. The *Shidiack* approach could be applied even where the statute specified the grounds on which the discretion was to be exercised: *Farah* v *Johannesburg Municipality* 1928 TPD 169 at 177–8.

[52] 1933 TPD 477.

[53] Joshi op cit 192.

[54] *Supra* note 52 at 486.

of refusal; but this difficulty . . . is due to the effect of the legislation which confers an absolute discretion on the board. The court is not concerned with the wisdom of this legislation and must give effect to its necessary implications.'

Notwithstanding this disclaimer, there is some evidence that the judiciary, more particularly the Appellate Division, was not altogether reluctant to abandon judicial intervention between what were apparently irrevocably opposed forces. In *Feinstein* v *Baleta*,[55] for example, Roos JA said that it was 'fortunate' that the courts were not required to investigate the reasons for decisions by administrative agencies. In *Sachs* v *Minister of Justice*[56] Stratford ACJ reaffirmed the *Shidiack* approach in terms that showed clear disapproval of the trend which had manifested itself in the lower courts.

It is not without significance that *Jooma* was overruled in part by the Appellate Division in *Pretoria North Town Council* v *A1 Electric Ice-cream Factory (Pty) Ltd*.[57] In a unanimous judgment delivered by Schreiner JA, the court held that, notwithstanding the 'absolute' character of the discretion granted by the 1932 ordinance, it had to be exercised 'according to the rules of reason and justice', and there was thus an obligation to disclose any adverse information on which a refusal might be based. This reassertion of rationality is not the only similarity between the period covered by the life of the ordinances and the early nineteen-fifties. Both saw an intensification of the policy of apartheid and a significant challenge to that policy in the courts. In both cases it became obvious that electoral support for the policy amongst the White electorate would continue, and a judicial withdrawal followed.[58] There are also striking similarities between the approach adopted by the courts in both periods. The broader issues surrounding the litigation arising under the ordinances are hardly apparent from the reported cases. With one or two rare exceptions,[59] the obvious bias of the authorities was ignored.[60] Much the same is true of allegations of racism. Yet the challenge, for as long as it lasted, was apparently effective. Cer-

[55] 1930 AD 319 at 326. The reason given for this view was that such an approach was bound to produce inconsistencies and anomalies.

[56] 1934 AD 11 at 37. The judgment contains this significant sentence: '*In this division, at all events*, no decision affirms the right of a court to interfere with the honest exercise of a duly conferred discretion' (my emphasis).

[57] 1953 (3) SA 1 (A).

[58] On the early nineteen-fifties, see John Dugard *Human Rights and the South African Legal Order* (1978) 316–19 and 328–32.

[59] Joshi (op cit 192) claims that one of the exceptions (viz remarks by Krause J in *Bitcon* v *City Council of Johannesburg and Arenow Behrman & Co* 1931 WLD 273 at 297) so offended those involved in local government that it was the direct cause of the repeal of the 1926 ordinance.

[60] Indeed, on the assumption that the courts could 'only trust that the members of local bodies [would] act conscientiously and . . . not for the purpose of discriminating unfairly on the grounds of colour or class' (*Lambat* v *Reciever of Revenue* 1926 TPD 520 at 526), applications were regularly referred back for reconsideration by the licensing authority rather than disposed of by the court itself.

tainly the Indian community saw judicial intervention as its one protection in an otherwise hostile environment.[61] The instruments employed by the courts were the technical tools of the lawyer's trade, in particular careful analysis of statutory language, an even more careful scrutiny of the evidence, and, above all, an examination of the rational basis for the decisions reached to expose the fallacies almost inevitably inherent in the arguments based on sheer prejudice. Although the decisions broke new ground and generally favoured the Indian traders, they could hardly be faulted for technical reasons or support a charge of partiality.

This technique has been criticized principally on the ground that it often obscures the real (moral) issues or, worse still, that it allows the judiciary (consciously or not) to avoid these issues or to decide them without appearing to do so.[62] The validity of such criticism should not lead one to ignore the essential value of the technique as a method of exposing prejudice while at the same time protecting the legal process from both internal[63] and external threats,[64] thus preserving its integrity as a whole for the future in circumstances in which its essential character and even its very existence may be in danger.[65]

The litigation under the 1925 and 1926 ordinances is at bottom an illustration of the relationship between reason and prejudice in the legal process. Legal systems and lawyers' reasoning operate within and assume the existence of a system of values. There is sometimes a tendency to assume that the former are almost wholly subordinate to the latter. The litigation considered in this article, it is submitted, shows that the relationship is not entirely one-sided. Lawyers' reasoning cannot be dismissed as mere rationalization used to justify predetermined conclusions. To treat it as such may simply make it easier to substitute one form of prejudice for another. The

[61] Representations on behalf of the Indian community consistently called for limitations of the kind that would require reasons to be given for decisions and provide for 'appeal' to the courts (Joshi op cit 128, 134 and 163–4).

[62] For criticism of this kind bearing on the South African situation in particular, see Edward McWhinney 'The Union Parliament, the Supreme Court, and the "Entrenched Clauses" of the South Africa Act' (1952) 30 *Canadian Bar Rev* 692 at 713–18; John Dugard 'The Judicial Process, Positivism and Civil Liberty' (1971) 88 *SALJ* 181 and *Human Rights and the South African Legal Order* ch 11; and Antony S Mathews *Law, Order and Liberty in South Africa* (1971) 301.

[63] On the value of these techniques as limiting the discretion of the judges, see Lord Devlin 'Judges and Lawmakers' (1976) 39 *Modern LR* 1, especially at 11. Is it not surprising, having regard to the personal background of the members of the South African Bench, that the judiciary has so often adopted views inconsistent with the current mainstream of public thinking in South Africa, and could this not be due (in part, at least) to the restraints imposed by the traditional techniques of lawyering rather than the 'values' espoused by individual judges?

[64] Although there is no suggestion of any attempt to 'pack' the Bench in the period under discussion, such a threat became real, and, in the view of some, a reality in the nineteen-fifties.

[65] Most critics make little attempt to discuss these issues, although they are obviously aware of them; see, for example, Edward McWhinney *Judicial Review* 4 ed (1969) 121–2.

legal process (with its emphasis on rational analysis and individual cases) is structurally inconsistent with ideological commitment. This does not mean that lawyers should be unconcerned with morality, but that rational analysis, by exposing injustice, has the potential for developing and changing values and, in particular, can be an effective weapon against prejudice. Had the dice been less heavily loaded,[66] the outcome of the litigation under discussion might have been significantly different.[67]

The truly remarkable feature of the whole episode is perhaps that twenty years later the South African courts were willing and able to try yet again, against even greater odds. The late Mr Justice Schreiner's role in that effort is well known, and it is to the memory of a man who, above all, was a champion of reason against prejudice, that this article is humbly dedicated.

[66] Robert A Dahl *Pluralist Democracy in the United States* (1967) 157, after reviewing the performance of the United States Supreme Court, concludes that that court 'would be least successful in blocking a determined and persistent law making majority on a major policy'. There is a useful analysis of the political environment within which the American Supreme Court operates in Dahl's *Democracy in the United States: Promise and Performance* (1972) ch 16.

[67] An article of this kind cannot even begin either to assess the role played by the South African judiciary in the political process or to deal with the question whether it is possible for a judicial process as conceived in the Western tradition to continue to function effectively (*whatever view is taken of the proper role of the judiciary*) in a legal system large parts of which are inherently unjust—an issue highlighted by the recent decision of the Appellate Division in *S* v *Adams; S* v *Werner* 1981 (1) SA 187 (A). This article is concerned only to illustrate the use and assert the value of traditional legal techniques both in the achievement of justice and the maintenance of the judicial process.

INTERNATIONAL HUMAN-RIGHTS NORMS IN DOMESTIC COURTS: CAN SOUTH AFRICA LEARN FROM BRITAIN AND THE UNITED STATES?

JOHN DUGARD*

The application of international human-rights norms by domestic courts largely postdates the judicial career of Oliver Deneys Schreiner. Oliver Schreiner did, however, in his judicial office and in his public life—particularly in his important contribution to the work of the South African Institute of Race Relations—display a deep concern for human rights.[1] Similarly, he was greatly interested in the international order, as shown by his active support for the activities of the South African Institute of International Affairs. An examination of the manner in which domestic courts in other countries have applied international human-rights norms and a discussion of the prospects for such a development in South Africa is therefore, it is believed, not an inappropriate subject for an essay that seeks to pay tribute to the memory of a great judge and a true South African.

In Britain and the United States, in particular, domestic courts have in recent times started to apply international human-rights norms in the interstices of municipal law. In South Africa an attempt was made in *S* v *Werner*[2] to persuade the Appellate Division to interpret the Group Areas Act[3] in the light of South Africa's obligations under the Charter of the United Nations, but the court failed to pay serious attention to the argument. Despite this setback, it is believed that South African courts might well learn from the experience of their British and American counterparts.

Together, the United States, Britain and South Africa present an interesting paradigm, for, despite the fact that South Africa is the

* BA LLB (Stell) LLB Diploma in International Law LLD (Cantab), Advocate of the Supreme Court of South Africa, Professor of Law in and Director of the Centre for Applied Legal Studies at the University of the Witwatersrand, Johannesburg.

[1] For an examination of Schreiner JA's decisions on human rights, see John Dugard *Human Rights and the South African Legal Order* (1978) 464 (index references).

[2] Reported in *S* v *Adams; S* v *Werner* 1981 (1) SA 187 (A).

[3] Act 36 of 1966.

odd man out in its general attitude towards human rights, the legal systems of the three countries have certain features in common. First, they share a common-law tradition; secondly, all three have a judiciary, with security of tenure, not drawn from the ranks of the bureaucracy; thirdly, their legal systems display a common approach to the relationship between municipal law and customary international law and to the domestic relevance of the human-rights provisions of the Charter of the United Nations.

The final assertion probably requires elaboration. The courts of all three countries have accepted the doctrine of incorporation and will ascertain and administer the appropriate rule of customary international law, except where it conflicts with a statutory provision.[4] The position of treaties in municipal law does, however, differ fundamentally. In both Britain and South Africa a treaty requires an act of legislative incorporation before it forms part of municipal law,[5] while in the United States art VI of the Constitution makes treaties part of 'the supreme Law of the Land' without the necessity for any statutory incorporation—*except where the treaty is judged by the courts to be non-self-executing.*[6] The Charter of the United Nations has not been incorporated by Act of Parliament into either the law of the United Kingdom or that of South Africa. In the United States certain provisions of the Charter have been held to be self-executing,[7] but the human-rights provisions have been found to be not self-executing by several courts,[8] although the Supreme Court itself has yet to pronounce on this issue. Consequently all three legal systems view the human-rights provisions of the United Nations Charter as binding on the international plane only.[9] Neither the United States nor South Africa has ratified any other major international human-rights convention. Britain, on the other hand, has signed and ratified both the European Convention

[4] *The Paquete Habana* 175 US 677 at 700 (1900); *Trendtex Trading Corporation Ltd* v *Central Bank of Nigeria* [1977] QB 529 (CA), [1977] 1 All ER 881; *Nduli* v *Minister of Justice* 1978 (1) SA 893 (A) at 906.

[5] *Republic of Italy* v *Hambros Bank Ltd* [1950] Ch 314, [1950] 1 All ER 430; *The Parlement Belge* (1879) 4 PD 129 at 154–5; *Pan American World Airways Inc* v *SA Fire and Accident Insurance Co Ltd* 1965 (3) SA 150 (A) at 161.

[6] *Foster* v *Neilson* 27 US (2 Pet) 253 at 314 (1829). See, further, Stefan Riesenfeld 'The Doctrine of Self-Executing Treaties and US v Postal: Win at Any Price?' (1980) 74 *American J of International Law* 892.

[7] For example, art 104, concerning the legal capacity of the United Nations: *Curran* v *City of New York* 191 Misc 299, 77 NYS 2d 206 (Sup Ct 1947).

[8] *Sei Fujii* v *State* 38 Cal 2d 718, 242 P 2d 617 (1952); *Hitai* v *Immigration and Naturalization Service* 343 F 2d 466 (2d Cir 1965).

[9] For many years there was some dispute over the question of the legal effect of the human-rights clauses in the Charter (notably arts 55 and 56). In 1971, however, the International Court of Justice confirmed that these provisions are legally binding on states: see its advisory opinion in *Legal Consequences for States of the Continued Presence of South Africa in Namibia (South West Africa) notwithstanding Security Council Resolution 276 (1970)* 1971 ICJ Reports 16.

on Human Rights and the International Covenant on Civil and Political Rights, but as these conventions have not been translated into municipal law by Act of Parliament, they are binding on the international level only.[10]

The United Kingdom

In the United Kingdom a court may invoke an unincorporated treaty in order to interpret legislation enacted *subsequent* to the treaty. The rationale for this rule is that Parliament is presumed to intend to legislate in accordance with, and not contrary to, its international obligations. Thus 'if one of the meanings which can reasonably be ascribed to the legislation is consonant with the treaty obligations and another or others are not, the meaning which is consonant is to be preferred'.[11] Acting in accordance with this principle, British courts have in recent years invoked unincorporated treaties such as the United Nations Charter and, particularly, the European Convention on Human Rights, as an aid to the interpretation of ambiguous statutes affecting fundamental rights.[12]

In 1974, in *Waddington* v *Miah*,[13] the House of Lords held that certain words of a provision in the 1971 Immigration Act were ambiguous and that the penal provision in the legislation in question should not be given retrospective effect. In reaching this conclusion, Lord Reid referred to the prohibition on retrospective legislation contained in art 7 of the European Convention on Human Rights and, after so doing, stated 'so it is hardly credible that any government department would promote or that Parliament would pass retrospective criminal legislation'.[14]

For a more comprehensive discussion of this issue, see John Dugard 'The Human Rights Clauses in the United Nations Charter and South African Law' (1980) 13 *De Jure* 297 at 297–8.

[10] Britain is, in addition, a party to the treaty establishing the European Economic Community, which confers several rights on individuals. For example, art 119 provides that men and women should receive equal pay for equal work. The European Community Act 1972 provides for the incorporation of certain articles of the treaty into the municipal law of the United Kingdom. See D Lasok and J W Bridge *An Introduction to the Law and Institutions of the European Communities* (1973) 220; *Amies* v *Inner London Education Authority* [1977] 2 All ER 100 (EAT) at 103; *Charles Early & Marriott (Witney) Ltd* v *Smith*; *Snoxell* v *Vauxhall Motors Ltd* [1978] QB 11 (EAT) at 33, [1977] 3 All ER 770 at 782; *O'Brien* v *Sim-Chem Ltd* [1980] 2 All ER 307 (CA) at 316, [1980] 1 WLR 734 at 745. As this treaty enjoys a special status in municipal law, thereby distinguishing it from the human-rights conventions, no further reference will be made to it.

[11] *Salomon* v *Commissioners of Customs and Excise* [1967] 2 QB 116 (CA) at 143, [1966] 3 All ER 871 at 875, per Diplock LJ. See too *Post Office* v *Estuary Radio* [1968] 2 QB 740 (CA) at 757, [1967] 3 All ER 663 at 682; P Wallington 'The European Convention on Human Rights and English Law' (1975) 34 *Cambridge LJ* 9.

[12] For a survey of these decisions, see P J Duffy 'English Law and the European Convention on Human Rights' (1980) 29 *International & Comparative LQ* 584 and A Drzemczewski 'The Implementation of the United Kingdom's Obligations under the European Convention on Human Rights: Recent Developments' 1979 *Human Rights Journal* 95.

[13] [1974] 2 All ER 377 (HL), [1974] 1 WLR 683.

[14] At 379, 694. See too the dictum of Stephenson LJ in the Court of Appeal in [1974] 1 WLR 683 at 690–1, *sub nom R* v *Miah* [1974] 1 All ER 1110 (CA) at 1116.

Lord Denning MR was still more explicit on the status of the European Convention on Human Rights in *R* v *Secretary of State for Home Affairs: Ex parte Bhajan Singh*[15] when he stated:

> 'What is the position of the Convention in our English law? . . . The courts can and should take the Convention into account. They should take it into account whenever interpreting a statute which affects the rights and liberties of the individual. It is to be assumed that the Crown, in taking its part in legislation, would do nothing which was in conflict with treaties.'

This approach has received substantial support from British judges,[16] particularly from Lord Scarman, who has also invoked 'our obligations under the Charter of the United Nations' for the purpose of interpreting statutes affecting discriminatory treatment and individual rights.[17]

On most occasions English courts have simply relied on the European Convention as a guide to statutory interpretation. Recent decisions, however, suggest that it may also be invoked where the common law is uncertain. In *Attorney-General* v *British Broadcasting Corporation*[18] Lord Fraser stated in relation to the offence of contempt of court:

> 'This House, and other courts in the United Kingdom, should have regard to the provisions of the Convention for the Protection of Human Rights and Fundamental Freedoms (1953) (Cmd 8969) and to the decisions of the Court of Human Rights in cases, of which this is one, where our domestic law is not firmly settled.'[19]

Moreover, in the same case, Lord Scarman, after referring to 'a presumption, albeit rebuttable, that our municipal law will be consistent with our international obligations',[20] declared that in deciding whether to depart from one of its own previous decisions, the House of Lords could properly have regard to the United Kingdom's international obligations under the European Convention, as interpreted by the European Court of Human Rights.[21]

[15] [1976] QB 198 (CA) at 207, [1975] 2 All ER 1081 at 1083. See too the dicta of Lord Denning MR in *R* v *Chief Immigration Officer, Heathrow Airport: Ex parte Salamat Bibi* [1976] 3 All ER 843 (CA) at 847, [1976] 1 WLR 979 at 984; *Ahmad* v *Inner London Education Authority* [1978] QB 36 (CA) at 41, [1978] 1 All ER 574 at 577. For a recent affirmation of Lord Denning's approach, see *Williams* v *Home Office (No 2)* [1981] 1 All ER 1211 (QB) at 1244–5.

[16] The Northern Ireland Court of Criminal Appeal has also endorsed this new approach: *R* v *Deery*, reported in (1977) 20 *European Convention on Human Rights Yearbook* 827, and *R* v *McCormick* [1977] NI 105, (1978) 21 *European Convention on Human Rights Yearbook* 789.

[17] *Ahmad* v *Inner London Education Authority* [1978] QB 36 (CA) at 48, [1978] 1 All ER 574 at 583. See too the dictum of Scarman LJ in *Pan-American World Airways Inc* v *Department of Trade* [1976] 1 Lloyd's Rep 257 at 261.

[18] [1981] AC 303 (HL), [1980] 3 All ER 161.

[19] At 352, 176. See too at 353, 177 where Lord Fraser sees the Convention as a 'reinforcement measure'.

[20] At 353, 177.

[21] At 354, 177.

This development constitutes some advance on Lord Scarman's previously expressed view that the European Convention might be invoked as a *reinforcement* of the common law where fundamental rights are in issue.[22]

Human-rights conventions may also be taken into account for the purpose of determining public policy. In 1976, in *Blathwayt* v *Lord Cawley*, Lord Wilberforce stated, with reference to the European Convention on Human Rights:

> '. . . I do not doubt that conceptions of public policy should move with the times and that widely accepted treaties and statutes may point the direction in which such conceptions, as applied by the courts, ought to move.'[23]

There are suggestions, albeit tentative, that administrative action may be reviewed against the obligations contained in unincorporated human-rights treaties. In 1975, in *R* v *Secretary of State for Home Affairs: Ex parte Bhajan Singh*,[24] Lord Denning MR gave strong support to the view that a state's international obligations are to guide administrative action. Here he held that immigration officers and the Secretary of State, in exercising their powers under the immigration laws, ought to have regard to the right to family life contained in the European Convention. 'They ought, consciously or subconsciously, to have regard to the principles in it [the European Convention]—because, after all, the principles stated in the Convention are only a statement of the principles of fair dealing; and it is their duty to act fairly.'[25] Lord Denning MR later retracted this statement in *R* v *Chief Immigration Officer, Heathrow Airport: Ex parte Salamat Bibi*,[26] in which he stated that it would be asking too much of immigration officers to know or apply the European Convention in the exercise of their duties.

While one may agree with Lord Denning that subordinate officials cannot be expected to apply human-rights conventions in their daily decision-making, it does not follow that senior officers of state are likewise exempted from considering a state's international obligations. Surely it is not asking too much of such officers to have regard to these obligations. In any event, Lord Denning's retraction of his earlier statement should not be construed as a total rejection of the notion that human-rights conventions may be used as a standard by which to judge administrative

[22] *R* v *Secretary for the Home Department: Ex parte Phansopkar; R* v *Secretary of State for the Home Department: Ex parte Begum* [1976] QB 606 (CA) at 626, [1975] 3 All ER 497 at 510–11.

[23] [1976] AC 397 (HL) at 426, [1975] 3 All ER 625 at 636. See, further, Duffy op cit note 12 at 605.

[24] [1976] QB 198 (CA), [1975] 2 All ER 1081.

[25] At 207, 1083.

[26] [1976] 3 All ER 843 (CA) at 847–8, [1976] 1 WLR 979 at 984. See too *R* v *Secretary of State for the Home Department: Ex parte Hosenball* [1977] 3 All ER 452 (CA) at 457, [1977] 1 WLR 776 at 778.

action. As James Crawford has suggested in the *British Year Book of International Law*:

> 'It may be then that outside the area of immigration law, there is still room for the argument that human rights standards accepted in binding terms by Her Majesty's Government . . . are relevant considerations in the judicial review of discretion conferred by subsequent statutes.'[27]

Generally, it may be said that the British courts have adopted an orthodox attitude towards the European Convention on Human Rights, for in effect they have used it mainly as a guide to the interpretation of ambiguous statutes. Certainly they cannot be accused of judicial activism in their reliance on the European Convention, although the dicta in *Attorney-General* v *British Broadcasting Corporation* hold out some prospect that the courts may be prepared to rely on the Convention in a greater number of situations. Lord Denning MR came closest to overstepping the line of orthodoxy in his suggestion that administrative action should be guided by the Convention, but he was quick to retreat. That judicial restraint prevails in this field is well illustrated by *Malone* v *Metropolitan Police Commissioner*,[28] in which the court refused to fill in an important gap in the common law by invoking the European Convention.

Malone concerned the lawfulness of telephone tapping in police investigations. As English law does not specifically prohibit such conduct, the plaintiff, who had been subjected to telephone taps, sought a number of declarations on the illegality of telephone tapping. In support of his main contention that it was unlawful to monitor a telephone conversation without consent, the plaintiff invoked art 8 of the European Convention, which guarantees the right to respect for private life.[29] Here he argued, first, that it conferred a direct right on the citizen, and, secondly, that it should be used to guide the court in a case of ambiguity and lack of clarity in English law. In addition, the plaintiff claimed declarations to the effect that both the tapping of his telephone and the failure of English law to provide an effective remedy violated the Convention. All the plaintiff's claims were dismissed by Sir Robert Megarry V-C.

It is difficult to question the court's refusal, in the light of existing authority,[30] to make a declaration that an unincorporated

27 'Decisions of British Courts during 1976–1977' (1976–7) 48 *BYIL* 351. See too Duffy op cit note 12 at 597–8.

28 [1979] Ch 344, *sub nom Malone* v *Commissioner of Police of the Metropolis (No 2)* [1979] 2 All ER 620.

29 Article 8 reads: '(1) Everyone has the right to respect for his private and family life, his home and his correspondence.'

30 *Malone* v *Metropolitan Police Commissioner* [1979] Ch 344 at 353–4, *sub nom Malone* v *Commissioner of Police of the Metropolis (No 2)* [1979] 2 All ER 620 at 627–8.

treaty had been violated. Sir Robert was also on firm ground in holding that an unincorporated treaty did not confer rights directly on the citizen.[31] On the other hand, it is arguable that the learned judge adopted an unduly cautious approach to the role of international law in the filling-in of gaps in domestic law. Here the court's refusal to use the Convention as a guide to the formulation of the law was premissed on the absence of a statutory provision requiring interpretation. Megarry V-C stated:

> 'I readily accept that if the question before me were one of construing a statute enacted with the purpose of giving effect to obligations imposed by the Convention, the court would readily seek to construe the legislation in a way that would effectuate the Convention rather than frustrate it. However, no relevant legislation of that sort is in existence. It seems to me that where Parliament has abstained from legislating on a point that is plainly suitable for legislation, it is indeed difficult for the court to lay down new rules of common law or equity that will carry out the Crown's treaty obligations, or to discover for the first time that such rules have always existed.'[32]

This dictum takes no account of the way in which English judges have in the past developed the common law by reference to general principles of law and legal values. Moreover, it fails to consider the question whether treaties such as the European Convention on Human Rights and the International Covenant on Civil and Political Rights,[33] and other instruments such as the Universal Declaration of Human Rights[34]—all of which recognize a right to privacy —have generated a rule of customary international law that would be cognizable by an English court.[35] Surely a municipal court faced with a lacuna in its own common law in the field of fundamental rights is entitled to enlist the aid of treaties reflecting generally recognized rights, either on the ground that these rights have become part of customary law or because they provide evidence of widely accepted principles of law worthy of incorporation into a fertile common-law system. Sir Robert Megarry V-C's judgment in *Malone* is in many ways reminiscent of the majority judgment of the International Court of Justice in the 1966 *South West Africa Cases*:[36]

> 'It may be urged that the court is entitled to engage in a process of "filling in the gaps". . . . The court need not here enquire into the scope of a principle the exact bearing of which is highly controversial, for it is

[31] Idem at 366, 378, 638, 647. [32] Idem at 379, 647–8.

[33] Article 17(1): 'No one shall be subjected to arbitrary or unlawful interference with his privacy, family, home or correspondence. . . .'

[34] Article 12: 'No one shall be subjected to arbitrary interference with his privacy, family, home or correspondence. . . .'

[35] See further on this subject, Duffy op cit note 12 at 599–605.

[36] 1966 ICJ Reports 6.

clear that it can have no application in circumstances in which the court would have to go beyond what can reasonably be regarded as being a process of interpretation, and would have to engage in a process of rectification or revision. Rights cannot be presumed to exist merely because it might seem desirable that they should.'[37]

This judicial philosophy has been widely condemned at the international level,[38] and one hopes that it will not be resurrected at the domestic level. The subsequent dicta of Lords Fraser and Scarman in *Attorney-General* v *British Broadcasting Corporation*,[39] which acknowledge that a court may invoke international obligations in the field of human rights where 'domestic law is not firmly settled', seem to contradict Sir Robert Megarry V-C's approach and to act as an encouragement to judges determined to develop the common law in accordance with contemporary human-rights norms.

The United States

International human-rights norms got off to a good start in the United States in *Oyama* v *California*,[40] in which four Supreme Court Justices[41] relied on the human-rights provisions in the United Nations Charter to buttress a finding that a discriminatory Californian statute violated the Fourteenth Amendment's requirement of 'equal protection of the laws'. This initial success was, however, short lived, as in 1952 the California Supreme Court in *Sei Fujii* v *State*[42] held that the human-rights clauses were not self-executing and thus were not justiciable by domestic courts. This judgment has been echoed in other decisions,[43] and although the question has yet to be addressed by the Supreme Court, there is no denying that *Sei Fujii* has obstructed the impact of the human-rights clauses on American jurisprudence.

The ghost of *Sei Fujii* still haunts the courts.[44] In 1980 the Court of Appeals for the Fifth Circuit followed this decision in *In re Alien Children Ed Litigation*,[45] in which it held that art 47 of the Charter of the Organization of American States, as amended by the 1967 Protocol of Buenos Aires, providing for the promotion of the right to free public education, was not self-executing.

[37] Idem at 48.
[38] See John Dugard *The South West Africa/Namibia Dispute* (1973) 357.
[39] At notes 18–21.
[40] 332 US 633 at 649–50, 673 (1948).
[41] Justices Black, Douglas, Murphy and Rutledge.
[42] 38 Cal 2d 718, 242 P 2d 617 (1952).
[43] *Comacho* v *Rogers* 199 F Supp 155 (SONY 1961); *Hitai* v *Immigration and Naturalization Service* 343 F 2d 466 (2d Cir 1965).
[44] R Lillich and F Newman *International Human Rights: Problems of Law and Policy* (1979) 100; B Schlüter 'The Domestic Status of the Human Rights Clauses of the United National Charter' (1973) 61 *California LR* 110.
[45] 501 F Supp 544 (1980). See too *Doe* v *Plyler* 628 F 2d 448 (1980).

While the attitude of domestic courts towards human-rights treaty obligations of the United States can be characterized as cautious, there are signs of judicial activism in the approach to the customary international law of human rights. For years scholars have argued that the more widely accepted principles of the Universal Declaration of Human Rights of 1948 have acquired binding force as rules of customary international law.[46] The International Court of Justice, however, successfully 'ducked' this issue in 1966 in the *South West Africa Cases*,[47] when it avoided pronouncing on the question whether the Universal Declaration and subsequent resolutions of the General Assembly had generated a norm of non-discrimination.[48] As domestic courts are understandably more sensitive to considerations of state sovereignty, and hence to the need for clear evidence of consent as a prerequisite to the creation of customary law, a similar approach might have been expected from the domestic courts of the United States. Yet two decisions handed down in 1980 display an awareness of the evolving nature of customary international law that holds out much hope for the future.

In *Filartiga* v *Pena-Irala*[49] two Paraguayan plaintiffs brought an action in a federal court against another Paraguayan citizen—a retired senior police official—for damages arising out of the torture and death of their son and brother in a Paraguayan prison. Here the Court of Appeals for the Second Circuit held that it had jurisdiction under the Alien Tort Act,[50] a federal statute dating back to 1789, which provides for jurisdiction over 'any civil action by an alien for a tort only, committed in violation of the law of nations . . .', where an alleged torturer is found within the territorial jurisdiction of the United States. In order to reach this finding, the court held that torture committed by a state official against a detainee violates customary international law, as evidenced by the human-rights clauses of the United Nations Charter, the Universal Declaration of Human Rights,[51] the Declaration on the Protection of All Persons from Being Subjected to Torture,[52] the American Convention on Human Rights,[53] the International Covenant on Civil and Political Rights,[54] the European Convention on Human Rights[55] and the Constitutions of many states. The court's attitude towards the legal

[46] J Humphrey 'The International Bill of Rights: Scope and Implementation' (1976) *William & Mary LR* 527 at 529; M G K Nayar 'Human Rights: The United Nations and United States Foreign Policy' (1978) 19 *Harvard International LJ* 813 at 817; H Waldock 'Human Rights in Contemporary International Law and the Significance of the European Convention' *International & Comparative LQ* Supp Publ No 11 at 15 (1965).

[47] 1966 ICJ Reports 6.

[48] For a thorough examination of this subject, see S Slonim *South West Africa and the United Nations* (1973) 249–77.

[49] 630 F 2d 876 (2d Cir 1980), (1980) 19 *International Legal Materials* 966.

[50] 28 USC § 1350.

[51] Article 5.

[52] General Assembly Resolution 3452, 30 UN GAOR Supp (ch 34) 91.

[53] Article 5.

[54] Article 7.

[55] Article 3.

effect of resolutions of the General Assembly went beyond that of many more cautious scholars. Commenting on the Universal Declaration of Human Rights and the Declaration on the Protection of All Persons from Being Subjected to Torture, the court stated:

> 'These UN declarations are significant because they specify with great precision the obligations of member nations under the Charter.'[56]

This development was taken one step further by Judge Rogers in a United States district court in Kansas in *Fernandez* v *Wilkinson*.[57] The petitioner in this case was a Cuban refugee, who the United States immigration authorities determined was ineligible for admission into the United States on the ground that he had previously been convicted of a crime involving moral turpitude. Pending deportation, he was detained in a maximum security prison, where he remained for over six months while the United States Government tried unsuccessfully to arrange his return to Cuba. In an application for a writ of *habeas corpus*, the court held that, while the Constitution offered no protection to an alien being held indefinitely pending deportation, customary international law did secure 'to petitioner the right to be free of arbitrary detention'.[58] As in *Filartiga*, evidence for a customary rule against arbitrary detention was found in the human-rights provisions of the United Nations Charter, the Universal Declaration of Human Rights,[59] the American Convention on Human Rights,[60] the European Convention on Human Rights[61] and the International Covenant on Civil and Political Rights.[62] Although he recognized that the Universal Declaration is 'not technically binding', Judge Rogers added that 'it appears that the Declaration has evolved into an important source of international human rights law'.[63] On appeal, the Tenth Circuit Court of Appeals affirmed the district court's judgment on constitutional grounds that made it unnecessary for the court to consider Judge Roger's recourse to international law.[64] Nevertheless, citing the Universal Declaration of Human Rights, it acknowledged that '[n]o principle of international law is more fundamental than the concept that human beings should be free from arbitrary imprisonment'[65] and declared that its construction of the statute in question in favour of the rights of deportable aliens was 'consistent with accepted international law principles that individuals are entitled to be free of arbitrary imprisonment'.[66] Consequently, while the court did not rely on international law directly, it invoked principles of international law as a guide to statutory interpretation *in favorem libertatis*.

[56] (1980) 19 *International Legal Materials* at 973. [57] 505 F Supp 787 (1980).
[58] At 795. [59] Articles 3 and 9. [60] Articles 5 and 7.
[61] Article 5. [62] Article 9. [63] At 796–7.
[64] 654 Federal Reporter 2d series 1382 (1981). [65] At 1388.
[66] At 1390.

Both *Filartiga* and, especially, *Fernandez* stand in sharp contrast to the judgment of Sir Robert Megarry V-C in *Malone*.[67] For in these cases the courts were prepared to rely on the provisions of unincorporated (and, in most instances, unratified) treaties and declarations in order to fill gaps in or to give substance to municipal law. These judgments illustrate clearly the manner in which an innovative judiciary, committed to the promotion of human rights, may invoke international human-rights norms in the domestic legal process.

Two other recent decisions, involving the rights of prisoners, pursue a line of reasoning which, on the face of it, is similar to the orthodox interpretative method of the British courts. Here international human-rights conventions and the Universal Declaration of Human Rights were relied on, not as evidence of customary international law but as support for a human-rights oriented interpretation of the United States Bill of Rights and of the Oregon Bill of Rights. In substance, however, these decisions go well beyond the British cases referred to above, as they use human-rights treaties that the United States has not ratified and non-binding General Assembly resolutions as a guide to the interpretation of domestic law.

In *Lareau* v *Manson*[68] Judge Cabranes, in the United States District Court of Connecticut, held that overcrowding in a correctional centre violated the Eighth Amendment's prohibition on 'cruel and unusual punishments'. In reaching this conclusion, Judge Cabranes invoked the United Nations Standard Minimum Rules for the Treatment of Prisoners,[69] the Universal Declaration of Human Rights[70] and the International Covenant on Civil and Political Rights[71] as evidence of the 'evolving standards of decency' basic to Eighth Amendment jurisprudence.[72] At the same time the learned judge gave his approval to the view of the Second Circuit that the precepts of the Univeral Declaration of Human Rights constitute basic principles of international law.[73] Employing a similar method of reasoning, the Supreme Court of the State of Oregon, in *Sterling* v *Cupp*,[74] held that in deciding whether there had been a violation of the dignity and privacy of prisoners, the court might have regard to the principles contained in the Universal Declaration of Human Rights,[75] the European Convention on Human Rights,[76] the International Convenant on Civil and Political

[67] *Supra* note 28. [68] 507 F Supp 1177 (1980).

[69] These Rules were adopted by the First United Nations Congress on the Prevention of Crime and the Treatment of Offenders in 1955, and approved by the Economic and Social Council of the United Nations in Resolution 663 (XXIV) C, 24 UN ESCOR Supp (No 1) 11, UN DOC E/3048 (1957) and Resolution 2076, 62 UN ESCOR Supp (No 1) 35, UN DOC E/5988 (1977).

[70] Article 5 prohibits 'cruel, inhuman or degrading treatment or punishment'.

[71] Article 7. [72] At 1193n18. [73] Ibid. [74] Or 625 P 2d 123.

[75] Article 5. [76] Article 3.

Rights,[77] the American Convention on Human Rights[78] and the United Nations Standard Minimum Rules for the Treatment of Prisoners 'as contemporary expressions of the same concern with minimizing needlessly harsh, degrading or dehumanizing treatment of prisoners that is expressed in article 1(13) [of the Oregon Constitution]'.[79]

The above decisions demonstrate a new awareness on the part of American courts of the place of international human-rights norms in municipal law. Like the British courts, American courts have invoked such norms or standards as a guide to the interpretation of or reinforcement of domestic law. But, by deciding that human-rights conventions and declarations have generated customary rules, they have gone much further. *Filartiga* and *Fernandez* hold out the hope that other core provisions of the Universal Declaration of Human Rights and the various human-rights conventions may receive the imprimatur of customary law by domestic courts. In this way international human-rights law might be employed in an activist manner in the interstices of statute and common law. On the other hand, an obvious note of warning must be sounded. Some rights, particularly those falling into the category of 'civil and political', are more susceptible to acceptance as recognized rules of customary law than others—particularly those that may be classified as 'economic and social'.[80] This is illustrated by *In re Alien Children Ed Litigation*,[81] currently on appeal to the United States Supreme Court, in which the court, while apparently accepting that '[t]he Universal Declaration is considered as authoritative interpretation of Article 55 of the UN Charter', refused to recognize the right to education, contained in art 26 of the Universal Declaration of Human Rights, as a rule of customary international law.[82]

South Africa

Does the experience of British and American courts in relation to the application of international human-rights norms have any relevance to South Africa? In answering this question, it is necessary to examine the relationship between international law and South African law as enunciated by our courts. This may best be done by means of a number of propositions.

(a) South African courts are strongly influenced by the approach of English and American courts to the relationship between international law and municipal law.[83]

[77] Articles 7 and 10. [78] Article 5.

[79] At 131. Article 1(13) reads: 'No person arrested, or confined in jail, shall be treated with unnecessary rigor.'

[80] Schlüter op cit note 44 at 142–3, 146. [81] *Supra* note 45.

[82] Idem at 593, 596.

[83] See, for example, *South Atlantic Islands Development Corporation Ltd* v *Buchan* 1971 (1) SA 234 (C) at 238; *Inter-Science Research and Development Services (Pty) Ltd* v *Republica Popular de Moçambique* 1980 (2) SA 111 (T); *Kaffraria Property Co (Pty) Ltd* v *Government of*

(*b*) Customary international law forms part of South African law without any act of legislative incorporation.[84] However, as it is part of our common law, it must give way to legislation in the case of conflict.[85]

(*c*) Treaties signed and ratified by the executive do not automatically become part of our law. They require legislative incorporation in order to form part of our law.[86]

(*d*) Ambiguous statutes should be interpreted to accord with South Africa's international treaty obligations,[87] that is, even where the treaty in question has not been incorporated into South African law by legislative enactment.

(*e*) There is some authority for the proposition that subordinate legislation is unreasonable—and hence invalid—if it violates South Africa's international obligations.[88]

From the above propositions it is clear that in theory there is no reason why a South African court should not follow the reasoning of Anglo-American courts, as the principles embodied in these propositions are the very principles upon which the Anglo-American courts have premissed their decisions. It is thus open to our courts to apply international human-rights norms in the following situations.

(1) Where there is a lacuna in our common law a court may 'fill the gap' by recourse to customary international law. Although not all the provisions of the Universal Declaration of Human Rights qualify as customary international law, there are certain key provisions, such as the prohibitions on torture (*Filartiga* v *Pena-Irala*) and arbitrary detention (*Fernandez* v *Wilkinson*), which now form part of customary international law as a result of their wide

the Republic of Zambia 1980 (2) SA 709 (E); John Dugard 'The "Purist" Legal Method, International Law and Sovereign Immunity' in *J C Noster: 'n Feesbundel* (1979) (ed J J Gauntlett) 36 at 40, 45.

[84] *Nduli* v *Minister of Justice* 1978 (1) SA 893 (A) at 906; *South Atlantic Islands Development Corporation Ltd* v *Buchan* 1971 (1) SA 234 (C) at 238; *Inter-Science Research and Development Services (Pty) Ltd* v *Republica Popular de Moçambique* 1980 (2) SA 111 (T) at 124; *Kaffraria Property Co (Pty) Ltd* v *Government of the Republic of Zambia* 1980 (2) SA 709 (E) at 712, 715.

[85] *Inter-Science Research and Development Services (Pty) Ltd* v *Republica Popular de Moçambique* 1980 (2) SA 111 (T) at 124.

[86] *Pan American World Airways Inc* v *SA Fire and Accident Insurance Co Ltd* 1965 (3) SA 150 (A) at 161.

[87] This principle has yet to be pronounced upon by a South African court. It has, however, been accepted by Hiemstra CJ of the Supreme Court of Bophuthatswana in *Maluleke* v *Minister of Internal Affairs* 1981 (1) SA 707 (B) at 713. H R Hahlo and Ellison Kahn assume that such a rule of statutory interpretation would be followed by our courts:

> 'Our courts, though they do not appear to have been faced with the question, will surely follow the rule of construction applied generally in civilized States that statutes that are ambiguously framed are to be interpreted so as not to conflict with the established canons of international law' (*The South African Legal System and its Background* (1968) 114; see too at 211, 311).

[88] See John Dugard 'The Human Rights Clauses in the United Nations Charter and South African Law' (1980) 13 *De Jure* 297 at 302. This proposition is discussed below in paragraph (5).

acceptance in international human-rights treaties and state constitutions.[89] In practice, one fears, there will be little scope for the application of this method of reasoning, as South Africa's discriminatory and repressive statutes, which take precedence over customary international law (and common law), leave little room for judicial ingenuity and creativity.

(2) South Africa's international obligations, both under customary law and convention, may be invoked to reinforce common-law principles that are not firmly settled. Here the dicta of Lords Fraser[90] and Scarman,[91] discussed above, are highly apposite.

(3) The Appellate Division, which is not absolutely bound by precedent, might, in deciding whether to depart from a particular precedent, have regard to the country's international obligations—in accordance with the suggestion of Lord Scarman in *Attorney-General* v *British Broadcasting Corporation*.[92]

(4) South African courts should be guided by unincorporated treaty obligations in interpreting an ambiguous statutory provision.

South Africa has signed and ratified the Charter of the United Nations, but the Charter has not been incorporated into our law by legislative enactment. In terms of the Charter South Africa has undertaken, in the human-rights clauses, to promote 'universal respect for, and observance of, human rights and fundamental freedoms'.[93] Although international lawyers were initially divided over the legal effect of these clauses,[94] it is now generally accepted, as a result of the decision of the International Court of Justice in its 1971 Advisory Opinion on Namibia/South West Africa,[95] that they do impose some legal obligation—however weak and ill defined—upon member states to encourage respect for human rights in their own jurisdictions. South Africa, as a signatory to the Charter of the United Nations, is therefore bound by the human-rights provisions at the international level. As far as the present

[89] See text to notes 46–63. [90] Note 19. [91] Note 22.

[92] Note 21.

[93] A number of provisions in the Charter emphasize the protection of human rights as an important aim of the United Nations. The preamble reaffirms 'faith in fundamental human rights, in the dignity and worth of the human person'; art 1 includes among the purposes of the United Nations the promotion and encouragement of 'respect for human rights and for fundamental freedoms for all without distinction as to race, sex, language or religion'; and art 13 commits the General Assembly to 'assisting in the realization of human rights'. The most important human-rights provisions are arts 55 and 56. In art 55 the United Nations pledges itself to promote a number of goals, including 'universal respect for, and observance of, human rights and fundamental freedoms for all without distinction as to race, sex, language or religion'. Then, in art 56, '*All members* pledge themselves to take a joint and separate action in co-operation with the Organization for the achievement of the purposes set forth in Article 55' (italics added).

[94] See Dugard op cit note 88 at 298.

[95] *Legal Consequences for States of the Continued Presence of South Africa in Namibia (South West Africa) notwithstanding Security Council Resolution 276 (1970)* 1971 ICJ Reports 16 at 56–7 (paras 129–31). See the comment on this aspect of the Court's Opinion by Egon Schwelb 'The International Court of Justice and the Human Rights Clauses of the Charter' (1972) 66 *American J of International Law* 337 at 346.

writer is aware, this has not been denied by the South African Government since the International Court of Justice pronounced on the subject in 1971.

Although the human-rights provisions of the Charter fail to describe in detail the obligations of member states, there is growing support for the view that, in determining the extent of a state's obligations, recourse should be made to the Universal Declaration of Human Rights and to conventions such as the European Convention on Human Rights, the American Convention on Human Rights and the International Covenant on Civil and Political Rights. Thus in *Filartiga* the court stated that the Universal Declaration of Human Rights is 'significant', because it specifies 'with great precision the obligations of member nations under the Charter'.[96]

A South African court might therefore legitimately invoke the human-rights clauses of the Charter of the United Nations, as elaborated upon by the Universal Declaration of Human Rights and international human-rights conventions to which South Africa (like the United States) is not a party, in the interpretation of an ambiguous statute affecting human rights. That this is a proper method of statutory construction is clear from the decisions of both British[97] and American[98] courts.

Professor Hercules Booysen of the University of South Africa has questioned the above line of reasoning.[99] While he accepts the wisdom of Diplock LJ's dictum in *Salomon* v *Commissioners of Customs and Excise*[100] that 'if one of the meanings which can reasonably be ascribed to the legislation is consonant with the treaty obligations and another or others are not, the meaning which is consonant is to be preferred', he qualifies this acceptance by adding:

> 'Daar moet in gedagte gehou word dat bogenoemde beginsels slegs geld indien dit duidelik is dat die bepaalde statuut dit as doel het om aan die staat se internasionale verpligtinge effek te gee. Daar bestaan geen algemene vermoede in ons reg dat elke statuut beoog om met die volkereg in ooreenstemming te wees nie.'[101]

This qualification, for which no authority is cited,[102] seriously undermines the view that there is a general presumption that the legislature intends to comply with its international obligations,

[96] Note 56. [97] Notes 11–17. [98] Notes 66, 68 and 74.

[99] In *Volkereg: 'n Inleiding* (1980).

[100] [1967] 2 QB 116 (CA) at 143, [1966] 3 All ER 871.

[101] Op cit note 99 at 328.

[102] In another section of his study (at page 311) Booysen cites *S* v *Bock* 1968 (2) SA 658 (A) at 665 for the proposition that '[v]olgens ons reg kan die uitvoerende gesag nie deur die sluiting van 'n ooreenkoms 'n vermoede skep dat die wetgewer bedoel het om die verpligtinge wat in die ooreenkoms vervat is, na te kom nie'. *Bock's* case did not involve a *treaty* but simply an agreement between the Administrator of South West Africa and a tribal leader (see Booysen op cit 252–4). This case therefore does not support the proposition in question in so far as it refers to treaties.

unless it expressly or by necessary implication indicates a contrary view. In practical terms it means that a court may interpret an ambiguous statute designed to incorporate a treaty into municipal law so as to accord with the terms of the treaty itself; but may not interpret an ambiguous statute, not purporting to incorporate a treaty, in accordance with general principles of international law or in accordance with a state's treaty commitments. For example, to illustrate this argument, while it would be permissible to have regard to the terms of the Hague Convention for the Suppression of Unlawful Seizure of Aircraft (1970) in interpreting the Civil Aviation Offences Act of 1972[103] (which seeks to incorporate this treaty into South African law), it would not be permissible to have regard to the human-rights provisions of the Charter in interpreting an ambiguous statute invading human rights.

It is submitted that Professor Booysen takes too narrow a view of this matter and that, as Hahlo and Kahn suggest,[104] there is a general presumption of legislative intent in favour of compliance with international law and treaty commitments. This is supported by the English decisions discussed above, in which the European Convention on Human Rights was invoked as a guide to statutory interpretation. In a recent study of these cases P J Duffy states:

> 'If the meaning of a legislative provision is clear and unambiguous, this interpretation must be adopted even if it is contrary to the Convention; in such cases no presumption of compliance may be used. By contrast, where the meaning of legislation is unclear or ambiguous, the presumption may be invoked and the provision interpreted in accordance with the Convention. Furthermore, *the authorities clearly establish that the presumption may be used although the legislator in question sought neither expressly nor impliedly to incorporate the Convention into English law.*'[105]

Both English and American courts have invoked *unincorporated* treaties in the interpretation of *any* statute affecting human rights. There is no reason why a South African court should not follow this example. Where a statute enacted after 1945[106] (when the Charter of the United Nations was signed by South Africa) invades human rights or undermines the notion of equality before the law in unclear or equivocal terms, it is submitted that a South African court may legitimately invoke the human-rights provisions of the Charter as a guide to statutory interpretation. As these provisions reinforce common-law principles of equality before the law and the allocation of fundamental rights without distinction on grounds of race, they should act as a real obstruction in the way of an interpretation in favour of unequal treatment or the restriction of individual liberty.

[103] Act 10 of 1972. [104] Note 87. [105] Note 12 at 589. Italics added.

[106] It is generally believed that the presumption applies only to legislation enacted *subsequent* to the treaty in question. Cf Duffy op cit note 12 at 591–3.

(5) A South African court may set aside subordinate legislation as being *ultra vires* on the ground of unreasonableness. Generally our courts have followed the dictum of Lord Russell of Killowen CJ in *Kruse* v *Johnson*[107] in this regard, but at the same time they have stressed that the species of unreasonableness described in that well-known dictum do not exhaust the forms of unreasonableness known to our law.[108] It is suggested that our courts might legitimately find that subordinate legislation is unreasonable (in the specialized sense) if it violates South Africa's international obligations. No doubt this suggestion will seem far-fetched at first, but a closer examination of the concept of reasonableness and a study of decisions in South Africa show, it is believed, that there is merit in the suggestion.[109]

As has been shown above, one of the presumptions of legislative intent is that the legislature, in enacting a law, did not intend to violate South Africa's international obligations. Presumptions of this kind are inextricably linked with the concept of reasonableness[110] and contribute substantially to the content of this concept. Thus the presumptions against manifest injustice and partial and unequal treatment constitute the main species of unreasonableness known to our law. Logically, therefore, there is good reason to view the presumption against deviation from a state's international commitments as a form of unreasonableness against which the validity of subordinate legislation may be measured.

This argument receives some support from two decisions of the Appellate Division that suggest that a proclamation (but not an Act of Parliament) may be set aside if it conflicts with an *unincorporated* treaty to which South Africa is a party. In both *Winter* v *Minister of Defence*[111] and *S* v *Tuhadeleni*[112] the Appellate Division left open the question whether proclamations might be tested for validity against the terms of the Mandate for South West Africa, which, like the Charter of the United Nations, is a treaty that has not been incorporated into municipal law.

It is not suggested that the state's international obligations should bind ordinary administrative officials in the exercise of their

[107] [1898] 2 QBD 91 at 99: '. . . there may . . . be cases in which it would be the duty of the court to condemn by-laws . . . as invalid because unreasonable. But unreasonable in what sense? If, for instance, they were found to be partial and unequal in their operation as between different classes; if they disclosed bad faith; if they involved such oppressive or gratuitous interference with the rights of those subject to them as could find no justification in the minds of reasonable men, the court might well say "Parliament never intended to give authority to make such rules; they are unreasonable and ultra vires".'

[108] *Minister of Posts and Telegraphs* v *Rasool* 1934 AD 167 at 180; *R* v *Carelse* 1943 CPD 242 at 252; L C Steyn *Die Uitleg van Wette* 5 ed (1981) 242.

[109] Hercules Booysen appears to give approval to this approach in 1976 *South African Yearbook of International Law* at 235, where he states that the provision of a treaty may 'play a role in ascertaining the reasonableness of the exercise of the administration's discretions'.

[110] Hahlo and Kahn op cit note 87 at 202, 208; Steyn op cit note 108 at 101, 235.

[111] 1940 AD 194 at 198.

[112] 1969 (1) SA 153 (A) at 176, 173–4.

administrative discretion—as was initially suggested by Lord Denning MR in *R* v *Secretary of State for Home Affairs: Ex parte Bhajan Singh*[113] (but later withdrawn[114]). What is suggested is that where senior executive officers, such as the State President or ministers of state, have the power to make subordinate legislation, they should be guided by the country's international commitments unless the enabling statute expressly or by necessary implication frees them from this duty.

This view is disputed by Professor Booysen, who states:

> 'Volgens ons reg kan die uitvoerende gesag nie deur die sluiting van 'n *ooreenkoms* 'n vermoede skep dat die wetgewer bedoel het om die verpligting wat in die ooreenkoms vervat is, na te kom nie. Aangesien die meeste administratiewe verpligtinge en diskresies uit wetgewing voortvloei, kan 'n mens dus aanvaar dat die amptenaar by die uitleg van die wetgewing nie hoef te vermoed dat dit sy plig is om die wetgewing so te interpreteer dat die staat se verpligtinge ingevolge enige verdrae nagekom word nie.'[115]

The authority upon which Professor Booysen relies for this proposition is *S* v *Bock*,[116] which concerned, *not an international agreement or treaty between states*, but ''n ooreenkoms wat in Augustus 1923 tussen die Administrateur van die Suidwes gebied as verteenwoordiger van die Unie regering aan die een kant, en die Kaptein en Raad van die Rehoboth-gemeenskap aan die ander kant, aangegaan is. . . .'[117] It is submitted that this decision, dealing as it does with a domestic, political agreement not governed by international law, can hardly serve as authority for the proposition that a treaty fails to create a presumption in favour of compliance on the part of both the legislature and the executive.

Ultimately, the inquiry into the reasonableness of subordinate legislation is related to the question whether the enabling statute has authorized such legislation.[118] Consequently, the argument that a court may insist on compliance with a state's international obligations as a requisite for the validity of subordinate legislation is intimately connected with the presumption in favour of interpreting statutes in accordance with such obligations. Nevertheless, reasonableness (in the specialized sense) remains a criterion for the determination of the validity of subordinate legislation, and it is submitted that this concept may legitimately be interpreted to encompass respect for international obligations. This would allow a South African court to invoke the human-rights provisions of the

[113] Note 24. [114] Note 26.

[115] *Volkereg: 'n Inleiding* 311 (italics added). See too at 324–5.

[116] 1968 (2) SA 658 (A) at 665.

[117] At 664. For a description of the status of such an agreement, see Booysen op cit note 115 at 52–4.

[118] *Sinovich* v *Hercules Municipal Council* 1946 AD 783 at 802.

Charter in an inquiry into the validity of subordinate legislation that undermines 'universal respect for, and observance of human rights and fundamental freedoms for all without distinction as to race, sex, language or religion'. This treaty obligation reinforces the principles of justice, respect for fundamental freedoms[119] and equality of treatment enunciated in *Kruse* v *Johnson* as components of the requirement for the validity of subordinate legislation, and should therefore be seriously considered by our courts when they are required to pronounce upon the validity of subordinate legislation.

The Judicial Setback in S v Werner

The reasoning contained in (4) and (5) above was advanced in support of a challenge to the validity of a proclamation establishing exclusive racial zones under the Group Areas Act for the city of Johannesburg in *S* v *Werner* (reported in the Appellate Division in *S* v *Adams*; *S* v *Werner*[120]). As this was the first occasion on which South Africa's obligations under the human-rights provisions of the Charter of the United Nations were raised in a domestic court, the case requires closer consideration—despite the failure of the trial court and the Appellate Division to give the arguments serious attention.

One of South Africa's most controversial race laws is the Group Areas Act,[121] which provides for the zoning of urban areas into different 'group areas' for each of the four statutory racial groups —Whites, Coloureds, Indians and Blacks. The Act itself does not define the geographical limits of each 'group area', but leaves this to be accomplished by the executive by means of proclamation by the State President. Despite its avowed segregationist purpose, the enabling Act does not expressly authorize the executive to treat the different racial groups unequally in its delimitations of the respective group areas. In Johannesburg a housing crisis resulted from the operation of the Group Areas Act in the late 1970s. Coloured persons and Indians, unable to find any accommodation whatsoever in their own group areas, moved into houses and flats in the White group area, where there was then an oversupply of accommodation. Over 600 Coloured and Indian families were accordingly prosecuted under the Group Areas Act in order to secure their eviction. At this stage the validity of the proclamation zoning central Johannesburg 'White' was challenged. As the Group Areas Act does not expressly authorize discrimination (in the sense of a 'substantial inequality of treatment'), it was argued, *inter alia*, that it should be interpreted to comply as closely as possible with South

119 *R* v *Slabbert* 1956 (4) SA 18 (T) at 21–2.

120 *S* v *Werner* 1980 (2) SA 313 (W); *S* v *Adams; S* v *Werner* 1981 (1) SA 187 (A).

121 Act 36 of 1966.

Africa's obligations under the human-rights provisions of the United Nations Charter, and that this required the court to insist on an equality of treatment of the races in the implementation of the Act.[122] As the races were treated substantially unequally in the implementation of the proclamation, it was contended that the proclamation should be held to be *ultra vires* the enabling Act. In addition, it was argued that the proclamation was invalid on the grounds of unreasonableness. Unreasonableness, it was submitted in accordance with the reasoning described in (5) above, occurs where a subordinate legislative authority acts without regard to the state's international obligations contained in the United Nations Charter.

Despite the fact that they were referred to recent British developments in this field, neither the trial court nor the Appellate Division seriously considered the arguments. Both courts simply held that the Group Areas Act was unambiguous and that by implication it allowed discrimination and manifest injustice. Consequently, they refused to examine the question whether reference to South Africa's treaty commitments might produce a more benevolent interpretation. Le Roux J in the court *a quo* stated that it was unnecessary to consider the arguments on the ground that '[a]s 'n Wet van ons eie Parlement iets magtig, kan dit na my mening nie deur 'n omstrede verpligting in die Verenigde Volke se Handves beïnvloed word nie'.[123] In a similar vein, Rumpff CJ, in the Appellate Division, declared:

> 'Die betoog dat internasionale verhoudings, b v die Handves van die Verenigde Volke, as toetssteen gebruik moes word is, in die omstandighede, onaanvaarbaar. 'n Proklamasie ingevolge die Wet op Groepsgebiede moet getoets word aan die bepaling van die Wet, 'n Wet wat uitdruklik voorsiening maak vir die skepping en ontwikkeling van groepsgebiede vir verskillende etniese groepe.'[124]

Neither the trial court nor the Appellate Division in *S* v *Werner* rejected the argument that an *ambiguous* statute might be interpreted in accordance with a state's international obligations under the human-rights provisions of the Charter. Both courts simply held that the Act in question was not ambiguous and therefore did not allow recourse to a presumption of compliance with international obligations. While opinions may differ as to whether the Group Areas Act does unambiguously allow unequal treatment of the races,[125] it is clear that a finding of non-ambiguity does, according to the English decisions, exclude the operation of the presumption

[122] For a summary of this argument, see *S* v *Adams; S* v *Werner* 1981 (1) SA 187 (A) at 208–11.

[123] *S* v *Werner* 1980 (2) SA 313 (W) at 328.

[124] *S* v *Adams; S* v *Werner* 1981 (1) SA 187 (A) at 225.

[125] See J D van der Vyver 'Qu'ils Mangent de la Brioche!' (1981) 98 *SALJ* 135 at 147–8.

of compliance. The argument based on this presumption still stands, however, and may accordingly be advanced in support of a benevolent statutory interpretation where the statute in question is unclear. Unfortunately, the judgment in *S* v *Werner* suggests that courts will all too readily accept the clarity and unambiguity of a statute invading human rights—a suggestion that is confirmed by the more recent decision of the Appellate Division in *S* v *Meer.*[126]

Some Concluding Comments on the Role of Courts and Lawyers

In the United States and, to a lesser extent, Britain, international human-rights lawyers have found a new receptivity to their arguments in domestic courts. This may be ascribed to a number of factors. The rhetoric of human rights occupies an increasingly important role in foreign-policy pronouncements in both the United States and Britain, and inevitably this has some impact on judicial awareness and sensitivity to human-rights arguments. Furthermore, the introduction of international human-rights courses in many law schools in both countries has probably contributed to the quality of the arguments presented and, possibly, to judicial knowledge. In Britain the European Convention on Human Rights has at last penetrated the practice of the legal profession, and a growing number of lawyers today approach their clients' problems in the context of the European Convention. In the United States a number of public-interest-law groups, focusing on international human-rights issues, have recently been established, which have had a considerable impact. In most of the American cases discussed in this article a public-interest-law group submitted an *amicus curiae* brief.[127] The *amicus* brief, which is not permitted in either Britain or South Africa, is, of course, an invaluable instrument for the advancement of human-rights arguments, as it allows qualified and concerned parties to contribute to the formulation of the judicial decision in a manner that is denied British and South African groups not directly involved in the litigation before the court. For example, there can be little doubt that the State Department's *amicus curiae* memorandum[128] in *Filartiga* greatly assisted the Second Circuit Court of Appeals.

[126] *S* v *Meer* 1981 (4) SA 604 (A), reversing the decision of the Natal Provincial Division in *S* v *Meer* 1981 (1) SA 739 (N).

[127] In *Filartiga* (*supra* n 49) the plaintiffs–appellants were partly represented by the Centre for Constitutional Rights, and *amicus* briefs were filed by the Department of State, Amnesty International-USA, the International League of Human Rights, the Lawyers' Committee for International Human Rights, the International Human Rights Law Group, the Council on Hemispheric Affairs and the Washington Office on Latin America. In *Fernandez* (*supra* n 57) Kansas Legal Services Inc submitted an *amicus* brief. In *Lareau* (*supra* n 68) the plaintiffs were assisted by the Connecticut Civil Liberties Union Foundation, the Prisoners' Legal Assistance Association and the Legal Services Organization, Yale Law School. In *In re Alien Children Ed Litigation* and *Doe* v *Plyler* (*supra* n 45) the International Human Rights Law Group filed an *amicus* brief.

[128] This memorandum, which was requested by the court itself, appears in (1980) 19 *International Legal Materials* 585.

English courts have not gone as far in the adoption of international human-rights norms as their American counterparts. *Malone* is disappointing, as it suggests that the courts are not prepared to do more than use international conventions as a guide to statutory interpretation or as a reinforcement of common-law principles. The courts of the United States have shown in *Filartiga* and *Fernandez* that international human-rights conventions and declarations may, in addition, be viewed as evidence of customary international law, and that this source of law has a far greater potential for filling in the gaps of municipal law with international human-rights norms.[129] English courts are traditionally less activist than American courts in respect of the protection of human rights under constitutional law. This is understandable, as the Bill of Rights and the principle of judicial review compel American courts to play a more creative role than English courts, restrained by the doctrine of Parliamentary supremacy. But in the field of international human-rights norms the shoe is on the other foot. The United Kingdom has ratified several major international human-rights conventions in addition to the Charter of the United Nations. The United States, on the other hand, has ratified only the Charter and has yet to ratify the International Convention on Civil and Political Rights and the American Convention on Human Rights. In these circumstances English courts might be expected to pursue a more activist role than those of the United States. One fears, however, that traditional self-imposed restraints on judicial lawmaking constitute the main obstacle in the way of a more positive approach on the part of the English judiciary.

South African courts have considered international human-rights-law arguments in only one case: *S* v *Werner*. They have consequently had little opportunity to respond to this new development in Anglo-American jurisprudence. Yet one cannot be hopeful that they will respond positively, as many judges are out of sympathy with arguments premissed on human rights and do not differ substantially from the executive[130] in their attitude towards such issues. And, as is well known, the South African Government is not part of the mainstream of the human-rights movement: it has yet to formulate either domestic or international policy pronouncements in the language of human rights. Furthermore, one cannot anticipate the raising of international human-rights arguments as a frequent occurrence in legal proceedings. For, although many South African lawyers are deeply concerned about the erosion of equality and individual liberty in the legal system and

[129] See Schlüter op cit note 44 at 145–6.

[130] John Dugard *Human Rights and the South African Legal Order* (1978) 380; John Dugard 'Some Realism about the Judicial Process and Positivism—A Reply' (1981) 98 *SALJ* 372 at 383.

frequently advance human-rights arguments in the context of municipal law, few are familiar with the international dimension, as international law does not feature prominently in law-school curricula. Public-interest law, in the American sense, is a recent phenomenon in South Africa, but is one that may contribute to the use of human-rights arguments.[131]

Current developments in human-rights law in the United States and Britain demonstrate that the lacunae of municipal law are susceptible to international norms, and that an innovative judiciary may contribute substantially to the unity of international law and municipal law in the promotion of human rights. International lawyers have an important role to play in this process, as domestic lawyers, not versed in international law, will often fail to recognize the opportunity for the application of international human-rights law when it arises. The message that emerges from the cases discussed in this article is clear: international lawyers are as much needed on the domestic legal scene as they are on the international legal scene.

[131] The Centre for Applied Legal Studies of the University of the Witwatersrand was responsible for raising the international human-rights arguments in *S* v *Werner*. This Centre is primarily engaged in research but, on occasion, it participates in litigation in the public interest.

COHABITATION, CONCUBINAGE AND THE COMMON-LAW MARRIAGE[1]

H R HAHLO*

The term 'common-law marriage' (*alias* 'putative marriage', '*de facto* marriage', 'quasi-marriage', 'extra-marital cohabitation' or 'concubinage') connotes the relationship of a man and a woman who live together as man and wife without having gone through a legal ceremony of marriage. The relationship of a couple who have gone through a legal ceremony of marriage but whose marriage is for some reason null and void, for example, because it is bigamous or the parties are related to each other within the prohibited degrees, does not fall within the definition of concubinage, and is governed by its own rules.[2]

* Dr Jur (Halle) LLB LLD Hon LLD (Witwatersrand), Advocate of the Supreme Court of South Africa, Associate Member of the International Academy of Comparative Law, Paris, Visiting Professor of Law, University of Toronto, formerly Director, Institute of International and Comparative Law, McGill University, Montreal, Professor of Law Emeritus in the University of the Witwatersrand, Johannesburg.

[1] Of the rapidly growing literature on this subject, reference may be made to John M Eekelaar and Sanford N Katz (eds) *Marriage and Cohabitation in Contemporary Societies* (1980), which contains a number of articles by leading experts from all over the world on the 'common-law marriage' and its consequences; the full report on 'Legal Problems Concerning Unmarried Couples' submitted by Wolfram Müller-Freienfels to the 11th Colloquy on European Law, held under the auspices of the Council of Europe in July 1981 (CJ-DE/11 (81)3); John L Dwyer (1977) 93 *LQR* 386; Rebecca J Bailey (1978) 52 *Australian LJ* 174; H A Finlay (1978) 52 *Australian LJ* 613; David Pearl (1978) 37 *Cambridge LJ* 252; Graham Douthwaite *Unmarried Couples and the Law* (1979); A A S Zuckerman (1980) 96 *LQR* 248; Anders Agell 1980 *Scandinavian Studies in Law* 9; Marvin Mitchelson *Living Together* (1981); Jacob W F Sundberg (1971) 20 *International and Comparative LQ* 223. See also H R Hahlo (1972) 89 *SALJ* 321; H Samuels (1976) 6 *Family Law* 152; Marianne Jennings and Bruce K Childers (1979) 6 *Community Property J* 258; Case Comment (1978) 62 *Minnesota LR* 449; Judith M Masson 1979 *Conveyancer* 184; Erwin Spiro (1979) 42 *THRHR* 403; Frank Bates (1980) 13 *CILSA* 131; Nicholas Bala (1980) 6 *Queen's LJ* (Canada) 72; I J Hardingham (1980) 12 *Melbourne University LR* 356; H W Strätz (1980) 27 *Zeitschrift für das Gesamte Familienrecht* 301, 434; Charles F Crutchfield (1981) 19 *Journal of Family Law* (University of Louisville School of Law) 247; Mary Ann Glendon in Jean Dabin (ed) *Famille, droit et changement social dans les sociétés contemporaines, travaux des VIII Journées d'études juridiques* (Brussels and Paris 1978) 18–28; Robert R Bell *Marriage and Family Interaction* 5 ed (1979) 89ff.

[2] See H R Hahlo *The South African Law of Husband and Wife* 4 ed (1975) 483ff (cited hereafter as Hahlo); John H Wade (1981) 9 *Sydney LR* 356. If a couple whose marriage is void *ab initio*, for example because one of them is already married, continue to live together after they know that their marriage is null and void, their relationship becomes concubinage. As a general rule, parties to a void marriage cannot be worse off, but may in certain circumstances be better off, than parties who live together as man and wife without having gone through a ceremony of marriage.

The 'common-law marriage' is not a legal marriage.[3] The term is a euphemism which harks back to the days before the Church Council of Trent (1545–63), when at canon law, which was then Europe's law of marriage, a legal marriage could be contracted by informal consent.[4] Not long ago the relationship for which the term stands was commonly referred to as 'concubinage', 'illicit liaison' or, even more scathingly, as 'living in sin', and many people still so refer to it. The change in popular usage to the term 'common-law marriage', which carries no pejorative implications, but, on the contrary, suggests that there is a marriage of a sort, signifies a profound change in mores. In Europe, North America, Australia, New Zealand and, to a lesser extent, even in conservative South Africa extra-marital cohabitation has lost much of its former moral and social stigma, and has become almost respectable.

As Bridge LJ remarked in *Dyson Holdings Ltd* v *Fox*:[5]

> '. . . between 1950 and 1975 there has been a complete revolution in society's attitude to unmarried partnerships. . . . Such unions are far commoner than they used to be. The social stigma that attached to them has almost, if not entirely, disappeared. The inaccurate but expressive phrases "common law wife" and "common law husband" have come into general use to describe them.'

In similar terms, the German *Landgericht* Bonn declared in 1976:

> 'These days . . . the conception of what is moral has changed. It corresponds to the conception of . . . a portion of all social classes that unmarried cohabitation does not run counter to the prevailing legal and social order. Accordingly, the landlord cannot enforce his own moral view contrary to the opinion of the tenant and compel him to either discontinue the concubinage or vacate. . . .'[6]

This change in social realities could not but affect the law. In almost all Western legal systems it is still true that most of the consequences, and in particular of the proprietary consequences, of a legal marriage do not attach to a common-law marriage. However, there is scarcely a country left that does not afford some

[3] For reasons of convenience, the terms 'common-law marriage', 'common-law husband' and 'common-law wife' will be used throughout this exposition, occasionally interspersed with terms such as 'putative marriage', 'putative husband', or 'wife', or, simply, 'relationship' and 'man and mistress'. The term '*de facto* marriage', while legally unobjectionable, is rarely used. The 'common-law marriage', as dealt with here, must not be confused with the common-law marriage of the handful of American jurisdictions where the informal consent marriage is still, or was until recently, recognized as a legal marriage. In West Germany and France it is still customary to speak of 'concubinage'; see K C Horton (1980) 10 *Family Law* 252.

[4] Hahlo 4,5.

[5] [1976] QB 503 (CA) at 512–13, [1975] 3 All ER 1030 at 1036. See also *Helby* v *Rafferty* [1978] 3 All ER 1016 (CA), [1979] 1 WLR 13, noted (1979) 95 *LQR* 161, and *Davis* v *Johnson* [1979] AC 264 (HL), [1978] 1 All ER 1132.

[6] 1976 *Neue Juristische Wochenschrift* 1690, quoted from Müller-Freienfels op cit note 1 at 10.

measure of recognition to a *de facto* marriage, always provided that the relationship is not of a casual or intermittent character, but has such a degree of 'apparent permanence and stability' that the ordinary man would say that the parties live together as man and wife.[7] Whether the parties hold themselves out as husband and wife is only one of the factors to be taken into account.

'Living common law' is not a privilege of the unmarried. A man may live with his mistress and not with his legal wife, he may share his time between his wife and his mistress, or he may live, 'harem fashion', with his legal wife and his mistress, or a bevy of mistresses.

Where the rights of a common-law spouse come into conflict with those of a legal spouse, the tendency in most systems is to prefer the legal spouse to the common-law spouse, but this is not universal. Where property and rights of succession are concerned, some legal systems give, in certain circumstances, the common-law spouse preference; others provide for equal division among the claimants or leave the division to judicial discretion.

For most purposes, South African law does not afford any recognition to a common-law marriage, no matter how long it has endured. There is no reciprocal duty of support between the parties. There exist no rights of intestate succession between them. On the other hand, there is nothing to preclude a man from leaving his estate to his mistress to the exclusion of his legal wife, or from leaving it to his illegitimate children to the exclusion of his legitimate ones.[8] However, where a man who has a legal wife and legitimate children as well as a mistress and illegitimate children leaves something in his will to 'my wife' or 'my children', there is a rebuttable presumption that he meant his legal wife[9] and his legitimate children.[10]

Neither party, unless appointed as agent by the other, can bind the other by contract with a third person. However, if the couple live ostensibly together as husband and wife, either of them can bind the other by contracts for household necessaries to the same extent as if they were legally married.[11]

A contract by which a man undertakes to pay a woman (or vice versa) for the commencement or continuance of sexual relations is null and void, as being against public policy.[12] On the other hand, the mere fact that a man and a woman live together as husband and

[7] *Helby* v *Rafferty* (*supra* note 5) at 1020, 18 per Stamp LJ; also James LJ in *Dyson Holdings Ltd* v *Fox* [1976] QB 503 (CA) at 511, [1975] 3 All ER 1030 at 1036.

[8] *Millward* v *Glaser* 1949 (4) SA 931 (A); *Momeen* v *Bassa* 1976 (4) SA 338 (D).

[9] See, for example, *Momeen* v *Bassa* 1976 (4) SA 338 (D).

[10] Voet 36.1.13; *In re Russo* (1896) 13 SC 185; *Du Plessis* v *Estate Meyer* 1913 CPD 1006; *Brey* v *Secretary for Inland Revenue* 1978 (4) SA 439 (C) at 442–3. See also *Wilkinson* v *Wilkinson's Estate* (1907) 24 SC 602; cf T F Yunken (1971) 8 *Melbourne University LR* 174.

[11] Cf *Thompson* v *Model Steam Laundry Ltd* 1926 TPD 674.

[12] *The Lady Cox's Case* (1734) 3 P Wms 339 (24 ER 1091).

wife without being legally married does not vitiate a contract which has nothing to do with their sexual relationship. Thus, a man cannot refuse to repay his girl-friend a loan or withhold from her wages due to her as his secretary or housekeeper. The position is different where the contract of employment was entered into for the sole purpose of enabling the man to pay his mistress, under the guise of a (tax-deductible) salary, 'wages of sin'.

In America it has been held that illicit intercourse which lies wholly in the past does not invalidate a promise or contract, even where it has been the underlying reason for making the promise or entering into the contract:

> 'Although the woman is not considered guiltless from a moral point of view, the law will not on that account prohibit the person who has caused or perhaps has only contributed to her misfortune from doing her that justice to which he may consider her entitled. The turpitude is in the act, and not in the compensation.'[13]

It is submitted that this is the law in South Africa also.

There is no rule in our law prohibiting donations between a man and his common-law wife, but if he has a legal wife to whom he is married in community he may not make to his mistress (or, for that matter, any third party) donations in fraud of his wife's rights in the joint estate.[14]

Where a man and his mistress have pooled their means for the purchase of a house which was registered in the man's name, and it is clear that the mistress did not intend a donation, she may be entitled to a share in it or, at least, to repayment of her contribution on grounds of unjust enrichment. And where a man and his mistress have built up a business by their joint efforts or collaborated in some other enterprise, the court may infer that they intended partnership.[15]

The parties to a common-law union can sue each other for damages in delict, for instance, where the man has assaulted the

[13] 17 *American Jurisprudence 2d* sv 'Contracts' § 184. The law is the same in France. Commenting on art 902 CC, *Les Petits Codes Dalloz* (1979–80) states: 'Gifts between persons living in concubinage must be annulled if they have been a means of corruption or the wages of vice, if they are the price of a shameful deal or if the condition of the continuation of illicit relations has been imposed. However, the mere fact that the donor had illicit, or even adulterous, relations with the donee is not sufficient to invalidate the transaction, which ought to be upheld if it was inspired by the wish to secure the future of the concubine or to repair the material and moral prejudice she has suffered.' (My translation.)

[14] Hahlo 162ff.

[15] See *V (also known as L)* v *De Wet NO* 1953 (1) SA 612 (O). And see 258 below. *Contra: Khoza* v *Sedibe*, an unreported judgment of the High Court of Swaziland, on appeal, 27 November 1968 (1969) 2 *CILSA* 162, where the *ex turpi causa non oritur actio* rule was applied, barring the plaintiff's claim. It is submitted that where the claim is not based on the illicit relationship it ought to succeed. In France the court will construe the business relationship between the parties as a *société en fait*, akin to, though not quite the same as, an implied partnership. In West Germany, too, the courts are beginning to apply partnership principles: K C Horton (1980) 10 *Fam Law* 252.

woman or she has been injured in an accident caused by his negligence. Neither party is liable to a third party for the other's delict, unless the wrongdoer committed the delict while acting within the scope of his or her employment as the other's servant, say, the woman as the man's housekeeper or the man as the woman's woodsman or chauffeur. If the man is killed through the wrongful act of a third party, his common-law wife cannot claim damages for loss of support from the wrongdoer, since the deceased did not owe her a duty of support.[16] Again, a clause in a motor-car insurance policy that confers special benefits (for example, life cover) on passengers who are members of the insured's family, or excludes them from certain benefits, does not, presumably, operate to the advantage or detriment of a mistress.[17]

There are a number of statutory provisions in South African law that, for certain purposes, treat a woman who was living with a man as his common-law wife as if she were legally married to him, at least where he has no legal wife. And there are several decided cases in which South African courts were called upon to consider the effects of a common-law marriage.

Of statutory provisions, mention may be made (the list does not profess to be exhaustive) of s 4(1) of the Workmen's Compensation Act 1941,[18] which includes in the definition of 'dependant' for the purposes of workmen's compensation,

> 'if there is no widow who, at the time of the accident, was wholly or partly dependent upon the deceased workman for the necessaries of life any woman with whom the workman was in the opinion of the commissioner living as man and wife at the time of the accident',

provided she was 'at the time of the accident . . . wholly or partly dependent on the workman for the necessaries of life'.[19]

Section 21 of the Insolvency Act 1936[20] provides that if the separate estate of one of two spouses who are not living apart is sequestrated, the estate of the solvent as well as that of the insolvent spouse vests first in the Master, and then in the trustee, but that the

[16] See, for example, *Zulu* v *Minister of Justice* 1956 (2) SA 128 (N); *Suid-Afrikaanse Nasionale Trust en Assuransie Maatskappy Bpk* v *Fondo* 1960 (2) SA 467 (A); *Nkabinde* v *SA Motor & General Insurance Co Ltd* 1961 (1) SA 302 (D); also *Ex parte Seti* 1963 (4) SA 962 (SR). In respect of a man and woman joined in a Black customary union, this was changed by s 31 of the Black Laws Amendment Act 76 of 1963.

[17] Cf *Lopez* v *Santiago* (1972) 93 S Ct 8, 294A 2d 272 (Dist Ct Essex County, New Jersey).

[18] Act 30 of 1941.

[19] Where a widow claims compensation, there is a rebuttable presumption that she was at the time of the accident dependent upon the workman. This does not apply to a common-law wife, who has to prove dependency unaided by any presumption. As far as Blacks are concerned, the term 'widow' in the Workmen's Compensation Act includes a woman who was associated to the deceased workman in a conjugal relationship according to Black law and custom, where neither the man nor the woman was a party to a subsisting legal marriage: s 4(3).

[20] Act 24 of 1936.

estate of the solvent spouse has to be released if he proves that it was acquired by him by a title which cannot be assailed by the creditors of the insolvent spouse. Subsection (13) of s 21 includes in the definition of 'spouse' for the purposes of the section a woman who is living with a man as his wife or a man who is living with a woman as her husband, who are not married to one another. In *Chaplin NO* v *Gregory (or Wyld)*[21] the insolvent lived with his mistress, apart from his legal wife. The court held that the estate of his legal wife, and not of his common-law wife, vested in the trustee, a ruling for which the common-law wife was, no doubt, grateful.

Whereas in *Chaplin NO* v *Gregory* the preference of the law for legal wives worked out to the disadvantage of the legal wife, in *Momeen* v *Bassa*[22] it worked out to her advantage. Here, the testator died survived by two wives: one to whom he was legally married, and one to whom he was married by Muslim rites not legally recognized. In his will he left certain benefits to 'my wife', without making it clear which one he meant. The court held that in the absence of indications to the contrary, it had to be assumed that he meant his legal wife.[23]

Another example of a statutory recognition of a common-law marriage is s 9(1)(*c*) of the Aliens Act 1937,[24] which lays down that a woman who lives with a man as his 'putative wife' may assume his surname without requiring authorization by the State President.

Of cases on the subject, mention may be made of *Drummond* v *Drummond*,[25] where the Appellate Division gave effect to an agreement embodied in a divorce decree under which the ex-husband's obligation to pay his former wife (defendant) maintenance was to cease not only on her death or remarriage but also 'should the plaintiff [husband] prove that the defendant [wife] is living as man and wife with a third person on a permanent basis'.

Dealing with the question whether the evidence was sufficient to establish such a relationship, Trengove AJA stressed the need for duration and continuity. He said:[26]

> 'To conclude on this aspect of the case. Looking at the evidence as a whole, I am satisfied that it has been established that the appellant and Bosch were living together as man and wife on a permanent basis, at the time when the motion proceedings were initiated, and thereafter.
>
> 'Counsel for the appellant also submitted that, in considering whether the respondent had discharged the onus resting on him, the court *a quo* should have disregarded the evidence of the appellant's relationship with Bosch subsequent to the date on which the motion proceedings were

[21] 1950 (3) SA 555 (C). [22] 1976 (4) SA 338 (D).

[23] A reference in the same will to the testator's children was interpreted to refer to the children of both unions.

[24] Act 1 of 1937. [25] 1979 (1) SA 161 (A). [26] At 170B–F.

launched, ie 3 December 1974. He contended that the court *a quo* erred in taking that evidence into account in its consideration of the issues between the parties because it was not relevant to the facts in issue and because it fell outside the scope of the inquiry as indicated by the affidavits. There is no substance in the first contention. The evidence of the subsequent conduct of the appellant and Bosch has a very legitimate and material bearing on the question whether they were living together as man and wife at the time in question. Evidence by which the existence of this sort of relationship is proved is seldom, if ever, direct; generally speaking it is usually impossible to prove it except by circumstantial evidence. A relationship of this nature involves an element of continuity, it is one that must of necessity have some duration, and its existence at any particular time can, therefore, only be established by facts illustrating the preceding or subsequent relation of the parties. And, in this regard, evidence of the subsequent conduct of the parties concerned is usually admissible for the purpose of showing what inference ought to be drawn from the evidence of previous acts of familiarity.'

Again, in *Ex parte Dessels*,[27] where the testator had left to his widow an annuity payable until death or remarriage subject to the condition, *inter alia*, that payments were to cease if the wife lived a life that would be regarded as immoral or if she permitted any strange person to live with her except one regarded as a visitor who stayed no longer than one week a year and who, if a male person, was accompanied by his wife, the court upheld the validity of the condition, which was obviously intended to ensure that the annuity would cease not only on the widow's remarriage, but also if she cohabited with a man as his wife without marrying him. It held that the condition was neither *contra bonos mores* nor so vague as to be unenforceable.

Ex parte Dessels and *Drummond* v *Drummond* confirm that, failing a condition specifically dealing with the matter, a divorcee or widow entitled to maintenance until death or remarriage does not lose her claim automatically if she assumes life with a man as his common-law wife. However, if her new man provides her with support, it would presumably be a good ground for the variation, rescission or suspension of the maintenance order.

In *Basetti* v *Louw*[28] the applicant and the respondent had had a 'relationship', resulting in the birth of a boy. Having decided that marriage between them would not be a success, they entered into an agreement whereunder the applicant acknowledged that he was the natural father of the child and obliged to maintain it. He also made provision for the maintenance of the child in terms of an insurance policy. The agreement further provided that the child was not to be removed from the Republic without the applicant's

[27] 1976 (1) SA 851 (D).

[28] 1980 (2) SA 225 (W).

written consent and that the respondent would not give up the custody or allow the child to be adopted without the prior consent of the applicant. The court, on application by the applicant, made the agreement an order of court.

In *S* v *Vengetsamy*[29] the court applied the common-law rule that the spouse of an accused person is not a compellable witness for the prosecution in the case of an invalid Hindu marriage.

Other countries have gone much further than South Africa in extending rights and duties that used to be the privileges and burdens of legally married couples to couples cohabiting as husband and wife in a relationship of 'apparent permanence and stability', without having gone to the trouble of contracting a legal marriage. This has been achieved partly by innovative legislation, partly by creative judicial law-making. Within the scope of this article it is not possible to mention more than a few examples, selected at random from French, English, American, Canadian and Australian law.[30]

An example of how adaptation of the law to changing mores can be achieved by judicial law-making is the 1970 decision of the *Cours de Cassation*, France's highest court in civil cases, in *Gaudras* c *Dangereux*.[31] Prior to this case it was settled law in France, as it still is in South Africa,[32] that a woman who lives with a man as his wife without being legally married to him has, unlike a legal wife, no action for damages for loss of support if he is killed as the result of the wrongful act of a third party. In *Gaudras* c *Dangereux* the *Cours de Cassation* reversed its previous stand. It decided that where 'concubinage' offered '*des garanties de stabilité*' and was not '*delictual*' in character (meaning, apparently, that neither of the parties was married to someone else), the mistress was entitled to claim damages for loss of support from the wrongdoer. In argument before the *Cours de Cassation*, counsel for the plaintiff, in referring to the judgment of the Second Chamber of the Appeal Court of Paris, which, in conformity with the earlier jurisprudence, had dismissed the plaintiff's claim, argued:

> '*Est-ce à dire que la deuxième Chambre civile considère le concubinage comme immoral, contraire aux bonnes moeurs?*
>
> '*Si cela était, ce serait, je pense, une erreur, car les moeurs sont, par nature, une chose qui évolue grandement, et il ne semble pas que le concubinage, stable et non entaché d'adultère, soit contraire aux moeurs d'aujourd'hui.*'

[29] 1972 (4) SA 351 (D). The Saskatchewan Court of Appeal in *Ex parte Cote* (1972) 22 DLR (3d) 353, noted (1973) 19 *McGill LJ* 577, on similar facts arrived at the opposite result. There was one difference between the two cases: the union in the Canadian case was not a marriage by the rites of any creed or denomination.

[30] For a wide-ranging survey, see the various articles in John M Eekelaar and Sanford N Katz (eds) *Marriage and Cohabitation in Contemporary Societies* (1980); and W Müller-Freienfels op cit note 1 above.

[31] *Cours Ch Mixte* 27 fev 1970, [1970] *Semaine Juridique* 16305.

[32] See note 16.

It was, apparently, this argument that caused the *Cours de Cassation* to change course.

And in 1978, in a case where a man killed in an accident had divided his life between his wife and his mistress and there were children of both unions, the Riom Court of Appeal awarded full damages to both women and their children.[33]

In England it has been held in several cases that a woman who has lived with a man for a number of years without being legally married to him is a 'member of his family' for the purpose of the rent legislation. The leading case is *Dyson Holdings Ltd* v *Fox*,[34] where the court decided that it was entitled to take the change in the meaning of the word 'family' to the ordinary man into account.

In *Kokosinski* v *Kokosinski*[35] the parties had lived together as husband and wife for 23 years before getting legally married. Their marriage lasted only a few months. In determining the financial provision to be made for the wife under the Matrimonial Causes Act 1973, the court took the pre-marital relationship of the parties into account.

English social benefit laws generally place common-law wives on the same basis as legal wives; see, for example, s 17(1) of the Family Income Supplements Act 1970, which defines a 'single woman' as 'any woman other than one who is a member of the same household as a man to whom she is married or with whom she is living as his wife', and para 3(1)(*b*) of Schedule 1 to the Supplementary Benefits Act 1976, which treats two persons 'cohabiting as man and wife' (save where there are exceptional circumstances) the same way as a legally married couple.

In *Re Evers's Trust, Papps* v *Evers*[36] an application for immediate sale under s 30 of the Law of Property Act 1925 was refused to the joint tenant of property in which his former mistress and their children still wished to live. The formerly cohabiting couple received the same treatment which a legally married couple would have received under s 24 of the Matrimonial Causes Act 1973.

Section 1(1) of the Domestic Violence and Matrimonial Property Proceedings Act 1976 empowers a county court on application by a spouse to grant an injunction restraining the other spouse from molesting the applicant or from excluding her from the matrimonial home, or requiring the other spouse to permit the applicant to enter and remain in the matrimonial home. Subsection (2) extends this provision to a man and a woman who are living with

[33] JCP 79 II 19107 (1979). The decision has met with criticism.

[34] [1976] QB 503 (CA), [1975] 3 All ER 1030. See also *Helby* v *Rafferty* [1978] 3 All ER 1016 (CA), [1979] 1 WLR 13, noted (1979) 95 *LQR* 161, and *Watson* v *Lucas* [1980] 3 All ER 647 (CA), [1980] 1 WLR 1493.

[35] [1980] Fam 72, [1980] 1 All ER 1106, noted (1980) 96 *LQR* 331. But see also *Campbell* v *Campbell* [1976] Fam 347, [1977] 1 All ER 1.

[36] [1980] 3 All ER 399 (CA), [1980] 1 WLR 1327.

each other in the same household as husband and wife. In *Davis* v *Johnson*,[37] where the respondent had caused his mistress by his violence to leave the common household, the court held that under this section it could exclude the man from the common home, of which he was a joint tenant, and allow his 'battered mistress' to enter and remain in it.

Under s 1 of the Inheritance (Provision for Family and Dependants) Act 1975 the English courts can make reasonable financial provision, by the award of periodical payments, payment of a lump sum or a property transfer, out of a deceased's estate not only for a widow or widower or a former spouse of the deceased, but also for any person 'who immediately before the death of the deceased was being maintained, either wholly or partly, by the deceased'. In terms of this section, the court can make provision for a mistress of the deceased (whence the Act has also been referred to as 'the Mistress's Charter'). There is, however, this difference: In the case of a surviving spouse, reasonable financial provision means such provision as it would be reasonable for him or her to receive, irrespective of whether or not the provision is required for his or her maintenance; in the case of any other person, including a mistress, it means such financial provision as it would be reasonable for the applicant to receive for his or her maintenance: subsec (2) of s 1.[38]

In South Australia, s 11 of the Family Relationships Act 1975 (SA) provides that, if it is satisfied that on a certain date a person was cohabiting with another person as husband or wife *de facto* and either *(a)* so cohabited with that other person continuously for five years immediately preceding that date or during the period of six years immediately preceding that date so cohabited with that other person for periods aggregating not less than five years; or *(b)* has had sexual relations with that other person resulting in the birth of a child, the court must make a declaration that on that date that person was the 'putative spouse' of that other person. Such a declaration has far-reaching consequences. If the partner of the putative spouse dies without having made reasonable provision for her, she can claim maintenance out of the deceased's estate.[39] If the deceased has died intestate, without being survived by a legal spouse, the putative spouse takes the intestate portion of a legal spouse; and if there is a legal spouse as well as a putative spouse, the

[37] [1978] 2 WLR 553 (HL), [1978] 1 All ER 1132, noted by A A S Zuckerman (1978) 94 *LQR* 324. See also *Harding* v *Harding* (1979) 10 *Fam Law* 146 (CA) and Judith M Masson [1979] *Conveyancer* 184.

[38] *Malone* v *Harrison* [1979] 1 WLR 1353, noted by M W Bryan (1980) 96 *LQR* 165, illustrates the principles which will guide the court in making provision for a mistress. On the interpretation of subsec (3) of s 1, which specifies in what circumstances a person is deemed to have been maintained by the deceased, see *Re Wilkinson (Deceased)* [1978] Fam 22, [1978] 1 All ER 221.

[39] Inheritance (Family Provision) Act 1972 (SA) s 4.

two share a spouse's intestate portion equally.[40] Again, a putative spouse is included among the persons entitled to recover damages from a third party whose wrongful act has caused the deceased's death, and if there is a legal as well as a putative spouse, they share the award equally.[41]

In Ontario, one of Canada's nine common-law provinces, and the most populous one, s 14 of the Family Law Reform Act 1978 includes in the definition of a spouse for purposes of support 'either of a man and woman not being married to each other who have cohabited continuously for a period of not less than five years, or who have cohabited in a relationship of some permanence where a child has been born of their union, and who in either case have so cohabited within the year preceding the application for support'. Section 60 of the same Act provides that, subject to the same conditions, a common-law spouse whose partner is injured or killed by the fault or neglect of another may recover damages from the wrongdoer. Under s 52 a man and a woman who are cohabiting without being married to each other may enter into an agreement in which they agree on their respective rights and obligations during cohabitation, or upon their ceasing to cohabit or death, including *(a)* ownership in or division of property; *(b)* support obligations; *(c)* the right to direct the education and moral training of their children, but not the right to custody of or access to their children; and *(d)* any other matter in the settlement of their affairs. And under s 53 a man and a woman who have cohabited but are now living apart may enter into a separation agreement regarding the same matters, but including as well the right to custody of and access to their minor children. To be enforceable, such cohabitation or separation agreements, whether entered into between legal or common-law spouses, must be made in writing, and signed by the persons to be bound, and witnessed: s 54. Finally, under s 64(*d*)(i) of the Ontario Succession Law Reform Act, relief out of a deceased's estate may be awarded to a common-law spouse who has cohabited with the deceased continuously for a period of not less than five years or in a relationship of some permanence where a child has been born of the union. The requirement under s 14 of the Family Law Reform Act 1978 that the parties must have so cohabited within the year preceding the application does not apply in this case.

In British Columbia, another of Canada's common-law provinces,[42] s 85 of the Estate Administration Act[43] includes in the definition of a 'common law spouse' a person who has lived and

[40] Administration and Probate Act 1919–1975 (SA) s 72h(2).
[41] Wrongs Act 1936–75 (SA) ss 3(*a*) and 20(4).
[42] On the position in the other provinces, see H R Hahlo *Nullity of Marriage in Canada* (1979) 48ff.
[43] RSBC 1979 c 114.

cohabited with another person as a spouse and has been maintained by that other person for a period of not less than two years immediately preceding his death. Where an intestate leaves surviving him a common-law spouse (or an illegitimate child), the court may order that there be applied for the support, maintenance and benefit of the common-law spouse (or the illegitimate child or both) so much of the net estate of the intestate as the court sees fit.

It is only fair that in a legal system where a couple who cohabit without entering into a legal marriage enjoy the same social benefits (unemployment benefits, the old-age pension, workmen's compensation) as a legally married couple, they should also share in the disadvantages attendant upon a legal marriage. There are a number of jurisdictions in which this is the law. To take again Ontario, regulations published under the Family Benefits Act[44] disentitle in certain circumstances a person from benefits if he or she is dependent upon a spouse not eligible for the old-age pension, 'spouse(s)' being defined for the purpose as including persons living together 'as if they were husband and wife'. On similar lines, the regulations published under the General Welfare Assistance Act,[45] which provide that no person shall be eligible for certain allowances who is not living as a 'single person', result in a common-law marriage having the same effect as a 'legal marriage' in rendering a person (in practice, invariably the woman) disentitled to, or ineligible for, these benefits.[46] Similar problems arise in connection with taxation. Taxation systems in which a man and a woman with substantial independent incomes are taxed more highly if they are married than if they cohabit without being married provide lovers with an incentive to live 'common law' rather than to get married. Thus, in the Income Tax Law of Belgium married and unmarried couples are jointly assessed in the same manner.[47]

The progressive extension by statute of rights and duties formerly restricted to legally married couples to couples joined in a 'common-law' union has been accompanied by a change in the judicial approach to contracts and other transactions between a man and his mistress. There has been no change in the basic rules *(a)* that, in accordance with the *ex turpi causa non oritur actio* doc-

[44] RSO 1970 c 151. [45] RSO 1970 c 192.

[46] See, for example, *Re Proc and Minister of Community and Social Services* (1975) 53 DLR (3d) 512 (Ont) and *Re Warwick and Minister of Community and Social Services* (1979) 21 OR 528 (Ont CA). Unfortunately, enforcement is difficult, and inevitably involves 'snooping'. There have been many cases in which women were prosecuted for welfare fraud because they continued to draw benefits, sometimes for years, after they were living with a man as his wife. One suspects that the cases in which the fraud was discovered constitute only the tip of the iceberg.

[47] *Code des impôts sur les revenues* arts 66 and 73, referred to by Müller-Freienfels op cit note 1 at 40. See also s 65 of the Swedish Communal Income Tax Act: 'The rules applicable to a married taxpayer will also be applied to those who live together without being married, if they have been married to each other previously or if they have had children together': Jacob W F Sundberg (1975) 23 *Am J Comp L* 39.

trine, an immoral contract will not be enforced; and *(b)* that a 'money for sex' contract falls within this category. The change in judicial attitudes that has occurred relates to the approach which the courts will adopt in determining whether the contract is a 'money for sex' contract.

Symptomatic of the old order was Lord Wright's statement in the 1938 House of Lords case of *Fender* v *St John-Mildmay*:[48]

> 'The law will not enforce an immoral promise, such as a promise between a man and woman to live together without being married or to pay a sum of money or to give some other consideration in return for immoral association.'

Of course, even in those more moralistic (though not necessarily more moral) days, the courts enforced a contract that was not connected with the sexual relationship of the parties. But once it was established that there existed an extra-marital relationship between the parties, the courts tended to regard any dealings even remotely connected with it as immoral, and refused to differentiate between prostitution and a quasi-marital relationship.[49] It is here that the change has taken place. Today, the courts recognize that, just as there is more to a legal marriage than sex—love, companionship, mutual support in sickness and health—so sex is only one element, and not necessarily the most important one, in a common-law union.

The much-discussed Californian case of *Michelle Marvin* v *Lee Marvin*[50] illustrates this trend. The plaintiff and the defendant had lived together as husband and wife for six years. Though they had not held themselves out as legally married, the plaintiff had assumed her lover's name (hence '*Marvin* v *Marvin*'). When the defendant abandoned the plaintiff to marry his former college sweetheart, the plaintiff sued him for $1,8 million, alleging that he had promised her half of his earnings, which for the six years of their cohabitation amounted to $3,6 million. The Los Angeles Superior Court, which tried the case, rejected the plaintiff's claim out of hand, holding that the alleged agreement was unenforceable as being tainted by immorality. The Supreme Court of California reversed and referred the matter back to the trial court. It held that

> 'the fact that a man and woman live together without marriage and engage in a sexual relationship, does not in itself invalidate agreements between them relating to their earnings, property or expenses. Neither is such an agreement invalid merely because the parties may have contemplated the creation or continuation of a non-marital relationship when they entered into it. Agreements between non-marital parties fail only to the extent that they rest upon a consideration of meretricious

[48] [1938] AC 1 (HL) at 42.
[49] See A A S Zuckerman (1980) 96 *LQR* 249.
[50] 557 P 2d 106.

sexual services, and not on the ground that the agreement is "involved in" or made "in contemplation of" a non-marital relationship.'[51]

Adults who voluntarily live together and engage in sexual relations, the court said, may agree to pool all or part of their earnings or property, form a partnership or joint venture, hold property acquired in common, or agree to any other such arrangement.

Said Mr Justice Tobriner, who delivered the judgment of the Supreme Court:

> '. . . we believe that the prevalence of nonmarital relationships in modern society and the social acceptance of them, marks this as a time when our courts should by no means apply the doctrine of the unlawfulness of the so-called meretricious relationship to the instant case. As we have explained, the nonenforceability of agreements expressly providing for meretricious conduct rested upon the fact that such conduct, as the word suggests, pertained to and encompassed prostitution. To equate the nonmarital relationship of today to such a subject matter is to do violence to an accepted and wholly different practice.
>
> 'We are aware that many young couples live together without the solemnization of marriage, in order to make sure that they can successfully later undertake marriage. This trial period, preliminary to marriage, serves as some assurance that the marriage will not subsequently end in dissolution to the harm of both parties. We are aware, as we have stated, of the pervasiveness of nonmarital relationships in other situations.
>
> 'The mores of the society have indeed changed so radically in regard to cohabitation that we cannot impose a standard based on alleged moral considerations that have apparently been so widely abandoned by so many.'

He hastened to add:

> 'Lest we be misunderstood, however, we take this occasion to point out that the structure of society itself largely depends upon the institution of marriage, and nothing we have said in this opinion should be taken to derogate from that institution. The joining of the man and woman in marriage is at once the most socially productive and individually fulfilling relationship that one can enjoy in the course of a lifetime.'

On remand from the Supreme Court, the Los Angeles Superior Court found on the facts that the plaintiff had failed to prove a sharing agreement, express or implied, and that the promise alleged by the plaintiff amounted to no more than 'lover's talk'. It consequently dismissed the action in so far as it was based upon an agreement. However, it granted the plaintiff on equitable ground a lump sum of $104 000 ($1 000 a week for two years) as 'palimony' for rehabilitation purposes, 'so that she may have the economic

[51] 557 P 2d 106 at 113.

means to re-educate herself and to learn new, employable skills or to refurbish those utilized, for example, during her most recent employment so that she may return from her status as a companion of a motion picture star to a separate, independent, but perhaps more prosaic existence'. I understand that on appeal by Mr Marvin, this award was set aside by the Court of Appeal, on the ground that there was no rule in the law of California on which it could be based, and that this has now been confirmed by the Supreme Court of California.[52]

It will be noted that the decision of the Supreme Court did not depart from the principle that a contract whereby one party undertakes to pay the other for sexual services is immoral and hence unenforceable. What it did hold was that adults who voluntarily live together and engage in sexual relations are as competent as any other persons to contract respecting their earnings and property rights. So long as their agreement does not rest upon an illicit, meretricious consideration, they may order their economic affairs as they choose, and no policy considerations preclude the court from enforcing such agreement.

What made *Marvin* v *Marvin* newsworthy was not its novelty but its Hollywood setting, and the magnitude of the plaintiff's claim. The laws of France and England have long been moving in the same direction. In the 1959 French case of *Venutolo* c *Dlle Bertoit*[53] the *Cours de Cassation* held that a promissory note which the defendant had given to his mistress was enforceable, dismissing his defence that it was vitiated by immorality. And in the English case of *Tanner* v *Tanner*,[54] where a man had provided his mistress, after she had given birth to twin daughters, with a house for herself and the children, the Court of Appeal held that he had by implication granted her a contractual licence to have accommodation in the house for herself and the children so long as the children were of school age and reasonably required the accommodation. J L Barton comments:[55]

> 'There may well come a time when the suggestion that it is inherently improper that a woman should expect to be remunerated for her favours will seem as odd to our posterity as the outburst of that medieval judge who characterized an agreement for the payment of a marriage portion as an attempted sale of the sacraments seems to us. . . .'

In *Pascoe* v *Turner*[56] the plaintiff had told his common-law wife that the house in which they were living and its contents were hers,

[52] At the time of writing, neither the judgment of the Court of Appeal nor that of the Supreme Court was available to me.

[53] D 1960 515 note Malaurie.

[54] [1975] 3 All ER 776 (CA), [1975] 1 WLR 1346, noted by J L Barton (1976) 92 *LQR* 168.

[55] At 171.

[56] [1979] 2 All ER 945 (CA), [1979] 1 WLR 431.

but no conveyance was ever drawn up. The court, holding that he was obliged to perfect the gift, made an order directing him to transfer the house and furniture to her.

Equally significant is the readiness of English, American, Canadian and Australian courts to find a resultant or constructive trust in favour of a common-law wife who has contributed money, money's worth or labour to the acquisition of property by her paramour.[57] It has long been settled law in England that if a wife makes financial contributions to the acquisition of property by her husband or helps him in building up his business or farm, she is entitled in equity to a beneficial share in the property, business or farm in proportion to her contribution.[58] The same rules are now being applied as between a man and his common-law wife.

Cooke v *Head*[59] and *Eves* v *Eves*[60] exemplify this trend. In *Cooke* v *Head* Mr Head, a married man, and Miss Cooke, his mistress, decided to buy some land and build a bungalow on it, in the expectation that Mr Head's wife would divorce him and that they could then set up home together. Mr Head purchased a vacant stand, paying a deposit and raising the rest of the purchase price on mortgage. The conveyance was taken in his name. Miss Cooke did not contribute to the purchase price, but worked hard at helping Mr Head with planning and building the bungalow. By the time the bungalow was practically finished the loving relationship between Mr Head and Miss Cooke was finished, too. Mr Head occupied the bungalow for almost two years. Thereafter he sold it. The trial court held that Miss Cooke was entitled to one-twelfth of the proceeds of the sale; the Court of Appeal raised her share to one-third. It held that Mr Head as the legal owner of the bungalow held it on trust for himself and Miss Cooke beneficially. Lord Denning MR said:[61]

> 'If this case had come up thirty or forty years ago, I do not suppose Miss Cooke would have had any claim to a share. . . . But that has all been altered now. . . . It is now held that, whenever two parties by their joint efforts acquire property to be used for their joint benefit, the courts may impose or impute a constructive or resulting trust. . . . This trust does not need any writing. . . . It applies to husband and wife, to engaged couples, and to man and mistress, and may be to other relationships too.'

The same principles were applied in *Eves* v *Eves*, where Lord Denning MR pungently remarked:[62]

[57] On the position in South Africa, see note 15.

[58] See, for example, *Pettitt* v *Pettitt* [1970] AC 777 (HL), [1969] 2 All ER 385 and *Gissing* v *Gissing* [1971] AC 886 (HL), [1970] 2 All ER 780.

[59] [1972] 2 All ER 38 (CA), [1972] 1 WLR 518.

[60] [1975] 3 All ER 768 (CA), [1975] 1 WLR 1338.

[61] [1972] 2 All ER 38 (CA) at 41, [1972] 1 WLR 518 at 520.

[62] [1975] 3 All ER 768 (CA) at 771, [1975] 1 WLR 1338 at 1341.

'In strict law she [the mistress] has no claim on him whatever. She is not his wife. He is not bound to provide a roof over her head. He can turn her into the street. She is not entitled to any maintenance from him for herself.. . . And a few years ago even equity would not have helped her. But things have altered now. Equity is not past the age of child bearing. One of her latest progeny is a constructive trust of a new model. Lord Diplock brought it into the world and we have nourished it.'

In *Pettkus* v *Becker*[63] the Supreme Court of Canada took the matter to its logical conclusion. The parties had lived together 'common law' for nearly 20 years. During that time the appellant (man), through toil and thrift, had acquired three farms and developed a bee-keeping business. Through her labour and earnings, the respondent, his common-law wife, had contributed substantially to the success of what the court found was in effect a common enterprise. When the relationship of the parties broke up, the appellant owned three farms and a prosperous bee-keeping business, the respondent nothing. The Supreme Court unanimously decided that the respondent was entitled to a half-interest in the farms and the business.

Mr Justice Dickson, who spoke for the majority, based his decision on constructive trust. 'Mr Pettkus has had the benefit of nineteen years of unpaid labour, while Miss Becker has received little or nothing in return.'[64] He did not regard the absence of a marital bond as presenting any problems:

'I see no basis for any distinction, in dividing property and assets, between marital relationships and those more informal relationships which subsist for a lengthy period. This was not an economic partnership nor a mere business relationship, nor a casual encounter. Mr Pettkus and Miss Becker lived as man and wife for almost twenty years. Their lives and their economic well-being were fully integrated. The equitable principle on which the remedy of constructive trust rests is broad and general; its purpose is to prevent unjust enrichment in whatever circumstances it occurs.'[65]

Conjuring up the ghosts of the Roman *concubinatus*,[66] overseas developments suggest that, trailing changing mores, the law is

[63] (1981) 117 DLR (3d) 257 (SC). See also the Canadian case of *Holub* v *Holub et al* (1977) 71 DLR (3d) 698 (Man CA); the American cases of *In re Marriage of Cary* 109 Cal Reptr 862 (Cal App 1973) and *In re Thornton* 81 Wash (2d) 72 (1972); and the Australian cases of *Napier* v *Public Trustee* (1980) 32 ALR 153, (1981) 55 ALJR 1 (High Court of Australia) and *Hohol* v *Hohol* [1981] VR 221. The same applies, of course, in reverse. In the Californian case of *Contreras* v *Guzman* (citation elusive) it was the woman who had accumulated a fortune (more than one million dollars) while living and working in a *de facto* partnership with her common-law husband. The court ordered her to share her wealth with him. Similarly, in the Canadian case of *Riess* v *Riess* (1981) 22 RFL (2d) 152 (Sask), where property had been acquired with the woman's money and the man's labour, the court decided that the woman, in whose name the property stood, held half of it on constructive trust for the man.

[64] At 274. [65] At 275–6.

[66] The Roman concubinage was a union short of marriage, which was usually entered into between a man of rank with a woman of lower status. Marriageable age and consent were required, and a man who had a concubine could not have a legal wife or another concubine, but there was no *dos*, as in marriage. Unlike a promiscuous union, the *concubinatus* carried no social stigma. Children were 'natural children', not 'bastards'.

moving towards the recognition of the quasi-marital union as a distinct legal institution, somewhere between a 'one-night stand' or transitory affair, which has no legal consequences whatsoever (unless, of course, a child is born of it), and a lawful marriage. 'There is a variety of possibilities, from the casual encounter to the life-long cohabitation.'[67] The difficulty is to determine at what stage and subject to what conditions an informal union ripens into a common-law marriage. Some legal systems leave the decision to judicial or administrative discretion,[68] others require a minimum period of continuous cohabitation, the birth of a child, or a combination of minimum duration and the birth of a child.

How far should the law go in extending the consequences of a legal marriage to a common-law marriage? There is, it is suggested, a good case for treating the parties to a common-law marriage for purposes of workmen's compensation and social assistance as if they were lawfully married, at least if neither of them has a legal spouse.[69] A good case can also be made out for allowing a party to a common-law marriage whose partner was killed as a result of the unlawful act of a third person to recover from the wrongdoer damages for loss of support. Nor is it equitable that an agreement as to maintenance, payment of a lump sum, or a property transfer entered into between common-law spouses, either during the subsistence of their union or after its termination, should be struck down as immoral, merely because sex entered into their relationship.

> '[I]t is difficult to see how the public morals are served by finding the parties equally guilty of immoral conduct but then, in effect, punishing one party while awarding the other a windfall.'[70]

To refuse enforcement of an agreement between common-law spouses on the *ex turpi causa non oritur actio* principle results, in the vast majority of cases, in benefiting the man at the expense of the woman who was naïve enough to trust his promises. Said Finley J, an American judge, in *West* v *Knowles*:[71]

> '[T]he unannounced but inherent rule is simply that the party who has title, or in some instances who is in possession, will enjoy the right of ownership of the property concerned. The rule often operates to the great advantage of the cunning and the shrewd, who wind up with the possession of property, or title to it in their names, at the end of a so-called meretricious relationship.'

Whether it is desirable, from the point of public policy, to extend the recognition of common-law marriages any further may be

[67] Müller-Freienfels op cit note 1 at 4.

[68] See, for example, s 4(1)(*b*) of the South African Workmen's Compensation Act 30 of 1941. See text to note 18.

[69] See, for example, s 14 of the Ontario Family Law Reform Act 1978, 254 above.

[70] (1978) 62 *Minnesota LR* 453.

[71] 311 P (2d) 689 at 692–3 (1957).

doubted. It has been suggested that any recognition extended to it is liable to undermine the sanctity and attractions of the legal marriage, but it may well have the opposite effect. Once men (and women) realize that by entering into a common-law union they cannot escape the obligations flowing from a legal marriage, they may decide that they might as well get married.

The fundamental objection to placing a common-law marriage on the same, or nearly the same, legal footing as a lawful marriage is that as long as marriage is retained as a legal institution parties who choose to cohabit without entering into a marriage exercise a deliberate choice. As it was put by Robert R Bell in *Marriage and Family Interaction*:[72]

> 'When "living together" couples look at their emotional commitment and role, it is typical that they do not see themselves in a relationship closely linked to marriage. . . . They do not usually see themselves as essentially wife and husband living together as a married couple and only different from the married because they have not met the legal requirements. The roles they play relative to one another are usually seen as quite different from the traditional roles of marriage.'

There is, it is suggested, no justification for attaching to the union of a couple who lack the *animus maritandi* all or most of the consequences of a legal marriage.

> 'If parties refrain from marrying because they do not want to incur the legal and financial obligations of marriage, then the law should be slow to impose those obligations on them.'[73]

Homer H Clark Jr in his article 'The New Marriage'[74] puts the same point thus:

> 'Whatever the social reality may be, it may still be efficient and not inequitable to retain conventional marriage as the criterion for property rights and duties. Individuals who wish to undertake those rights and duties then have a clearly defined method for doing so. Those who do not wish to undertake them have an equally clearly defined method for avoiding them, that is, by not marrying. Those who advocate the freedom that accompanies the refusal to marry but who at the same time wish the law to impose property rights and duties upon cohabiting but unmarried people are indulging in the great American dream of wishing to have their cake and eat it too. This is a common natural desire, but not one that the law is equipped to fulfill. The meaning of freedom in this context is the absence of legal regulation. Its virtue is that it leaves with individuals the power to work out their own personal relation-

[72] 5 ed (1979) 99.

[73] Final Report of the South Australian Royal Commission on Human Relationships (1977) IV 73.

[74] (1976) 12 *Williamette LJ* 441 at 452. The case against recognition of the 'common-law marriage' was persuasively put by Ruth Deech in her article on 'The Case Against Legal Recognition of Cohabitation' in *Marriage and Cohabitation* op cit note 1 at 300.

ships. Its defect is that they alone are responsible when those relationships become painful.'

I am inclined to agree with Professor Anders Agell when he says:[75]

'. . . [I]t would be better if (1) the legislation was so far as possible restricted to a contract type which already exists, embodied as it is in the current legislation on marriage, which now is purely secular, (2) the state encouraged the contracting of marriages, and (3) legislation on free cohabitation was carried through as restrictively as possible instead of being based on the notion of neutrality [as it is in Swedish law] on the part of society.'

[75] 1980 *Scandinavian Studies in Law* at 47–8.

CUSTOMARY LAW IN THE APPELLATE DIVISION 1945–1960

A J KERR*

Few, if any, of our judges of appeal have had to deal with as many problems concerning customary law[1] as the late Mr Justice O D Schreiner. The reports for the period during which he was a judge of appeal[2] contain fourteen decisions of the Appellate Division in this field.[3] Mr Justice Schreiner was on the bench in all but three[4] of them. In five of the eleven in which he sat his opinion was concurred in by all the other members of the court.[5] Questions of fundamental importance relating to the choice of law; judicial

* BA (SA) LLB (Witwatersrand) LLM PhD (Natal), Advocate of the Supreme Court of South Africa, Professor of Law in Rhodes University.

[1] The term 'customary law' is used with the meaning given in the present writer's *The Customary Law of Immovable Property and of Succession* 2 ed (1976) 7–8. This work is referred to hereafter as *Customary Law*.

[2] 1 January 1945–29 December 1960. (*R* v *Dumezweni*, reported in 1961 (1961 (2) SA 751 (A)) was heard in 1960.)

[3] *Ex parte Minister of Native Affairs: In re Molefe* v *Molefe* 1946 AD 315; *R* v *Mpanza* 1946 AD 763; *Ex parte Minister of Native Affairs: In re Yako* v *Beyi* 1948 (1) SA 388 (A); *Ratsialingwa and another* v *Sibasa* 1948 (3) SA 781 (A); *Tushini and others* v *Mzobe and another* 1949 (3) SA 623 (A); *Nkambula* v *Linda* 1951 (1) SA 377 (A); *Umvovo* v *Umvovo* 1953 (1) SA 195 (A); *Mosii* v *Motseoakhumo* 1954 (3) SA 919 (A); *Ex parte Minister of Native Affairs: In re Magqabi* v *Magqabi and Mngonjane* v *Mngonjane* 1955 (2) SA 428 (A); *Saliwa* v *Minister of Native Affairs* 1956 (2) SA 310 (A); *Ex parte Minister of Bantu Administration and Development: In re Jili* v *Duma and another* 1960 (1) SA 1 (A); *Matshali* v *Gwala* 1960 (1) SA 597 (A); *Suid-Afrikaanse Nasionale Trust en Assuransie Maatskappy Bpk* v *Fondo* 1960 (2) SA 467 (A); *R* v *Dumezweni* 1961 (2) SA 751 (A).

Cases which are only marginally concerned with customary law, for example, *R* v *Kumalo and others* 1952 (1) SA 381 (A) (see especially at 386E–F), fall outside the scope of this essay.

To understand why three of the cases are *Ex parte Minister of Native Affairs* and one *Ex parte Minister of Bantu Administration and Development*, it is necessary to remember that s 14 of Act 38 of 1927, first called the Native Administration Act, later the Bantu Administration Act, now the Black Administration Act (hereafter referred to as 'the Act'), empowered the Minister (originally of Native Affairs, later of Bantu Administration and Development, now of Co-operation and Development) to submit a decision on questions of law arrived at by a Native Appeal Court, later the Bantu Appeal Court, now the Appeal Court of Commissioners' Courts, to the Appellate Division for its determination, if he doubted the correctness of the decision.

[4] The three in which he did not sit are *Tushini and others* v *Mzobe and another*; *Nkambula* v *Linda*; *Suid-Afrikaanse Nasionale Trust en Assuransie Maatskappy Bpk* v *Fondo* (all *supra* n 3).

[5] The five are *Ex parte Minister of Native Affairs: In re Yako* v *Beyi*; *Ratsialingwa and another* v *Sibasa*; *Umvovo* v *Umvovo*; *Ex parte Minister of Native Affairs: In re Magqabi* v *Magqabi and Mngonjane* v *Mngonjane*; *Ex parte Minister of Bantu Administration and Development: In re Jili* v *Duma and another* (all *supra* n 3).

It may be noted in passing that all fourteen decisions were unanimous.

notice of, or proof of, customary law; jurisdiction; and topics within the law of persons, property and succession[6] were brought before the court. Each of these subjects will be discussed in turn.

I The Choice of Law

Ex parte Minister of Native Affairs: In re Yako v *Beyi*,[7] usually referred to as *Yako's* case or as *Yako* v *Beyi*, ranks high in any list of important decisions. Section 11(1) of the Black Administration Act 1927,[8] with the interpretation of which the case is principally concerned,[9] read at the time, and still reads, with the exception that the term 'Native' is now 'Black':

> 'Notwithstanding the provisions of any other law, it shall be in the discretion of the courts of native commissioners in all suits or proceedings between Natives involving questions of customs followed by Natives, to decide such questions according to the native law applying to such customs except in so far as it shall have been repealed or modified: Provided that such native law shall not be opposed to the principles of public policy or natural justice: Provided further that it shall not be lawful for any court to declare that the custom of lobola or bogadi or other similar custom is repugnant to such principles.'

The history of this provision is long and involved.[10] After its enactment many interpretations were put forward;[11] but no common ruling could be found until the Natal and Transvaal Division of the Native Appeal Court in *Mashego* v *Ntombela*[12] followed the decision of the Cape and Orange Free State Division given the previous year in *Yako* v *Beyi*.[13] Of the various questions of law on which rulings were given in these two cases, the Minister referred three to the Appellate Division, namely:

(a) 'whether a Native female has the right under common law to sue for damages for seduction';

(b) 'if so, whether the damages claimable by her under the common law must be limited to the amount which her guardian is entitled to claim under Native law'; and

[6] Persons, property, and succession are the three branches of customary law in which distinctive rules are most likely to endure: see, for example, D S Koyana *Customary Law in a Changing Society* (1980) 158 and the present writer in a review of that work in (1981) 98 *SALJ* 442 at 447.

[7] 1948 (1) SA 388 (A).

[8] Act 38 of 1927: see note 3.

[9] It is also concerned with s 11(3), as to which see the section below on the Law of Persons.

[10] See G B M Whitfield *South African Native Law* 2 ed (1948) 1ff; S M Seymour *Bantu Law in South Africa* 3 ed (1970) 1ff; N J J Olivier (Jnr) 'Artikel 11(1) van die Bantoe-administrasiewet, Wet 38 van 1927' (1976) 9 *De Jure* 284; (1977) 10 *De Jure* 141. See also A J Kerr 'The Reception and Codification of Systems of Law in Southern Africa' (1958) 2 *Journal of African Law* 82 at 89–100.

[11] See Julius Lewin 'The Conflict of Native Law and Common Law in South Africa' (1941) 58 *SALJ* 365 and the cases before 1948 mentioned in N J J Olivier, N J J Olivier (Jnr) and W H Olivier *Die Privaatreg van die Suid Afrikaanse Bantoetaalsprekendes* (1981) 596–612.

[12] 1945 NAC (N & T) 117.

[13] 1944 NAC (C & O) 72. McLoughlin P sat as President in both cases.

(*c*) 'whether the interpretation placed on subsec (3) of sec 11 of Act 38 of 1927, as amended by sec 5 of Act 21 of 1943, by the Native Appeal Court (Natal and Transvaal) in its judgment in the case of *Phillip Mashego* v *Agrineth Ntombela* is correct.'[14]

The first of the three questions was the most fundamental: is South African common law[15] available to all inhabitants of the country of whatever race? Both divisions of the Native Appeal Court had held that 'a Native litigant cannot ignore the system of law peculiar to himself to the detriment of his adversary'.[16] Schreiner JA (with whom Watermeyer CJ and Tindall, Centlivres and Greenberg JJA concurred) must have felt that the answer to the first question was obviously in the affirmative. He reframed the question, saying:[17] 'The matter that is really sought to be determined is whether a Native woman as such is debarred from bringing an action for damages for seduction against a Native man in a Native Commissioner's court.' Dealing with this problem, the learned judge of appeal pointed out that

> 'the Native Commissioners' courts are expressed to be courts of law (sec 10(2)); in the absence of any further provision the law that they would have to apply would be the general law of the land',[18]

and said:[19]

> 'I can find no support in the language of [the Native Administration] Act 38 of 1927 for the President's view that Native law should be treated as prima facie applicable in cases between Natives. On the contrary, the indications are rather that common law was intended to be applied unless the Native Commissioner in his discretion saw fit in a proper case to apply Native law. . . . But I do not find it necessary for the purpose of deciding the present matter to hold that such a prima facie preference for the use of common law exists; and as there are various factors which the Native Commissioner would in one case or another have to take into account and which would ordinarily outweigh any such preference I think that I should assume, what leads for present purposes to the same result, that the Native Commissioner should exercise his discretion without regarding either of the systems of law as prima facie applicable. In each case he has at some stage to determine which system of law it would be fairest to apply in deciding the case between the parties.'

[14] See *Yako's* case 1948 (1) SA 388 (A) at 392–3, where the first two are grouped together. Why the Minister referred only these questions is not apparent. Another question, namely, that where there is a breach of promise of a contract to enter into the South African common-law marriage any loss is the father's and not the daughter's (1944 NAC (C & O) 72, point (d)), is as questionable as those which were referred.

[15] Using this term with the meaning explained in *Customary Law* 10.

[16] *Yako* v *Beyi* 1944 NAC (C & O) 72 at 80; *Mashego* v *Ntombela* 1945 NAC (N & T) 117 at 122.

[17] At 393.

[18] At 394.

[19] At 397.

Attention is drawn to the technique, in marked contrast to that in the courts *a quo*, by which Schreiner JA solved the problem: the preliminary careful examination of the statute in question; consideration of the context in which the statute applied; the decision not to go further than the case before the court required; and the statement of the final goal, namely, fairness in deciding the case between the parties.[20]

The importance of achieving a just result was referred to again later, where Schreiner JA said:[21]

> '. . .[I]t would not necessarily and in all cases lead to a juster result to apply the system of law which alone gives the plaintiff a remedy or which gives him or her the more adequate remedy. Generally, no doubt, if a remedy exists under one of the two systems but not under the other this would be a reason for applying the former, since the existence of a remedy, especially under the more advanced system of law, itself provides some ground for believing that its general application would probably be in the interests of justice. But in some cases it may seem to be preferable to give effect to a defence that the defendant has under the one system and not under the other. . . .
>
> '. . .[T]he Native Commissioner must of course pay principal regard to the facts of the case before him since the dominant consideration is his own reasoned view as to the best system of law to apply in order to reach a just decision between the parties.'

These remarks were misunderstood by the Native Appeal Court in *Mtolo* v *Poswa*,[22] where it was said:

> '[T]he Native Commissioner has the choice of applying the one or the other system of law only when the wrong complained of is actionable under both systems of law; otherwise the law which provides the remedy should be applied.'

Mtolo's case came up for consideration in the Appellate Division in *Umvovo* v *Umvovo*,[23] a case that has a complicated history of its own. Schreiner JA (with whom Centlivres CJ and Fagan JA concurred) said:[24]

> '[A]lthough the existence of a remedy under one legal system and not under the other would be a major factor in the exercise of the discretion, it must not be treated as if it were the only consideration, leading automatically to the application of the system providing the remedy.'

[20] Cf statements in other contexts which show Mr Justice Schreiner's concern for what is right, fair and just, for example, *R* v *Kumalo* 1952 (1) SA 381 (A) at 385E–H; *Daniels* v *Daniels* 1958 (1) SA 513 (A) at 522F–G; *National and Overseas Distributors Corporation (Pty) Ltd* v *Potato Board* 1958 (2) SA 473 (A) at 479E–G; *R* v *Sillas* 1959 (4) SA 305 (A) at 311A–B; and in his Hamlyn Lectures on *The Contribution of English Law to South African Law; and the Rule of Law in South Africa* (1967) 19–20.

[21] At 399–401. [22] 1950 NAC (S) 253 at 255.

[23] 1953 (1) SA 195 (A). On its history, see the present writer's article 'Choosing a System of Law by the Exercise of Discretion' 1977 *Acta Juridica* 95 at 99–100.

[24] At 201pr–B.

The main principles established by *Yako's* and *Umvovo's* cases are that South African common law is available to all inhabitants; and that when action is brought in a Commissioner's court consideration is to be given to all the factors in the case, some being of major and others of lesser importance. The exercise of the discretion and the nature of the different factors are discussed elsewhere.[25]

If South African common law is applied in a Commissioner's court, the Minister's second question in *Yako* v *Beyi*[26] arises: are the damages claimable limited to the amount which her guardian is entitled to claim under customary law? In *Yako's* case and *Mashego's* case the courts *a quo* answered in the affirmative, McLoughlin P saying:[27]

> 'A Native litigant cannot force his opponent into a worse position than that in which Native Law places him. By so doing he would unjustly enrich himself at the expense of the other in contravention of the rule of equity.'

Schreiner JA dealt with the matter as follows:[28]

> '. . .[R]eference may be made to a feature that bulks largely in the two judgments under review. The President speaks with disapproval of the plaintiff's having recourse to common law to obtain a greater benefit than would be allowed under Native law. By seeking a remedy at common law, where only a less favourable one, or possibly even where none at all, would be obtainable under Native law, the President considers that the plaintiff is trying to enrich himself or herself unjustly at the expense of the defendant. It may have been found convenient for a Native plaintiff to indicate in his statement of claim on which system of law he relies, but I cannot think that it should be necessary for him to do so. Apart from any rule of court that may have been introduced in this connection it would seem that the plaintiff should only be required to allege, and later to prove, the facts which he claims entitle him to relief. It is for the Native Commissioner to decide what relief, if any, the plaintiff should receive, and in order to arrive at that decision he will generally, or at least often, have to decide which system of law to apply. But it is not a question of the plaintiff's forcing his action into a European mould, or ignoring the system of law peculiar to himself to the detriment of his adversary or compelling the court to deviate from that system by the mere form of his claim—to quote some of the expressions used by the President. This language seems to me to lose

[25] By the present writer in the article referred to in note 23, by T W Bennett 'The Application of Common Law and Customary Law in Commissioners' Courts' (1979) 96 *SALJ* 399 and by N J J Olivier, N J J Olivier (Jnr) and W H Olivier op cit note 11 at 621–9. See also Erwin Spiro 'Internal Conflicts' (1981) 98 *SALJ* 231 at 235–7. The present writer's article contains a discussion, at 97, of the problem in *Mokhesi* v *Nkenjane* 1962 BAC 70 (S), which is relevant if the question raised in *Matshali* v *Gwala* 1960 (1) SA 597 (A) recurs.

[26] 265 above.

[27] 1944 NAC (C & O) 72 at 79; 1945 NAC (N & T) 117 at 122.

[28] At 397–8.

sight of the fact that it is the Native Commissioner's duty to give judgment for that one of the litigants who is in the right according to the legal system which, in the exercise of his discretion, the Native Commissioner decides to apply in the case. The litigants are entitled to the due exercise of that discretion and neither of them can be criticized because he claims, or claims successfully, that the discretion should be exercised in the manner most favourable to his action or his defence.'

Summing up on this question, he said[29]

> 'there appears to be no reasonable ground for limiting the damages recoverable by the woman under common law to the flat rate amounts[30] recoverable by her guardian under Native law'.

Thus it is clear that damages are to be assessed according to the rules of the system of law under which liability is determined, that is, the system of law applied in the case. This does not mean that the amount awarded under South African common-law rules will always be more than that which would be awarded if customary-law rules were to be applicable. In customary law damages for seduction read in head of cattle, or, in the alternative, their value. The value is the amount that would enable the successful plaintiff to buy live animals of average quality in or near the court's area at the time of action.[31] This varies from place to place and from time to time. Professor D S Koyana says[32] that in the Republic of Transkei in 1980 the amount normally claimed per beast was R160. If the tribal law in question allows five head of cattle for seduction, and if the value in the area equals that in the Republic of Transkei (it may well increase as time passes), the total (R800) may in some cases exceed, and in other cases fall short of, the amount claimable under South African common law.

Difficulties persist, however. As late as 1969, in *Mdolo* v *Vanda*,[33] the court cited with approval[34] a statement in a Native Appeal Court decision before *Yako's* case to the effect that 'the damages awarded under Common Law should have some relation to the amount recoverable under [customary] law' and said that 'this principle is a good one to follow provided it is regarded as a guide and not as a fixed rule'. With respect, it is suggested that when

[29] At 401.

[30] See S M Seymour op cit note 10 at 327–9; N J J Olivier, N J J Olivier (Jnr) and W H Olivier op cit note 11 at 282–8.

[31] *Matolengwe* v *Pateni* 1949 NAC (S) 106; *Mdinge* v *Kotshini* 1951 NAC (S) 270; *Moni* v *Ketani* 1961 NAC 58 (S) at 59.

[32] *Customary Law in a Changing Society* (1980) 7. (The learned author says that the sum he mentions (R160) was 'fixed' by the Transkei Attorneys' Association. Presumably, as in South Africa, only the court can fix a value, but a plaintiff may claim an alternative value in his summons. If this value is not put in issue by the defendant, it is the value given by the court: *Sgatya and another* v *Mbane* 1956 NAC 48 (S); *Mtuzula* v *Nkokla* 1964 BAC 41 (S).) See also G Seymour Wood in (1968) 4 *Speculum Juris* 65 at 68.

[33] 1969 BAC 25 (S). [34] At 26.

South African common law is applied there is no reason to depart from, or to modify, its rules for the recovery of damages. Further, it has been recognized in a number of cases on seduction that two actions may be brought, one in South African common law by the girl and the other in customary law by her guardian.[35] In whichever action it is that is brought second, if the court applies the system of law which gives the plaintiff a remedy, and if that system allows the recovery of an amount greater than that awarded in the first action, the successful plaintiff in the second case gets the difference between the two amounts.[36] If the statement approved in *Mdolo's* case were to be the law, there would be little scope for an award of damages under South African common law to the girl if her father had already sued and been awarded the damages allowed in customary law.

II Judicial Notice of, or Proof of, Customary Law

So far as the present writer is aware, no one has ever doubted that Commissioners' courts and the Appeal Court for Commissioners' Courts take judicial notice of all written sources of customary law, whether statutory or non-statutory. Although the titles of these courts have varied in the past, the rule that judicial notice is taken of written sources of customary law has been uniformly applied. The reason given in *Yako's* case,[37] reaffirmed in *Mosii's*[38] and *Dumezweni's*[39] cases, is that when the Act was passed the legislature took account of the fact that Native Commissioners' courts (as they were to be called) would be staffed by experts who would not need the existence of a custom to be proved in each case. There may well have been a number of experts in 1927[40] with knowledge of customs gathered from sources other than legal ones, and there may be isolated instances of experts with such knowledge today;[41] but it is clear from the references to authority in the reports of the Native Appeal Court, later the Bantu Appeal Court, now the Appeal Court for Commissioners' Courts, that the normal method by which judicial officers in these courts and in Native Commissioners' courts, later Bantu Commissioners' courts, now Commissioners' courts, have in the past acquired and developed, and now acquire and develop, their expertise in customary law is by studying and applying statutory customary law,[42] precedents, the early Commission reports, and books.

[35] A J Kerr 'Choosing a System of Law by the Exercise of Discretion' 1977 *Acta Juridica* 95 at 98.

[36] Ibid. [37] *Supra* note 3 at 394–5. [38] *Supra* note 3 at 930E–F.

[39] *Supra* note 3 at 756C–D. [40] The year in which the Act was passed.

[41] That a Commissioner is entitled to use such knowledge is clear from what is said in *Dumezweni's* case (*supra*) at 756G–757C.

[42] On the point that certain statutes are, or contain, statutory customary law, see *Customary Law* 86–8. *R* v *Mpanza* 1946 AD 763 at 771 is the main Appellate Division authority from the period under discussion in this essay. *R* v *Ngcobo* 1941 AD 412 at 421 is an earlier instance.

The Appellate Division 1945 or 1946. *Left to right:* Oliver D Schreiner JA, B A Tindall JA, E F Watermeyer CJ, Leopold Greenberg JA, R P B Davis AJA. Albert v d S Centlivres JA was absent, serving as Chairman of the Public Service Commission of Inquiry

The Appellate Division 1949 or 1950. *Left to right:* F P (Toon) van den Heever JA, Oliver D Schreiner JA, Albert v d S Centlivres JA, E F Watermeyer CJ, Leopold Greenberg JA, Oscar H Hoexter JA

Whether judicial notice is taken by the Supreme Court of such sources does not seem to have received detailed consideration by the Appellate Division.[43] It is thought that the answer is in the affirmative,[44] but the question is not entirely free from doubt.[45]

III Jurisdiction

When Parliament established special courts empowered to apply customary law, some wondered whether it was the intention that cases between Black South Africans should no longer be brought before any other court.[46] As the Act expressly took away the jurisdiction of magistrates' courts in civil cases within the jurisdiction of Native Commissioners' courts,[47] the question came to this: is the Supreme Court open to Black South Africans, or has its jurisdiction also been ousted? The point was raised in *Yako's* case[48] and decided in *Mosii* v *Motseoakhumo*,[49] where it was held that the Supreme Court's jurisdiction has not been ousted.

Commissioners' courts hear cases in which both parties are Black South Africans.[50] Have they jurisdiction to hear a claim for the transfer of immovable property when the registrar of deeds, or the corresponding person in cases of unsurveyed land, is not a Black South African? The answer given in *Tushini and others* v *Mzobe and another*[51] was in the affirmative, it being noted that what the plaintiff had claimed was an order that the defendants be ordered to sign all documents necessary to pass transfer. Whether the Commissioners' courts can in the alternative authorize a messenger of the court to execute documents was a matter not before the court, the question not having been put by the Native Appeal Court, but was referred to,[52] because there was such a claim in the summons.[53] It seems to be clear from two later decisions, one of the Native

[43] The question is discussed by the present writer in 'The Application of Native Law in the Supreme Court' (1957) 74 *SALJ* 313. Of the cases in the Appellate Division that fall within the scope of this essay, the following are discussed in the article: *R* v *Mpanza* (*supra* n 42); *Ex parte Minister of Native Affairs: In re Yako* v *Beyi*; *Mosii* v *Motseoakhumo*; *Saliwa* v *Minister of Native Affairs*; and *Nkambula* v *Linda* (all *supra* n 3).

[44] See the article referred to in the previous note.

[45] The reason why the question is not entirely free from doubt is that some statements are made in wide terms. It must be remembered that judicial statements are always to be read against the background of the case in which they are made. Hence the statement in *R* v *Dumezweni* 1961 (2) SA 751 (A) at 756E–F, reaffirming the statement in *Mosii's* case to the effect that 'in the ordinary courts of law Native custom must be proved in the same manner as any other custom' (per Hoexter JA, who relied on *Yako's* case as his authority), is to be read as referring to customs on which written sources are meagre or lacking. In other words, as cases accumulate, unwritten 'customs' are recorded and become part of written customary law: see the article referred to in note 43 above.

[46] See *Njapa* v *Njapa* 1932 NLR 421; *Seneloe* v *Thloloe and others* 1935 TPD 290; *Sigcau* v *Sigcau* 1941 CPD 71; *Ntisana NO* v *Ntisana* 1944 EDL 69.

[47] Section 17(4) of the Act.

[48] 1948 (1) SA 388 (A) at 393.

[49] 1954 (3) SA 919 (A) at 929A–B.

[50] Section 10(1) of the Act.

[51] 1949 (3) SA 623 (A).

[52] At 626.

[53] See 624.

Appeal Court[54] and the other of the Bantu Appeal Court,[55] that a Commissioner's court has such jurisdiction.

IV The Law of Persons

The Act recognizes two forms of union: a 'marriage', which in its terminology[56] means

> 'the union of one man and one woman in accordance with any law for the time being in force in any Province governing marriages, but does not include any union contracted under Black law and custom . . .',

and a 'customary union', which in its terminology[57] means

> 'the association of a man and a woman in a conjugal relationship according to Black law and custom, where neither the man nor the woman is party to a subsisting marriage'.

Special provision is made concerning the proprietary consequences of marriages between Black South Africans. Section 22(6) reads, and read in 1945 with minor changes in terminology relating to the word 'Native':

> 'A marriage between Blacks, contracted after the commencement of this Act, shall not produce the legal consequences of marriage in community of property between the spouses: Provided that in the case of a marriage contracted otherwise than during the subsistence of a customary union between the husband and any woman other than the wife it shall be competent for the intending spouses at any time within one month previous to the celebration of such marriage to declare jointly before any magistrate, Commissioner or marriage officer (who is hereby authorized to attest such declaration) that it is their intention and desire that community of property and of profit and loss shall result from their marriage, and thereupon such community shall result from their marriage except as regards any land in a location held under quitrent tenure such land shall be excluded from such community.'

It will have been noted that the Act does not say what the proprietary regime shall be if no joint declaration of intention is made before marriage. It contains only the negative statement that such a marriage 'shall not produce the legal consequences of marriage in community of property between the spouses'. When Abraham Molefe died intestate in 1942 he was survived by a son born of his first marriage, which was in community of property, and by his

[54] *Skey* v *Mzamo* 1962 NAC 44 (S) at 49–50.

[55] *Mallie* v *Messenger of the Court and Mtimkulu* 1964 BAC 94 (N–E) at 95–6. As regards the reference in this case to *Sacks NO and Molope* v *Mdhluli* 1956 NAC 43 (C), see now the definition of 'Black' in s 35 of the Act as amended. The amendment, effected by s 4 of the Black Laws Amendment Act 70 of 1974, adopts the point of view put forward by M J D Francis 'Civil Jurisdiction of Native Commissioners' Courts' (1964) 81 *SALJ* 117 and H Balk 'Jurisdiction of Bantu Affairs Commissioners' Civil Courts' (1964) 81 *SALJ* 375.

[56] Section 35 of the Act.

[57] Ibid.

wife in his second marriage, to which the terms of s 22(6) applied.[58] His widow claimed to be heir, saying that she had been married in community of property; but it was found that s 22(6) applied.[59] As the succession regulations then read, the property devolved 'as if [the deceased] had been a European'.[60] If the widow was a surviving spouse who had been 'married out of community of property' she was heir to the entire estate in terms of the Succession Act 1934,[61] the amount involved being less than £600.

In the Native Appeal Court Braatvedt P said:[62]

> 'It appears to me that the intention of the legislature [in enacting s 22(6) of the Act] was that native law should apply to native women on marriage, except where the parties specially declare their desire for community of property; and native law is that the husband is the sole owner. . . .
>
> 'That Act [the Succession Act 1934] undoubtedly applies only to common law marriages, i.e. marriages either in or out of community of property. It does not apply to native customary unions. Plaintiff's marriage does not fall under the common law. She is in the same position as far as property rights are concerned, as a wife of a customary union. Everything belongs to her husband. Her marriage is neither in nor out of community of property. In my opinion she cannot succeed to the estate under Act No. 13 of 1934.'

Johnson M said:[63]

> 'Section 22(6) is clear and unequivocal. *Unless* an antenuptial written declaration is entered into by the spouses concerned, the consequences of their marriage are governed by their "recognised" native laws and customs obtaining between them.'

Morgan M dissented, saying:[64]

> 'It has been suggested that the marriage between the late Abraham Molefe and Adelina [the plaintiff, his second wife] was not necessarily a marriage *out of* community of property merely because it was *not in* community of property, and that for this reason the provisions of [the Succession] Act No. 13 of 1934 are inoperative.
>
> 'The common law consequences of marriage (i.e. community of property) may be specifically altered by an antenuptial contract providing, *inter alia*, for the exclusion of community of property as well as of profit and loss.
>
> 'The common law consequences of marriage may also be altered by operation of law. This is indeed the case with Native marriages (not customary unions) where no declaration in terms of section 22(6) of [the Native Administration] Act No. 38 of 1927 has been made by the parties.

[58] See *Molefe* v *Molefe* 1944 NAC (T & N) 8.
[59] Ibid.
[60] *Customary Law* 277n1.
[61] Act 13 of 1934. [62] 1944 NAC (T & N) 8 at 10.
[63] At 11. Italics by the learned member of the court.
[64] At 12. Italics by the learned member of the court.

'The result in either case is the exclusion of community of property. It seems to follow that if a marriage is not *in* community of property that it must be *out of* community of property.'

This, then, was the origin of the problem which the Minister referred to the Appellate Division. He omitted any reference to the Succession Act of 1934, and, concerning a marriage under s 22(6) where there is no existing customary union and no joint antenuptial declaration, asked: 'are the proprietary rights of the parties the same as those of [parties to] any legal marriage out of community of property, or are their rights regulated by native law and custom?'[65] The Appellate Division, with respect correctly, held that the nature of the union was more important than its proprietary consequences. Watermeyer CJ (with whom Tindall, Greenberg JA, Schreiner JA and Davis AJA concurred), after quoting the definition of 'marriage' in the Act, said:

'In the case of a legal marriage, . . . the proprietary rights of the spouses resulting therefrom must be governed by the common law of South Africa except in so far as specific provisions have been introduced by statute, which alter the common law.'[66]

'[S]ec 22(6) has altered the common law by providing that community of property shall not result from a marriage between Natives. The Act has not provided that such Native custom, as would regulate the proprietary rights of the spouses if the marriage were a customary union, shall take the place of the common law. Consequently the common law must be applied, with the specific modification that community of property does not result from such a marriage unless a contract in terms of sec 22(6) is entered into.'[67]

'If a marriage does not introduce community of property between spouses such marriage is necessarily, in the absence of special legislative provision, a marriage out of community of property.'[68]

It is clear from the above and from what is said elsewhere in the judgment[69] that there are three proprietary regimes open to Black South Africans when they marry,[70] if neither is a partner in an existing customary union: *(a)* community of property and of profit and loss introduced by joint antenuptial declaration in terms of s 22(6); *(b)* whatever arrangements the parties make by antenuptial contract; and *(c)* in the absence of *(a)* and *(b)*, by virtue of s 22(6), no community of property or of profit and loss,[71] control of the property of both spouses being vested in the husband by virtue of his marital power.[72]

[65] *Ex parte Minister of Native Affairs: In re Molefe* v *Molefe* 1946 AD 315 at 317. As to the addition of the words 'parties to', see at 317–18.

[66] At 318. [67] At 318–19. [68] At 320. [69] At 319–20.

[70] Using the word as defined in the Act, that is, the parties enter into a South African common-law union. They also have the option, if they so desire, of entering into a customary union.

[71] For the reference to profit and loss, see at 319.

[72] For the reference to the husband's marital power, see at 320.

A man cannot be a partner in a polygamous union and in a monogamous one at the same time. The first allows him to have two or more lawful wives; under the second he may have only one, and any purported conjugal relationship with another is unlawful. This is the basis of the decision in *Nkambula* v *Linda*.[73] It follows that where, as in South African law,[74] monogamous unions are preferred to polygamous ones, if a man who is a partner in a customary union marries[75] another, he terminates his customary union with his first wife and forfeits the *ikhazi*.[76]

Concern for widows not considered as majors by virtue of any statutory provision[77] led to the amendment of s 11(3) of the Act in 1943.[78] It is so framed that it applies to minors as well.[79] It lays down that, subject to two provisos, the capacity of a Black South African 'to enter into any transaction or to enforce or defend his rights in any court of law shall . . . be determined as if he were a European'. The first proviso lays down that if the existence or extent of any right held or alleged to be held by, or of any obligation resting or alleged to be resting on, a Black South African depends upon or is governed by customary law, the capacity of the person in question must be determined by customary law. The Native Appeal Court in *Mashego* v *Ntombela*[80] appeared to think that the subsection supplied 'the governing factor' in determining the choice of law under s 11(1).[81] Schreiner JA commented:[82]

> 'I am not sure that I understand the reasoning underlying this passage in the President's judgment. As I read sub-sec (3) it has no bearing on the question what law the Native commissioner is to apply in the exercise of his discretion under sub-sec (1). . . . [T]he issue whether or not the question (whether a Native has a right or not) does depend upon or is governed by Native law has to be decided independently of the question whether the Native has or had capacity in relation to any matter affecting the right. . . . Once the system of law is decided upon this will determine questions of capacity in relation both to the party in whom the right is or is claimed to be vested and to the party on whom the obligation rests or is alleged to rest.'

There is another problem relating to customary unions and to the guardianship of children of such unions. Does South African common law *recognize* (in the sense in which the word is used in the

[73] 1951 (1) SA 377 (A). See especially at 380H–381C, 382H–383A.

[74] Transkei law differs: see s 3 of the Transkei Marriage Act 21 of 1978.

[75] Using the word with the meaning in the Act.

[76] *Nkambula* v *Linda* 1951 (1) SA 377 (A).

[77] For statutory provisions see *Mlanjeni* v *Macala* 1947 NAC (C & O) 1 at 2–3.

[78] Black Administration (Amendment) Act 21 of 1943. See A J Kerr 'Does a Minor Need Two Natural Guardians in Two Systems of Law to Assist Him at the Same Time?' (1965) 82 *SALJ* 487 at 492–3.

[79] See the article in the previous note.

[80] 1945 NAC (N & T) 117.

[81] At 122, per McLoughlin P.

[82] In *Yako's* case (*supra* n 3) at 402.

conflict of laws, whether inter-personal or inter-territorial), as distinct from *enforce*, the rights and obligations of the parties and the rights of guardianship arising from such unions?[83] The Appellate Division case bearing on this problem within the period dealt with in this essay is *Suid-Afrikaanse Nasionale Trust en Assuransie Maatskappy Bpk* v *Fondo*,[84] which, it is suggested with due respect, was wrongly decided.[85] The point need not be laboured with reference to the wife, because Parliament, recognizing that the resulting situation required changes to be made, enacted s 31 of the Black Laws Amendment Act 1963.[86] This, however, left the position relating to guardianship of children untouched. If the decision in *SANTAM* v *Fondo* were to be considered to be correct, and if the husband and wife were to be living together,[87] the court would, in effect, have to say to the father: 'We do not recognize your guardianship over your children. We do, however, recognize your guardianship over your wife. We treat her as guardian of your children, though we know she is not such in customary law, which is the system of law under which you are united. Although we treat her as the guardian of the children, as she is considered to be a minor subject to your guardianship[88] you are entitled to exercise rights of guardianship over the children.'[89] Schreiner JA was not on the bench in *SANTAM* v *Fondo*. How different this chapter in the history of our law might have been if he had had to deal with the issues raised.

V The Law of Property

Section 11(1) of the Act gives Commissioners' courts a discretion to decide a question in issue according to the law applying to the relevant custom(s). This confines the application of customary law to substantive matters.[90] The remedies of South African common law are used in whichever system of law the right originates.[91] The same holds true of a case involving customary law brought in the Supreme Court, because there the custom is proved in the same

[83] See A J Kerr 'Liability in Delict for Wrongfully Causing the Death of a Native Man Married According to Native Law' (1956) 73 *SALJ* 402; Ellison Kahn 'Dependant's Action Brought by Native Customary Wife' (1960) 77 *SALJ* 279; A J Kerr 'Guardianship of Children of Bantu Customary Unions: The Inter-personal Conflict of Laws Problem' (1973) 90 *SALJ* 4; Reep verLoren van Themaat 'Voogdy van 'n Swart Minderjarige Gebore uit 'n Gebruiklike Verbinding (Die Gewoonteregtelike Huwelik van Swartes)—Die Nie-erkenning van Inheemse Gewoontereg in die Gewone Howe van Suid-Afrika' (1979) 42 *THRHR* 112; and, in general, Joan Church 'Guardianship as an Incident of the Customary Law of Parent and Child—With Reference to Transkei' (1979) 12 *CILSA* 326.

[84] 1960 (2) SA 467 (A). [85] See (1973) 90 *SALJ* 4. [86] Act 76 of 1963.

[87] See proviso *(b)* to s 11(3) of the Act. [88] See (1973) 90 *SALJ* 4.

[89] See (1973) 90 *SALJ* 4 at 5, 8–11.

[90] A J Kerr 'Choosing a System of Law by the Exercise of Discretion' 1977 *Acta Juridica* 95 at 96.

[91] Ibid.

way as any other custom would be proved, and no question of procedure, or of the law in which the remedy is found, arises. The appellant in *Mosii* v *Motseoakhumo*[92] had built a house on a plot of land 'which had been allotted to him for residential purposes according to Native law and custom'.[93] The respondent was the chief of his tribe. It was claimed that the respondent did not have the sanction of his tribe for what he proposed to do,[94] namely, to compel the residents of the area to move elsewhere.[95] Whether or not the tribe had sanctioned the move was in dispute. The appellant applied in the Griqualand West Local Division for an interdict. Pending resolution of the dispute concerning the tribe's sanction, a temporary interdict was granted,[96] a decision which was upheld by the Appellate Division with a slight modification.[97] Hoexter JA (with whom Centlivres CJ, Greenberg, Schreiner and Van den Heever JJA concurred) said:[98]

> 'On the material before me I am not in a position to define, nor shall I attempt to define the exact nature of the right of possession acquired by the appellant in respect of the land allotted to him, but I have no doubt that his actual possession, as evidenced by his occupation and improvement of that land, entitles him at common law to the ordinary possessory remedies and in the present case to the remedy against disturbance of possession which may owe its origin to the *interdictum uti possidetis* of the Roman law. (See eg Voet 43.17 and Grotius 2.2.6.)'

On the ownership of land in customary law, the leading case came before the Appellate Division in 1948: *Ratsialingwa and another* v *Sibasa*.[99] In 1946 the Government had dismissed Sibasa from the chieftainship of his section of the Bavenda tribe and had appointed Ratsialingwa in his place. To what property, if any, previously owned or controlled by Sibasa was Ratsialingwa entitled? This was the question brought before the Transvaal Provincial Division[100] and then, on appeal, before the Appellate Division. In so far as immovable property was concerned, there were two problems: *(a)* Sibasa's residence, referred to, when he was the chief, as the Great Place;[101] and *(b)* the *dzunde* lands, which were lands cultivated and reaped for the chief by the tribesmen, the chief supplying the seed.[102] If, as Roper J thought in the court *a quo*, 'there is no individual ownership of land in Native law',[103] the inquiry would be limited to rights of possession or occupation.[104] In the Appellate

92 1954 (3) SA 919 (A).
93 Per Hoexter JA at 923G–H.
94 At 924A–C.
95 At 924pr–B.
96 At 925E–H.
97 At 931D–F.
98 At 930pr–A.
99 1948 (3) SA 781 (A).
100 *Sibasa* v *Ratsialingwa and Hartman NO* 1947 (4) SA 369 (T).
101 1948 (3) SA 781 (A) at 794–5. It was his 'residence' even though he was compelled by Government order to live elsewhere: at 795.
102 1947 (4) SA 369 (T) at 393.
103 1947 (4) SA 369 (T) at 385.
104 Note the grant (at 398) of prayer (d) of the petition, which asked for a declaration that Sibasa was 'entitled under tribal law and custom to occupy the site of his present dwelling . . .' (at 378).

Division, however, Schreiner JA (with whom Tindall ACJ and Greenberg JA concurred) took the view, which is in accord with other authority,[105] that there is ownership in residential (other authorities add 'and arable') land in customary law, although the incidents of such ownership are not necessarily the same in all respects as those of ownership in South African common law.[106] The learned judge of appeal said:[107]

> '. . . [O]ne must start from the principle that, if a system of law recognizes that a man may own property, the property which he had received by a recognized system of succession or which he has acquired by lawful transactions belongs to him, subject only to such rights of other persons as the system of law also recognizes.'

And:[108]

> '. . . [O]n the evidence the "Great Place" in question in this case must be regarded as Sibasa's dwelling, which he inherited from his father, and not as a public building or group of buildings used for the carrying on of the business of the tribe. Subject to such limitations as native law may impose in favour of his family it was his property and he was entitled to an order declaring it to be his as against Ratsialingwa.'

The *dzunde* lands, on the other hand, had not been occupied by Sibasa personally and were not his property:

> '[T]hey are not held by him but are part of the tribal lands which are set aside to be worked by the tribesmen to provide the chief for the time being with the means of carrying out his duties.'[109]

VI THE LAW OF SUCCESSION

It does not often happen that a court finds that legislation, even subordinate legislation, is so badly framed that it (the court) has to substitute its own formulation for one or more of the propositions contained in it. This was the position in *Ex parte Minister of Native Affairs: In re Magqabi* v *Magqabi and Mngonjane* v *Mngonjane*.[110] Section 23(2) of the Act reads:

> 'All land in a location held in individual tenure upon quitrent conditions by a Black shall devolve upon his death upon one male person, to be determined in accordance with tables of succession to be prescribed under sub-section (10).'

The tables in question in *Magqabi's* case were those in Proclamation 142 of 1910. In essence those in force at present in the Cape

[105] *Customary Law* 54–94.

[106] *Customary Law* 75–6. See also Roper J in the court *a quo* at 385–6. It is suggested, with due respect, that Roper J went too far both when he said that 'there is no individual ownership of land in Native law' and when he said, referring to movables, that 'there was originally no power of testation'. On the earlier statement, see above, and on the latter, see *Customary Law* 143–51.

[107] At 791–2. [108] At 795. [109] Per Schreiner JA at 796.

[110] 1955 (2) SA 428 (A).

Province[111] are the same. The main problem was that the tables give the deceased's 'eldest son of the principal house' as the heir first in rank,[112] and the definition of a 'house' in the Act[113] clearly specifies a family unit arising out of a customary union. It being recognized that a South African common-law marriage does not give rise to a 'house' in this sense,[114] does it follow that no son of a South African common-law union, often the only form of union his father had, can succeed to quitrent land of which his father died possessed? Schreiner JA (with whom Van den Heever and Hoexter JJA concurred), without taking refuge in any talk of ambiguities or hidden specialized meanings (apart from a reference to a certain 'looseness of usage'),[115] pointed out the shortcomings in the regulations,[116] and reframed the one with which the case was concerned.[117] The fact that the reframed version can, with respect, be improved upon[118] does not detract from one's tribute to the forthright manner in which Schreiner JA dealt with the problem.

The decision[119] clears up some of the difficulties in relation to s 23(2). It does not dispose of similar but more widespread difficulties with reg 2 of Government Notice R34 of 1966.[120] It is to be regretted that the Department responsible for the subordinate legislation in question has not dealt comprehensively with the problems in the more than twenty-five years that have elapsed since the decision was given.[121]

When the Act was first promulgated, s 23(3), which deals with liberty to bequeath property that is neither house property[122] nor quitrent land,[123] read:

> 'All other property of whatsoever kind belonging to a Native shall be capable of being devised by will. Any such property not so devised shall devolve and be administered according to Native law and custom.'

There was also s 23(10), which gave the Governor-General power to make regulations, not inconsistent with the Act,

> '*(a)* prescribing the manner in which the estates of deceased Natives shall be administered and distributed . . .'.

In 1929 the second sentence of s 23(3) was repealed. Later in the same year Government Notice 1664 of 1929, which purported to have been made by virtue of the powers given in s 23(10), was promulgated. It dealt not only with the administration of estates

[111] See *Customary Law* 273–5.
[112] The whole table is clearly statutory customary law: *Customary Law* 224–5.
[113] Section 35. [114] At 432H–433B, 436pr–A. [115] At 436A–D.
[116] At 433C–434C, 436E–F. [117] At 435H–fine. [118] *Customary Law* 227.
[119] With the suggestion in *Customary Law* 227 as to the words of items 1–2 of the table of succession.
[120] See *Customary Law* 235–40.
[121] Some suggestions for improvement are to be found in *Customary Law* 239–40.
[122] Dealt with in s 23(1). [123] The subject of s 23(2).

but also with rules concerning the choice of law.[124] This raised the question whether rules of choice of law fell within the reference to 'distribution' in s 23(10). If so, the regulations and their successors were valid; if not, they were beyond the powers conferred by that subsection and invalid. In 1957 the North-Eastern Native Appeal Court, despite five decisions in other courts indicating that the regulations were valid,[125] by a two to one majority held them to be *ultra vires*.[126] The Minister then referred the question of validity to the Appellate Division, and asked what rules applied if those in the regulations were *ultra vires*: *Ex parte Minister of Bantu Administration and Development: In re Jili* v *Duma and another*.[127] After a careful examination of the history of choice-of-law rules governing succession to Black South Africans and of the intention disclosed by the amendments introduced by the Native Administration Act, 1927, Amendment Act 1929,[128] Schreiner JA (with whom Beyers, Malan and Ogilvie Thompson JJA and Botha AJA concurred) said:[129]

> '. . . [I]t seems to me to be quite clear that Parliament, when it passed the 1929 Act, did not intend by the repeal of the second sentence of sub-sec (3) to reapply to Native intestate estates the [South African] common-law rules of intestacy.
>
> 'Nevertheless it seems to be equally clear that after the repeal[130] and before the publication of the 1929 regulations[131] it was the common-law rules that applied. For there were no other rules that could apply.
>
> 'But there was nothing to prevent that position from being changed by another Act or by regulations duly made within the enabling provision. No further Act was passed but the 1929 regulations if they were valid could effectively achieve the same result. . . .
>
> '. . . [E]ven in the unamended Act the wording of sec 23(10)(*a*) was wide enough to cover regulations that provided rules of devolution. Our attention was drawn to pre-Union provisions in which the expression "administration and distribution", as applied to the estates of deceased Natives, was apparently used to include the laying down of rules of devolution (see e.g. [the Native Successions] Act 18 of 1864 (C) secs 2 and 5; [the Administration of Estates] Proc 28 of 1902 (T) sec 70). There can be no doubt that the expression can be used in a wide sense of the sort indicated, but there is also no doubt that it can be used in a relatively narrow sense, to connote the procedural steps by which estates are reduced into possession, liquidated and paid out to the persons entitled. The correct sense must depend on the context. . . .'

The learned judge of appeal then mentioned that there was doubt whether before the 1929 amendment there was power under

[124] Cf its successor, reproduced in *Customary Law* 276–83.
[125] See *Customary Law* 231–2. In some of the five the question was not discussed in detail.
[126] *Jili* v *Duma and another* 1957 NAC 129 (N–E).
[127] 1960 (1) SA 1 (A) at 6F–H. [128] Act 9 of 1929. See at 9C–11B.
[129] At 11B–H. [130] On 3 April 1929: see at 8pr–A.
[131] On 20 September 1929: see at 8C–D.

s 23(10)(*a*) to make regulations relating to devolution. One argument not put before the court merits consideration. With the subsection in its unamended state, the regulations could not have altered the system of law by which devolution was to take place, because that would have been inconsistent with the Act as it then read and the regulations would have fallen outside the scope of the opening words of s 23(10). But could regulations not have laid down the order of succession in customary law for the purposes of s 23(3) as it then read, just as other regulations did for the purposes of s 23(2)?

The learned judge of appeal continued:[132]

> 'Assuming this doubt to be well-founded, the second answer to the argument advanced in support of the majority judgment [of the North-Eastern Native Appeal Court] must now be considered. It is that when the 1929 Act repealed the second sentence of sub-sec (3) it so changed the context of sec 23(10)(*a*) as to give it a wider meaning. On principle that seems to be correct. The second sentence of sub-sec (3) completed the system of devolution provided by sub-secs (1), (2) and (3) and it was because of the completeness of the system that the regulating power in sec 23(10)(*a*) had to be interpreted narrowly. Consequently when Parliament removed the second sentence of sub-sec (3) it enabled sec 23(10)(*a*) to be given the wider meaning that could support a regulation providing rules of devolution. In order to ascertain whether the 1929 regulations (as amended) are valid one should read sec 23 in its amended form. (Cf *New Mines Ltd* v *Commissioner for Inland Revenue* 1938 AD 455 at 463, referred to in *R* v *Correia* 1958 (1) SA 533 (AD) at 540.) So reading the section, and having regard to what has been said about the apparent intention of Parliament when it enacted the 1929 Act, it seems to me that sec 23(10)(*a*) in its changed context is wide enough to support reg 2.'

And, after considering an argument about delegation:

> 'The answer to the Minister's first question is that reg 2 of Government Notice 1664 of 1929 is not *ultra vires* either on the ground that it lays down substantive rules of devolution or on the ground of delegation.'[133]

Thus the Minister and countless others, both in his department and in the legal profession, were relieved of their anxieties about the estates which, over a period of thirty years, had been wound up in terms of the regulations.

[132] At 12B–E. [133] At 13C–D.

REFLECTIONS ON SOME ASPECTS OF THE JUDICIAL FUNCTION

C S MARGO*

I

In our judicial system, can the outcome of cases differ according to the background or personality of individual judges? Aside from differences in result *(a)* occasioned by judicial error, or *(b)* caused by dissenting opinions on questions of principle where each conclusion is based on objective reasoning, or *(c)* within the narrow range possible in the exercise of a judicial discretion, the determination of particular issues of fact and of law should in general, and at least in theory, be the same, irrespective of the identity of the judge or judges who decide those issues.

That proposition appears to be justified by solid reasons. First, South Africa, like England, enjoys a monolithic common-law base. Secondly, the judge's oath of office,[1] which is no mere formality, requires him to 'administer justice to all persons alike, without fear, favour or prejudice, and, as the circumstances of any particular case may require, in accordance with the law and customs of the Republic of South Africa'. Thirdly, and perhaps this is the predominating factor, the professional training, experience and outlook of almost all the judges are the product of the same crucible and the same mould, namely, practice at the Bar and the attainment of silk, achieved in the demanding conditions of the adversary system and under the unforgiving scrutiny of the courts, of other members of the Bar and of the attorneys. In those rare instances of the judicial appointment of a silk from the ranks of non-practitioners, the individual has invariably strained to conform to the established modes. Through these pressures and influences, the requirements and traditions of fairness, integrity, application to duty and antiseptic detachment from political or other controversy touching the parties to a case have become part of the system.

In England, where the system is similar, there are a few who refer with disdain to these matrices of the judicial character. The

* BA LLB (Witwatersrand), Judge of the Supreme Court of South Africa, Transvaal Provincial Division.

[1] See s 10(2) of the Supreme Court Act 59 of 1959.

critics are not to be found only among the ranks of unsuccessful litigants. J A G Griffith in *The Politics of the Judiciary* insists that there is judicial partiality, which, he says, 'stems from a strikingly homogeneous collection of attitudes, beliefs and principles which the policy-making judges have acquired by their education, training and pursuit of their profession as barristers'.[2]

A similar distortion of image is that presented by Paul Foot in *Why You Should be a Socialist*.[3] In asserting that there is a class bias on the part of English judges, he says:

> 'No one can be a judge who hasn't been a barrister. And no one can be a barrister without some form of "independent means"[4] and an initiation into a curious, spooky world of "dinners", inns of court and cranky uniforms. Eighty-six per cent of judges were educated at public school.'

These are viewpoints that betray lack of knowledge and experience of the fierce independence, moral fearlessness and sense of duty that are generally characteristic of the Bar and of the judiciary, which stems from the Bar.

The paradigm of the judicial character appears from Steyn CJ's eulogy in the Appellate Division on 19 February 1963, upon the death of Benjamin Arthur Tindall, former judge of appeal.[5] In the course of his speech, the Chief Justice said:

> 'Perfect and absolute detachment, even in a judge, may humanly be unattainable, but it is said of him—and I believe with justification—that he unerringly maintained an objective approach, unblemished by personal preference for any party or for any conflicting interest which might induce a predisposed appraisal, and that he was commendably free from the preoccupations of irrelevant knowledge, sentiment and opinion, which sometimes invade the true merits of a case and tend to confuse impartial judgment.
>
> 'I never had the privilege of making his acquaintance. In our legal literature I have found a surprising dearth of comment. That, perhaps, is how he wished it to be. By all accounts of those who knew him, he was a courteous, modest and unassuming man, of a retiring disposition, without any pretension to any art of a showman which would draw attention to himself or his work. On the Bench he was unruffled, not given to lively passages with counsel, and disinclined to avail himself of the advantage arising from the fact that counsel is precluded from sharp retort.
>
> 'For more than a quarter of a century, he has been one of those whose work and conduct have defined for us all the qualities of a judge, and he

[2] (1977). I have quoted the synopsis by Paul Watchman in the first essay in Peter Robson and Paul Watchman (eds) *Justice, Lord Denning and the Constitution* (1981) 18.

[3] (SWP Publications 1977) 26, as quoted by Peter Robson in the second essay op cit note 2 at 46.

[4] Those in this country who might be encouraged by these remarks to extend financial credit to junior advocates should be cautioned that Foot's excogitation has no application to the South African Bar.

[5] See (1963) 80 *SALJ* 164.

has added to our jurisprudence a wealth of opinion upon which all members of the profession will continue to draw for many years to come.'

The near-perfection of judicial qualities ascribed to Tindall JA (sometime ACJ) is not unique. There are many other examples in our judicial history, among them Schreiner JA, but the judges, like any other company of believers in high principles, must inevitably have their weaker brethren. Judges are not above the ordinary human traits of personal beliefs, likes, dislikes, and disapproval of certain views or conduct, although by their training and experience, and the pressures of our judicial system, they contrive in general to eliminate conscious prejudices.

It would be unrealistic not to recognize that, at least at the frontiers of judicial lawmaking, that is, in those areas where new questions of law have to be solved, the background and personality of the judges must from time to time influence developments. Mr Justice Saul Solomon was wont to recount the story that Sir Henry de Villiers, after learning in 1909 that he was to become the Union's first Chief Justice, manoeuvred to obtain a 'Cape majority' in the Appellate Division, so that when the question of valuable consideration in contract came up, as it was certain to do, the view of the Cape Supreme Court in *Mtembu* v *Webster*[6] should prevail over that of the Transvaal Supreme Court in *Rood* v *Wallach*.[7] As it happened, the issue was not raised in the Appellate Division until 1919,[8] by which time Lord De Villiers, as he became, was no longer in office, and the Transvaal view was upheld. Though not an example of a judicial decision influenced by the background or personality of a judge, the story (if true) is near enough to illustrate the possible effects on some legal decisions of the beliefs and convictions of individual judges. More striking illustrations may be found in Edwin Cameron's recent article in the *South African Law Journal* on the judicial career of Steyn CJ.[9]

In *The Nature of the Judicial Process*[10] United States Supreme Court Justice Cardozo offered an analysis of the considerations and motives that influence judicial decisions. He distinguished the conscious factors from what he termed the subconscious ones.[11] The first category consisted of the acknowledged guiding principles of conduct. The second comprised the inherited instincts, traditional beliefs and acquired convictions, with a resultant outlook on life and conception of social needs.

[6] (1904) 21 SC 323. [7] 1904 TS 187.
[8] See *Conradie* v *Rossouw* 1919 AD 279. [9] See (1982) 99 *SALJ* 38.
[10] This is the title of the published addresses delivered by Justice Benjamin N Cardozo to the Law School of Yale University in 1921, as part of the William L Storrs Lecture Series.
[11] At 11.

Referring to the judicial interpretation of codes and practices, Justice Cardozo observed:[12]

> 'There are gaps to be filled. There are doubts and ambiguities to be cleared. There are hardships and wrongs to be mitigated if not avoided. Interpretation is often spoken of as if it were nothing but the search and the discovery of a meaning which, however obscure and latent, had none the less a real and ascertainable pre-existence in the legislator's mind. The process is, indeed, that at times, but it is often something more. The ascertainment of intention may be the least of a judge's troubles in ascribing meaning to a statute. "The fact is", says Gray in his lectures on the "Nature and Sources of the Law", that the difficulties of so-called interpretation arise when the legislature has had no meaning at all; when the question which is raised on the statute never occurred to it; when what the judges have to do is not to determine what the legislature did mean on a point which was present to its mind, but to guess what it would have intended on a point not present to its mind if the point had been present.'

According to Justice Cardozo,[13] the judge as the interpreter for the community of its sense of law and order must supply omissions, correct uncertainties and harmonize results with justice through a method of free decision. He quoted Ehrlich[14] on the point that in the long run 'there is no guaranty of justice except the personality of the judge', and he commented:[15]

> 'Interpretation, thus enlarged, becomes more than the ascertainment of the meaning and intent of lawmakers whose collective will has been declared. It supplements the declaration, and fills the vacant spaces, by the same processes and methods that have built up the customary law. Codes and other statutes may threaten the judicial function with repression and disuse and atrophy. The function flourishes and persists by virtue of the human need to which it steadfastly responds. Justinian's prohibition of any commentary on the product of his codifiers is remembered only for its futility.'

Justice Cardozo concluded[16] that the judicial process, in its highest reaches, is not discovery but creation. The forces that shape the form and content of judgments in that process are not only those consciously recognized, but also those deep below consciousness, such as the likes and dislikes, the predilections and the prejudices, the complex of instincts and emotions and habits and convictions, which make the man.

The extent to which an individual judge's beliefs and personality can influence not only his own decisions in developmental areas of the law, but also the decisions of other members of the appellate

[12] At 14. [13] At 16.
[14] *Freie Rechtsfindung und freie Rechtswissenschaft* (1905) (Modern Legal Philosophy Series IX). 'Guaranty' is so spelt.
[15] At 17–18. [16] At 166–7.

court on which he sits, is the subject of a growing number of recent publications.[17] There is no better illustration of the phenomenon than the history of the constitutional decisions of the United States Supreme Court over the last fifty years, with alignments of conservative and liberal opinions and split decisions on civil rights.

The popular concept (which does not embrace views such as those of J A G Griffith or Paul Foot) being that justice and the judges are totally objective and impersonal, there is a reluctance to acknowledge the role of the background and personality of the judges in the judicial law-making process, 'as if judges must lose respect and confidence by the reminder that they are subject to human limitations'.[18] There can be no advantage in this fiction. On the contrary, in the judicial process, the cause of truth and objectivity, and of judicial detachment itself, can only be advanced by candid recognition of these elements.

II

Judge Harold R Medina, of the United States Court of Appeals for the Second Circuit, in a light-hearted address delivered in 1952,[19] claimed that when he became a judge he discovered with surprise that there were cases in which counsel, by 'the cogency of . . . [his] argument, the skill and ingenuity with which he built up his propositions in logical sequence and the research he brought to bear upon his presentation of the case really did much more than merely clarify the issues and then leave the case for me to decide'. Judge Medina noted that certain judges were unwilling to admit that counsel was able to persuade the judge to decide a certain way when, if left to himself, he might well have decided the contrary. Judge Medina was only too ready to confess that judges could be so persuaded. He declared:[20]

> 'Assuming that at least some judges hate to admit that a lawyer has argued them into deciding a case on a certain theory, why does the judge act this way? Perhaps he is beginning to get an exaggerated notion of his relative importance in the general scheme of things. I don't say he is; I only say *quaere*. . . .
>
> 'After all is said and done, we cannot deny the fact that a judge is almost of necessity surrounded by people who keep telling him what a wonderful fellow he is. And if he once begins to believe it he is a lost soul.'

As to the points referred to in the last sentence of this quotation, it may at once be said that in South Africa, as elsewhere, respon-

[17] See, for example, H N Hirsch's *The Enigma of Felix Frankfurter* (1981) and the publications listed there in note 1 to chapter 1 at 214.

[18] *The Nature of the Judicial Process* 168.

[19] 'Some Reflections on the Judicial Functions: A Personal Viewpoint' (1952) 38 *American Bar Association J* 107.

[20] Idem at 108.

sible and well-informed academic criticism seems to play a particularly sanitary role in protecting judges from any such belief and from the denial of eternal salvation by reason thereof. However, as is found in even the best of hygienic systems, the protection is not one hundred per cent effective.

The concept of persuasion in the full sense is too wide to be accepted. No doubt an advocate, by sheer oratory, by emotional eloquence, by playing on the heart-strings of the court, could sometimes induce a wrong decision in a jury trial. It would be disturbing indeed if judges could likewise be influenced to decide wrongly on sentimental or emotional grounds alone.

While such a possibility cannot be denied, an analysis of the basis upon which the trained judicial mind yields to persuasion in argument shows that the main inducing factors are not purely visceral, but are *(a)* a presentation of the case that puts equity on its side, or that, at least, satisfies the needs of equity; *(b)* the harmonization or reconciliation of the case with the legal principles applicable; and *(c)* a reasoned analysis that accords with logic. The general rule is obviously, as Medina J indicated, that the persuasive force lies in the quality of the argument.

Fagan CJ once remarked to junior counsel (who, when introducing himself before appearing in a difficult appeal, had said that he would be as brief as possible in argument): 'That would be a mistake. My experience is that, especially in difficult matters, the decision is greatly facilitated by a thorough discussion of the case between counsel and the court.' That was no commendation of long-winded or irrelevant argument. The interaction between the minds of counsel and the judge or judges is best induced by pointed submissions presented simply, lucidly, logically and in a form that enables every material proposition to be tested in discussion.

There are, of course, cases in which important points do not yield to this formula. Judge Medina provided an amusing solution to such problems in the following reminiscence:[21]

> 'I remember when I was a young law clerk working in one of the big law offices here in New York. Several of us boys were working on the different points in a brief and we got all of them in pretty good shape except one which related to the Statute of Frauds. We went in together to report to the member of the firm in charge of the case and said that we just could not figure out any answer for that point. "Oh", he said, "that is easy." And he took the brief and, without making a separate point of it, added the following words in the conclusory paragraph: "The Statute of Frauds is obviously inapplicable." We didn't think much of this until the opinion of the Court of Appeals came down and there to our utter amazement we found repeated the words "The Statute of Frauds is obviously inapplicable".'

[21] Idem at 109.

III

In a recent address[22] Justice Stanley Mosk of the California Supreme Court discussed 'judicial activism', both in appellate tribunals and at the trial court level. The term 'activist court' is illustrated by the United States Supreme Court's change of approach from 1953. Said Justice Mosk:

> 'In this new period the Supreme Court abandoned an apathetic approach to overt injustice in society and elected to employ the federal Constitution to achieve a liberating and egalitarian impact in the areas of political opportunity, criminal justice, and racial equality.'

He concluded:

> 'In the final analysis, there is only one sure curb on judicial activism: that is executive and legislative activism in defense of constitutional liberties. It may be said, I believe, that the courts possess only so much power as is relinquished by the other branches in abdication of their responsibilities.'

In South Africa some academic writers have recently been urging the judges to take a stand on security legislation, to adopt a teleological approach, and to interpret certain provisions benevolently in favour of those whose rights are affected, regardless of plain language to the contrary in the statute. However, in South Africa and in other countries where the doctrine of parliamentary supremacy confines the courts to a lesser constitutional role than that accorded under the Constitution of the United States, the scope for judicial activism of the kind discussed above is restricted. Nevertheless, the phenomenon is present in a more general form, where judicial impatience with outworn rules causing hardship and even injustice has upon occasion resulted in reformative decisions in the teeth of plain statutory language or binding precedent to the contrary.

We have had our judicial reformers in this country. This story is told of Mr Justice Blackwell, sitting alone in the Transvaal Provincial Division in a case in which all the previous decisions were against the proposition favoured by him during the arguments. When leading counsel cautioned: 'My lord, there is not a single decision the other way', Blackwell J answered: 'Well, there will be one by this afternoon.'

The shining example of the teleological approach is that of Lord Denning MR, undoubtedly one of the greatest judges of this century, whose judicial philosophy emerges from the following passage in *Liverpool City Council* v *Irwin:*[23]

[22] Delivered to the Conference on the Role of the Judges in the 1980s, held by the Judicial Administration Division of the American Bar Association at Washington DC, on 19–20 June 1981.

[23] [1976] QB 319 (CA) at 332, [1975] 3 All ER 658 at 666.

'I am confirmed in this view [of the duties of a landlord] by the fact that the Law Commission, in their codification of the law of landlord and tenant, recommend that some such term should be implied by statute. . . . But I do not think we need wait for a statute. We are well able to imply it now in the same way as judges have implied terms for centuries. Some people seem to think that now that there is a Law Commission the judges should leave it to them to put right any defect and to make any new development. The judges must no longer play a constructive role. They must be automatons applying the existing rules. Just think what this means. The law must stand still until the Law Commission have reported and Parliament passed a statute on it; and, meanwhile, every litigant must have his case decided by the dead hand of the past. I decline to reduce the judges to such a sterile role. They should develop the law, case by case, as they have done in the past; so that the litigants before them can have their differences decided by the law as it should be and is, and not by the law of the past.'

Strong stuff indeed, but not generally accepted as the right stuff.

There are of course the novel situations in which neither authority nor principle is apparent, and in which the courts are called upon to lay down new rules. Lord Shaw once said:[24]

'The *casus improvisus* is always with us: and in ninety-nine cases out of a hundred it must be settled before Parliament can act. The appeal is not made to laws, for there are none, but to law: call it what you like—the common law, the principles of jurisprudence—anything from the *jus divinum* to common sense, from *recta ratio* to a square deal: it is on and by and with that stuff that judges have to work, and they must do so not as bondmen but as free.'

So, too, in *Jones* v *Secretary of State for Social Services*[25] Lord Simon of Glaisdale, under the heading of 'Afterthoughts', reflected that

'[i]n this country it was long considered that judges were not makers of law but merely its discoverers and expounders. The theory was that every case was governed by a relevant rule of law, existing somewhere and discoverable somehow, provided sufficient learning and intellectual rigour were brought to bear. But once such a rule had been discovered, frequently the pretence was tacitly dropped that the rule was pre-existing. . . . Nevertheless, the theory, however unreal, had its value—in limiting the sphere of lawmaking by the judiciary (inevitably at some disadvantage in assessing the potential repercussions of any decision, and increasingly so in a complex modern industrial society), and thus also in emphasising that central feature of our constitution, the sovereignty of Parliament. But the true, even limited, nature of judicial lawmaking has been more widely acknowledged of recent years. . . .'[26]

In the task of developing the law to meet new problems, our courts have not always been confined by the old law. The adapta-

[24] *Legislature and Judiciary* (1914) 13–14, quoted in Louis L Jaffe's *English and American Judges as Lawmakers* (1969) 21.

[25] [1972] AC 944 (HL), [1972] 1 All ER 145.

[26] At 1026, 198.

bility of the Roman-Dutch law to modern conditions, through, *inter alia*, the adoption of certain principles and features of English law, is a fact of life in this country. As Holmes JA once observed in a now celebrated passage,[27]

> '[t]he original sources of the Roman-Dutch law are important, but exclusive preoccupation with them is like trying to return an oak tree to its acorn. It is looking ever backwards. Lot's wife looked back. Our national jurisprudence moves forward where necessary, laying aside its swaddling clothes.'[28]

However, the need for judicial enterprise and wisdom to accommodate developments in the social, economic and financial order, where the existing law does not provide for such, is not to be confused with judicial 'legislation' whereby the existing law is discarded or changed in the face of binding precedent or statutory provisions. If the judge is to be free to reform the law as he thinks fit, the overall results might well be worse than the ills they are intended to cure. Depending on the zeal of the individual reformer, rapid-fire developments could be expected at a tempo which would leave the most ardent advocates of teleological tribunals reeling, while the law reports would become congested with controversy.

Some of the consequences, if Lord Denning's approach to judicial law reform were to be adopted, were examined by Lord Scarman in *Lim Poh Choo* v *Camden and Islington Area Health Authority*,[29] and again in *Duport Steels Ltd* v *Sirs*.[30] In the former case he said:[31]

> 'For so radical a reform . . . raises issues of social, economic and financial policy not amenable to judicial reform, which will almost certainly prove to be controversial and can be resolved by the legislature only after full consideration of factors which cannot be brought into clear focus, or be weighed and assessed, in the course of the forensic process. The judge—however wise, creative, and imaginative he may be—is "cabin'd, cribb'd, confin'd, bound in" not, as was Macbeth, to his "saucy doubts and fears" but by the evidence and arguments of the litigants. It is this limitation, inherent in the forensic process, which sets bounds to the scope of judicial law reform.'

In his speech in the latter case Lord Scarman said:[32]

> 'For, if people and Parliament come to think that the judicial power is to be confined by nothing other than the judge's sense of what is right (or, as Selden put it, by the length of the Chancellor's foot), confidence in the judicial system will be replaced by fear of it becoming uncertain and arbitrary in its application.'

[27] While he was still Holmes J, in *Ex parte De Winnaar* 1959 (1) SA 837 (N) at 839D–E.

[28] See also *Smith NO and Lardner-Burke NO* v *Wonesayi* 1972 (3) SA 289 (RAD), per Beadle CJ at 314, and J W Wessels *History of the Roman-Dutch Law* (1908) ch XXXV pp 386ff.

[29] [1980] AC 174 (HL), [1979] 2 All ER 910.

[30] [1980] 1 All ER 529 (HL), [1980] 1 WLR 142.

[31] At 183B, 914.

[32] At 551, 169.

IV

We, like the common-law countries, take the integrity and independence of our judges for granted. That is also the position in Britain, where the present standards of the judges have instilled general confidence in the quality of British justice. However, integrity and independence, and the added qualities of competence and experience, are not the only fundamental attributes required of a judge in our system. Equally necessary is a sense of propriety in the conduct of judicial proceedings. It goes without saying that most cases are of great importance to the parties, and that judicial determinations frequently and unavoidably result in hardship and even humiliation for the losing party. It is not enough that in the actual result justice is done. Litigants are also entitled to see and hear in the conduct of the proceedings that they have been given a full and fair hearing, and that every bona fide and proper contention has received patient and careful attention by a conscientious and considerate judge. That is of the essence of the judicial process and of confidence in the administration of justice.

In Britain there are abundant examples, a few within the last fifty years, of judicial arrogance and eccentricity, of judges ostentatiously reading newspapers or writing letters on the bench to show disapproval of a particular argument, or making impulsive and high-handed orders causing unreasonable interference and inconvenience (such as grounding all aircraft at an aerodrome near the court, and diverting motor traffic from a main highway passing the court building), of partisan behaviour, of coercing a jury into a hurried verdict, and of jesting in bad taste.[33]

We have had some examples of aberrations in our own judicial history, although instances of arrogance or discourtesy have been very rare indeed. Sir Etienne de Villiers, as a member of the Appellate Division, occasionally left the court during argument, and during one case was observed writing a letter, placing it in a stamped envelope and handing it to his clerk for mailing. There was no malice or churlishness in De Villiers JA, but merely an element of eccentricity which did not seem to impair his exceptional ability as a lawyer and a judge.

Some years ago the Johannesburg Bar Council lodged an informal complaint with the Judge President against the judicial conduct of a newly appointed judge. It was claimed that, in a number of separate episodes, the judge had shown gross discourtesy and

[33] For example, see in Simon Shetreet's *Judges on Trial* (1976) the numerous episodes discussed in Part V—'Standards of Judicial Behaviour'. See also the examples cited in E S Turner's *May It Please Your Lordship* (1971) at 225 and 236. With regard to jesting or being witty at the expense of a litigant or a witness, Justice Mosk (see text to note 22), in an article entitled 'On Being a Controversial Judge', published in the *Los Angeles Lawyer* April 1982 p 3, says: 'My first advice to a judge is to be semantically wary. Never shoot from the quip.'

unreasonable impatience towards counsel. The Judge President declined to intervene. It seemed that it was no part of his duties to instruct individual judges in good manners or deportment. It must be recorded that the judge concerned mellowed, and that he came to be highly respected not only for his erudition and wisdom, but also for his compassion. His barbs, once aimed at counsel, became exquisite and finely-honed specimens of sarcasm, directed at litigants whose conduct was deserving of censure. A well-known example was his comment on the defence of a burly policeman, who was sued for damages for assault by an elderly and slightly built Black plaintiff. The plea was that the policeman had acted in self-defence and that he had had great difficulty in subduing the plaintiff. The judge said that the defendant's evidence 'conjured up the epic of a titanic struggle between this emaciated policeman, only six feet in height and weighing barely 250 pounds, and a pocket Hercules, in his prime at 60 years of age'. It may be that, after the passage of the years, a review of the complaints by the Bar would reveal that there was a good deal less incivility and a good deal more wit than was originally appreciated.

Justice delayed is justice denied, but there have been some (again, happily, rare) instances of prolonged delay in rendering judgment. In one case, many years ago, the judge presiding over the Special Court for hearing Income Tax Appeals seemed to be quite unable to produce the judgment, despite several requests from the parties. After two years, he was notified of an application to the Provincial Division for a mandamus directing the Special Court to deliver its judgment, which notice had the desired effect. In another case, many years ago, an order was given with reasons to follow. An appeal was noted against the order, but the reasons were not forthcoming. Some two and a half years later the appeal was set down for hearing in the Appellate Division, still without the reasons. During the hearing of the appeal in Bloemfontein, a motor cyclist, described by counsel as a 'despatch rider', arrived with the reasons, which had been sent by the judge personally and at his own expense. It is said that the Appellate Division noted the arrival of the document, but that the appeal was argued and decided without regard to it. In yet another case the judge reserved judgment and shortly afterwards retired. Three years passed, but no judgment was delivered. The parties finally settled the matter *inter se*.

These various instances of judicial failings are *de minimis* when compared with the recent episode involving a new magistrate in a new state in southern Africa. While presiding at a trial he observed an elderly spectator leaving the court with his hat on his head. Without bothering to adjourn, the magistrate left the bench, pursued the spectator, arrested him, brought him back to the court, and then tried, convicted and sentenced him for contempt of court. It is scarcely necessary to add that the conviction and sentence did not survive on review.

Fortunately, such phenomena have largely disappeared from today's courts. The requisite standards have been firmly laid down by appellate courts, which have not tolerated any material departures from the basic standards of justice. In a country such as ours, with its different races and language groups, those standards are of particular importance. Universal confidence in the judiciary, and in the 'square deal' given by the courts, is an essential prerequisite, *inter alia*, of racial harmony.

V

The community's respect for and confidence in the administration of justice cannot be based only on the personal qualifications of the judges. Among the other indispensable elements are, first, a strong and independent legal profession, which, because of its own high standards of probity and professional competence, enjoys the respect and the trust of the community. Secondly, justice must as far as possible be in the open; as Edmund Burke said, where mystery begins, justice ends. Thirdly, cases must be heard and decided with reasonable despatch. Lastly, though by no means least, the status of the courts and of judicial proceedings must be maintained.

The status of the courts and of judicial proceedings also involves the status and privileges of the judges. In this modern, democratic age, these things are not provided and are not sought after as the prizes of office. Such status and privileges are a necessary concomitant of our judicial system, not only because they lend a better image to the administration of justice, but also because they make a judicial appointment attractive to persons of the necessary calibre; because they enable the judges to maintain their independence from outside influences; and because they enable the judges, as a matter of public interest, to perform their highly responsible and onerous duties in a proper working environment, and without the distractions and pressures of inadequate facilities and inadequate time.

THE RULE OF LAW—A REASSESSMENT

A S MATHEWS*

The Rule of Law, an expression coined in the nineteenth century and popularized[1] by the Victorian jurist Albert Venn Dicey, is without doubt an enduring concept. Ivor Jennings unjustly and unwisely condemned it as a transitory phenomenon expressive of little more than 'Whig politics'.[2] While we may agree with Jennings that Dicey's concept was influenced by his own political philosophy, it has long been obvious that Dicey, as one writer put it, has 'conquered something for everybody, as an achievement of mankind'.[3] What has turned out to be ephemeral is the condemnation of the Rule of Law as an ephemeral doctrine.

It is the association of the Rule of Law with freedom and justice that largely accounts for its enduring quality. Freedom in modern society is in some measure dependent upon the Rule of Law, though whether it should be directly linked to freedom, and to what kind of freedom, are disputed questions. The principle of the Rule of Law is also expressive of justice, not in the broadest sense but in the sense of justice as regularity.[4] The function of the Rule of Law as an element of justice and as a buttress to freedom will ensure that it has a permanent place in political, philosophical and legal discourse. It has held this place of distinction, though not as a rounded theory, since classical Greek times. Elements of the rounded theory, such as the principles of generality and certainty in law, were incorporated by Aristotle into his theory of justice,[5] and were reasserted in the form of constitutionalism in the Middle Ages and after.[6] Dicey reconstructed the basic elements into a full-blown doctrine and thereby unintentionally created what was to become a

* BA LLB PhD (Natal), Professor and Head of the Department of Private Law of the University of Natal, Durban.

[1] In his recent biography of Dicey Richard A Cosgrove acknowledges that the expression was first used by W E Hearn in 1876 and credits Dicey with popularizing rather than coining the phrase. See *The Rule of Law: Albert Venn Dicey, Victorian Jurist* (1980) 67, 87n70.

[2] W Ivor Jennings *The Law and the Constitution* 5 ed (1959) 42ff, 305ff.

[3] G Treves 'The Rule of Law in Italy' in *Annales de la Faculté de Droit d'Istanbul* (1959) IX 113, 118.

[4] John Rawls *A Theory of Justice* (1972) § 38.

[5] *The Nichomachean Ethics of Aristotle* (trans Browne) (1914) bk V ch 10 § 4.

[6] See Charles Howard McIlwain *Constitutionalism: Ancient and Modern* (1940).

banner in the crusade against repressive political systems throughout the world.

'Banner' is hardly an appropriate expression for all theories of the Rule of Law, not even for those, like Dicey's, which associate it with a limited and clearly defined concept of freedom. Some of the theories are formalistic and are deliberately constructed so as to avoid the contamination of political concepts such as freedom. Others consciously strive for a banner-like quality by an avowed association with justice and freedom in the broadest sense. Viewed on a spectrum, they range between dry legalism at one end and value-charged sloganizing at the other. All theories, with a little bit of Procrustean distortion here and there, can be grouped under one of four heads or categories of doctrine. The four are:

(a) Law-enforcement theories;
(b) theories of the Rule of Law as procedural justice;
(c) Dicey's approach: the protection of the basic rights of the citizen through preannounced rules administered by the ordinary courts;
(d) the Rule of Law as justice in the substantive sense.

These categories begin with the narrowest and broaden out towards the widest, and some are implicit in the others; for example, the first theory is an element in the other three. Despite this overlap, they may be viewed as constituting separate approaches to the meaning of the Rule of Law and will be so discussed in this essay.

The Law-enforcement Theory

According to this approach, a government rules according to law when its actions towards the citizens are legally authorized. The test of whether the Rule of Law is being observed is whether the proceeding, decision or action in question is backed by a law that is valid and enforceable in terms of the Constitution of the relevant state. This is a theory of rule by law; not of rule *under* law. It confines the citizen who feels aggrieved by prejudicial government action, or by private action for that matter,[7] to an appeal to *ultra vires*; and a showing by the official or government concerned that the citizen was dealt with in terms of a valid legal rule is a complete answer. What we have here is Kelsen's theory of law turned into the Rule of Law.

The achievement of the Rule of Law in this narrow sense marks the transition from a state of anarchy to that of the ordered society. While such an achievement is not to be underestimated, as Hobbes has forcefully demonstrated in his *Leviathan*, it is clearly one of

[7] The Rule of Law is concerned primarily with the relation between officialdom and the private citizen.

strictly limited value. We have come to learn, even if it took the Biko tragedy to drive the lesson home, that life in a society ruled only *by* law may also be 'solitary, poor, nasty, brutish, and short'. It ought to be a sobering thought to adherents of the law-enforcement theory that Hitler covered most, if not all, of his actions during the Third Reich by an enabling Act passed on 23 March 1933 and entitled 'Law for the Relief of the People and the Reich'. This Act conferred legislative authority on the National-Socialist Cabinet and even gave it power to deviate from the Constitution itself.[8] Ironically, an apologist of the Nazi Party wrote in 1934 of *der deutsche Rechtsstaat Adolf Hitlers*,[9] thereby illustrating both the danger of the narrow theory and the value which dictatorial regimes attach to having the imprimatur of the Rule of Law.

The problem about the law-enforcement theory is that it has nothing whatever to say either about the content of laws or about their form—it is silent on both substantive and procedural justice. The laws may deny the most fundamental rights of humanity and be expressed in either vague or retrospective form, and yet they will exemplify the Rule of Law, if they have been validly enacted. Rules that have been validly enacted which abolish all procedural rights and safeguards will likewise conform to the Rule of Law. This theory may be designated the lowest common denominator of doctrines of the Rule of Law, and, as such, it has the widest appeal to governments of the world, but simultaneously the smallest significance for their citizens.

Procedural-justice Theories

It is a common feature of these theories and those of the first type (law-enforcement theories) that they do not address themselves to the *content* of the laws of a society. But, while they avoid any attempt to define or prescribe the substantive rights of the citizen in his relations with the state, the theories now under discussion have much to say about the *form* of the laws which govern that relationship and the procedures by which they have to be administered. Therefore, though the first two approaches have in common the avoidance of any entanglement, at least directly, with the meaning of justice in the material sense, they are fundamentally different, because theories of the second type are, unlike those of the first, concerned with justice, though with justice in the limited sense of procedural due process. Expressed differently, the movement from theories of the first type to those of the second is a transition from legalism[10] to legality.

[8] Arthur T Vanderbilt *The Doctrine of the Separation of Powers and its Present-Day Significance* (1953) 17.

[9] See Kenneth H F Dyson *The State Tradition in Western Europe* (1980) 108.

[10] 'Legalism' stands in this context for a theory of formal validity.

Legality is a vitally important concept in legal discourse. According to some writers, of whom Lon L Fuller[11] is the outstanding example, it is at the centre of the idea of the legal ordering of a society. The idea of legality is captured by a number of expressions such as 'procedural due process', the '*Rechtsstaatsprinzip*', 'justice according to law' and 'justice as regularity'. Though I share Fuller's view that the concept reflected by these expressions is one related to the essence of law itself, it is unnecessary to enter into the debate on this point between Fuller and his critics such as H L A Hart. Legality, if not a defining characteristic of law itself, is without doubt a notion that lies right at the heart of the Rule of Law. Unravelling the doctrine of the Rule of Law includes, but is not according to all theories exhausted by, the exposition of the principle of legality.

There is a wealth of material to guide (and confuse!) the writer seeking to elucidate the principle of legality. A recent attempt appears in an illuminating article by Joseph Raz,[12] who restates the doctrine of the Rule of Law in the form of eight main principles, which, although Raz himself does not directly say so, are simultaneously an extended discussion of the legality notion. These principles, in summarized form, are:

(i) Laws should be prospective, open and clear. According to Raz's explanation the requirement that the laws should be clear also means that they should be precise.[13]
(ii) Laws should be relatively stable in the sense that they are not changed too often.
(iii) Open, stable, clear and general rules should govern subordinate legislation and orders having legal effect.
(iv) There should be an independent judiciary charged with the application of the law to cases brought before it.
(v) The principles of natural justice should be observed.
(vi) The courts should have review powers to ensure the implementation of the above principles.[14]
(vii) The courts should be easily accessible to subjects of the state.
(viii) The discretion of crime-preventing agencies must not be allowed to pervert the law.

In commenting generally on his eight principles, Raz observes that the first three principles require that the laws should be so

[11] Especially in his *The Morality of the Law* revised edition (1969).

[12] 'The Rule of Law and its Virtue' (1977) 93 *LQR* 195.

[13] The requirement that laws should be precise will be examined below. Much writing on legality emphasizes the requirement of the *generality* of laws, which Raz does not offer as a principle of the Rule of Law, but which seems to be central to the notion and only achievable if the laws that are generally applicable are framed in reasonably precise terms.

[14] Raz includes review power over parliamentary legislation 'merely to ensure conformity to the rule of law'. This presumably means that review will touch the form, not the content, of laws. Most expositions of legality do not include review of parliamentary laws.

framed as to constitute an effective guide to action and that the next five are meant to provide a legal machinery that will ensure undistorted application of these laws and the availability of remedies in cases of deviation.

The cluster of principles that constitute Raz's reformulation of the Rule of Law may be summed up in the following more succinct proposition: The Rule of Law means government according to preannounced, clear rules faithfully administered by independent and accessible courts according to fair-trial procedures. This approach is characterized by several noteworthy features. First, his theory applies to all areas of governing and not just, for example, the laws touching upon the basic liberties of the citizen. He has formulated it, in other words, to make it applicable to all the laws of the society. Secondly, perhaps for this very reason, his theory omits the requirement that the laws which must provide a clear and prospective guide to action should also be general in application.[15] In this respect his approach differs from other formulations of legality in which generality of the laws is given a prominent place. Christopher Zimmerli, for example, has argued that the Rule of Law prescribes three basic requirements:

> '[F]irst, the generality of the law; secondly, the limitation of those powers of the administration and of the judiciary by that law; and thirdly, an independent judiciary for the implementation of these requirements.'[16]

In the third place, Raz's theory incorporates the proposition that the courts should have review powers, including the authority to review parliamentary legislation to ensure that the laws conform to the requirements of legality. Though the review of Parliament's laws which he envisages does not touch the content of legislation and is limited to guaranteeing procedural justice, the theory again diverges from other doctrines of legality, particularly on the Continent, where the Rule of Law is not generally related to the operations of parliaments.

The Rule of Law in the form of legality has a much greater richness than the theory which would limit it to the application of legally valid rules; there is a 'power and fruitfulness' in the formal theory, as Raz himself says.[17] But even this more meaningful theory has its limitations, and Raz appears to be guilty of making greater claims for it than are warranted. While he is careful to dissociate his theory of the Rule of Law from political freedom and

[15] Generality is brought in only under the third principle, which governs delegated authority to make regulations or issue legal orders.

[16] Christopher H Zimmerli 'Human Rights and the Rule of Law in Southern Rhodesia' (1971) 24 *International and Comparative LQ* 239 at 247.

[17] (1977) 93 *LQR* 195 at 202.

to state 'that it has no bearing on the existence of spheres of activity free from governmental interference and is compatible with gross violations of human rights', he does assert that freedom in another sense is promoted by the formal theory. Because it is a central principle of his theory that the law should provide a clear guide to human conduct, it presupposes that men are 'rational autonomous creatures' and enlarges their freedom in the sense of 'an effective ability to choose between as many options as possible'.[18] However, the claim that legality promotes freedom in this limited sense of broadening the options of human choice is not borne out by all experience and, especially, by experience of that system of laws collectively known as apartheid. Some of these laws demonstrate that a denial of freedom in the restricted sense of an ability to choose between options is compatible with the observance of all the principles which Raz associates with the Rule of Law. This compatibility is well illustrated by the influx-control legislation for Blacks that is contained in the Black (Urban Areas) Consolidation Act of 1945.[19] In terms of this law, a Black (that is, an African) has residential rights in an urban area if he can prove that

(1) he has resided in such area continuously since birth; or
(2) he has worked continuously in such area for the same employer for ten years; or
(3) he has lawfully resided continuously in such area for fifteen years; or
(4) he or she is the wife, married daughter or minor son of a male who qualifies under (1), (2) or (3) above, and is, in addition, lawfully resident[20] in the area.

A person who does not qualify under one of the above heads may not remain in an urban area for longer than 72 hours unless he has a permit granted by a labour bureau; and if he does so remain, he commits an offence punishable by a fine, imprisonment and 'repatriation'.[21] Even a person who does qualify for residence in a proclaimed urban area may lose his rights if, after a hearing conducted by a Commissioner, he is found to be 'idle' (on the ground that he is habitually unemployed) or 'undesirable' (on the ground that he has committed one or more of certain offences).[22] A finding that a person is 'idle' or 'undesirable' is subject to judicial review.

[18] Op cit 204–5.

[19] Act 25 of 1945. Another example of this compatibility is the law prohibiting sexual relations between White and 'non-White' persons in South Africa: s 16 of the Immorality Act 23 of 1957. This is manifestly a law that narrows human choice.

[20] The requirement that the dependant must be *lawfully* resident in the area was imposed in *Komani NO* v *Bantu Affairs Administration Board, Peninsula Area* 1979 (1) SA 508 (C), and means that being a dependant of a qualified person does not confer an additional basis for residential rights in a proclaimed area. Lawfulness as a requirement was reaffirmed in the subsequent Appellate Division decision: see 1980 (4) SA 448 (A) at 472.

[21] Section 10. [22] Section 29.

The legal position of Blacks in proclaimed urban areas is governed by a prospective, open and clear law. The law is stable (in this case that is the problem, rather than the virtue, of the law), and administrative decisions under it are guided by open, clear and general rules, that is, by the criteria prescribed by the Act and enumerated above. Prosecutions for being in an urban area without lawful authority take place before the ordinary courts applying fair-trial procedures. The only clear deviation from legality is that legal aid is not generally available to the mainly indigent Africans who are prosecuted under this law. However, this one deviation does not detract from the point that while legality is substantially preserved, freedom of choice is narrowed—not broadened—for persons subject to this law; and it is hardly a piece of legislation that deals with its victims as rational, autonomous human beings. The only choice it appears to offer unqualified Africans is to remain in the prohibited area and face prosecution or to leave and be jobless. A very large number of Africans are unqualified to live in urban areas under this law. The conclusion must follow that legality is compatible with the denial of all kinds of freedom, even the denial of liberty in the narrow sense of freedom to choose. In different words, repression may be achieved under a system that adheres to legality, but, in contrast to the direct repression that the law-enforcement theories of the Rule of Law permit, where freedom is denied by laws that conform to legality the result (repression) is achieved by a more roundabout, cumbersome and therefore *disguised* method.

Diceyan Theories

Whereas it is a characteristic of the first two approaches to the Rule of Law that they have no bearing upon the content of laws, Dicey's theory is concerned with justice in the material sense, but (and this is crucial) only with *one* aspect of substantive justice. The particular aspect with which he was concerned is stated quite clearly in his treatise on the Rule of Law, where he says that for him the concept means 'the security given under the English constitution to the rights of individuals'.[23] His discussion of the rights protected under the Constitution centres upon freedom of the person, freedom of expression, freedom of movement and the right to hold meetings. In more modern terminology, his theory stands for the legal protection of civil liberties.[24] Civil liberties are today defined more broadly than in Dicey's writings, and a contemporary Diceyan approach would advocate the protection through law of

[23] *Introduction to the Study of the Law of the Constitution* 10 ed (1959) 184.

[24] 'Civil liberties' is used in a narrow sense in this context, and excludes social and political rights.

the freedoms of person, conscience, speech, movement, meeting and association.[25] A society is governed according to the Rule of Law if its legal institutions guarantee justice in the sense that these basic rights of the subject will be protected. In brief, the modern Diceyan doctrine expresses the principle of legally guaranteed justice in the restricted sense of individual liberty.

The famous three related principles into which Dicey divided his exposition of the meaning of the Rule of Law do not refer directly to basic rights; but they clearly have to be read in the context of his discussion of individual freedoms. What kind of approach to the Rule of Law do the three principles express when considered simply as they stand, without reference to context? The principles, concisely reformulated, are the following:

(a) The principle that no one shall be subject to pains and penalties except for a distinct breach of law established before the ordinary courts;
(b) the principle of equality before the law;
(c) the principle that the subject is more effectively protected when rights and remedies are incorporated into the ordinary law of the land.

The answer to the question just posed is that Dicey was attempting to set out, though in a form that was both rudimentary and incomplete, the basic requirements of the principle of legality. The phrase 'distinct breach of the law' was his way of expressing the notion of clear, preannounced rules or standards as a guide to conduct. The principle of equality meant that the standards would be equally, and hence *generally*, applicable. Finally, as most formulations of legality insist, the rules or standards will be applied by impartial tribunals. Dicey being a pioneer, his description of legality is not as sophisticated as that of Raz or of even of earlier writers such as Jerome Hall;[26] and since he was a common lawyer, it lacked the theoretical approach characteristic of Continental discourses on the topic. Nevertheless, his three principles, in part explicitly and in part implicitly, express the basic ideas of legality that others have elaborated on and refined in more extended expositions.

Dicey's theory and modern restatements of it constitute a combination of formal and substantive justice, which may be reformulated in the following propositions:

(a) The Rule of Law requires the observance of legality in the form of general and clear preannounced rules administered by independent courts.

[25] At its first congress on the Rule of Law, the International Commission of Jurists adopted a modern version of Dicey's doctrine, but expanded it further by including political rights.

[26] Jerome Hall *General Principles of Criminal Law* 2 ed (1960) 35ff.

(*b*) It also requires that the citizens should actually enjoy the basic civil liberties of person, conscience, speech, movement, meeting and association.

(*c*) The substantive rights described in paragraph (*b*) are best secured by the procedural mechanisms described in paragraph (*a*) as the principle of legality. These rights therefore constitute the sphere of operation of the rules of procedural justice referred to in paragraph (*a*).

The third proposition (paragraph (*c*)) is crucial, although it is seldom spelt out in descriptions of Diceyan theories. Its effect is to confine legality to the achievement of justice in a limited sense (the protection of basic civil rights) and to avoid its application to the broad areas of economic, social and political justice.

Before discussing the non-applicability of legality in the full sense to the search for justice in these other areas (the economic, the social and the political), it will be helpful to record how legality secures justice in the limited field of civil liberties. In all countries which by popular acknowledgement observe the Rule of Law, the subject enjoys freedom of the person, speech, movement and so on, except to the extent that these liberties are actually limited by law. Whether the source of the liberties is the common law or a constitutional declaration, the citizen has a kind of antecedent right to them which he may exercise as fully as the law permits. Since rights are never (or hardly ever) absolute, they require qualification either for the purpose of reconciliation with one another[27] or with the rights of others.[28] Legality requires that the qualifications or limitations on the basic freedoms should be general, prospective, open and clear. Expressed differently, restrictions on liberty that are over-broad, vague or discriminatory will violate the legality principle and facilitate the erosion of civil liberties. Where the restrictions are imposed by the criminal law, legality is expressed in the maxim *nullum crimen sine lege*; but the principle of a narrow and precise definition of legal inroads into freedom is equally applicable when they are imposed outside the criminal law by executive action or in terms of private law. Freedom through legality means, in a nutshell, that the law's constraints will be narrow and precise. Moreover, it is part of the legality rule that the constraining rules will be subject to adjudication by independent courts to ensure that they are kept in bounds and applied in a consistent and even-handed way. This is a task with which courts are familiar and which forms part of their traditional and known competence as judicial bodies.

[27] For example, freedom of movement, if absolutely protected, would invade personal freedom.

[28] Speech, for example, is everywhere limited, either to protect other individual interests (for example, the interest in not having one's character unjustly defamed) or social interests (for example, the interest in public peace).

The Appellate Division September 1954, at the time of the visit of Sir Alfred Denning, then a lord justice of appeal, subsequently Master of the Rolls. See page 128. *Seated, left to right:* Sir Alfred Denning, Albert v d S Centlivres CJ, Leopold Greenberg JA. *Standing, left to right:* Oscar H Hoexter, JA, Oliver D Schreiner JA, F P (Toon) van den Heever JA, Henry A Fagan JA

The Appellate Division's Wednesday afternoon bowls at Bloemfontein in the early fifties. *Left to right:* Albert v d S Centlivres CJ, Leopold Greenberg JA, Oliver D Schreiner JA

The entire Appellate Division at the Wednesday afternoon bowls at Bloemfontein in the early fifties. *Left to right:* Oscar H Hoexter JA, Oliver D Schreiner JA, Albert v d S Centlivres CJ, Leopold Greenberg JA, F P (Toon) van den Heever JA, Henry A Fagan JA

Dicey did not extend the principle of legality to the search for justice in other areas such as the economic sphere, and modern exponents of his doctrine can now demonstrate rationally the wisdom of a restraint which for him was probably intuitive. The basis of that demonstration is the proposition that the principle of legality is either inapplicable or only partially applicable to the achievement of justice in the social and economic sphere. This proposition may be expressed differently by saying that there are certain governmental tasks which either cannot, or should not, be solved by adherence to legality. This argument can be more effectively presented in the consideration of the final of the four theories of the Rule of Law—the theory that it stands for justice in the substantive sense.

The Rule of Law as Substantive Justice

The International Commission of Jurists has become the chief exponent of the most expansive theory of the Rule of Law by making the doctrine stand for the achievement of justice in the fullest sense. While the Commission supported a more circumscribed approach at its first congress on the subject at Athens,[29] it adopted a vastly extended approach at the 1959 Delhi Congress, where it declared that the Rule of Law stands for the values of a free society in which the 'supreme value of human personality' is accorded the fullest possible respect. It was made explicit at Delhi that the recognition of the supreme value of human personality involved the Rule of Law in the protection not just of man's 'spiritual and political freedom', but also of his economic and social needs.[30] This led subsequently to the grand statement at the Lagos Conference:

> '. . . [T]he Rule of Law is a dynamic concept which should be employed to safeguard and advance the will of the people and the political rights of the individual and to establish social, economic, educational and cultural conditions under which the individual may achieve his dignity and realize his legitimate aspirations in all countries, whether dependent or independent.'[31]

It has rightly been said that this approach advances 'the cause of justice in the widest sense'[32] and that it 'propounds a complete social philosophy' and the view that 'good should triumph'.[33] The

[29] *The Rule of Law in a Free Society: A Report on the International Congress of Jurists, New Delhi, India, 1959* 194–6.

[30] Idem 193.

[31] *African Conference on the Rule of Law: A Report on the Proceedings of the International Congress of Jurists held at Lagos, Nigeria, in 1961* 11.

[32] O D Schreiner *The Contribution of English Law to South African Law; and the Rule of Law in South Africa* (1967) 82–4.

[33] Joseph Raz 'The Rule of Law and its Virtue' (1977) 93 *LQR* 195 at 195–6.

function of the Rule of Law has become the full achievement of justice in the material or substantive sense.

There are several good reasons for not equating substantive justice with the Rule of Law. One of these is that there are numerous and often completely opposed theories of social justice, all of which will be legitimate competitors for the seemingly objective imprimatur of the title Rule of Law. The doctrine is thereby placed at the centre of ideological conflict and loses all chance of a broad acceptance and of trans-cultural recognition. But the most important reason of all for avoiding the equation is that the notion of legality, the core meaning of the expression Rule of Law, is either submerged or lost in theories that are over-charged with social and political values. 'Justice as regularity' is transformed into 'justice', and thereby forfeits any claim to the title of Rule of Law. The precise reasons for that forfeiture require some elaboration.

A central role is envisaged for the courts by the theory that the Rule of Law stands for legality, as well as by followers of Dicey who associate legality with the protection of individual liberty. Whether the envisaged role can be fulfilled by the courts is directly related to the kind of function that is assigned to them in terms of the governing doctrine of the Rule of Law. Dicey's doctrine requires the courts to carry out traditional operations that are well within judicial competence. In contrast, the International Commission of Jurists, while not de-emphasizing the role of the courts, has burdened them with tasks which they cannot realistically be expected to carry out. Whereas Dicey's theory requires the courts to restrict encroachment on individual freedom by the even-handed application of clear legal rules to whomever is in breach of them, the International Commission contemplates judicial protection of *positive* demands for economic and social justice. The Rule of Law, and hence the courts, are looked to as the guarantors of the right of the citizen to employment and adequate remuneration, to a stable roof over his head, to an adequate standard of education, and the like. While it is not to be denied that the law will inevitably be involved in the creation and fulfilment of such rights, they are more essentially tasks for the legislative and executive branches rather than the judicial branch. A court decree may effectively protect personal liberty by authorizing a writ of *habeas corpus* and the investigation of the legality of detention; but the mind boggles at the idea of a court's creating and maintaining a decent standard of education by judicial decrees and orders.[34] Restraining the excesses

[34] This point is not invalidated by judgments such as *Brown* v *Board of Education of Topeka* 347 US 483 (1954), requiring the integration of existing educational facilities. As profoundly important as that decision was, the court's function in the provision of decent educational facilities remains marginal.

of aberrant officials is a manageable judicial task; the creation of a decent educational system or housing policy goes beyond what may reasonably be expected of a judiciary.

The reason why the fulfilment of the citizens' positive demands[35] on the state cannot be entrusted to the courts is not simply that they lack the power and resources of the other arms of government. The more fundamental reason is that most, perhaps all, of these rights cannot be expressed in the form of clear and precise rules. The task of providing a good education, for example, is not one for which relatively fixed and stable legal rules can or should be devised. The judicial function assumes the existence of preannounced rules or norms, and areas not susceptible to regulation by rules or norms lie outside the limits of adjudication. Lon L Fuller, in his remarkable paper entitled 'The Forms and Limits of Adjudication',[36] has described these limits in the following passage:

> 'If, however, we regard a formal definition of rights and wrongs as a nearly inevitable product of the adjudicative process, we can arrive at what is perhaps the most significant of all limitations on the proper province of adjudication. Adjudication is not a proper form of social ordering in these areas where the effectiveness of human association would be destroyed if it were organized about formally defined "rights" and "wrongs".'

Apart from the spheres of social activity in which formal ordering would be destructive of the law's purposes, there are others in which the formulation of clear, general and durable rules is neither conceivable nor realistic. Fuller describes these as the areas of 'polycentric tasks', a concept which he employs with great imagination to sketch the boundaries of the judicial process. A polycentric task is one which cannot be settled by proofs and arguments related to established claims of right and wrong, either because of the multiplicity of parties involved, or because the context of the problem is fluid and rapidly changing, or because of the complex and wide-ranging repercussions of a decision on any aspect of the problem.[37] A concrete example of a polycentric task is offered by Fuller in the following passage:

> 'As a second illustration suppose in a socialist regime it were decided to have all wages and prices set by courts which would proceed after the usual forms of adjudication. It is, I assume, obvious that there is a task that could not successfully be undertaken by the adjudicative method. The point that comes first to mind is that courts move too slowly to

[35] As distinct from their negative freedom—freedom in the sense of protected area in which conduct is free.

[36] (1978) 92 *Harvard LR* 353 at 370–1.

[37] This description attempts to draw together the various elements which Fuller attributes to polycentric tasks in an extended discussion of the concept: see 'The Forms and Limits of Adjudication' (1978) 92 *Harvard LR* 353 at 394–404.

keep up with a rapidly changing economic scene. The more fundamental point is that the forms of adjudication cannot encompass and take into account the complex repercussions that may result from any change in prices or wages. A rise in the price of aluminium may affect in varying degrees the demand for, and therefore the proper price of, thirty kinds of steel, twenty kinds of plastics, an infinitude of woods, other metals, etc. Each of the separate effects may have its own complex repercussions in the economy.'[38]

Fixed rules, or in Fuller's terms, 'formal claims of right and wrong', and court adjudication are clearly out in respect of such matters as wages and prices, interest rates, governmental resource allocations, foreign policy determination, and the like. The most that adjudication or the law can accomplish in such areas is to declare certain 'ground rules' applicable to those activities. The process applicable to the solution of polycentric tasks is not adjudicative; rather, as Fuller says, it is managerial or contractual.[39]

Neither law nor legality is completely excluded from the solution of polycentric tasks or from the achievement of justice in the broadest sense. In these areas the law will inevitably set a broad framework, and elements of the principle of legality, such as the duty to afford a fair hearing, may be applicable. A delicate question, and a central problem in administrative law, is to determine when and how far the courts may intervene in public administration. Because the rules of natural justice[40] have acquired a certain rigidity, especially as regards their sphere of operation, the courts in some jurisdictions have evolved a new principle in the form of the duty to act fairly.[41] This concept is less precise than the rules of natural justice and is likewise only an element of the legality principle. Where the courts impose a duty to act fairly on the administration, they are not introducing the Rule of Law into the area of economic and social justice. Rather, elements of procedural justice, which by no means comprise the whole of what legality means, are being injected into the administrative process with a view to curbing administrative discretion. If this is what is meant by the so-called material *Rechtsstaat*,[42] it may be welcomed and

[38] Idem 394. [39] Idem 398.

[40] Which constitute only a part of what we mean by legality.

[41] L G Baxter 'Fairness and Natural Justice in English and South African Law' (1979) 96 *SALJ* 607.

[42] Zimmerli, for example, declares that the material *Rechtsstaat* incorporates a demand for the recognition of human rights: op cit note 16 at 244. H J van Eikema Hommes, an enthusiastic supporter of the material *Rechtsstaat*, after lamenting the inability of the formal *Rechtsstaat* to withstand political movements that reject traditional human values of Western culture, demands that 'materiële rechtsbeginselen' should determine the inner boundaries of state power and govern the development of public law from top to bottom. See 'De Materiële Rechtsstaatsidee' 1978 *TSAR* 42 at 46–7; but except to say that the material *Rechtsstaat* is fully reconcilable with the welfare state (at 51–2), he nowhere elucidates the basic principles of justice which will inform his material *Rechtsstaat*. While

encouraged, without, however, designating the process as an extension of the Rule of Law. Where the material *Rechtsstaat* stands for more than this; where it means that legality in the full sense (general, clear, preannounced and precise rules administered by ordinary courts) is applicable to the general search for economic and social justice, including polycentric tasks, then it must be rejected as Utopian and unworkable. In this extended sense, the material *Rechtsstaat* assumes an unattainable consensus on the goals of public administration, and would have the effect, to the extent that goals are actually transcribed into formal law, of freezing social development[43] and putting an unmanageable strain on the adjudicative process.

We can now see that the actual difficulty in the approach of the International Commission of Jurists to the Rule of Law is not that it prescribes undesirable social goals; indeed, the achievement of justice in the broader sense (encompassing both material and 'spiritual' needs) is admirable and a desirable corrective to the near exclusive concentration of the developed world on political and intellectual freedom. The problem is that many of the reforms envisaged by the Commission are not adjudicative or Rule-of-Law tasks. Close legal ordering in these areas is either unworkable or undesirable, or both. When a concept such as the Rule of Law is packed with almost all the ingredients of social justice, it is transformed into an ideology, and the central notion of legality is likely to be submerged or lost. Without legality, any claim to the title 'Rule of Law' is without foundation.

Conclusions

Neither the first nor the last of the four approaches to the Rule of Law surveyed in this paper is a serious contender for the title. Making the doctrine synonymous with law and order is as unacceptable as equating it with the good life. This leaves, as challengers in the field, Dicey's approach and the theory of legality. There are cogent reasons for preferring theories cast in the Diceyan mould. Perhaps the most obvious is that the Rule of Law is a doctrine of constitutional law, and Diceyan-type theories retain its public-law character. What these theories attempt to achieve is the prevention of governmental encroachment on civil rights by means of preannounced and relatively fixed rules administered by independent courts. Their concern with a legally defined and controlled

one may fully share his belief in Western human values and welfare state programmes, there are cogent reasons (outlined in this paper) for not incorporating this entire package into the Rule of Law.

[43] See 310 below, where the effect of excessive legalism is discussed, and where excessive legalism is rejected on account of its tendency to divorce the law from contemporary social realities.

relationship between citizen and state is squarely within the realm of public law. In contrast, theories of legality tend to have no specific reference and to be potentially applicable to any area of the social life. John Finnis, whose approach to the Rule of Law is very close to that of Raz, writes of the virtue of the doctrine in the realm of 'consumer–supplier relations'.[44] While this may well be an area in which definite rules administered by the regular courts can secure substantial justice between the two sides, the relationship referred to is essentially one of private law. In such a context the Rule of Law loses its constitutional and public-law character, and is being employed in a metaphorical sense.

Dicey and his followers have been accused of the pursuit of moral or political goals under the rubric of the expression Rule of Law, which is supposed to have value-free connotations. This accusation is misguided. There is no meaningful theory of the Rule of Law that is without moral implications. As Judith N Shklar has justly observed, the adherents of legalism[45] 'fail to recognize that they too have made a choice among political values'.[46] Moreover, while writers such as Raz and Finnis are careful not to associate legality with any specific set of moral objectives, they do claim that its observance has a kind of spin-off benefit of moral significance. Finnis, for example, says that legality is premissed upon the right of human beings to 'respectful consideration' and to the dignity of being 'responsible agents'.[47] Earlier reference to the system of apartheid has shown that there is no necessary relation between observance of the requisites of legality and human autonomy or dignity. However, when one considers that there are methods of social organization other than legality, it is certainly true that the choice between them is at base a value decision. The error of the adherents of the pure legality theory of the Rule of Law does not lie in the assertion that their approach has moral implications, but rather in the excessive claims made for it in the promotion of human dignity and autonomy as a specific moral virtue. Dicey's doctrine, to a far greater extent than theirs, secures individual freedom of action and choice by making the principle of legality serve precisely those values. When a citizen's civil rights are secured by law, he is guaranteed a substantial measure of recognition as a rational and autonomous human being.

The proposition that civil liberties constitute the prime sphere for formal justice has stood the test of time and has recently found reaffirmation in the writings of John Rawls. His exposition of social justice centres on two fundamental principles, the first of which is that 'each person is to have an *equal* right to the most extensive

[44] John Finnis *Natural Law and Natural Rights* (1980) 272.

[45] By which she means 'legality' as the term is used in this paper.

[46] Judith N Shklar *Legalism* (1964; reprint 1971) 8.

[47] Op cit note 44 at 272–3.

basic liberty compatible with a similar liberty for others'.[48] Rawls defines what he means by basic liberties in the following passage:

> 'The basic liberties of citizens are, roughly speaking, political liberty (the right to vote and to be eligible for public office) together with freedom of speech and assembly; liberty of conscience and freedom of thought; freedom of the person along with the right to hold (personal) property; and freedom from arbitrary arrest and seizure as defined by the concept of the rule of law.'[49]

In his chapter on the Rule of Law, Rawls underlines the necessary association between liberty (as defined above) and formal justice or, as he prefers to call it, justice as regularity: 'The principle of legality has a firm foundation, then, in the agreement of rational persons to establish for themselves the greatest equal liberty. To be confident in the possession and exercise of these freedoms, the citizens of a well-ordered society will normally want the rule of law maintained.'[50] The fact that these rights are to be equally available to all gives full scope to the principle of generality, which is a central idea in legality.[51]

The second principle of justice formulated by Rawls is that 'social and economic inequalities are to be arranged so that they are both (a) reasonably expected to be to everyone's advantage, and (b) attached to positions and offices open to all'.[52] This principle has been described as a theory of just inequalities and, as such, is one in which justice as regularity has a greatly diminished scope. Rawls does not link formal justice with his second principle, perhaps because generality and inequality are logically inconsistent. His writings appear to support the argument expressed earlier in this paper that formal justice has a greatly diminished significance in the economic and social spheres of societal relations.[53]

In his description of basic rights, Rawls includes the right to vote and to hold public office, which is one of the civil liberties that has not been incorporated into the Rule of Law by most supporters of Dicey's theory.[54] On balance, it seems preferable to limit the basic rights protected by the doctrine to all except the purely political. The right to vote is, in contrast to the other civil liberties, a positive liberty, which lends itself less to exact formulation and judicial

[48] John Rawls *A Theory of Justice* (1972) § 11 p 60 and § 46 p 302 (my italics).

[49] Idem § 11 p 61. [50] Idem § 38 pp 239–40.

[51] See, for example, Franz Neumann 'The Change in the Function of Law in Modern Society' in *The Democratic and the Authoritarian State* (1906) 29.

[52] Op cit note 48 at 60.

[53] This is not to suggest that formal legal ordering is inappropriate to all economic relations. Clearly, however, many policy decisions of government, whether economic or otherwise, do not lend themselves to precise legal rules or court adjudication. In administrative law, for example, there is a constant tension between the need to permit an area of free discretion for government bodies and officials, and the opposite need to tie down discretion by appropriate legal controls.

[54] Nor did Dicey include it in the liberties discussed in his chapter on the Rule of Law.

enforcement. It is significant that the Supreme Court of the United States long avoided entanglement in the reapportionment 'thicket'; and when it intervened in *Baker* v *Carr*,[55] it merely declared that the system of apportionment under challenge violated the equal protection clause. It may safely be predicted that no court would undertake the positive task of reapportionment of boundaries, and the decision in the *Baker* case amounts to the prescription of ground rules to guide the legislature in the performance of that task. Reapportionment is too complex a task for the prescription of exact standards or rules.[56] In an illuminating analysis of the 'elements' of citizenship by Ralf Dahrendorf,[57] the wisdom of excluding the political right to vote and hold office from the ambit of legality is incidentally demonstrated by the author. He divides citizenship into three parts:

(a) The 'civil element', in which is included primarily the rights necessary for individual freedom, such as liberty of 'the person, speech, thought and faith'. The institutions most directly associated with civil rights are the courts of justice.

(b) The 'political element', which means 'the right to participate in the exercise of political power, as a member of a body vested with political authority or as an elector of the members of such a body'. In this case, the corresponding institutions are Parliament and the councils of local government.

(c) The 'social element', covering 'the whole range from the right to a modicum of economic welfare and security to the right to share to the full in the social heritage and the life of a civilized being . . .'. The institutions connected with this element are the educational system and the social services.

Since, as Lon Fuller has said, '[a]ll are agreed that courts are essential to the "rule of law"',[58] and courts in the above classification are directly involved only in the civil element of citizenship, it seems sensible to exclude protection of the other elements from the ambit of the Rule of Law.

There is one final reason for preferring Dicey's doctrine to the principle of legality as the most authoritative statement of the Rule of Law. According to his doctrine, law is conclusively elevated above politics only in the sphere of civil liberties. Under theories of legality the supremacy of law is potentially, at least, applicable to social tasks other than the guarantee of equal liberty in Rawls's sense. If legality acquires too broad a scope of operation, the result may be what Nonet and Selznick[59] describe as its 'affliction'—legalism. Legalism they describe as a condition in which the 'focus on

[55] 369 US 186 (1962).

[56] It appears to qualify as a polycentric task in Fuller's terms.

[57] In *Society and Democracy in Germany* (1968) 70.

[58] Op cit note 37 at 372.

[59] Philippe Nonet and Philip Selznick *Law and Society in Transition* (1978) 64.

rules tends to narrow the range of legally relevant facts, thereby detaching legal thought from social reality'. This produces a rigidity in which rule application 'ceases to be informed by a regard for purposes, needs and consequences',[60] and in which formal justice 'is consistent with serving existing patterns of privilege and power'.[61] It is the great virtue of Dicey's doctrine that, by making legality supreme only in the area of basic rights, and leaving unstated its relevance to other social tasks, he avoids the charge of rigidity and entrenchment of the *status quo*. If the basic liberties are legally guaranteed, the citizen is free to support or attack the *status quo*, and to argue that its preservation in the forms of positive law is undesirable. In fact, the legal guarantee of the basic liberties facilitates the constant reassessment of the *status quo* and the redefinition of social 'purposes, needs and consequences'.

O D Schreiner, in whose memory this volume has been compiled, was clearly right to support 'the relatively narrow earlier meaning' of the Rule of Law which Dicey advocated.[62] Its strength lies in its moderation, and while so restricted its banner, 'torn, but flying', will continue to 'stream like the thunder-storm *against* the wind'.

[60] Ibid. [61] Idem 67.

[62] The Diceyan approach to the Rule of Law is not linked to any general theory of law and the state, except that it is entirely consonant with the 'constitutional state', that is, with the state in which constitutionalism is a prime value.

THE TWO CARDINAL RULES OF LOGIC IN REX v *BLOM*

H C NICHOLAS*

Shortly after 10 pm on Friday 29 April 1938 a train travelling from Rosmead to Graaff Reinet in the Cape ran over and severely mutilated the body of a woman lying across one of the rails. At the trial of the accused, Blom, on a charge of murdering her, medical opinion was that she was already dead at the time. The trial court concluded from the medical evidence that her death was due to a sudden shock. Such a shock causing death might have been caused by a blow on the head or by chloroform applied in concentrated form to the face. The doctors were, however, unable to say which of these two was the cause: the head had been crushed by the train after death, and it was not possible to say whether a head injury had been inflicted before the train ran over the body; and if death was caused by the application of chloroform to the face, no trace of it could be expected after the time that elapsed between the death and the post-mortem examination. The case against the accused was based entirely on circumstantial evidence. It was proved that he had a motive to kill the deceased. He had had illicit sexual relations with her; she was five to six months pregnant; and he had tried to assist her to procure an abortion. He had a design to kill someone: that was proved by the fact that he bought chloroform under an assumed name on the afternoon of the murder and gave a false reason for the purchase. He had an opportunity to kill the deceased: at about 5.30 pm on 29 April he was seen riding a bicycle at a place about eight miles from where the body was found at 10 pm. There was evidence of his conduct after the event showing a guilty conscience. Evidence was given by a doctor that the accused consulted him two days after the woman was killed with regard to the recurrence of an injury in the nature of a strain in his right side. This strain had first been caused a month earlier by his falling down a cliff, and he explained the recurrence by saying that he had ridden a motor cycle to Aberdeen. About a week later he again consulted the doctor, and he then said that the recurrence had been caused by lifting a sack of quinces, and he denied that he had previously told

* BA LLB (Witwatersrand), Judge of the Supreme Court of South Africa, Transvaal Provincial Division.

him that it was caused by a ride on a motor cycle to Aberdeen. The inference suggested from this was that he had injured himself in carrying the body of the dead woman, and was afraid that the story of a ride on a motor cycle might be proved to be false. There was also evidence that three weeks after the death of the woman a police officer showed him a search warrant and said that he was looking for a chloroform bottle, and the accused then lied, saying that he had never had a chloroform bottle in his possession. In this way he tried to hide from the police the fact that he had had chloroform in his possession on the day of the murder, and the inference could be drawn that he had used it for some unlawful purpose.

The accused did not give evidence in his own defence. He was convicted and sentenced to death.

At the conclusion of the trial three questions of law were reserved for the decision of the Appellate Division. In the appeal[1] the court was mainly concerned with the first of the questions, namely, whether there was evidence on which a reasonable man could convict.

It was held that there was undoubtedly evidence justifying the conclusion that the deceased was murdered; that she was dead when her body was placed across the line; and that the murderer was the person who so placed the corpse after having perpetrated the crime. If the woman died from the administration of chloroform, there was ample evidence upon which the accused could be convicted, but if she died in any other way, the verdict could not be sustained. The cause of death was therefore the paramount issue in the case.

The unanimous conclusion was that, having regard to all the circumstances of the case, including the conduct of the accused and his failure to give an explanation, there was evidence upon which a reasonable man could come to the conclusion that death was due to the administration of chloroform.

Separate judgments were given by four of the five members of the court. They included Watermeyer JA, who, after stating that the determination of the cause of death was entirely a matter of inference from a number of circumstances, said:[2]

> 'In reasoning by inference there are two cardinal rules of logic which cannot be ignored:
>
> '(1) The inference sought to be drawn must be consistent with all the proved facts. If it is not, the inference cannot be drawn.
>
> '(2) The proved facts should be such that they exclude every reasonable inference from them save the one sought to be drawn. If they do not exclude other reasonable inferences, then there must be a doubt whether the inference sought to be drawn is correct.'

These rules were nothing new. Similar rules had often been stated and discussed by logicians and legal writers. But with their

[1] *R* v *Blom* 1939 AD 188. [2] At 202–3.

succinct formulation in a few lapidary lines they quickly became received doctrine in the courts of South Africa. Two years after the decision in *Blom*, Watermeyer JA's dictum was applied by the full court of the Appellate Division in *R* v *Magatuse*.[3] Since then, it has been referred to, quoted and paraphrased in a number of cases decided in the Appellate Division[4] and in many cases decided in the various provincial divisions. The rules have not, however, always been properly understood or applied. In particular, counsel, harassed by strongly inculpatory evidence, have come to resort to them as a last-ditch argument.[5] It may therefore be useful to essay a more detailed consideration of the rules than they have hitherto received.

Although the methods of logic are seldom referred to in terms by judges and advocates, the logical rules underlie the process of proof, as they do all forms of human reasoning. They have their main application in the concept of relevancy and in reasoning by inference. In neither field, however, are the logical powers employed those of trained logicians. Schreiner JA stated the approach in these words:

> 'Relevancy is based upon a blend of logic and experience lying outside the law. The law starts with this practical or common sense relevancy and then adds material to it or, more commonly, excludes material from it, the resultant being what is legally relevant and therefore admissible.'[6]

'The process of drawing inferences', said Van den Heever J in *R* v *Erasmus*,[7]

> 'is not a pure or abstract one, like problems in mathematics. The fact that an accused person ran away from the scene of a crime has no physical or mathematical bearing on the question whether the man who ran away committed the crime. It only acquires probative force, by way of inference, in the light of common or human experience.'

The methods employed in legal reasoning are

> 'those untechnical ways of all sound reasoning, of the logical process in its normal and ordinary manifestations; and the rules that govern it here are the general rules that govern it everywhere, the ordinary rules of human thought and human experience, to be sought in the ordinary sources, and not in law books. And so a knowledge of these processes and methods is presupposed in all judges and lawyers.'[8]

Where the evidence against an accused person is of a circumstantial nature, a conclusion must be reached by inductive inference—

[3] 1941 AD 201 at 202.
[4] See, for example, *R* v *Du Plessis* 1944 AD 314; *S* v *Dlodlo* 1966 (2) SA 401 (A); *S* v *ffrench-Beytagh* 1972 (3) SA 430 (A); and *S* v *Sesetse* 1981 (3) SA 353 (A).
[5] See *S* v *Mlambo* 1957 (4) SA 727 (A) at 737.
[6] *R* v *Matthews and others* 1960 (1) SA 752 (A) at 758.
[7] 1945 OPD 50 at 71–2.
[8] J B Thayer *A Preliminary Treatise on Evidence at the Common Law* (1898) 275.

the process of inferring some kind of order among phenomena or observations (which in a criminal trial are the evidentiary facts). In that process there lurks a special danger of fallacy. The untrained and the unwary may easily be beguiled by circumstances

> 'which, however they may excite conjecture, do not warrant belief. Occurrences may be mysterious and justify even vehement suspicion, and yet the supposed connection between them may be but imaginary, and their coexistence indicative of accidental concurrence merely, and not of mutual correlation.'[9]

And again:

> 'Where the evidence is direct, and the testimony credible, belief is the immediate and necessary result; whereas, in cases of circumstantial evidence, processes of inference and deduction are essentially involved,—frequently of a delicate and perplexing character,—liable to numerous causes of fallacy, some of them inherent in the nature of the mind itself, which has been profoundly compared to the distorting power of an uneven mirror, imparting its own nature to the true nature of things. . . . Mr Baron Alderson, upon a trial of this kind, said, "It was necessary to warn the jury against the danger of being misled by a train of circumstantial evidence. The mind was apt to take a pleasure in adapting circumstances to one another, and even straining them a little, if need be, to force them to form parts of one connected whole; and the more ingenious the mind of the individual, the more likely was it, in considering such matters, to overreach and mislead itself, to supply some little link that is wanting, to take for granted some fact consistent with its previous theories and necessary to render them complete" (*Reg* v *Hodge* (1838) 2 Lewin CC 227).[10] The learned Baron's remarks are taken from a contemporaneous MS report).'[11]

The canons of logic provide tools for the guidance of our reasoning as safely as possible through the dangers to which it is exposed.[12] Thomas Starkie, an early writer on the law of evidence,[13] enumerated rules 'essential to circumstantial proof', some of which were rules of logic and others rules of policy:

> 'First, *that the circumstances from which the conclusion is drawn should be fully established*. If the basis be unsound, the superstructure cannot be secure.'[14]
>
> 'Secondly: It is essential *that all the facts should be consistent with the hypothesis*.'[15]
>
> 'Thirdly: It is essential *that the circumstances should be of a conclusive nature and tendency*.'[16]

[9] *Wills' Principles of Circumstantial Evidence* 7 ed (1936) edited by V R N Gattie and M Krishnamachariar 297. 'The strongest suspicions founded on circumstantial evidence have turned out before now to have been unfounded': *R* v *Dube* 1915 AD 557 at 564.

[10] 168 ER 1136. [11] *Wills* op cit note 9 at 44–5.

[12] See Alfred Sidgwick *Fallacies: A View of Logic from the Practical Side* 3 ed (1901) 17.

[13] Thomas Starkie *A Practical Treatise of the Law of Evidence* 2 ed (1833).

[14] At 507. [15] At 509. [16] At 510.

Fourthly: It is essential *that the circumstances should, to a moral certainty, actually exclude every hypothesis but the one proposed to be proved.*'[17]

'Lastly: It seems that mere circumstantial evidence ought in no case to be relied on where direct and positive evidence, which might have been given, is wilfully withheld by the prosecutor.'[18]

Wills devotes Chapter VI of his book to 'Rules of Induction Specially Applicable to Circumstantial Evidence'. The first paragraph reads:

> 'All reasoning concerning human conduct is essentially a process of induction, of which it is the object, by means of generalizations founded upon a knowledge of the faculties, emotions, and laws of the mind, to discover the moral qualities and causal origin of the voluntary actions of our fellow-men; whence it follows that the rules for the conduct of inductive inquiry belong formally to the province of LOGIC, or the science of the laws of thought. The rules of evidence are therefore a selection of maxims tacitly assumed and acted upon by all men in the ordinary affairs of life, and recognized by philosophical wisdom and judicial experience as the best means of discovering truth.'[19]

There follows a discussion of five rules:

> 'RULE 1.—*The facts alleged as the basis of any legal inference must be clearly proved, and beyond reasonable doubt connected with the* factum probandum.'[20]
>
> 'RULE 2.—*The burden of proof is always on the party who asserts the existence of any fact which infers legal accountability.*'[21]
>
> 'RULE 3.—*In all cases, whether of direct or circumstantial evidence, the best evidence must be adduced which the nature of the case admits.*'[22]
>
> 'RULE 4.—*In order to justify the inference of guilt, the inculpatory facts must be incompatible with the innocence of the accused, and incapable of explanation upon any other reasonable hypothesis than that of his guilt.*'[23]
>
> 'RULE 5.—*If there be any reasonable doubt of the guilt of the accused, he is entitled as of right to be acquitted.*'[24]

The first rule in *Blom* is a formulation of Starkie's second rule, and the second rule in *Blom* is a formulation of the fourth rule of Starkie and Wills.

It is to be observed that in his dictum in *Blom* Watermeyer JA used the word 'inference' in two senses: as a process of reasoning ('[i]n reasoning by inference') and as a conclusion ('the inference sought to be drawn'). Inference regarded as a process is an ambiguous word. It is capable of being applied to Discovery, when we proceed from premisses to conclusion, arriving at new truths by means of old ones: and it is capable of being applied to Proof,

[17] At 512.
[18] At 515. In each of these quotations the emphasis is that of the author of the book.
[19] Op cit note 9 at 296. [20] At 296. [21] At 313. [22] At 318.
[23] At 320.
[24] At 329. The emphasis in all these quotations is that of the author of the book.

when, having a thesis (or assertion or proposition) before us, we ask whether it has been established on a sound basis. In the former sense it is the process of reaching a belief; in the latter sense it is the process of establishing a proposition on a fair foundation. Instead of asking at large, 'What conclusion may be drawn?' Proof asks, 'Is such and such a conclusion warranted?' Proof has come to mean establishment on a sound basis, establishment by means of tests, establishment in the face of hostile criticism.[25]

The rules in *Blom* are rules for Proof—rules for testing whether the 'inference sought to be drawn' can validly be drawn. They are rules of logic, not legal precepts. They are instruments for detecting and avoiding fallacy, for testing the logical validity of the conclusion. The failure to recognize this has led to misconception and misapplication of the rules.

The first rule was given striking expression by T H Huxley: 'The great tragedy of Science—the slaying of a beautiful hypothesis by an ugly fact.'[26] The rationale of the rule was stated by Starkie:[27]

> 'For as all things which have happened were necessarily congruous and consistent, it follows, that if any one established fact be wholly irreconcilable with the hypothesis, the latter cannot be true. Such an incongruity and inconsistency is sufficient to negative the hypothesis, even although it coincide and agree with all the other facts and circumstances of the case to the minutest extent. . . . [I]f the incongruity cannot eventually be removed, the hypothesis must fall, although no other can be suggested. . . .'

The case of *R* v *Hodge* has been referred to above, in a quotation from Wills. According to the report of that case contained in the English Reports,[28] Alderson B referred in his address to the jury to

> '. . . the proneness of the human mind to look for—and often slightly to distort the facts in order to establish such a proposition—forgetting that a single circumstance which is inconsistent with such a conclusion, is of more importance than all the rest, inasmuch as it destroys the hypothesis of guilt.'[29]

In *Lejzor Teper* v *The Queen*[30] Lord Normand said:

> 'It is . . . necessary before drawing the inference of the accused's guilt from circumstantial evidence to be sure that there are no other co-existing circumstances which would weaken or destroy the inference.'

[25] See Sidgwick op cit note 12 at 32–5, on which I have freely drawn in this paragraph. The distinction is illustrated by the process of inference used by the investigator of a crime and the process used by the trier of fact. The process used by the investigator is that of Discovery—it leads him to the solution of the crime. The process used by the trier of fact is that of Proof.

[26] Quoted in *The Oxford Dictionary of Quotations* 3 ed 269.

[27] Op cit note 13 at 509–10.

[28] (1838) 168 ER 1136.

[29] 168 ER 1136 at 1137 (being 2 Lewin CC 227 at 228). In referring in *McGreevy* v *Director of Public Prosecutions* [1973] 1 All ER 503 (HL), [1970] 1 WLR 276 to the passage from which this quotation is taken, Lord Morris said that no one could doubt that 'the wise words used by the learned judge were helpful and admirable and as such were worthy of being recorded' (at 508, 282).

[30] [1952] AC 480 (PC) at 489.

A discussion by a logician of the rule formulated as the second rule in *Blom* is contained in Sidgwick.[31] He says:

> '. . . [I]f we accept a conclusion without considering how far the facts will support an opposite one, we do so at our peril. . . . [I]n establishing an explanation, a law of nature, or a prediction not yet verifiable by the event, the important point is to exclude all alternative theories. . . . [B]efore we can consider any theory proved, whether such theory be a sweeping law, like that of gravitation, or an explanation or prediction of some one actual event, we must have sound reasons for excluding every possible rival theory.'

And again:[32]

> 'The important point is always, to show that all other possible theories are weighed in the balance and found wanting; that is to say, that all precautions have been taken against that crudest kind of unchecked generalization which the least trained mind possesses ever in greatest abundance.'

Wills[33] says of this rule:

> 'It is not enough, however, that a particular hypothesis will explain all the phenomena; nothing must be inferred merely because, if true, it would account for the facts; and if the circumstances are equally capable of solution upon any other reasonable hypothesis, it is manifest that their true moral cause is not exclusively ascertained, but remains in uncertainty; and they must therefore be discarded as affording conclusive presumptions of guilt. Every other reasonable supposition by which the facts may be explained consistently with the hypothesis of innocence must therefore be rigorously examined and successively eliminated; and only when no other supposition will reasonably account for all the conditions of the case can the conclusion of guilt be legitimately adopted. . . .'

Although Watermeyer JA treated the two rules as applying generally to 'reasoning by inference', the second rule as formulated in *Blom* is applicable only when the standard of proof is proof beyond a reasonable doubt. The rule is more rigorous where the standard is complete proof or certainty, when every possible inference must be excluded, and less rigorous where the standard is

[31] Op cit note 12 at 39–40.

[32] At 275–6.

[33] Op cit note 9 at 322. In *R* v *Tshabangu* 1934 AD 514 at 519 Curlewis JA said that one of the rules of induction which Wills lays down 'is that, in order to justify the inference of guilt, the inculpatory facts must be incompatible with the innocence of the accused and incapable of explanation upon any other reasonable hypothesis than that of his guilt. That is what I have understood as the principle that should guide one in dealing with circumstantial evidence, and it has always guided me in addressing a jury or when sitting alone.'

See also James Fitzjames Stephen *General View of the Criminal Law of England* 2 ed (1890), quoted in *R* v *Kumalo and another* 1930 AD 193 at 214; J P Taylor *A Treatise on the Law of Evidence* 12 ed (1931); *Halsbury's Laws of England* 4 ed XI (1976) §§ 361–2 pp 198–9.

proof on a balance of probabilities, where 'one may . . . by balancing probabilities select a conclusion which seems to be the more natural, or plausible, conclusion from amongst several conceivable ones, even though that conclusion be not the only reasonable one'.[34]

The view has been expressed that the second rule in *Blom* is another way of stating the criminal standard of proof.[35]

It is submitted that this view is erroneous, and is the result of confusing what is a rule of logic with a legal precept. If, of course, the proved facts are consistent not only with guilt but some other reasonable inference, then the conclusion of guilt cannot validly be drawn. But, on the other hand, even though the inference of guilt can validly be drawn, it does not follow that the trier of fact must find that the accused's guilt has been proved beyond a reasonable doubt. In *R* v *Ndhlovu*[36] Davis AJA said:

> 'No one doubts that the person mentioned by Voet (22.3.14) who was at enmity with the deceased, and at the time of his death was seen coming from the room where he had been killed, with a bloody sword, in great agitation and with a wild look on his face, if he gives no explanation, may be found guilty of murder. But the judge could not direct the jury that as a matter of law they were bound to return that verdict. . . . But, of course, if the accused gives no explanation, when he might fairly be expected to do so, a jury may, and probably would, drawn the inference of guilt.'

There was, it is respectfully submitted, some blurring in the judgment in the case of *R* v *De Villiers*[37] of the distinction between the second rule in *Blom* and the concept of proof beyond a reasonable doubt. Davis AJA in that judgment was dealing with an argument pressed upon the court by counsel for the appellant that, in a case depending upon circumstantial evidence, 'the court must take each factor separately, and, if each of them is possibly consistent with innocence, then it must discard each in turn'.[38] The learned judge said:[39]

> 'This argument is entirely fallacious. It is in the first place inconsistent with the statement of my brother Watermeyer, in *R* v *Blom* (1939 AD at p 202): "The proved facts should be such that they exclude every reasonable inference from them save that one sought to be drawn." It is not each proved fact which must exclude all other inferences; the facts as a whole must do so.'

He went on to say that the argument was also inconsistent with the reasoning of the Appellate Division in all the cases where convic-

[34] *Govan* v *Skidmore* 1952 (1) SA 732 (N) at 734C–E; *Ocean Accident and Guarantee Corporation Ltd* v *Koch* 1963 (4) SA 147 (A) at 159C–D; *South British Insurance Co Ltd* v *Unicorn Shipping Lines (Pty) Ltd* 1976 (1) SA 708 (A) at 713F–G.

[35] So, L H Hoffmann and D T Zeffertt *The South African Law of Evidence* 3 ed (1981) 464. Cf *S* v *Cooper* 1976 (2) SA 875 (T) at 890; *S* v *Matsaneng* 1966 (1) SA 46 (O) at 50.

[36] 1945 AD 369 at 386. [37] 1944 AD 493 at 508–9. [38] At 508.

[39] Ibid.

tions upon circumstantial evidence had been called into question. He stated:[40]

> 'The court must not take each circumstance separately and give the accused the benefit of any reasonable doubt as to the inference to be drawn from each one so taken. It must carefully weigh the cumulative effect of all of them together, and it is only after it has done so that the accused is entitled to the benefit of any reasonable doubt which it may have as to whether the inference of guilt is the only inference which can reasonably be drawn. To put the matter in another way: the Crown must satisfy the court, not that each separate fact is inconsistent with the innocence of the accused, but that the evidence as a whole is beyond reasonable doubt inconsistent with such innocence.'

Counsel's argument was clearly erroneous, but not, it is respectfully submitted, for the first of the reasons given by Davis AJA. The argument was a legal submission as to the meaning of 'proof beyond a reasonable doubt', and had nothing to do with the second rule in *Blom*, which, as stated above, is not a legal precept, but a rule of logic, an instrument for the avoidance of fallacious inference. If the law were as submitted by counsel, it would in no way be 'inconsistent' with that rule.

In a criminal case the ultimate proposition to be proved, the *factum probandum*, is the guilt of the accused. Where the case is one depending upon circumstantial evidence, the *factum probandum* is established as a matter of inference from the proved facts, the *facta probantia*. But a *factum probans* may itself be a proposition to be proved by way of inference from other facts.[41]

In considering whether the *factum probandum* has been established in a criminal case depending upon circumstantial evidence, the trier of fact must decide two questions: whether the inference of guilt can on the proved facts logically be drawn; and whether guilt has been proved beyond a reasonable doubt. The latter requirement does not necessarily mean that 'every factor bearing on the question of guilt must be treated as if it were a separate issue to which the test of reasonable doubt must be distinctly applied'.[42] But the question remains whether the second rule in *Blom* applies to the drawing of intermediate inferences.

It is submitted that it does apply.

Watermeyer JA's dictum applies generally to reasoning by inference in criminal cases, and not only to the drawing of the ultimate inference of guilt. In *Blom* itself the court was primarily concerned with an intermediate inference, namely, as to the cause of death of the deceased. Similarly, in the case of *R* v *Du Plessis*,[43] which was referred to by Davis AJA in *De Villiers*, the accused had been

[40] At 508–9. [41] See J H Wigmore *A Treatise on Evidence* 3 ed I 6.
[42] *R* v *Mtembu* 1950 (1) SA 670 (A) at 679, per Schreiner JA. [43] 1944 AD 314.

convicted of the theft of a motor car. The conviction was based on an inference drawn by the trial court, from the fact of the fingerprint of the accused on the bumper of the car, that the accused must necessarily have been working on the car in some way. It was held on appeal that there were a number of innocent explanations for the presence of the fingerprint which were reasonably possible, and it followed that the inference that the accused 'did something to the car' was not one which could be reasonably drawn, to the exclusion of all others, from the presence and position of the fingerprint. It was accordingly held that there was no legal evidence to support the finding of the trial court that the accused was guilty of theft.

In order to apply the second rule, the trier of fact must consider what other possible inferences can be drawn from the proved facts. If any of them is a reasonable inference, then the inference sought to be drawn cannot validly be drawn.

This does not mean, as has sometimes been suggested, that the trier of fact is entitled to speculate as to the possible existence of facts which, together with the proved facts, would justify a conclusion that the accused may be innocent.

In *R* v *Erasmus*[44] the appellant had been convicted on a statutory charge of harbouring two persons who had escaped, one (Richter) from a prison, the other from an internment camp. The appeal centred on the question whether the accused had knowledge that the two, whom he was proved to have accommodated at his farm house, were escapees. De Beer J posed the question whether the investigation of this issue should be confined to the bare fact that the fugitives were found on the premises of the accused or whether the court could go beyond the recorded evidence. He referred to certain dicta in *Blom* and in the case of *R* v *Du Plessis*,[45] and said that not only was the court not precluded from considering suppositions, possibilities and hypotheses, but was expressly enjoined to do so. He said:[46]

> 'To apply, then, the second cardinal rule, as enunciated above by Watermeyer JA in the light of these dicta, can the inference be excluded that on his arrival at the farm, say two months ago, Richter made some such statement to the accused:—"I was informed by the doctor on the Mazuma mine where I work, that I strained a heart muscle and was advised to have a complete rest till July. Could you accommodate me until then? I am prepared to assist in supervising your farming operations and to pay for my keep."'

He then said:[47]

> 'If the proved facts are such that the accused knew or ought to have known that Richter was an escapee, he is clearly guilty: but unless the

[44] 1945 OPD 50. [45] Op cit note 43 at 321. [46] Op cit note 44 at 83.
[47] At 84.

possibilty or probability be ruled out that Richter on his arrival told the accused some fictitious story designed to mislead him, I fail to see how it could be reasonably inferred merely from the length of his stay that Richter subsequently disclosed the true facts or that the accused may or should have gathered this therefrom.'

With respect, the learned judge failed to distinguish between speculation as to possible inferences from the proved facts (which is legitimate and indeed necessary in applying the second rule in *Blom*), and speculation as to matters of fact not supported by the evidence (which is not legitimate).

One cannot test the validity of an inference drawn from facts A, B and C by considering what inference can be drawn from facts A, B and C, and hypothesis X. The second rule in *Blom* concerns the inferences to be drawn from 'the proved facts', and those alone. When the trier of fact writes a scenario of what might have happened, he is exercising his powers of imagination, not applying a rule of logic.

The rule against speculation has frequently been stated in judgments of the Appellate Division. For example,

> '. . . the jury should not speculate on the possible existence of matters upon which there is no evidence, or the existence of which cannot reasonably be inferred from the evidence'.[48]
>
> 'An accused's claim to the benefit of a doubt when it may be said to exist must not be derived from speculation but must rest upon a reasonable and solid foundation created either by positive evidence or gathered from reasonable inferences which are not in conflict with, or outweighed by, the proved facts of the case.'[49]

There is therefore no warrant in the second rule in *Blom* for an argument that, because the State has not excluded every reasonably conceivable constellation of facts consistent with innocence, the conclusion of guilt cannot be drawn.

It was presumably such an argument that called forth the trenchant observations of Malan JA in *R* v *Mlambo*:[50]

> 'It is argued that this conclusion is erroneous because the Crown is said to have failed to eliminate every hypothesis which is inconsistent with the appellant's guilt or which, as it is also expressed, is consistent with his innocence.
>
> 'This method of stating the rule that the Crown must discharge the onus resting upon it beyond reasonable doubt has gradually gained in popularity, especially at the Bar where it is a recognized refuge for

[48] *R* v *Ndhlovu* 1945 AD 369 at 386, per Davis AJA. See also *R* v *Dhlumayo* 1948 (2) SA 677 (A) at 687.

[49] *R* v *Mlambo* 1957 (4) SA 727 (A) at 738B. See also *S* v *Sauls* 1981 (3) SA 172 (A) at 182H–183B.

[50] 1957 (4) SA 727 (A) at 737F–738A. Noted with approval by Rumpff JA in *S* v *Rama* 1966 (2) SA 395 (A) at 401. See also *S* v *Sauls* 1981 (3) SA 172 (A) at 182H–183B.

counsel for the defence who are harassed by strongly inculpatory evidence and attempts are frequently made to interpret it as an intention to depart from the rule.

'It is obviously impossible to formulate the principle in language which will produce any measure of certainty and endeavours are made to afford more definite and reliable guidance to those engaged in the solution of tantalizing problems by unravelling inferences from circumstantial evidence. The language employed in the more popular way of enunciating the principle does not appear to offer much relief. It is no more precise than, and it is exposed to the same dangers of misinterpretation and misapplication as, the form which at one time found almost universal favour and which has served the purpose so successfully for generations.

'In my opinion, there is no obligation upon the Crown to close every avenue of escape which may be said to be open to an accused. It is sufficient for the Crown to produce evidence by means of which such a high degree of probability is raised that the ordinary reasonable man, after mature consideration, comes to the conclusion that there exists no reasonable doubt that an accused has committed the crime charged. He must, in other words, be morally certain of the guilt of the accused.'

In *Mlambo* the accused had been convicted by a judge and assessors of murdering one Martha Nkosi. He was sentenced to death. The facts in outline were these.

The accused and the deceased were both employed by one Van Kraayenburg at his house at Volksrust, he mainly as a gardener, she as a domestic servant. They occupied adjoining rooms on the premises. Martha was in the kitchen of the Van Kraayenburg residence at about 8.30 pm on the night of 1 December 1956. She was not seen alive again. On the following morning her room was found to be bare of her possessions. It had been swept as clean as if it had never been occupied. On 11 December the body of a black female was dug out of a compost heap, which was controlled by the accused. It was naked and in an advanced state of decomposition, so that its identity could not be ascertained from the features, and the cause of death could not be determined.

All five members of the Appellate Division were agreed that it had been proved beyond reasonable doubt that the body was that of Martha, and that the accused had at least had a share in causing her death. The accused's evidence denying that he was concerned was rejected. Nothing, however, was known as to the circumstances of her death, and there was disagreement among the members of the court on the question whether it could be inferred beyond a reasonable doubt that the accused had had the intent to kill.

In his judgment Steyn JA (with whom D O K Beyers JA concurred) said:[51]

[51] At 732H–733A.

> 'Na my mening is moord met die oog op diefstal dan ook nie die enigste redelike afleiding uit die bewese feite nie. Die feite sou bv ook daarmee bestaanbaar wees dat Martha in die loop van 'n seksuele aanranding omgekom het sonder dat die appellant die nodige opset vir moord gehad het, dat hy daarna haar kamer aan kant gemaak het om die spore van die worsteling uit te wis, en dat hy haar naakte lyk versteek het en haar goed gevat het om dit te laat voorkom dat sy met haar goed weg is. So 'n verloop van sake sou tot dieselfde skuldige gedrag aanleiding kon gegee het, en ek kan geen gewese feit vind wat nie daarmee bestaanbaar sou wees nie.'

He accordingly considered that the appeal should succeed and the verdict should be altered to one of guilty of culpable homicide and the matter referred back to the trial court to impose another sentence after hearing any further evidence.

In his judgment Schreiner JA considered that on the facts proved he could find no more than a probability that in the circumstances the killing amounted to murder. He agreed with the order proposed by Steyn JA.

In a dissenting judgment, Malan JA (with whom Price AJA concurred) considered that the absence of proof of a motive for the killing did not present an insurmountable obstacle to a finding that the accused had intended to kill the deceased, because

> '. . . even if motive is held not to have been established there remains the fact that an assault of so grievous a nature was inflicted upon the deceased that death resulted either immediately or in the course of the same night. If an assault—using the term in its widest possible acceptation—is committed upon a person which causes death either instantaneously or within a very short time thereafter and no explanation is given of the nature of the assault by the person within whose knowledge it solely lies, a court will be fully justified in drawing the inference that it was of such an aggravated nature that the assailant knew or ought to have known that death might result. The remedy lies in the hands of the accused person and if he chooses not to avail himself thereof he has only himself to blame if an adverse verdict is given.'[52]

It is respectfully submitted that Steyn JA engaged in a piece of illegitimate speculation. There was no evidence (apart possibly from the fact that Martha's body was naked when it was found in the compost heap) that an assault was committed in order to facilitate sexual intercourse before the act had taken place, or after intercourse in order to remove Martha from the scene, and with her the only direct evidence against the accused. It was not enough that the proved facts were not inconsistent with a sexual assault: there was no evidence of such an assault. As Malan JA observed,[53] it was unrealistic to have regard to the realm of conjecture when there was at hand material which furnished 'a perfectly sound, rational, common-sense solution of the problem'.

[52] At 737D–F. [53] At 738E–F.

It is not possible to define what is meant in the second rule by 'a reasonable inference': that depends partly on logic and partly on human experience. All that can be said is that it must be an inference which on the basis of current knowledge and experience can be regarded as a reasonable one.[54] Generally speaking, the body of current knowledge and experience applicable to the usual run of criminal cases is common to all judges and lawyers, and ordinarily there will be a measure of general agreement among them as to the reasonableness of a possible inference.[55]

The investigation into other possible hypotheses is not an academic exercise. It is conditioned by the nature of the task in hand—the practical business of deciding a criminal trial. Legal reasoning works in an atmosphere and not in a vacuum.[56] And in considering whether there are other reasonable inferences, the fact that the accused has given an explanation, or the fact that, although an explanation was called for in the circumstances, the accused failed to give one, may considerably narrow the inquiry.

Where the accused does give an explanation, whether extra-judicially or in the evidence at his trial, 'its effect may be to narrow the question to the consideration whether that statement be or be not excluded and falsified by the evidence'.[57] If the explanation is a reasonable one, then unless it is negatived by the State (or it can be said that it cannot reasonably be true), the inference of guilt cannot be drawn.[58] If the explanation is negatived by the State, then ordinarily the court will not investigate the possibility of other inferences not mentioned by the accused. So, in *R* v *Bhardu*[59] Davis AJA said:

> 'It must not be overlooked that the accused has given an explanation which has been rejected—one which cannot even possibly be true. . . . The court should not, as it seems to me, find on his behalf some explanation which, if given, might perhaps have been true, but which he himself has not given.'[60]

In *Mlambo*[61] again Malan JA said:

> 'Moreover, if an accused deliberately takes the risk of giving false evidence in the hope of being convicted of a less serious crime or even, perchance, escaping conviction altogether and his evidence is declared to

[54] Cf *S* v *Glegg* 1973 (1) SA 34 (A) at 38–9, dealing with 'reasonable doubt'.

[55] In *R* v *Erasmus* 1945 OPD 50 De Beer J said at 81: 'A "reasonable inference" is of course a flexible expression incapable of exact definition and dependent on and closely correlated to the facts of each individual case and will vary with individual judges or magistrates.' And in *S* v *Rama* 1966 (2) SA 395 (A) at 401 Rumpff JA said, with reference to *R* v *Mlambo* (*supra* note 50), 'In my opinion this court should not have held that the trial court was wrong, even though this court, as the original *judex facti*, might not have arrived at the trial court's conclusion'.

[56] Thayer op cit note 8 at 273.

[57] Starkie op cit note 13 at 513.

[58] *R* v *Kumalo* 1930 AD 193 at 213; *R* v *Difford* 1937 AD 370 at 373.

[59] 1945 AD 813 at 822–3.

[60] See too *S* v *Rubenstein* 1964 (3) SA 480 (A) at 487–8.

[61] 1957 (4) SA 727 (A) at 738. This paragraph was approved in *S* v *Nkomo* 1966 (1) SA 831 (A) at 833D–F and in *S* v *Rama* 1966 (2) SA 395 (A) at 401B–C.

be false and irreconcilable with the proved facts a court will, in suitable cases, be fully justified in rejecting an argument that, notwithstanding that the accused did not avail himself of the opportunity to mitigate the gravity of the offence, he should nevertheless receive the same benefits as if he had done so.'

Where the facts are such as to call for an explanation by the accused and he does not give one, the trier of fact may conclude that any hypothesis consistent with his innocence should be discarded as not reasonably possible.[62]

So, where the evidence against an accused on a charge of theft consists in his possession of property recently stolen, his silence as to the way he acquired possession points strongly to the absence of an innocent explanation for the possession. If his possession was an innocent one, as the facts are within his knowledge, he should be able to show that fact by statement if not by proof.[63]

Again, in a case where the fingerprint of an accused was found inside a house which has been broken into, it would not be enough for him to say, 'I may have been inside that house by mistake, but innocently'. He could fairly be expected to say when and how he came to enter the house.[64]

The rationale of this approach is that experience teaches that in important affairs of life a man is likely to act as best he can for his own preservation and will tend to serve his own best interests, so that if there is an innocent explanation for facts seriously incriminatory, he will give it. Starkie[65] stated:

> 'If, on the supposition that a charge or claim is unfounded, the party against whom it is made has evidence within his reach by which he may repel that which is offered to his prejudice, his omission to do so supplies a strong presumption that the charge or claim is well founded; it would be contrary to every principle of reason, and to all experience of human conduct, to form any other conclusion.'

This approach derives support from the case of *R* v *Ismail.*[66]

The appellant, a man living in a small house in the yard of another house, had been convicted of possessing 80 bottles of wine

The qualification '*in suitable cases*' is an important one. Caution must be exercised, because experience shows that a weak but innocent man will sometimes, when appearances are against him, take refuge in an invented story, because he does not think that the truth alone will be sufficient to carry conviction. See *Maharaj* v *Parandaya* 1939 NPD 239 at 243.

[62] See *R* v *Padhla* 1948 (1) PH H87 (A); *S* v *Essack* 1974 (1) SA 1 (A) at 11.

[63] See *R* v *Du Plessis* 1944 AD 314 at 321–2. In *R* v *Kumalo* 1930 AD 193 at 214 Stratford JA said with reference to such a case: '. . . [I]f the possessor will not explain his possession the existence of explanations consistent with innocence are by that fact (ie, of silence or refusal) thus rendered improbable and it is not incumbent on the prosecution therefore to imagine all possible explanations and to negative them. But if a probable explanation has been given the Crown must negative it.' (It would perhaps be more accurate to substitute for 'a probable explanation', 'an explanation which may reasonably be true'.) See also *S* v *Rama* 1966 (2) SA 395 (A) at 401.

[64] *R* v *Du Plessis* op cit note 63 at 322.

[65] Op cit note 13 at 499.

[66] 1952 (1) SA 204 (A).

in contravention of the Liquor Act.[67] It was clear that the appellant possessed the 80 bottles, and that he also had 87 bottles in a locked store some distance from his house. He did not give evidence. The question was whether he possessed the 80 bottles of wine for the purpose of sale. It was argued that the proved facts did not exclude every reasonable inference save that which the Crown sought to draw.

In his judgment (in which three of the other members of the court concurred) Centlivres CJ said:[68]

> 'In the absence of any explanation by the appellant as to why he was in possession of the 80 bottles of wine plus the 87 found in his store and having regard to the humble position he occupied in the community, it is asking too much of human credulity to draw from the facts proved in his case any inference other than that the appellant was in possession of the 80 bottles of wine for the purpose of sale.'

Schreiner JA dealt with the failure of the accused to give evidence in a somewhat different way, saying:[69]

> 'That this fact may be given weight in deciding on the guilt of an accused person is of course clear. That too much weight should not be given to it has often been stated but the statement, though it may sometimes serve as a salutary warning, is not very helpful, since undue weight should naturally not be given to any factor in arriving at a decision. Since the absence of evidence from the accused is not one of the facts that make up the transaction itself under investigation at the trial, but is a consideration which may point, in a general way, to guilt, it is often difficult to decide what weight, if any, should be given to it in any particular case.'

It is respectfully submitted that not only may the absence of evidence from the accused point in a general way to guilt, but the absence of any explanation, when one is called for, may point specifically, in the application of the second rule in *Blom*, to the inference that there is no reasonable hypothesis consistent with his innocence.

Although a court *may* conclude that, in the absence of an explanation where one is called for in the circumstances, there is no innocent explanation, it will not necessarily do so. In this regard account may have to be taken of such matters as those referred to by Schreiner JA in *Ismail* in dealing with the weight to be given to the failure of an accused to give evidence:[70]

[67] Act 30 of 1928. [68] At 206. [69] At 209G–fine.

[70] At 210B–C. See *S* v *Matsiepe* 1962 (4) SA 708 (A) at 716; *S* v *Mthetwa* 1972 (3) SA 766 (A) at 769. In *R* v *Ndhlovu* 1945 AD 369 Davis AJA said at 387–8: 'It is true that the accused, as I have already mentioned earlier, gave no explanation of what occurred. This must, of course, be taken into account against him—indeed, I have done so. But it must be remembered that once he decided to say, quite untruthfully, that he was not there at all, he could thereafter give no explanation. And his deciding to do so is not altogether surprising in an ignorant native, who felt that he would be involved in serious trouble, no matter what he said, if once he admitted that he was there. In these circumstances, the

> 'Each case has to be dealt with in relation to is own circumstances; considerations which may have to be taken into account in any particular case are the strength or weakness of the Crown case, the apparent certainty with which the accused could have answered that case, if he were innocent, and the probability or improbability of the accused's failure to testify being explainable on some hypothesis unrelated to his guilt on the charge in question.'

To summarize: The second rule of logic in *Blom* is a salutary rule, whose field of application is limited by its nature. It is a tool for detecting and avoiding fallacy, for testing the logical validity of a conclusion. It is no more than that. It is not a legal precept. It is not another way of stating the criminal standard of proof. It does not in itself provide an automatic answer to the question whether guilt has been proved beyond a reasonable doubt. Even if the rule is satisfied, it does not follow that the trier of fact *must* convict the accused. It does not license speculation as to facts not proved by the evidence, nor does it mean that the State is obliged to close every avenue of escape which might otherwise be open to an accused. In investigating other reasonable inferences, the field of inquiry may be limited by the fact that the accused has given an explanation, or by the fact that he has failed to give an explanation where one was called for in the circumstances.

Attorney-General exercised a wise discretion in offering no opposition to the alteration of the conviction to one of culpable homicide. There is a doubt whether the accused was guilty of murder, and the accused must receive the benefit of that doubt.'

CLINICAL INDEPENDENCE OF THE DOCTOR IN THE TREATMENT OF PRISONERS: A CRITICAL SURVEY OF OUR LAW[1]

S A STRAUSS*

INTRODUCTION

Any unnatural death of a prisoner when he is in official custody is a matter of the gravest concern to the system of criminal justice. If such a death occurs whilst the prisoner is being, or ought to be, medically treated, it becomes a matter of the utmost importance to the medical profession as well, from the point of view both of professional ethics and the potential legal liability of the medical practitioner.

The truth of these statements has never been better manifested in South Africa than by the death of Mr S B Biko in 1977 and the circumstances surrounding that tragic event. As is known, Mr Biko, a young Black Consciousness leader, was detained under security legislation. He went into detention a healthy man and 26 days later, whilst still in detention and under the general care of medical personnel, died in consequence of a head injury which he had probably sustained during a scuffle[2] with members of the Security Branch of the South African Police a few days before his death. The sequelae—bitter indignation on the part of large segments of our population, embarrassed and embarrassing ministerial explanations, denunciation of South Africa internationally, painful self-examination on the part of the medical profession,[3] a protracted

* BA (Stell) LLB (UOVS) LLD (SA), Advocate of the Supreme Court of South Africa, Professor of Law in the University of South Africa.

[1] The law set forth in this paper is that which obtained on 30 September 1981. [I have added references to certain later legislation, in particular the Internal Security Act 74 of 1982.—Ed.]

[2] The word 'scuffle' was used by the inquest magistrate in his finding, the gist of which I have given in the text. It has been contended by an observer (Sir David Napley) that the magistrate was wrong in having added the rider that the injuries causing death were probably sustained in a 'scuffle'. See (1979) 3 *SACC/SASK* 99.

[3] In 1981 the South African Medical Association appointed an *àd hoc* committee, consisting of Mr I A Maisels QC and Professor J N de Villiers, to consider medico-ethical issues flowing from the *Biko* case. The committee made important recommendations for amendment of the law. Its report was published, after the text of this paper had been written, as a supplement to *The South African Medical Journal* of 22 August 1981. The report contains a useful summary of the facts of the *Biko* case.

inquest, litigation,[4] an intense public debate ever since—are matters of public record.

The treatment meted out to men behind bars—and I am not referring in this context to medical treatment only—in the modern world has become a touchstone for some of the most basic values adhered to by democratic societies. A special dimension was added to this by the spectacular advances made by medical science in our century. Today, medical treatment is no longer regarded as a privilege of the affluent few, but has come to be viewed by some as nothing less than a human right[5] accorded, or ideally to be accorded, to all.[6] Health care has become one of the most important duties of the state.

The mere fact that a man becomes a prisoner, whether as a subject of preventive detention, as a subject of detention for the purposes of interrogation (so far as this is at all compatible with democratic ideals), as a suspect awaiting trial or as a convict, is not regarded as divesting him of the right to receive adequate health care, however heinous his crime or suspected crime may be. On the contrary, the modern view is that a special duty is cast upon police and prison authorities, and upon medical officers, because in conse-

[4] It was reported in the press that Mr Biko's widow sued the Government for damages and that the case was settled out of court. The only reported case dealing (peripherally) with the death of Biko is *Tucker and another* v *SA Medical and Dental Council and others* 1980 (2) SA 207 (T). The issue in that case was the legal nature of certain preliminary procedural steps after a complaint against a doctor had been lodged with the Council.

[5] See, for example, the opening address by Professor H J J Leenen (of the Netherlands), entitled 'The Right to Health Care and the Right to Self-Determination', delivered at the Fifth World Congress on Medical Law held at Ghent, Belgium, in 1979. According to Leenen, health law is based on two pillars, namely, the right to health care, which he describes as a 'social human right', and the right of self-determination of man, which he describes as an 'individual right'. The latter type of right is in principle enforceable in a court of law, but Leenen concedes that social human rights can only be enforced in so far as a right of action has been laid down in positive law. He makes the point that an individual right may be meaningless unless the relative social right is satisfied. The right to health care, he says, includes *inter alia* the right to expert care and the availablity of such care to everyone. See also 'Health Aspects of Human Rights' (1976) 30 *WHO Chronicle* 347. (As to whether medical treatment is a 'right' a South African gaol prisoner has, or merely a 'privilege', see text to note 59.)

[6] A warning note must be sounded against overemphasis of 'a human right to medical treatment' to the point that the individual looks solely to the state for the provision of health-care services. In the free-enterprise society the citizen may be expected to make provision for his own medical care, within such limits at least as may be regarded as reasonable, considering his personal and social circumstances (cf W M P Fennell 'The Role of the State in Curative Medicine' (1981) 3 *Free Market* 8). And in no society is it unreasonable to expect the citizen to render his own contribution to the maintenance of personal and public health, especially by collaborating in preventive-medicine programmes. As far as the prisoner is concerned, there is an undeniable duty on the state to provide him with reasonable medical care. But even he (the prisoner) may be expected to do his duty to maintain his own health and to collaborate with the authorities in the maintenance of a prison health programme. If a prisoner were to make it impossible for the authorities to provide him with health care (for example, by refusing medical services, by deliberately inflicting injuries upon himself or by starving himself to death in an obstinate hunger-strike), it may be argued that the state's duty falls away *pro tanto*. (I am indebted to Professor J N de Klerk for the benefit of his views on the limits of the right to medical care, expressed in correspondence with me, which assisted me in shaping my own views on the subject.)

quence of the deprivation of his liberty the prisoner no longer has free access to medical practitioners and health-care facilities.[7]

These views have been given powerful expression in international documents. In 1955 the first United Nations Congress on the Prevention of Crime and the Treatment of Offenders was held.[8] This congress adopted 'Standard Minimum Rules for the Treatment of Prisoners'.[9] Rules 22 to 26,[10] inclusive, refer to medical services specifically, but many of the other rules relate to matters that have a direct bearing on the health of prisoners, and some of these make specific mention of the role of the medical officer in various situations. There have been further congresses in this series. As a result of the initiative taken by the World Health Organization, the World Medical Association in 1975 in Tokyo adopted a set of 'Guide-lines for Medical Doctors concerning Torture and other Cruel, Inhuman or Degrading Treatment or Punishment in relation to Detention and Imprisonment'. These guide-lines became known as the 'Declaration of Tokyo'.[11]

The Declaration of Tokyo deals primarily with the ethical position of the doctor vis-à-vis torture of prisoners and other forms of cruel, inhuman or degrading treatment. Article 4[12] contains the following injunction:

> 'A doctor must have complete clinical independence in deciding upon the care of a person for whom he or she is medically responsible. The doctor's fundamental role is to alleviate distress of his or her fellow men, and no motive whether personal, collective or political shall prevail against this higher purpose.'

Irrespective of the political system of a society, the efficacious realization of these exalted ideals is certainly not without problems.

[7] A facet of imprisonment as a form of sentence that is not always borne in mind is that imprisonment itself may be dangerous to the health of prison inmates. See the interesting study by D A Jones *The Health Risks of Imprisonment* (1976).

[8] The background to this congress and further developments following it were set forth fully in a circular letter dated 6 December 1976 of the executive secretary of the Council for International Organizations of Medical Sciences (established under the auspices of the World Health Organization and Unesco). This letter was widely circulated internationally and was the subject of intensive discussion in medico-legal circles in South Africa.

[9] The rules were formulated as part of a movement to give effect to art 5 of the Universal Declaration of Human Rights, adopted by the United Nations General Assembly on 10 December 1948, which reads: 'No one shall be subjected to torture or to cruel, inhuman or degrading treatment or punishment.'

[10] Rules 4 to 26, 44 and 45, 62, 71, 82, 83 and 91 were reproduced in a bilingual publication, the English title of which is *The Medical Practitioner in the Health Service*, published in March 1981 by the South African Department of Health and Welfare (at pp 56–9 of the English text).

[11] For the historical background to this declaration, see the source referred to in note 8.

[12] The six articles of the Tokyo Declaration are reproduced in the publication referred to in note 10 (at pp 48–9 of the English text). It is to be noted that some other sources indicate that there are eight articles, but the contents are exactly the same; the apparent difference is only a difference in arrangement and numbering of the individual paragraphs. I quote from the publication referred to in note 10.

A substantial percentage of prisoners are 'difficult' people—psychopaths, activists, habitual offenders, malingerers—and the life of the prison warder is not an easy one. Prison authorities may be forgiven for being sceptical towards measures that might be abused by prisoners, thereby undermining institutional discipline. On the other hand, the validity of these ideals is beyond dispute, and any civilized community should strive towards their effectuation in practice. The consensus in the medical profession is that when it comes to medical treatment, the doctor, by virtue of his specialized knowledge, skill and experience, is the only person who can make a proper clinical assessment of how serious the prisoner's condition is, whether medical treatment is indicated, how urgent it is and what form it should take, and that a professional assessment should not be capable of being vetoed by a non-medical officer in the service of the state. It is further to be noted that part of the medical assessment may be whether or not the facilities in a prison or other place of detention are suitable or adequate for the treatment of a particular prisoner and whether a prisoner should not be taken to a hospital or other health-care facility outside the walls of the prison. Finally, there is the question whether the state of health of a prisoner is such that he can safely be conveyed to an outside facility, how far he can travel and under what conditions he should be conveyed. In the unlikely event of a difference of opinion arising between custodial staff and the medical officer, the medical officer should have the conclusive say on these matters as well.

In this article it is proposed to examine our law, in order to assess to what extent these ideals have been, or are capable of being, attained.[13] Special attention will be given to statutory provisions relating to the medical treatment of detainees and other prisoners. The laws bearing upon the subject are the Police Act,[14] security legislation, and the Prisons Act[15] and regulations under it. Some observations will also be made, however, on common-law principles relevant to the subject.

A few words about terminology: In the strict legal sense of the word, 'detainee'—in the South African context, at any event—refers to a person detained under security legislation.[16] But there are of course other types of detainees as well, such as persons detained

[13] There are several other legal issues regarding the medical treatment of prisoners, for example, the issue of consent, in particular the question whether a prisoner may be treated against his will (including the question of force-feeding); the treatment of prisoners who are minors; medical examinations against the will of the prisoner; the participation of doctors in the treatment of patients subjected to corporal punishment and other harsh forms of punishment; medical experimentation upon prisoners; organ and tissue donation by prisoners. It is not proposed to deal with any of these questions in the present paper.

[14] Act 7 of 1958. [15] Act 8 of 1959.

[16] [Such as the former Internal Security Act 44 of 1950 s 10(1)(*a*)*bis*, the General Law Amendment Act 62 of 1966 s 22 and the Terrorism Act 83 of 1967 s 6, now replaced by ss 28 and 29 of the Internal Security Act 74 of 1982.—Ed.]

under the Abuse of Dependence-producing Substances and Rehabilitation Centres Act 1971.[17] In a strictly legal sense, 'prisoner', again, may refer specifically to a person held in custody under the Prisons Act. 'Prisoner' is defined in s 1 of the latter statute; the material part of this definition is quoted below, and from that it will be apparent that 'prisoner' may in particular circumstances include a 'detainee' in the sense mentioned above. Whether a person in custody belongs to the one or the other, or both, of these categories may be important in determining his rights. But where general observations are made in this paper, they are really intended to deal with any person held in official police custody or in prison, irrespective of the strict statutory terminology that may apply to him, and whatever the cause of, or objective for, his detention or incarceration may be.

The Police Act

There are no provisions in the Police Act itself or the regulations[18] under it governing medical treatment of detainees and prisoners. There are, however, important instructions to the police contained in paragraphs (18) to (23) of standing order 319 of the South African Police,[19] as well as a newly introduced[20] standing instruction ('staande opdrag') specially relating to the treatment of persons detained under security legislation.

Standing orders and instructions, it must be noted, derive their legal power from reg 6 of the Police Regulations promulgated under s 33 of the Police Act.[21] As is indicated by the terminology, these orders are in the nature of departmental orders and instructions given by the Commissioner of Police and directed to members of the Police Force. Unlike regulations made by the State President under an Act of Parliament, they are not published in the *Government Gazette* (or otherwise made known to the public at large), and accordingly are not law in the generally accepted sense of the word.[22] They are legally significant, however, in the sense

[17] Act 41 of 1971 s 13.

[18] The Police Regulations are contained in GN R203 *GG* 719 of 14 February 1964 (*Reg Gaz* 299). The Government Notice has been amended from time to time.

[19] I am grateful to the Headquarters of the South African Police in Pretoria for kindly furnishing me with the text of the standing orders as they existed in March 1981. I have since established that up to the date when this paper was finalized (30 September 1981) no further changes were brought about.

[20] The standing instruction is dealt with below under 'Security Legislation'. It is to be noted that it was introduced by the Commissioner of Police after the death of Mr Biko.

[21] See note 18. The Commissioner is given the general power of issuing orders and instructions. Orders and instructions of a permanent nature are known as 'standing' or 'Force' orders (reg 6(2)).

[22] I fully realize that with this statement I am venturing into an area where angels fear to tread: the concept and definition of law. There is, of course, the view that law exists if there is a certain degree of enforceability and if there is some specific mechanism for securing compliance (George Whitecross Paton *A Text-book of Jurisprudence* 4 ed (1972) edited by G W Paton and David P Derham at 78). 'Die konstabel wat die samedrom-

that failure on the part of a policeman to obey any particular order may expose him to disciplinary action being taken against him under the Police Act.[23] It is also a criminal offence for a member of the Police Force to fail to comply with an order issued in terms of the Police Act.[24] It is further submitted that a suspect, prisoner or another person who feels himself aggrieved by police action in violation of a standing order affecting a right of his (such as a right of personality or proprietary right) may at common law apply to court for an interdict or a *mandamus* (as the circumstances may be) to enforce compliance with the order. Moreover, the duties imposed by standing orders upon policemen may be relevant in regard to potential delictual or criminal liability on the part of the state, where it is alleged that a policeman committed an act in breach of an official duty that resulted in damage to (or the death of) another person.[25] Lastly, there is the question of judicial review of police decisions taken in disregard of standing orders, but as is pointed out below in connection with review of prison decisions, this is a remedy not without problems.

From the provisions of standing order 319 it is clear that there is a duty upon the police to call in the district surgeon or another medical practitioner to attend to seriously injured or ill prisoners.[26]

mende massa beveel om aan te stap', says Professor J D van der Vyver ('Die Regsbegrip' (1962) 25 *THRHR* 1 at 7–8), 'positiveer deur sy bevel net soseer objektiewe reg . . . as die parlement wat openbare geweldpleging verbied.' If this view is correct, then the Commissioner of Police who, by virtue of a police regulation made in terms of an Act of the sovereign legislature, issues general written orders to members of the Force, would *a fortiori* be 'positivering' law. Perhaps I should therefore play it safe and qualify my statement in the text by saying that the body of standing orders does not constitute *statutory law*, because there is no promulgation. Of some consolation to me is the case of *R* v *Koenig* 1917 CPD 225, also quoted by Van der Vyver in his erudite article. In that case the court, per Gardiner J (at 241), regarded the order 'to move on', made by a policeman, as an administrative act and not as a law, because it does not require promulgation in the *Gazette*. In *Union Government* v *Thorne* 1929 TPD 380 at 380, 383 it was held that police standing orders have no 'statutory force'. See also *E Rosenberg (Pty) Ltd* v *Union Government (Minister of Justice)* 1945 TPD 225; *Khoza* v *Minister of Justice* 1965 (4) SA 286 (W) at 291.

[23] See police reg 58(1). [24] See s 9 of the Act.

[25] See, for example, the argument by counsel in *S* v *Van As* 1967 (4) SA 594 (A) at 595B–C; *Weir-Mason* v *Minister of Justice* 1958 (3) SA 299 (N) at 302H–fine; the reference by counsel in *Mhlongo and another NO* v *Minister of Police* 1978 (2) SA 551 (A) at 558C–D to 'specific instructions'. See also *Minister van Polisie en 'n ander* v *Gamble en 'n ander* 1979 (4) SA 759 (A) at 767B–C, where Joubert JA referred to 'wettige opdragte' given to a policeman by his superiors. Compare *Sahanga* v *Dupont NO* 1965 (2) SA 404 (SRAD), in which the court referred to police standing orders to determine whether or not injuries sustained by a policeman could properly be said to have been occasioned in the course of his official duties. (The delictual liability of the state for actions of a policeman naturally does not depend on the mere question whether he was performing a statutory or official duty. The decisive question is whether he acted within the scope of his employment. See *Union Government (Minister of Justice)* v *Thorne* 1930 AD 47 at 50–1; *Mhlongo* (*supra*) at 567–8; *Gamble* (*supra*).)

[26] Standing order 319(18) provides as follows: 'Whenever a prisoner is seriously injured or shows signs of serious illness, the district surgeon shall be sent for by the speediest means available and requested to attend, first aid being applied meanwhile.' Certain entries must be made in the occurrence book (319(1)), and standing order 319(20) then

('Prisoner' is not defined in the subparagraphs of the standing order, but is presumably used in the general sense of any person in police custody following an arrest.) Of special significance is the provision[27] whereby policemen are ordered to carry out without delay '[a]ny instructions given by the district surgeon or medical practitioner called in to act for him'. This provision intimates that it is the district surgeon (or other doctor) who has the final say in regard to the medical treatment of such a prisoner, and this is most laudable in the light of the need for clinical independence adumbrated above. Moreover, explicit mention is made of the possibility of treatment in an 'outside' hospital.[28] Equally commendable is the right given to a prisoner to be treated by his own doctor. The standing order[29] provides as follows:

> 'Should a prisoner elect to be examined or treated by his own medical practitioner, his request shall be acceded to provided the prisoner himself defrays the costs and it does not entail additional expense to the Government.'[30]

The following observations must, however, be made regarding standing order 319(18) to (23): First, it is submitted that these provisions are of such importance that they should not be relegated to standing orders but should be accorded proper statutory status either in the Police Act itself or, at the very least, in regulations promulgated by the State President under s 33 of that statute. Secondly, some of these provisions seem to be contradicted to a certain extent by the standing instruction relating to detainees in terms of security legislation (discussed below) and in particular by the Prisons Act and the regulations under it. As is indicated below, *any* police prisoner may in certain circumstances be considered a 'prisoner' in terms of the latter Act and its regulations, which clearly give the Commissioner of Prisons the effective say over medical treatment of prisoners. It can be argued that because of the fact that they are (promulgated) statutory regulations, the regulations under the Prisons Act must prevail in the event of their provisions conflicting with standing orders of the South African Police. For the sake of legal certainty, any possible contradiction between these various sets of provisions should be cleared up by the legislature.

goes on to provide: 'If the district surgeon is not available, any other medical practitioner may, in serious and urgent cases, be called in to attend to the prisoner pending the arrival of the district surgeon.' An appropriate entry must then be made in the occurrence book.

[27] Contained in standing order 319(21).

[28] Para (21) contains the following provision: 'If removal to a hospital other than a gaol hospital or sickbay is ordered, all precautions shall be made to guard [the prisoner] en route and while detained in hospital.'

[29] Para (22)(*a*).

[30] The other provisions of standing order 319(18) to (23) deal with tuberculotic patients, and the notification of the death or serious illness of a patient.

District Surgeons

At this point something must be said about the legal status of the district surgeon, who will ordinarily be responsible for the medical treatment of detainees and prisoners. The district surgeon, whether full-time (as in the cities) or part-time (as in country towns), is not an employee of the Department of Police or the Prisons Service. District surgeons are medical practitioners employed by the Department of Health and Welfare, and in general their conditions of service and official duties are determined by the Minister of Health and Welfare. In performing the functions of prison medical officers,[31] however, they are to a certain extent subject to the prison regulations—as is described below.

As far as the Department of Health and Welfare is concerned, a recent (March 1981) official publication of the department, entitled *The Medical Practitioner in the Health Service*,[32] lists a number of obligations on the part of doctors (and in particular district surgeons) in regard to patients in police custody who are examined at the request of the police. Thus it is described as 'imperative that the District Surgeon or his deputy have access to the patient at all times'.[33] The manual also states that '[w]here the district surgeon has reason to believe that his instructions are not being complied with, he shall report this to the appropriate Commanding Officer at the same time notifying the Regional Director, State Health Services of the action he has taken'.[34] Other instructions embodied in the manual that relate to the treatment of patients in police custody which should be mentioned here are the following: The doctor must ascertain whether the prisoner 'is in a fit condition for transfer by specified means of transport to the consulting room(s) or other appropriate nearby place suitable for the examination of the person in private'.[35] Should the person be removed into the care of another doctor, the latter must be fully informed as expeditiously as possible of his condition.[36] The district surgeon should not hesitate to call for a second medical opinion should this in his opinion be necessary.[37] Where the detainee requests his own doctor, 'this must be considered as a privilege and not as a right,[38] but in any case the district surgeon should not fail to consult with such medical practioner . . .'.[39] It is further stated that the doctor 'should inform the officer commanding the prison of any inadequacy regarding the health of the prisoners or any other matter concerning the prison. This should be done in the form of a written report and a copy

[31] By virtue of s 6 of the Prisons Act, read with prison reg 6(2). See further below.
[32] See also note 6. [33] Page 52 item 5. [34] Page 53 item 8.
[35] Page 52 item 2. [36] Page 52 item 5. [37] Page 53 item 6.
[38] This statement appears to be in conflict with police standing order 319(22)(*a*) quoted in the text above, which clearly accords the prisoner a right and not merely a privilege.
[39] Page 53 item 7.

should be sent to the Regional Director of the Department of Health and Welfare. If the report does not create the desired reaction the physician should himself bring it under the regional director's attention.'[40] (The manual then proceeds[41] to set forth extracts from a decision taken by the First United Nations[42] Congress on the Prevention of Crime and the Treatment of Transgressors of 30 August 1955,[43] containing 'practical suggestions for the health care of prisoners and other persons in custody',[44] as well as an extract from the Association of State Correctional Administrators policy guide-lines.[45] It is clear that these extracts are not in the nature of regulations or even departmental instructions applying to South African health-care personnel, but were included in the above-mentioned publication of the Department of Health and Welfare merely as general guide-lines.)

Security Legislation

At the beginning of 1982 the most important enactments pertaining to the safety of the state and security were the Internal Security Act 1950,[46] the General Law Amendment Act 1962[47] (s 21, the so-called sabotage clause), the General Law Amendment Act 1966[48] (s 22, governing 'the detention of terrorists and certain other persons for interrogation') and the Terrorism Act 1967.[49] In several other Acts of Parliament there were also provisions relating to security matters, for example, the Criminal Procedure Act 1977.[50] None of these laws contain any provisions dealing with the medical treatment of prisoners.

It has been suggested that the Terrorism Act, which in s 6 made provision for the indefinite detention of suspected terrorists, effectively prevented access of medical practitioners to detainees held

[40] Page 55. This item is under the general heading 'The patient in prison and other places of custody'.

[41] Pages 55ff.

[42] The word 'National' is used in the text instead of 'Nations', and is clearly a misprint.

[43] The date given in the text is 1953, but this must be a misprint. To the best of my knowledge the correct date is 1955.

[44] The suggestions are classified under the following heading: 'Minimum stipulated regulations for the treatment of prisoners.' Those in Part I are described as 'regulations for general application' (accommodation; personal hygiene; clothes and bedding; food; medical services; notification of death; disease; transfer, etc; transport of prisoners). Those in Part II are described as 'regulations applicable to certain specific categories' (prisoners on trial; mentally disturbed and mentally abnormal prisoners; and prisoners in detention or awaiting trial).

[45] These guide-lines deal with medical services in general, preventive measures and medical experiments. The extracts published in the departmental guide were reproduced from a publication indicated as *Medical Care of Prisoners and Detainees—Ciba Geigy Foundation Symposium* (Elsevier 1973).

[46] Act 44 of 1950. [47] Act 76 of 1962. [48] Act 62 of 1966.

[49] Act 83 of 1967. [All these statutes were repealed by the Internal Security Act 74 of 1982, which contains similar provisions. The important changes will be referred to later.—Ed.]

[50] Act 51 of 1977.

under that statute. But this interpretation is mistaken. Subsection (6), the 'sealing off' provision of s 6, read as follows:

> 'No person, other than the Minister [of Justice] *or an officer in the service of the State acting in the performance of his official duties*,[51] shall have access to any detainee, or shall be entitled to any official information relating to or obtained from any detainee.'[52]

The Terrorism Act should, of course, not be read in isolation. As is pointed out below, detainees held under security legislation may also legally be 'prisoners' under the Prisons Act, and the latter enactment, together with its regulations, provides in detail for medical treatment of prisoners. It is submitted that the Terrorism Act must be read with the Prisons Act; and, on the hypothesis that there is a conflict of provisions, inasmuch as the latter Act makes provision for medical treatment whereas the former prohibits access to a detainee by 'outsiders' generally, which would presumably include medical practitioners, account must be taken of the basic canon of construction that statutory provisions must be reconciled with one another.

Neat arguments may perhaps be advanced to the effect that a later 'special' enactment (the Terrorism Act) repealed or modified the earlier 'general' enactment (the Prisons Act).[53] Quite apart from difficulties in characterizing the one Act as 'special' and the other as 'general' legislation,[54] it is submitted that such a debate would be quite pointless. The fact of the matter is that the basic assumption is erroneous. Section 6(6) of the Terrorism Act did *not* exclude access of certain medical practitioners to detainees. The phrase italicized in the quotation of the subsection above clearly envisages certain officials having access to a detainee. In my opinion there can be no doubt that prison medical officers and a district surgeon or other 'approved' doctor[55] belong to the category 'officers in the service of the State' who, in rendering medical services to persons in custody,

[51] My italics.

[52] [The corresponding provision of the Internal Security Act 1982 is s 29(7). It reads:

> 'No person other than the Minister [of Law and Order] or a person acting by virtue of his office in the service of the State—
>
> *(a)* shall have access to any person detained in terms of the provisions of this section, except with the consent of and subject to such conditions as may be determined by the Minister or the Commissioner [of the South African Police]; or
>
> *(b)* shall be entitled to any official information relating to or obtained from such person.'

Subsection (9) of s 29 states that any person so detained 'shall . . . be not less than once in a fortnight . . . visited in private by a district surgeon'.—Ed.]

[53] I have here in mind the principles of interpretation of statutes brought home under the well-known doctrine of *generalia specialibus non derogant.*

[54] In so far as such a debate may be at all relevant to the present discussion, I would suggest that both the Terrorism Act and the Prisons Act are 'general' enactments. In particular, it is submitted, the Terrorism Act—albeit a harsh measure in several respects —was never intended to regulate medical treatment of detainees or to restrict the rights and duties of medical or prison officers under the Prisons Act (and the rights of prisoners under the latter Act to receive medical treatment).

[55] ie in terms of s 6(3) of the Prisons Act, read with prison reg 6(2).

are 'acting in the performance of their official duties'.[56] As is argued below, such medical officers and district surgeons (or specially appointed doctors) do not only have the right to treat prisoners medically, but in fact have a duty to do so. The same reasoning, it is submitted, applies to persons detained under other security laws.[57, 58]

It is further to be noted that the official 'Warrant for Detention/Transfer' relating to the 'Place and Conditions of Detention/Transfer under Section 6 of the Terrorism Act, 1967 (Act 83 of 1967)' issued by the Commissioner of the South African Police in the case of these detainees in fact contains the following directions,[59] *inter alia*:

> 'The detainee shall, if necessary, receive medical treatment from any medical officer designated under section 6 of the Prisons Act, 1959, or any District Surgeon. Any medical or dental prescription given by such medical officer or District Surgeon shall be given effect to forthwith.'

A warrant ('lasbrief' or 'lasgewing') is, of course, a document authorizing police action under a legal provision, but it may also—as is the case with the warrant referred to here—contain directions to the police or other officials. Significantly, the warrant in question authorizes the detention of a detainee in the following terms:

> 'The detainee shall be transferred to and detained in a prison as defined in section 1 of the Prisons Act, 1959 (Act 8 of 1959), namely the prison at . . . from the prison at . . . on . . . (hereinafter referred to as the place of detention).'

[56] Compare *Ngxale* v *Minister of Justice of the Ciskei and others* 1981 (2) SA 554 (E). In this case the mother of a young woman detained by the Ciskeian Police applied to court for an order which, *inter alia*, would have authorized a medical officer or specialist of her choice, or a district surgeon in the area where her daughter was kept, to visit her in order to conduct a thorough and detailed medical examination of her and to compile a report. The girl was detained under reg 8 of Proc R252 (Regulations for the Administration of the Ciskei). Subregulation (4) provides as follows: 'No person shall, except with the consent of the Minister, have access to any person detained in terms of sub-reg (2): Provided that no less than once each week such person shall be visited by the magistrate, additional magistrate, or assistant magistrate of the district in which he is detained.' The court held that the doctors whom it was suggested should be given access to examine the girl 'are not persons who fall within the class of persons permitted access to her in terms of the proviso to sub-reg (4)' (at 562B–C). (It is to be noted that the wording of subreg (4) is not identical to that of s 6(6) of the Terrorism Act.)

[57] As far as the Internal Security Act 44 of 1950 was concerned, this was affirmed *pro tanto* at least—and *ex abundanti cautela*, it is submitted—by the Minister of Justice in GN R1281 of 16 July 1976 (*GG* 5228, *Reg Gaz* 2340) containing the regulations made in terms of s 12B(2) of the Internal Security Act 1950, reg 2 of which reads as follows: 'Subject to the provisions of section 12B of the Act and these regulations, the provisions of the Prisons Act, 1959 (Act 8 of 1959), and the regulations promulgated under section 94 thereof, the Prisons Service Orders and official instructions of the Commissioner of Prisons, in so far as these apply to unconvicted prisoners awaiting trial for an alleged offence, shall apply *mutatis mutandis* to all detainees.'

[58] This part of my discussion is confined to security legislation. It goes without saying that there are several other laws which also contain provisions on arrest and detention, for example, s 13 of the Abuse of Dependence-producing Substances and Rehabilitation Centres Act 41 of 1971 (detention of persons for interrogation under warrant issued by magistrate). The latter Act likewise has no provisions referring to the medical treatment of detainees. What is said in this paper about prisoners other than detainees under security legislation would naturally apply to prisoners arrested or held in custody under Act 41 of 1971 or any other statute. This applies in equal measure to detention of witnesses under s 185 of the Criminal Procedure Act 1977 (the so-called 180-days clause).

[59] In para 8.

Finally, mention must be made of the recently introduced standing instruction specially relating to the treatment of persons detained under security legislation to which I have already made reference above, and which I shall now quote in full:[60]

'*Complaints and symptoms of illness ("ongesteldheid") of a detainee*

'(i) The services of a competent medical practitioner must be obtained forthwith.

'(ii) Effect must be given to the instructions of the medical practitioner, but should it be necessary for the detainee to be removed for treatment in a hospital other than a prison hospital and such a removal is regarded as involving a security risk, Head Office[61] must first be consulted.

'(iii) The fact of any illness must without delay be reported to Head Office by telex, so that the Minister can be informed if necessary.

'(iv) No sick detainee must without Head Office's approval be removed from one city or town to another city or town.

'(v) Sick detainees must in regard to sleeping and eating facilities enjoy special attention and must be visited more often than in normal circumstances.

'(vi) Save in exceptional cases, for instance where disclosure of the fact of detention of a terrorist will harm the investigation, the nearest blood relation ("bloedverwant") or relation by marriage ("aanverwant") must be notified of such a condition of illness, which in any way may be regarded as serious. Visits to the sick detainee must, however, not be permitted without permission having been granted by Head Office.'

The introduction of this standing instruction is to be commended. It evidences special concern about the medical treatment of detainees and an earnest endeavour to avoid a situation such as arose in the case of Mr Biko. But what I have said above regarding the legal status of standing order 319(18)–(23) likewise applies to this standing instruction: if not ensconced in parliamentary legislation itself, these provisions should at the very least be embodied in promulgated regulations and should leave no doubt that a bona fide clinical assessment by the doctor concerned and his subsequent directions shall be decisive. Moreover, what applies to security detainees should be of equal application to all other categories of persons in custody.

The Prisons Act

A study of definitional provisions of s 1 of the Prisons Act reveals that the definitions of 'prison' and 'prisoner', respectively,

[60] The standing instruction, which was kindly made available to me by the Headquarters of the South African Police in Pretoria, is available only in Afrikaans. The translation is mine.

[61] This is clearly a reference to the Security Branch of the Police Headquarters in Pretoria.

are wide enough to embrace not only convicted persons or awaiting-trial prisoners, but also in many cases—although not invariably—persons detained under security legislation.

'Prison' is defined *inter alia* as 'any place established or deemed to have been established under . . . [the Prisons Act] as a place for the reception, detention, confinement, training or treatment of persons liable to detention in custody . . .; and for the purposes of any offence under this Act or any contravention of or failure to comply with any provision of this Act further includes every place used as a police cell or lock-up'.[62] 'Prisoner' is generally defined as 'any person, whether convicted or not, who is detained in custody in any prison or is being transferred in custody or is en route in custody from one prison to another prison . . .'.[63] ('This Act', it is ot be noted, is defined as including the regulations under the Act.)

From these definitions it is clear that if any person who has been arrested or detained by the Police is brought to a prison established under the Prisons Act, he falls squarely within the ambit of the latter statute and, of course, the regulations under it. He need not have been convicted—in fact, he need not even necessarily be an awaiting-trial detainee (in terms of the Terrorism Act, for instance, persons could be—and were in fact ordinarily—arrested for interrogation and were not always charged ultimately). As I have mentioned above, the official warrant for detention/transfer of detainees under the Terrorism Act makes express mention of detention of such detainees *in prisons as defined in s 1 of the Prisons Act.* It would therefore seem that such detainees would ordinarily at an early stage after arrest fall under the latter Act as far as their conditions of detention are concerned.

Police cells and lock-ups, on the other hand, generally do not qualify as 'prisons' under the Prisons Act. It is only for the relatively narrow purposes of the offences created by the Prisons Act or 'any contravention or failure to comply with any provision of this Act' that police cells and lock-ups qualify as prisons. The legislature's intention with these provisions, it would seem, is that where any person commits an offence under the Act—such as escaping from custody or giving illegal publicity to prison affairs—it is irrelevant whether the offence was committed in or in respect of a cell or lock-up, and he may be charged under the Act; the same applies to enforcement of any other statutory duty under the Act.

The Prisons Act as such contains several provisions directly relevant to medical treatment, and these provisions are amplified by a number of regulations promulgated under the Act. It is submitted

[62] Section 1 of the Prisons Act 8 of 1959.

[63] Ibid. The general definition is followed by a specific definition for the purpose of s 44(1)(*e*) of the Act (relating to forbidden publication of certain prison matters).

that the Act and its regulations create a right to health care on the part of the prisoner, and not merely a privilege to be granted or refused at will by the prison authorities.[64] This does not mean, of course, that the prisoner can prescribe to the Prisons Service exactly what form the medical treatment should take or under what conditions it should be given. Nor does it necessarily mean that the prisoner can enforce his right by means of judicial review of decisions taken by the prison authorities concerning the nature and scope of medical treatment to be given to him.[65]

As far as the Prisons Act is concerned, an important section that must be mentioned at the outset is s 6, which makes provision for the appointment of medical officers in the following terms in subsec (1): 'For every prison there shall be a medical officer who shall perform such duties as are assigned to him by or under this Act.' The Minister of Justice is empowered[66] to appoint resident medical officers whose whole time must be given to the duties of the post to which they were appointed. If no resident medical officer is appointed (or where his post is temporarily vacant), the duties assigned to him must be performed by the district surgeon for the area in which the prison is situated, or by another doctor approved by the Director-General: Health and Welfare.[67]

As was noted above, district surgeons, whether full-time or part-time, are employees of the latter department. But in so far as they work as medical officers in a prison, there can, in my opinion, be no doubt that by virtue of the Prisons Act they fall within the general control and direction of the Commissioner of Prisons.[68]

This is suggested by s 77 of the Prisons Act, which provides as follows:

> 'Every prisoner sentenced to imprisonment, and detained in a prison, including a hospital prison for psychopaths, shall, subject to the provisions of this Act and subject also to any special order of the court, be employed, trained and treated[69] in such manner as the Commissioner [of

[64] The Prisons Service takes the view—and correctly so, it is submitted—that a prisoner is entitled to medical care as a matter of right and not merely as a matter of privilege. See *Goldberg and others* v *Minister of Prisons and others* 1979 (1) SA 14 (A) at 22C–D. But in *Goldberg* (at 30H–fine) the Appellate Division in its majority ruling (per Wessels ACJ) considered it unnecessary for the purposes of its decision to distinguish between 'necessaries or basic rights' on the one hand, and 'privileges or comforts' on the other. On prisoners' rights in general, see further the quartet of notes (by D H van Wyk, Barend van Niekerk, R G Nairn and Jerold Taitz, respectively) on *Goldberg* in (1979) 3 *SACC/SASK* 52ff; Harold G Rudolph '"Man's Inhumanity to Man Makes Countless Mourn." Do Prisoners have Rights?' (1979) 96 *SALJ* 640; and J H van Rooyen 'Aspekte van Reg en Geregtigheid met Betrekking tot Gevangenes' (1981) 44 *THRHR* 1 at 9.

[65] The question of review of prison decisions is touched upon below.

[66] By s 6(2).

[67] Section 6(3). The subsection refers to the Secretary for Health, which must now be construed as a reference to the Director-General.

[68] 'Medical officer' is defined s 1 of the Prisons Act 1959 so as to include district surgeons and other 'approved' doctors.

[69] The word used in the Afrikaans text of the Act is 'behandel'.

Oliver Schreiner receiving the honorary degree of Doctor of Laws at the graduation ceremony of the University of Cape Town on 27 June 1958. *Seated:* Albert v d S Centlivres, Chancellor of the University, and Dr J P Duminy, Principal and Vice-Chancellor.

(Photograph by courtesy of *The Argus*)

On the occasion of the conferring of the honorary degree of Doctor of Laws on Albert van de Sandt Centlivres by the University of the Witwatersrand, Johannesburg, on 4 April 1964. *Left to right:* The Hon Oliver D Schreiner (Chancellor of the University), Centlivres, Professor I D MacCrone (Vice-Chancellor and Principal), Mr B L Bernstein (Chairman of the Council of the University)

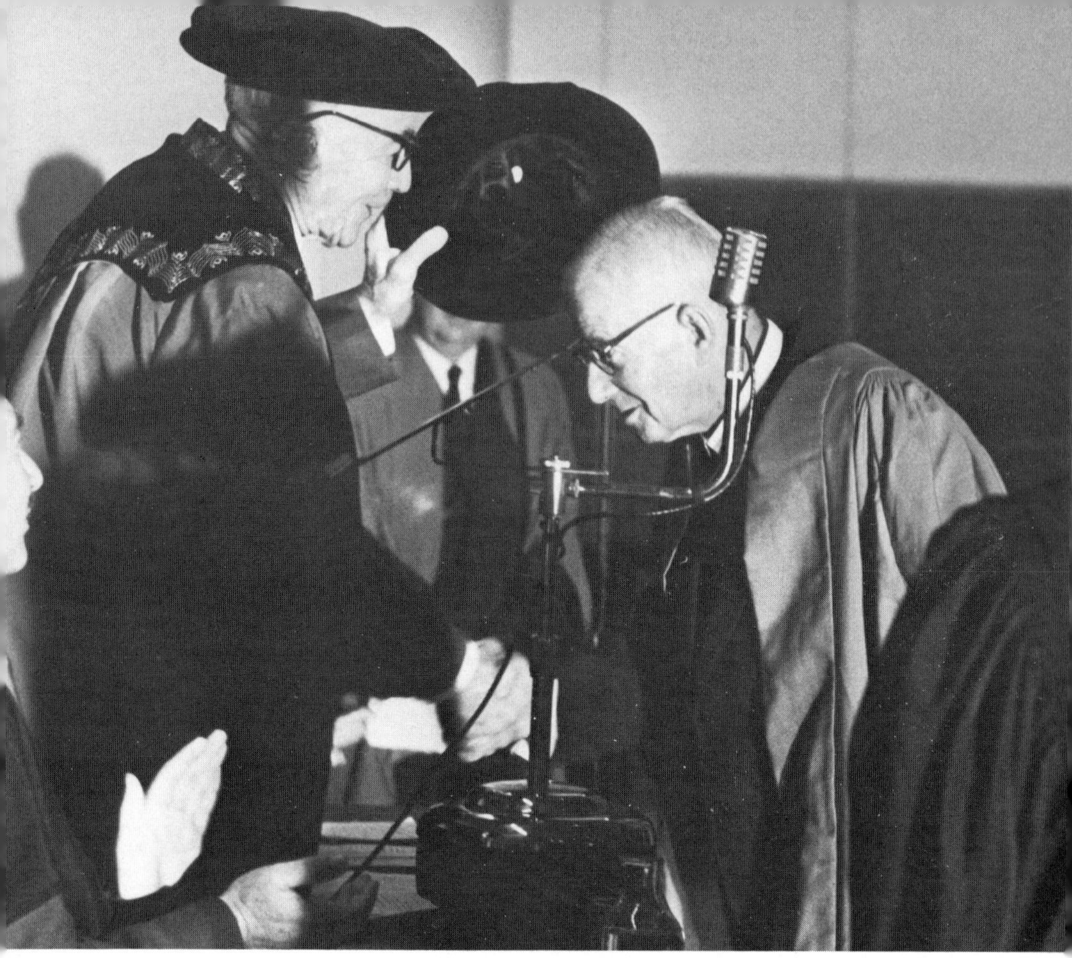

Oliver Schreiner being capped by Richard Feetham, Chancellor of the University of the Witwatersrand, Johannesburg, on receiving the honorary degree of Doctor of Laws of that university on 8 April 1961

Reception during the session of the Court of Appeal of Lesotho, Maseru, April 1971. On the left is Oliver D Schreiner, President of the Court of Appeal. In the centre foreground is Chief Leabua Jonathan, Prime Minister. Behind him is Mr Justice H R Jacobs, then Chief Justice of Swaziland. Next to Chief Jonathan is Mr Justice A Milne, judge of the Court of Appeal, and behind him, partly obscured, is Mr Justice I A Maisels, judge of the Court of Appeal

> Prisons] may determine, and such a prisoner shall at all times perform such labour, tasks and other duties as may be assigned to him for the purpose of such employment, training or treatment[70] or for any purpose connected with such prison, by any member of the Prisons Service.'

Without a doubt the words 'treated' and 'treatment' used in s 77 do not primarily or even materially refer to medical treatment, but are used in the more general sense of acting towards, of dealing with, a person with a view to obtaining a particular result.[71] But it goes without saying that the word 'treated' is wide enough to include the provision of medical services, and the Commissioner will, in my opinion, be within his rights if he were to rely on this section to justify the provision or determination of the scope of medical treatment within prison walls. (Section 77 is a section contained in Chapter VII of the Act, the heading of which is 'Removal, Training and Treatment of Prisoners'.)

Another section falling under Chapter VII is s 73, subsec (1) of which reads as follows:

> 'Any prisoner detained in any prison may, on the authority of the Commissioner, be removed to any other prison or to a police cell or lock-up, or in the case of serious illness or of a woman who is about to give birth to a child, and if adequate facilities do not exist for the treatment of such prisoner in such prison, to any other place.'

This section enables the Commissioner to order the removal of a seriously ill prisoner to an outside hospital or other health-care facility. It is to be noted that no right is given in the section (or elsewhere in the Act) to a prison medical officer independently to authorize or order such removal. Whatever the position in actual prison practice may be, the legal position clearly seems to be that the medical officer exercises his functions under the general control and direction of the Commissioner; in theory, at least, the Commissioner can overrule an instruction, order or decision issued or made by the medical officer.

Section 3 of the Act provides that the Commissioner is in charge of the Prisons Service, subject to the direction and control of the Director-General: Justice (who in turn is subject to the direction and control of the Minister of Justice).[72] Section 22(2), again, gives the Commissioner the right, in his discretion, to 'grant such privileges and indulgences as he may think fit to any prisoner'. This provision clearly would enable the Commissioner to allow a prisoner to undergo special medical treatment inside and outside a prison, but there is nothing in the Act to indicate that the medical

[70] The word used in the Afrikaans text of the Act is 'behandeling'.

[71] See *The Shorter Oxford English Dictionary* 3 ed revised (1977) sv 'treat'.

[72] See GN 2302 of 31 October 1980 (GG 7288), read with s 1 of the Regulation of Functions of Officers in the Public Service Act 19 of 1980.

officer is vested with the power independently to order such special treatment. However, I have been assured by experienced district surgeons who work as prison medical officers that the prison staff take a sympathetic view of recommendations made by them for special medical treatment to be given to prisoners, whether inside or outside the prisons.

Finally, as far as the Prisons Act itself is concerned, mention must be made of s 81(3), which makes provision *inter alia* that a President's patient[73] and any person detained in a hospital prison for psychopaths 'shall receive such treatment' as the Commissioner may determine. 'Treatment' here ostensibly includes medical treatment,[74] although it is not confined to this narrow meaning.

The regulations[75] under the Prisons Act contain a number of provisions governing medical treatment of prisoners and the duties of medical officers. Thus provision is made[76] for the establishment of a hospital at every prison, to be equipped according to local requirements to provide sick prisoners with accommodation for their care and medical treatment by the medical officer. It is provided that all the essential services at a prison hospital are to be performed by trained staff only. Reg 111(2)(*a*) imposes a duty upon the medical officer to visit sick prisoners as often as necessary, and to examine and treat them. This applies to prisoners who complain that they are ill, as well as any other prisoner to whom his attention is specially drawn. Strict duties of inspection and reporting are imposed upon medical officers.[77] Special provision is also made for consultation with other medical practitioners; as far as serious operations are concerned, there is in fact a duty upon the medical officer to do so before the operation is performed.[78]

The general duties of resident medical officers are outlined in reg 6. Apart from their duties to attend prison staff members and their dependants, they are charged in mandatory terms to attend prisoners. The wording of reg 6(1)(*b*) is significant:

> 'The resident medical officer shall comply with the provisions of this Act as well as the instructions issued by the Commissioner.'

The plain meaning of this subregulation is that the Commissioner has the power to give instructions to the medical officer, and not

[73] A President's patient is a person who, because of mental illness or defect, is found to be incapable of being tried by a criminal court, or is found to be criminally non-responsible, and is detained by order of a court pending the signification of a decision of the State President. See s 1 of the Prisons Act, read with s 1 of the Mental Health Act 18 of 1973 and ss 77(6) and 78(6) of the Criminal Procedure Act.

[74] It is to be noted that s 81(3) empowers a prison medical officer to certify that the performance of any specified work will be injurious to such a patient, in which case the Commissioner may not compel such work to be done.

[75] The current prison regulations are contained in GN R2080 of 31 December 1965 (*GG* 1326, *Reg Gaz* 604), as amended over the years.

[76] Reg 111(1). [77] Reg 111(2)(*b*). [78] Reg 111(3)(*a*).

vice versa (whatever actual prison practice may be), and this appears to be in accordance with the provisions of the Prisons Act itself, referred to above. Reg 6(2) deals with the duties of the district surgeon (or other 'approved' medical practitioner) and provides *inter alia* that he must 'pay such visits and hold such inspections at such times and as often as may be stipulated in his conditions of appointment or as *the Commissioner*[79] or circumstances require and he shall generally perform the duties of the resident medical officer as set out in subregulation (1)'. These provisions are not quite as emphatic as those of reg 6(1)(*b*), but the reference to the Commissioner cannot leave much doubt that he is entitled to issue instructions regarding visitation and inspection; moreover, the last part of the subregulation seems to put the district surgeon virtually in the shoes of the resident medical officer with regard to his legal obligations concerning medical treatment of prisoners.

Allowing a prisoner to make use of the services of a private doctor likewise is a matter within the exclusive discretion of the Commissioner. Reg 132(7) provides as follows:

> 'Subject to security measures, the Commissioner, at his discretion, on request of a prisoner awaiting trial or sentence, may authorise him to employ the services of a private medical practitioner or dentist on such conditions as are specially or generally prescribed: Provided that no additional cost to the State is incurred by such private medical or dental services.'

It is to be noted that this subregulation makes mention only of prisoners awaiting trial or sentence. No reference is made to convicted prisoners who have already been sentenced. It is submitted, however, that, in view of the clear provisions of s 73(1) of the Act, this regulation should not be interpreted as preventing the Commissioner from allowing sentenced prisoners to be attended to in cases of serious illness by private practitioners, in 'outside' facilities. This does in fact occur in practice. As far as treatment of such prisoners by private practitioners *inside* a prison is concerned, it may be argued on the basis of *inclusio unius est exclusio alterius* that this is not permitted by the Act (or the regulations); if this is the correct interpretation of the Act, the Commissioner would nevertheless be entitled to allow this in cases of dire emergency by application of the common-law principle of *nood breek wet*. It is none the less submitted that the legislature might consider *ex abundanti* to give expression to the latter principle in the Act itself.

As the Act and regulations now stand, it is submitted that the conclusion is inescapable that the prison medical officer as well as the district surgeon or specially appointed ('approved') doctor

[79] The italics are mine.

attending prisoners in gaol carry out their functions under the general direction of the Commissioner of Prisons. Obviously this does in practice not mean the Commissioner himself; in practice the Commissioner must of necessity delegate many of his functions to prison personnel. Should a difference of opinion arise between the medical officer and a non-medical prison official as to the medical treatment of a particular prisoner, the doctor would obviously be entitled to appeal to the Commissioner himself for a decision. In the unlikely event of the Commissioner's refusing to give effect to the medical officer's recommendation, the latter could approach the Director-General: Justice or the Minister of Justice for a ruling. As we have seen, the Commissioner works under the direction and control of these two functionaries (in the line of authority as indicated).

In extreme cases the medical officer or the prisoner himself may conceivably approach the Supreme Court with an application for a review of the Commissioner's decision.[80] But from a practical point of view this is highly unlikely to be an effective remedy. Quite apart from the time factor and considerations of cost, a review can take place only on limited grounds, such as mala fides, ulterior or improper motive on the part of the respondent, failure by him to apply his mind or to exercise his discretion, or his disregarding the express provisions of a statute.[81] The 'wide range of powers' to be exercised by the prison authorities and the 'great latitude of choice . . . left to the person charged with the duty of exercising a . . . discretionary power', which may lead to the conclusion that 'he may virtually have complete freedom in the exercise of his discretion as to whether, when and in what manner he will act', may make a court reluctant to interfere with prison rulings of an administrative nature—as is apparent from the majority ruling of the Appellate Division (per Wessels ACJ) in *Goldberg and others* v

[80] This in fact occurred in *Harris* v *Commissioner of Prisons* 1965 (2) SA 645 (T). In this case the applicant, a prisoner who had been condemned to death, applied to court for an order that the Commissioner reconsider a decision that a psychiatrist be not allowed to visit him. The applicant hoped that information given by the psychiatrist could influence those responsible for exercising clemency in his case. The applicant relied on reg 111 (the gist of which I quoted in the text above), which imposes a duty upon the prison medical officer to attend prisoners. Clayden J (in whose judgment De Wet JP and Hill J concurred) drew attention to the fact that reg 111 deals primarily with the medical treatment of a sick prisoner. *In casu* the examination by a psychiatrist was not sought because the applicant was in need of medical treatment; it was sought because the applicant wished to put further information before those concerned with his appeal for clemency. In so far as the Commissioner made a decision under reg 111, there was accordingly no ground to interfere with it on the basis of its unreasonableness. However, the applicant also relied on prison reg 139(7)(*c*), which in the widest terms allows visits to a condemned prisoner by any person with the approval of the Commissioner, and the court held that the Commissioner had not directed his attention at all to the latter regulation. An order along these lines was therefore made.

[81] This is trite law. See, for example, *Shidiack* v *Union Government* 1912 AD 642 at 651; *Divisional Commissioner of SA Police, Witwatersrand Area, and others* v *SA Associated Newspapers Ltd and another* 1966 (2) SA 505 (A).

Minister of Prisons and others,[82] from which the phrases quoted have been culled. As regards persons detained under s 6 of the Terrorism Act and its successor statute, there is, further, the extremely discouraging factor that such detainees have no right of access to legal practitioners.[83]

The Common Law

It is not proposed to go fully into delictual rights and liabilities surrounding the medical treatment of detainees and prisoners. The prison medical officer may, of course, on the basis of negligence be held liable for damages in his personal capacity for failure to treat a sick prisoner properly. The state may also be held liable vicariously for the negligence of the medical officer.[84] If a medical officer were dutifully to bring to the attention of the prison authorities the necessity or urgency of special treatment to be given to a particular prisoner, and this were disregarded by the authorities, the state might be held liable in damages. The same would apply were a medical officer to warn non-medical prison or police officials that a prisoner was not in a fit condition to be conveyed to an outside facility or to be safely conveyed beyond a specified distance.

The 1975 decision of the Appellate Division in *Minister van Polisie* v *Ewels*,[85] apart from its significance in starkly underlining the principle that delictual liability may be based upon a mere *omissio*, highlighted the special duty owed by the police to persons in their custody. This case did not involve medical treatment at all, but in a subsequent 1977 decision, *Minister of Police* v *Skosana*,[86] the state was held liable in damages to the dependants of a drunken driver who had been held in custody by the police and who had died in consequence of a negligent delay in the furnishing of medical treatment for injuries sustained in a road accident.[87]

[82] 1979 (1) SA 14 (A). The quotations in the text are from pages 31–2 of the decision.

[83] An aggrieved detainee might possibly also be deterred by s 6(5) [now s 29(6) of the Internal Security Act 1982], which precludes a court of law from pronouncing 'on the validity of any action taken under this section'. There can be no doubt, however, that a decision taken in terms of the Prisons Act as to the medical treatment of a detainee cannot be categorized as 'action taken under this section'. Compare the Transkei decisions in *Sigaba* v *Minister of Defence and Police and another* 1980 (3) SA 535 (Tk); *Honey and another* v *Minister of Police and others* 1980 (3) SA 800 (Tk).

[84] The resident medical officer will in my opinion undoubtedly qualify as an employee of the Department of Prisons. However, whether or not a district surgeon and 'approved' medical officer will qualify as employees for the purposes of vicarious liability is a question that falls beyond the scope of this paper.

[85] 1975 (3) SA 590 (A). [86] 1977 (1) SA 31 (A).

[87] The facts of the case, very briefly stated, were as follows: T, whilst heavily under the influence, drove his car off the road and landed in a ditch, as a result of which he and some of his passengers were injured. T was removed in a police van to the charge office and taken from there to the consulting rooms of the district surgeon for the usual tests and the taking of a blood specimen. He complained of a pain in the chest, but after a thorough examination no internal injury could be detected. The next morning he complained of a severe pain over the abdomen and was taken two hours later to the district surgeon, who attended to him immediately. The doctor wrote a note for the

Conclusion

As far as the medical treatment of detainees and prisoners is concerned, the position in South Africa is satisfactory in so far as extensive provision has been made for the establishment of adequate prison hospitals and the appointment of qualified medical officers, either on a full-time or part-time basis. Senior and reputable medical practitioners with long experience of prison medical work have publicly praised the high quality of medical care available in prisons. Statutory law imposes a firm duty on prison authorities and medical officers to provide medical services to sick prisoners. Moreover, the common law provides a remedy to an aggrieved person, or his dependants, in the form of an action for delictual damages.

There are deficiencies in our statutory law, however. First, provisions relating to the medical treatment of detainees and prisoners are presently scattered in a variety of instruments, ranging from parliamentary legislation, to regulations and police standing orders, to guide-lines issued to district surgeons. The legal status of some of these provisions is not that of promulgated statutory law. The subject of medical treatment of detainees and prisoners is so important that rights and duties should be set forth clearly and in detail, in a single set of legislative provisions embodied in an Act of Parliament[88] or statutory regulations, which should be of equal application to all categories of persons in custody.

Secondly, it is submitted that it is untenable in principle that a medical practitioner in the prison situation, in taking a clinical decision regarding medical treatment of a prisoner—which may be a matter of life or death to the prisoner—can legally be overruled by a non-medical police or prison official. Even if it were the declared policy of the Commissioner of Prisons and the Commissioner of Police that immediate effect should be given to decisions or recommendations of medical officers, the mere fact that the executive officer of the state in law has a veto may inhibit medical

hospital and instructed the constable to arrange for him to be taken there. There was a further delay of two hours before the ambulance arrived. At the hospital he was found to be in a very serious condition. An attempt at resuscitation was made and a laparotomy performed, revealing the viscus to be ruptured with severe general peritonitis. T died shortly after leaving the theatre. The Appellate Division sustained a finding of the trial court that the constables had been negligent *(a)* in not immediately summoning the district surgeon and *(b)* in not causing T to be taken to hospital immediately.

[88] There is a lamentable tendency in our time for more and more statutory law to take the form of regulations, emanating from the executive, rather than in proper statutory form, debated and passed by Parliament. Perhaps it is largely unavoidable. But making laws affecting *basic* rights of the individual should be the work of Parliament and not of the executive. Quite apart from these considerations, an important advantage of embodying basic principles relating to medical treatment of prisoners in the Prisons Act itself is to be found in s 85 of the latter Act, which obliges the Commissioner to make available to prisoners, immediately after admission to a prison, the provisions of the Act relating to the treatment and conduct of prisoners.

officers in carrying out their duties. Clinical independence of the prison doctor should be legislatively guaranteed in express terms.

Finally, it is observed that s 6 of the Terrorism Act, which precluded a security detainee from having access to a legal adviser without official permission, could render whatever rights such a detainee might have in regard to medical treatment nugatory in practice from the point of view of their enforcement by means of judicial intervention. Quite apart from having created the possibility of indefinite detention of suspected terrorists, the Act in this respect offended against basic democratic notions valued in the Western world. The successor statute[89] to the Terrorism Act has not changed the position.

[89] The Internal Security Act 1982. [The last sentence of the text and this note have been added.—Ed.]

LAW AND MORALITY

J D VAN DER VYVER*

Perplexities appertaining to the relationship between law and morality have intrigued legal philosophers since the infancy of Western jurisprudence. The leading analysts of juridical phenomena more or less agreed that one could construct some form of symbiosis and concrescence or a degree of mutual impregnation of law and morality, but opinions differed greatly as to the exact foundation, nature, extent and implications of the evident interaction between these two aspects of reality.

The many instances of legal provisions with a definite ethical foundation furnish ample evidence of the law's affinity with morality.[1] As far as South African law is concerned, such ethically based rules of law include the following examples:

(a) By virtue of s 4(2)(*b*) of the Divorce Act of 1979[2] adultery constitutes one of the facts that may in certain circumstances be regarded by the court as proof of the irretrievable breakdown of a marriage, which in turn would warrant a decree of divorce.

(b) In terms of the common law, contracts with an immoral purport are unenforceable.

(c) Section 47(2)(*a*) of the Publications Act of 1974[3] provides that a publication or object, film and public entertainment or intended public entertainment would be undesirable and may therefore be banned if it is found to be 'indecent or obscene or offensive or harmful to public morals'.

(d) The criminal law proscribes various manifestations of immoral conduct, such as sodomy, bestiality, prostitution, public indecency, possession of indecent or obscene photographic matter, and sexual intercourse between a White person and a person of colour, or involving female idiots or imbeciles, or with girls under the age of 16 or boys under the age of 18.

* BCom LLB BAHons (PU vir CHO) LLD (Pret), Advocate of the Supreme Court of South Africa, Professor of Law in the University of the Witwatersrand, Johannesburg.

[1] See, in general, L M du Plessis *Die Juridiese Relevansie van Christelike Geregtigheid* (unpublished LLD thesis Potchefstroom University for Christian Higher Education 1978) 803–35.

[2] Act 70 of 1979.

[3] Act 42 of 1974.

(e) Administrative proceedings are required to comply with certain basic directives of natural justice, such as the principle of *audi alteram partem* and *nemo iudex in re sua*.

(f) The rules governing the interpretation of statutory law include a rebuttable presumption that the legislature did not intend its enactments to have unjust, inequitable or unreasonable consequences.

How, then, should one construct the bond between law and morality?

Certain textbook writers give a purely empirical account of the relationship between law and morality. W J Hosten, A B Edwards, Carmen Nathan and Francis Bosman, for instance, merely assert the simple truism that certain rules of South African law afford legal sanction to particular principles of morality, while other rules are clearly incompatible with the established norms of morality.[4] Many legal provisions may, furthermore, be classified as morally neutral. One may, therefore, conclude that the law does to some extent take cognizance of moral values, but that it would be wrong to identify the law with morality.[5]

These simplistic observations do not, of course, expose the basic fundamentals of the connection between and diversity of the law and morality. In the elaborate literature on the subject the matter has been debated in greater depth on the basis of the following elementary questions:

(a) Does any moral principle enjoy legal validity per se; that is to say, are there certain ethical norms that must be enforced by a court of law even though the norms in question have not been formally promulgated by a competent law-creating agent?

(b) Must the law necessarily comply with certain minimum ethical standards; that is to say, is the validity of the law dependent upon the incorporation into the legal system of particular moral values?

(c) Is it a function or the duty of the depositaries of state authority to enforce the current code of good moral behaviour?

I The Legality of Moral Principles

The question whether or not certain norms of morality as such are, without more ado, legally valid and enforceable was answered in the affirmative by many proponents of the doctrine of natural law. Per se validity of the principles of natural justice in fact emerged as an essential element of the traditional (pre-nineteenth century) concept of natural law.

[4] *Introduction to South African Law and Legal Theory* (1980) 17–19.

[5] See also H R Hahlo and Ellison Kahn *The South African Legal System and its Background* (1968) 6–13.

Cicero (104–43 BC) defined natural law accordingly as a true decree of right reason, which applies to all people at all times, which is eternal and unchangeable and of which God himself is the inventor, interpreter and promulgator.[6]

Natural lawyers were, however, not at all in agreement as to the exact contents of the preferred moral norms that would qualify for automatic legal validity. For instance, Aristotle (384–322 BC) identified the moral directives of natural law with the concept of justice, which, broadly speaking, requires the equal treatment of all the subjects of a given community by and before the law;[7] Ulpian (*c* 300 BC) sought to capture the gist of natural law in the well-known maxim: live honourably, do not injure others, and give to everyone his due;[8] and Grotius (1583–1645) reduced the dictates of natural law to four basic functions of the law, to wit, the protection of property rights, the enforcement of agreements, the granting of compensation for harm caused by fault, and the sanctioning of punishment for violations of the principles already mentioned.[9]

Positivism, on the other hand, clearly and consistently rejected the primary assumptions of natural law. Jeremy Bentham (1748–1832) accordingly described natural law as 'nothing but a phrase',[10] and added: 'All this talk about nature, natural rights, natural justice and injustice proves two things and two things only, the heat of the passions, and the darkness of the understanding';[11] John Austin (1790–1859) referred to the traditional classification of the law into positive law and natural law as 'utterly unintelligible' and 'senseless';[12] Hans Kelsen (1881–1973) rejected the notion of the social compact and of natural law as merely a fiction,[13] and further stated: '. . . the natural law doctrine is based on the illusion that it is

[6] *De Re Publica* 3 22: '*Est quidem vera lex recta ratio, naturae congruens, diffusa in omnes, constans, sempiterna, quae vocet ad officium iubendo, vetando a fraude deterreat, quae tamen neque probos frustra iubet aut vetat, nec improbos iubendo aut vetando movet. Huic legi nec obrogari fas est, neque derogari ex hac aliquid licet, neque tota abrogari potest. Nec vero aut per senatum aut per populum solvi hac lege possumus: neque est quaerendus explanator aut interpres eius alius: nec erit alia lex Romae, alia Athenis, alia nunc, alia posthac; sed et omnes gentes et omni tempore una lex, et sempiterna et immutabilis, continebit, unusque erit communis quasi magister et imperator omnium Deus; ille legis huius inventor, disceptator, lator; cui qui non parebit, ipse se fugiet, ac, naturam hominis aspernatus, hoc ipso luet maximas poenas, etiam si cetera supplicia, quae putantur, effugerit.*'

[7] See, in general, M Salomon *Der Begriff der Gerechtigkeit bei Aristotelés* (1937); P Trude *Der Begriff der Gerechtigkeit in der aristotelischen Rechts- und Staatsphilosophie* (1955); H Dooyeweerd 'Een Nieuwe Studie over het Aristotelisch Begrip der Gerechtigheid' 1958 *Rechtsgeleerd Magazijn Themis* 3ff; J D van der Vyver 'Die Regsleer van Aristotelés (384–322 vC): 'n Probleemstelling' 1962 *Koers* 224ff.

[8] Inst 1.1.3; D 1.1.10.1: '*honeste vivere, alterum non laedere, suum cuique tribuere.*'

[9] *De Iure Belli ac Pacis* prol 8: '*quo pertinent alieni abstinentia, et, si quid alieni habeamus aut lucri inde facerimus, restitutio; promissorum implendorum obligatio; damni culpa dati reparatio; et poenae inter homines meritum.*'

[10] *A Fragment on Government* (1931) 4.19.

[11] *The Limits of Jurisprudence Defined* (with an Introduction by C W Everett) (1945) 84.

[12] *The Province of Jurisprudence Determined and the Uses of the Study of Jurisprudence* (with an Introduction by H L A Hart) (1954) 102.

[13] *Principles of International Law* (1952) 310–11.

possible to obtain from our insight in nature, that is, from our knowledge of facts, a knowledge of what is right and wrong';[14] and others spoke in similar vein.

Positivists were equally emphatic in repudiating the postulate of natural-law theorists regarding the per se legality of moral principles.

Austin circumscribed the law properly so called as a command, issued by a sovereign power, entailing a duty on the part of the subordinates of state authority and backed by a sanction.[15] It follows that all rules of human conduct which do not comply with any of these supposed *essentialia* of positive law—for instance, those norms that did not emanate from the formal enactments of a political superior[16]—are not part of the 'law simply and strictly so called', but can at best be classified as instances of positive morality.[17]

John Chipman Gray (1839–1915), an early representative of the American realist movement, was of the same mind—at least as far as the ajuridical nature of moral norms is concerned. Said he: 'The Law of a country or other organized body of men is composed of the rules for conduct that its courts follow and that it holds itself out as ready to enforce; no ideas, however just, that its courts refuse to follow are Law, and all rules which they follow and to which it enforces obedience are Law.'[18]

The South African judiciary has on several occasions pronounced opinions that, in the present context, support the positivistic approach. In *Preston and Dixon* v *Biden's Trustee*[19] Laurence J, while considering whether or not certain creditors had renounced their claim to particular assets of an insolvent estate, remarked: 'That would have been a very honourable thing to do. . . . But a judge is not a *censor morum*.' In *Executors of McCorkindale* v *Bok NO*[20] Kotzé CJ, rejecting a submission of an advocate in the case, explained: 'This most eloquent argument confounds two extremely different things. It mixes up the legal and the moral. A matter may be quite in accordance with law, and yet be morally objectionable—*non omne quod licitum honestum est.* Our notions of morality may differ, but the simple question for a Court of Justice is "What is the law?"' In *Kent* v *Transvaalsche Bank*[21] Innes CJ said: 'The court has again and again had occasion to point out that it does not administer a system of equity, as distinct from a system of law.' In *R* v *K and F*[22] Gutsche J declared: 'The courts are not *custodes morum populi* in that

[14] Idem 310.

[15] See his *Lectures on Jurisprudence* 5 ed by R Campbell (1885) I 86–103.

[16] Austin idem I 86 defined the law as 'a rule laid down for the guidance of an intelligent being by an intelligent being having power over him'.

[17] Idem I 182ff.

[18] *The Nature and Sources of the Law* (1927) 308–9.

[19] (1883) 1 Buch AC 322 at 333.

[20] (1884) 1 SAR 202 at 216.

[21] 1907 TS 765 at 774.

[22] 1932 EDL 71 at 77.

they do not administer the moral but the judicial law. . . .' And in *S* v *Adams*[23] King J stated (with reference to the Group Areas Act of 1966[24]): 'An Act of Parliament creates law but not necessarily equity.'

South African courts are therefore not entitled to apply norms merely on account of their moral laudability. Legal tribunals are required to implement the law; and the concept of law includes juridical norms only. Legality of norms presupposes, *inter alia*, the formation of law in a recognized manner and through the medium of a competent lawmaking organ, such as a legislature (in the case of statutory law) or the community (in the case of customary law).

Nothing, however, prevents a legislature or other law-creating authority from transforming, by means of the appropriate law-making procedure, moral principles into positive law, in which event the courts will be obliged to give effect to the legal provisions in question—not because of their moral content, but as part and parcel of positive law.

The doctrine of natural law quite rightly assumed that positive law is founded upon certain principles—including the normative directives of legal ethics—but erred in supposing that such principles could of their own accord acquire the quality of legal validity. Positivism, again, was correct in maintaining that positive law presupposes a particular formative act recognized by law as an effective means for the creation of law in the juridical sense, and executed by a competent law-making instrument. The positivistic approach may, on the other hand, be criticized for its denial or underrating of the reality or significance of pre-positive legal principles.

The truth is that one can identify a variety of principles—including those with a moral foundation—which lend themselves to being transformed into positive law. Those principles do not without further ado possess the validity of rules of law, but must, in order to become positive law, be laid down as law in the prescribed manner and by a competent law-creating agent.

II The Morality of Positive Law

Which brings us to the question whether or not the law, in order to be valid law, must also reflect certain moral standards. This problem constituted the subject-matter of the celebrated Fuller-Hart debate.

The theory of natural law was espoused by a school of thought that directly inferred positive law from the norms of natural law. This view clearly suggested that discrepancy between man-made (positive) law and natural law was not at all possible. Aurelius

[23] 1979 (4) SA 793 (T) at 801. [24] Act 36 of 1966.

Augustine (353–430) declared along these lines: 'In my opinion a law cannot be present where there is no justice';[25] and again: '. . . where true justice does not exist, the law also cannot be.'[26] This view was subsequently endorsed by Thomas Aquinas (1224(5)–1274).[27]

Positivism naturally denied the existence of an essential link between law and morality. Referring to the Austinean concept of law, Buckland tellingly made the point: 'Law is law since it is made by the Sovereign. The Sovereign is sovereign because he makes the law.'[28] Validity of the law is therefore determined by the decree of a legislature and is not necessarily conditioned by moral considerations. Hans Kelsen, the neo-Kantian legal philosopher who nevertheless was influenced considerably by positivistic notions, expressed this point of view in clear language: 'The validity of a legal norm cannot be questioned on the ground that its contents are incompatible with some moral or political value. A norm is a valid legal norm by virtue of the fact that it has been created according to a definite rule and by virtue thereof only.'[29]

In April 1957 H L A Hart (1907–), Professor of Jurisprudence at Oxford, delivered an address at the Harvard Law School in which he advocated the positivistic conception of a clear dividing line between law and morality.[30] Hart admitted, as an historical fact, that the law has over the ages been influenced by moral ideas (and vice versa), and that certain rules of law do indeed coincide with, or afford legal validity to, particular moral principles, but said that that does not mean that the force of law of juridical norms is determined by their compatibility with moral standards. Referring to certain decrees of the Nazi regime in Germany, Hart furthermore recognized the right of the people to disobey substantially immoral laws, but in his opinion the legal provisions in question would nevertheless remain part of positive law.[31] Hart in fact also conceded the proposition that systems of law must comply with certain minimum standards relating to 'survival', such as adequate protection of one's person and property in order that one may live and eat (including safeguards against murder, violence and theft) and a certain degree of equal protection and impartiality in the administration of justice,[32] but, said he, it is equally true that a system of law, while satisfying these minimum requirements, may

[25] *De Libero Arbitrio* 1.11: '*Nam mihi lex esse non videtur, quae iusta non fuerit.*'
[26] *De Civitate Dei* 19.21.1: '. . . *ubi ergo iustitia vera non est, nec ius potest esse.*'
[27] See *Summa Theologica* 1.2 q 96 a 4.
[28] *Some Reflections on Jurisprudence* (1974) 48.
[29] *General Theory of Law and State* (1961) 113.
[30] 'Positivism and the Separation of Law and Morals' (1958) 71 *Harvard LR* 593.
[31] See idem 620, where he asserted his own preference for the proposition '. . . laws may be law but too evil to be obeyed' over the proposition '. . . certain rules cannot be law because of their moral iniquity'.
[32] In his famous essay 'Are there Any Natural Rights?' in (1955) 64 *Philosophical Review* 175 Hart maintained that there is at least one natural right, namely, the right to equal personal freedom of each individual.

nevertheless, from the moral point of view, remain highly untenable. The crux of his conclusion can be summarized in his own words: '. . . there are laws which may have any degree of iniquity or stupidity and still be laws. And conversely there are rules that have every moral qualification to be laws and yet are not laws.'[33]

Subsequently, in *The Concept of Law*,[34] Hart dealt with the problem of law and morality in somewhat greater detail. He outlined several juridical substrata that may, subject to certain reservations, be regarded as 'the minimum content of Natural Law'. They include the following:[35]

(a) In the prevailing circumstances of our time *human vulnerability* may tempt one to regard legal provisions for the protection of life and limb as an essential constituent element of the law; but if man were to develop immunity against bodily injury (including exoskeletons or a carapace), the moral proscription of homicide (and assault) would become juridically irrelevant.

(b) The personal differences between man and man are not so great as to allow, for an indefinite period, the domination and suppression of one human being by another;[36] and this principle of *approximate equality* requires, both in morality and in law, a fundamental basis of mutal forbearance and compromise.

(c) Although people are not by nature dominated by a wish to exterminate each other, the human person is on the other hand not exactly possessed of a 'disinterested interest' in the survival and welfare of his fellow man; and the tendency towards aggression, which stems from this *limited altruism*, is frequent enough in man to warrant legal provisions to control it.

(d) *Limited resources* (food, clothes and shelter) necessitate the protection in one form or another of property rights—though not necessarily on the basis of private ownership—and, with the emergence of division of labour, also the regulation of exchange founded upon the principle that promises are binding; but if circumstances were to be different so that, for instance, the human organism would acquire the capacity of plants to extract nutrition from air, or the essential means of livelihood would become available in limitless abundance, this 'minimum material requirement' of legal systems would also disappear.

(e) In every society one encounters people who, on account of *limited understanding and strength of will*, seek to obtain the advantages of the system without submitting to its obligations, and consequently coercion in the form of sanction becomes essential to protect those who are faithful to their legal obligations against the ones who are not.

[33] Op cit note 30 at 626. [34] 1961. [35] *The Concept of Law* 189–95.

[36] In this context Hart (*The Concept of Law* 191) paraphrased a striking truism: 'Even the strongest must sleep at times and, when asleep, loses temporarily his superiority.'

Hart emphatically rejected the supposition that the above minimum conditions signify an essential link between law and morality. The doctrine of natural law, however, is based on further assumptions which clearly involve morality in the strict sense. Hart summarized his point of view with regard to those 'minimum moral standards' under six heads of argument:[37]

(i) It is often said that the coercive power of state authority is in itself not enough to ensure maintenance of the law and order, and that the law must in addition be supported by the community's moral consciousness. Hart agreed that the legal order requires the support of the bulk of society who accept the juridical decrees of state authority as law. He pointed out, however, that it would not be possible to determine with certainty why some legal subjects obey the law. Some may be influenced by coercion to do so, and in many instances obedience to the law is not at all attributable to moral considerations or a person's ethical sense of duty.

(ii) Morality does influence the law, and Hart was even willing to concede that law to a large extent derives stability from the moral foundation of many of its provisions. This does not, however, imply that the validity of law is conditional upon its reflection of a moral content.

(iii) Interpretation of the law is a creative activity, which involves the formation of new law. Interpretation of the law furthermore almost invariably involves a choice between different possible meanings of the provision in question, and the rules of interpretation leave ample scope for judges to elect the moral alternative. It would, however, be wrong to assume that judges always interpret the law in conformity with moral directives.[38] Hart stated in this regard: '. . . we need to remember that the same principles have been honoured nearly as much in the breach as in the observance.'[39]

(iv) It may be said that there are fixed ethical standards for evaluating the law, but it is also true that many systems of law particularly noted for their sanctioning of injustices have long endured.

(v) Certain principles of legality (pre-conditions for the validity of the law) are often made out to be of a moral character, for instance, the notion that the law must apply generally and impartially, that it must be intelligible and practicable, and that as a general rule it must not be retroactive, as legal subjects

[37] Idem 198–207.

[38] The fact that South African judges do not always prefer the moral alternatives was the theme of John Dugard's inaugural lecture 'The Judicial Process, Positivism and Civil Liberty' (1971) 88 *SALJ* 181.

[39] *The Concept of Law* 201.

should have an opportunity to obey its commands. Realization of these principles, said Hart, may be attended with profound iniquities, and therefore they should not be classified as specimens of morality.

(vi) Resistance to injustice is according to Hart always justified. One could base the right of resistance on the assumption that unjust provisions do not constitute positive law, or, alternatively, that such provisions are law, but law which is too iniquitous to be applied or obeyed. For several reasons Hart preferred the latter view. Among the reasons are the following: if one were to assume that unjust provisions do not form part of the law, they would not fall within the jurisdiction of legal science; and the assumption that morally iniquitous stipulations do not belong to the law would provoke anarchy.

Hart therefore endorsed the view that draws a clear distinction between the validity and morality of positive law. In his opinion the concept of law embraces 'all rules which are valid by the formal tests of a system of primary and secondary rules,[40] even though some of them offend against a society's own morality or against what we may hold to be an enlightened or true morality'.[41]

Lon L Fuller (1902–), Professor of Jurisprudence at Harvard, immediately responded to Hart's lecture of April 1957.[42] He defined the law as follows: 'Law is the enterprise of subjecting human conduct to the governance of rules.'[43] According to Fuller there is an intimate relationship between law and morality, and that relationship finds expression in eight constituent elements of the law, which Fuller recapitulated under the heading of 'the internal morality of the law'. They comprise the following supposed requirements of legality:[44]

(a) The law must be of a general nature and apply equally to all the subjects of a particular legal system.

(b) The law must be promulgated and be made known to all its subjects.

(c) Laws must not be introduced retroactively.

(d) The law must be clear and intelligible.

(e) There must be no contradictions in the law; that is, the law must not burden the subjects with conflicting obligations.

[40] See idem 78–9 regarding primary and secondary rules. A primary rule of law, according to Hart, creates an obligation to do something or to refrain from doing something; a secondary rule bestows on legal subjects the competence to enact, amend or repeal primary rules.

[41] Idem 205.

[42] 'Positivism and Fidelity to Law—A Reply to Professor Hart' (1958) 71 *Harvard LR* 630; and see also *The Morality of Law* revised edition (1969) 133–45 and 187, where he analysed and criticized Hart's views.

[43] *The Morality of Law* (for instance) 106.

[44] Idem 46–91.

(f) The law must not require the impossible; that is, it must be practicable.

(g) The law should remain relatively static; that is, it should not be changed too frequently.

(h) Congruence between the law and official action (application and administration of the law by state authority) is of the utmost importance.

Fuller developed the basic assumptions of his notion of 'the internal morality of the law' on the basis of the neo-Kantian philosophy.

The most outstanding feature of neo-Kantian thought centres upon an endeavour to apply Kant's theory of knowledge to the domain of ethics (the province—in Kantian semantics—of the *Oughts*). Giorgio del Vecchio (1878–1970), for instance, sought to construct the concept of law by means of 'purely reasonable reflection'[45] (vis-à-vis empirical or sensual perception). It may be noted in passing that del Vecchio's concept of law clearly denotes an intimate relationship between law and morality. The law, he said, regulates human conduct according to a basic moral norm, which determines its exercise and excludes its prevention.[46] According to del Vecchio, morality thus constitutes an integral part of the law.

The legal theory of Fuller follows the Baden or Freiburg school of neo-Kantianism.[47] The members of the school of Baden/Freiburg were particularly noted for their emphasis on the value structures of reality and as disciples of relativism in philosophy.

Perhaps the best-known contemporary exponent of the Baden/Freiburg variety of neo-Kantianism was Gustav Radbruch (1878–1949), and it should be emphasized at the outset that Fuller was particularly influenced by Radbruch.

In imitation of the Baden/Freiburg School, Radbruch defined the subject-matter of jurisprudence in terms of the value structure of the legal idea: 'It [jurisprudence] has to do with the value and purpose of the law, with the idea of the law and with the ideal law, and it extends to legal politics, which has as its subject-matter the eventuality of implementing the ideal law.'[48] The legal idea (ideal law) entails, according to Radbruch, three value ideas, to wit justice, efficacy and legal certainty.

[45] *Lehrbuch der Rechtsphilosophie* 2e Aufl übergesetzt von F Darmstaedter (1951) 348: '*eine reine Vernunftüberlegung.*'

[46] Idem 371: '*Das Recht ist die objektive Einordnung der unter einer Mehrzahl von Subjekten möglichen Handlungen nach einem ethischen Grundsatz, der ihre Entfaltung bestimmt und ihre Behinderung ausschlieszt.*'

[47] Neo-Kantian philosophy is commonly divided into the Marburg school (which emphasized the natural sciences, the domain of *Sein*) and the Baden/Freiburg school (which focused its analyses on the humanities, the area of *Sollen*).

[48] *Vorschule der Rechtsphilosophie* 2e Aufl (1959) 19: '*Sie handelt also von dem Werten und Zielen des Rechts, von der Idee des Rechts und vom idealen Recht, und findet ihre Fortsetzung in der Rechtspolitik, welche die Verwirklichungsmöglichkeiten des idealen Recht zu ihrem Gegenstand hat.*'

The *form* of legal norms is determined by the idea of justice, which, according to Radbruch, requires the equal treatment of equals and the unequal treatment of unequals.[49] The *material contents* of the law, on the other hand, derive from the idea of efficacy, which entails three value systems, namely:

(i) the individualistic value system, which refers to whatever is of value to the singular person ('*Einzelpersönlichkeit*');
(ii) the super-individualistic value system, which refers to whatever is of value to collective persons ('*Gesamtpersönlichkeiten*'); and
(iii) the transpersonal value system, which refers to the value of cultural objects.

The law, finally, owes its *validity* to the idea of legal certainty.

Legal certainty may require the subordinates of a particular legal system to endure a certain degree of iniquity contained in the positive law of that system. Radbruch pointed out in this regard that the various value ideas of the law may in particular instances contradict one another. But in cases of excessive injustice, legal certainty would no longer be decisive and the provisions in question would in fact forfeit their validity, leaving the subjects at large to arrange their conduct on the basis of *das übergesetzliche Recht* (natural law).[50]

The neo-Kantian obsession with values resulted, *inter alia*, in attempts to moralize various amoral aspects of reality. In the legal theory of Radbruch the inaccurate and simplistic pretence that certain such non-moral phenomena in fact belong to the sphere of ethics is evidenced by the supposed transformation of (non-moral) conditions of legality (legal certainty and efficacy) as specimens, on a par with justice, of the truly ethically based legal idea.

The same misconception appears from the concept of law enunciated by Fuller. He identified morality with all teleological (purposeful) activities (every human act aimed at achieving a particular purpose), and he consequently labelled various non-ethical elements of legality, such as the principle of legal certainty—which, incidentally, may be evident in morally untenable systems of law—as part of morality. Friedmann typified Fuller's eight principles of legality as no more than 'the minimum components of an efficiently functioning modern legal system';[51] and it would in my opinion be fair to say that the Fuller–Hart polemic resulted in the Oxford professor having the last say when he exposed Fuller's interpolation

[49] Idem 26: '*Sie bedeutet Gleichbehandlung Gleicher, Ungleichbehandlung Ungleicher nach gleichem Maszstab. . . .*'

[50] Idem 32–3 and 37; and see also *Rechtsphilosophie* 8e Aufl von Erik Wolf and Hans-Peter Schneider (1973) 345–6.

[51] *Legal Theory* 5 ed (1967) 18.

of the concept of morality:[52] '. . . the classification of these eight principles as a form of morality breeds confusion.'[53]

Fuller's legal theory also bears testimony of the relativism of neo-Kantian philosophy. Friedmann captured the core of the relativistic approach, as expressed in the teaching of Radbruch, when he wrote: 'This legal relativism is . . . concerned with the ultimate meaning of legal systems but does not see its task in suggesting a choice between opposite values. This choice is a matter for personal decisions; a matter not of science but of conscience. Relativism does not evade political decisions, but does not wish to give them a scientific cloak.'[54]

In support of neo-Kantian relativism, Radbruch for instance denied the existence of universally valid and immutable norms of natural law, and also of static human rights.[55] Natural law, he said, has a variable content; justice is dependent on the temporal and local *Natur der Sache*;[56, 57] the hierarchy of the three value systems included in the idea of efficacy cannot be fixed verifiably and with certainty;[58] and he made other similar observations.

Similar traces of relativism are to be found in the legal theory of Fuller. The eight conditions of legality, which he singled out as the 'internal morality of the law', cannot—according to him—be classified in a fixed order, may contradict one another, need not in all circumstances be applied with the same measure of fastidiousness, and must occasionally be sacrificed for the sake of other of those values.[59] For instance: if a particular rule of law corresponds to the sense of justice of the community, the principle of publicity and the proscription of retroactive legislation become of less importance; the rule against retroactive enactments is more important in criminal law than in taxation; if the principle of publicity has been disregarded, retroactive legislation may be necessary to remedy that

52 See Hart's review of Fuller's *The Morality of Law* in (1965) 78 *Harvard LR* 1281ff, especially at 1283–8.

53 Idem 1284; and see also 1285: '. . . the author's insistence on classifying these principles of legality as a "morality" is a source of confusion both for him and his readers.'

54 Op cit note 51 at 192.

55 Op cit note 48 at 20.

56 Cf idem 21, where he defined *die Natur der Sache* as '. . . *die natürlichen, sozialen und rechtlichen Zustände, welche der Gesetzgeber vorfindet und seiner Regeln unterwirft*' ('. . . the natural, social and juridical circumstances that confront the legislator and to which he must subject his decrees').

57 See idem 23, where he said: '*Jede Wertidee ist für einen bestimmten Stoff und deshalb auch durch diesen Stoff bestimmt*' ('Every value-idea is destined to serve a particular object and therefore it is also determined *by* that object').

58 Idem 28: '*Die höchsten Zwecke und Werte des Rechts sind nicht nur verschieden nach Maszgabe der sozialen Zustände der verschiedenen Völker und Zeiten, sie werden auch subjektiv von Mensch zu Mensch verschieden beurteilt, je nach Rechtsgefühl, Staatsauffassung und Parteistandpunkt, Religion oder Weltanschauung*' ('The supreme purpose and value of the law does not only differ according to the social conditions of different peoples and times, but are also subjectively and differently evaluated by different people according to their (distinct) sense of justice, idea of the state, party-political conviction, religion or world view').

59 See *The Morality of Law* 41–5, 91–4 and 104.

neglect; if the law were often to be amended, the principle of publicity would have to be applied meticulously. Fuller summarized the matter in the following words: '. . . the Utopia of legality cannot be viewed as a situation in which each desideratum of the law's special morality is realized to perfection. . . . In every human pursuit we shall always encounter the problem of balance at some point as we traverse the long road that leads from the abyss of total failure to the heights of human excellence.'[60]

At first glance these statements seem to constitute an anomaly in Fuller's teaching. The assumption that circumstances could arise in which a certain principle may be disregarded or would apply less stringently is apparently in conflict with the assertion that the same principle constitutes a condition of legality—that is, an essential precedent requirement for the validity of the law. Fuller, however, resolved the ostensible anomaly on the basis of relativism.[61] One should not regard the law as an inflexible or rigid entity that either exists or does not exist; the existential being of the law may operate more or less, half-and-half or so-so. Fuller stated the matter as follows: '. . . the existence of a legal system is a matter of degree';[62] and again: '. . . both rules of law and legal systems can and do half exist.'[63]

As far as the relationship in general between law and morality is concerned, one should, in my opinion, acknowledge the existence of juridical substrata: that is, principles which precede and are foundational to positive law. Those conditions of legality are not, however, necessarily moral in character.

Nineteenth-century positivism entertained the popular notion that a legislature was omnipotent and that any wish of Parliament could, by the stroke of a lawgiver's pen, be transformed into positive law. This, of course, is a misconception. The capacity of the law to appease the social appetite of the people upon the basis of order and stability, or to manipulate social conditions in the process of 'social engineering', is indeed not unlimited. This inaptitude of the law stems from various essential limitations inherent in the very concept of law, as well as from certain other ('external') conditions of legality.[64] It includes the following categories of pre-positive *constitutive legal principles*, which, as such, are presupposed by every rule of law and legal system:

(*a*) the law must evidently accommodate within itself the characteristic essence of the juridical aspect of reality; that is to say, in

[60] Idem 45–6.

[61] Idem 122–3. [62] Idem 122. [63] Ibid.

[64] See P J Laubscher 'The Foundation of Sovereignty—Parliament as a Law-making Body' (1981) 98 *SALJ* 529 for an extremely interesting recent exposition of the same thesis—albeit from quite a different angle, and with (fairly one-sided) emphasis of acquiescence of the electorate in the enactments of the legislature as (it would seem) the overriding condition of legality.

order to qualify as law in the juridical sense, the enactments of a legislature or other law-creating agency must remain within the confines and bear the stamp of that vital element which causes the law to be law[65]—whatever that element may be.[66]

(b) The law is furthermore based on certain foundational substrata that in fact constitute an integral part of the structural make-up of the law. These accessories of the concept of law include territorial limits (South Africa cannot legislate for Zimbabwe), a basic power structure to support the implementation machinery of the law (law without effective means of enforcement is useless) and a social setting (the law regulates human relations and will therefore be meaningless in a Robinson Crusoe situation).

(c) The feasibility of social control through law is also dependent upon a category of impediments that may collectively be described as 'external circumstances'. Under this label one may list a great variety of extra-juridical phenomena that would to a greater or lesser extent determine the contents and practicability of the law, such as the geographical setting, mineral wealth and weather conditions of the territory in which the law is to operate, the composition of the local population, the political predilections, moral consciousness and religious convictions of the people, and the prevailing social conditions, cultural refinement and economic structure.[67]

(d) Conditions of legality may finally be curtailed by the law's self-imposed substantive and procedural restraints, which may include material limitations enunciated in a Bill of Rights or extraordinary formalities for the enactment of statutory law, such as two-thirds-majority support in Parliament, consensus of decision-taking authorities, or sanctioning by means of referendum.[68]

The above conditions of legality are by and large not moral in character. Moral directives, in fact, constitute regulative principles of what the law ought to be; they do not modify the concept of law

[65] For that reason, the provision contained in s 2 of the Republic of South Africa Constitution Act 32 of 1961 ('The people of the Republic of South Africa acknowledge the sovereignty and guidance of Almighty God') does not in my opinion constitute positive law. See J D van der Vyver 'The Function of Legislation as an Instrument for Social Reform' (1976) 83 *SALJ* 56 at 62 and *Seven Lectures on Human Rights* (1976) 44.

[66] According to the Calvinistic legal philosopher, Herman Dooyeweerd (1894–1977), the distinguishing feature of the law is to be found in the modal aspect of retribution in the sense of 'an irreducible mode of balancing and harmonizing individual and social interests' (*A New Critique of Theoretical Thought* (1969) II 129).

[67] The influence of such external circumstances upon the law is evidence of the simple truism that the law functions within, and must therefore take cognizance of, the facts and contingencies of empirical reality. An enactment prohibiting fishing in the Namib, or segregating Eskimos in the Makwassie magisterial district, would for that reason not constitute what Rudolph Stammler (1856–1938) referred to as *richtiges Recht*.

[68] See J D van der Vyver 'The Section 114 Controversy—and Governmental Anarchy' (1980) 97 *SALJ* 363.

as such, but compose the essence of the legal idea. Immoral legal provisions are consequently not invalid, though they would be censurable—and I, for one, would not wager one cent on the chances of eventual survival of a legal system that deviates substantially from the ethically based pointers of the legal idea.

III The Moral Function of State Authority

The question whether or not incumbents of political power ought to enforce by means of legal compulsion the prevailing standards of praiseworthy behaviour was elaborately canvassed in the Devlin–Hart debate.

As a sworn disciple of positivism, H L A Hart, relying heavily on John Stuart Mill (1806–1873), gave a negative answer to this proposition.[69] Mill summarized his own basic premiss regarding the function of the law as follows: 'The only purpose for which power can be rightfully exercised over any member of a civilized community, against his will, is to prevent harm to others. His own good, either physical or moral, is not a sufficient warrant. He cannot rightfully be compelled to do or forbear because it will be better for him to do so, because it will make him happier, because, in the opinion of others, to do so would be wise, or even right.'[70] Subscribing to this view, Hart maintained that (state-imposed) law should not be utilized for the purpose of upholding moral principles.

Hart was responding to a lecture delivered in 1959 by the English judge, Patrick A (Lord) Devlin (1905–), in which Devlin dealt with the relationship between criminal law and morality and addressed himself in particular to the question whether it would be proper for the legislature to prohibit homosexual practices.[71] His argument can be summarized in several main points:

(a) a community is justified in protecting itself against internal and external dangers;
(b) such dangers include moral debasement;
(c) for legal purposes immorality entails what every right-minded person is presumed to consider to be immoral, and the law ought not to enforce disputed standards;
(d) it is not possible to set theoretical limits to the power of the state to combat immorality, and one cannot, for instance, meaningfully distinguish in this regard between private and public morality;
(e) the legislature must bear certain 'elastic principles' in mind when deciding upon the enforcement of moral values, for instance:

[69] See in particular *Law, Liberty and Morality* (1968).
[70] 'On Liberty' in *Three Essays by John Stuart Mill* (with an Introduction by M G Fawcett) (1963) 15.
[71] The lecture was included and elaborated upon in *The Enforcement of Morals* (1965).

(i) the legislature must make allowance for the greatest degree of individual freedom that would be compatible with the integrity of society;

(ii) the legislature must also take account of the fact that the level of tolerance of the community may shift,[72] and since the law is less susceptible to change it should not, when new moral issues arise, intervene precipitately;

(iii) privacy of the individual must be respected as far as possible, but it would be wrong to assume that the state may not take action in cases where immorality is practised 'in private'; and even where all the participants in immoral activity are consenting parties, 'public interest in the moral order' should nevertheless be balanced against the claims of privacy; and, finally,

(iv) the mere fact that certain behaviour is reprehensible does not necessarily mean that such behaviour should be proscribed by criminal law: 'There is much in the Sermon on the Mount', said Devlin,[73] 'that would be out of place in the Ten Commandments'—but the dividing line that should apply in this regard cannot be determined on the basis of 'clear-cut principle'.[74]

Towards the end of the nineteenth century James Fitzjames Stephen (1829–1894), while attacking the positivistic assumptions of John Stuart Mill, advanced similar arguments to those of Devlin in support of the contention that the state has a positive duty to enforce moral standards by means of legal coercion.[75]

There is, however, an important distinction between the respective premisses of the arguments put forward by Devlin and Stephen.[76] Devlin regarded morality as the 'cement of society', and consequently made state-imposed proscriptions of immoral conduct conditional upon the adverse effect of such conduct on society. Stephen, on the other hand, assumed that the combating of immorality by the state was in itself good, and therefore he defended coercive measures against immorality, regardless of the negative effect which it may or may not have on society. Stephen thus subscribed to 'the doctrine that public opinion ought to put a restraint upon vice, not to such an extent merely as is necessary for definite self-protection, but generally on the ground that vice is a bad thing from which men ought by appropriate means to restrain

[72] Devlin (idem 18) emphasized that moral standards in fact remain static, but that the limits of tolerance may vary—and he added that 'tolerance' does not amount to 'approval'.

[73] Idem 19. [74] Idem 21–2.

[75] *Liberty, Equality and Fraternity* (1873), in particular at 123–88. In *The Enforcement of Morals* vii Devlin, however, denied knowledge of Stephen's treatise at the time of his (Devlin's) 1959 lecture.

[76] See Hart *Law, Liberty and Morality* 48–52.

each other';[77] the purpose of legal injunctions against immorality is simply 'to make people better than they would be without compulsion'.[78]

Stephen nevertheless conceded that the furthering of moral objectives by means of legal restraints is subject to limitations. He explained in this regard[79] that the law ought not to concern itself with trivialities; that the moral behaviour of others ought not to be judged on insufficient or secondary evidence; that the law ought to confine its prohibitions to the prevailing moral standards of a given time and place and should forbid only such conduct as is 'strenuously and unequivocally' denounced by society; and that privacy of the subjects ought definitely to be respected.[80]

The idea of state responsibility in matters of ethics was strongly contested by Hart. In response to Devlin's reasoning in this regard, he made the following points:

(a) The question whether or not the state should enforce moral norms is in itself a moral problem; that is to say, *ought* the state to act as custodian of morals?

(b) Devlin's basic premiss that society has a moral right to safeguard its own survival is disputable. Should one, morally speaking, demand such a right in the case of morally deplorable communities, such as those practising religious intolerance or racial discrimination? Would the disintegration of such communities not, morally speaking, be preferable to their survival? Hart added: 'In asking the question, we are assuming the legitimacy of a standpoint which permits criticism of the institutions of any society, in the light of general principles and knowledge of the facts.'[81]

(c) There are two sides to criminal sanction: on the one hand it decrees punishment of wrongdoers; and on the other hand it compels those who do not violate the law to conduct themselves in the prescribed manner—which they would in other circumstances perhaps not have done. In the latter sense the criminal injunction limits the freedom of the subjects, and

[77] *Liberty, Equality and Fraternity* 134–5; and see also idem 148–9: '. . . these acts have in fact been forbidden and subjected to punishment not only because they are dangerous to society, and so ought to be prevented, but also for the sake of gratifying the feeling of hatred—call it revenge, resentment, or what you will—which the contemplation of such conduct excites in healthily constituted minds.'

[78] Idem 137. [79] Idem 138–60.

[80] There are—if I understand Stephen correctly—two sides to the matter: The law ought, first, not to concern itself with what happens in the privacy of a person's inner chambers (see idem 162: '. . . there is a sphere, none the less real because it is impossible to define its limits, within which law and public opinion are intruders likely to do more harm than good'); but at the same time the present limitation also refers to the fact that A's immoral conduct may infringe the privacy of B (see, for instance, idem 160: 'Conduct which can be described as indecent is always in one way or another a violation of privacy').

[81] *Law, Liberty and Morality* 20.

therefore its introduction would require special justification. Many reasons may be advanced why the moral behaviour of individuals should not be made subject to criminal-law regulation: for instance, because freedom of choice in such matters is in itself a virtue, because people should be left free to develop experimentally their own sense of values, and because sexual impulse and desires cannot be regulated by legal provisions.

(d) Opinions regarding morality differ greatly, and the problem therefore is not simply *whether* morality ought to be enforced by law, but *which* moral code should be sanctioned by the legislature.

(e) Criminal-law proscription of victimless immoral acts has a distinct paternalistic foundation. Hart found the idea that individuals should be protected against themselves, or that A should be punished simply because B condemns his conduct, totally unacceptable.[82] He said in this regard: 'The fundamental objection surely is that a right to be protected from the distress which is inseparable from the bare knowledge that others are acting in ways you think wrong, cannot be acknowledged by anyone who recognizes individual liberty as a value.'[83]

(f) Although Devlin based his standpoint on the supposition that morality was 'the cement' of society, he did not give sufficient account of the actual effect on society of those instances of immorality that should in his opinion be prohibited by law. If one were to concede Devlin's supposition that the survival of society is conditioned by the maintenance of moral standards, it follows that every immoral act, however 'private', would in the long run be detrimental to a political community; and this conclusion would lead one to Stephen's supposition that morality ought to be enforced for the sake of morality alone: *la moralité pour la survivance de la société* then becomes *la moralité pour la moralité.*

(g) An act derives its moral value from the motive that inspired its perpetrator, and by enforcing conduct believed to be conformable to moral standards the legislature in fact converts noble intention to performance of duty, thereby depriving the deed of its moral quality. Hart added: '. . . where there is no harm to be prevented and no potential victim to be protected . . ., it

[82] Norval Morris (1923–) 'The Overreach of the Criminal Law' 1975 *Acta Juridica* 40 took a similar stand against the morally based criminal prohibitions on what he preferred to call 'complainantless crimes' (the next of kin of habitual perpetrators of moral indecency are in a sense victims of such immorality but would normally not qualify as complainants in the legal sense). Morris did not, however, advocate a policy of *laissez-faire* in so far as immoral behaviour is concerned, but criminal sanctions are not in his opinion the answer to the social problems engendered by, for instance, the abuse of drugs and alcohol, gambling or sexual perversity. Instead, he championed a system of administrative control backed by criminal deterrents.

[83] *Law, Liberty and Morality* 46.

is difficult to understand the assertion that conformity, even if motivated by fear of the law's punishment, is a value worth pursuing, notwithstanding the misery and sacrifice of freedom which it involves. The attribution of value to mere conforming behaviour, in abstraction from both motive and consequence, belongs not to morality but to taboo.'[84]

My own view regarding the moral function of state authority rests on two basic suppositions:

(i) It is not the function of the state to enforce moral principles by means of legal coercion.
(ii) The law—including state-imposed enactments—ought to embody the morally based directives of the legal idea.

These two seemingly conflicting propositions are not really incompatible.

When one considers the desirablity of state intervention to avert a particular social evil, one should approach the matter on the basis of two distinct questions:

(1) Would it be proper (legitimate) for the state to regulate the matter in question through the medium of state-imposed legal provisions?
(2) If—and only if—one answers the first question in the affirmative, the further problem arises: What ought the contents of such legal provisions to be?

One's answer to the first question will evidently be influenced by one's primary conviction regarding the structural nature and basic destiny of the body politic. This intricate and controversial problem of political science cannot be debated within the confines of these pages. My own view in this regard, founded upon the fundamental premiss of the Calvinistic philosophy of the Cormonomic Idea,[85] may, in somewhat simplified terms, be summarized in these words:

The dominant function of the state is to establish and to maintain a legal order within the defined limits of a particular territory;[86] and

[84] Idem 57.

[85] The inventor and major proponent of this philosophy is Herman Dooyeweerd (1894–1970), his principal work being *A New Critique of Theoretical Thought* (in four volumes, Presbyterian & Reformed Publishing Co 1969)—see vol III ch 3 regarding the state. See also F J van Zyl and J D van der Vyver *Inleiding tot die Regswetenskap* 2 ed (1982), particularly at 15–45 for a general outline of the foundational notions of the philosophy of the Cosmonomic Idea and at 440ff regarding the state.

[86] See Dooyeweerd *A New Critique of Theoretical Thought* III 438: 'The integration of the citizens into the political unity of a people is in principle bound to the typical structure of the body politic, in which the leading function is that of a public legal community. This is an unparalleled, unique structural principle enabling the State to organize within its territory a truly universal legal communal bond transcending all non-juridically qualified legal societal relations.' Dooyeweerd (idem III 414) defined the foundational function of the state as '. . . an internal monopolistic organization of the power of the sword over a particular cultural area within territorial boundaries'. See also L M du Plessis *Die Juridiese Relevansie van Christelike Geregtigheid* (op cit note 1) 812: 'Die staat is 'n menslike instelling binne (of beter: oor) 'n bepaalde grondgebied wat deur 'n juridiese

a legal order is in the main destined to balance and harmonize conflicting interests of the subordinates of the political community among themselves and of society and its members.[87] The *juridical* function of the state[88] is accordingly focused upon arbitration and settlement of conflict situations in a legal community.

In view of the state's predestined design as arbitrator of inter-individual conflicts in human society, one must inevitably conclude that furtherance of moral virtues for the sake of morality *an sich* does not fall within the scope of the state's appropriate functions. The moral attribute of human behaviour rests on *conviction*, which in turn may be animated by *persuasion*; morality is, in a word, not a matter of compulsion backed by coercion. There is, therefore, particular merit in Hart's argument that state-imposed constraint would deprive one's good conduct of its moral quality.

This does not mean that state authority should deny its subjects the protection of the law in all instances that may involve moral behaviour. The state's primary function and obligation is to resolve conflict situations, and whenever a *de facto* conflict of interests requiring arbitration arises, the state may and ought to intervene with a view to balancing and harmonizing the competing interests in question. The fact that a particular conflict of interests may have a bearing on moral conduct should not preclude state intervention. The state legislature may in such instances find it expedient to proscribe immoral acts, but would do so in the process of regulating the conflict of interests and not as a supposed custodian of moral values.

Once it appears that a conflict of interests does warrant the enactment of state law, the second question mentioned above arises: How should the state regulate the interests of its subjects so as to promote harmony in society; or, what ought the contents of such enactment to be? In answer to this question one would affirm the normative propriety of the legal idea: The law ought always to conform with the morally based directives that signify the *oughts* of legal relations.

The core of those directives is centred upon the concept of justice, which, broadly, requires the equal treatment of all the subjects of a given political society by and before the law.

bestemming (die verwesenliking van die ampsgeborgenheid van alle mense binne daardie grondgebied) gekwalifiseer (of "gelei") word', and also 'Menseregte in Konfliksituasies' 1979 *Koers* 340: 'Die staat se aard en struktuur word deur die feit dat dit op die handhawing van 'n openbare regsorde binne 'n bepaalde (gewoonlik grond-) gebied bedag is, bepaal.'

[87] See note 66.

[88] The state also has cultural, social, economic and other functions, though its leading function is juridically qualified.

FACTUAL CAUSATION IN PERSPECTIVE

ROGER WHITING*

Lawyers are frequently faced with the problem of having to determine whether certain human conduct, A, must for legal purposes be regarded as the cause of a certain later occurrence or state of affairs, X. According to the view now generally taken both in South Africa and elsewhere, such questions of causation must be considered in two stages. On this approach, there must be an initial inquiry into whether the conduct in question, A, is what is commonly called a factual cause of the later occurrence or state of affairs in question, X. If this inquiry yields a negative result, that is an end of the matter: A cannot be considered a cause of X. If, on the other hand, the initial inquiry shows A to be a factual cause of X, there must then be a further inquiry into whether there is a sufficient connection between A and X for A to be regarded also as the legal cause of X.[1]

As the title I have chosen indicates, I shall be concerned in this paper only with the preliminary stage of the overall inquiry into legal causation, that is to say, with an examination of the nature of so-called factual causation. This will involve a consideration of the different tests that have been propounded to determine the existence of factual causation and an endeavour to place each of these tests in its proper perspective. My main purpose will be to show that the meaning of 'factual cause'—and consequently also the appropriate test to determine factual causation—differs according as to which of two different types of result is involved. In elaborating on this, my main, theme, I shall also seek to show, though somewhat incidentally, that it is wrong to see so-called factual causation as being concerned purely with factual questions, and that, particularly in certain instances, legal considerations play a not insignificant part in its determination.

* MA (Oxon), Advocate of the Supreme Court of South Africa, Professor of Law in the University of the Witwatersrand, Johannesburg.

[1] See, for instance, A M Honoré *International Encyclopaedia of Comparative Law* XI ch 7 (general); John G Fleming *The Law of Torts* 5 ed (1977) 179 (Anglo-American law). For South Africa, see in particular *Minister of Police* v *Skosana* 1977 (1) SA 31 (A) at 34–5; *The Law of South Africa* (ed W A Joubert) VIII (1979) para 47 (delict); and P M A Hunt *South African Criminal Law and Procedure* II: *Common-law Crimes* 2 ed (1982) by J R L Milton 344ff (criminal law).

Much the best known and most widely used of the theories of factual causation is that of the *conditio sine qua non* or necessary condition.[2] In terms of this theory factual cause is equated with necessary condition, so that conduct will be a factual cause of a particular result if, but for such conduct, the result would not have occurred.[3] It is usual to employ two different forms of the *conditio sine qua non* test, one for acts and the other for omissions. Where the conduct in question takes the form of a positive act, it is usual to employ a hypothetical elimination test, in terms of which the act in question is notionally eliminated from the actual factual complex of which it forms part. If the result would not have occurred in the absence of the act in question, then the act must be considered a necessary condition, and therefore a factual cause, of the result; otherwise not.[4] Where the conduct in question takes the form of an omission or failure to act, it is usual to employ a hypothetical addition test, in terms of which the act which should have been performed is notionally added to the actual factual complex. If the result in question would not have occurred if such act had been performed, then the omission or failure to perform such act must be considered a necessary condition, and therefore a factual cause, of the result; otherwise not.[5]

There are some who reject the *conditio sine qua non* theory in whole or in part and apply what may be called a contribution theory of factual causation, in which factual cause is equated with 'contributory factor'.[6] In its simplest form, the contribution theory states that an act is a factual cause of a result if it in some way contributes to the occurrence of the result.[7] Other forms are essentially the same as this, except that they adopt what is perhaps the more convenient course of building the *de minimis non curat lex* principle into the inquiry into factual causation. They state that conduct is a factual cause of a result if it is a 'substantial factor' in producing it or makes a 'material contribution' to it.[8] The formulation in terms of 'material contribution' seems preferable, as 'substantial factor' is more likely to be misunderstood in a way which would overstate the degree of contribution required. The contribution theory is, therefore, perhaps best seen as identifying causality of a result with the making of a material contribution to its occurrence.

In endeavouring to place the *conditio sine qua non* and contribution theories in their proper perspective, one should notice two important

[2] See, generally, Honoré op cit note 1 at para 107.

[3] See, for instance, Fleming op cit note 1 at 180; *The Law of South Africa* VIII para 48; Hunt note 1 loc cit.

[4] *The Law of South Africa* loc cit. [5] Ibid.

[6] See, generally, Honoré op cit note 1 at para 108; and, particularly for South Africa, A D J van Rensburg 'Nog Eens *Conditio sine qua non*' 1977 *TSAR* 101.

[7] Van Rensburg op cit 103, 111–12, 115.

[8] Honoré loc cit, and the authorities there cited.

points at the outset. The first is that, contrary to what is sometimes asserted,[9] the two theories are essentially opposed to each other, because, as will appear more fully later, 'necessary condition' and 'contributory factor' are not the same thing. Although in many cases both theories will produce the same answer to the inquiry into factual causation, the notion of 'contributory factor' is clearly wider than that of 'necessary condition'. A necessary condition will always be a contributory factor, but the converse is not true. There are quite a number of cases in which a contributory factor will not also be a necessary condition, and in which therefore the two theories will produce conflicting answers to the causal inquiry. The second important point to notice is that, as will be demonstrated later, neither theory is correct for all situations. There are certain situations in which only the *conditio sine qua non* theory will produce the right answer, and others in which only the contribution theory will produce the right answer.

Thus, both theories have an indispensable role to play in determining factual causation. In order to assign to each its proper place in such inquiries, it is necessary to establish in what circumstances factual cause means 'necessary condition' and in what circumstances it means merely 'contributory factor'. I shall seek to show that the key lies in the type of result which is involved, and that the solution—in slightly over-simplified form—is as follows. In relation to a positive result, factual cause means merely 'contributory factor'. In relation to a negative result, factual cause means 'necessary condition'.

To distinguish causes as positive or negative according to whether they consist in the presence or absence of something is common enough.[10] But the idea of making a similar distinction with regard to results is perhaps unusual, and therefore, simple though it is, requires some explanation. One causes a positive result where one causes something to happen, as where one causes injury or death, or damage to or destruction of property. One causes a negative result where one causes something not to happen or prevents something from happening. In the legal context, causing a negative result typically consists in causing some advantage not to eventuate. Negative results are thus common in the field of damages, as where one causes loss of profits, loss of earnings or loss of support. They are also common as initial or intermediate stages in the causation of positive results, as where one causes the

[9] Thus, in *Skosana's* case (*supra* n 1) Corbett JA says in effect that the question whether a negligent act or omission has caused or materially contributed to the harm must be determined by the *sine qua non* test (at 34–5).

[10] For example, where a crop is destroyed by flood, we say the flood is a positive cause, but where it is destroyed by drought, we say the drought or absence of water is a negative cause. Again, causal conduct is commonly distinguished as positive or negative according to whether it consists in an act or an omission.

death of a child through failure to feed it, or where one causes a car to crash by sabotaging its braking system.

So much for terminology. It is now necessary to examine what justification there is for the assertion that in relation to negative results factual cause means 'necessary condition', whereas in relation to positive results it means merely 'contributory factor'.

Causation of a negative result involves interfering with the course of events in such a way that something which would otherwise have happened does not happen. Determining the cause of a negative result thus necessarily involves a hypothetical inquiry into what course events would have taken but for the alleged cause. In particular, it involves an inquiry into whether, but for the alleged cause, that which has not happened would have happened, in other words a *sine qua non* inquiry.

It is characteristic of causation of a negative result that it involves no change in reality, indeed, that such a change is prevented. Herein lies the fundamental difference between it and causation of a positive result, which involves bringing about a change in reality, not preventing it. Thus, whereas the connection between cause and negative result is merely hypothetical, based on what would have happened, the connection between cause and positive result is essentially[11] real or actual, based on what has actually happened. A real or actual connection is properly determined simply by enquiring whether the alleged cause has materially contributed to the happening of the result in question. There is no need to resort to a hypothetical inquiry such as that involved in the *conditio sine qua non* test. Such an inquiry would at best provide a convoluted way of arriving at the same conclusion as that provided by the contribution test. Moreover, at worst the use of the *conditio sine qua non* test to determine causation of a positive result will actually produce wrong answers to the causal inquiry. This is because, as has previously been mentioned, 'necessary condition' and 'contributory factor' are not the same thing, and, as will now be demonstrated, there are certain situations in which a cause of a positive result will not also be a necessary condition of that result.

The first situation one may mention in this regard is where two or more independently sufficient causes take effect simultaneously, as in the commonly cited example where A and B simultaneously shoot X dead. Here neither A's act nor B's act is by itself a necessary condition of X's death, because the act of either would on its own have produced this result. Yet each act has materially contributed to X's death, and is clearly a cause of it.[12]

[11] The qualification inherent in the word 'essentially' is necessary, because, as will be seen more fully later, there are certain situations in which negative results form essential links in the causal chain connecting conduct with a positive result, in which therefore the connection between the causal conduct and the positive result is partly hypothetical.

[12] See, for example, Honoré op cit note 1 at para 132; Hunt op cit note 1 at 345.

A second such situation occurs with combining causes—where two or more causes become consolidated before they take effect. An example is where A and B each place poison in X's coffee, and X dies as a result of drinking the poisoned coffee. Of course, where the dose which each puts in is insufficient by itself to cause death, the act of each is not merely a contributory factor but also a necessary condition of X's death. And where each puts in a lethal dose, we merely have another example of the first situation, in which two or more independently sufficient causes take effect simultaneously. But where A puts in, say, half a lethal dose, and B a lethal dose, A's act, though neither a necessary condition nor an independently sufficient cause of X's death, is still a cause of it, because the death is due to a single dose of poison to which A has materially contributed. Although B's contribution would have been sufficient on its own to cause X's death and A's contribution would not have been, the fact is that X has actually died not merely from B's contribution but from both contributions in combination.[13] On the same principle, where a fire started by A merges with a fire started by B and the resulting conflagration causes X's death, A must be held to be a cause of X's death as long as his contribution to the conflagration was a material one. It will not matter that A's fire would not have been sufficient on its own to cause X's death, nor that B's fire would have been sufficient by itself to produce this result. Again the point is that X has actually died not merely from B's contribution but from both contributions in combination.[14]

Combining causes may also be of importance in the field of what has been called psychic[15] or interpersonal[16] causation. In this type of causation, A's causality of X's action arises from the influence he has exerted on X's mind. Examples are where A induces X to enter into a contract or persuades X to shoot someone. In the simple case where X's sole reason for acting is the inducement provided by A, no question of combining causes will arise. But often X's motivation may be more complex. His decision to act may have been influenced not merely by A's conduct but also by a further factor or further factors, such as his own predisposition to do the act or a further inducement provided by B. Here one is again in the field of combining causes, where two or more causes become consolidated

[13] Cf the (unpublished) LLD thesis of A D J van Rensburg *Juridiese Kousaliteit en Aspekte van Aanspreeklikheidsbeperking by die Onregmatige Daad* (University of South Africa 1970) 48–50.

[14] Some writers appear a little hesitant about this conclusion, but it seems to be supported clearly enough by what is said by William L Prosser *Handbook of the Law of Torts* 4 ed (1971) 239–40.

[15] The term 'psigiese veroorsaking' is used by Afrikaans writers, for example J C de Wet 'Opmerkings oor die Vraagstuk van Veroorsaking' (1941) 5 *THRHR* 126 at 134; and cf *S* v *Maxaba en andere* 1981 (1) SA 1148 (A) at 1156.

[16] H L A Hart and A M Honoré *Causation in the Law* (1959), particularly at 48, prefer to speak of 'interpersonal transactions'.

Official opening on 6 December 1967 of the Neutrino Laboratory of the University of the Witwatersrand, Johannesburg at 77 level Hercules Shaft ERPM Boksburg, 11 000 feet below the surface

Oliver Schreiner looking at the MO, who is pretending to be another type of MO—a mine official—and trying to hide his medical bag. See page 95

Oliver Schreiner inspecting the equipment at the Neutrino Laboratory on 6 December 1967

Link with the past: Oliver Schreiner with the bemedalled Charles F Stallard QC at Stallard's farm, Hope Woolith, 16 kilometres south-east of Johannesburg, on Stallard's 95th birthday on 4 June 1966. On Stallard's right is Brother Norwood E Coaker (Coaker QC), and on Coaker's right (*far left in the photograph*) is the Hon E R Roper, previously a Transvaal judge

Link with the past: Oliver Schreiner talking to the former Chief Justice, Sir James Rose Innes (*far left in the photograph*). The man in the centre is not identified. Date unknown; probably in the mid-thirties

before they take effect. Just as in the poisoning example previously mentioned X dies as a result of a single dose of poison to which A and B have each contributed, so here X acts as a result of a single decision, which separate influences, including A's conduct, have combined to produce. And just as in the poisoning case A's causality is established simply by his having materially contributed to the dose which caused X's death, so here A's causality must be considered established simply by the fact that he has materially contributed to X's decision to do the act. It should not matter that X would still have done the act even if A had not influenced him. In other words, it should not matter that A's act was not a necessary condition of X's act.[17] And indeed the Appellate Division has held that where X commits suicide after being encouraged to do so by A, A's conduct must be regarded as causally linked with X's death unless X's suicide was a completely independent act having no connection with A's encouragement.[18]

A third situation in which a cause of a positive result will not also be a necessary condition of that result involves what have been called alternative causes and occurs where, had one cause not operated to produce a result, another would have operated to produce the same result at least as soon. The following is an example. A injures X at his home, and X is removed to hospital, where he later dies of the wound. In the meantime, X's home is engulfed by an avalanche which would have killed him had he not already been removed to hospital. Here A's act is obviously a cause of X's death, although but for A's act X would actually have died sooner.[19]

A fourth situation in which one may have a cause of a positive result which is not also a necessary condition of that result involves what may be called causation by facilitation, as where A makes it easier for B to kill X. An example is where A holds X while B stabs X to death. Here A will be a cause of X's death, even if B would have succeeded in killing X in exactly the same way without A's assistance.[20]

Having dealt with the method of determining A's causality of X's death, one may now contrast with it the method of determining A's causality of the loss of support suffered by X's dependants following his death. The contrast lies in the fact that, loss of support being a negative result, its cause will fall to be determined not by the contribution test but by the *sine qua non* test. Thus, in

[17] Cf Honoré op cit note 1 at para 121.

[18] *Ex parte die Minister van Justisie: In re S* v *Grotjohn* 1970 (2) SA 355 (A), particularly at 363–4.

[19] Cf Hart and Honoré op cit note 16 at 118–19 and 225–6; Fleming op cit note 1 at 183.

[20] Supported inferentially by *S* v *Williams en 'n ander* 1980 (1) SA 60 (A), particularly at 64, where it appears to have been assumed to be irrelevant to A's causality whether B might have succeeded in killing X in exactly the same way without A's assistance.

order to determine whether the loss of support suffered by X's dependants was caused by A's act, one must ask whether, but for A's act, the dependants would have received support from X. The mere fact that A's act may be said to have contributed to the loss of support will not be enough. This may conveniently be illustrated by the avalanche example already mentioned in dealing with alternative causes, where it was seen that A's causality of X's death was not affected by the fact that, but for A's act, an alternative cause, the avalanche, would have produced the same result. The point that must now be noticed is that the existence of the alternative cause, though irrelevant to A's causality of X's death, will nevertheless operate to exclude A's causality of the loss of support suffered by X's dependants following his death. This is because, by preventing A's act from being a *conditio sine qua non* of X's death, it also necessarily prevents A's act from being a *conditio sine qua non* of the loss of support suffered by X's dependants. In this example, A's act was not even a necessary condition of X's death. But of course it would make no difference in principle if A's act was a necessary condition of X's death if it was not also a necessary condition of the loss of support suffered by X's dependants. Thus, if shortly before A killed him, X had contracted an incurable debilitating disease which would have prevented him from continuing to work, A's act, though a necessary condition of X's death, would still not have been a cause of the loss of support suffered by X's dependants, because it would not have been a necessary condition of such loss of support.[21]

From what has been said, it would seem that conduct ought never to be regarded as a cause of a negative result if it was not a necessary condition of that result. However, the unqualified application of such a principle would lead to conclusions which are legally unacceptable. For example, it would mean that, where A and B simultaneously shoot X dead in circumstances in which each would be liable for causing his death, neither would be liable for the consequential loss of support suffered by X's dependants, because neither's act would have been a necessary condition of such loss of support. In order to avoid inequitable results such as this, the law must intervene to override ordinary causal principles by modifying the application of the *sine qua non* test to the extent necessary to prevent one wrongdoer from sheltering behind another. The rule must be that, where the conduct of each would,[22] but for the conduct of the other, have been a factual cause of the result in question, and each would, but for the other's conduct,

[21] Cf Hart and Honoré op cit note 16 at 226–7; Fleming op cit note 1 at 183.

[22] The rule applies only where the conduct of each is not an actual cause of the result. Thus, for absolute clarity the words 'is not but' should be inserted between the words 'each' and 'would'.

have been legally liable for causing that result, then each must be held legally liable as if his conduct had been a factual cause of that result.[23]

It should be noticed that, although in the situation just mentioned the *sine qua non* test has to be applied in a modified form, it is still the *sine qua non* test (or a variant of it), and not the contribution test, which is being applied. Indeed, it is true to say that the contribution test has no part whatever to play in determining the causation of a negative result. One might expect that it would also be true to say that the *conditio sine qua non* test has no part to play in determining the causation of a positive result. However, if one thought this, one would be wrong. There are certain circumstances in which the *sine qua non* test will have a part to play in determining the causation of a positive result.

In order to demonstrate the truth of this statement, one may start with the following example. Let us say that A sabotages the braking system of a train, so that when the driver, on encountering a red-light signal to stop, attempts to apply the brakes, they do not work, and the train crashes into the back of a stationary train further down the line, with consequent loss of life. Here it is obvious that the death of the occupants of the trains has been caused by A's act of sabotaging the braking system. However, the correct method of explaining this conclusion is not so obvious. On a superficial view, it might seem that, as the death of the victims was a positive result, A's causality must be considered established simply by his having materially contributed to that result. But this would be wrong. The correct explanation involves a closer analysis of the causal chain by which A's act is linked with the death of the victims. Such an analysis would reveal that there were certain negative results which were essential links in the causal chain by which the ultimate positive result was reached. In a situation like this the proper procedure is to divide the causal chain, and with it the inquiry into factual causation, into two distinct stages. The dividing line between the two stages must be drawn at the latest negative result, in this case the failure of the train to stop. In the first stage, one is *ex hypothesi* concerned with a negative result and one therefore applies the *sine qua non* test in order to determine whether A's act was a cause of the train's failure to stop. Only if one receives an affirmative answer to this inquiry does one proceed to the second stage. Here one is *ex hypothesi* concerned with a positive result, and one therefore applies the contribution test in order to determine whether the failure of the train to stop was a cause of the ultimate result, the death of the victims.

The correctness of this approach may be more fully demonstrated by adapting the facts of the example just mentioned. Let us say that not only does A sabotage the braking system of the train but also the signal

[23] Honoré op cit note 1 at para 132 *in fine*; cf Hart and Honoré op cit note 16 at 227–8, and Arno C Becht and Frank W Miller *The Test of Factual Causation in Negligence and Strict Liability Cases* (1961) § 9(3). Glanville Williams in 'Causation in the Law' 1961 *Cambridge LJ* 62 at 76 states the rule too widely.

is defective, so that when the train reaches it, it still shows green. As a result, the driver does not even attempt to apply the brakes (which in any event are not working) until he sees the stationary train in front of him, and the same disastrous consequences ensue as before. Let us assume also that the warning the driver had of the presence of the stationary train was so limited that, even if the brakes had been in proper working order, there would have been no material difference in the resultant collision and its effects.

Here there are again the same two stages in the causal chain as were present in the original example, but the first stage is now complicated by there being a further factor bearing on the train's failure to stop, namely, the faulty operation of the signal. The existence of this further factor makes a vital difference to A's causality of the death of the victims, because it prevents A's act of sabotaging the braking system from being a necessary condition of the train's failure to stop. While A's act may be said—just as much as the defective signal—to have contributed to the train's failure to stop, this will not be sufficient to establish his causality. This is because, as the failure to stop is a negative result, causation of this stage of the causal chain must be determined not by the contribution test but by the *sine qua non* test. Consequently, A's act will not be regarded as a cause of the death of the victims unless the circumstances were such as to bring into play the special legal rule mentioned earlier. For example, if the failure of the signal to show red were due to the fault of B, the law would not allow either A or B to shelter behind the other's wrongdoing. And, as the conduct of each would but for the conduct of the other have been a necessary condition of the failure of the train to stop, each would be held legally liable for causing the death of the victims as if his conduct had been a necessary condition of the train's failure to stop.[24]

In elaborating on how the causation of positive and negative results must be tested, we have thus far been concerned only with causation by a positive act. It is now necessary to consider causation by an omission, and how it fits into the overall causal scheme.

The first point to notice about causation by an omission is that, unlike causation by a positive act, it is fundamentally a normative concept. To say of a person that he has caused a result by a positive act does not necessarily imply that he has done anything wrong. Where A shoots X dead, the description of A as the cause of X's death is no less apt for the fact that he may have been acting in self-defence. But when one speaks of causation by an omission or failure to act, what one really means is causation by a wrongful omission, causation by failing to comply with a duty to act. To say of a person that he has caused a result by an omission necessarily

[24] The train crash examples are entirely my own, but cf Becht and Miller op cit note 23 at § 9(3), which may be seen as providing inferential support for my conclusions.

connotes a neglect of duty on his part.[25] This may be illustrated by the following example. Where a level-crossing keeper fails to lower the booms when a train is approaching, and a car then enters the level crossing and is hit by the train coming through, we would say the level-crossing keeper has caused the accident through his failure to lower the booms. But if he had his girl-friend with him in his cabin, we would not say that she had caused the accident, notwithstanding that she could equally well have lowered the booms herself. The reason for differentiating between them is simply that the level-crossing keeper was under a duty to lower the booms, whereas the girl-friend was not.

Thus, whenever it is necessary for legal purposes to determine whether a person has caused a result by an omission, there must always be a preliminary inquiry into whether, firstly, he was under a legal duty to act in a way which might have prevented that result, and, secondly, he has committed a breach of that duty. Only once one has received affirmative answers to these questions can one proceed to the actual causal inquiry, namely, whether the necessary factual nexus exists between the breach of duty and the result.

This causal inquiry will be governed by the same basic principles as govern the determination of causation by a positive act. However, the application of these principles, and with it the nature of the inquiry, will to some extent be affected by the fact that the conduct initiating the causal chain consists in a failure to comply with a duty instead of in a positive act. Thus, there is a difference in the way results are produced by a failure to act. A failure to act, if it produces any result at all, will in the first instance always produce a negative result, though that negative result may in turn produce a positive result. For example, if A fails to feed her child, her failure to act will have no effect at all if someone else feeds the child. If her failure to act has any effect, it will always in the first instance be that the child receives no food, a negative result. But the fact that the child receives no food may in due course lead to its death, a positive result.

We saw earlier, in dealing with the examples involving the train crash, that, where a causal chain includes one or more negative results, the causation of that part of the causal chain up to the latest negative result must be determined by the *sine qua non* test. And we have just seen that a causal chain which starts with an omission must always include at least an initial negative result. It therefore follows that the causation of at least the first stage of a causal chain starting with an omission must be determined by the *sine qua non* test.

[25] This is true not only of legal, but also of lay, parlance; but while the layman might be satisfied with moral wrongfulness, the lawyer is of course concerned only with legal wrongfulness.

Where one uses the *sine qua non* test to determine causation by a positive act, one adopts the method of elimination: one asks whether, without the act, the result would not have occurred. However, this method cannot be applied to causation by an omission for the simple reason that there is here no act to eliminate. For causation by an omission the appropriate method is that of addition or substitution. One substitutes for the omission the act which should have been performed, and asks whether, if the person concerned had done his duty, the result would not have occurred.[26]

For the rest, causation by an omission falls to be determined in exactly the same way as causation by a positive act. In particular, the distinction between positive and negative results is just as much the primary determinant of causation by an omission as it is of causation by a positive act. This may be illustrated by two examples, the first involving a negative result and the second involving a positive result.

For the first example, we may take a case involving breach of contract. Let us say that A is to erect a building and, wishing to start work on 1 February, engages B to supply him on that date with the bricks he requires. However, B delivers the bricks only on 1 March, and the building work is started only on that date. The question then arises whether B's breach of his obligation to deliver on 1 February is a cause of the delay in the commencement of the work. The proper procedure will be to ask whether, if B had complied with his obligation and delivered the bricks on 1 February, the building work would have commenced on that date as scheduled. If the answer is that it would have, B's breach of contract will have been a necessary condition, and therefore a cause, of the delay. However, if A received delivery of the cement he required for the erection of the building also only on 1 March, this would prevent B's breach from being a necessary condition of the delay. Though B's breach might be said—just as much as the non-availability of the cement—to have contributed to the delay, this would not be sufficient to establish B's causality. This is because, as the delay is a negative result, its cause must be determined not by the contribution test but by the *sine qua non* test. Consequently, B's breach would not be regarded as a cause of the delay unless the circumstances were such as to bring into play the special legal rule preventing one wrongdoer from sheltering behind another. If, for example, C had agreed to supply A on 1 February with the cement he required, the law would not allow either B or C to shelter behind the other's breach of contract. Accordingly, if the wrongful conduct of each would, but for the wrongful conduct of the other, have been a necessary condition of the delay, each would

[26] See 371 above, and the authority cited in notes 4 and 5.

be treated as if his conduct had been a necessary condition of the delay.[27]

For our second example of causation by an omission, this time involving a positive result, we may take a case of combining causes. Let us say, adapting the facts of an earlier example, that A is under a legal duty to take steps to keep any fire which may break out on his property under proper control, but that a fire nevertheless breaks out on his property and spreads out of control. This fire, which we may call fire A, later combines with another fire of independent origin, which we may call fire B, and the resulting conflagration causes X's death. The question then arises whether A's failure to keep fire A under proper control is a factual cause of X's death. As a preliminary step, one must first ask whether A was in breach of his legal duty. Only once one has determined that A failed to do what his legal duty required of him can one proceed to the actual causal inquiry, namely, whether A's breach of duty was a factual cause of X's death.

We have already seen that a causal chain which starts with an omission will always include at least an initial negative result. We have also already seen that where a causal chain leading to a positive result includes one or more negative results, the proper procedure is to divide the causal inquiry into two distinct stages, the dividing line between the two stages being drawn at the latest negative result. In the first stage, one must apply the *sine qua non* test in order to determine whether the conduct in question was a cause of the latest negative result. If one receives an affirmative answer to this inquiry, one then proceeds to the second stage, in which one applies the contribution test in order to determine whether the latest negative result was itself a cause of the ultimate positive result. In the present example, the latest negative result is the lack of control over fire A. We must therefore ask whether, if A had taken the steps his legal duty required of him, fire A would have been kept under control. If the answer is that it would have been, then A's breach of duty was a necessary condition, and therefore a cause, of the lack of control over fire A. The final question will then be whether the lack of control over fire A materially contributed to X's death. As one is here concerned with a positive result, it will not matter that fire A would not have been sufficient on its own to produce X's death, nor that fire B would have been sufficient by itself to produce this result. In other words, it will not matter that fire A was not a necessary condition of X's death.[28]

[27] Cf the example given by Glanville Williams op cit note 23 at 76.

[28] *Arguendo* from the earlier example involving combining fires, and see also Becht and Miller op cit note 23 at § 2(4).

To conclude, one may sum up the overall position as follows:

(a) A positive act will be a factual cause of a negative result if it was a necessary condition of that result in the sense that the result would not have occurred if the act had not been committed.

(b) A wrongful omission will be a factual cause of a negative result if it was a necessary condition of that result in the sense that the result would not have occurred if the person concerned had done what his legal duty required of him.

(c) Subject to what is said in paragraph *(d)*, a positive act will be a factual cause of a positive result if it has materially contributed to the happening of that result.

(d) Where a negative result or two or more negative results are essential links in a causal chain leading to an ultimate positive result, the conduct initiating the causal chain will be a factual cause of the ultimate positive result only if—

(i) such conduct is in terms of the rules set out in paragraphs *(a)* and *(b)* a factual cause of the latest negative result in the causal chain, and

(ii) the latest negative result has materially contributed to the happening of the ultimate positive result.

(e) The above rules are subject to the qualification that, if the wrongful conduct of each of two or more people would, but for that of the other or others, have been a factual cause of the ultimate result in question and each would have been legally liable for causing that result, the wrongful conduct of each will be treated as if it were a factual cause of that result.

THE FUNDAMENTAL LAWS BEHIND OUR CONSTITUTION

REFLECTIONS ON THE JUDGMENT OF SCHREINER JA IN THE SENATE CASE[1]

MARINUS WIECHERS*

South Africa is a country rich in constitutional law but extremely poor in constitutional law theory.

Since we do not have a written, rigid Constitution with superior legal force or any formal protection of human rights, and since judicial review of parliamentary Acts is virtually non-existent, we do not have a large body of judicial precedent on constitutional matters. But it is remarkable how many constitutional laws we have. Apart from the Constitution itself, there is a myriad of laws creating separate institutions for the various population groups and separate citizenships for Blacks, and providing for the devolution of powers and functions to homelands, provinces and even ethnic bodies such as the Indian Council and, formerly, the Coloured Persons' Representative Council. Alongside these constitutional laws there are many enactments with a profound constitutional effect in so far as they create the foundations of the present governmental and political structures. These are the statutes relating to population registration, group areas, elections, local governments and other community authorities. It can be foreseen, as has happened over the past few years, that the number of constitutional laws will be ever increasing. Indeed, the impression is sometimes obtained that Parliament passes a multitude of constitutional laws deliberately to create an illusion or at least a climate of so-called evolutionary change.

Over the years a vast body of theory of political science has emerged to explain the nature of South African government and society, mainly on the basis of attitudes and behaviour, and by using models of conflict, suppression and accommodation. In this respect, it has become fashionable to discuss politics by analysing

* BA LLB LLD (Pret), Professor of Constitutional and Public International Law in the University of South Africa.

[1] *Collins* v *Minister of the Interior* 1957 (1) SA 552 (A).

the proposing various constitutional arrangements such as federations, confederations and consociations. It can truthfully be said that the South African politician nowadays readily talks constitutional law to impress upon his voters and supporters the needs for and possibilities of future political change.

However, relatively little has been done by constitutionalists to establish a theory of constitutional law that explores basic questions regarding the role of law in the state, the relationship between law and the state, and the nature of the laws on which the state and its government and institutions rest. Admittedly, the positivistic methods of our constitutional-law practice as well as our more Anglo-American approach to constitutional issues do not encourage a deeper search into the general relationship between law and the state. On the other hand, the constitutional reform that is imminent and the strongly felt desire for future stability in a broad framework of constitutionalism urge upon us the importance of a more profound and fundamental reflection on these issues.

For the constitutional lawyer the removal of the Coloureds from the common voters' roll in the early fifties and the ensuing decisions by the Appellate Division on the legality of these parliamentary actions not only represent the most important constitutional events in our legal history but still provide him with abundant food for thought and pondering. Rereading the *Vote* case,[2] the *High Court of Parliament* case[3] and the *Senate* case is not simply an escape into the political past, but a direct encounter with some of the most burning theoretical issues that confront us now. The sovereignty of Parliament, constitutional guarantees and their protection, institutional stability and judicial review are all aspects that played their part in those grand judgments and are just as relevant today as they were thirty years ago.

The facts that resulted in the constitutional crisis of the fifties are well known. In 1951 Parliament removed Coloured voters from the common voters' roll by an ordinary bicameral procedure. The Appellate Division declared the Act[4] which was so passed invalid, and Parliament then sought to create a High Court of Parliament to take the court's decision on review. The High Court of Parliament Act,[5] which was also passed by an ordinary majority in bicameral session, was also declared null and void by the Appellate Division. After having failed to obtain the two-thirds majority required by the Constitution, the Government then managed to get an Act[6] passed by Parliament in terms of which the membership of the Senate was enlarged to ensure that the Government had the neces-

[2] *Harris* v *Minister of the Interior* 1952 (2) SA 428 (A).
[3] *Minister of the Interior* v *Harris* 1952 (4) SA 769 (A).
[4] Separate Representation of Voters Act 46 of 1951.
[5] Act 35 of 1952. [6] Senate Act 53 of 1955.

sary two-thirds majority and to validate the previous Acts. In the *Senate* case the Appellate Division accepted the validity of Parliament's *démarche* and refused to declare the swamping of the Senate or the ensuing validation of the removal statute invalid. Only Schreiner JA gave a dissenting judgment, in which he strongly declared himself against the actions taken by the Government to attain its two-thirds majority.

All students of South African constitutional law, if asked what principle the three decisions establish, will reply that they ruled in favour of the legal proposition that Parliament, although it has plenary powers to pass Acts on any subject-matter, must comply with manner-and-form requirements. In other words, although Parliament is the supreme law-creating body, it is, as a collective institution, still answerable to the laws that define the manner and form in which it acts. Were these manner-and-form prescriptions to be ignored by Parliament, it would not act at all, and such 'action' could then be declared null and void by a court of law. Obviously, this is (in a very distilled form) the basic legal principle pronounced by the court in the three cases. It furnished constitutional lawyers here and abroad with a valuable understanding of and insight into the necessary conditions that accompany the exercise of Parliament's legislative supremacy.[7]

What is perhaps less appreciated is that these decisions are also a veritable gold-mine of other constitutional principles and issues which go to the heart of the great and timeless constitutional debate. Thus, it is not always realized that the *High Court of Parliament* case is our clearest vindication of and judicial pronouncement on the *trias politica* and the independence of the judiciary.[8]

The *Senate* case, which is the focus of this discussion, brings an even more important issue to the fore, namely, whether there exists in constitutional law a rule that forbids the abuse and even perversion by a parliamentary majority of those institutions that embody democratic government. For the real question in the case was whether the Constitution prevents a parliamentary majority from using its legislative power to overcome its own limitations and thereby, so to say, to usurp the institutions of the state. In other words, the question was whether there is a law that sustains the Constitution and that is immutable in the sense that it cannot be changed by the organs of state created under the Constitution. In order to appreciate and answer this question, it is necessary to have a closer look at the judgment in the *Senate* case, and, more

[7] Cf a recent article by G N Barrie 'Die Gebondenheid van die Parlement aan die Reg rakende sy Struktuur en Funksionering' 1981 *TSAR* 46 and the authorities quoted by him, and Marinus Wiechers *VerLoren van Themaat—Staatsreg* 3 ed (1981) 305 and the authorities quoted.

[8] Wiechers *VerLoren van Themaat—Staatsreg* op cit note 7 at 51.

particularly, to analyse the dilemma which Schreiner JA so clearly perceived and ventured to pronounce upon.

The Senate Case

To the court the true object of the Senate Act was clear: 'There can, however, be no doubt that the object of passing the Senate Act was to provide the Government with a two-thirds majority at a joint sitting of the two Houses in order to pass at that joint sitting an Act to validate [the Separate Representation of Voters] Act 46 of 1951. In other words, the object was to increase the membership of the Senate so as to provide the Government with a two-thirds majority of the members of both Houses—a majority which the Government did not command as long as the old Senate existed.'[9] But the majority of the court, as expressed in the judgment of Centlivres CJ, decided that '[i]f Parliament sitting bicamerally has plenary power to reconstitute the Senate, ie if its powers are not restricted by any other provision in the South African Act, then evidence as to the purpose of the Senate Act is irrelevant'.[10] Since the court could not find any restrictions on Parliament's plenary powers to reconstitute the Senate, it refused to take the legislative scheme of which it formed part as a nullifying factor into account and to declare the Senate Act invalid.

Steyn JA in his concurring judgment reiterated the views of the majority and went so far as to state that the 'procedural obstacle' of a two-thirds majority could be cleared in a lawful manner, as the result either of a general election or of legislation within the competency of Parliament in bicameral session.[11] Once this is brought about, he said, 'it is inept to speak, in any legal sense at any rate, of the frustration of the guarantee or the violation of any right flowing from it or protected by it'.[12] Whilst Steyn JA was not prepared to infer a 'supplemental restraint' on the plenary powers of Parliament as regards the composition of the Senate, he did surmise that '[t]here is, moreover, the circumstance that it [ie the constituent legislature, meaning the British Parliament] may well

[9] At 564F–G.

[10] At 565C–D. At 566B–D the court was, however, to find one restriction on the powers of Parliament in reconstituting the Senate, namely, that should Parliament enact that membership of the Senate is restricted to persons who can speak or write Afrikaans or speak or write English, then it would be an infringement of the protection of the equality of the official languages and therefore invalid. This is a curious admission. If the entrenched language rights can be affected by a change in the composition of the Senate, why can such a change not also affect the entrenched voting right? Also, the court at 569pr–A indulged in a kind of sophistry that cannot be left unnoticed: 'No doubt the effect of the Senate Act was to supply the Government with the two-thirds majority required by the proviso to sec 152 but it did not in any way purport to affect the appellant's rights and so it cannot be said to have rendered his rights nugatory. A further legislative step had to be taken in order to destroy appellant's rights and that step was in conformity with the proviso to sec 152.'

[11] At 583C–D. [12] Ibid.

have considered that the sanctions of the electorate would provide an adequate and more appropriate curb for the purposes which the limitation in question would serve, and that, if need be, these could be implemented by the powers in regard to the reservation and disallowance of Bills under sec 64 of the Act, exercised in accordance with the constitutional practices prevailing at the time the South Africa Act was passed'.[13] In other words, although Steyn JA refused to accept a limitation of Parliament's powers to reconstitute the Senate solely in order to obtain the required two-thirds majority, he did concede that other means could possibly have existed to thwart such a scheme. But in postulating these obstructions, he did not expound on their possible grounds or justification.

Schreiner JA disagreed with his ten colleagues who upheld the validity of the legislative scheme.

The crux of the whole matter and the reason for Schreiner's deepest concern is contained in this simple sentence: 'If an *ad hoc* Senate could be validly created, so could an *ad hoc* House of Assembly.'[14] He then asked whether the *ad hoc* Senate was a House of Parliament for the purposes of the entrenched sections. 'Prima facie it is not. The proviso [to s 152] was intended to furnish a real and not a merely theoretical protection against Parliamentary majorities acting bicamerally. Prima facie the framers of the Constitution did not intend that Parliament, that is, in effect, the Government acting through its majority, should have the power by bicameral legislation to convert an insufficient majority in a joint session into a sufficient one, merely by invoking the procedure of nomination or its equivalent.'[15]

Basing his premiss on the argument that '[o]nce legislation in the one field is used as a stage preparatory to legislation in the other, there ceases to be real separation and in substance they become one field',[16] Schreiner proceeded to deal with Commonwealth cases in which the Privy Council decided that where in a federal system there is a constitutionally entrenched limitation of powers of either the federal or state governments, a legislative scheme composed of two or more Acts to bypass such a limitation would be invalid. However, he had to concede that these cases dealt with the delimitation of powers and not with the composition of a legislature.[17] But then, he argued, 'in the restricted area of rigidity in our Constitution we have a situation that bears a fair analogy to the competing spheres in federations'.[18]

The gist of Schreiner's reasoning was that while Parliament in bicameral session has plenary powers to pass laws affecting its own composition, as soon as it uses its plenary powers to change the composition of one of the houses as part of a legislative scheme

[13] At 585G–H.
[14] At 571G–H.
[15] At 574pr–A.
[16] At 575B–C.
[17] At 576C–D.
[18] At 579F–G.

with the *purpose* of encroaching on the powers of Parliament in joint session regarding the entrenched sections, the Act that brings about the change in composition becomes invalid. The line of distinction is the purpose of the legislative scheme. Were the Senate to have been enlarged to conduct legislative business in ordinary bicameral session and not with the purpose of diminishing the powers of Parliament in unicameral session, the Act would not have been invalid.[19]

It has been observed that Schreiner's reasoning in reaching the conclusion that the Senate Act was invalid might well have been wrong, but that it is very difficult to point out where.[20] Schreiner's judgment went wrong simply because he tried to construe two spheres of competency, to distinguish between a bicameral Parliament legislating with an ordinary majority and a unicameral Parliament acting with a two-thirds majority. In fact and in law there were not two spheres of competency in Parliament. At the time of the Senate Act, Parliament, with its two houses, had plenary powers to change the South Africa Act in the prescribed manner and form. There could have been no competition between two Parliaments as far as spheres of competency were concerned.

So much for the purely legalistic point of view. The true question, however, was whether the Constitution—or a law behind the Constitution—prescribed a *certain kind* of Senate for purposes of both bicameral as well as unicameral sessions. Just as in the *High Court of Parliament* case, where the *nature* of the High Court of Parliament as a judicial institution was explored and found to be deficient,[21] the inquiry should have been directed to the nature of the Senate as a composite part of Parliament. Such an inquiry

[19] It is in this respect that Schreiner's reliance on the purpose of the Senate Act as being the distinguishing factor and reason for its invalidity becomes tenuous. In acknowledging the possibility that an enlarged Senate, although not originally instituted to obtain the two-thirds majority, could subsequently and validly participate in a joint session so as to remove the entrenchment of s 35, he had to concede that for the purposes of the constitutional guarantees there were not two different Senates operating in separate spheres of competency. To say that a 'difference in the purpose', as he did at 580A–B, could, as it were, create two different Senates, one valid and the other not, is not convincing.

[20] Cf Ellison Kahn 'Oliver Deneys Schreiner—The Man and his Judicial World' (1980) 97 *SALJ* 566 at 604: 'Alone among the judges of appeal, Schreiner JA found the enactment invalid. Perhaps the bulk of commentators have agreed with the majority decision that the end of the road had been reached; but none has inflicted more than the merest dent on the closely reasoned analysis of Schreiner JA.'

[21] As summed up by Centlivres CJ in the *Senate* case at 567E–F. 'In that case [ie the *High Court* case] it was held (at pp 779 and 780) that the method employed by sec 152 to entrench the rights conferred by secs 35 and 137 is the sanction of invalidity as determined by courts of law; that the so-called High Court of Parliament was not a court of law as it had *none of the characteristics of such a court* and that in any event the High Court of Parliament was in truth and in substance simply Parliament functioning under another name.' (My emphasis.)

Cf also Schreiner JA in the *High Court* case at 787F–G: 'The Constitution makes no express provision for the determination of questions of validity or invalidity and must therefore be taken to have left such determination to the courts of law of the land.'

should have gone back to the history and background of the Senate as a body of revision and control, the composition of which could not be altered for the first ten years after Union and which was proportionally constituted so as to reflect the electoral support both in the provinces and in the House of Assembly. Parliament's powers are conferred upon it by the political sovereign, the people.[22] It is an essential democratic principle that the people who confer power on Parliament should be freely represented in the legislature to participate through their representatives in the exercise and distribution of that power. A unilateral inflation by a parliamentary group of its own majority, either in the House of Assembly or in the Senate, therefore goes against the fundamental law on which Parliament is based and from which it derives its ultimate legitimacy.

The objection can immediately be raised that the above argument based on a supposed fundamental law of democracy has no actual application in our body of constitutional laws and belongs purely to the realms of theory and ideology. However, it is exactly this fundamental law that was postulated by Van den Heever J in her *obiter dictum* in *Cowburn* v *Nasopie (Edms) Bpk*[23] when she declared: 'Sou 'n gewone meerderheid van die Parlement—maak nie saak hoe hy dit regkry nie dalk omdat daar 'n epidemie woed en die opposisie sterk van gestel is—besluit dat alle toekomstige verkiesings afgeskaf word en die Staatspresidentskap voortaan 'n lewenslange en oorerflike amp met onbegrensde wetgewende, uitvoerende en regsprekende mag sal wees, *sou daar geen twyfel daaromtrent wees* dat die howe so 'n "wet" sou kon ongeldig verklaar nie.'[24]

FUNDAMENTAL LAWS OF DEMOCRACY

Are there laws of democracy—for instance, a law which prevents the usurpation of state institutions by a parliamentary majority—which are so fundamental that they cannot be changed unless by revolution? It is universally recognized that a head of state who suspends a Constitution and assumes all powers of state for himself is effecting a revolution. Can the same be said of a parliamentary majority that entrenches itself by destroying and usurping other institutions of state?

The concept of laws behind or above the Constitution that are unalterable in a democratic state is by no means unknown in constitutional-law systems. It is recognized by writers[25] that there

[22] Cf P J Laubscher 'The Foundation of Sovereignty—Parliament as a Law-making Body' (1981) 98 *SALJ* 529 at 540: 'The ruler's legal norms are valid not because they are valid (the *petitio principii* of illimitability), but because the governed acquiesce in the ruler's power. Its power is conferred. Conferred power is not habitual obedience.'

[23] 1980 (2) SA 547 (NC). [24] At 554H–555B. My emphasis.

[25] Pierre Wigny *Propos Constitutionnels* (1963) 24 poses the question: '*Faut-il creuser plus avant, découvrir des fondations plus profondes et plus immuables encore qui serait à l'abri même*

are rules of such a fundamental nature that they cannot be amended by any constitutional revision or change, not even if such revision or change is in itself very complicated and burdensome. It is said that these fundamental laws ensure the foundations on which the Constitution rests and are therefore immutable. Examples of such laws are those that prescribe the democratic nature of a state, its continuity and its unity, and in a federal state, the institutional and geographic bounds of federation and separate states.

The clearest illustration of the recognition of such a fundamental law that cannot be changed by any kind of revision of the Constitution is to be found in art 79(3) of the West German Republic, which declares the amendment of the Constitution so as to change the relationship between *Bund* and *Länder* and to alter the nature of the social, federal state to be totally impermissible. Commentators on this article draw the attention to the distinction between a *pouvoir constitué* and a *pouvoir constituant*,[26] the former being an authority that under the Constitution can amend or alter the Constitution, and the latter being an authority that can make a Constitution. No parliament, according to this theory, that derives its legislative power from the Constitution has authority to become a Constitution-maker itself and to change the laws that determine the identity and continuity of the Constitution. In pronouncing on the scope of art 79(3), the German Federal Constitutional Court has made it clear that the legislature may not, in any formal legalistic manner, affect the substance and fundamentals of the existing constitutional order under which it is constituted and operating.[27]

In the Norwegian Constitution[28] it is also expressly stipulated that no constitutional change may affect the fundamental principles of that Constitution. Constitutional theorists in most countries will defend the view that there are rules so basic that they precede the

d'une revision? En d'autre termes, y a-t-il des prescriptions supraconstitutionnelles?' And he comes to the conclusion: '*Mais dans l'organisation politique, certaines structures peuvent être si essentielles que pour elles, il n'est pas de "peaceful change". La nation souveraine peut les abandonner mais ce sera une décision revolutionnaire.*'

[26] Cf Klaus Stern *Das Staatsrecht der Bundesrepublik Deutschland* I (1977) 94, quoting the definition of the distinguished constitutionalist Carl Schmitt of a power to amend a Constitution, in contradistinction to the power to make a Constitution: '*Eine durch verfassungsgesetzliche Normierung erteilte Befugnis, die "Verfassung zu ändern", bedeutet, dass einzelne oder mehrere verfassungsgesetzliche Regelungen durch ander verfassungsgesetzliche Regelungen ersetzt werden können, aber nur unter der Voraussetzung, dass Identität und Kontinuität der Verfassung als ein Ganzes gewahrt bleiben. Die Befugnis zur Verfassungsänderung enthält also nur die Befugnis, unter Beibehaltung der Verfassung an verfassungsgesetzlichen Bestimmungen Änderungen, Zusätze, Ergänzungen, Streichungen usw. vorzunehmen, nicht aber die Befugnis, eine neue Verfassung zu geben.*'

[27] Cf the decision of the German Federal Constitutional Court of 15 December 1970, BVerfGE 30, 1 at 24, where it was ruled that art 79(3) imposes '*als Schranke für den verfassungsändererenden Gesetzgeber . . . den Sinn zu verhindern, dass die geltende Verfassungsordnung in ihrer Substanz, in ihren Grundlagen auf dem formal-legalistischen Weg eines verfassungsändererenden Gesetzes beseitigt und zur nachträglichen Legalisierung eines totalitären Regimes missbraucht werden kann*'.

[28] Article 112 of the Norwegian Constitution of 1814.

Constitution and cannot be removed by an amendment of the Constitution. As has been stated by C H McIlwain:[29] 'We must preserve and strengthen those bonds beyond which no free government ought ever to go, and make them limits beyond which no government can ever legally go. We must make *ultra vires* all exorbitant acts of government.' According to a well-known French author,[30] the Constitution of the Fifth Republic of 1958 is hailed exactly for the fact that it restored '*l'idée de l'État*', that it subtracted the unity and continuity of the state from the whims and autocratic tendencies of political parties and thereby managed '*triompher la démocratie contre l'usurpation représentative*'. It is left to the President to act as arbiter and guardian of the state to preserve the fundamentals of statehood. Even in Great Britain, a country which is not generally and traditionally known for a quest for legal principles more fundamental than the Diceyan fiat on parliamentary sovereignty, it has recently been argued that under the Constitution the Queen-in-Parliament is 'continuing' and 'self-embracing', and that the abolition of the House of Lords would go against the ultimate or fundamental rule of British constitutional law that Parliament is in essence a bicameral institution; therefore, should the House of Lords be abolished, it would be tantamount to a legal revolution.[31]

As regards the South African Constitution, the view has been advanced that the recognition of the sovereignty of the Almighty God in s 2 of the Constitution is not simply a mere declaration of faith but the embodiment of a legal norm.[32] It may well be that it is an example of the kind of fundamental law that cannot be altered or repealed by an Act of Parliament, since it would go against the basic nature of the state itself.

Turning to the *Senate* case, and taking into consideration the composite nature of Parliament as well as the then role and func-

[29] 'The Fundamental Law Behind the Constitution of the United States' in *Constitutionalism in the Changing World* (1939) 244. Cf also J D van der Vyver 'Rigidity and Flexibility in Constitutions: The Judiciary, the Rule of Law and Constitutional Amendment' in John A Benyon (ed) *Constitutional Change in South Africa* (1978) 52 at 61, where the author quotes the well-known dictum of Clark J in *Mapp* v *Ohio* (1961) 367 US 643 at 659: 'Nothing can destroy a government more quickly than its failure to observe its own laws, or worse, *its disregard of the character of its own existence*.' (My emphasis.)

[30] George Burdeau *Droit Constitutionnel et Institutions Politiques* 19 ed (1980) 499–50.

[31] Peter Mirfield 'Can the House of Lords Lawfully be Abolished?' (1979) 95 *LQR* 36; see, however, George Winterton 'Is the House of Lords Immortal?' (1979) 95 *LQR* 386 for the other, traditional view. See also, in support of the idea that the British Parliament is bound by more fundamental principles, the remarkable *esquisse* by L J du Plessis 'Wetgewersoewereiniteit' (1960) 23 *THRHR* 164 at 173: 'Die Engelse ideologie laat die "omnipotence of parliament" slegs toe so lank as die parlement of die heersende party "plays the game", dws sy perke erken, en dit is Germaanse en Christelike erfenis wat ook in ons Romeins-Hollandse reg oorgeneem is, maar by ons meer spesifiek en algemeen sy uitdrukking vind in die Christelike Nasionalisme wat sowel ons hoof-partye as ons parlement bely.'

[32] F Venter 'Die Staatsregtelike Soewereiniteit van God' 1977 *TSAR* 64; L Roeleveld 'Die Voorrede in die Begin van ons Grondwet' in *Huldigingsbundel Daniel Pont* (1970) 295 at 313.

tions of the Senate within the ambit of the entrenched procedure, one is inclined to think that it would perhaps have been more profitable and legally sounder to deny the enlarged Senate the status of and recognition as a house of Parliament. Just as the High Court of Parliament was denied the status of a court of law for the reason that it was merely Parliament acting in a judicial guise, the inflated Senate was not a house of Parliament but the majority of the House of Assembly posturing through their nominated and elected agents as an upper house. The fundamental rule of the Constitution which was involved and should have been held to be infringed in the *High Court of Parliament* case as well as in the *Senate* case would have simply been the rule that a majority in the House of Assembly is not allowed to usurp the roles and functions of the other institutions of state, thereby jeopardizing the democratic nature and continuity of the state itself.

The Senate Act of 1955 was the death-knell of the Senate. The disgrace inflicted upon the Senate by the Government's blatantly using it as a political instrument finally led to its abolition in 1980.[33] Had the courts been able to prevent the rape of the Senate at the time of the Senate Act, that body might have continued to exist as an honoured and stable institution of state in a way which ensured the protection of provincial and group interests as was intended. However, the vexed question remains whether, even if the rule against the abuse of authority by parliamentary majorities is accepted, the courts are capable of settling a controversy of such magnitude and profound political implications. This brings the ultimate problem of judicial review of political questions to the fore.

The Courts and Political Controversy

One cannot escape the feeling that the majority of the members of the court in the *Senate* case were becoming weary of, if not impatient with, the political implications of the controversy. Amongst the appellate judges, only Schreiner took up the cause of constitutionalism with enthusiasm. But the question remains whether a court of law could have come to grips with the political issues involved.

Notwithstanding Alexis de Tocqueville's famous belief that the courts in America remain the strongest bulwarks against the tyranny of political institutions,[34] it has since *Luther* v *Borden*[35] been

[33] Section 13 of the Republic of South Africa Constitution Fifth Amendment Act 101 of 1980; for the details of the abolition of the Senate and the retention of the entrenched language rights, see Wiechers *VerLoren van Themaat—Staatsreg* op cit note 7 at 268.

[34] *De la Démocratie en Amérique* I 14 ed (1864) 172: '*Resserré dans ses limites, le pouvoir accordé aux trinunaux américains de prononcer sur l'inconstitutionnalité des lois forme encore une des plus puissantes barrières qu'on ait jamais élevées contre la tyrannie des assemblées politiques.*'

[35] 7 How 1, 12 L Ed 581 (1849).

a settled rule in that country that the courts will not interfere with those controversies which a political power must settle.[36] Admittedly, as experience has shown, and as is explained by Shapiro and Tresolini,[37] '[t]he term *political question* cannot be defined precisely, because the Court may expand or contract the definition as it sees fit. In other words, a political question is whatever the Supreme Court says it is.'

Even in Germany, where as we have seen, the role of the Federal Constitutional Court as *Hüter der Verfassung* (guardian of the Constitution) has become extremely elevated and important, there are strong voices against the idea that the state and its highest representative institutions should be subjected to the same judicial scrutiny as all other subordinate bodies and authorities.[38] It is said that statehood, *Staatlichkeit*, itself is thereby undermined and that it necessarily leads to political justice, *politische Justiz*.[39] In political controversies, it is averred, the courts have to acknowledge a judicial deficit, *rechtliches Defizit*, which cannot be solved by the normative dialectics of the law.[40]

The arguments against judicial enforcement of the fundamental rules behind the Constitution are indeed very strong. It may very well be, in the words of Carl Schmitt, that 'in a system of judicial protection of the Constitution, politics has nothing to gain and the judiciary stands to lose everything'.[41]

Just as in the case of constitutional conventions, which are, for the greater part, rules of law governing the relationship between Parliament and the Government and are not justiciable in courts of law, fundamental laws, which sustain the Constitution and upon which the democratic nature of the state is founded, must perhaps be left to the state itself for their defence and enforcement. This could be achieved, as in the case of France, by investing the President with powers of guardianship and protection. In the ultimate sense, courts cannot be the protectors of the state and its

[36] Cf the dictum of Chief Justice Taney (at 47, 601), cited in Martin Shapiro and Rocco J Tresolini *American Constitutional Law* 4 ed (1975) 90: 'No one, we believe, has ever doubted the proposition, that, according to the institutions of this country, the sovereign in every State resides in the people of the State, and that they may alter and change their form of government at their own pleasure. But whether they have changed it or not by abolishing an old government, and establishing a new one in its place, is a question to be settled by the political power. And when that power has decided, the courts are bound to take notice of its decision, and to follow it.'

[37] Op cit note 36 at 69.

[38] Hugo J Hahn '*Uber die Gewaltenteilung in der Wertwelt des Grundgesetzes*' 1965 *Jahrbuch des Offentlichen Rechts* 15 at 38: '*[J]e mehr die Justiz zur Hüterin der rechtlichen Grundordnung des Staates wird, um so mehr auch muss die Besetzung der Gerichte zu einem politisches Anliegen werden, muss sie die organisierten Interessen ausserhalb des Parlaments in die Versuchung führen, durch die Personalpolitik auf die Gerichte Einfluss zu gewinnen.*'

[39] Ernst Forsthoff '*Rechtsstaat oder Richterstaat?*' *Rechtsstaat im Wandel* 2 ed (1976) 255; see also Ulrich Scheuner '*Verantwortung und Kontrolle in der demokratischen Verfassungsordnung*' *Staatstheorie und Staatsrecht* (1978) 293.

[40] Felix Ermacora *Grundriss einer Allgemeinen Staatslehre* (1979) 158, 162.

[41] As quoted by Ernst Forsthoff op cit note 39 at 249.

fundamental laws, since judges are not the representatives of the nation, the political sovereign, and do not control armies or other forces of coercion.

Taken in the context of the *Senate* case, the above ideas would make the remarks by Steyn JA very relevant, namely, that the sanction for the kind of abuse by the Parliamentary majority which led to the passing of the Senate Act is not to be supplied by the courts but by the electorate, or is to be found in the powers of reservation or disallowance which the Governor-General possessed at the time of the passing of the South Africa Act. Elaborating on that point of view, it is certainly not far-fetched to suggest that the Senate Act, being an infringement of the fundamental law against the abuse of democratic institutions and the continuity of the state, should have been a sufficient cause for the Governor-General to exercise his reserve powers of dissent. And it is likewise not too far-fetched to suggest that our State President should do the same if such an infringement of fundamental laws were to occur. Obviously, under our Constitution the refusal of the State President to assent to a Bill that to his mind encroaches upon the state's fundamental laws will probably result in the Parliamentary majority dismissing him on the grounds of misconduct. But in such an event the controversy will inevitably be referred to the nation, where the ultimate responsibility lies.

Conclusion

Every state, even one with the most flexible Constitution, has laws that precede its Constitution, upon which the state and its institutions are founded and which ensure the continuity of the state and its unity. In a democratic state one of these fundamental laws is the protection of the state against the abuses of parliamentary majorities.

Although there are countries, such as West Germany, where the courts are entrusted with the function of enforcing these fundamental, supra-constitutional laws, it is more in the nature of the democratic state to leave their enforcement in the hands of the political sovereign itself or to invest a popularly elected head of state with the powers of protector or guarantor.

The *Senate* case has impressed upon us the need for a true understanding of our fundamental, supra-constitutional laws, and the need for their effective protection and enforcement. In his dissenting judgment Schreiner JA, more than any other judge in that series of great constitutional judgments, has made us aware how frail and defenceless democracy and constitutional guarantees could become if these fundamental laws are ignored.

POINTING OUT

D ZEFFERTT*

A prisoner's confession, made to prevent his being suffocated or to avoid one more electric shock to his genitals, has dubious value as proof. That is why it has been said[1] that the fundamental reason for excluding improperly obtained statements is that they are unreliable.

Another approach is to look at the matter from what is good or bad for society. It is not in the interests of society to try a man on such evidence, because it would be unfair to do so—it is socially malignant to get a conviction by recklessly disregarding whether the accused is truly guilty. But there is another reason for getting rid of the tainted results of violence and deceit. A just society cannot exist if its policemen are violent, sadistic and corrupt. If the courts were to receive improperly obtained statements, they would encourage policemen to resort to vicious and evil practices.[2] Due process is essential to the well-being of society.

It would be no less malign to exclude involuntary statements but to allow them to poison due process by sly and oblique means. To allow the proof of facts discovered as a result of an inadmissible statement, at least when it has been induced by cruelty, is to encourage brutality; but to be myopic as regards their unreliability would be to disregard fairness as well. No South African judge saw this more acutely than the late Mr Justice Schreiner. I have, therefore, in paying tribute to that great jurist, thought it fitting to write about 'pointing out' and the discovery of facts as a consequence of the accused's having made an inadmissible statement or confession.

In one respect the South African law is better than the English as regards evidence of this kind. The English cases 'conflict so far as the admissibility of the part of the confession showing the accused's knowledge of those facts is concerned'.[3] For what it is worth, it is

* BA LLB (Witwatersrand), Advocate of the Supreme Court of South Africa, Professor of Law in the University of the Witwatersrand, Johannesburg.

[1] For instance in *R* v *Samhando* 1943 AD 608.

[2] For a full discussion, see A P Paizes 'Undue Influence and Involuntary Admissions and Confessions' (1981) 5 *SACC* 122; see, further, 1981 *Criminal LR* 92; Criminal Law Revision Committee 11th Report 'Evidence (General)' Cmnd 4991 (1972) § 55; 1977 *Criminal LR* 723; 1979 *Criminal LR* 412; 1981 *Criminal LR* 469.

[3] *Cross on Evidence* 5 ed (1979) 323.

submitted that the view, reflected in decisions such as *R* v *Warickshall*[4] and *R* v *Berriman*,[5] which holds that no part of the confession becomes admissible because it has been confirmed by the discovery of facts, is to be preferred. It is clear in South Africa that a court cannot receive a confession (or any part of it) in the guise of a pointing out. As Kotzé JA recently remarked in *S* v *Mbele*,[6] 'slegs die aanwysings en nie die voorlegging van 'n bekentenis onder die skyn van 'n aanwysing nie' is permissible. But in another respect the English law is very much better than ours. In England, 'facts discovered in consequence of inadmissible confessions may . . . be proved in evidence [only] if their relevance can be established without resorting to any part of the confession'.[7] Although this principle may encourage irregularities by the police by admitting their tainted results, it has, at the least, the virtue of eschewing unreliable evidence: the discovery of actual facts 'removes some of the risk that evidence [may have been] manufactured by [the accused's having been compelled] to perform self-incriminatory acts'.[8] The South African law, it will be submitted, lacks this virtue. That it does is in despite of Schreiner JA, who strove in vain to establish a South African rule that would insist on the reception of evidence of reliable discoveries only.

It is necessary to go back to 1943, when the leading case of *R* v *Samhando*[9] was decided. The appellant, who had been convicted of murder, had been forced by the use of considerable violence to admit that he had killed the deceased. After making this admission, he pointed out to his interrogators (they were not 'peace officers') where the blood-stained clothing of the deceased had been concealed in the branches of an orange tree about five hundred yards away from where an axe had been found. The presiding judge excluded the accused's admission, but admitted the following evidence:[10]

> '"He pointed out the clothing and blankets of the deceased in an orange tree" . . . .
>
> '"I missed the axe so I asked the accused where the axe was. He then took me there and pointed the axe out. At first we looked for the axe and could not find it, and then we asked him where it was and he knew where it was." . . .
>
> '"The accused showed us the axe". . . .
>
> '"We then went with the accused into the orchard; there we found a parcel of clothing, it was hanging in an orange tree, the accused showed it to us, this is the clothing before the court, that clothing belongs to the accused and deceased." . . .

4 (1783) 1 Leach 263 (168 ER 234). 5 (1854) 6 Cox CC 388.

6 1981 (2) SA 738 (A) at 743B–C. See, further, *S* v *Nkosi* 1980 (3) SA 829 (A).

7 *Cross on Evidence* 323.

8 Per Schreiner JA in *R* v *Tebetha* 1959 (2) SA 337 (A) at 344pr–A.

9 1943 AD 608. 10 At 611.

> '"The first time John and I saw the clothes in the tree was when the accused showed them to us."
>
> '"We went down to the orchard and found the clothing there in consequence of what the accused had said."'

It was not necessary to decide whether any part of the accused's statement could have been received, because no proof of what he had said was admitted. The evidence, which merely showed that the accused had pointed out the clothing and the axe, was admissible to prove that he knew where the clothing and the axe were to be found. The accused's knowledge of where the deceased's blood-stained clothing had been concealed was highly relevant to his guilt—it was very damaging evidence against him.

Samhando, it should be noted, was decided without the help of the provisions of s 274 of the Criminal Procedure and Evidence Act 1917,[11] which was then applicable and which said:

> 'It shall be lawful to admit evidence of any fact otherwise admissible in evidence, notwithstanding that such fact has been discovered and come to the knowledge of the witness who gives evidence respecting it only in consequence of information given by the person under trial in any confession or deposition which by law is not admissible in evidence against him on such trial, and notwithstanding that the fact has been discovered and come to the knowledge of the witness against the wish or will of the accused.'

Subsequently, in *R* v *Duetsimi*,[12] *Samhando's* case was explained and distinguished. The appellant in *R* v *Duetsimi* had been convicted of housebreaking with intent to rob and robbery. He had been found in possession of blankets which were alleged to have been stolen from a shop that had been broken into. At his trial the Crown had been permitted to lead evidence that the appellant had pointed out the shop. Schreiner JA, who delivered the judgment of the court (Van den Heever and Hoexter JJA concurring), remarked that the *ratio decidendi* of *Samhando's* case was not easy to discover, but its true basis was that *in statements not amounting to confessions* within the meaning of s 273 of the Criminal Procedure and Evidence Act 1917 the fact that a statement had not been freely and voluntarily made did not prevent the prosecution's proving not only things discovered as a result of such a statement (including the whereabouts of things connected with the crime) but also that the accused had pointed them out. In *Duetsimi* the pointing out of the shop was part of an inadmissible confession and should have been excluded by the trial court.

No mention was made of s 274 of the Criminal Procedure and Evidence Act 1917, probably because the *Samhando* rule had

[11] Act 31 of 1917. [12] 1950 (3) SA 674 (A).

extended the ambit of admissibility beyond what it had said to include the fact that there had been a pointing out and had been laid down irrespective of its provisions. Two questions were left open. The policeman to whom the shop had been pointed out had been ignorant of the crime at that time. It was not necessary to decide whether his ignorance 'could in any event have supported the contention that the whereabouts of the shop [had been] discovered in consequence of the pointing out by the appellant, so as to let in the rule in *Samhando's* case'.[13] It was also unnecessary 'to consider in what circumstances, if at all, that rule could be applied to the pointing out of the scene of a crime, as opposed to the disclosure of movables associated with the crime'.[14]

In 1955 the law was changed by Parliament. The Criminal Procedure and Evidence Amendment Act[15] of that year introduced a new subsec (2) into s 274 of the principal Act.[16] The old s 274 of the 1917 Act, with insignificant changes, became subsec (1), and a subsec (2) was added, which said:

> 'It shall be lawful to admit evidence that anything was pointed out by the person under trial or that any fact or thing was discovered in consequence of information given by such person notwithstanding that such pointing out or information forms part of a confession or statement which by law is not admissible against him on such trial.'

Later that year the consolidating Criminal Procedure Act[17] repeated these provisions in subsecs (1) and (2) of s 245.

There the matter rested until 1959, when the meaning of s 245 (which corresponds to s 218 of the present Criminal Procedure Act[18]) fell to be decided in *R* v *Tebetha*.[19]

On 4 September 1957 a panel van which was carrying tins containing money was stolen by robbers from a street in Johannesburg. Later that same day the van was found abandoned on a gravel road on mining property. The tins, emptied of money, were found the same evening in a hole near Van Wyk's Rust. *These discoveries were not made as a result of anything that had been said by the appellant.* He was arrested by Detective-Sergeant B only on 7 November. The crucial feature of the case against the appellant was that he had made a report which was inadmissible—presumably because it was a confession in terms of s 244 of the Criminal Procedure Act 1955 and had been made to a peace officer other than a magistrate or justice. As a result of this report, B took the appellant from the police station, and the appellant pointed out to him a place 40 to 60 yards from where the van had been found on 4 September. From there, according to B, the appellant had taken him to where the tins had been found.

[13] At 679A–B. [14] At 679B–C. [15] Act 29 of 1955.
[16] Criminal Procedure and Evidence Act 31 of 1917. [17] Act 56 of 1955.
[18] Act 51 of 1977. [19] 1959 (2) SA 337 (A).

In other words, no place or thing had been discovered as a result of what the appellant may have said or done. The evidence amounted merely to that B had discovered—and there was only his testimony to vouch for it—that the appellant had knowledge of where the van and the tins had been when they were found. It is much more dangerous to receive such evidence than to receive evidence that some corporeal thing was found as a consequence of the accused's having made an inadmissible statement or confession. Let us take these examples. Constable X assaults the accused, who makes an involuntary statement. As a result, the accused points out a stolen article, which is, consequently, discovered by the police. The fact that that thing was actually found gives the evidence of the discovery at least some circumstantial guarantee of trustworthiness. Let us now twist the facts. Mr Y finds the stolen article (that is, discovers it) and gives it to Constable X. Constable X arrests the accused some days afterwards and, after torturing the accused, makes him confess to the theft. This evidence cannot, of course, be received. But Constable X testifies that after the accused had confessed to the crime, he had pointed out the place where Y had found the thing. It is submitted that this evidence comes in so dubious a guise as to make its reception very dangerous: its admissibility would depend on the *ipse dixit* of the torturer; the circumstantial guarantee of trustworthiness, present in the first instance, would be missing. But according to the majority decision in *R* v *Tebetha* it would be admissible.[20] The decision of the majority was delivered by Hoexter JA[21] (Steyn, Malan and Ogilvie Thompson JJA concurring) in language so terse (and perhaps even opaque and cryptic to those of us who lack the scalpel-sharp intellect of Hoexter JA) that I propose to quote it in full—particularly because it is the *fons et origo mali* of our law on the subject:

> 'The facts and the relevant statutory provisions are set out in the judgment of my Brother Schreiner. I find myself unable to agree with his interpretation of sec 245(2) of the Criminal Procedure Act 56 of 1955. That section reads as follows:
>
> > "It shall be lawful to admit evidence that anything was pointed out by the person under trial or that any fact or thing was discovered in consequence of information given by such person notwithstanding that such pointing out or information forms part of a confession or statement which by law is not admissible against him on such trial."
>
> In my opinion it is doing violence to the clear words of that subsection to construe it as though it read as follows:
>
> > "It shall be lawful to admit evidence that any fact or thing was discovered in consequence of the pointing out of anything by the

[20] This was the meaning attributed to *R* v *Tebetha* in *S* v *Ismail (1)* 1965 (1) SA 446 (N); see below. A useful summary of the law is to be found in *S* v *Moumbaris* 1973 (3) SA 109 (T).

[21] *R* v *Tebetha* 1959 (2) SA 337 (A) at 345H–346H.

> person under trial or in consequence of information given by such person notwithstanding. . . ."

The subsection refers to (1) things pointed out by the person under trial, and (2) facts or things discovered in consequence of information given by such person. When a person points out a thing, the pointing out is his act and proves that he has knowledge of some fact relating to that thing. In the case of the discovery by the police of a thing there is no proof of knowledge of any fact in relation to that thing on the part of the person under trial unless there is proof that the discovery was made in consequence of information given by such person. In my opinion sec 245(1) by itself did not make it clear that evidence of knowledge on the part of the person under trial was admissible. But the enactment of subsec (2) has made it quite clear that such evidence is now admissible. In the case of the pointing out of a thing, the mere pointing out, which is the act of the person under trial himself, is sufficient by itself to prove his knowledge of the thing pointed out or of some fact connected with it. In the case of the discovery of a fact or thing, evidence merely of such discovery would prove no knowledge on the part of the person under trial, and therefore the subsection permits proof of such knowledge by making admissible the evidence that the discovery was made in consequence of information given by such person. It may very well be that the subsection would have achieved a better result if it had insisted on discovery of some thing as the result of the pointing out, but that does not entitle the court to do violence to the language of the legislature. *Jus dicere, non dare* is the function of the court and the language of an Act of Parliament

> "must neither be extended beyond its natural sense and proper limits in order to supply omissions or defects, nor strained to meet the justice of an individual case".

(See *Union Government* v *Thompson* 1919 AD 404 at p 425.)

'In the result I am of opinion that the challenged evidence given by Booysen was admissible in terms of sec 245(2) of the Criminal Procedure Act. In all other respects I agree with the reasons of my Brother Schreiner. The evidence of Booysen, coupled with the other incriminating factors referred to by my Brother, proves the guilt of the appellant beyond any doubt, and it follows that the appeal should be dismissed.'

It is submitted with respect that the dissenting judgment of Schreiner JA is much to be preferred to this strictly literal construction that has the effect of letting in dangerous and highly prejudicial evidence.

Schreiner JA argued convincingly, with respect, that all that s 245(1) (now s 218(1) of the Criminal Procedure Act 1977) did was directly to declare admissible a fact discovered in consequence of a confession or other statement that is inadmissible.[22] It also did not exclude 'proof that the appellant [in *Samhando*] pointed out the clothing and therefore, by inference, that he knew of its presence in

[22] At 343pr–B.

the tree and was connected with the crime'.[23] *Duetsimi's* case had held that *Samhando's* case, in extending admissibility to the fact of pointing out, was not applicable to a pointing out that formed part of a confession. The learned judge of appeal went on to say[24] that '[t]he suggestion naturally presents itself that the object of introducing s 245(2) [now s 218(2) of the 1977 Act] was to remove the effect of *Duetsimi's* case and to allow proof of facts like pointings out in cases of inadmissible confessions as freely as in cases of inadmissible self-criminatory statements falling short of confessions'. In his lordship's view the legislature had made no further change: '. . . *Samhando's* case was an example of confirmation of a self-criminatory statement by subsequently discovered facts, the facts having been discovered through the accused's pointing them out. This sort of confirmation, the theory underlying it and the extent of its operation, have been the subject of considerable investigation by writers of textbooks on evidence and articles in law periodicals. . . . So far as I can ascertain it has never been suggested that confirmation could be obtained by the act of pointing at something already known by the witness, in whose presence this is done, to be connected with the crime. The notion of discovery resulting from the confession is invariably present in the cases discussed.'[25] Why this is so is obvious—without discovery the inadmissible confession is not confirmed:

> 'The element of discovery, though it provides no absolute guarantee of the truthfulness of the inadmissible confession, removes some of the risk that evidence may be manufactured by compelling the accused to perform self-criminatory acts. It would generally be much easier to compel or induce the accused to point at something connected with the crime where the thing has already been discovered and is in his presence, than it would be to get him to disclose the unknown whereabouts of the thing.'[26]

Schreiner JA went on to show[27] that, from a linguistic point of view, the Crown's contention (which was accepted by the majority of the court) 'involves treating "aangewys is" as if it were "na gewys is" and "pointed out" as if it were "pointed at"'. The interpretation of the subsection was difficult—'it may even be conceded to be doubtful'.[28] When that is so 'the more lenient construction should be adopted'.[29]

It is submitted, with the very greatest respect, that the majority of the court put too much stress on the declaratory role of the judge, attached too great a belief in the semantic clarity of words taken in isolation and took too imperceptive a view of the linguistic difficulties of the section. Schreiner JA, on the other hand, realized

[23] At 343A–B. [24] At 343C–E. [25] At 343E–H. [26] At 344pr–B.
[27] At 344H–345C. [28] At 344F–345B. [29] At 344B–C.

that justice cried out for the court to search for a permissible basis that would warrant the application of the most lenient and sensible approach.[30]

A year later, he was able to write a gloss on *R* v *Tebetha*. In *R* v *Nhleko*[31] the appellant, who was charged with murder, had pointed out to Detective-Sergeant B a place, F, where he had left a body, or the body of the deceased, on marshy ground near water infested with crocodiles, which could easily have removed it. No body was found. 'That', said Schreiner JA, who delivered the judgment of the court, 'was clearly a most prejudicial statement and even though no objection was taken to it the Crown had to lay a foundation for its admission.'[32] The Crown had not done so. The fact that the evidence of B had been linked with the pointing out of point F suggested that the evidence had been received under s 245 of the Criminal Procedure Act 1955[33] (now s 218 of the Criminal Procedure Act 1977).[34] The learned judge of appeal, in rejecting this evidence, said:[35]

> 'This provision was considered in *R* v *Tebetha* . . . where the only evidence that was held to be admissible was that the appellant pointed out two places. . . . In the circumstances the inference could be drawn that he was pointing out two places where the stolen van and the tins had to his knowledge been after the robbery. And this inference it was held was properly drawn. But the case furnishes no support for the suggestion that this part of sec 245(2) allows anything more to be proved than the pointing out of a thing—be it a place or any other thing.'

There is, unfortunately, an ellipsis in the judgment. Schreiner JA did not say, in as many words, that the distinction between the two cases is that while, in *Tebetha*, the police had discovered that the appellant, by being able to point out a thing or place, had guilty knowledge, in *Nhleko* nothing had been discovered—the evidence of the pointing out did not demonstrate that the appellant had such knowledge, since the body had not been found. But this is the necessary inference from the decision, since the appellant had pointed out a place but the pointing out was, nevertheless, excluded.

A significant feature of Schreiner JA's judgment is that it left open the question whether a pointing out that had been induced by violence was admissible.[36] This glimmer was soon doused by Milne JP in *S* v *Ismail (1)*.[37]

The accused had pointed out where an act of sabotage had taken place. He had made an inadmissible confession. Milne JP, after

[30] Ibid. [31] 1960 (4) SA 712 (A). [32] At 720E–F.
[33] Act 56 of 1955. [34] Act 51 of 1977. [35] At 721pr–C.
[36] At 721B–C. [37] 1965 (1) SA 446 (N).

remarking that, 'even if it is quite clear that a statement, not amounting to a confession, was obtained by a policeman as a result of acts of physical violence committed upon the accused, such as to render the statement itself inadmissible, the evidence as to the pointing out, forming part of the statement, would nevertheless be admissible',[38] went on to hold that the legislature, by enacting s 245(2) of the Criminal Procedure Act 1955 (now s 218(2) of the Criminal Procedure Act 1977), intended to make admissible evidence of a pointing out that formed part of an inadmissible confession 'notwithstanding that it [had been] obtained in a fashion similar to the fashion in which the pointing out [had been] obtained in *Samhando's* case',[39] that is to say, even if it had been obtained as a result of considerable physical violence. Or, as submitted by the prosecutor, the section 'let in evidence as to a pointing out, even though the relative confession was obtained as a result of acts of gross cruelty inflicted upon the person making it'.[40]

One is sure that Parliament would be horrified to hear that our courts, not to mention a very senior public servant, have attributed to it so base an intention. Such are the fruits of an over-literal mind!

It has subsequently been held in the Transvaal in *S* v *Dladla*[41] that, although evidence of the discovery's having been made as a result of violence by the police does not prevent the proof of the discovery, it is admissible as being relevant to the credibility of the policemen. The Natal decision, *S* v *Nkwanyana*,[42] is to the same effect.

The question fell also to be decided in *S* v *Bvuure (1)*,[43] where it was held that the parallel Rhodesian provision[44] renders a pointing out admissible no matter how the pointing out was obtained.

A suggestion by Young J in an earlier Rhodesian decision, *R* v *Moyo*,[45] indicates that there is, possibly, another solution: a court might exclude a pointing out as a matter of discretion where there has been a serious breach of propriety and fair play. But the existence of a judicial discretion, in a criminal case, to reject admissible evidence is far from certain.

In the course of his advice in *R* v *Kuruma, son of Kaniu*[46] Lord Goddard LCJ observed:

> 'No doubt in a criminal case the judge always has a discretion to disallow evidence if the strict rules of admissibility would operate unfairly against an accused.'

Subsequently the Privy Council has again emphasized the existence of a judicial discretion to exclude evidence if the trial judge thinks

[38] At 450D–F. [39] At 451F–H. [40] At 449G–fine.
[41] 1975 (1) SA 811 (T). [42] 1978 (3) SA 404 (N).
[43] 1974 (1) SA 206 (R).
[44] Section 289(2) of the Criminal Procedure and Evidence Act Ch 31 (R).
[45] 1967 (4) SA 613 (R).
[46] [1955] AC 197 (PC) at 204, [1955] 1 All ER 236 at 239.

that its reception would be unfair to the accused.[47] And Rumpff CJ, in an *obiter dictum* in *S* v *Mushimba*,[48] quoted the passage from Lord Goddard's advice, which has been cited above, with apparent approval.

The difficulty with Lord Goddard's sweeping statement is, first, that the decisions on which his lordship relied did not support the existence of a general discretion to exclude admissible evidence that would operate unfairly against an accused. In the Canadian case of *R* v *Wray*[49] it was pointed out that '[t]he dictum of Lord Goddard, in the *Kuruma* case, appears to be founded on *Noor Mohamed*'[50] and that its basis was the rule that gives a judge a discretion to exclude similar-fact evidence whose probative value is outweighed by its potentiality to cause prejudice to the accused. Whatever the merits of such a discretionary power—it is submitted that it has had no significance in South Africa since the abolition of juries—it does not warrant the existence of a general discretion to exclude unfairly obtained admissible evidence. And, now, this has been recognized by the House of Lords. The *ratio* of *R* v *Sang*[51] is obscure,[52] but four out of the five members of the Appellate Committee appear to have been *ad idem* (*a*) that a trial judge has a discretion to reject evidence if its probative value is outweighed by it prejudicial effect and (*b*) that, except with regard to admissions and confessions and, generally, with regard to evidence obtained from the accused after his commission of the offence, *he has no discretion to refuse to admit relevant evidence on the ground that it had been obtained by unfair means.* Where the discretion exists, however, it is based on considerations of fairness.

In other jurisdictions[53] it has been considered that there should be a judicial discretion to exclude illegally obtained evidence when public policy demands such an exclusion. Thus, in the Irish case of *People* v *O'Brien*[54] Kingsmill Moore J said:

> '[I]n every [criminal] case a determination has to be made by the trial judge as to whether the public interest is best served by the admission or exclusion of evidence of facts ascertained as a result of, and by means of, illegal actions, and the answer to the question depends on a consideration of all the circumstances. On the one hand the nature and extent of the illegality have to be taken into account. Was the illegal action intentional or unintentional, and, if intentional, was it the result of an *ad hoc* decision or does it represent a settled or deliberate policy? Was the illegality one of a trivial or technical nature or was it a serious invasion

[47] *R* v *King* [1969] 1 AC 304 (PC), [1968] 2 All ER 610.
[48] 1977 (2) SA 829 (A) at 840. [49] (1970) 11 DLR 3d 673.
[50] *R* v *Noor Mohamed* [1949] AC 182 (PC), [1949] 1 All ER 365.
[51] [1980] AC 402 (HL), [1979] 2 All ER 1222.
[52] Cf *Cross on Evidence* 5 ed (1979) Addendum with J D Heydon 1980 *Criminal LR* 129.
[53] In Australia, see *Bunning* v *Cross* (1978) 19 ALR 641; J D Heydon op cit.
[54] [1965] IR 142 (cited by J D Heydon *Cases and Materials on Evidence* (1975) 238).

of important rights the recurrence of which would involve a real danger to necessary freedoms? Were there circumstances of urgency or emergency which provide some excuse for action?'

It is submitted that there is much to be said for this approach, which is similar to that found in Australia.[55] It appears to strike a satisfactory balance between the policy that all relevant evidence should be ventilated unless it be hit by an exclusionary rule and the policy that evidence should not be admitted if it is illegally obtained, because the police should be deterred from illegal conduct and the liberties of the citizen should be zealously fostered.

In South Africa there is some authority for the existence of a discretion in criminal cases to exclude admissible evidence,[56] but the matter has never been scrutinized with care. Should the matter fall to be considered, it is suggested that the approach of *People* v *O'Brien*[57] ought to be adopted: it is far less slippery and vague[58] than the general proposition in *Kuruma* and yet it strikes a just balance between the extremes of excluding or including unfairly or illegally obtained evidence. Valuable evidence will not be lost because of some technicality; but expression will be given to the public interest in curbing the excesses of the executive.

If South Africa would apply the principle in *People* v *O'Brien* to the reception of evidence of facts pointed out, or discovered, as a result of the accused's having made an inadmissible statement or confession through being subjected to cruelty or violence, then the South African law of evidence, in this regard, could once more reflect those high ideals exemplified by Schreiner JA. The majority decision in *R* v *Tebetha* was correctly construed in *S* v *Ismail (1)*[59] as allowing the reception of evidence discovered as a result of a statement or confession that has been obtained from an accused by the use of gross cruelty or violence. The recognition of a judicial discretion to exclude admissible evidence that has been illegally obtained, when the public interest demands its rejection, would go far towards drawing the rotten teeth of such a rule. That the evidence of a pointing out which has been induced by these means is allowed by statute should be no impediment. The South African law of evidence is statutory law—both when it is a local codification or the application of the English common law by virtue of a statute. And there is, it is submitted, nothing in our evidentiary statutes that expressly excludes such a discretion.[60] We should be slow to conclude that they have such an implication.

[55] See note 53.

[56] *S* v *Forbes* 1970 (2) SA 594 (C); *S* v *Mushimba* 1977 (2) SA 829 (A) at 840 (*obiter*), in which Rumpff CJ cited Lord Goddard's dictum in *Kuruma* (*supra*) with apparent approval.

[57] *Supra* note 54.

[58] See 1980 *Criminal LR* 129.

[59] 1965 (1) SA 446 (N); see 402–3 above.

[60] See further the *obiter* remarks of Miller JA in *S* v *Mphahlele* 1982 (4) SA 505 (A) at 512H–513E.